CODE OF FEDERAL REGULATIONS

Title 18

Conservation of Power and Water Resources

Part 400 to End

Revised as of April 1, 2018

Containing a codification of documents
of general applicability and future effect

As of April 1, 2018

Published by the Office of the Federal Register
National Archives and Records Administration
as a Special Edition of the Federal Register

Table of Contents

Cite this Code: CFR

To cite the regulations in this volume use title, part and section number. Thus, 18 CFR 401.0 *refers to title 18, part 401, section 0.*

Explanation

The Code of Federal Regulations is a codification of the general and permanent rules published in the Federal Register by the Executive departments and agencies of the Federal Government. The Code is divided into 50 titles which represent broad areas subject to Federal regulation. Each title is divided into chapters which usually bear the name of the issuing agency. Each chapter is further subdivided into parts covering specific regulatory areas.

Each volume of the Code is revised at least once each calendar year and issued on a quarterly basis approximately as follows:

Title 1 through Title 16..as of January 1
Title 17 through Title 27 ....as of April 1
Title 28 through Title 41 ....as of July 1
Title 42 through Title 50...as of October 1

The appropriate revision date is printed on the cover of each volume.

LEGAL STATUS

The contents of the Federal Register are required to be judicially noticed (44 U.S.C. 1507). The Code of Federal Regulations is prima facie evidence of the text of the original documents (44 U.S.C. 1510).

HOW TO USE THE CODE OF FEDERAL REGULATIONS

The Code of Federal Regulations is kept up to date by the individual issues of the Federal Register. These two publications must be used together to determine the latest version of any given rule.

To determine whether a Code volume has been amended since its revision date (in this case, April 1, 2018), consult the "List of CFR Sections Affected (LSA)," which is issued monthly, and the "Cumulative List of Parts Affected," which appears in the Reader Aids section of the daily Federal Register. These two lists will identify the Federal Register page number of the latest amendment of any given rule.

EFFECTIVE AND EXPIRATION DATES

Each volume of the Code contains amendments published in the Federal Register since the last revision of that volume of the Code. Source citations for the regulations are referred to by volume number and page number of the Federal Register and date of publication. Publication dates and effective dates are usually not the same and care must be exercised by the user in determining the actual effective date. In instances where the effective date is beyond the cutoff date for the Code a note has been inserted to reflect the future effective date. In those instances where a regulation published in the Federal Register states a date certain for expiration, an appropriate note will be inserted following the text.

OMB CONTROL NUMBERS

The Paperwork Reduction Act of 1980 (Pub. L. 96–511) requires Federal agencies to display an OMB control number with their information collection request.

Many agencies have begun publishing numerous OMB control numbers as amendments to existing regulations in the CFR. These OMB numbers are placed as close as possible to the applicable recordkeeping or reporting requirements.

PAST PROVISIONS OF THE CODE

Provisions of the Code that are no longer in force and effect as of the revision date stated on the cover of each volume are not carried. Code users may find the text of provisions in effect on any given date in the past by using the appropriate List of CFR Sections Affected (LSA). For the convenience of the reader, a "List of CFR Sections Affected" is published at the end of each CFR volume. For changes to the Code prior to the LSA listings at the end of the volume, consult previous annual editions of the LSA. For changes to the Code prior to 2001, consult the List of CFR Sections Affected compilations, published for 1949-1963, 1964-1972, 1973-1985, and 1986-2000.

"[RESERVED]" TERMINOLOGY

The term "[Reserved]" is used as a place holder within the Code of Federal Regulations. An agency may add regulatory information at a "[Reserved]" location at any time. Occasionally "[Reserved]" is used editorially to indicate that a portion of the CFR was left vacant and not accidentally dropped due to a printing or computer error.

INCORPORATION BY REFERENCE

What is incorporation by reference? Incorporation by reference was established by statute and allows Federal agencies to meet the requirement to publish regulations in the Federal Register by referring to materials already published elsewhere. For an incorporation to be valid, the Director of the Federal Register must approve it. The legal effect of incorporation by reference is that the material is treated as if it were published in full in the Federal Register (5 U.S.C. 552(a)). This material, like any other properly issued regulation, has the force of law.

What is a proper incorporation by reference? The Director of the Federal Register will approve an incorporation by reference only when the requirements of 1 CFR part 51 are met. Some of the elements on which approval is based are:

(a) The incorporation will substantially reduce the volume of material published in the Federal Register.

(b) The matter incorporated is in fact available to the extent necessary to afford fairness and uniformity in the administrative process.

(c) The incorporating document is drafted and submitted for publication in accordance with 1 CFR part 51.

What if the material incorporated by reference cannot be found? If you have any problem locating or obtaining a copy of material listed as an approved incorporation by reference, please contact the agency that issued the regulation containing that incorporation. If, after contacting the agency, you find the material is not available, please notify the Director of the Federal Register, National Archives and Records Administration, 8601 Adelphi Road, College Park, MD 20740-6001, or call 202-741-6010.

CFR INDEXES AND TABULAR GUIDES

A subject index to the Code of Federal Regulations is contained in a separate volume, revised annually as of January 1, entitled CFR INDEX AND FINDING AIDS. This volume contains the Parallel Table of Authorities and Rules. A list of CFR titles, chapters, subchapters, and parts and an alphabetical list of agencies publishing in the CFR are also included in this volume.

An index to the text of "Title 3—The President" is carried within that volume.

The Federal Register Index is issued monthly in cumulative form. This index is based on a consolidation of the "Contents" entries in the daily Federal Register.

A List of CFR Sections Affected (LSA) is published monthly, keyed to the revision dates of the 50 CFR titles.

REPUBLICATION OF MATERIAL

There are no restrictions on the republication of material appearing in the Code of Federal Regulations.

INQUIRIES

For a legal interpretation or explanation of any regulation in this volume, contact the issuing agency. The issuing agency's name appears at the top of odd-numbered pages.

For inquiries concerning CFR reference assistance, call 202–741–6000 or write to the Director, Office of the Federal Register, National Archives and Records Administration, 8601 Adelphi Road, College Park, MD 20740-6001 or e-mail *fedreg.info@nara.gov.*

SALES

The Government Publishing Office (GPO) processes all sales and distribution of the CFR. For payment by credit card, call toll-free, 866-512-1800, or DC area, 202-512-1800, M-F 8 a.m. to 4 p.m. e.s.t. or fax your order to 202-512-2104, 24 hours a day. For payment by check, write to: US Government Publishing Office – New Orders, P.O. Box 979050, St. Louis, MO 63197-9000.

ELECTRONIC SERVICES

The full text of the Code of Federal Regulations, the LSA (List of CFR Sections Affected), The United States Government Manual, the Federal Register, Public Laws, Public Papers of the Presidents of the United States, Compilation of Presidential Documents and the Privacy Act Compilation are available in electronic format via *www.ofr.gov.* For more information, contact the GPO Customer Contact Center, U.S. Government Publishing Office. Phone 202-512-1800, or 866-512-1800 (toll-free). E-mail, *ContactCenter@gpo.gov.*

The Office of the Federal Register also offers a free service on the National Archives and Records Administration's (NARA) World Wide Web site for public law numbers, Federal Register finding aids, and related information. Connect to NARA's web site at *www.archives.gov/federal-register.*

The e-CFR is a regularly updated, unofficial editorial compilation of CFR material and Federal Register amendments, produced by the Office of the Federal Register and the Government Publishing Office. It is available at *www.ecfr.gov.*

OLIVER A. POTTS,
Director,
Office of the Federal Register.
April 1, 2018.

THIS TITLE

Title 18—CONSERVATION OF POWER AND WATER RESOURCES is composed of two volumes. The first volume containing parts 1—399, includes all current regulations of the Federal Energy Regulatory Commission, Department of Energy. The second volume, containing part 400 to end, includes all current regulations issued by the Delaware River Basin Commission, the Water Resources Council, the Susquehanna River Basin Commission, and the Tennessee Valley Authority as of April 1, 2018.

The OMB control numbers for the Federal Energy Regulatory Commission, Department of Energy, appear in § 389.101 of chapter I.

For this volume, Ann Worley was Chief Editor. The Code of Federal Regulations publication program is under the direction of John Hyrum Martinez, assisted by Stephen J. Frattini.

Title 18—Conservation of Power and Water Resources

(This book contains part 400 to End)

1

CHAPTER III—DELAWARE RIVER BASIN COMMISSION

SUBCHAPTER A—ADMINISTRATIVE MANUAL

PART 400 [RESERVED]

PART 401—RULES OF PRACTICE AND PROCEDURE

officials, and other special government employees.

Subpart I—General Provisions

AUTHORITY: Delaware River Basin Compact (75 Stat. 688), unless otherwise noted.

SOURCE: 39 FR 25474, July 11, 1974, unless otherwise noted.

§ 401.0 Introduction.

(a) The Delaware River Basin Compact requires the Commission to formulate and adopt a Comprehensive Plan and Water Resources Program. In addition, the Compact provides in Section 3.8 that no project having a substantial effect on the water resources of the Basin shall be undertaken unless it shall have been first submitted to and approved by the Commission. The Commission is required to approve a project whenever it finds and determines that such project would not substantially impair or conflict with the Comprehensive Plan. Section 3.8 further provides that the Commission shall provide by regulation for the procedure of submission, review and consideration of projects and for its determinations pursuant to Section 3.8.

(b) The Comprehensive Plan consists of all public and those private projects and facilities which the Commission has directed be included therein. It also includes those documents and policies which the Commission has determined should be included with the Comprehensive Plan as being needed to insure optimum planning, development, conservation, use, management and control of the water resources of the Delaware Basin to meet present and future needs. The Comprehensive Plan is subject to periodic review and revision as provided in Sections 3.2 and 13.1 of the Compact.

(c) The Water Resources Program is based upon the Comprehensive Plan. It is required to be updated annually and to include a systematic presentation of the quantity and quality of water resources needs of the area to be served for such reasonably foreseeable period as the Commission may determine, balanced by existing and proposed projects required to satisfy such needs. The Commission's review and modification of the Water Resources Program is conducted pursuant to the provisions of Articles 3.2 and 13.2 of the Compact.

(d) The Commission's Rules of Practice and Procedure govern the adoption and revision of the Comprehensive Plan, the Water Resources Program, the exercise of the Commission's authority pursuant to the provisions of Article 3.8 and other actions of the Commission mandated or authorized by the Compact.

(e) These Rules of Practice and Procedure extend to the following areas of Commission responsibility and regulation:

Article 1—Comprehensive Plan.
Article 2—Water Resources Program.
Article 3—Project Review Under Section 3.8 of the Compact.
Article 4—(Reserved).
Article 5—Appeals or Objections to Decisions of the Executive Director in Water Quality Cases.
Article 6—Administrative and Other Hearings.
Article 7—Penalties and Settlements in Lieu of Penalties.
Article 8—Public Access to the Commission's Records and Information.
Article 9—General Provisions.

(f) These rules are subject to Commission revision and modification from time to time as the Commission may determine. The Commission reserves the right to waive any Rule of Practice and Procedure it determines should not be applicable in connection with any matter requiring Commission action. All actions by the Commission, however, shall comply fully with the applicable provisions of the Compact.

[62 FR 64154, Dec. 4, 1997]

Subpart A—Comprehensive Plan

SOURCE: 62 FR 64154, Dec. 4, 1997, unless otherwise noted.

§ 401.1 Scope.

This subpart shall govern the submission, consideration, and inclusion of projects into the Comprehensive Plan.

§401.2 Concept of the plan.

(a) The Comprehensive Plan shall be adopted, revised and modified as provided in Sections 3.2 and 13.1 of the Compact. It is the Commission's responsibility to adopt the Comprehensive Plan, after consultation with water users and interested public bodies, for the immediate and long-range development and uses of the water resources of the Basin. The Plan shall include the public and private projects and facilities which the Commission determines are required for the optimum planning, development, conservation, utilization, management and control of the water resources of the Basin to meet present and future needs. In addition to the included projects and facilities, the Comprehensive Plan consists of the statements of policies, and programs that the Commission determines are necessary to govern the proper development and use of the River Basin. The documents within the Comprehensive Plan expressing the Commission's policies and programs for the future, including the means for carrying them out, may be set forth through narrative text, maps, charts, schedules, budgets and other appropriate means.

(b) Specific projects and facilities and statements of policy and programs may be incorporated, deleted or modified from time to time to reflect changing conditions, research results and new technology. The degree of detail described in particular projects may vary depending upon the status of their development.

§401.3 Other agencies.

Projects of the federal agencies affecting the water resources of the Basin, subject to the limitations in Section 1.4 of the Compact, shall be governed by Section 11.1 of the Compact. Projects of the signatory states, their political subdivisions and public corporations affecting the water resources of the Basin, shall be governed by the provisions of Section 11.2 of the Compact.

§401.4 Project applications and proposed revisions and changes.

(a) Applications for inclusion of new public projects and the deletion or al-teration of previously included public projects may be submitted by signatory parties and agencies or political subdivisions thereof. Owners or sponsors of privately owned projects may submit applications for the inclusion of new private projects and the deletion or alteration of previously included private projects in which the applicant has an interest. The Commission may also receive and consider proposals for changes and additions to the Comprehensive Plan which may be submitted by any agency of the signatory parties, or any interested person, organization, or group. Any application or proposal shall be submitted in such form as may be required by the Executive Director to facilitate consideration by the Commission.

(b) Applications for projects shall include at least the following information:

(1) Purpose or purposes, including quantitative measures of physical benefit anticipated from the proposal;

(2) The location, physical features and total area required.

(3) Forecast of the cost or effect on the utilization of water resources;

(4) Relation to other parts of the existing Comprehensive Plan;

(5) A discussion of conformance with Commission policies included in the Comprehensive Plan; and

(6) A discussion of the alternatives considered.

§401.5 Review of applications.

Following staff study, examination, and review of each project application, the Commission shall hold a public hearing upon notice thereon as provided in paragraph 14.4(b) of the Compact and may take such action on a project application as it finds to be appropriate.

§401.6 Proposed revisions and changes.

Proposals for changes and additions to the Comprehensive Plan submitted by any agency of the signatory parties or any interested person, organization or group shall identify the specific revision or change recommended. In order to permit adequate Commission consideration of any proposal, the Executive Director may require such additional information as may be needed. Review or consideration of such proposals shall be based upon the recommendation of the Executive Director and the further direction of the Commission.

§ 401.7 Further action.

The Commission will review the Comprehensive Plan in its entirety at least once every six years from the date of the initial adoption of the Comprehensive Plan (March 28, 1962). Such review may include consideration of proposals submitted by the signatory parties, agencies or political subdivision thereof or other interested parties. The amendments, additions, and deletions adopted by the Commission will be compiled and the Plan as so revised shall be made available for public inspection.

§ 401.8 Public projects under Article 11 of the Compact.

(a) After a project of any federal, state or local agency has been included in the Comprehensive Plan, no further action will be required by the Commission or by the agency to satisfy the requirements of Article 11 of the Compact, except as the Comprehensive Plan may be amended or revised pursuant to the Compact and this part. Any project which is changed substantially from the project as described in the Comprehensive Plan will be deemed to be a new and different project for the purposes of Article 11 of the Compact. Whenever a change is made the sponsor shall advise the Executive Director who will determine whether the change is deemed substantial within the meaning of this part.

(b) Any public project not having a substantial effect on the water resources of the Basin, as defined in subpart C of this part, may proceed without reference to Article 11 of the Compact.

§ 401.9 Custody and availability.

The Comprehensive Plan shall be and remain in the custody of the Executive Director. The Plan, including all maps, charts, description and supporting data shall be and remain a public record

open to examination during the regular business hours of the Commission, under such safeguards as the Executive Director may determine to be necessary to preserve and protect the Plan against loss, damage or destruction. Copies of the Comprehensive Plan or any part or parts thereof shall be made available by the Executive Director for public sale at a price covering the cost of production and distribution.

Subpart B—Water Resources Program

§ 401.21 Scope.

This subpart shall govern the submission, consideration and inclusion of projects into the Water Resources Program.

§ 401.22 Concept of the Program.

The Water Resources Program, as defined and described in section 13.2 of the Compact, will be a reasonably detailed amplification of that part of the Comprehensive Plan which the Commission recommends for action within the ensuing six-year period. That part of the Program consisting of a presentation of the water resources needs of the basin will be revised only at such intervals as may be indicated to reflect new findings and conclusions, based upon the Commission's continuing planning programs.

§ 401.23 Procedure.

Each project included in the Water Resources Program shall have been previously included in the Comprehensive Plan, except that a project may be added to both the Plan and the Program by concurrent action of the Commission. The project's sponsor shall furnish the following information prior to the inclusion of the project in the Water Resources Program:

(a) The Comprehensive Plan data brought up-to-date for the period of the Water Resources Program.

(b) Specific location and dimension of a structural project, and specific language of a standard, policy or other non-structural proposal.

(c) The plan of operation of a structural project.

(d) The specific effects of a non-structural project.

(e) Sufficient data to indicate a workable financial plan under which the project will be carried out.

(f) A timetable for implementation.

§401.24 Preparation and adoption.

The Water Resources Program will be prepared and considered by the Commission for adoption annually. Projects required to satisfy the basin needs during the period covered by the Program may be classified as follows:

(a) *"A" list.* This shall include public projects which require no further review, and inclusion in such list shall be deemed to be approved for the purposes of section 3.8 of the Compact.

(b) *"B" list.* This shall include public projects not included in the "A" list and privately sponsored projects which are proposed or anticipated by the Commission.

§401.25 Alternatives for public projects.

Any publc project which has been included in the Comprehensive Plan but is not on the "A" list of the current Water Resources Program, at the option of the sponsor, may be submitted for review and approval under section 3.8 of the Compact in accordance with Subpart C of this part.

§401.26 Inventory of other projects.

Each Water Resources Program will include, for information purposes only, an inventory of projects approved during the previous year pursuant to section 3.8 of the Compact but which are not part of the Comprehensive Plan or Water Resources Program.

Subpart C—Project Review Under Section 3.8 of the Compact

SOURCE: 62 FR 64155, Dec. 4, 1997, unless otherwise noted.

§401.31 Scope.

This subpart shall govern the submission and review of projects under Section 3.8 of the Delaware River Basin Compact.

§401.32 Concept of 3.8.

Section 3.8 is intended to protect and preserve the integrity of the Comprehensive Plan. This section of the Compact provides:

"No project having a substantial effect on the water resources of the basin shall hereafter be undertaken by any person, corporation or governmental authority unless it shall have been first submitted to and approved by the Commission, subject to the provisions of Sections 3.3 and 3.5. The Commission shall approve a project whenever it finds and determines that such project would not substantially impair or conflict with the Comprehensive Plan and may modify and approve as modified, or may disapprove any such project whenever it finds and determines that the project would substantially impair or conflict with such Plan. The Commission shall provide by regulation for the procedure of submission, review and consideration of projects, and for its determinations pursuant to this section. Any determination of the Commission hereunder shall be subject to judicial review in any court of competent jurisdiction."

§401.33 Administrative agreements.

The Executive Director is authorized and directed to enter into cooperative Administrative Agreements with federal and state regulatory agencies concerned with the review of projects under federal or state law as follows:

(a) To facilitate the submission and review of applications and the determinations required under Section 3.8 of the Compact;

(b) To avoid unnecessary duplication of staff functions and hearings required by law; and

(c) For such other and different purposes as he may deem feasible and advantageous for the administration of the Compact or any other law.

§401.34 Submission of project required.

Any project which may have a substantial effect on the water resources of the Basin, except as provided in paragraph (d) of this section, shall be submitted to the Commission for a determination as to whether the project impairs or conflicts with the Comprehensive Plan, as follows:

(a) Where the project is subject to review by a state or federal agency which has entered into an Administrative Agreement with the Commission, such project will be referred to the Commission in accordance with the terms of the Administrative Agreement, and appropriate instructions will be prepared and issued by the Executive Director for guidance of project sponsors and applicants.

(b) Where no other state or federal agency has jurisdiction to review and approve a project, or no Administrative Agreement is in force, the project sponsor shall apply directly to the Commission.

(c) Any project proposal, which may have a substantial effect on the water resources of the Basin, may be received and reviewed by the staff informally in conference with the project sponsor during the preliminary planning phase to assist the sponsor to develop the project in accordance with the Commission's requirements.

(d) Whenever a project sponsored by one of the signatory parties, or by any agency, political subdivision or public corporation thereof, has been included in the Water Resources Program in the "A List" classification, the project, to the extent of such inclusion and as described in the Program, shall be deemed approved for the purposes of Section 3.8 of the Compact.

(e) Whenever a project is subject to review and approval by the Commission under this section, there shall be no substantial construction activity thereon, including related preparation of land, unless and until the project has been approved by the Commission; provided, however, that this prohibition shall not apply to the drilling of wells for purposes of obtaining geohydrologic data, nor to in-plant control and pretreatment facilities for pollution abatement.

§ 401.35 Classification of projects for review under Section 3.8 of the Compact.

(a) Except as the Executive Director may specially direct by notice to the project owner or sponsor, or as a state or federal agency may refer under paragraph (c) of this section, a project in any of the following classifications will be deemed not to have a substantial effect on the water resources of the Basin and is not required to be submitted under Section 3.8 of the Compact:

(1) The construction of new impoundments or the enlargement or removal of existing impoundments, for whatever purpose, when the storage capacity is less than 100 million gallons;

(2) A withdrawal from ground water for any purpose when the daily average gross withdrawal during any 30 consecutive day period does not exceed 100,000 gallons;

(3) A withdrawal from impoundments or running streams for any purpose when the daily average gross withdrawal during any 30 consecutive day period does not exceed 100,000 gallons;

(4) The construction of new domestic sewage treatment facilities or alteration or addition to existing domestic sewage treatment facilities when the design capacity of such facilities is less than a daily average rate of 10,000 gallons per day in the drainage area to Outstanding Basin Waters and Significant Resource Waters or less than 50,000 gallons per day elsewhere in the Basin; and all local sewage collector systems and improvements discharging into authorized trunk sewage systems;

(5) The construction of new facilities or alteration or addition to existing facilities for the direct discharge to surface or ground waters of industrial wastewater having design capacity of less than 10,000 gallons per day in the drainage area to Outstanding Basin Waters and Significant Resource Waters or less than 50,000 gallons per day elsewhere in the Basin; except where such wastewater contains toxic concentrations of waste materials;

(6) A change in land cover on major ground water infiltration areas when the amount of land that would be altered is less than three square miles;

(7) Deepening, widening, cleaning or dredging existing stream beds or relocating any channel, and the placement of fill or construction of dikes, on streams within the Basin except the Delaware River and tidal portions thereto, and streams draining more than one state;

(8) Periodic maintenance dredging;

(9) Encroachments on streams within the Basin caused by:

(i) Floating docks and anchorages and buoys and navigational aids;

(ii) Temporary construction such as causeways, cofferdams and falsework required to facilitate construction on permanent structures;

(10) Bridges and highways unless they would pass in or across an existing or proposed reservoir or recreation project area as designated in the Comprehensive Plan;

(11) Liquid petroleum products pipelines and appurtenances designed to operate under pressures less than 150 psi; local electric distribution lines and appurtenances; local communication lines and appurtenances; local natural and manufactured gas distribution lines and appurtenances; local water distribution lines and appurtenances; and local sanitary sewer mains, unless such lines would involve significant disturbance of ground cover affecting water resources;

(12) Electric transmission or bulk power system lines and appurtenances; major trunk communication lines and appurtenances; natural and manufactured gas transmission lines and appurtenances; major water transmission lines and appurtenances; unless they would pass in, on, under or across an existing or proposed reservoir or recreation project area as designated in the Comprehensive Plan; unless such lines would involve significant disturbance of ground cover affecting water resources;

(13) Liquid petroleum products pipelines and appurtenances designed to operate under pressures of more than 150 psi, unless they would pass in, on, under or across an existing or proposed reservoir or recreation project area as designated in the Comprehensive Plan, or in, on, under or across any stream within the Basin; unless such lines would involve significant disturbance of ground cover affecting water resources;

(14) Landfill projects, unless no state-level review and permit system is in effect; broad regional consequences are anticipated; or the standards or criteria used in state level review are not adequate to protect the water of the Basin for the purposes prescribed in the Comprehensive Plan;

(15) Draining, filling or otherwise altering marshes or wetlands when the area affected is less than 25 acres; provided; however, that areas less than 25 acres shall be subject to Commission review and action;

(i) Where neither a state nor a federal level review and permit system is in effect, and the Executive Director determines that a project is of major regional or interstate significance requiring action by the Commission, or

(ii) When a Commissioner or the Executive Director determines that the final action of a state or federal permitting agency may not adequately reflect the Commission's policy as to wetlands of the Basin. In the case of a project affecting less than 25 acres for which there has been issued a state or federal permit, a determination to undertake review and action by the Commission shall be made no later than 30 days following notification of the Commission of such permit action. The Executive Director, with the approval of the Chairman, may at any time within the 30-day period inform any permit holder, signatory party or other interested party that the Commission will decline to undertake review and action concerning any such project;

(16) The diversion or transfer of water from the Delaware River Basin (exportation) whenever the design capacity is less than a daily average rate of 100,000 gallons;

(17) The diversion or transfer of water into the Delaware River Basin (importation) whenever the design capacity is less than a daily average rate of 100,000 gallons except when the imported water is wastewater;

(18) The diversion or transfer of wastewater into the Delaware River Basin (importation) whenever the design capacity is less than a daily average rate of 50,000 gallons; and

(19) Temporary or short term projects determined to have non-substantial impact on the water resources of the Basin by the Executive Director.

(b) All other projects which have or may have a substantial effect on the water resources of the Basin shall be submitted to the Commission in accordance with this part for determination as to whether the project impairs or conflicts with the Comprehensive Plan. Among these are projects involving the following (except as provided in paragraph (a) of this section):

(1) Impoundment of water;

(2) Withdrawal of ground water;

(3) Withdrawal of water from impoundment or streams;

(4) Diversion of water into or out of the Basin;

(5) Deepening or widening of existing stream beds, channels, anchorages, harbors or tuning basins, or the construction of new or enlarged channels, anchorages, harbors or turning basins, or the dredging of the bed of any stream or lake and disposal of the dredged spoil, when the nature or location of the project would affect the quantity or quality of ground or surface waters, or fish and wildlife habitat;

(6) Discharge of pollutants into surface or ground waters of the Basin;

(7) Facilities designed to intercept and transport sewage to a common point of discharge; and pipelines and electric power and communication lines;

(8) Facilities for the direct discharge to surface or ground waters of industrial wastewater;

(9) Projects that substantially encroach upon the stream or upon the 100-year flood plain of the Delaware River or its tributaries;

(10) Change in land cover on major ground water infiltration areas;

(11) Hydroelectric power projects, including pumped storage projects;

(12) Projects or facilities of Federal, state and local agencies such as highways, buildings and other public works and improvements, affecting the water and related land resources of the Basin;

(13) Draining, filling or otherwise altering marshes or wetlands;

(14) Regional wastewater treatment plans developed pursuant to the Federal Water Pollution Control Act;

(15) Landfills and solid waste disposal facilities affecting the water resources of the Basin;

(16) State and local standards of flood plain regulation;

(17) Electric generating or cogenerating facilities designed to consumptively use in excess of 100,000 gallons per day of water during any 30-day period; and

(18) Any other project that the Executive Director may specially direct by notice to the project sponsor or land owner as having a potential substantial water quality impact on waters classified as Special Protection Waters.

(c) Whenever a state or federal agency determines that a project falling within an excluded classification (as defined in paragraph (a) of this section) may have a substantial effect on the water resources of the Basin, such project may be referred by the state or federal agency to the Commission for action under this part.

(d) Except as otherwise provided by § 401.39 the sponsor shall submit an application for review and approval of a project included under paragraph (b) of this section through the appropriate agency of a signatory party. Such agency will transmit the application or a summary thereof to the Executive Director, pursuant to Administrative Agreement, together with available supporting materials filed in accordance with the practice of the agency of the signatory party.

§ 401.36 Water supply projects—Conservation requirements.

Maximum feasible efficiency in the use of water is required on the part of water users throughout the Basin. Effective September 1, 1981 applications under Section 3.8 of the Compact for new water withdrawals subject to review by the Commission shall include and describe water-conserving practices and technology designed to minimize the use of water by municipal, industrial and agricultural users, as provided in this section.

(a) Applications for approval of new withdrawal from surface or ground water sources submitted by a municipality, public authority or private water works corporation whose total average withdrawals exceed one million gallons per day shall include or be in reference to a program prepared by the applicant consisting of the following elements:

(1) Periodic monitoring of water distribution and use, and establishment of a systematic leak detection and control program;

(2) Use of the best practicable water-conserving devices and procedures by all classes of users in new construction or installations, and provision of information to all classes of existing users

concerning the availability of water-conserving devices and procedures; and

(3) A contingency plan including use priorities and emergency conservation measures to be instituted in the event of a drought or other water shortage condition. Contingency plans of public authorities or private water works corporations shall be prepared in cooperation with, and made available to, all municipalities in the area affected by the contingency plan, and shall be coordinated with any applicable state-wide water shortage contingency plans.

(b) Programs prepared pursuant to paragraph (a) of this section shall be subject to any applicable limitations of public utility regulations of the signatory party in which the project is located.

(c) Applications for approval of new industrial or commercial water withdrawals from surface or ground water sources in excess of an average of one million gallons per day shall contain

(1) A report of the water-conserving procedures and technology considered by the applicant, and the extent to which they will be applied in the development of the project; and

(2) A contingency plan including emergency conservation measures to be instituted in the event of a drought or other water shortage. The report and contingency plan shall estimate the impact of the water conservation measures upon consumptive and non-consumptive water use by the applicant.

(d) Applications for approval of new agricultural irrigation water withdrawals from surface or ground water sources in excess of one million gallons per day shall include a statement of the operating procedure or equipment to be used by the applicant to achieve the most efficient method of application of water and to avoid waste.

(e) Reports, programs and contingency plans required under this section shall be submitted by the applicant as part of the permit application to the state agency having jurisdiction over the project, or directly to the Commission in those cases where the project is not subject to the jurisdiction of a state agency. State agencies having jurisdiction over a project that is subject to the provisions of this section shall

determine the adequacy and completeness of the applicant's compliance with these requirements and shall advise the Commission of their findings and conclusions.

§401.37 Sequence of approval.

A project will be considered by the Commission under Section 3.8 of the Compact either before or after any other state or federal review, in accordance with the provisions of the Administrative Agreement applicable to such project.

§401.38 Form of referral by State or Federal agency.

Upon approval by any State or Federal agency of any project reviewable by the Commission under this part, if the project has not prior thereto been reviewed and approved by the Commission, such agency shall refer the project for review under Section 3.8 of the Compact in such form and manner as shall be provided by Administrative Agreement.

(a) The Commission will rely on the appropriate agency in each state to review and regulate the potability of all public water supplies. Applications before the Commission should address the impact of the withdrawal, use and disposal of water on the water resources of the Basin.

(b) The Commission will rely on signatory party reviews as much as possible and generally the Commission will not review the performance standards of individual components of treatment processes but will require compliance with all policies in the Comprehensive Plan including all applicable Water Quality Standards.

§401.39 Form of submission of projects not requiring prior approval by State or Federal agencies.

Where a project does not require approval by any other State or Federal agency, or where such approval is required but an Administrative Agreement is not in force, the project shall be submitted directly to the Commission for review and determination of compatibility with the Comprehensive Plan, in such form of application, with such supporting documentation, as the

Executive Director may reasonably require for the administration of the provisions of the Compact. These shall include without limitation thereto:

(a) *Exhibits to accompany application.* The application shall be accompanied by the following exhibits:

(1) Abstract of proceedings authorizing project, where applicable;

(2) General map showing specific location and dimension of a structural project, or specific language of a standard or policy in the case of a non-structural proposal;

(3) Section of the United States Geological Survey topographic map showing the territory and watershed affected;

(4) Maps, drawings, specifications and profiles of any proposed structures, or a description of the specific effects of a non-structural project;

(5) Written report of the applicant's engineer showing the proposed plan of operation of a structural project;

(6) Map of any lands to be acquired or occupied;

(7) Estimate of the cost of completing the proposed project, and sufficient data to indicate a workable financial plan under which the project will be carried out; and

(8) Analyses and conclusions of regional water supply and wastewater investigations.

(b) *Letter of transmittal.* The application shall be accompanied by a letter of transmittal in which the applicant shall include a list of all enclosures, the names and addresses to which communications may be directed to the applicant, and the names and addresses of the applicant's engineer and counsel, if any.

(c) Unless otherwise ordered by the Commission, two copies of the application and accompanying papers shall be filed. If any application is contested, the Commission may require additional copies of the application and all accompanying papers to be furnished by the applicant. In such cases, certified copies of photographic prints or reproduction may be used.

§ 401.40 Informal conferences and emergencies.

(a) Whenever the Executive Director shall deem necessary, or upon request of the applicant, an informal conference may be scheduled to explain, supplement or review an application.

(b) In the event of an emergency requiring immediate action to protect the public interest or to avoid substantial and irreparable injury to any private person or property, and the circumstances do not permit a review, hearing and determination in the regular course of the regulations in this part, the Executive Director with the approval of the chairman of the Commission may issue an emergency certificate authorizing an applicant to take such action as the Executive Director may deem necessary and proper in the circumstances, pending review, hearing and determination by the Commission as otherwise required in this part.

§ 401.41 Limitation of approval.

(a) Approval by the Commission under this part shall expire three years from the date of Commission action unless prior thereto the sponsor has expended substantial funds (in relation to the cost of the project) in reliance upon such approval. An approval may be extended or renewed by the Commission upon application.

(b) Any application that remains dormant (no proof of active pursuit of approvals) for a period of three years from date of receipt, shall be automatically terminated. Any renewed activity following that date will require submission of a new application.

§ 401.42 One Permit Program.

(a) *Purpose.* The purpose of the One Permit Program set forth in this section is to provide the opportunity for the environmental agency and/or other administrative agency of a Signatory Party ("Signatory Party Agency") and the Commission to coordinate and collaborate in the administration of a single process for the review and adjudication of projects. The One Permit Program allows the Signatory Party Agency and Commission to incorporate requirements and determinations of both entities in a single permit or other approval instrument, pursuant to a duly adopted Administrative Agreement under paragraph (d) of this section.

(b) *Scope.* This section applies to all projects that:

(1) Are reviewable under the Compact;

(2) Meet the thresholds for review set forth in §401.35 of these *Rules of Practice and Procedure;*

(3) Are subject to review by a Signatory Party Agency under its own statutory authorities; and

(4) Are within regulatory programs that have been identified in a duly adopted Administrative Agreement between the Commission and a Signatory Party Agency under this section. For any project that requires an approval under the Compact that is outside the scope of the Signatory Party Agency's approval issued in accordance with an Administrative Agreement under this section, the project sponsor shall apply to the Commission in accordance with procedures established by the Commission.

(c) *Regulatory programs.* Regulatory programs eligible for administration under the One Permit Program may include but are not limited to those concerning: Basin discharges, Basin water withdrawals, and Basin flood plain requirements.

(d) *Procedure.* The categories of projects covered and the procedures for processing applications under the One Permit Program shall be set forth in one or more Administrative Agreements between the Commission and the Signatory Party Agency that have been adopted by the Commission following a duly noticed public hearing and are in form and substance acceptable to the Commission and the Signatory Party Agency, consistent with the following:

(1) Except as provided in paragraphs (b) and (e) of this section or in an Administrative Agreement that has been duly executed by the Commission and the Signatory Party Agency under this section, an application for initial approval, renewal or revision of any project subject to the One Permit Program shall be filed only with the Signatory Party Agency.

(2) To enable the Commission to compile and make available to the public a current list of pending applications for projects within the Basin subject to Commission jurisdiction, the Signatory Party Agency shall notify the Commission at least monthly of applications the Signatory Party has received during the preceding month that may be eligible for review under the One Permit Program.

(3) For those categories of projects identified in the Administrative Agreement as requiring Commission input, the Commission staff shall provide the Signatory Party Agency with such input, including where specified by the Administrative Agreement, a recommendation as to any conditions of approval that may be necessary or appropriate to include in the project review determination under Section 3.8 of the Compact as to those regulatory programs identified in an Administrative Agreement in accordance with paragraph (b) of this section.

(4) Unless the Signatory Party Agency disapproves the project or the Administrative Agreement provides for separate Commission action under Section 3.8 of the Compact, the Signatory Party Agency shall make the project review determination under Section 3.8 of the Compact, as specified in the Administrative Agreement, as to the regulatory program covered by the Signatory Party Agency's approval and include the determination and any associated conditions of approval within the permit or other approval instrument that it issues to the project sponsor. If in accordance with the applicable Administrative Agreement the determination under Section 3.8 of the Compact is made by the Commission, the Signatory Party Agency may include the determination together with any associated conditions of approval in its permit or other approval instrument covering the project.

(5) The Commission will maintain on its Web site a list of all projects being administered pursuant to the Program.

(e) *Comprehensive Plan projects.* Articles 11 and 13 of the Compact require certain projects to be included in the Comprehensive Plan. To add a project not yet included in the Comprehensive Plan, the project sponsor shall submit a separate application to the Commission. If following its review and public hearing the Commission approves the addition of the project to the Comprehensive Plan, the Commission's approval will include such project requirements as are necessary under the Compact and Commission regulations. All other project approvals that may be required from the Signatory Party Agency or the Commission under regulatory programs administered pursuant to this section may be issued through the One Permit Program. An application for renewal or modification of a project in the Comprehensive Plan that does not change the project so substantially as to render it a new and different project may be submitted only to the Signatory Party Agency unless otherwise specified in the Administrative Agreement.

(f) *Retention of Commission review and enforcement authorities.* Notwithstanding any other provision of this section, any Commissioner or the Executive Director may designate for Commission review any project that is reviewable under the Compact. Nothing in this section shall limit the authority of the Commission to exercise its review authority under the Compact and applicable Commission regulations. Similarly, although Administrative Agreements executed pursuant to this section may include collaborative and cooperative compliance and enforcement procedures, nothing in this section shall limit the authority of the Commission to exercise its enforcement authority under the Compact and applicable regulations.

(g) *Exhaustion of Signatory Party administrative remedies prerequisite to appeal.* Before commencing an action in a court of appropriate jurisdiction challenging any final action taken by a Signatory Party Agency under this section, the appellant must first exhaust its administrative remedies under the law of the Signatory Party whose agency issued the decision at issue.

(h) *Fees.* The Commission shall establish and maintain a schedule of fees for any or all of the services it renders pursuant to this section. The applicable fee(s) for Commission services rendered pursuant to this section shall be those set forth in DRBC Resolution No. 2009-2 (available at *http://www.nj.gov/drbc/library/documents/Res2009-2.pdf*) for the review and renewal of project approvals. Project sponsors shall pay such fees, if any, directly to the Commission in accordance with the current schedule and applicable rules.

(i) *Effect of One Permit Program on Commission dockets.* (1) Unless the Executive Director or Commission otherwise directs, if a docket holder submits, or has submitted, a timely application to a Signatory Party Agency for a project subject to review under an Administrative Agreement duly adopted under paragraph (d) of this section, the most recent docket for the project shall, upon expiration, be deemed administratively continued until final action is taken in accordance with paragraph (i)(2) of this section.

(2) Unless the Executive Director or Commission otherwise directs, upon a Signatory Party Agency's final action on an application for a project subject to the One Permit Program:

(i) Any existing or administratively continued docket for such project shall terminate as to all of its provisions and conditions that pertain to regulatory programs administered by the Signatory Party Agency under the Administrative Agreement ("the Covered Programs"); and

(ii) The docket shall continue in effect as to any provisions and conditions not pertaining only to Covered Programs, including, as applicable, the incorporation of the project in the Commission's Comprehensive Plan.

(j) *Modification of rules of practice and procedure to conform to this section.* Any project subject to review under an Administrative Agreement duly adopted under paragraph (d) of this section, shall be governed by this section and not §§ 401.4, 401.5, 401.6, 401.8, 401.34(a), (c) and (e), 401.37, 401.38 and 18 CFR part 401, subpart F, where they are inconsistent with the procedures provided in this section.

(k) *No interference with Supreme Court decree.* In accordance with Sections 3.3(a) and 3.5 of the Compact, nothing in this section shall grant the authority to any Signatory Party Agency to impair, diminish or otherwise adversely affect the diversions, compensating releases, rights, conditions, obligations and provisions for administration thereof provided in the United

States Supreme Court decree in *New Jersey* v. *New York*, 347 U.S. 995 (1954) ("Decree"). Any such action shall be taken only by the Commission with the unanimous consent of the parties to the Decree or upon unanimous consent of the members of the Commission following a declaration of a state of emergency in accordance with Section 3.3(a) of the Compact.

[81 FR 5587, Feb. 3, 2016]

§ 401.43 Regulatory program fees.

(a) *Purpose.* The purpose of this section is to provide an adequate, stable and reliable stream of revenue to cover the cost of the Commission's regulatory program activities, an important means by which the Commission coordinates management of the shared water resources of the Basin. Activities to be covered by the fees include the review of applications for projects that are subject to review under the Delaware River Basin Compact and implementing regulations; and ongoing activities associated with such projects, including but not limited to, effluent and ambient monitoring, data analysis, hydrodynamic and water quality modeling, and coordination with state and federal agencies.

(b) *Types of fees.* The following types of fees are established by this section:

(1) *Docket application fee.* Except as set forth in paragraph (b)(1)(iii) of this section, the docket application fee shall apply to:

(i) *Project requiring a DRBC-issued docket or permit.* Any project that, in accordance with the Delaware River Basin Compact and DRBC regulations, requires a Commission-issued docket or permit, whether it be a new or existing project for which the Commission has not yet issued an approval or a project for which the renewal of a previous Commission approval is required.

(ii) *Project requiring inclusion in the comprehensive plan.* Any project that in accordance with section 11 or section 13.1 of the *Delaware River Basin Compact* and DRBC regulations must be added to the Comprehensive Plan (also, "Plan"). In addition to any new project required to be included in the Plan, such projects include existing projects that in accordance with section 13.1 of the *Compact* are required to be included

in the Plan and which were not previously added to the Plan. Any existing project that is changed substantially from the project as described in the Plan shall be deemed to be a new and different project for purposes of this section.

(iii) *Exemptions.* The docket application fee shall not apply to:

(A) Any project for which the Signatory Party Agency serves as lead under the One Permit Program rule (§ 401.42), unless such project must be added by the Commission to the Comprehensive Plan.

(B) Any project for which an agency, authority or commission of a signatory to the Compact is the primary sponsor. Projects sponsored by political subdivisions of the signatory states shall not be included in this exemption. For purposes of this section "political subdivisions" shall include without limitation municipalities, municipal utility authorities, municipal development corporations, and all other entities not directly under the budgetary and administrative control of the Commission's members.

(2) *Annual monitoring and coordination fee.* (i) Except as provided in paragraph (b)(2)(ii) of this section, an annual monitoring and coordination fee shall apply to each active water allocation or wastewater discharge approval issued pursuant to the *Compact* and implementing regulations, regardless of whether the approval was issued by the Commission in the form of a docket, permit or other instrument, or by a Signatory Party Agency under the One Permit Program rule (§ 401.42). The fee shall be based on the amount of a project's approved monthly water allocation and/or approved daily discharge capacity.

(ii) For any withdrawal or diversion covered in part by a certificate of entitlement issued pursuant to §§ 420.31 and 420.32 of the water supply charges regulations (18 CFR part 420), the annual monitoring and coordination fee shall be based on the allocated amount, if any, in excess of the quantity specified in the entitlement.

(3) *Alternative review fee.* In instances where the Commission's activities and related costs associated with the review of an existing or proposed project

are expected to involve extraordinary time and expense, an alternative review fee equal to the Commission's actual costs may be imposed. The Executive Director shall inform the project sponsor in writing when the alternative review fee is to be applied and may require advance payment in the amount of the Commission's projected costs. Instances in which the alternative review fee may apply include, but are not limited to, matters in which:

(i) DRBC staff perform a detailed pre-application review, including but not limited to the performance or review of modeling and/or analysis to identify target limits for wastewater discharges.

(ii) DRBC staff perform or review complex modeling in connection with the design of a wastewater discharge diffuser system.

(iii) DRBC manages a public process for which the degree of public involvement results in extraordinary effort and expense, including but not limited to, costs associated with multiple stakeholder meetings, special public hearings, and/or voluminous public comment.

(iv) DRBC conducts or is required to engage third parties to conduct additional analyses or evaluations of a project in response to a court order.

(4) *Additional fees*—(i) *Emergency approval.* A request for an emergency certificate under § 401.40 to waive or amend a docket condition shall be subject to a minimum fee in accordance with paragraph (e) of this section. An alternative review fee also may be charged in accordance with paragraph (b)(3) of this section.

(ii) *Late filed renewal application.* Any renewal application submitted fewer than 120 calendar days in advance of the expiration date or after such other date specified in the docket or permit or letter of the Executive Director for filing a renewal application shall be subject to a late filed renewal application charge in excess of the otherwise applicable fee.

(iii) *Modification of a DRBC approval.* Following Commission action on a project, each project revision or modification that the Executive Director deems substantial shall require an additional docket application fee calculated in accordance with paragraph (e) of this section and subject to an alternative review fee in accordance with paragraph (b)(3) of this section.

(iv) *Name change.* Each project with a docket or permit issued by the DRBC or by a Signatory Party Agency pursuant to the One Permit Program rule (§ 401.42) will be charged an administrative fee as set forth in paragraph (e) of this section.

(v) *Change of ownership.* Each project that undergoes a "change in ownership" as that term is defined at 18 CFR 420.31(e)(2) will be charged an administrative fee as set forth in paragraph (e) of this section.

(c) *Indexed adjustment.* On July 1 of every year, beginning July 1, 2017, all fees established by this section will increase commensurate with any increase in the annual April 12-month Consumer Price Index (CPI) for Philadelphia, published by the U.S. Bureau of Labor Statistics during that year.[1] In any year in which the April 12-month CPI for Philadelphia declines or shows no change, the docket application fee and annual monitoring and coordination fee will remain unchanged. Following any indexed adjustment made under this paragraph (c), a revised fee schedule will be published in the FEDERAL REGISTER by July 1 and posted on the Commission's Web site. Interested parties may also obtain the fee schedule by contacting the Commission directly during business hours.

(d) *Late payment charge.* When any fee established by this section remains unpaid 30 calendar days after the payment due date provided on the Commission's invoice, an incremental charge equal to 2% of the amount owed shall be automatically assessed. Such charge shall be assessed every 30 days thereafter until the total amount owed, including any late payment charges has been paid in full.

[1] Consumer Price Index –U/Series ID: CUURA102SA0/Not Seasonally Adjusted/ Area: Philadelphia-Wilmington-Atlantic City, PA–NJ–DE–MD/Item: All items/Base Period 1982–84=100.

(e) *Fee schedules.* The fees described in this section shall be as follows:

TABLE 1 TO § 401.43—DOCKET APPLICATION FILING FEE

Project type	Docket application fee	Fee maximum
Water Allocation	$405 per million gallons/month of allocation,[1] not to exceed $15,190.[1] Fee is doubled for any portion to be exported from the basin.	Greater of: $15,190[1] or Alternative Review Fee.
Wastewater Discharge	Private projects: $1,013[1] .... Public projects: $506[1]	Alternative Review Fee.
Other	0.4% of project cost up to $10,000,000 plus 0.12% of project cost above $10,000,000 (if applicable), not to exceed $75,951[1].	Greater of: $75,951[1] or Alternative Review Fee.

[1] Subject to annual adjustment in accordance with paragraph (c) of this section.

TABLE 2 TO § 401.43—ANNUAL MONITORING AND COORDINATION FEE

	Annual fee	Allocation
Water Allocation	[1] $304	<4.99 mgm.
	[1] 456	5.00 to 49.99 mgm.
	[1] 658	50.00 to 499.99 mgm.
	[1] 835	500.00 to 9,999.99 mgm.
	[1] 1,013	>or = to 10,000 mgm.

	Annual fee	Discharge design capacity
Wastewater Discharge	[1] $304	<0.05 mgd.
	[1] 618	0.05 to 1 mgd.
	[1] 830	1 to 10 mgd.
	[1] 1,013	>10 mgd.

[1] Subject to annual adjustment in accordance with paragraph (c) of this section.

TABLE 3 TO § 401.43—ADDITIONAL FEES

Proposed action	Fee	Fee maximum
Emergency Approval Under 18 CFR 401.40.	$5,000	Alternative Review Fee.
Late Filed Renewal Surcharge	$2,000.	
Modification of a DRBC Approval	At Executive Director's discretion, Docket Application Fee for the appropriate project type.	Alternative Review Fee.
Name change	$1,013[1].	
Change of Ownership	$1,519[1].	

[1] Subject to annual adjustment in accordance with paragraph (c) of this section.

[81 FR 95861, Dec. 29, 2016, as amended at 82 FR 7647, Jan. 23, 2017; 82 FR 26989, June 13, 2017]

Subpart D [Reserved]

Subpart E—Appeals or Objections to Decisions of the Executive Director in Water Quality Cases

SOURCE: 62 FR 64158, Dec. 4, 1997, unless otherwise noted.

§ 401.71 Scope.

This subpart shall apply to the review, hearing and decision of objections and issues arising as a result of administrative actions and decisions taken or rendered by the Executive Director under the Compact and the regulations in this chapter. Any hearings shall be conducted pursuant to the provisions of subpart F of this part.

§ 401.72 Notice and request for hearing.

The Executive Director shall serve notice of an action or decision by him under the regulations in this chapter by personal service or certified mail, return receipt requested. The affected discharger shall be entitled (and the notice of action or decision shall so state) to show cause at a Commission hearing why such action or decision should not take effect. A request for such a hearing shall be filed with the Secretary of the Commission not more than 30 days after service of the Executive Director's determination. Failure to file such a request within the time limit shall be deemed to be an acceptance of the Executive Director's determination and a waiver of any further hearing.

[62 FR 64158, Dec. 4, 1997, as amended at 63 FR 45943, Aug. 28, 1998]

§ 401.73 Form of request.

(a) A request for a hearing may be informal but shall indicate the name of the individual and the address to which an acknowledgment may be directed. It may be stated in such detail as the objector may elect. The request shall be deemed filed only upon receipt by the Commission.

(b) Whenever the Executive Director determines that the request for a hearing is insufficient to identify the nature and scope of the objection, or that one or more issues may be resolved, reduced or identified by such action, he may require the objector to prepare and submit to the Commission, within such reasonable time (not less than 30 days) as he may specify, a technical report of the facts relating to the objection prior to the scheduling of the hearing. The report shall be required by notice in writing served upon the objector by certified mail, return receipt requested, addressed to the person or entity filing the request for hearing at the place indicated in the request.

§ 401.74 Form and contents of report.

(a) *Generally.* A request for a report under this subpart may require such information and the answers to such questions as may be reasonably pertinent to the subject of the action or determination under consideration.

(b) *Waste loading.* In cases involving objections to an allocation of the assimilative capacity of a stream, wasteload allocation for a point source, or load allocation for a new point source, the report shall be signed and verified by a technically qualified person having personal knowledge of the facts stated therein, and shall include such of the following items as the Executive Director may require:

(1) A specification with particularity of the ground or grounds for the objection; and failure to specify a ground for objection prior to the hearing shall foreclose the objector from thereafter asserting such a ground at the hearing;

(2) A description of industrial processing and waste treatment operational characteristics and outfall configuration in such detail as to permit an evaluation of the character, kind and quantity of the discharges, both treated and untreated, including the physical, chemical and biological properties of any liquid, gaseous, solid, radioactive, or other substance composing the discharge in whole or in part;

(3) The thermal characteristics of the discharges and the level of heat in flow;

(4) Information in sufficient detail to permit evaluation in depth of any in-plant control or recovery process for which credit is claimed;

(5) The chemical and toxicological characteristics including the processes and/or indirect discharges which may be the source of the chemicals or toxicity;

(6) An analysis of all the parameters that may have an effect on the strength of the waste or impinge upon the water quality criteria set forth in the regulations in this chapter, including a determination of the rate of biochemical oxygen demand and the projection of a first-stage carbonaceous oxygen demand;

(7) Measurements of the waste as closely as possible to the processes where the wastes are produced, with the sample composited either continually or at frequent intervals (one-half hour or, where permitted by the Executive Director, one hour periods), so as to represent adequately the strength and volume of waste that is discharged; and

(8) Such other and additional specific technical data as the Executive Director may reasonably consider necessary and useful for the proper determination of a wasteload allocation.

[62 FR 64158, Dec. 4, 1997, as amended at 63 FR 45943, Aug. 28, 1998]

§401.75 Protection of trade secrets; Confidential information.

No person shall be required in such report to divulge trade secrets or secret processes. All information disclosed to any Commissioner, agent or employee of the Commission in any report required by this part shall be confidential for the purposes of Section 1905 of Title 18 of the United States Code which provides:

Whoever, being an officer or employee of the United States or of any department or agency thereof, publishes, divulges, discloses, or makes known in any manner or to any extent not authorized by law any information coming to him in the course of his employment or official duties or by reason of any examination or investigation made by, or return, report or record made to or filed with, such department or agency or officer or employee thereof, which information concerns or relates to the trade secrets, processes, operations, style of work, or apparatus, or to the identity, confidential statistical data, amount or source of any income, profits, losses, or expenditures of any person, firm, partnership, corporation or association; or permits any income return or copy thereof to be seen or examined by any persons except as provided by law; shall be fined not more than $1,000 or imprisoned not more than one year, or both; and shall be removed from office or employment. June 25, 1948, C.645, 62 Stat. 791.

§401.76 Failure to furnish report.

The Executive Director may, upon five days' notice to the objector dismiss the request for a hearing as to any objector who fails to file a complete report within such time as shall be prescribed in the Director's notice.

§401.77 Informal conference.

Whenever the Executive Director deems it appropriate, he may cause an informal conference to be scheduled between an objector and such member of the Commission staff as he may designate. The purpose of such a conference shall be to resolve or narrow the ground or grounds of the objections.

§401.78 Consolidation of hearings.

Following such informal conferences as may be held, to the extent that the same or similar grounds for objections are raised by one or more objectors, the Executive Director may in his discretion and with the consent of the objectors, cause a consolidated hearing to be scheduled at which two or more objectors asserting that ground may be heard.

Subpart F—Administrative and Other Hearings

Source: 62 FR 64159, Dec. 4, 1997, unless otherwise noted.

§401.81 Hearings generally.

(a) *Scope of subpart.* This subpart shall apply to contested cases required to be held under subparts C and E of this part, to the conduct of other administrative hearings involving contested cases and to proceedings which Commission regulation or the Commission directs be conducted pursuant to this subpart.

(b) *Definition of contested case.* "Contested case" means a proceeding in which the legal rights, duties, obligations, privileges, benefits or other legal relations of specific parties are involved. Such a proceeding may involve personnel matters, project applications and docket decisions but shall not extend to the review of any proposed or adopted rule or regulation of the Commission.

(c) *Requests for hearings.* Any person seeking a hearing to review the action or decision of the Commission or the Executive Director may request a hearing pursuant to the provisions of this subpart provided such a request is received by the Commission within thirty (30) days of the action or decision which is the subject of the requested hearing. Requests shall be submitted in writing to the Secretary of the Commission and shall identify the specific action or decision for which a hearing is requested, the date of the action or decision, the interest of the person requesting the hearing in the subject matter of the proposed hearing and a summary statement setting forth the basis for objecting to or seeking review of the action or decision. Any request filed more than thirty days after an action or decision will be deemed untimely and such request for a hearing shall be considered denied unless the Commission by unanimous vote otherwise directs. Receipt of requests for hearings, pursuant to this subpart, whether timely filed or not, shall be submitted by the Secretary to the Commissioners for their information.

(d) *Optional joint hearings.* Whenever designated by a department, agency or instrumentality of a signatory party, and within any limitations prescribed by the designation, a Hearing Officer designated pursuant to this subpart may also serve as a Hearing Officer, examiner or agent pursuant to such additional designation and may conduct joint hearings for the Commission and for such other department, agency or instrumentality. Pursuant to the additional designation, a Hearing Officer shall cause to be filed with the department, agency or instrumentality making the designation, a certified copy of the transcript of the evidence taken before him and, if requested, of his findings and recommendations. Neither the Hearing Officer nor the Delaware River Basin Commission shall have or exercise any power or duty as a result of such additional designation to decide the merits of any matter arising under the separate laws of a signatory party (other than the Delaware River Basin Compact).

(e) *Schedule.* The Executive Director shall cause the schedule for each hearing to be listed in advance upon a "hearing docket" which shall be posted in public view at the office of the Commission.

(f) *Notice of hearing.* Notice of any hearing to be conducted pursuant to this subpart shall comply with the provisions of Section 14.4(b) of the Compact relating to public notice unless otherwise directed by the Commission.

§ 401.82 Authorization to conduct hearings.

(a) *Written requests for hearings.* Upon receipt of a written request for a hearing pursuant to this subpart, the Executive Director shall review the record available with regard to the action or decision for which a hearing is requested. Thereafter, the Executive Director shall present the request for a hearing to the Commission for its consideration. The Commission shall grant a request for a hearing pursuant to this subpart if it determines that an adequate record with regard to the action

or decision is not available, the contested case involves a determination by the Executive Director or staff which requires further action by the Commission or that the Commission has found that an administrative hearing is necessary or desirable. If the Commission denies any request for a hearing in a contested case, the party seeking such a hearing shall be limited to such remedies as may be provided by the Compact or other applicable law or court rule.

(b) *Commission directed hearings.* This subpart shall be applicable to any proceeding which Commission regulation or the Commission directs be conducted in accordance with the provisions, of this subpart.

§ 401.83 Hearing Officer.

(a) *Generally.* Hearings shall be conducted by one or more members of the Commission, by the Executive Director, or by such other Hearing Officer as the Chairman may designate, except as provided in paragraph (b) of this section.

(b) *Wasteload allocation cases.* In cases involving the allocation of the assimilative capacity of a stream:

(1) The Executive Director shall appoint a hearing board of at least two persons. One of them shall be nominated by the water pollution control agency of the state in which the discharge originates, and he shall be chairman. The board shall have and exercise the powers and duties of a Hearing Officer;

(2) A quorum of the board for purposes of the hearing shall consist of two members; and

(3) Questions of practice or procedure during the hearing shall be determined by the Chairman.

§ 401.84 Hearing procedure.

(a) *Participation in the hearing.* In any hearing, the person requesting the hearing shall be deemed an interested party and shall be entitled to participate fully in the hearing procedure. In addition, any person whose legal rights may be affected by the decision rendered in a contested case shall be deemed an interested party. Interested parties shall have the right to be represented by counsel, to present evidence and to examine and cross-examine witnesses. In addition to interested parties, any persons having information concerning a contested case or desiring to present comments concerning the subject matter of the Hearing for inclusion in the record may submit a written statement to the Commission. Any interested party may request the right to examine or cross-examine any person who submits a written statement. In the absence of a request for examination of such person, all written statements submitted shall be included within the record and such statements may be relied upon to the extent determined by the Hearing Officer or the Commission.

(b) *Powers of the Hearing Officer.* The Hearing Officer shall:

(1) Rule upon offers of proof and the admissibility of evidence, regulate the course of the hearings, hold conferences for the settlement or simplification of procedures or issues, and shall schedule submission of documents, briefs and the time for the hearing.

(2) Cause each witness to be sworn or to make affirmation.

(3) Limit the number of times any witness may testify, limit repetitious examination or cross-examination of witnesses or the extent to which corroborative or cumulative testimony shall be accepted.

(4) Exclude irrelevant, immaterial or unduly repetitious evidence, but the interested parties shall not be bound by technical rules of evidence and all relevant evidence of reasonably probative value may be received.

(5) Require briefs and oral arguments to the extent determined necessary which shall be included as part of the record unless otherwise ordered by the Hearing Officer.

§ 401.85 Staff and other expert testimony.

(a) *Presentation on behalf of the Commission.* The Executive Director shall arrange for the presentation of testimony by the Commission's technical staff and other experts, as he may deem necessary or desirable, to incorporate in the record or support the ad-

ministrative action, determination or decision which is the subject of the hearing.

(b) *Expert witnesses.* An interested party may submit in writing to the Hearing Officer the report and proposed testimony of an expert witness. No expert report or proposed testimony, however, shall be included in the record if the expert is not available for examination unless the report and proposed testimony shall have been provided to the Commission and all interested parties prior to the hearing and the Commission and interested parties have waived the right of cross-examination.

(c) The Executive Director may designate for inclusion in the record those records of the Commission which the Executive Director deems relevant to a decision in a contested case or to provide an understanding of applicable Commission policies, regulations or other requirements relating to the issues in the contested case. The designation of such Commission documents shall be provided to all interested parties prior to the hearing.

§ 401.86 Record of proceedings.

A record of the proceedings and evidence at each hearing shall be made by a qualified stenographer designated by the Executive Director. Where demanded by the applicant, objector, or any other person who is a party to these proceedings, or where deemed necessary by the Hearing Officer, the testimony shall be transcribed. In those instances where a transcript of proceedings is made, two copies shall be delivered to the Commission. The applicant, objector, or other persons who desire copies shall obtain them from the stenographer at such price as may be agreed upon by the stenographer and the person desiring the transcript.

§ 401.87 Assessment of costs; Appeals.

(a) Whenever a hearing is conducted under this subpart, the costs thereof, as defined in this subpart, shall be assessed by the Hearing Officer to the party requesting the hearing unless apportioned between the interested parties where cost sharing is deemed fair and equitable by the Hearing Officer.

For the purposes of this section costs include all incremental costs incurred by the Commission, including, but not limited to, hearing examiner and expert consultants reasonably necessary in the matter, stenographic record, rental of a hearing room and other related expenses.

(b) Upon scheduling of a matter for hearing, the Secretary shall furnish to the applicant and/or interested parties a reasonable estimate of the costs to be incurred under this section. The applicant and/or interested parties may be required to furnish security for such costs either by cash deposit or by a surety bond of a corporate surety authorized to do business in a signatory state.

(c) An appeal of the assessment of costs may be submitted in writing to the Commission within ten (10) days of the assessment. A copy of the appeal shall be filed with the Secretary and served on all interested parties. The filing of said appeal shall not stay the Hearing.

§ 401.88 Findings, report and Commission review.

(a) The Hearing Officer shall prepare a report of his findings and recommendations. In the case of an objection to a waste load allocation, the Hearing Officer shall make specific findings of a recommended allocation which may increase, reduce or confirm the Executive Director's determination. The report shall be served by personal service or certified mail (return receipt requested) upon each party to the hearing or its counsel unless all parties have waived service of the report. The applicant and any objector may file objections to the report within 20 days after the service upon him of a copy of the report. A brief shall be filed together with any objections. The report of the Hearing Officer together with objections and briefs shall be promptly submitted to the Commission. The Commission may require or permit oral argument upon such submission prior to its decision.

(b) The Executive Director, in addition to any submission to the Hearing Officer, may also submit to the Commission staff comments upon, or a response to, the Hearing Officer's findings and report and, where appropriate, a draft docket or other recommended Commission action. Interested parties shall be served with a copy of such submission and may have not less than ten (10) days to respond before action by the Commission.

§ 401.89 Action by the Commission.

(a) The Commission will act upon the findings and recommendations of the Hearing Officer pursuant to law.

(b) Commission Counsel shall assist the Commission with its review of the hearing record and the preparation of a Commission decision to the extent directed to do so by the Chairman.

(c) The determination of the Commission will be in writing and shall be filed together with any transcript of the hearing, report of the Hearing Officer, objections thereto, and all plans, maps, exhibits and other papers, records or documents relating to the hearing. All such records, papers and documents may be examined by any person at the office of the Commission, and shall not be removed therefrom except temporarily upon the written order of the Secretary after the filing of a receipt therefor in form prescribed by the Secretary. Copies of any such records and papers may be made in the office of the Commission by any person, subject to such reasonable safeguards for the protection of the records as the Executive Director may require.

§ 401.90 Appeals from final Commission action; Time for appeals.

Any party participating in a hearing conducted pursuant to the provisions of this subpart may appeal any final Commission action. To be timely, such an appeal must be filed with an appropriate federal court, as provided in Article 15.1(p) of the Commission's Compact, within forty-five (45) days of final Commission action.

Subpart G—Penalties and Settlements in Lieu of Penalties

SOURCE: 52 FR 37602, Oct. 8, 1987, unless otherwise noted.

§401.91 Scope of subpart.

This subpart shall be applicable where the Commission shall have information indicating that a person has violated or attempted to violate any provision of the Commission's Compact or any of its rules, regulations or orders (hereafter referred to as possible violator). For the purposes of this subpart, person shall include person, partnership, corporation, business association, governmental agency or authority.

§401.92 Notice to possible violators.

Upon direction of the Commission the Executive Director shall, and in all other instances, the Executive Director may require a possible violator to show cause before the Commission why a penalty should not be assessed in accordance with the provisions of these rules and section 14.17 of the Compact. The notice to the possible violator shall:

(a) Set forth the date on which the possible violator shall respond; and

(b) Set forth any information to be submitted or produced by the possible violator.

§401.93 The record for decision-making.

(a) *Written submission.* In addition to the information required by the Commission, any possible violator shall be entitled to submit in writing any other information that it desires to make available to the Commission before it shall act. The Executive Director may require documents to be certified or otherwise authenticated and statements to be verified. The Commission may also receive written submissions from any other persons as to whether a violation has occurred and the adverse consequences resulting from a violation of the Commission's Compact or its rules, regulations and orders.

(b) *Presentation to the Commission.* At the date set in the Notice, the possible violator shall have the opportunity to supplement its written presentation before the Commission by any oral statement it wishes to present and shall be prepared to respond to any questions from the Commission or its staff or to the statements submitted by persons affected by the possible violation.

§401.94 Adjudicatory hearings.

(a) An adjudicatory hearing, which may be in lieu of or in addition to proceedings pursuant to §401.93 at which testimony may be presented and documents received shall not be scheduled unless:

(1) The Executive Director determines that a hearing is required to have an adequate record for the Commission; or

(2) The Commission directs that such a hearing be held.

(b) If an adjudicatory hearing is scheduled, the possible violator shall be given at least 14 days written notice of the hearing date unless waived by consent. Notice of such a hearing may be given to the general public and the press in the manner provided in section 14.4(b) of the Compact but may be waived by the Executive Director.

(c) Except to the extent inconsistent with the provisions of this subpart adjudicatory hearings shall be conducted in accordance with the provisions of §§491.83 through 401.88 (including §401.86 *et seq.*).

§401.95 Assessment of a penalty.

The Executive Director may recommend to the Commission the amount of the penalty to be imposed. Such a recommendation shall be in writing and shall set forth the basis for the penalty amount proposed. Based upon the record submitted to the Commission, the Commission shall decide whether a violation has occurred that justifies the imposition of a penalty pursuant to §14.17 of the Compact. If it is found that such a violation has occurred, the Commission shall determine the amount of the penalty to be paid.

§401.96 Factors to be applied in fixing penalty amount.

(a) Consideration shall be given to the following factors in deciding the amount of any penalty or any settlement in lieu of penalty:

(1) Previous violation, if any, of the Commission's Compact and regulations;

(2) Whether the violation was unintentional or willful and deliberate;

(3) Whether the violation caused adverse environmental consequences and the extent of any harm;

(4) The costs incurred by the Commission or any signatory party relating to the failure to comply with the Commission's Compact and regulations;

(5) The extent to which the violator has cooperated with the Commission in correcting the violation and remediating any adverse consequences or harm that resulted therefrom; and

(6) Whether the failure to comply with the Commission's Compact and regulations was economically beneficial to the violator.

(b) The Commission retains the right to waive any penalty or reduce the amount of the penalty should it determine that, after consideration of the factors in paragraph (a) of this section, extenuating circumstances justify such action.

§ 401.97 Enforcement of penalties.

Any penalty imposed by the Commission shall be paid within 30 days or such further time period as shall be fixed by the Commission. The Executive Director and Commission counsel are authorized to take such action as may be necessary to assure enforcement of this subpart. If a proceeding before a court becomes necessary, the action of the Commission in determining a penalty amount shall constitute the penalty amount recommended by the Commission to be fixed by the court pursuant to § 14.17 of the Compact.

§ 401.98 Settlement by agreement in lieu of penalty.

A possible violator may request settlement of a penalty proceeding by agreement. If the Executive Director determines that settlement by agreement in lieu of a penalty is in the best interest of the Commission, he may submit to the Commission a proposed settlement agreement in lieu of a penalty. No settlement will be considered by the Commission unless the possible violator has indicated to the Commission acceptance of the terms of the agreement and the intention to comply with all requirements of the settlement agreement including payment of any settlement amount within the time period provided. If the Commission determines not to approve a settlement agreement, the Commission may proceed with a penalty action in accordance with this subpart.

§ 401.99 Suspension or modification of penalty.

The Commission may postpone the imposition of a penalty or provide for reconsideration of the penalty amount imposed pending correction of the condition that gave rise to the violation or pending a satisfactory resolution of any adverse consequences that resulted from the violation.

Subpart H—Public Access to Records and Information

AUTHORITY: 5 U.S.C. 552.

SOURCE: 40 FR 14056, Mar. 28, 1975; 40 FR 17987, Apr. 24, 1975, unless otherwise noted. Redesignated at 52 FR 37602, Oct. 8, 1987.

§ 401.101 Policy on disclosure of Commission records.

The Commission will make the fullest possible disclosure of records to the public, consistent with the rights of individuals to privacy, the property rights of persons in trade secrets and confidential commercial or financial information, and the need for the Commission to promote frank internal policy deliberations and to pursue its regulatory activities without disruption.

§ 401.102 Partial disclosure of records.

If a record contains both disclosable and nondisclosable information, the nondisclosable information will be deleted and the remaining record will be disclosed unless the two are so inextricably intertwined that it is not feasible to separate them or release of the disclosable information would compromise or impinge upon the nondisclosable portion of the record.

§ 401.103 Request for existing records.

(a) Any written request to the Commission for existing records not prepared for routine distribution to the public shall be deemed to be a request for records pursuant to the Freedom of Information Act, whether or not the Freedom of Information Act is mentioned in the request, and shall be governed by the provisions of this part.

(b) Records or documents prepared by the Commission for routine public distribution, e.g., pamphlets, speeches, public information and educational materials, shall be furnished free of charge upon request as long as the supply lasts. The provisions of this part shall not be applicable to such requests.

(c) All existing Commission records are subject to routine destruction according to standard record retention schedules.

§ 401.104 Preparation of new records.

The Freedom of Information Act and the provisions of this part apply only to existing records that are reasonably described in a request filed with the Commission pursuant to the procedures herein established. The Commission shall not be required to prepare new records in order to respond to a request for information.

§ 401.105 Indexes of certain records.

(a) Indexes shall be maintained, and revised at least quarterly, for the following Commission records:

(1) Final opinions and orders made in the adjudication of cases.

(2) Statements of policy and interpretation adopted by the Commission and still in force and not published in the FEDERAL REGISTER or official minutes of Commission meetings.

(3) Administrative staff manuals and instructions to staff that affect members of the public.

(b) A copy of each such index is available at cost of duplication from the FOIA Officer.

§ 401.106 FOIA Officer.

The Executive Director shall designate a Commission employee as the FOIA Officer. The FOIA Officer shall be responsible for Commission compliance with the Freedom of Information Act and these regulations. All requests for agency records shall be sent in writing to:

FOIA Officer
Delaware River Basin Commission

P.O. Box 7360
West Trenton, NJ 08628–0360

[40 FR 14056, Mar. 28, 1975; 40 FR 17987, Apr. 24, 1975. Redesignated at 52 FR 37602, Oct. 8, 1987, as amended at 63 FR 45943, Aug. 28, 1998]

§ 401.107 Permanent file of requests for Commission records.

The Commission shall maintain a permanent file of all requests for Commission records and all responses thereto, incuding a list of all records furnished in response to a request. This file is available for public review during working hours.

§ 401.108 Filing a request for records.

(a) All requests for Commission records shall be filed in writing delivered to the FOIA Officer, or by mailing it to the Commission. The Commission will supply forms for written requests.

(b) A request for Commission records shall reasonably describe the records being sought, in a way that they can be identified and located. A request should include all pertinent details that will help identify the records sought. A person requesting disclosure of records shall be permitted an opportunity to review them without the necessity for copying them where the records involved contain only disclosable data and information.

(1) If the description is insufficient to locate the records requested, the FOIA Officer will so notify the person making the request and indicate the additional information needed to identify the records requested.

(2) Every reasonable effort shall be made by the staff to assist in the identification and location of the records sought.

(3) In any situation in which it is determined that a request for voluminous records would unduly burden and interfere with the operations of the Commission, the person making the request will be asked to be more specific and to narrow the request, and to agree on an orderly procedure for the production of the requested records.

(c) Upon receipt of a request for records, the FOIA Officer shall enter it in a public log (which entry may consist of a copy of the request). The log shall state the date and time received, the name and address of the person making the request, the nature of the records requested, the action taken on the request, the date of the determination letter sent pursuant to § 401.99(b), the date(s) any records are subsequently furnished, the number of staff-hours and grade levels of persons who spent time responding to the request, and the payment requested and received.

(d) A denial of a request for records, in whole or in part, shall be signed by the FOIA Officer. The name and title or position of each person who participated in the denial of a request for records shall be set forth in a letter denying the request. This requirement may be met by attaching a list of such individuals to the letter.

§ 401.109 Time limitations.

(a) All time limitations established pursuant to this section shall begin as of the time at which a request for records is logged in by the FOIA Officer pursuant to § 401.98(c). An oral request for records shall not begin any time requirement. A written request for records sent elsewhere within the Commission shall not begin any time requirement until it is redirected to the FOIA Officer and is logged in accordance with § 401.98(c). A request that is expected to involve fees in excess of $50 will not be deemed received until the requester is promptly notified and agrees to bear the cost or has so indicated on his request.

(b) Within ten (10) working days (excepting Saturdays, Sundays, and legal public holidays) after a request for records is logged by the FOIA Officer, the record shall be furnished or a letter shall be sent to the person making the request determining whether, or the extent to which, the Commission will comply with the request, and, if any records are denied, the reasons therefor.

(1) If all of the records requested have been located and a final determination has been made with respect to disclosure of all of the records requested, the letter shall so state.

(2) If all of the records have not been located or a final determination has not yet been made with respect to disclosure of all of the records requested, the letter shall state the extent to which the records involved shall be disclosed pursuant to the rules established in this part.

(3) In the following unusual circumstances, the time for sending this letter may be extended by the Executive Director for up to an additional ten (10) working days by written notice to the person making the request setting forth the reasons for such extension and the time within which a determination is expected to be dispatched:

(i) The need to search for and collect the requested records from field facilities or other establishments that are separate from the Commission's Headquarters.

(ii) The need to search for, collect and appropriately examine a voluminous amount of separate and distinct records which are demanded in a single request.

(iii) The need for consultation, which shall be conducted with all practicable speed, with another agency having a substantial interest in the determination of the request or among two or more components of the Commission having substantial subject-matter interest therein.

(c) If any record is denied, the letter shall state the right of the person requesting such records to appeal any adverse determination to the Executive Director of the Commission. Such an appeal shall be filed within thirty (30) days from receipt of the FOIA Officer's determination denying the requested information (where the entire request has been denied), or from the receipt of any information made available pursuant to the request (where the request has been denied in part). Within twenty (20) working days (excepting Saturdays, Sundays, and legal public holidays) after receipt of any appeal, or any authorized extension, the Executive Director or his designee shall make a determination and notify the appellant of his determination. If the appeal is decided in favor of the appellant the requested information shall be promptly supplied as provided in this part. If on appeal the denial of the request for records is upheld in whole or in part, the appellant shall be entitled to appeal to the Commission at its next regular meeting. In the event that the Commission confirms the Executive

Director's denial the appellant shall be notified of the provisions for judicial review.

(d) If the request for records will result in a fee of more than $25, determination letter under § 401.99 shall specify or estimate the fee involved and may require prepayment, as well as payment of any amount not yet received as a result of any previous request, before the records are made available. If the fee is less than $25, prepayment shall not be required unless payment has not yet been received for records disclosed as a result of a previous request.

(e) Whenever possible, the determination letter required under § 401.99(b), relating to a request for records that involves a fee of less than $25.00, shall be accompanied by the requested records. Where this is not possible, the records shall be forwarded as soon as possible thereafter. For requests for records involving a fee of more than $25.00, the records shall be forwarded as soon as possible after receipt of payment.

§ 401.110 Fees.

(a) Unless waived in accordance with the provisions of § 401.111, the following fees shall be imposed for production of any record pursuant to this part.

(1) *Administrative fees.* (i) Charges for administrative fees include staff time associated with:

(A) Processing FOIA requests;

(B) Locating and reviewing files;

(C) Monitoring file reviews;

(D) Generating computer records (electronic print-outs); and

(E) Preparing logs of records deemed non-public.

(ii) Administrative charges will be calculated as follows: Administrative charges will be billed to the requester per quarter hour following the first quarter hour. These charges will be billed at the current, hourly paygrade rate (pro-rated for quarter hour increments) of the personnel performing the service. Administrative charges will be in addition to any copying charges.

(iii) Appointment rescheduling/cancellation. Requesters that do not reschedule or cancel appointments to view files at least one full business day in advance of the appointment may be subject to the administrative charges

incurred by the Commission in preparing the requested records. The Commission will prepare an itemized invoice of these charges and mail it to the requester for payment.

(2) *Photocopying fees.* The following are charges for photocopies of public records made by Commission personnel:

(i) *Standard sized, black and white copies.* The charge for copying standard sized, black and white public records shall be $0.15 per printed page (*i.e.*, single-sided copies are $0.15 and double-sided copies are $0.30). This charge applies to copies on the following standard paper sizes:

(A) 8.5″ × 11″;

(B) 8.5″ × 14″;

(C) 11″ × 17″.

(ii) *Color copies/printouts.* The charge for color copies or color printouts shall be as follows:

(A) 8.5″ × 11″—$1.00 per page;

(B) 8.5″ × 14″—$1.50 per page;

(C) 11″ × 17″—$2.00 per page;

(D) The charge for all color copies larger than 11″ × 17″ (including, but not limited to: photographic imagery, GIS print-outs, and maps) shall be calculated at the rate of $2.50 per square foot.

(iii) *Electronically generated records.* Charges for copying records maintained in electronic format will be calculated by the material costs involved in generating the copies (including, but not limited to: magnetic tape, diskette, or compact disc costs) and administrative costs.

(iv) *Other copying fees.* The Commission, at its discretion, may arrange to have records copied by an outside contractor if the Commission does not have the resources or equipment to copy such records. In this instance, the requester will be liable for payment of these costs.

(3) *Forwarding material to destination.* Postage, insurance, and special fees will be charged on an actual cost basis.

(b) No charge shall be made for the time spent in resolving legal or policy issues or in examining records for the purpose of deleting nondisclosable portions thereof.

(c) Payment shall be made by check or money order payable to "Delaware

River Basin Commission'' and shall be sent to the FOIA Officer.

[40 FR 14056, Mar. 28, 1975; 40 FR 17987, Apr. 24, 1975. Redesignated at 52 FR 37602, Oct. 8, 1987, as amended at 67 FR 56753, Sept. 5, 2002]

§ 401.111 Waiver of fees.

(a) No fee shall be charged for disclosure of records pursuant to this part where:

(1) The records are requested by a congressional committee or subcommittee or the General Accounting Office.

(2) The records are requested by an agency of a signatory party.

(3) The records are requested by a court of competent jurisdiction.

(4) The records are requested by a state or local government having jurisdiction thereof.

(b) No fee shall be charged if a record requested is not found or for any record that is totally exempt from disclosure.

§ 401.112 Exempt information.

The following materials and information covered by this part shall be exempt from disclosure; that is, information that is:

(a) Related solely to the internal personnel matters of the Commission;

(b) Specifically exempted from disclosure by statute;

(c) Trade secrets and commercial or financial information obtained from a person and privileged or confidential. (For purposes of this section a trade secret may consist of any formula, pattern, device, or compilation of information which is used in one's business and which gives him an opportunity to obtain an advantage over competitors who do not know or use it. Commercial or financial information that is privileged or confidential means valuable data or information which is used in one's business and is of a type customarily held in strict confidence or regarded as privileged and not disclosed to any member of the public by the person to whom it belongs.)

(d) Inter-agency or intra-agency memorandums or letters other than purely factual compilations, which would not be available by law to a party other than an agency in litigation with the Commission;

(e) Personnel and medical files and similar files the disclosure of which would constitute a clearly unwarranted invasion of personal privacy; and

(f) Investigatory records compiled for law enforcement purposes, but only to the extent that the production of such records would (1) interfere with enforcement proceedings, (2) deprive a person of a right to a fair trial or an impartial adjudication, (3) constitute an unwarranted invasion of personal privacy, (4) disclose the identity of a confidential source, (5) disclose investigative techniques and procedures, or (6) endanger the life or physical safety of law enforcement personnel.

[40 FR 14056, Mar. 28, 1975; 40 FR 17987, Apr. 24, 1975. Redesignated at 52 FR 37602, Oct. 8, 1987, as amended at 63 FR 45943, Aug. 28, 1998]

§ 401.113 Segregable materials.

Any reasonably segregable portion of a record shall be provided to any person requesting such record after deletion of the portions which are exempt under this part, except as provided in § 401.92.

§ 401.114 Data and information previously disclosed to the public.

Any Commission record that is otherwise exempt from public disclosure pursuant to this part is available for public disclosure to the extent that it contains data or information that have previously been disclosed in a lawful manner to any member of the public, other than an employee or consultant or pursuant to other commercial arrangements with appropriate safeguards for secrecy.

§ 401.115 Discretionary disclosure by the Executive Director.

(a) The Executive Director may, in his discretion, disclose part or all of any Commission record that is otherwise exempt from disclosure pursuant to this part. The Executive Director shall exercise his discretion to disclose such records whenever he determines that such disclosure is in the public interest, will promote the objectives of the Commission, and is consistent with the rights of individuals to privacy, the property rights of persons in trade secrets, and the need for the Commission to promote frank internal policy deliberations and to pursue its regulatory activities without disruption.

(b) Discretionary disclosure of a record pursuant to this section shall invoke the requirement that the record shall be disclosed to any person who requests it pursuant to §401.98, but shall not set a precedent for discretionary disclosure of any similar or related record and shall not obligate the Executive Director to exercise his discretion to disclose any other record that is exempt from disclosure.

§401.116 Disclosure to consultants, advisory committees, State and local government officials, and other special government employees.

Data and information otherwise exempt from public disclosure may be disclosed to Commission consultants, advisory committees, state and local government officials, and other special government employees for use only in their work in cooperation with the Commission. Such persons are thereafter subject to the same restrictions with respect to the disclosure of such data and information as any other Commission employee.

§401.117 Disclosure to other Federal government departments and agencies.

Any Commission record otherwise exempt from public disclosure may be disclosed to other Federal Government departments and agencies, except that trade secrets may be disclosed only to a department or agency that has concurrent jurisdiction over the matter and separate legal authority to obtain the specific information involved. Any disclosure under this section shall be pursuant to an agreement that the record shall not be further disclosed by the other department or agency except with the written permission of the Commission.

§401.118 Disclosure in administrative or court proceedings.

Data and information otherwise exempt from public disclosure may be revealed in Commission administrative or court proceedings where the data or information are relevant. The Commission will request that the data or information be held in camera and that any

other appropriate measures be taken to reduce disclosure to the minimum necessary under the circumstances.

§401.119 Disclosure to Congress.

All records of the Commission shall be disclosed to Congress upon an authorized request.

Subpart I—General Provisions

SOURCE: 40 FR 14059, Mar. 28, 1975; 40 FR 17987, Apr. 24, 1975, unless otherwise noted. Redesignated at 52 FR 37602, Oct. 8, 1987.

§401.121 Definitions.

For the purposes of this part, except as the context may otherwise require:

(a) All words and phrases which are defined by section 1.2 of the Compact shall have the same meaning herein.

(b) Words and phrases which are defined by part I of the Administrative Manual (section 1–3) shall have the same meaning for the purposes of this part 401.

(c) *Application* shall mean a request for action by the Commission in any written form, including without limitation thereto, a letter, referral by any agency of a signatory party, or an official form prescribed by the Commission; provided that whenever an official form of application has been duly required, an application shall not be deemed to be pending before the Commission until such time as such form, together with the information required thereby, has been completed and filed.

(d) *Applicant* shall mean any sponsor or other person who has submitted an application to the Commission.

(e) *Sponsor* shall mean any person authorized to initiate, construct or administer a project.

§401.122 Supplementary details.

Forms, procedures and supplementary information, to effectuate these regulations, may be provided or required by the Executive Director as to any hearing, project or class of projects.

§401.123 Waiver of rules.

The Commission may, for good cause shown, waive rules or require additional information in any case.

§ 401.124 Construction.

This part is promulgated pursuant to section 14.2 of the Compact and shall be construed and applied subject to all of the terms and conditions of the Compact and of the provisions of section 15.1 of Pub. L. 87–328, 75 Stat. 688.

PART 410—BASIN REGULATIONS; WATER CODE AND ADMINISTRATIVE MANUAL—PART III WATER QUALITY REGULATIONS

AUTHORITY: Delaware River Basin Compact, 75 Stat. 688.

§ 410.1 Basin regulations—Water Code and Administrative Manual—Part III Water Quality Regulations.

(a) The Water Code of the Delaware River Basin is a codification of regulations of the Delaware River Basin Commission applicable to public and private water projects and programs within the Delaware River Basin. Article I of the water code sets forth general policies of the Commission. Article II concerns the conservation, development and utilization of Delaware River Basin water resources, including during periods of drought. Article III sets forth water quality standards and guidelines for the Delaware River Basin. Article IV contains rules relating to application of water quality standards within the Basin. The Commission's Administrative Manual—Part III, Water Quality Regulations, applies to all public and private entities that discharge waste to waters of the Delaware River Basin.

(b) Article III of the water code consists of Article III of the water quality regulations. Article IV of the water code consists of portions of Article IV of the water quality regulations.

(c) Work, services, activities and facilities affecting the conservation, utilization, control, development or management of water resources within the Delaware River Basin are subject to regulations contained within the Delaware River Basin Water Code with Amendments Through December 4, 2013 and the Administrative Manual—Part III Water Quality Regulations with Amendments Through December 4, 2013. Both the Delaware River Basin Water Code and the Administrative Manual—Part III Water Quality Regulations are incorporated by reference into this part with the approval of the Director of the Federal Register under 5 U.S.C. 552(a) and 1 CFR part 51. You may obtain or inspect copies at the Delaware River Basin Commission (DRBC), 25 State Police Drive, West Trenton, New Jersey 08628–0360, 609–883–9500, *http://www.drbc.net*, or at the National Archives and Records Administration (NARA). For information on the availability of this material at NARA, call 202–741–6030 or go to *http://www.archives.gov/federal_register/code_of_federal_regulations/ibr_locations.html.*

[73 FR 55750, Sept. 26, 2008, as amended at 74 FR 60155, Nov. 20, 2009; 76 FR 16285, Mar. 23, 2011; 79 FR 26615, May 9, 2014]

PART 415—BASIN REGULATIONS—FLOOD PLAIN REGULATIONS

GENERALLY

Sec.
415.1   Short title.
415.2   Definitions.
415.3   Purpose and findings.

TYPES OF PROJECTS AND JURISDICTION

415.20   Class I projects.
415.21   Class II projects.

STANDARDS

415.30   Regulations generally.
415.31   Prohibited uses.
415.32   Permitted uses generally.
415.33   Uses by special permit.

ADMINISTRATION

415.40   Administrative agency.
415.41   Special permits.
415.42   Technical standards.
415.43   Mapped and unmapped delineations.

ENFORCEMENT

415.50   General conditions.
415.51   Prior non-conforming structures.
415.52   Violations.

AUTHORITY: Pub. L. 87–328 (75 Stat. 688).

SOURCE: 42 FR 13541, Mar. 11, 1977, unless otherwise noted.

GENERALLY

§415.1 Short title.

This part shall be known and may be cited as the "Flood Plain Regulations."

§415.2 Definitions.

For the purposes of this part, except as otherwise required by the context:

Project means the same word as defined by section 1.2(g) of the Delaware River Basin Compact.

Floodway means the channel of the watercourse and those portions of the adjoining flood plains which are reasonably required to carry and discharge the regulatory flood. For this purpose the limit of the floodway shall be established by allowing not more than a one-foot rise of the water surface elevation of the regulatory flood as a result of encroachment. Wherever practical, equal conveyance reduction from each side of the flood plain shall be used. (See Figure 1.)

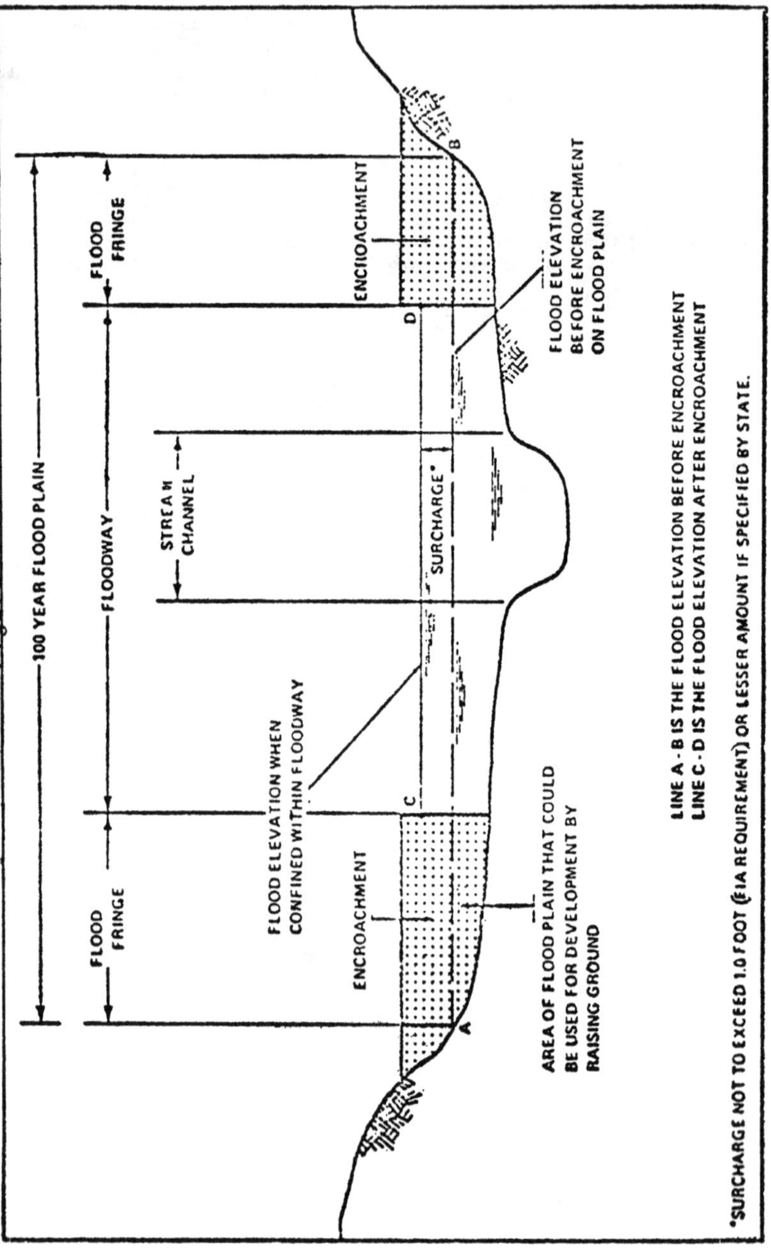

Figure 1

Flood fringe means that portion of the flood hazard area outside the floodway.

Flood hazard area means the area inundated by the regulatory flood.

Flood plain means the area adjoining the channel of a stream which has been or hereafter may be covered by flood water.

Floodproofing means any combination of structural and nonstructural additions, changes, or adjustments to properties and structures which reduce or eliminate flood damage to lands, water and sanitary facilities, structures, and contents of buildings.

Flood protection elevation means one foot above the elevation of the flood that has a one percent chance of occurring in any one year. (The 100-year flood).

Major tributary means the mainstem of the following streams:

PENNSYLVANIA

Brandywine Creek, Brodhead Creek, Big Bushkill Creek, Lackawaxen, Lehigh, Schuylkill, Neshaminy.

DELAWARE

Brandywine Creek, Christina.

NEW YORK

East Branch, Mongaup, Neversink, West Branch.

NEW JERSEY

Assunpink, Musconetcong, Paulins Kill, Rancocas, Pequest.

Official flood plain map means a map showing the flood plain area of a community prepared pursuant to the National Flood Insurance Act, or a map recognized by the Executive Director as meeting equivalent hydraulic or engineering criteria.

Regulatory flood means the flood which has a one percent chance of occurring in any one year. (The 100-year flood.)

Structure means any assembly of material above or below the surface of land or water, including but not limited to, buildings, dams, fills, levees, bulkheads, dikes, jetties, embankments, causeways, culverts, roads, railroads and bridges.

§415.3 Purpose and findings.

(a) The Commission hereby finds and determines that the use of flood plains is affected with a public interest due to:

(1) The danger to life and property due to increased flood heights or velocities caused by encroachments.

(2) The danger that materials may be swept onto other lands or downstream to the injury of others.

(3) The requirements of a facility for a waterfront location.

(b) In order to protect the public interest, the following principles and goals have been determined:

(1) The overall goal is prudent land use within the physical and environmental constraints of the site.

(2) The principle of equal and uniform treatment shall apply to all flood plain users who are similarly situated.

(3) Flood plain use shall not result in nuisance to other properties.

(4) Flood plain use shall not threaten public safety, health and general welfare.

(5) Future land uses in private flood plains shall not result in public expense to protect the property and associated public services from flood damage.

(6) All future public and private flood plain users shall bear the full direct and indirect costs attributable to their use and actions.

(7) Restrictions on flood plain use, and flood hazard information shall be widely publicized.

(8) Land and water use regulations of responsible units of government shall not impair or conflict with the flood plain use standards duly adopted for the basin, except as provided for in §415.42(a) of this part.

(9) Plans for land and water use adopted by responsible agencies shall not impair or conflict with these flood plain use standards.

(10) No action of any unit of government shall impair or conflict with these flood plain use standards.

TYPES OF PROJECTS AND JURISDICTION

§415.20 Class I projects.

Projects described in paragraphs (a) and (b) of this section shall be subject to review by the Commission under standards provided by this section and in accordance with the provisions of §§415.30 through 415.33 of this part, as follows:

(a) All projects subject to review by the Commission under section 3.8 of the Compact and the regulations thereunder.

(b) State and local standards of flood plain regulation.

§ 415.21 Class II projects.

Class II projects, subject to review in accordance with §§ 415.40 through 415.43 of this part, include all projects other than Class I projects, in non-tidal areas of the basin, which involve either:

(a) A development of land, either residential or non-residential within a flood hazard area which:

(1) Includes one or more structures covering a total land area in excess of 50,000 square feet; or

(2) Contains in excess of 25 residential building lots or 25 dwelling units as part of an integrated development plan whether or not such development is included in a single application; or

(b) A development of land in the flood hazard area to mine, manufacture, process, store or dispose of materials which, if flooded, would pollute the waters of the basin or threaten damage to off-site areas, including, without limitation thereto, materials which are poisonous, radioactive, biologically undesirable or floatable.

STANDARDS

§ 415.30 Regulations generally.

The uses of land within a flood hazard area shall be subject to regulation within one of the following categories:

(a) Prohibited uses;

(b) Permitted uses generally;

(c) Uses by special permit.

§ 415.31 Prohibited uses.

(a) Within the floodway, except as permitted by special permit, the following uses are prohibited:

(1) Erection of any structure for occupancy at any time by humans or animals.

(2) Placing, or depositing, or dumping any spoil, fill or solid waste.

(3) Stockpiling or disposal of pesticides, domestic or industrial waste, radioactive materials, petroleum products or hazardous material which, if flooded, would pollute the waters of the basin.

(4) The storage of equipment or of buoyant materials, except for purposes of public safety.

(b) Within the flood fringe, except as permitted by special permit, the following uses are prohibited:

(1) Stockpiling or disposal of pesticides, domestic or industrial waste, radioactive materials, petroleum products or hazardous material which, if flooded, would pollute the waters of the basin.

(2) Any use which will adversely affect the capacity of channels or floodways of any tributary to the main stream, drainage ditch, or any other drainage facility.

§ 415.32 Permitted uses generally.

(a) Within the floodway, the following uses are permitted to the extent that they do not require structures, fill or storage of materials or permanently installed equipment, and do not adversely affect the capacity of the floodway:

(1) Agricultural uses such as general farming, livestock, and dairy farming, horticulture, truck farming, sod farming, forestry, wild crop harvesting, and normal operating practices associated therewith.

(2) Industrial-commercial uses such as loading areas, parking areas and airport landing strips.

(3) Private and public recreational uses such as golf courses, driving ranges, archery ranges, picnic grounds, boat launching ramps, swimming areas, parks, wildlife and nature preserves, game farms, shooting preserves, target ranges, trap and skeet ranges, hunting and fishing areas, hiking and horseback riding trails.

(4) Uses such as lawns, gardens, parking areas and play areas.

(b) Within the flood fringe, the following uses are permitted:

(1) Any use permitted in the floodway.

(2) Residences and other structures constructed so that the first floor, including basement, is above the Flood Protection Elevation. When fill is used the finished fill elevation shall be no lower than the Flood Protection Elevation for the particular area and shall extend at least 15 feet beyond the limits of any structure or building erected thereon.

§415.33   Uses by special permit.

(a) Within the floodway the following uses by special permit may be authorized under the standards hereinafter provided:

(1) Uses or structures accessory to open space use.

(2) Circuses, carnivals and similar transient enterprises.

(3) Drive-in theaters, signs and billboards.

(4) Extraction of sand, gravel and other non-toxic materials.

(5) Marinas, boat liveries, docks, piers, wharves and water control structures.

(6) Fish hatcheries.

(7) Railroads, streets, bridges, utility transmission lines and pipelines.

(b) Within the flood fringe the following uses by special permit may be authorized under standards hereinafter provided:

(1) *Non-residential uses generally.* Structures other than residence shall ordinarily be elevated as herein provided but may in special circumstances be otherwise flood proofed to a point above the Flood Protection Elevation.

(2) *Commercial uses.* Commercial structures shall be elevated so that no first floor or basement floor is below the Flood Protection Elevation; or such structures may be flood proofed to the Flood Protection Elevation. Accessory land uses, such as yards, railroad tracks and parking lots may be at lower elevations. However, a permit for such facilities to be used by the general public shall not be granted in the absence of a flood warning system, if the area is inundated to a depth greater than two feet or subject to flood velocities greater than four feet per second upon the occurrence of the Regulatory Flood.

(3) *Manufacturing and industrial uses.* Manufacturing and industrial buildings, structures, and appurtenant works shall be elevated so that no first floor or basement floor is below the Flood Protection Elevation; or such structures may be flood proofed to the Flood Protection Elevation. Measures shall be taken to minimize flood water interference with normal plant operations especially for streams having protracted flood durations. Certain accessory land uses as yards and parking lots may have lesser protection subject to the flood warning requirements set out in 2 above.

(4) *Utilities, railroad tracks, streets and bridges.* Public utility facilities, roads, railroad tracks and bridges shall be designed to minimize increases in flood elevations and shall be compatible with local comprehensive flood plain development plans to the extent applicable. Protection to the Flood Protection Elevation shall be provided where failure or interruption of these public facilities would result in danger to the public health or safety, or where such facilities are essential to the orderly functioning of the area. Where failure or interruption of service would not endanger life or health, a lesser degree of protection may be provided for minor or auxiliary roads, railroads or utilities.

(5) *Water supply and waste treatment.* No new construction, addition or modification of a water supply or waste treatment facility shall be permitted unless the lowest operating floor of such facility is above the Flood Protection Elevation, or the facility is flood proofed according to plans approved by the Commission, nor unless emergency plans and procedures for action to be taken in the event of flooding are prepared. Plans shall be filed with the Delaware River Basin Commission and the concerned state or states. The emergency plans and procedures shall provide for measures to prevent introduction of any pollutant or toxic material into the flood water or the introduction of flood waters into potable supplies.

ADMINISTRATION

§415.40   Administrative agency.

(a) Class I projects as defined by §415.20 of this part shall be subject to review and approval by the Commission.

(b) Class II projects as defined by §415.21 shall be subject to review and approval by a duly empowered state or local agency; and if there be no such state or local agency at any time on and after January 1, 1978, and only during such time, the Commission may review any such project which has been identified by the Executive Director as having special flood hazards, and:

(1) Is located along the mainstem Delaware River or a major tributary thereof, or

(2) An agency of a signatory party requests such review.

§ 415.41   Special permits.

A special permit may be granted, or granted on stated conditions, provided:

(a) There is a clear balance in favor of the public interest in terms of the following environmental criteria:

(1) The importance of a facility to the community.

(2) The availability of alternative locations not subject to flooding for the proposed use.

(3) The compatibility of the proposed use with existing development and development anticipated in the foreseeable future.

(4) The relationship of the proposed use to any applicable comprehensive plan or flood plain management program for the area.

(5) The safety of access to the property in times of flood for ordinary and emergency vehicles.

(6) The expected heights, velocity, duration, rate of rise and sediment transport of the flood water expected at the site.

(7) The degree to which the proposed activity would alter natural water flow or water temperature.

(8) The degree to which archaeological or historic sites and structures, endangered or rare species of animals or plants, high quality wildlife habitats, scarce vegetation types, and other irreplaceable land types would be degraded or destroyed.

(9) The degree to which the natural, scenic and aesthetic values at the proposed activity site could be retained.

(b) The project shall not:

(1) Endanger human life.

(2) Have high flood damage potential.

(3) Obstruct flood flows nor increase flood heights or velocities unduly whether acting alone or in combination with other uses.

(4) Degrade significantly the water carrying capacity of any delineated floodway or channel.

(5) Increase significantly the rate of local runoff, erosion, or sedimentation.

(6) Degrade significantly the quality of surface water or the quality or quantity of ground water.

(7) Be susceptible to flotation.

(8) Have service facilities installed below the elevation of the regulatory flood without being adequately flood proofed.

§ 415.42   Technical standards.

(a) Standards used by state and local governments shall conform in principle to Commission standards but may vary in detail provided that resulting flood plain use will not be less restrictive than would result from the application of Commission standards. The Commission will review proposed state and local flood plain regulations to determine their compliance with Commission standards.

(b) Because of the variety and diversity of presently recognized hydrologic procedures, no one procedure or method is prescribed for determining the peak flow in cubic feet per second for the 100-year storm (Q 100) on which profiles for the delineation of flood hazard areas are based. The following may be used:

(1) A uniform Technique for Determining Flood Flow Frequencies—Bulletin No. 15—Water Resources Council, December 1967.

(2) Basin-Wide Program for Flood Plain Delineation—Delaware River Basin Commission—Anderson-Nichols & Co., Inc., June 1973.

(3) Magnitude and Frequency of Floods in New Jersey with Effects of Urbanization—Special Report 38 U.S.G.S.—New Jersey Department of Environmental Protection, 1974.

(4) Guidelines for Determining Flood Flow Frequency—Bulletin No. 17—Water Resources Council, March 1976.

State and local agencies may use methods resulting in Q 100s which are in reasonable agreement with those of the Commission. Any significant difference shall be reviewed with and subject to approval by the Executive Director.

(c) Methods and procedures shall be uniform, so far as practicable, within sub-basins which have a major effect on the larger basins of which they are a part. To assist in achieving this objective the Commission staff will periodically provide to the various interested governmental agencies and others Q 100 data as developed by the Delaware River Basin Commission Hydrology Coordinating Committee for key locations in the Delaware River Basin. These will be based on a Log Pearson Type 3 analysis of data from the U.S.G.S. gaging stations using station skew, regional skew, or weighted skew, depending on the scope of data at each station.

§ 415.43 Mapped and unmapped delineations.

(a) Whenever an official flood plain map providing the pertinent information is available with respect to a given project, the map shall be used for the delineation of the flood hazard area, floodway, flood fringe and determination of flood protection elevation.

(b) Whenever an official flood plain map providing the required information is not available with respect to a given project, the administrative agency shall require the project landowner to submit details concerning the proposed uses as needed to determine the floodway and flood fringe limits at the proposed site, including: cross-sections of the stream channel and overbanks, stream profile, and factors involved in determining obstructions to flow. From the data submitted, soil surveys, historic flood maps, high water marks and other empirical data, the applicant, subject to verification by the administrative agency, shall calculate flood hazard areas, and establish the flood protection elevation for the particular site.

(c) Pending the preparation and completion of flood plain mapping, a "general flood plain" area shall be prescribed by the administrative agency to delineate for public guidance the areal limits of site locations which are required to be submitted for review under this regulation.

ENFORCEMENT

§ 415.50 General conditions.

On and after January 1, 1978, where:
(a) The flood hazard at the site is clear, present and significant, or the local government having jurisdiction has special flood hazard areas identified pursuant to the National Flood Insurance Act; and

(b) The site is not subject to an approved state or municipal regulatory system having the same or similar effect on the flood hazard as this regulation, the Commission may condition its approval on any local governmental project under section 3.8 of the Compact upon the adoption and enforcement of flood plain regulations, approved hereunder, by the state or local government having jurisdiction.

§ 415.51 Prior non-conforming structures.

A structure which was lawful before the adoption of this regulation but which is not in conformity with the provisions hereof, shall be subject to the following conditions (to be enforced by the appropriate authority as to Class I and Class II projects, respectively, under §§ 415.40 through 415.43 of this part):

(a) A non-conforming structure in the floodway may not be expanded, except that it may be modified, altered or repaired to incorporate flood proofing measures provided such measures do not raise the level of the 100-year flood.

(b) A non-conforming structure in the floodway which is destroyed or damaged by any means, including a flood, to the extent of 50 percent or more of its market value at that time may not be restored, repaired, reconstructed or improved except in conformity with the provisions of these regulations.

§ 415.52 Violations.

Any violation of this regulation shall be subject to penalties imposed by the Compact.

PART 420—BASIN REGULATIONS— WATER SUPPLY CHARGES

GENERAL

39

420.24 Effective date of rates.

AUTHORITY: Delaware River Basin Compact, 75 Stat. 688.

SOURCE: 42 FR 13544, Mar. 11, 1977, unless otherwise noted.

GENERAL

§ 420.1 Definitions.

For the purposes of this part 420, except as otherwise required by the context:

Person means any person, corporation, partnership, association, trust, or other entity, public or private.

Water user means any person who uses, takes, withdraws or diverts surface waters within the Delaware River Basin.

Executive Director means the Executive Director of the Delaware River Basin Commission.

Consumptive use means the water lost due to transpiration from vegetation in the building of plant tissue, incorporated into products during their manufacture, lost to the atmosphere from cooling devices, evaporated from water surfaces, exported from the Delaware River Basin, or any other water use for which the water withdrawn is not returned to the surface waters of the basin undiminished in quantity.

WATER SUPPLY POLICY

§ 420.21 Policy.

The provisions of this part 420 implement Commission Resolution No. 71–4 (Comprehensive Plan) relating to water supply charges.

§ 420.22 Prohibition; sanctions.

Any person, firm, corporation or other entity, including a public corporation, body or agency, who shall use, withdraw or divert surface waters of the basin, shall pay such charges therefor as may be required by this resolution. Any violation of this resolution shall be subject to penalty as prescribed under Article 14.17 of the Compact. The Commission may also recover the value (according to the established water pricing schedules of the Commission) of any such use, withdrawal or diversion, and invoke the jurisdiction of the courts to enjoin any further use, withdrawal or diversion, unless all charges under this resolution are paid in full when due.

§ 420.23 Exempt uses under the Compact.

(a) Section 15.1(b) of the Delaware River Basin Compact provides that "no provision of section 3.7 of the Compact shall be deemed to authorize the Commission to impose any charge for water withdrawals or diversions from the basin if such withdrawals or diversions could lawfully have been made without charge on the effective date of the Compact; * * *" In compliance with this provision: There shall be no charge for water withdrawn or diverted in quantities not exceeding the legal entitlement of the user, determined as of October 27, 1961. Each water user may submit proof satisfactory to the Commission of the factors constituting legal entitlement, as defined in paragraph (b) thereof. In the absence of such proof of these conditions as of October 27, 1961, the quantity of water exempt from charge to each user will be the legal entitlement of the user determined as of March 31, 1971.

(b) For the purposes of paragraph (a) of this section:

(1) *Legal entitlement* means the quantity or volume of water expressed in million gallons per month determined by the lesser of the following conditions:

(i) A valid and subsisting permit, issued under the authority of one of the signatory parties, if such permit was required as of October 27, 1961, or thereafter;

(ii) Physical capability as required for such taking; or

(iii) The total allocable flow without augmentation by the Commission, using a seven-day, ten-year, low-flow criterion measured at the point of withdrawal or diversion.

(2) *Physical capability* means the capacity of pumps, water lines and appurtenances installed and operable, determined according to sound engineering principles. The physical capability specifically includes plant facilities actually using water, but excludes facilities which may have been installed in anticipation of future plant expansion not yet realized.

(c) Whenever adequate records of legal entitlement for agricultural irrigation purposes are not available to the Commission, such legal entitlement shall be measured by the maximum number of acres under irrigation by the water user at any time during the year ending March 31, 1971, allowing one acre-foot of surface water annually per acre irrigated.

(d) Notwithstanding the provisions of paragraphs (a), (b) and (c) of this section, there shall be no charge for water made available from storage where:

(1) The cost of the storage facility has or will be otherwise paid for by the user,

(2) Such storage controls a drainage area, and

(3) The use does not exceed the yield of such storage without augmentation from other surface water of the basin.

§ 420.24 Effective date of rates.

Rates and charges shall apply to all water users not exempt hereunder on and after the date of the first impoundment of water for water supply purposes at the Beltzville Reservoir (February 8, 1971), or the effective date hereof, whichever is later.

ENTITLEMENT; MEASUREMENT; BILLING

§ 420.31 Certificate of entitlement.

(a) The Executive Director will issue to each known water user a certificate of entitlement within 30 days after the effective date of these regulations subject to the provisions of paragraph (b). In addition, any other water user may apply for a certificate of entitlement at any time. A preliminary notice of entitlement shall be issued to each user. Such entitlement shall become final and take effect, unless the user shall file with the Commission, within 20 days after the service of the notice of entitlement, a request for hearing by the Commission. At such hearing the water user may show cause why the proposed entitlement shall not take effect.

(b) The Executive Director shall schedule a hearing to be held not less than ten days after receipt of a request for a hearing by the Commission. Hearings shall be conducted and the results thereof subject to review in accordance with Article 5 of the Commission's rules of practice and procedure.

(c) A final certificate of entitlement will be issued either upon expiration of the time to request a hearing, where there has been no request, or in accordance with the determination of a hearing where one is held.

(d) *Limitations.* (1) A certificate of entitlement is granted to a specific user for water withdrawals or diversions at a specific facility in the amount of the Legal Entitlement as defined in § 420.23(b).

(2) A certificate of entitlement shall not be applied, transferred or modified to apply to a facility other than the facility initially specified in the certificate.

(3) A certificate of entitlement may not be transferred from the certificate holder to another user, except as provided in the exceptions set forth in paragraph (f) of this section.

(4) A certificate of entitlement does not exempt the certificate holder from paying water supply charges for any portion of water withdrawals or diversions used outside the facility specified in the certificate and any additional service area to which the facility supplied water as of October 27, 1961 or at the facility specified in the certificate by a user other than the certificate holder. For purposes of this paragraph (d)(4), a certificate holder claiming an exemption from charges for water supplied within a service area shall submit proof satisfactory to the Commission identifying the facility's service area as of October 27, 1961. In the absence of proof of the service area as of October

27, 1961, the service area defined in the Commission docket, if any, for the facility in effect at the time the certificate was issued shall be deemed to be the facility's service area. In the absence of proof of a service area, the certificate shall only exempt the certificate holder from paying water supply charges for water used at the facility.

(e) *Termination of certificate.* (1) A certificate of entitlement terminates pursuant to this section and without the need for Commission action if at least one of the following occurs:

(i) The certificate holder dissolves or otherwise ceases to exist;

(ii) The certificate holder ceases the withdrawals or diversions at the facility to which the certificate of entitlement applies, or abandons the intake, provided that a shutdown of the facility for maintenance or improvement, or a replacement of the intake, that is performed at the earliest practicable commercially reasonable time following commencement of the shutdown or replacement, shall not be deemed to be a cessation of withdrawal or diversion;

(iii) The certificate holder through contract, lease or other agreement ceases to be the user or public water system supplier of the water withdrawn or diverted at the facility; or

(iv) There is a change in the ownership or control of the facility. Once terminated, a certificate of entitlement may not be reinstated or reissued.

(2) A change in ownership or control of the facility includes, but is not limited to, any transaction, acquisition, merger or event (collectively "transaction") resulting in at least one of the following:

(i) A transfer of title to the facility;

(ii) A person or entity or the shareholders or other owners of an entity becoming the beneficial owner, directly or indirectly, or acquiring alone or in concert the power or right to vote at least 20 percent of any class of ownership interest in a certificate holder or any of its parent entities, regardless of the tier in the corporate or entity structure at which the transaction occurs;

(iii) A change in ownership or control for purposes of any of the certificate holder's or any of its parent corporations' employee agreements; or

(iv) A change of the de facto controlling interest in a certificate holder or any of its parent entities, regardless of the tier in the corporate or entity structure at which the change occurs.

(3) A change of the de facto controlling interest in an entity includes, but is not limited to, a change of the persons or entities with the ability or authority, expressed or reserved, to direct the management or policies of an entity and/or to take at least one of the following actions:

(i) Amend or change the entity's identity (*e.g.* joint venture agreement, unincorporated business status);

(ii) Appoint or remove at least 50% of the members of the Board of Directors or Trustees of a corporation, general partner of a partnership, or a similar member of the governing body of an entity;

(iii) Amend or change the by-laws, constitution, or other operating or management direction of the entity;

(iv) Control the sale of, use of or access to any or all of the entity's assets;

(v) Encumber the entity's assets by way of mortgage or other indebtedness;

(vi) Control any or all of the assets or other property of the entity upon the sale or dissolution of the entity;

(vii) Dissolve the entity;

(viii) Arrange for the sale or transfer of the entity to a new ownership or control;

(ix) Select or change the management of the entity or determine management compensation; or

(x) Set operating policies, financial policies or budgets.

(4) For purposes of applying paragraph (e)(3) of this section, consideration may be given to circumstances particular to the person or entity and certificate holder involved, including without limitation the ability of that person or entity to take actions in light of the number of shares in the certificate holder or its parent entities that are actively voted, the practice of any majority shareholder in exercising or refraining from exercising majority rights, and any agreements giving the person or entity the right to control votes of others.

(5) A series of transactions undertaken pursuant to a plan or that are otherwise related shall be considered a single transaction for purposes of this section. For purposes of calculating the twenty percent threshold in paragraph (e)(2)(ii) of this section, the securities, shares or other interests held immediately prior to the transaction shall be added to the securities, shares or other interests acquired in the transaction.

(f) *Exceptions*—(1) *Agricultural exception.* (i) Whenever ownership or possession of land in agricultural use is transferred, any certificate of entitlement with respect to such land shall be deemed to run with the land, if but only if within sixty days following the land transfer the new user demonstrates to the Executive Director that it will continue to use the water withdrawn or diverted for agricultural irrigation. Following any such timely demonstration, the Executive Director shall transfer the certificate of entitlement to the new user. The Executive Director may extend the sixty day period for good cause shown.

(ii) A certificate of entitlement that has been transferred pursuant to paragraph (f)(1)(i) of this section relieves the user of the obligation to pay water supply charges only with respect to the quantity of water in fact used by the new certificate holder for agricultural irrigation up to the Legal Entitlement specified in the certificate, and not with respect to the quantity of water used for any other purposes. The provisions of §420.43 shall apply to water uses outside the scope of the certificate of entitlement.

(iii) A certificate of entitlement that has been transferred pursuant to paragraph (f)(1)(i) of this section terminates pursuant to this paragraph (f)(1) and without the need for Commission action if and when the certificate holder ceases using the water for agricultural irrigation, provided that if the cessation occurs in conjunction with a transfer of ownership or possession of the land in agricultural use, the certificate of entitlement may be transferred to a new user pursuant to paragraph (f)(1)(i). Once terminated, a certificate of entitlement may not be reinstated or reissued.

(2) *Corporate reorganization exceptions.* The following provisions apply where a corporate parent directly or indirectly owning 100% of each class of shares of all of its subsidiary corporations decides to reorganize those subsidiary corporations without affecting the corporate parent's 100% ownership interest.

(i) Whenever a corporate reorganization consists solely of a change of the name, identity, internal corporate structure, or place of organization of a corporate certificate holder or any of its parent corporations, the Executive Director may reissue a certificate of entitlement in the name of the new owner of the facility, provided that the reorganization does not affect ownership and/or control by the certificate holder's corporate family of companies within the meaning of paragraphs (e)(2) through (5) of this section and does not alter the ultimate corporate parent's 100% ownership interest.

(ii) A merger or other plan, transaction or series of transactions that effectuates a change of ownership or control within the meaning of paragraphs (e)(2) through (5) does not fall within the exemption of paragraph (f)(2)(i) of this section on the basis that a corporate reorganization constitutes part of the merger, plan, transaction or series of transactions.

[42 FR 13544, Mar. 11, 1977, as amended at 59 FR 64571, Dec. 15, 1994; 81 FR 35608, June 3, 2016]

§420.32 Measurement and billing of water taken.

(a) The quantity and volume of waters used by each person shall be determined by meters, or other methods approved by the Commission, installed, maintained and read by or on behalf of the taker. Meters or other methods of measurement shall be subject to approval and inspection by the Commission as to installation, maintenance and reading.

(b) Each user of surface water who is not exceeding the quantity specified in his "certificate of entitlement" shall annually, on or before January 31, file with the Commission, on a form to be prescribed by the Executive Director, a report of the user's physical capability, as defined, permit limitations, and the volume of water used during the preceding year.

(c) Each user of surface water who is taking a quantity of water greater than the amount specified in his "certificate of entitlement" shall report his usage to the Commission on or before April 30, July 31, October 31 and January 31, of each year covering the next preceding calendar quarter, respectively, on forms to be prescribed by the Executive Director. The amount due for water usage in excess of the legal entitlement for each of the first three quarters of a calendar year shall be computed and paid by the user, together with the report.

(d) The Commission will render a statement of the net amount due based on the fourth quarter report, including a negative or positive adjustment, so that the net total billing and payment for four quarters will equal the total water used during the four quarters less the user's legal entitlement, if any.

§ 420.33   Payment of bills.

The amount due for each quarter shall bear interest at the rate of 1 percent per month for each day it is unpaid beginning 30 days after the due date of the quarterly report for the first three quarters and 30 days after the bill is rendered for the fourth quarter.

CHARGES; EXEMPTIONS

§ 420.41   Schedule of water charges.

The schedule of water charges established in accordance with § 420.22 shall be as follows:

(a) $81.01 per million gallons for consumptive use, subject to paragraph (c) of this section; and

(b) $0.81 per million gallons for non-consumptive use, subject to paragraph (c) of this section.

(c) On July 1 of every year, beginning July 1, 2017, the rates established by this section will increase commensurate with any increase in the annual April 12-month Consumer Price Index (CPI) for Philadelphia, published by the U.S. Bureau of Labor Statistics

during that year.[1] In any year in which the April 12-month CPI for Philadelphia declines or shows no change, the water charges rates will remain unchanged. Following any indexed adjustment made under this paragraph (c), revised consumptive and non-consumptive use rates will be published in the FEDERAL REGISTER by July 1 and posted on the Commission's Web site. Interested parties may also obtain the rates by contacting the Commission directly during business hours.

[81 FR 95863, Dec. 29, 2016, as amended at 82 FR 26990, June 13, 2017]

§ 420.42   Contracts; minimum charge.

Subject to the exclusions for certificates of entitlement and exempt uses, the Executive Director may require contracts for any taking, use, withdrawal or diversion of waters of the basin. Each contract shall provide for a minimum annual payment in accordance with an estimated annual demand schedule, regardless of use, withdrawal or diversion. The failure of any person to execute a contract under this section shall not affect the application of other requirements of this resolution.

§ 420.43   Exempt use.

The following uses shall be exempt from charge:

(a) Non-consumptive uses of less than 1,000 gallons during any day, and less than 100,000 gallons during any quarter.

(b) Ballast water used for shipping purposes.

(c) Water taken, withdrawn or diverted from streams tributary to the river master's gauging station at Montague.

(d) Water taken, withdrawn or diverted below R.M. 38 (the mouth of the Cohansey River) and such proportion of waters taken, diverted or withdrawn above R.M. 38 and below R.M. 92.4 (the mouth of the Schuylkill River) as the Executive Director may determine, on the basis of hydrologic studies, would have no discernible effect upon the

---

[1] Consumer Price Index—U/Series ID: CUURA102SA0/Not Seasonally Adjusted/Area: Philadelphia-Wilmington-Atlantic City, PA–NJ–DE–MD/Item: All items/Base Period 1982–84=100.

maintenance of the salt front below the mouth of the Schuylkill River.

§420.44 Cooling water.

Water used exclusively for cooling purposes which is returned to the stream in compliance with the effluent requirements of applicable water quality standards, shall be charged at the non-consumptive use rate except that losses due to in-stream evaporation caused by cooling uses will be charged as consumptive use.

§420.45 Historical use.

A person who or which could not for any reason use, take, withdraw or divert waters of the basin from the place in question on March 31, 1971, shall not be entitled to a certificate of entitlement.

HYDROELECTRIC POWER WATER USE CHARGES

§420.51 Hydroelectric power plant water use charges.

(a) *Annual base charges.* Owners of conventional run-of-river hydroelectric power plants that benefit from water storage facilities owned or partially owned by the Commission shall pay an annual base charge to the Commission. The amount of the base annual charge shall be one dollar per kilowatt of installed capacity.

(b) *Annual variable charges.* In addition to the base charge established in (a) of this section, annual charges based on power generated at each facility will be assessed as follows:

(1) Owners of hydroelectric power plants that benefit from increased hydraulic head available to the hydroelectric project as a result of investments by the Commission shall be charged one mill per kilowatt-hour of energy produced.

(2) Owners of hydroelectric power plants that derive additional benefits from increased flows available to the hydroelectric project that would not have been available without the Commission-sponsored project shall be charged one-half mill per kilowatt-hour of energy produced. No charges for increased flows will be required when charges for increased hydraulic head are in effect.

(3) Charges for the use of any facilities such as pipe conduits, outlet works, and so on, installed in, on or near a Commission-sponsored project that benefit the hydroelectric project in any way will be determined on a case-by-case basis as approved by the Commission.

(c) *Credits.* The owner of any hydroelectric generating facility shall receive a credit against the current year water use fee otherwise payable to the Commission for any amount which the Commission receives from the U.S. Army Corps of Engineers or from the Federal Energy Regulatory Commission for each calendar year.

(d) *Exemptions.* No payment will be required when hydroelectric power facility water use charges would amount to less than $25 per year. Retroactive charges will not be assessed for facilities which have already obtained Commission approval pursuant to Section 3.8 of the Delaware River Basin Compact. All hydroelectric generating projects that do not benefit from storage owned or partially owned by the Commission are exempt from these Commission water charges.

(e) *Payment of bills.* The amount due each year shall bear interest at the rate of 1% per month for each day it is unpaid beginning 30 days after the due date. Payments are due within 30 days of the end of each calendar year. Annual base charges will be prorated for periods less than a year.

[53 FR 45260, Nov. 9, 1988]

SUBCHAPTER B—SPECIAL REGULATIONS

PART 430—GROUND WATER PROTECTION AREA: PENNSYLVANIA

AUTHORITY: Pub. L. 87–328 (75 Stat. 688).

SOURCE: 46 FR 24, Jan. 2, 1981, unless otherwise noted.

§ 430.1 Policy.

The provisions of this part implement Commission Resolutions 80–18 and 80–27 relating to ground water protection in southeastern Pennsylvania.

§ 430.3 Purpose.

The purpose of this regulation is to protect the ground water resources in the Triassic lowland and adjacent area of southeastern Pennsylvania and the public interest in those resources. In particular this regulation is to:

(a) Assure the effective management of water withdrawals to avoid depletion of natural stream flows and ground waters and to protect the quality of such water.

(b) Assure that ground water withdrawals are undertaken consistent with the policies stated in the Comprehensive Plan.

(c) Protect the just and equitable interests and rights of present and future lawful users of water resources, giving due regard to the need to balance and reconcile alternative and conflicting uses in view of present and threatened shortages of water of the quality required to serve such uses.

(d) Provide a mechanism for the acquisition of additional information necessary to more accurately plan and manage water resources.

(e) Encourage all water users to adopt and implement reasonable water conservation measures and practices, to assure efficient use of limited water supplies.

§ 430.5 Definitions.

For purposes of this regulation, except as otherwise required by the context:

Aquifer means waterbearing formation that contains sufficient ground water to be important as a source of supply.

Comprehensive Plan means the plans, policies and programs adopted as part of the Comprehensive Plan of the Delaware Basin in accordance with section 3.2 and Article 13 of the Delaware River Basin Compact.

Ground water means all water beneath the surface of the ground.

Ground water basin means a subsurface structure having the character of a basin with respect to the collection, retention and outflow of water.

Ground water protected area means the areas declared and delineated by the Commission to be a ground water protected area pursuant to Article 10 of the Delaware River Basin Compact and this regulation.

Ground water recharge means the addition of water to an aquifer by infiltration of precipitation through the soil, infiltration from surface streams, lakes or reservoirs, flow of ground water from another aquifer, or pumpage of water into the aquifer through wells.

Project means the same word as defined by section 1.2(g) of the Delaware River Basin Compact.

Protected area permit means a permit to divert or withdraw ground water within the ground water protected area for domestic, municipal, agricultural or industrial uses, granted pursuant to section 10.3 of the Delaware River Basin Compact and this regulation.

§430.7 Determination of protected areas and restriction on water use.

In consideration of the foregoing facts and for the purposes cited above:

(a) The Commission hereby determines and delineates the following area to be a protected area within the meaning and for the purpose of Article 10 of the Delaware River Basin Compact:

Southeastern Pennsylvania Ground Water Protected Area

The "Southeastern Pennsylvania Ground Water Protected Area" shall consist of those portions of the following listed counties and political subdivision located within the Delaware Basin:

Townships
Berks County .... Douglass, Hereford, Union.
Bucks County .... Bedminster, Buckingham, Doylestown, East Rockhill, Hilltown, Lower Southampton, Middletown, Milford, New Britain, Newtown, Northampton, Plumstead, Richland, Upper Southampton, Warminster, Warrington, Warrick, West Rockhill, Wrightstown.

Boroughs
Chalfont, Doylestown, Dublin, Hulmeville, Ivyland, Langhorne, Langhorne Manor, New Britain, Newtown, Penndel, Perkasie, Quakertown, Richlandtown, Sellersville, Silverdale, Telford, Trumbauersville.

Townships
Chester County .... Birmingham, Charlestown, East Coventry, East Bradford, East Goshen, East Pikeland, Easttown, East Vincent, East Whiteland, North Coventry, Schuylkill, South Coventry, Thornbury, Tredyffrin, Warwick, West Bradford, West Goshen, Westtown, Willistown, West Whiteland.

Boroughs
Elverson, Malvern, Phoenixville, Spring City, West Chester.

Townships
Lehigh County .... Lower Milford.
Montgomery County ..... All of the area within the county boundary.

(b) The Commission hereby determines that within the Southeastern Pennsylvania Ground Water Protected Area demands upon available ground water supplies have developed or threaten to develop to such a degree as to create a water shortage or to impair or conflict with the requirements or effectuation of the Comprehensive Plan. Accordingly, no person, firm, corpora-

tion or other entity within the area shall withdraw ground water for any purpose at a rate exceeding 10,000 gallons per day, except as prescribed by this regulation.

§430.9 Comprehensive plan policies.

The water resources within the Southeastern Pennsylvania Ground Water Protected Area shall be managed consistent with the Comprehensive Plan policies. For purposes of this ground water protected area, section 2.20.4 of the Water Code of the Delaware River Basin shall be applied using the following definition of the term "withdrawal limits":

(a) *Withdrawal limits.* Except as may be otherwise determined by the Commission to be in the public interest, withdrawals from the underground waters of the basin shall be limited to the maximum draft of all withdrawals from a ground water basin, aquifer, or aquifer system that can be sustained without rendering supplies unreliable, causing long-term progressive lowering of ground water levels, water quality degradation, permanent loss of storage capacity, or substantial impact on low flows of perennial streams.

(b) [Reserved]

§430.11 Advance notice of exploratory drilling.

The Commission encourages consultation with any project sponsor who is considering development of a new or expanded ground water withdrawal that is being planned for any purpose when the daily average withdrawal during any calendar month exceeds 10,000 gallons to insure proper implementation of this regulation and to reduce the possibility of investment in new ground water development facilities which may not be approved hereunder. Such consultation should occur early in the planning stage of a new project and prior to initiation of exploratory drilling.

(a) Any person, firm corporation or other entity planning a new or expanded ground water withdrawal that may be operated at a daily average withdrawal during any calendar month in excess of 10,000 gallons shall notify the Executive Director not less than 30 days prior to initiation of exploratory drilling. Such notice shall be in writing and shall specify the location of proposed new facility, the anticipated rate of withdrawal, and the general purpose of the proposed water use. The notice shall also state the location of existing wells within the radius set forth in § 430.21(a).

(b) Whenever the Executive Director shall deem necessary, or upon request of a party proposing a new or expanded withdrawal of ground water, an informal conference may be scheduled to review the nature of the proposed withdrawal, the applicability of the Commission's standards relating to ground water, and the requirements of a protected area permit under this regulation.

§ 430.13 Protected area permits for new withdrawals.

Any person, firm, corporation or other entity who proposes to develop a new ground water withdrawal or expand an existing ground water withdrawal for any purpose within the Southeastern Pennsylvania Ground Water Protected Area shall be required to obtain a protected area permit under this regulation if the proposed new or increased rate of withdrawal from a well or group of wells operated as a system average more than 10,000 gallons per day over a 30-day period. Whenever the Executive Director, upon investigation or upon a reference from a state or federal agency, determines that a new or increased withdrawal from a group of wells within the protected area, whether or not such wells are operated as a system, may have a substantial effect on the water resources of the basin or is likely to have a significant adverse effect on other water uses within the protected area, the Commission may direct a notice to the owners or sponsors of such wells, and require such owners or sponsors to apply for and obtain a protected area permit under this regulation.

(a) Applications for a protected area permit shall be submitted to the Commission on forms approved by the Executive Director. Each application shall be accompanied by the following information:

(1) A map indicating the location of existing wells and perennial streams.

(2) A written report prepared by a hydrogeologist describing the expected effects of the proposed withdrawal on existing wells, flows of perennial streams and the long-term lowering of ground water levels.

(3) A log showing the nature of subsurface material encountered during the construction and installation of the exploratory or production well(s).

(4) The detailed results of extended pump tests, of not less than 48 hours duration, and records of observations during such pump tests from representative monitoring wells.

(b) Applications for a protected area permits whose daily average withdrawal during any calendar month is in excess of 10,000 gallons shall be accompanied by an application fee of $100. Government agencies shall be exempt from such application fee.

(c) If the application for a protected area permit is for a daily average withdrawal during any calendar month in excess of 100,000 gallons, it shall be accompanied by such other information or exhibits required by Article 3 of the Commission's Rules of Practice and Procedure. In such cases, only the application fee required by the Rules will be assessed.

(d) To qualify for approval of a protected area permit, the owner or sponsor of the proposed withdrawal shall demonstrate that:

(1) The proposed withdrawal is consistent with the Commission's Comprehensive Plan and the policies and purposes of these regulations.

(2) Opportunities to satisy water requirements on a timely basis from existing available supplies and facilities have been explored and found infeasible.

(3) The proposed withdrawal, in conjunction with other withdrawals in the applicable ground water basin, will not exceed withdrawal limits of a ground water basin, aquifer or aquifer system.

(4) The proposed withdrawal will not significantly impair or reduce the flow of perennial streams in the area.

(5) Existing ground and surface water withdrawals will not be adversely impacted, or will be otherwise assured of adequate supplies in accordance with the requirements of § 430.19 of this part.

(6) The proposed withdrawal will not cause substantial, permanent adverse impact to the overlying environment.

(7) The owner or sponsor has adopted and will implement conservation and management programs as required by §430.15 of this part.

(e) Ground water withdrawals for space heating or cooling purposes that are less than 100,000 gallons per day shall be exempt from obtaining a protected area permit provided that the water withdrawn is returned locally, and to the same ground water basin and aquifer system from which it is withdrawn, undiminished in quantity and quality (except temperature). Ground water withdrawals for space heating or cooling that are subsequently used for commercial or industrial water supply purposes are subject to Commission withdrawal and wastewater discharge regulations. Ground water withdrawals exempted pursuant to this subsection shall be subject to the registration requirements of §430.17.

(f) All ground water withdrawal projects exempted by subsection "e" above shall be constructed in conformance with accepted industry practice and as a minimum shall comply with the following standards:

(1) All wells shall be drilled by a Pennsylvania licensed well driller and a Water Well Inventory Report shall be completed and filed with the Pennsylvania Department of Environmental Resources (PADER);

(2) No wells shall be located within a 100-year floodway;

(3) All wells shall have top of casing extended a minimum of one foot above the 100-year flood elevation;

(4) All wells shall have the casing protruding a minimum of six inches above the immediate surrounding grade;

(5) The area around all wells or well pits shall be constructed and/or graded to prevent the entrance of surface waters;

(6) All wells shall be accessible for inspection and shall have an access hole for water level measurements;

(7) In order to protect against significant leaks of refrigerant, all ground water heat pump systems shall be equipped with an automatic shutdown device that senses abnormally low or abnormally high refrigerant pressures;

(8) Any drilled well holes that are abandoned shall be sealed with a minimum of ten feet of cement grout. Additional seals may be required to separate different water-bearing zones.

(g) Protected area permits shall be approved or disapproved by the Executive Director with the concurrence of the Pennsylvania member of the Commission or his alternate.

(h) Dockets and protected area permits may be issued for a duration of up to ten years and shall specify the maximum total withdrawals that must not be exceeded during any consecutive 30-day period. Such maximum total withdrawals shall be based on demands projected to occur during the duration of the docket or protected area permit.

(i) Ground water withdrawal limits shall be defined for subbasins in accordance with the provisions of (i)(1) or (2) of this section. The limits for specific subbasins are set forth in (i)(3) of this section.

(1) Baseflow frequency analyses shall be conducted for all subbasins in the Southeastern Pennsylvania Ground Water Protected Area. The analyses shall determine the 1-year-in-25 average annual baseflow rate. The 1-year-in-25 average annual baseflow rate shall serve as the maximum withdrawal limit for net annual ground water withdrawals for subbasins. If net annual ground water withdrawals exceed 75 percent of this rate for a subbasin, such a subbasin shall be deemed "potentially stressed." The Commission shall maintain a current list of net annual ground water withdrawals for all subbasins. "Net" annual ground water withdrawals includes total ground water withdrawals less total water returned to the ground water system of the same subbasin.

(2) Upon application by the appropriate governmental body or bodies, the withdrawal limits criteria set forth in (i)(1) of this section may be revised by the Commission to provide additional protection for any subbasin identified in (i)(3) of this section with streams or stream segments designated by the Commonwealth of Pennsylvania as either "high quality," or "exceptional value," or "wild," or "scenic,"

or "pastoral," or to correspond with more stringent requirements in integrated resource plans adopted and implemented by all municipalities within a subbasin identified in (i)(3) of this section. Integrated resource plans shall be developed according to sound principles of hydrology. Such plans shall at a minimum assess water resources and existing uses of water; estimate future water demands and resource requirements; evaluate supply-side and demand-side alternatives to meet water withdrawal needs; assess options for wastewater discharge to subsurface formations and streams; consider stormwater and floodplain manage-

ment; assess the capacity of the subbasin to meet present and future demands for withdrawal and nonwithdrawal uses such as instream flows; identify potential conflicts and problems; incorporate public participation; and outline plans and programs including land use ordinances to resolve conflicts and meet needs. Integrated resource plans shall be adopted and implemented by all municipalities within a subbasin and incorporated into each municipality's Comprehensive Plan.

(3)(i) The potentially stressed levels and withdrawal limits for all delineated basins and subbasins are set forth below:

Subbasin	Potentially Stressed (mgy) [1]	Withdrawal Limit (mgy)
Neshaminy Creek Basin		
West Branch Neshaminy Creek Basin	1054	1405
Pine Run Basin	596	795
North Branch Neshaminy Creek	853	1131
Doylestown Subbasin Neshaminy Creek	710	946
Warwick Subbasin Neshaminy Creek	889	1185
Warrington Subbasin Little Neshaminy Creek	505	673
Park Creek Basin	582	776
Warminster Subbasin Little Neshaminy Creek	1016	1355
Mill Creek Basin	1174	1565
Northampton Subbasin Neshaminy Creek	596	794
Newtown Creek	298	397
Core Creek Basin	494	658
Ironworks Creek Basin	326	434
Schuylkill River Basin	3026	4034
Lower Section Subbasin Neshaminy Creek		
Hay Creek	974	1299
Lower Reach Manatawny-Ironstone Creek	1811	2414
Pigeon Creek	611	815
Schuylkill-Crow Creek	1157	1543
Schuylkill-Mingo Creek	671	895
Schuylkill-Plymouth-Mill Creeks	4446	5929
Schuylkill-Sixpenny Creek	1490	1987
Schuylkill-Sprogels Run	1091	1455
Schuylkill-Stony Creek	687	916
Schuylkill-Trout Creek	1082	1443
Stony Creek	1242	1655
Valley Creek	1865	2486
French and Pickering Creek Subbasins		
Lower Reach French Creek	634	845
Lower Reach Pickering Creek	1716	2288
Middle Reach French Creek	1608	2145
South Branch French Creek	1044	1393
Upper Reach French Creek	1295	1726
Upper Reach Pickering Creek	1358	1811
Perkiomen and Skippack Creek Subbasins		
East Branch Perkiomen-Indian Creeks	633	844
East Branch Perkiomen-Mill Creeks	720	961
East Branch Perkiomen-Morris Run	1214	1619
Hosensack-Indian Creeks	1257	1676
Lower Reach Skippack Creek	1069	1426
Perkiomen-Deep Creeks	1047	1396
Perkiomen-Lodal Creeks	1200	1600

Subbasin	Potentially Stressed (mgy) [1]	Withdrawal Limit (mgy)
Perkiomen-Macoby Creek	1252	1669
Swamp-Middle Creeks	1423	1898
Swamp-Minister Creeks	547	730
Swamp-Scioto Creeks	746	994
Towamencin Creek	466	622
Unami-Licking Creeks	992	1322
Unami-Ridge Valley Creeks	1068	1424
Upper Reach Perkiomen Creek	1223	1631
Upper Reach Skippack Creek	813	1084
West Branch Perkiomen Creek	1566	2088

Delaware River Basin

Subbasin	Potentially Stressed	Withdrawal Limit
Jericho Creek	421	562
Mill Creek	1600	2134
Paunnacussing Creek	513	684
Pidcock Creek	563	751
Upper Reach Cobbs Creek	871	1161
Upper Reach Crum Creek	1290	1721
Upper Reach Darby Creek	1625	2167
Upper Reach East Branch Chester Creek	1865	2487
Upper Reach Frankford Creek	1414	1886
Upper Reach Poquessing Creek	1008	1344
Upper Reach Ridley Creek	1707	2275

Tohickon Subbasin

Subbasin	Potentially Stressed	Withdrawal Limit
Tohickon-Beaver-Morgan Creeks	1156	1541
Tohickon-Deep Run	956	1274
Tohickon-Geddes-Cabin Runs	602	803
Tohickon-Lake Nockamixon	556	741
Tohickon-Three Mile Run	726	968

Pennypack and Wissahickon Subbasins

Subbasin	Potentially Stressed	Withdrawal Limit
Lower Reach Wissahickon Creek	2750	3666
Upper Reach Wissahickon Creek	1302	1736
Middle Reach Pennypack Creek	1295	1727
Upper Reach Pennypack Creek	1358	1811

Brandywine Creek Subbasin

Subbasin	Potentially Stressed	Withdrawal Limit
East Branch Brandywine-Taylor Run	1054	1405
Middle Reach Brandywine Creek	823	1098
Upper Reach Brandywine Creek	1614	2153
West Branch Brandywine-Beaver Run	2110	2813
West Branch Brandywine-Broad Run	2380	3173
West Valley Creek	1673	2231

Lehigh Subbasin

Subbasin	Potentially Stressed	Withdrawal Limit
Upper Reach Saucon Creek	946	1262

[1] mgy means million gallons per year.

(ii) Subject to public notice and hearing, this section may be updated or revised based upon new and evolving information on hydrology and streamflow and ground water monitoring or in accordance with paragraph (i)(2) of this section.

(j) Upon its determination that a subbasin is potentially stressed, the Commission shall notify all ground water users in the subbasin withdrawing 10,000 gallons per day or more during any 30-day period of its determination. If any such users have not obtained a docket or protected area permit from the Commission, they shall be required to apply to the Commission within 60 days of notification.

(k) In potentially stressed subbasins, dockets and protected area permit applications for new or expanded ground water withdrawals must include one or more programs to mitigate the adverse impacts of the new or expanded ground water withdrawal. The eligible programs are noted below. If the remainder of the application and the program(s) submitted are acceptable, the withdrawal may be approved by the Commission for an initial three-year period. The applicant shall implement the program(s) immediately upon Commission approval. If after the three-year period the program(s) is deemed successful by the Commission, the docket or permit duration may be extended for up to 10 years. The project sponsor shall be required to continue the program(s) for the duration of the docket or permit.

(1) A conjunctive use program that demonstrates the applicant's capability to obtain at least 15 percent of its average annual system usage from a reliable surface water supply. An acceptable program shall include either reservoir storage or an interconnection with a surface water supplier and an agreement or contract to purchase water from the supplier for the duration of the docket or permit.

(2) A water conservation program that exceeds the requirements of § 430.15. For existing water utilities, the program shall reduce average annual per capita water usage by at least five percent. All conservation programs shall include water conservation pricing, either inclining block rates, seasonal rates, or excess-use surcharges, and plumbing fixture rebate or retrofit components. For self-supplied users, the program shall include water efficient technologies such as recycling, reuse, xeriscaping, drip or micro irrigation, or other innovative technology approved by the Commission.

(3) A program to monitor and control ground water infiltration to the receiving sewer system. The program must quantify ground water infiltration to the system and document reductions in infiltration. The program should include such measures as leakage surveys of sewer mains, metering of sewer flows in mains and interceptors, analysis of sewer system flows to quantify infiltration, and remedial measures such as repair of leaks and joints, main lining, and main replacement.

(4) An artificial recharge or spray irrigation program that demonstrates a return of at least 60 percent of the total new or expanded annual withdrawal to the same ground water basin and aquifer system from which it is withdrawn. The program shall not impair ground water quality.

(5) An alternative program approved by the Commission to mitigate the adverse impacts of the new or expanded ground water withdrawal.

(l) The durations of all existing dockets and protected area permits may be extended by the Commission for an additional five years if the docket or permit holder successfully implements in either (k)(1) or (k)(2) of this section. If the docket or permit holder successfully implements both options, the docket or permit may be extended for an additional ten years. The Executive Director shall notify all docket and permit holders potentially affected by this resolution of their right to file an application to determine their eligibility for extension.

(m) It is the policy of the Commission to prevent, to the extent reasonably possible, net annual ground water withdrawals from exceeding the maximum withdrawal limit. An application for a proposed new or expanded ground water withdrawal that would result in net annual ground water withdrawals exceeding the maximum withdrawal limit established in paragraph (i)(3) of this section shall set forth the applicant's proposal for complying with the Commission's policy, with such supporting documentation as may be required by the Executive Director. Notification of the application shall be given to all affected existing water users who may also submit comments or recommendations for consideration by the Commission on the pending application. In taking action upon the application, the Commission shall give consideration to the submissions from the applicant and affected water users. If the Commission determines that it is in the public interest to do so, it may reduce the total of proposed and existing ground water withdrawals within a subbasin to a level at or below the withdrawal limit. Unless otherwise determined by the Commission, docket and permit holders shall share equitably in such reductions.

[46 FR 24, Jan. 2, 1981, as amended at 50 FR 5973, Feb. 13, 1985; 63 FR 6477, Feb. 9, 1998; 64 FR 35566, July 1, 1999]

§430.15 Conservation requirements.

The following conservation requirements shall apply to all existing, new or expanded ground water withdrawals for municipal, public, industrial or commercial water supply whose cumulative daily average withdrawal from one or more wells during any calendar month exceeds 10,000 gallons.

(a) Each person, firm, corporation or other entity withdrawing ground water within the Southeastern Pennsylvania Ground Water Protected Area for purposes of municipal or public water supply shall comply with the following conservation requirements:

(1) Water connections shall be metered, and water charges collected shall be based on metered usage.

(2) A water conservation program shall be initiated and diligently pursued within the service area of the municipal or public water supply. Such program shall include a program for leakage control providing for the monitoring, prevention and repair of significant leakage, and the provision of customer information relating to water-saving devices.

(3) Interconnections with adjacent water systems shall be considered to assure more reliable supplies of water during emergencies.

(4) A drought emergency plan specifying actions which would be taken to reduce demand and assure supplies to priority uses in the event of drought conditions shall be prepared in cooperation with the municipalities in the service area. The plan shall be filed with the Commission.

(b) Each person, firm, corporation or other entity withdrawing ground water within the Southeastern Pennsylvania Ground Water Protected Area for purposes of industrial or commercial water supply shall comply with the following conservation requirements:

(1) Opportunities for water conservation shall be investigated and all feasible conservation measures shall be implemented at the earliest practicable time.

(2) Water uses shall be monitored, and a systematic process shall be adopted and implemented to provide for the detection and expeditious correction of leakage.

(3) A drought emergency plan specifying the actions to be taken to reduce demand in the event of drought conditions shall be prepared and filed with the Commission.

(c) Permits issued pursuant to these regulations shall be conditioned upon compliance with the requirements of this section.

§430.17 Registration of existing withdrawals.

(a) Existing users of ground water within the Southeastern Pennsylvania Ground Water Protected Area whose lawful use commenced prior to the effective date of this regulation, whose cumulative monthly average daily withdrawal from one or more wells exceeds 10,000 gallons and whose withdrawal has not previously been approved by DRBC, pursuant to section 3.8 of the Compact, shall, prior to July 1, 1981, register their use with the Pennsylvania Department of Environmental Resources acting as agent for the Commission. Registration is required as a condition for such existing users being eligible for the protection afforded by this regulation. Such registration shall include withdrawals from quarries that are not fed by surface streams.

(b) Registrations shall be filed on forms approved by the Executive Director of the Commission. Each registrant shall provide, without limitation thereto, the following:

(1) A description of the location, size and depth of each well and the pump facilities installed therein.

(2) The estimated quantity of water withdrawn from each well, or related group of wells, during each month of 1980.

(3) The purposes for which the water is withdrawn, its place of use, and the approximate quantity of water used for each purpose.

(4) The location and method of wastewater disposal and discharge.

(5) A registration fee of $5 for each well.

§ 430.19 Ground water withdrawal metering, recording, and reporting.

(a) Each person, firm, corporation, or other entity whose cumulative daily average withdrawal of ground water from a well or group of wells operated as a system exceeds 10,000 gallons per day during any 30-day period shall meter or measure and record their withdrawals and report such withdrawals to the Pennsylvania Department of Environmental Resources. Withdrawals shall be measured by means of an automatic continuous recording device, flow meter, or other method, and shall be measured to within five percent of actual flow. Meters or other methods of measurement shall be subject to approval and inspection by the Pennsylvania Department of Environmental Resources as to type, method, installation, maintenance, calibration, reading, and accuracy. Withdrawals shall at a minimum be recorded on a daily basis for public water supply use and on a biweekly basis for all other water uses, and reported as monthly totals annually. More frequent recording or reporting may be required by the Pennsylvania Department of Environmental Resources or the Commission.

(b) The following water uses and operations are exempt from the metering or measurement requirements of paragraph (a): Agricultural irrigation; snowmaking; dewatering incidental to mining and quarrying; dewatering incidental to construction; and space heating or cooling uses that are exempt from permit requirements in § 430.13. Except for space heating and cooling uses described herein, persons engaged in such exempt withdrawals in excess of 10,000 gallons per day during any 30-day period shall record the pumping rates and the dates and elapsed hours of operation of any well or pump used to withdraw ground water, and report such information as required in paragraph (a). Space heating and cooling uses that are exempt from permit requirements in § 430.13 shall also be exempt from the requirement for recording and reporting.

(c) Pursuant to section 11.5 of the Compact, the Pennsylvania Department of Environmental Resources shall administer and enforce a program for metering, recording, and reporting ground-water withdrawals in accordance with this regulation.

(Delaware River Basin Compact, 75 Stat. 688)

[51 FR 25031, July 10, 1986]

§ 430.21 Protection of existing users.

(a) Protected area permits issued under this regulation for new or expanded withdrawals of ground water shall include conditions to protect the owners of existing wells in accordance with the provisions of this section.

(b) Any person, firm, corporation or other entity who commences a new or expanded withdrawal of ground water that is subject to the requirement of a protected area permit under this regulation shall provide mitigating measures if the withdrawal significantly affects or interferes with any existing well. Mitigation measures may consist of:

(1) Providing an alternative water supply, of adequate quantity and quality, to the effected well owner(s);

(2) Providing financial compensation to the affected well owner(s) sufficient to cover the costs of acquiring an alternative water supply of adequate quantity and quality; or

(3) Such other measures as the Commission shall determine to be just and equitable under the circumstances present in the case of any individual application.

[46 FR 24, Jan. 2, 1981. Redesignated at 51 FR 25031, July 10, 1986]

§ 430.23 Technical determinations and procedures.

(a) The radius to be considered in assessing the potential impact of a proposed new or expanded ground water withdrawal, as required by §§ 430.11 and 430.13 of this part shall be as follows:

Quantity of cumulative proposed withdrawal (gpd)	Radius from the proposed withdrawal to be considered (miles)
10,000 to 50,000	0.5
50,000 to 100,000	0.75
In excess of 100,000	1.0

(b) Ground water withdrawal limits, as defined in section 2.20.4 of the Water Code of the Delaware River Basis and § 430.9 of this part, shall be calculated on the basis of the average recharge rate to the basin, aquifer, or aquifer system during repetition of a period which includes the worst recorded drought.

(c) The requirement of paragraph (a) or (b) of this section may be modified or waived by the Executive Director or the Commission if an applicant adopts and implements a program for coordinated use of ground and surface water, and the applicant demonstrates that operation of the coordinated program will be consistent with the policies contained in the Comprehensive Plan and the purposes of these regulations.

[46 FR 24, Jan. 2, 1981. Redesignated at 51 FR 25031, July 10, 1986]

§430.25 Other permit requirements.

(a) Except to the extent provided in these regulations, registration of existing ground and surface water withdrawals and the issuance of withdrawal permits hereunder shall not create any private or proprietary rights in the water of the basin and the Commission reserves the right to amend, alter, or repeal these regulations and to amend, alter or rescind any actions taken hereunder in order to insure the proper control, use and management of the water resources of the basin.

(b) Neither the obligation to obtain a protected area permit under this regulation, nor the receipt thereof, shall relieve the sponsor of a new or expanded ground water withdrawal project of the obligation to obtain any other applicable permits required by Federal, state or local government agencies.

(c) A new or expanded ground water withdrawal subject to the requirement of a protected area permit under this regulation shall not require any further approval by the Commission if the daily average withdrawal during any calendar month is less than 100,000 gallons. If the new or expanded withdrawal exceeds a daily average of 100,000 gallons during any calendar month, the project shall be subject to review and approval by the commission pursuant to section 3.8 of the Delaware River Basin Compact, and the requirement of a protected area permit for such a project shall be in addition to other requirements of the Commission

and its Rules of Practice and Procedure.

[46 FR 24, Jan. 2, 1981. Redesignated at 51 FR 25031, July 10, 1986]

§430.27 Emergencies.

In the event of an emergency requiring immediate action to protect the public health and safety or to avoid substantial and irreparable injury to any private person or property, and the circumstances do not permit full review and determination in accordance with these regulations, the Executive Director, with the concurrence of the Pennsylvania member of the Commission or his alternate, may issue an emergency permit authorizing an applicant to take such action relating to these regulations as the Executive Director may deem necessary and proper. In such cases, the applicant shall be fully responsible for protecting existing ground water users, as prescribed in §430.19 of this part. The Executive Director shall report at the next meeting of the Commission on the nature of the emergency and any action taken under this section.

[47 FR 21776, May 20, 1982. Redesignated at 51 FR 25031, July 10, 1986]

§430.29 Appeals.

Any person aggrieved by any action or decision of the Executive Director taken under these regulations shall be entitled upon timely filing of a request therefor, to a hearing in accordance with Article 6 of the Commission'a Rules of Practice and Procedure.

[46 FR 24, Jan. 2, 1981. Redesignated at 51 FR 25031, July 10, 1986]

§430.31 Sanctions: Civil and criminal.

(a) Any person, association, corporation, public or private entity who or which violates or attempts or conspires to violate any provision of this regulation, or any order, regulation or permit issued in furtherance thereof, shall be punishable as provided in section 14.17 of the Compact.

(b) General Counsel of the Commission may, in his discretion, request the appropriate law enforcement officers of the Commonwealth of Pennsylvania to prosecute any or all violations of this regulation in accordance with the Compact and the laws of the Commonwealth, and for recovery of the fines fixed by section 14.17 of the Compact, in the name and on behalf of the Commission. The Commonwealth of Pennsylvania and its law enforcement officers are hereby requested pursuant to sections 10.1 and 11.5 of the Compact, to provide such technical, professional and administrative services as may be required for such enforcement.

(c) In addition to such penal sanctions as may be imposed pursuant to this section, any violation of this regulation shall be subject to such civil remedies by injunction and otherwise as provided by law.

[46 FR 24, Jan. 2, 1981. Redesignated at 51 FR 25031, July 10, 1986]

§ 430.33 Duration.

The delineation and declaration of the Southeastern Pennsylvania Ground Water Protected Area made pursuant to this regulation, and the requirements established hereby, shall continue until terminated by specific action of the Commission.

[46 FR 24, Jan. 2, 1981. Redesignated at 51 FR 25031, July 10, 1986]

§ 430.35 Amendments.

Upon request by any interested party, or on its own motion, the Commission may consider amendment of this regulation, and modify the geographic boundaries of the protected area, in accordance with Article 10 of the Compact.

[46 FR 24, Jan. 2, 1981. Redesignated at 51 FR 25031, July 10, 1986]

PARTS 431–499 [RESERVED]

CHAPTER VI—WATER RESOURCES COUNCIL

PART 700 [RESERVED]

PART 701—COUNCIL ORGANIZATION

Subpart A—Introduction

AUTHORITY: Sec. 402, Pub. L. 89–80; 79 Stat. 244, as amended (42 U.S.C. 1962–1962d–5), unless otherwise noted.

Subpart A—Introduction

SOURCE: 43 FR 25944, June 15, 1978, unless otherwise noted.

§ 701.1 General.

This part describes the organization established by the Water Resources Council in discharging its duties and responsibilities. The organization is designed to assure that Council Members will meet at least quarterly and consider and decide major matters before the Council. It provides that the Director can take action when necessary and appropriate; provided, that in the preparation of agenda items for the Council meetings, the Director shall consult with the Interagency Liaison Committee. It also provides that the Council Members shall be continuously advised of the significant actions of the Council staff. Council Members expect to participate personally in the work of the Council.

§ 701.2 Creation and basic authority.

The Water Resources Council was established by the Water Resources Planning Act of 1965 (Pub. L. 89–80, 79 Stat. 244, as amended (42 U.S.C. 1962–1962d–5)). The rules and regulations of this part are promulgated by authority of

59

section 402 of the Act (42 U.S.C. 1962d–1).

[41 FR 20548, May 19, 1976]

§ 701.3 Purpose of the Water Resources Council.

It is the purpose of the Water Resources Council to effectuate the policy of the United States in the Water Resources Planning Act (hereinafter the Act) to encourage the conservation, development, and utilization of water and related land resources of the United States on a comprehensive and coordinated basis by the Federal Government, States, localities, and private enterprise with the cooperation of all affected Federal agencies, States, local governments, individuals, corporations, business enterprises, and others concerned, within the limitations set forth in section 3 of the Act (42 U.S.C. 1962–1).

§ 701.4 Functions.

The functions of the Water Resources Council are:

(a) To maintain a continuing study and prepare periodically an assessment of the adequacy of supplies of water necessary to meet the water requirements in each water resource region in the United States and of the national interest therein.

(b) To maintain a continuing study of the relation of regional or river basin plans and programs to the requirements of larger regions of the Nation.

(c) To appraise the adequacy of administrative and statutory means for coordination and implementation of the water and related land resources policies and programs of the several Federal agencies and to make recommendations to the President with respect to Federal policies and programs.

(d) To establish, after consultation with appropriate interested Federal and non-Federal entities, and with approval of the President, principles, standards, and procedures for Federal participation in the preparation of comprehensive regional or river basin plans and for the formulation and evaluation of Federal water and related land resources projects, including primary direct navigation benefits as defined by section 7a, Pub. L. 89–670.

(e) To coordinate schedules, budgets, and programs of Federal agencies in comprehensive interagency regional or river basin planning.

(f) To carry out its responsibilities under Title II of the Act with regard to the creation, operation, and termination of Federal-State river basin commissions.

(g) To receive plans or revisions thereof submitted by river basin commissions in accordance with section 204(3) of the Act (42 U.S.C. 1962b(3)), and to review and transmit them, together with its recommendations, to the President in accordance with section 104 of the Act (42 U.S.C. 1962a–3).

(h) To assist the States financially in developing and participating in the development of comprehensive water and related land resources plans in accordance with Title III of the Act.

(i) To perform such other functions as the Council may be authorized by law, executive orders, regulations, or other appropriate instructions to perform.

(j) To take such actions as are necessary and proper to implement the Act and to carry out the functions enumerated herein.

§ 701.5 Organization pattern.

(a) The Office of the Water Resources Council is composed of the Water Resources Council, the Chairman of the Water Resources Council, the Water Resources Council Staff headed by a Director, and Field Organizations within its jurisdiction.

(b) The Water Resources Council consists of the following Members: The Secretary of Agriculture; the Secretary of the Army; the Secretary of Commerce; the Secretary of Energy; the Secretary of Housing and Urban Development; the Secretary of the Interior; the Secretary of Transportation; and the Administrator of the Environmental Protection Agency.

(c) The Chairman of the Council is designated by the President.

(d) The Water Resources Council staff is employed, assigned duties and responsibilities, and supervised by the Director.

(e) The Council Members shall establish an Interagency Liaison Committee. Task forces may be established and assigned duties by the Director with the concurrence of the Members, and/or action of the Council. Any Council Member may provide each task force with whatever representation he or she deems necessary.

(f) Field organizations are established by or operate under the Council and include field committees formerly under the Inter-Agency Committee on Water Resources and the offices of the Chairmen of Federal-State River Basin Commissions established under Title II of the Act.

§701.6 Location of office.

The Headquarters is located in the Washington, DC area.

Subpart B—Headquarters Organization

SOURCE: 43 FR 25945, June 15, 1978, unless otherwise noted.

§701.51 The Council.

Decisions of the Council are made as hereinafter described in §§701.53 and 701.54.

§701.52 Definitions.

As used in this part the term *Member* means the Secretary of Agriculture, the Secretary of the Army, the Secretary of Commerce, the Secretary of Energy, the Secretary of Housing and Urban Development, the Secretary of the Interior, the Secretary of Transportation, and the Administrator of the Environmental Protection Agency, or Alternate appointed in accordance with §701.53(a) when the alternate is acting for one of the above-named.

§701.53 Council decisions by Members.

Council decisions by Members may be made by direct vote at Council meetings or by a written communication which may provide for either a written or telephone response. Written communications shall state the time limit for voting on issues which they contain; however, extensions of time may be granted by the Director or Chairman when it is deemed necessary. Issues raised at Council meetings shall be decided by majority vote of Members present and voting. Issues identi-

fied in written communications must receive approval of all Members. If an action item does not receive approval of all Members, it will be considered as an agenda item at the next Council meeting. For purposes of this section, approval of all Members shall be defined as approval without a negative vote within the time limit for voting provided within each action memorandum. Decisions affecting the authority or responsibility of a Member, within the meaning of section 3(b) of the Act, (42 U.S.C. 1962–1(b)), can be made only with that Member's concurrence.

(a) Each of the Members in §701.5(b) shall designate in writing to the Chairman, with a copy to the Director, those individuals who may act as their Alternates in fulfilling the duties as a Member. Each Member shall designate one Alternate and one second Alternate to represent the Member on the Council.

(b) A quorum for the transaction of business at Council meetings shall consist of five or more Members and a majority shall consist of at least four votes.

(c) Each Member has equal responsibility and authority in all decisions and actions of the Council. Each Member may place an item on a meeting agenda or, acting through the Director, circulate in writing an item for Council action. Each Member, as well as each Associate Member and each Observer, shall have full access to all information relating to the performance of his duties and responsibilities.

(d) No vote shall be taken at Council meetings until each Member and Associate Member present has had full opportunity to express his views.

(e) Members shall meet regularly at least quarterly, upon the call of the Chairman, or when requested by a majority of Members.

(f) Matters specifically reserved for Council decision by Members are:

(1) Actions requiring Presidential action or approval.

(2) Approval of Annual Budget requests and the Annual Operating Program of the Office of the Water Resources Council.

(3) Decisions involving substantial policy issues.

(4) Delegations of authority.

(5) Determination that testimony taken or evidence received shall be taken under oath.

(6) Issuance of invitations to become Associate Members or Observers.

(7) Appointment and termination of the appointment of the Director.

[43 FR 25945, June 15, 1978, as amended at 45 FR 24460, Apr. 10, 1980]

§ 701.54 Interagency Liaison Committee.

There is established within the Council an Interagency Liaison Committee (hereafter referred to as ILC).

(a) The ILC shall be composed of one representative for each Member, Associate Member, and Observer. Additional agency representatives may participate in the ILC meeting whenever necessary.

(b) The chairmanship of the ILC shall rotate quarterly among the Members' representatives. Secretarial assistance shall be the responsibility of the ILC Chairman.

(c) The function of the ILC will be to provide a forum for discussion of agenda items prior to Council meetings to advise the Director of the Members' views on such agenda items, and with the Director, to develop the final agenda. It shall be the duty of the Director or his representative to brief the ILC on each agenda item at these meetings.

(d) The ILC may meet at other times upon the call of the Chairman or Director, to consider other items.

(e) Draft agenda items shall be submitted to ILC representatives at least 30 days prior to the Council meeting. The ILC shall meet at least 20 days prior to the Council meeting. Final Council agenda material shall be submitted to the Members at least 7 days prior to the Council meeting.

(f) All ILC meetings will be open except when privileged information is discussed. At such meetings only representatives of Members shall be present.

[43 FR 25945, June 15, 1978, as amended at 45 FR 58834, Sept. 5, 1980]

§ 701.55 Associate Members.

(a) The Chairman, with concurrence of the Council, may invite the heads of other Federal agencies having authorities and responsibilities relating to the work of the Council to become Associate Members. Associate Members, on the same terms and conditions as Members, may designate persons, in accordance with the same procedure identified in § 701.53(a), to serve for them as Associate Members.

(b) Associate Members may participate with Members in consideration of all matters relating to their areas of responsibility, except that their concurrence on a decision of the Council is not required.

§ 701.56 Observers.

(a) Chairmen and Vice-Chairmen of River Basin Commissions established under Title II of the Act shall be Observers.

(b) The Chairman, with the concurrence of the Council, may invite the heads of offices or other officials of the Executive Office of the President or other Federal agencies to become Observers.

(c) Observers may designate persons to attend Council meetings of Members. Observers will be furnished agenda and other materials on the same basis as Associate Members.

§ 701.57 Official decisions of the Council.

Official decisions of the Council shall be of record. Such decisions shall be recorded in accepted minutes of duly called regular or special meetings or set forth in resolutions, memoranda, or other documents approved by Members. Decisions which would affect the authority and responsibilities of heads of other Federal agencies, including Associate Members, within the meaning of section 3(b) of the Act, shall only be made during a regular or special meeting of Members and recorded in the minutes thereof.

§ 701.58 Task forces.

The Director with Council concurrence or the Council may establish task forces from time to time to aid in the preparation of issues for presentation to the Council.

(a) Any Member, Associate Member, or Observer may provide representation on each task force.

(b) The Director or the Council may designate the chairman of each task force.

(c) For each task force, the Director or the Council shall set forth the purpose and specific functions of each task force and their termination dates in establishing such task forces. Such charter documents shall also identify the relationship of each task force to functions of the Council.

(d) Each duly constituted task force will be provided administrative and secretarial support by the Water Resources Council Staff to the extent possible, directly or through arrangements with other Federal agencies.

§ 701.59 Advisory committees.

The Council may establish standing and ad hoc advisory committees. The establishment, operation, and termination of such committees shall be in accordance with the Federal Advisory Committee Act (Pub. L. 92–463) and other pertinent law and directives.

§ 701.60 Procedures for revision of rules and regulations.

Revisions proposed by the Water Resources Council Members to the Principles and Standards Manual of Procedures promulgated as rules and regulations by the Water Resources Council are to be submitted in writing by one or more Members of the Water Resouces Council to the Director, Water Resources Council, to be handled as an action item in accordance with § 701.53. Proposed revisons adopted by the Council in accordance with § 701.53 will be published in the FEDERAL REGISTER as proposed interim, or final changes. Proposed or interim changes shall be subject to a minimum 60-day public comment period; after the comment period, the Water Resources Council will publich notice that the revision is final as written or as changed to reflect comment or is revoked. Final changes will not be subject to a public comment period following publication in the FEDERAL REGISTER and will become effective when published or at specified date.

[44 FR 72584, Dec. 14, 1979]

§ 701.71 The Chairman.

(a) The Chairman shall preside at Council Meetings of Members.

(b) The Chairman is the official spokesman of the Council and represents it in its relations with the Congress, the States, Federal agencies, persons, or the public. He shall from time to time report, on behalf of the Council, to the President. He shall keep the Council apprised of his actions under this section.

(c) The Chairman shall request the heads of other Federal agencies to participate with the Council when matters affecting their responsibilities are considered by the Council.

(d) In the case of absence, disability, or vacancy, the acting Chairman shall be, in order of precedence, as designated (1) by the President (2) by the Chairman from among the Members, or (3) by the Council from among the Members.

§ 701.76 The Water Resources Council Staff.

The Water Resources Council Staff (hereinafter the Staff) serves the Council and the Chairman in the performance of their functions and in the exercise of their authorities in accordance with the Act, the rules and regulations and other decisions of the Council, and all other laws, rules, regulations, and orders applicable to the Water Resources Council, and will be organized in accordance with a structure approved by the Council.

§ 701.77 Director—duties and responsibilities.

The Director shall serve as the principal executive officer for the Council and as the head of the staff, and shall see to the faithful execution of the policies, programs, and decisions of the Council; report thereon to the Council from time to time or as the Council may direct; administer the office and staff of the Council within the limits of the Annual Budget and the Annual Operating Program related thereto; make recommendations to the Council and the Chairman relating to the performance of their functions and the exercise of their authorities; and facilitate the work of the Council and the Chairman.

His duties and responsibilities include, but are not limited to, the following:

(a) Acting for the Chairman, represents the Council in its relations with the Congress, States, Federal agencies, persons, or the public under the general supervision and direction of the Council.

(b) Establishes the line of succession as Acting Director among the other officers of the Council below the Deputy Director.

(c) Directs the Staff in its service to the Council and the Chairman in the performance of their functions and in the exercise of their authorities. The Director is responsible to the council for the organization of the Staff, employment and discharge of personnel, training and personnel development program, assignment of duties and responsibilities, and the conduct of its work.

(d) Insures that the quality of the work of the Staff in its studies, reports, and in other assignments is high that the professional integrity of its personnel is respected, and that its overall perspective and independence of judgment with regard to water and related land resources matters is approximately maintained within the context of the inter-agency, intergovernmental, and other staff collaboration that is both necessary and desirable in the fulfillment of the purpose of the Council as set forth in § 701.3.

(e) Prepares and recommends reports on legislation, Executive orders, and other documents requested of the Council.

(f) Prepares and recommends an Annual Budget request in accordance with policies, rules, and regulations applicable thereto. During its consideration by the Office of Management and Budget the President and the Congress, the Director shall seek acceptance of the proposed Annual Budget by every appropriate means. On behalf of the Council, he is authorized in his descretion to make appeals and agree to adjustments. However, to the extent that time and circumstances permit, he shall consult with and obtain the approval of the Council on all substantial appeals and adjustments.

(g) Prepares and recommends the Annual Operating Program to carry out the work of the Council, within the appropriations provided by the Congress and allowances approved by the Office of Management and Budget.

(h) Prepares and recommends proposed rules and regulations, including proposed delegations of authority, for carrying out the provisions of the Act, or other provisions of law which are administered by the Council.

(i) Prepares and recommends reports and materials for public information that are explanatory of the work and accomplishments of the Council.

(j) Appoints staff representatives to each task force established pursuant to § 701.58.

(k) Establishes and enforces administrative rules and regulations pertaining to the Staff consistent with applicable laws, Executive Orders, Budget Circulars, and other regulations and orders.

§ 701.78 Director—delegation of authorities.

(a) Under the authority of section 403 of the Act (42 U.S.C. 1962d–2), the Director is delegated authority to:

(1) Hold hearings, sit and act at such times and places, take such testimony, receive such evidence, and print or otherwise reproduce and distribute so much of its proceedings and reprints thereon as he may deem advisable.

(2) Acquire, furnish, and equip such office space as is necessary.

(3) Use the U.S. mails in the same manner and upon the same conditions as other departments and agencies of the United States.

(4) Employ and fix compensation of all personnel as the Director deems advisable in accordance with the civil service laws and the Classification Act of 1949, as amended; assign duties and responsibilities among such personnel and supervise personnel so employed.

(5) Procure services as authorized by section 15 of the Act of August 2, 1946 (5 U.S.C. 3109), at rates not in excess of the daily equivalent of the rate prescribed for grade GS–18 under section 5332 of Title 5 of the United States Code in the case of individual experts or consultants.

(6) Purchase, hire, operate, and maintain passenger motor vehicles.

(7) Utilize and expend such funds as are deemed advisable for proper administration of the authorities delegated herein. However, contract and individual modifications there of in excess of $100,000 or which involve significant policy decisions shall be submitted to the Council for approval before execution.

(8) Request any Federal department or agency (i) to furnish to the Council such information as may be necessary for carrying out its functions and as may be available to or procurable by such department or agency, and (ii) to detail personnel to temporary duty with the Council on a reimbursable basis.

(9) Make available for public inspection during ordinary office hours all appropriate records and papers of the Council.

(10) Compute and certify for payment funds to the States in accordance with standards and formula approved by the Council, and perform related functions of the Council contained in section 305 of the Act.

(11) Serve as a duly authorized representative of the Chairman of the Council for the purpose of audit and examination of any pertinent books, documents, papers, and records of the recipient of a grant under Title III of the Act, and recommend to the Chairman the appointment of further representatives as may be necessary for such function.

(12) Review, for compliance, State programs approved under Title III; conduct full inquiries as the Council may direct; and recommend for Council decision such withholding or reinstatement of payments as is appropriate and authorized by section 304 of the Act.

(13) Serve as the "responsible agency official" under part 705 of these rules and regulations.

(b) The authorities delegated in this section may be redelegated by the Director to the extent determined by him to be necessary and desirable for proper administration.

§ 701.79 Selection policy for professional personnel.

In the selection for employment of the professional staff as a whole, the Director shall be guided by the following criteria:

(a) Outstanding character and competence—both personal and professional.

(b) Spread and balance of training and experience in the several relevant professions—ecology; economics; economic geography; engineering; fish and wildlife biology; forestry; hydrology; irrigation; landscape architecture; law; political science; recreation; sanitary engineering; soil conservation; urban and other land planning; etc.

(c) Diversity of prior identification and experience, both planning and operating in Washington and in the field; including personnel with prior identification and experience with Federal, State, or local government, private enterprise, or university teaching and research.

Subpart C—Field Organization

SOURCE: 39 FR 20590, June 12, 1974, unless otherwise noted.

§ 701.100 Field Directors.

The Council may employ as professional staff Field Directors who shall be designated as chairmen of committees or groups established by the Council to develop and prepare regional or river basin assessments or plans. Such Field Directors shall perform their official functions at locations established by the Council.

§ 701.101 Field committees.

The Council may establish or continue already established regional committees to carry out assigned functions at field level.

§ 701.102 Existing committees.

Field Committees operating under the Water Resources Council (formerly under the Inter-Agency Committee on Water Resources) are as follows:

Pacific Southwest Inter-Agency Committee
Arkansas-White-Red Inter-Agency Committee
Southeast Basins Inter-Agency Committee

Subpart D—Availability of Information

AUTHORITY: 5 U.S.C. 552 as amended by Pub. L. 93–502, 88 Stat. 1561; 42 U.S.C. 1962d–1.

SOURCE: 40 FR 7253, Feb. 19, 1975, unless otherwise noted.

§ 701.200 Statement of policy.

Water Resources Council records and informational materials are available to the fullest extent possible consistent with 5 U.S.C. 552, as amended, and will be promptly furnished to any member of the public.

§ 701.201 Availability of records and informational materials.

(a) Except for records and materials exempted from disclosure pursuant to paragraph (b) of this section, any person may inspect and copy any document in the possession and custody of the Water Resources Council in accordance with the procedure provided in § 701.202.

(b) The provisions of 5 U.S.C. 552 which require that agencies make their records available for public inspection and copying do not apply to matters which are:

(1)(i) Specifically authorized under criteria established by an Executive order to be kept secret in the interest of national defense or foreign policy and

(ii) Are in fact properly classified pursuant to such Executive order;

(2) Related solely to the internal personnel rules and practices of an agency;

(3) Specifically exempted from disclosure by statute;

(4) Trade secrets and commercial or financial information obtained from a person and privileged or confidential;

(5) Inter-agency or intra-agency memorandums or letters which would not be available by law to a party other than an agency in litigation with the agency;

(6) Personnel and medical files and similar files the disclosure of which would constitute a clearly unwarranted invasion of personal privacy;

(7) Investigatory records compiled for law enforcement purposes but only to the extent that the production of such records would (i) interfere with enforcement proceedings, (ii) deprive a person of a right to a fair trial or an impartial adjudication, (iii) constitute an unwarranted invasion of personal privacy, (iv) disclose the identity of a confidential source and, in the case of a record compiled by a criminal law enforcement authority in the course of a criminal investigation, or by an agency conducting a lawful national security intelligence investigation, confidential information furnished only by the confidential source, (v) disclose investigative techniques and procedures, or (vi) endanger the life or physical safety of law enforcement personnel;

(8) Contained in or related to examination, operating, or condition reports prepared by, on behalf of, or for the use of an agency responsible for the regulation or supervision of financial institutions; or

(9) Geological and geophysical information and data, including maps, concerning wells.

Any reasonably segregable portion of a record shall be provided to any person requesting such record after deletion of the portions which are exempt under this subsection.

§ 701.202 Procedure for requests for information.

(a) A member of the public who requests records or materials from the Water Resources Council must provide a reasonable description of the records or materials sought so that such records or materials may be located without undue search or inquiry.

(b) Requests which reasonably describe the records or materials sought should be directed to the Public Information Officer, Water Resources Council, Suite 800, 2120 L Street NW., Washington, DC 20037.

(c) To insure that requests for information are processed as expeditiously as possible, all Freedom of Information Act (FOIA) requests should be clearly identified by the requester as such on the envelope and in the letter.

(d) Records or materials will be available for inspection and copying in person during normal business hours or by mail.

(e) Requests for records which originate in or concern matters which originate in another department or agency may be forwarded to the department or agency primarily concerned and the requester so notified.

§ 701.203 Schedule of fees.

(a) The Public Information Officer will to the extent practicable, encourage the widest possible distribution of information by permitting requests for inspection or copies of records or materials to be met without cost to the person making the request.

(b) Fees will be charged in the case of requests which are determined by the Public Information Officer to involve a burden on staff or facilities significantly in excess of that normally accepted by the Council in handling routine requests for information.

(c) In all instances where the Public Information Officer determines that a request for information can be considered as primarily benefiting the general public (despite a § 701.203 determination of burden), such request shall be met either without cost wherever practicable or at a reduced cost to the requester. Any such reduction shall be determined by the Public Information Officer on the basis of the balance between the benefit to the general public and the cost to the Water Resources Council.

(d) Fees shall be limited to recovery of only direct costs of search and duplication but in no event shall the fee for search and duplication exceed $2.50 per half hour, nor shall the fee for copying exceed $0.25 per page (maximum per page dimension of 8 × 14 inches).

(e) Unless a request for information specifically states that whatever cost is involved will be acceptable, or acceptable up to a specified limit that covers anticipated costs, a request that is expected to involve an assessed fee in excess of $50.00 will not be deemed to have been received until the requester is advised promptly upon physical receipt of the request of the anticipated cost and agrees to bear it.

(f) When anticipated fees exceed $50.00, a deposit for 25% of the amount must be made within 10 days of the notice to the requester of the initial determination.

(g) The Council reserves the right to limit the number of copies of any document that will be provided to any one person.

§ 701.204 Time limits for WRC initial determinations regarding requests for information.

(a) An initial determination to grant or deny each request for information will be made within ten (10) working days of receipt of such request.

(b) The requester shall be notified immediately of the initial determination and the reasons therefor.

(c) The Public Information Officer will make initial determinations to grant requests for information.

(1) In those instances where the initial determination by the Public Information Officer is to grant the request and the information is immediately supplied such action will serve as both notice of determination and compliance with the request.

(2) In those instances where the initial determination by the Public Information Officer is to grant the request, but the information is not immediately available, the Public Information Officer will send immediate notice of the determination to comply, and the approximate date the information will be forwarded.

(d) The Public Information Officer will make initial determination to deny the requests only with the concurrence of the General Counsel. The requester shall be notified immediately of the initial adverse determination, the reasons therefor, and the right to appeal the initial adverse determination to the Director.

§ 701.205 Time limit for requester to appeal an initial adverse determination.

(a) The requester shall have thirty (30) calendar days to file with the Director an appeal from an initial adverse determination. The appeal must be in writing.

(b) The thirty (30) day period of appeal shall run from receipt of the initial adverse determination (in cases of denials of an entire request) and from receipt of any records being made available pursuant to the initial adverse determination (in cases of partial denials).

§ 701.206 Time limit for WRC final determinations regarding requests for information appealed by the requester from an initial adverse determination.

The Director shall make a final determination with respect to any appeal within twenty (20) working days after receipt of such appeal. If the initial adverse determination is in whole or in part upheld by the Director, the requester shall be notified of the final adverse determination and the provisions for judicial review of that determination as stated in the Freedom of Information Act, as amended (see 5 U.S.C. 552(a)(4) *et seq.*; as amended by Pub. L. 93–502).

§ 701.207 Extension of time limits for WRC initial and final determinations.

(a) In unusual circumstances, as specified in this section, the time limits prescribed in either § 701.203 or § 701.204 may be extended by written notice from the responsible WRC official (i.e., the Public Information Officer in instances of initial requests and the Director in instances of appeals) to the requester setting forth the reasons for such extension and the date on which a determination is expected to be dispatched. No such notice shall specify a date that would result in an extension for more than ten (10) working days, and in no event shall the total extended time exceed ten (10) working days with respect to a particular request.

(b) As used in this section, *unusual circumstances* means, but only to the extent reasonably necessary to the proper processing of the particular request:

(1) The need to search for and collect the requested records from field facilities or other establishments that are separate from the office processing the request;

(2) The need to search for, collect, and appropriately examine a voluminous amount of separate and distinct records which are demanded in a single request; or

(3) The need for consultation, which shall be conducted with all practicable speed, with another agency having a substantial interest in the determination of the request or among two or more components of the agency having substantial subject-matter interest therein.

§ 701.208 WRC petition for judicial extension of time.

The provisions of § 701.206 notwithstanding, the Director may petition for judicial extension of time when exceptional circumstances warrant such action.

§ 701.209 River basin commissions and field committees.

(a) River basin commissions established pursuant to Title II of the Water Resources Planning Act are encouraged to establish, pursuant to section 205(c) of that Act, procedures for public availability of information that are consistent with 5 U.S.C. 552, as amended, and this subpart.

(b) Field committees will be governed by the procedures adopted by the lead Federal agency to implement 5 U.S.C. 552, as amended; except that if the lead agency of a field committee is a non-Federal entity, the standards of this subpart shall apply.

(c) Requests for documents and informational materials may be made to the chairmen of the field committees and river basin commissions at the following addresses:

(1) River Basin Commissions:

Great Lakes Basin Commission, P.O. Box 999, Ann Arbor, Michigan 48106;
New England River Basins Commission, 55 Court Street, Boston, Massachusetts 02108;
Ohio River Basin Commission, 36 East 4th Street, Suite 208–220, Cincinnati, Ohio 45202;
Pacific Northwest River Basins Commission, P.O. Bqx 908, Vancouver, Washington 98660;
Upper Mississippi River Basin Commission, Federal Office Building, Room 510, Fort Snelling, Twin Cities, Minnesota 55111;
Missouri River Basin Commission, 10050 Regency Circle, Suite 403 Omaha, Nebraska 68114.

(2) Field Committees:

Arkansas-White-Red Inter-Agency Committee, Room 4030, Federal Building, Albuquerque, New Mexico 87101;

Pacific Southwest Inter-Agency Committee, 630 Sansome Street, Room 1216, San Francisco, California 94111;

Southeast Basins Inter-Agency Committee, 402 New Walton Building, Atlanta, Georgia 30303.

[40 FR 7253, Feb. 19, 1975, as amended at 40 FR 10668, Mar. 7, 1975]

Subpart E—Protection of Privacy

AUTHORITY: Sec. 402, Water Resources Planning Act of 1965 (Sec. 402, Pub. L. 89–80; 79 Stat. 254, as amended (42 U.S.C. 1962d–1)) and the Privacy Act of 1974 (Pub. L. 93–579; 88 Stat. 1896 (5 U.S.C. 552a)).

SOURCE: 40 FR 45676, Oct. 2, 1975, unless otherwise noted.

§ 701.300 Purpose and scope.

(a) The purpose of this subpart is to set forth rules to inform the public about information maintained by the U.S. Water Resources Council relating to identifiable individuals and to inform those individuals how they may gain access to and correct or amend information about themselves.

(b) The regulations in this subpart implement the requirements of the Privacy Act of 1974 (Pub. L. 93–579; 88 Stat. 1896 (5 U.S.C. 552a)).

(c) The regulations in this subpart apply only to records disclosed or requested under the Privacy Act of 1974, and not requests for information made pursuant to the Freedom of Information Act, as amended (5 U.S.C. 552, as amended by Pub. L. 93–502).

§ 701.301 Definitions.

For the purposes of this subpart, unless otherwise required by the context:

(a) *Council* means the U.S. Water Resources Council;

(b) *Individual* means a citizen of the United States or an alien lawfully admitted for permanent resident;

(c) *Maintain* means maintain, collect, use or disseminate;

(d) *Record* means any item, collection, or grouping of information about an individual that is maintained by the Council, including, but not limited to, his education, financial transactions, medical history and criminal or employment history, and that contains his name, or the identifying number, symbol, or other identifying particular assigned to the individual, such as a finger or voice print or a photograph;

(e) *Adverse determination* means a decision by the proper Council official to deny, in whole or in part, a request from an individual for a correction or amendment of a record concerning the individual and maintained by the Council; and

(f) *Record system* means *system of records* as defined in the Act, i.e., a group of any records under the control of the Council from which information is retrieved by the name of the individual or by some identifying particular assigned to the individual.

§ 701.302 Procedures for notification of existence of records pertaining to individuals.

(a) The systems of records, as defined in the Privacy Act of 1974, maintained by the Council are listed annually in the FEDERAL REGISTER as required by that Act. Any individual may request the Council to inform him or her whether a particular record system named by the individual contains a record pertaining to him or her. The request may be made in person during business hours or in writing at the location and to the person specified in the notice describing that record system.

(b) An individual who believes that the Council maintains records pertaining to him or her but who cannot determine which records system contains those records, may request assistance by mail or in person at the Division of Program Coordination and Management, 2120 L Street, NW., Washington, DC 20037, during business hours (8:00 A.M. through 4:30 P.M., Monday through Friday, excluding legal holidays).

(c) The Council will attempt to respond to a request as to whether a record exists within 10 working days from the time it receives the request or to inform the requestor of the need for additional time or additional information within 10 working days. If a request is complied with within 10 working days, no separate acknowledgment will be made.

[40 FR 45676, Oct. 2, 1975, as amended at 41 FR 8343, Feb. 26, 1976]

§ 701.303 Conditions of disclosure.

(a) Subject to the conditions of paragraphs (b) and (c) of this section, the Council will not disclose any record which is contained in a system of records, by any means of communication to any person who is not an individual to whom the record pertains.

(b) Upon written request or with prior written consent of the individual to whom the record pertains, the Council may disclose any such record to any person or other agency.

(c) In the absence of a written consent from the individual to whom the record pertains, the Council may disclose any such record provided such disclosure is:

(1) To those officers and employees of the Council who have a need for the record in the performance of their duties;

(2) Required under the Freedom of Information Act (5 U.S.C. 552);

(3) For a routine use compatible with the purpose for which it was collected;

(4) To the Bureau of Census for purposes of planning or carrying out a census or survey or related activity under the provisions of Title 13 of the United States Code;

(5) To a recipient who has provided the Council with adequate advance written assurance that the record will be used solely as a statistical research or reporting record, and the record is to be transferred in a form that is not individually identifiable;

(6) To the National Archives of the United States as a record which has sufficient historical or other value to warrant its continued preservation by the United States government, or for evaluation by the Administrator of General Services or his designee to determine whether the record has such value;

(7) To another agency or to an instrumentality of any governmental jurisdiction within or under the control of the United States for a civil or criminal law enforcement activity authorized by law: *Provided,* The head of the agency or instrumentality has made a prior written request to the Assistant Director Program Coordination and Management specifying the particular record and the law enforcement activity for which it is sought;

(8) To a person pursuant to a showing of compelling circumstance affecting the health or safety of an individual: *Provided,* That upon such disclosure notification is transmitted to the last known address of such individual (and see § 701.306);

(9) To either House of Congress, and to the extent of a matter within its jurisdiction, any committee or subcommittee, or joint committee of Congress;

(10) To the Comptroller General, or any of his authorized representatives in the course of the performance of the duties of the GAO; or

(11) Under an order of a court of competent jurisdiction.

§ 701.304 Procedures for identification of individuals making requests.

(a) Each individual requesting the disclosure of a record or copy of a record will furnish the following information with his or her request:

(1) The name of the record system containing the record;

(2) Proof as described in paragraph (b) of this section that he or she is the individual to whom the requested record relates; and

(3) Any other information required by the notice describing the record system.

(b) Proof of identity as required by paragraph (a)(2) of this section will be provided as described in paragraph (b)(1) and (2) of this section. Requests made by an agent, parent, or guardian will include the authorization described in § 701.310(a) and (b).

(1) Requests made in writing will include a statement, signed by the individual and properly notarized, that he or she appeared before a notary public and submitted proof of identification in the form of a drivers license, birth certificate, passport or other identification acceptable to the notary public. In any case in which, because of the extreme sensitivity of the record sought to be seen or copied, the agency determines that the identification is not adequate, it may request the individual to submit additional proof of identification.

(2) If the request is made in person, the requester will submit proof of identification similar to that described in

paragraph (b)(1) of this section, acceptable to the Council.

[41 FR 8343, Feb. 26, 1976]

§ 701.305 Procedures for requests for access to or disclosure of records pertaining to individuals.

(a) After being informed by the Council that a system of records contains a record pertaining to him or her, an individual may request the Council for access to or disclosure of that record to him or her in the manner described in this section. Each such request of a record or a copy of it will be made at the place specified in the notice describing that system of records, either in writing or in person. Requests may be made by agents, parents, or guardians of individuals as described in § 701.310(a) and (b).

(b) The request for access to or disclosure of a record should specifically identify the systems of records involved.

(c) The Council will attempt to affirm or deny a request within 10 working days from the time it receives the request or to inform the requester of the need for additional time, additional information, identification, or the tendering of fees (as specified in § 701.312), within 10 working days; except that if the request for access was not preceded by a notification request as provided in § 701.302, then the 10-day period will not begin until after such time as it has been determined that the record exists. If a request is complied with within 10 working days, no separate acknowledgement will be made.

[41 FR 8343, Feb. 26, 1976]

§ 701.306 Special procedure: Medical records.

(a) An individual requesting disclosure of a record which contains medical or psychological information may name a medical doctor or other person to act as his agent as described in § 701.310(a). Records containing medical or psychological information may be disclosed to that agent rather than to the individual at the individual's request.

(b) If the individual has not named a medical doctor as agent, the Council may determine, after consultation with a medical doctor, that disclosure of the information would have an adverse effect on the requester. The Council may then disclose that information to a medical doctor specified by the individual, rather than to that individual, either in person or by mail.

[40 FR 45676, Oct. 2, 1975, as amended at 41 FR 8343, Feb. 26, 1976]

§ 701.307 Request for correction or amendment to record.

(a) Any individual who has reviewed a record pertaining to him that was furnished to him under this subpart, may request the agency to correct or amend all or any part of that record.

(b) Each individual requesting a correction or amendment will send the request to the agency official who furnished the record to him.

(c) Each request for a correction or amendment of a record will contain the following information:

(1) The name of the individual requesting the correction or amendment;

(2) The name of the system of records in which the record sought to be corrected or amended is maintained;

(3) The location of that record in the system of records;

(4) A copy of the record sought to be corrected or amended or a description of that record;

(5) A statement of the material in the record requested to be corrected or amended;

(6) A statement of the specific wording of the correction or amendment sought; and

(7) A statement of the basis for the requested correction or amendment, including any material that the individual can furnish to substantiate the reasons for the correction or amendment sought.

§ 701.308 Council review of request for correction or amendment of record.

(a) Not later than 10 days (excluding Saturdays, Sundays, and legal holidays) after the receipt of the request for the correction or amendment of a record under § 701.307, the Council will acknowledge receipt of the request and inform the individual whether further information is required before the correction or amendment can be considered.

(b) The Council will promptly review the request and either make the requested correction or amendment or notify the individual of the initial adverse determination, including in the notification the reasons for the adverse determination and the appeal procedure provided by § 701.309.

(c) The Assistant Director, Program Coordination and Management, or his designee, will, after consulting with the General Counsel, or his designee, have the primary authority to make an initial adverse determination.

(d) The Council will make each requested correction or amendment to a record if that correction or amendment will correct anything that is not accurate, relevant, timely, or complete, within the record.

(e) If the requested correction or amendment to a record is agreed to by the Council, the Council will, within 30 working days:

(1) Advise the individual;

(2) Correct the record accordingly; and

(3) Where an accounting of disclosures had been made (as provided in § 701.311), advise all previous recipients (including the individual) of the record of the fact that the correction was made and the substance of the correction.

[40 FR 45676, Oct. 2, 1975, as amended at 41 FR 8343, Feb. 26, 1976]

§ 701.309 Appeal of initial adverse determination.

(a) Any individual whose request for a correction or amendment, requested by him, to a record has been denied, in whole or in part, may appeal that decision to the Director of the Council.

(b) The appeal will be in writing and will:

(1) Name the individual making the appeal;

(2) Identify the record sought to be amended;

(3) Name the record system in which that record is contained;

(4) Contain a short statement describing the amendment sought; and

(5) State the name and location of the Council official who made the initial adverse determination.

(c) Not later than 30 days (excluding Saturdays, Sundays, and legal holidays) after the date on which the Council received the appeal, the Director will complete his review of the appeal and make a final decision thereon. However, for good cause shown, the Director may extend that 30 day period by not more than an additional 30 working days. If the Director so extends the period, he will promptly notify the individual requesting the review that the extension has been made and the reasons therefor.

(d) After review of an appeal request, the agency will send a written notice to the requester containing the following information:

(1) The decision and, if the denial is upheld, the reasons for the decision; and

(2) The specific civil remedies available to the requester as per section 2(g) of Pub. L. 93–579, as well as notice that additional remedies may be appropriate and available to enable the full exercise of the requester's rights at law.

(3) The right to file with the Council a concise statement setting forth the requester's reasons for disagreement with the Council's refusal to correct or amend the record.

[40 FR 45676, Oct. 2, 1975, as amended at 41 FR 8344, Feb. 26, 1976]

§ 701.310 Disclosure of record to person other than the individual to whom it pertains.

(a) Any individual who desires to have a record covered by this subpart disclosed to or mailed to a person other than that individual may authorize that person to act as his agent for that specific purpose. The authorization will be in writing, signed by the individual, and will be notarized. The agent will submit with the authorization proof of the individual's identity as required by § 701.304(b).

(b) The parent of any minor individual or the legal guardian of any individual who has been declared by a court of competent jurisdiction to be incompetent due to physical or mental incapacity or age, may act on behalf of that individual in any matter covered by this subpart. A parent or guardian who desires to act on behalf of such an individual will present suitable evidence of parentage or guardianship, by birth certificate, certified copy of a court order, or similar documents, and proof of the individual's identity in a form that complies with § 701.304(b).

(c) An individual to whom a record is to be disclosed in person pursuant to this subpart, may have a person of his own choosing accompany the individual when the record is disclosed.

§ 701.311 Accounting for disclosures.

(a) *Maintenance of an accounting.* (1) Where a record is disclosed to any person, or to another agency, under any of the provisions of § 701.303 except § 701.303(c)(1) and (2), an accounting will be made.

(2) The accounting will record (i) the date, nature, and purpose of each disclosure of a record to any person or to another agency and (ii) the name and address of the person or agency to whom the disclosure was made.

(3) Accountings prepared under this section will be maintained for at least five years or the life of the record, whichever is longer, after the disclosure for which the accounting is made.

(b) *Access to accounting.* (1) Except for accounting of disclosures made under § 701.303(c)(1) and (2), accountings of all disclosures of a record will be made available to the individual to whom the record relates at his or her request.

(2) An individual desiring access to accountings of disclosures of a record pertaining to him or her will submit his request by following the procedures of § 701.305.

(c) *Notification of disclosure.* When a record is disclosed pursuant to § 701.303(c)(11) as the result of the order of a court of competent jurisdiction, reasonable efforts will be made to notify the individual to whom the record pertains as soon as the order becomes a matter of public record.

[41 FR 8344, Feb. 26, 1976]

§ 701.312 Fees.

(a) The Council will not charge an individual for the costs of making a search for a record or the costs of reviewing the record. When the Council makes a copy of a record as a necessary part of the process of disclosing the record to an individual, the Council will not charge the individual for the cost of making that copy.

(b) If an individual requests the Council to furnish him with a copy of the record (when a copy has not otherwise been made as a necessary part of the process of disclosing the record to the individual), the Council will charge a maximum fee of $0.25 per page (maximum per page dimension of 8 × 14 inches) to the extent that the request exceeds $5.00 in cost to the Council. Requests not exceeding $5.00 in cost to the Council will be met without cost to the requester.

[40 FR 45676, Oct. 2, 1975. Redesignated at 41 FR 8344, Feb. 26, 1976]

§ 701.313 Penalties.

Title 18 U.S.C. 1001, Crimes and Criminal Procedures, makes it a criminal offense, subject to a maximum fine of $10,000 or imprisonment for not more than 5 years or both, to knowingly and willfully make or cause to be made any false or fraudulent statements or representations in any matter within the jurisdiction of any agency of the United States. Section 552a(i)(3) of the Privacy Act (5 U.S.C. 552a(i)(3)) makes it a misdemeanor, subject to a maximum fine of $5,000, to knowingly and willfully request or obtain any record concerning an individual under false pretenses. Section 552a(i)(1) and (2) of the Privacy Act (5 U.S.C. 552a(i)(1) and (2) provide penalties for violations by agency employees of the Privacy Act or regulations established thereunder.

[40 FR 45676, Oct. 2, 1975. Redesignated at 41 FR 8344, Feb. 26, 1976]

§ 701.314 Exemptions.

No Council records system or systems are exempted from the provisions of 5 U.S.C. 552a as permitted under certain conditions by 5 U.S.C. 552a(j) and (k).

[40 FR 45676, Oct. 2, 1975. Redesignated at 41 FR 8344, Feb. 26, 1976]

PART 704—PLAN FORMULATION STANDARDS AND PROCEDURES

Subparts A–D [Reserved]

Subpart E—Standards for Plan Formulation and Evaluation

AUTHORITY: Sec. 402, 79 Stat. 254; 42 U.S.C. 1962d-1.

§ 704.39 Discount rate.

(a) The interest rate to be used in plan formulation and evaluation for discounting future benefits and computing costs, or otherwise converting benefits and costs to a common time basis, shall be based upon the average yield during the preceding fiscal year on interest-bearing marketable securities of the United States which, at the time the computation is made, have terms of 15 years or more remaining to maturity: *Provided, however,* That in no event shall the rate be raised or lowered more than one-quarter of 1 percent for any year. The average yield shall be computed as the average during the fiscal year of the daily bid prices. Where the average rate so computed is not a multiple of one-eighth of 1 percent, the rate of interest shall be the multiple of one-eighth of 1 percent nearest to such average rate.

(b) The computation shall be made as of July 1 of each year, and the rate thus computed shall be used during the succeeding 12 months. The Executive Director shall annually request the Secretary of the Treasury to inform the Water Resources Council of the rate thus computed.

(c) Subject to the provisions of paragraphs (d) and (e) of this section, the provisions of paragraphs (a) and (b) of this section shall apply to all Federal and federally assisted water and related land resources project evaluation reports submitted to the Congress, or approved administratively, after the close of the second session of the 90th Congress.

(d) Where construction of a project has been authorized prior to the close of the second session of the 90th Congress, and the appropriate State or local governmental agency or agencies have given prior to December 31, 1969, satisfactory assurances to pay the required non-Federal share of project costs, the discount rate to be used in the computation of benefits and costs for such project shall be the rate in effect immediately prior to the effective date of this section, and that rate shall continue to be used for such project until construction has been completed, unless the Congress otherwise decides.

(e) Notwithstanding the provisions of paragraphs (a) and (b) of this section, the discount rate to be used in plan formulation and evaluation during the remainder of the fiscal year 1969 shall be 4⅝ percent except as provided by paragraph (d) of this section.

(f) Section V. G. 2 of the interagency agreement dated May 15, 1962, approved by the President on May 15, 1962, entitled "Policies, Standards, and Procedures in the Formulation, Evaluation, and Review of Plans for Use and Development of Water and Related Land Resources," and published on May 29, 1962, as Senate Document No. 97, 87th Congress, 2d Session, is superseded by the provisions of this section.

[33 FR 19170, Dec. 24, 1968]

PART 705—NONDISCRIMINATION IN FEDERALLY ASSISTED PROGRAMS—EFFECTUATION OF TITLE VI OF THE CIVIL RIGHTS ACT OF 1964

Sec.
705.1 Purpose.
705.2 Definitions.
705.3 Application of this part.
705.4 Discrimination prohibited.
705.5 Assurance required.
705.6 Compliance information.
705.7 Conduct of investigations.
705.8 Procedure for effecting compliance.
705.9 Hearings.
705.10 Decisions and notices.
705.11 Judicial review.
705.12 Effect on other regulations.

AUTHORITY: Sec. 602 of Pub. L. 88-352, 78 Stat. 252, (42 U.S.C. 2000 d—1), and sec. 402 of Pub. L. 89-80, 79 Stat. 254, (42 U.S.C. 1962 d—1).

SOURCE: 39 FR 41521, Nov. 29, 1974, unless otherwise noted.

§ 705.1 Purpose.

The purpose of this subpart is to implement the provisions of Title VI of the Civil Rights Act of 1964, 78 Stat. 252 (hereafter referred to as the "Act"), to the end that no person in the United States shall, on the ground of race, color, or national origin, be excluded from participation in, be denied the benefits of, or otherwise be subjected to discrimination under any program or activity receiving Federal financial assistance from the Water Resources Council.

§705.2 Definitions.

As used in this part:

(a) *Applicant* means one who submits an application, request, or plan required to be approved by the Water Resources Council, or by a primary recipient, as a condition to eligibility for Federal financial assistance, and the term *application* means such an application, request, or plan.

(b) *Facility* includes all or any part of structures, equipment, or other real or personal property or interests therein, and the provision of facilities includes the construction, expansion, renovation, remodeling, alteration or acquisition of facilities.

(c) *Federal financial assistance* includes:

(1) Grants and loans of Federal funds;

(2) The grant or donation of Federal property and interests in property;

(3) The detail of Federal personnel;

(4) The sale and lease of, and the permission to use (on other than a casual or transient basis), Federal property or any interest in such property without consideration or at a nominal consideration, or at a consideration which is reduced for the purpose of assisting the recipient, or in recognition of the public interest to be served by such sale or lease to the recipient; and

(5) Any Federal agreement, arrangement, or other contract which has as one of its purposes the provision of assistance.

(d) *Primary recipient* means any recipient that is authorized or required to extend Federal financial assistance to another recipient for the purpose of carrying out a program.

(e) *Program* includes any program, project, or activity for the provision of services, financial aid, or other benefits to individuals (including education or training, health, welfare, rehabilitation, housing, or other services, whether provided through employees of the recipient of Federal financial assistance or provided by others through contracts or other arrangements with the recipient, and including work opportunities), or for the provision of facilities for furnishing services, financial aid or other benefits to individuals. The services, financial aid, or other benefits provided under a program receiving Federal financial assistance shall be deemed to include any services, financial aid, or other benefits provided with the aid of Federal financial assistance or the aid of any non-Federal funds, property, or other resources required to be expended or made available for the program to meet matching requirements or other conditions which must be met in order to receive the Federal financial assistance, and to include any services, financial aid, or other benefits provided in or through a facility provided with the aid of Federal financial assistance or such non-Federal resources.

(f) *Recipient* may mean any State, territory, possession, the District of Columbia, or Puerto Rico, or any political subdivision thereof, or instrumentality thereof, any public or private agency, institution, or organization, or other entity, or any individual, in any State, territory, possession, the District of Columbia, or Puerto Rico, to whom Federal financial assistance is extended, directly or through another recipient, for any program, including any successor, assignee, or transferee thereof, but such term does not include any ultimate beneficiary under any such program.

(g) *Responsible agency official* means the Director of the Water Resources Council or his designee.

§705.3 Application of this part.

This part applies to any program for which Federal financial assistance is authorized under a law administered by the Water Resources Council. It applies to money paid, property transferred, or other Federal financial assistance extended under any such program after the date of this part pursuant to an application whether approved before or after such date. This part does not apply to (a) any Federal financial assistance by way of insurance or guaranty contracts, or (b) any employment practice except to the extent described in §705.4(c).

§ 705.4 Discrimination prohibited.

(a) *General.* No person in the United States shall, on the grounds of race, color, or national origin be excluded from participation in, be denied the benefits of, or be otherwise subjected to discrimination under, any program to which this part applies.

(b) *Specific discriminatory actions prohibited.* (1) A recipient under any program to which this part applies may not directly or through contractual or other arrangements, on the grounds of race, color, or national origin:

(i) Deny a person any service, financial aid, or other benefit provided under the program;

(ii) Provide any service, financial aid, or other benefit to a person which is different, or is provided in a different manner, from that provided to others under the program;

(iii) Subject a person to segregation or separate treatment in any matter related to his receipt of any service, financial aid, or other benefit under the program;

(iv) Restrict a person in any way in the enjoyment of any advantage or privilege enjoyed by others receiving any service, financial aid, or other benefit under the program;

(v) Treat a person differently from others in determining whether he satisfies any admission, enrollment, quota, eligibility, membership, or other requirement or condition which persons must meet in order to be provided any service, financial aid, or other benefit provided under the program; or

(vi) Deny a person an opportunity to participate in the program through the provision of services or otherwise or afford him an opportunity to do so which is different from that afforded others under the program.

(vii) Deny a person the opportunity to participate as a member of a planning or advisory body which is an integral part of the program.

(2) A recipient, in determining the types of services, financial aid, or other benefits, or facilities which will be provided under any such program, or the class of persons to whom, or the situations in which, such services, financial aid, other benefits, or facilties will be provided under any such program, or the class of persons to be afforded an opportunity to participate in any such program, may not, directly or through contractual or other arrangements, utilize criteria or methods of administration which have the effect of subjecting persons to discrimination because of their race, color, or national origin, or have the effect of defeating or substantially impairing accomplishment of the objectives of the program with respect to individuals of a particular race, color, or national origin.

(3) As used in this section, the services, financial aid, or other benefits provided under a program receiving Federal financial assistance include any service, financial aid, or other benefit provided in or through a facility provided with the aid of Federal financial assistance.

(4) The enumeration of specific forms of prohibited discrimination in this paragraph does not limit the generality of the prohibition in paragraph (a) of this section.

(5) This part does not prohibit the consideration of race, color, or national origin if the purpose and effect are to remove or overcome the consequences of practices or impediments which have restricted the availability of, or participation in, the program or activity receiving Federal financial assistance, on the grounds of race, color, or national origin. When previous discriminatory practice or usage tends, on the grounds of race, color, or national origin, to exclude individuals from participation in, to deny them the benefits of, or to subject them to discrimination under any program or activity to which this part applies, the applicant or recipient has an obligation to take reasonable action to remove or overcome the consequences of the prior discriminatory practice or usage, and to accomplish the purposes of the Act.

(c) *Employment practices.* (1) Where a primary objective of a program of Federal financial assistance to which this part applies is to provide employment, a recipient or other party subject to this part shall not, directly or through contractual or other arrangements, subject a person to discrimination on the grounds of race, color, or national origin in its employment practices under such program (including recruitment or recruitment advertising, hiring, firing, upgrading, promotion, demotion, transfer, layoff, termination, rates of pay or other forms of compensation or benefits, selection for training or apprenticeship, use of facilities, and treatment of employees). Such recipient shall take affirmative action to insure that applicants are employed, and employees are treated during employment, without regard to their race, color, or national origin. The requirements applicable to construction employment under any such program shall be those specified in or pursuant to part III of Executive Order 11246 or any Executive Order which supersedes it.

(2) Where a primary objective of the Federal financial assistance is not to provide employment, but discrimination on the grounds of race, color, or national origin in the employment practices of the recipient or other persons subject to the regulation tends, on the grounds of race, color, or national origin, to exclude individuals from participation in, to deny them the benefits of, or to subject them to discrimination under any program to which this regulation applies, the provisions of paragraph (c)(1) of this section shall apply to the employment practice of the recipient or other persons subject to the regulation, to the extent necessary to assure equality of opportunity to, and nondiscriminatory treatment of, beneficiaries.

(d) *Location of facilities.* A recipient may not make a selection of a site or location of a facility if the purpose of that selection, or its effect when made, is to exclude individuals from participation in, to deny them the benefits of, or to subject them to discrimination under any program or activity to which this rule applies, on the grounds of race, color, or national origin; or if the purpose is to, or its effect when made will, substantially impair the accomplishment of the objectives of this part.

§705.5 Assurance required.

(a) *General.* Every application for Federal financial assistance to carry out a program to which this part applies, and every application for Federal

financial assistance to provide a facility shall, as a condition to its approval and the extension of any Federal financial assistance pursuant to the application, contain or be accompanied by an assurance that the program will be conducted or the facility operated in compliance with all requirements imposed by or pursuant to this part. In the case of an application for Federal financial assistance to provide real property or structures thereon, or personal property or equipment of any kind, such assurance shall obligate the recipient, or, in the case of a subsequent transfer, the transferee, for the period during which the property is used for a purpose for which the Federal financial assistance is extended or for any other purpose involving the provisions of similar services or benefits. In all other cases, such assurance shall obligate the recipient for the period during which Federal financial assistance is extended pursuant to the application. The responsible agency official shall specify the form of the foregoing assurances for each program, and the extent to which like assurances will be required of subgrantees, contractors, and subcontractors, transferees, successors in interest, and other participants in the program. Any such assurance shall include provisions which give the United States a right to seek its judicial enforcement.

(b) *Planning grants to States.* Each designated State agency must submit the assurance specified in §703.5(n) of these rules and regulations.

(c) *River basin commissions.* Each river basin commission is required to submit, along with its annual budget request, written assurance of its continuing compliance with §705.4 of this part.

§705.6 Compliance information.

(a) *Cooperation and assistance.* The responsible agency official shall, to the fullest extent practicable, seek the cooperation of recipients in obtaining compliance with this part and shall provide assistance and guidance to recipients to help them comply voluntarily with this part.

(b) *Compliance reports.* Each recipient shall keep such records and submit to the responsible agency official timely, complete, and accurate compliance reports at such times, and in such form and containing such information, as the responsible agency official may determine to be necessary to enable him to ascertain whether the recipient has complied or is complying with this part. In the case of any program under which a primary recipient extends Federal financial assistance to any other recipient or subcontracts with any other person or group, such other recipient shall also submit such compliance reports to the primary recipient as may be necessary to enable the primary recipient to carry out its obligations under this part.

(c) *Access to sources of information.* Each recipient shall permit access by the responsible agency official during normal business hours to such of its books, records, accounts, and other sources of information, and its facilities, as may be pertinent to ascertain compliance with this part. Whenever any information required of a recipient is in the exclusive possession of any other agency, institution, or person and that agency, institution, or person fails or refuses to furnish that information, the recipient shall so certify in its report and set forth the efforts which it has made to obtain the information.

(d) *Information to beneficiaries and participants.* Each recipient shall make available to participants, beneficiaries, and other interested persons such information regarding the provisions of this part and its applicability to the program under which the recipient receives Federal financial assistance, and make such information available to them in such manner, as the responsible agency official finds necessary to apprise such persons of the protections against discrimination assured them by the Act and this part.

§ 705.7   Conduct of investigations.

(a) *Periodic compliance reviews.* The responsible agency official shall from time to time review the practices of recipients to determine whether they are complying with this part.

(b) *Complaints.* Any person who believes himself or any specific class of individuals to be subjected to discrimination prohibited by this part may by himself or by a representative file with the responsible agency official a written complaint. A complaint must be filed not later than 180 days from the date of the alleged discrimination, unless the time for filing is extended by the responsible agency official.

(c) *Investigations.* The responsible agency official will make a prompt investigation whenever a compliance review, report, complaint, or any other information indicates a possible failure to comply with this part. The investigation should include, whenever appropriate, a review of the pertinent practices and policies of the recipient, the circumstances under which the possible noncompliance with this part occurred, and other factors relevant to a determination as to whether the recipient has failed to comply with this part.

(d) *Resolution of matters.* (1) If an investigation pursuant to paragraph (c) of this section indicates a failure to comply with this part, the responsible agency official will so inform the recipient and the matter will be resolved by informal means whenever possible. If it has been determined that the matter cannot be resolved by informal means, action will be taken as provided for in § 705.8.

(2) If an investigation does not warrant action pursuant to subparagraph (1) of this paragraph, the responsible agency official will so inform the recipient and the complainant, if any, in writing.

(e) *Intimidatory or retaliatory acts prohibited.* No recipient or other person shall intimidate, threaten, coerce, or discriminate against any individual for the purpose of interfering with any right or privilege secured by section 601 of the Act or this part, or because he has made a complaint, testified, assisted, or participated in any manner in an investigation, proceeding, or hearing under this part. The identity of complainants shall be kept confidential except to the extent necessary to carry out the purpose of this part, including the conduct of any investigation, hearing, or judicial proceeding arising thereunder.

§ 705.8 Procedure for effecting compliance.

(a) *General.* If there appears to be a failure or threatened failure to comply with this part and if the noncompliance or threatened noncompliance cannot be corrected by informal means, the responsible agency official may suspend or terminate, or refuse to grant or continue, Federal financial assistance, or use any other means authorized by law, to induce compliance with this part. Such other means include, but are not limited to, (1) a reference to the Department of Justice with a recommendation that appropriate proceedings be brought to enforce any rights of the United States under any law of the United States (including other titles of the Act), or any assurance or other contractual undertaking, and (2) any applicable proceeding under State or local law.

(b) *Noncompliance with assurance requirement.* If an applicant or recipient fails or refuses to furnish an assurance required under § 705.5 or fails or refuses to comply with the provisions of the assurance it has furnished, or otherwise fails or refuses to comply with any requirement imposed by or pursuant to Title VI or this part, Federal financial assistance may be suspended, terminated, or refused in accordance with the procedures of Title VI and this part. The Water Resources Council shall not be required to provide assistance in such a case during the pendency of administrative proceedings under this part, except that the Council will continue assistance during the pendency of such proceedings whenever such assistance is due and payable pursuant to a final commitment made or an application finally approved prior to the effective date of this part.

(c) *Termination of or refusal to grant or to continue Federal financial assistance.* No order suspending, terminating, or refusing to grant or continue Federal financial assistance shall become effective until:

(1) The responsible agency official has advised the applicant or recipient of his failure to comply and has determined that compliance cannot be secured by voluntary means;

(2) There has been an express finding on the record, after opportunity for hearing, of a failure by the applicant or recipient to comply with a requirement imposed by or pursuant to this part;

(3) The action has been approved by the Chairman of the Water Resources Council pursuant to § 705.10(e); and

(4) The expiration of 30 days after the responsible agency official has filed with the committee of the House and the committee of the Senate having legislative jurisdiction over the program involved, a full written report of the circumstances and the grounds for such action. Any action to suspend or terminate or to refuse to grant or to continue Federal financial assistance shall be limited to the particular political entity, or part thereof, or other applicant or recipient as to whom such a finding has been made and shall be limited in its effect to the particular program, or part thereof, in which such noncompliance has been so found.

(d) *Other means authorized by law.* No action to effect compliance with Title VI of the Act by any other means authorized by law shall be taken until:

(1) The responsible agency official has determined that compliance cannot be secured by voluntary means;

(2) The recipient or other person has been notified or its failure to comply and of the action to be taken to effect compliance; and

(3) The expiration of at least 10 days from the mailing of such notice to the recipient or other person. During this period of at least 10 days, additional efforts shall be made to persuade the recipient or other person to comply with the regulation and to take such corrective action as may be appropriate.

§ 705.9 Hearings.

(a) *Opportunity for hearing.* Whenever an opportunity for a hearing is required by § 705.8(c), reasonable notice shall be given by registered or certified mail, return receipt requested, to the affected applicant or recipient. This notice shall advise the applicant or recipient of the action proposed to be taken, the specific provision under which the proposed action against it is to be taken, and the matters of fact or law asserted as the basis for this action, and either (1) fix a date not less than 20 days after the date of such notice within which the applicant or recipient may request of the responsible agency official that the matter be scheduled for heaing or (2) advise the applicant or recipient that the matter in question has been set down for hearing at a stated place and time. The time and place so fixed shall be reasonable and shall be subject to change for cause. The complainant, if any, shall be advised of the time and place of the hearing. An applicant or recipient may waive a hearing and submit written information and argument for the record. The failure of an applicant or recipient to request a hearing under this paragraph or to appear at a hearing for which a date has been set shall be deemed to be a waiver of the right to a hearing under section 602 of the Act and § 705.8(c) and consent to the making of a decision on the basis of such information as is available.

(b) *Time and place of hearing.* Hearings shall be held at the offices of the Water Resources Council in Washington, DC, at a time fixed by the responsible agency official unless it determines that the convenience of the applicant or recipient or of the Council requires that another place be selected. Hearings shall be held before the responsible agency official or at its discretion, before a hearing examiner appointed in accordance with section 3105 of Title 5, U.S.C., or detailed under section 3344 of Title 5, U.S.C.

(c) *Right to counsel.* In all proceedings under this section, the applicant or recipient and the Water Resources Council shall have the right to be represented by counsel.

(d) *Procedures, evidence, and record.* (1) The hearing, decision, and any administrative review thereof shall be conducted in conformity with the Administrative Procedure Act (5 U.S.C. 554–557) and with such other regulations that may be necessary or appropriate for the conduct of hearings pursuant to this part.

(2) Technical rules of evidence do not apply to hearings conducted pursuant to this part, but rules or principles designed to assure production of the most credible evidence available and to subject testimony to test by cross-examination shall be applied where reasonably necessary by the officer conducting the hearing. The hearing officer may exclude irrelevant, immaterial, or unduly repetitious evidence. All documents and other evidence offered or taken for the record shall be open to examination by the parties and opportunity shall be given to refute facts and arguments advanced on either side of the issues. A transcript shall be made of the oral evidence except to the extent the substance thereof is stipulated for the record. All decisions shall be based upon the hearing record and written findings shall be made.

(e) *Consolidated or joint hearings.* In cases in which the same or related facts are asserted to constitute noncompliance with this part with respect to two or more programs to which this part applies, or noncompliance with this part and the regulations of one or more other Federal departments or agencies issued under Title VI of the Act, the responsible agency official may, by agreement with such other departments or agencies, where applicable, provide for the conduct of consolidated or joint hearings, and for the application to such hearings of rules or procedures not inconsistent with this part. Final decisions in such cases, insofar as this regulation is concerned, shall be made in accordance with § 705.10.

§ 705.10   Decisions and notices.

(a) Procedure on decisions by hearing examiner. If the hearing is held by a hearing examiner, the hearing examiner shall either make an initial decision, if so authorized, or certify the entire record including his recommended findings and proposed decision to the responsible agency official for a final decision, and a copy of such initial decision or certification shall be mailed to the applicant or recipient. Where the initial decision is made by the hearing examiner, the applicant or recipient may, within 30 days after the mailing of such notice of initial decision, file with the responsible agency official his exceptions to the initial decision, with his reasons therefor. In the absence of exceptions, the responsible agency official may, on his own motion, within 45 days after the initial decison, serve on the applicant or recipient a notice that he will review the decision. Upon the filing of such exceptions or of notice of review, the responsible agency official shall review the initial decision and issue his own decision thereon including the reasons therefor. In the absence of either exceptions or a notice or review the initial decision shall, subject to paragraph (e) constitute the final decision of the responsible agency official.

(b) *Decisions on record or review by the responsible agency official.* Whenever a record is certified to the responsible agency official for decision or its reviews the decision of a hearing examiner pursuant to paragraph (a) of this section or whenever the responsible agency official conducts the hearing, the applicant or recipient shall be given reasonable opportunity to file with it briefs or other written statements of its contentions and a written copy of the final decision of the responsible agency official shall be sent to the applicant or recipient and to the complainant, if any.

(c) *Decisions on record where a hearing is waived.* Whenever a hearing is waived pursuant to §705.9, a decision shall be made by the responsible agency official on the record and a written copy of such decision shall be sent to the applicant or recipient, and to the complainant, if any.

(d) *Rulings required.* Each decision of a hearing examiner or the responsible agency official shall set forth his or its ruling on each finding, conclusion, or exception presented, and shall identify the requirement or requirements imposed by or pursuant to this part with which it is found that the applicant or recipient has failed to comply.

(e) *Approval by the Chairman.* Any final decision by the responsible agency official provides for the suspension or termination of, or the refusal to grant or continue Federal financial assistance, or the imposition of any other sanction available under this part or the Act, shall promptly be transmitted to the Chairman of the Water Resources Council, who may approve such decision, may vacate it, or remit or mitigate any sanction imposed.

(f) *Content of orders.* The final decision may provide for suspension or ter-

mination of, or refusal to grant or continue Federal financial assistance, in whole or in part, under the program involved, and may contain such terms, conditions, and other provisions as are consistent with and will effectuate the purposes of the Act and this part, including provisions designed to assure that no Federal financial assistance will thereafter be extended under such programs to the applicant or recipient determined by such decision to be in default in its performance of an assurance given by it pursuant to this part, or to have otherwise failed to comply with this part, unless and until it corrects its noncompliance and satisfies the responsible agency official that it will fully comply with this part.

(g) *Post termination proceedings.* (1) An applicant or recipient adversely affected by an order issued under paragraph (f) shall be restored to full eligibility to receive Federal financial assistance if it satisfies the terms and conditions of that order for such eligibility or if it brings itself into compliance with this part and provides reasonable assurance that it will fully comply with this part.

(2) Any applicant or recipient adversely affected by an order entered pursuant to paragraph (f) of this section may at any time request the responsible agency official to restore fully its eligibility to receive Federal financial assistance. Any such request shall be supported by information showing that the applicant or recipient has met the requirements of paragraph (g)(1) of this section. If the responsible agency official determines that those requirements have been satisfied, he shall restore such eligibility.

(3) If the responsible agency official denies any such request, the applicant or recipient may submit a request for a hearing in writing, specifying why it believes the responsible agency official to have been in error. It shall thereupon be given an expeditious hearing, with a decision on the record. The applicant or recipient will be estored to such eligibility if it proves at such a hearing that it satisfied the requirements of paragraph (g)(1). While proceedings under this paragraph are pending, the sanctions imposed by the

order issued under paragraph (f) of this section shall remain in effect.

§ 705.11 Judicial review.

Action taken pursuant to section 602 of the Act is subject to judicial review as provided in section 603 of the Act.

§ 705.12 Effect on other regulations.

(a) Nothing in this part shall be deemed to supersede any other order, regulation, or instruction which prohibits discrimination on the grounds of race, color, or national origin in any program or situation to which this part is inapplicable, or prohibit discrimination on any other ground.

(b) *Forms and instructions.* The responsible agency official shall issue and promptly make available to all interested persons forms and detailed instructions and procedures for effectuating this part as applied to programs to which this part applies and for which he is responsible.

(c) *Supervision and coordination.* The responsible agency official may from time to time assign to officials of other departments or agencies of the Government with the consent of such departments or agencies, responsibilities in connection with the effectuation of the purposes of Title VI of the Act and this part (other than responsibility for final decision as provided in § 705.10), including the achievement of effective coordination and maximum uniformity within the Water Resources Council and within the Executive Branch of the Government in the application of Title VI and this part to similar programs and in similar situations. Any action, taken, determination made, or requirements imposed by an official of another department or agency acting pursuant to an assignment of responsibility under this paragraph shall have the same effect as though such action had been taken by the responsible agency official.

PART 706—EMPLOYEE RESPONSIBILITIES AND CONDUCT

Subpart A—General Provisions

Subpart B—Conduct and Responsibilities of Employees

Subpart C—Conduct and Responsibilities of Special Government Employees

Subpart D—Statements of Employment and Financial Interests

AUTHORITY: Water Resources Planning Act, 1965 (Sec. 402, Pub. L. 89–80, 79 Stat. 254 (42 U.S.C. 1962d–1)); E.O. 11222 (30 FR 6469, 3 CFR Proc. 3279; as amended); 5 CFR part 735 (33 FR 12487).

SOURCE: 40 FR 32818, Aug. 4, 1975, unless otherwise noted.

Subpart A—General Provisions

§ 706.101 Purpose.

The maintenance of unusually high standards of honesty, integrity, impartiality, and conduct by employees and special Government employees is essential to assure the proper performance of the Water Resources Council's (hereafter referred to as the Council) business and the maintenance of confidence by citizens in their Government. The avoidance of misconduct and conflicts of interest on the part of employees and special Government employees through informed judgment is indispensable to the maintenance of these standards. To accord with these concepts, this part sets forth the Council's regulations prescribing standards of conduct and responsibilities and governing statements of employment and financial interests for employees and special Government employees.

§ 706.102 Definitions.

In this part:

(a) *Employee* means the Director and an employee of the Council employed by the Director under the authority of § 701.78(a)(4) of this chapter.

(b) *Special Government employee* means a special Government employee as defined in section 202 of Title 18 of the United States Code who is employed by the Council.

§ 706.103 Remedial action.

(a) A violation of this part by an employee or special Government employee may be cause for remedial action. Remedial action may include, but is not limited to:

(1) Changes in assigned duties;

(2) Divestment by the employee or special Government employee of his conflicting interest;

(3) Disciplinary action which may be in addition to any penalty prescribed by law; or

(4) Disqualification for a particular assignment.

(b) Remedial action, whether disciplinary or otherwise, shall be effected in accordance with any applicable laws, Executive orders, and regulations.

§ 706.104 Interpretation and advisory service.

The General Counsel will serve as Counselor for the purpose of providing interpretation and advisory assistance to the Council staff on matters covered in this part 706.

Subpart B—Conduct and Responsibilities of Employees

§ 706.201 Proscribed actions.

An employee shall avoid any action which might result in, or create the appearance of:

(a) Using public office for private gain;

(b) Giving preferential treatment to any person;

(c) Impeding Government efficiency or economy;

(d) Losing complete independence or impartiality;

(e) Making a Government decision outside official channels; or

(f) Affecting adversely the confidence of the public in the integrity of the Government.

§ 706.202 Gifts, entertainment, and favors.

(a) Except as provided in paragraphs (b) and (c) of this section, an employee shall not solicit or accept, directly or indirectly, any gift, gratuity, favor, entertainment, loan, or any other thing of monetary value, from a person who:

(1) Has, or is seeking to obtain, contractual or other business or financial relations with the Council;

(2) Conducts operations or activities that are regulated by the Council; or

(3) Has interests that may be substantially affected by the performance or nonperformance of his official duty.

(b) The restrictions set forth in paragraph (a) of this section do not apply to:

(1) Obvious family or personal relationships, such as those between the employee and his parents, children, or spouse, when the circumstances make it clear that those relationships rather than the business of the persons concerned are the motivating factors;

(2) The acceptance of food and refreshments of nominal value on infrequent occasions in the ordinary course of a luncheon or dinner meeting or other meeting or on an inspection tour where an employee may be properly in attendance;

(3) The acceptance of loans from banks or other financial institutions on customary terms to finance proper and usual activities of employees, such as home mortgage loans; and

(4) The acceptance of unsolicited advertising or promotional material, such as pens, pencils, note pads, calendars, and other items of nominal intrinsic value.

(c) An employee shall not solicit a contribution from another employee for a gift to an official superior, make a donation as a gift to an official superior, or accept a gift from an employee receiving less pay than himself (5 U.S.C. 7351). However, this paragraph does not prohibit a voluntary gift of nominal value or donation in a nominal amount made on a special occasion such as marriage, illness, or retirement.

(d) An employee shall not accept a gift, present, decoration, or other thing from a foreign government unless authorized by Congress as provided by the Constitution and in 5 U.S.C. 7342.

(e) Neither this section nor § 706.203 precludes an employee from receipt of bona fide reimbursement, unless prohibited by law, for expenses of travel and such other necessary subsistence as is compatible with this part for which no Government payment or reimbursement is made. However, this paragraph does not allow an employee to be reimbursed, or payment to be made on his behalf, for excessive personal living expenses, gifts, entertainment, or other personal benefits, nor does it allow an employee to be reimbursed by a person for travel on official business under Council orders when reimbursement is proscribed by Decision B–128527 of the Comptroller General dated March 7, 1967.

§ 706.203 Outside employment and activity.

(a) An employee shall not engage in outside employment or other outside activity not compatible with the full and proper discharge of the duties and responsibilities of his Government employment. Incompatible activities include, but are not limited to:

(1) Acceptance of a fee, compensation, gift, payment of expense, or any other thing of monetary value in circumstances wherein acceptance may result in, or create the appearance of, a conflict of interest;

(2) Outside employment or activity which tends to impair his mental or physical capacity to perform the duties and responsibilities of his position in an acceptable manner;

(3) Outside employment or activity which is in violation of a statute, Executive order, or regulation, including applicable State and local statutes and ordinances.

(b) Employees are encouraged to engage in teaching, lecturing, and writing that is not prohibited by law, Executive Order 11222 of May 11, 1965, as amended by Executive Order 11590 of April 27, 1971, this part or other Council regulations. However, an employee shall not, either for or without compensation, engage in teaching, lecturing, or writing, including teaching, lecturing, or writing for the purpose of the special preparation of a person or class of persons for an examination of the Civil Service Commission or Board of Examiners for the Foreign Service, that depends on information obtained as a result of his Government employment, except when that information has been made available to the general public or will be made available on request, or when the agency head gives written authorization for use of nonpublic information on the basis that the use is in the public interest.

(c) An employee shall not receive any salary or anything of monetary value from a private source as compensation for his services to the Government.

(d) An employee shall not engage in outside work or activity which may be construed by the public to be official acts of the Council, or of a nature closely paralleling the work of the Council.

(e) An employee who engages in any kind of outside paid employment on a substantially regular basis shall submit to his immediate supervisor a memorandum describing the employment and stating approximately how many hours per week he is so employed. The immediate supervisor shall forward the memorandum through the Director for inclusion in the employee's Official Personnel Folder.

(f) This section does not preclude an employee from:

(1) Participation in the activities of national or State political parties not proscribed by law;

(2) Participation in the local self-government activities in the community in which he resides to the extent permitted by law; or,

(3) Participation in the affairs of, or acceptance of an award for meritorious public contribution or achievement given by, a charitable, religious, professional, social, fraternal, nonprofit educational, recreational, public service, or civic organization.

§706.204 Financial interests.

(a) An employee shall not:

(1) Have a direct or indirect financial interest that conflicts substantially, or appears to conflict substantially, with his Government duties and responsibilities; or

(2) Engage in, directly or indirectly, a financial transaction as a result of or primarily relying on, information obtained through his Government employment.

(b) This section does not preclude an employee from having a financial interest or engaging in financial transactions to the same extent as a private citizen not employed by the Government so long as it is not prohibited by law, Executive Order 11222, as amended, 5 CFR part 735, or this part.

§706.205 Misuse of information.

For the purpose of furthering a private interest an employee shall not, except as provided in §706.203(b), directly or indirectly use, or allow the use of, official information obtained through or in connection with his Government employment which has not been made available to the general public.

§706.206 Support of Council programs.

(a) When a Council program is based on law or Executive order, every employee has a positive obligation to make it function as efficiently and economically as possible and to support it as long as it is a part of recognized public policy. An employee may, therefore, properly make an address explaining and interpreting such a program, citing its achievements, defending it against uninformed or unjust criticism, pointing out the need for possible improvements, or soliciting views for improving it.

(b) An employee shall not, either directly or indirectly, use appropriated funds to influence a Member of Congress to favor or oppose legislation in violation of 18 U.S.C. 1913. However, an employee is not prohibited from:

(1) Testifying as a representative of the Council on pending legislation proposals before congressional committees on request; provided, that the relevant provisions of the current OMB Circular A-14 ("Legislation Coordination and Clearance") are complied with; or

(2) Assisting congressional committees in drafting bills or reports on request, when it is clear that the employee is serving solely as a technical expert under the direction of committee leadership.

§706.207 Use of Government property.

An employee shall not directly or indirectly use, or allow the use of, Government property of any kind, including property leased to the Government, for other than officially approved activities. An employee has a positive duty to protect and conserve Government property including equipment, supplies, and other property entrusted or issued to him.

§706.208 Indebtedness.

(a) An employee shall pay each just financial obligation in a proper and timely manner, especially one imposed by law, such as Federal, State, or local taxes. For the purpose of this section, a "just financial obligation" means one acknowledged by the employee or reduced to judgment by a court or one imposed by law such as Federal, State or local taxes.

(b) When an employee has a levy placed against his salary for failure to pay an indebtedness for Federal income taxes, he shall be issued a written reprimand stating that failure to make satisfactory arrangements regarding future tax liabilities will be grounds for removal.

(c) When an employee is the subject of a letter of complaint stating that he has not paid his State or local taxes and has failed to make satisfactory arrangements regarding the debt, he shall be interviewed by the Assistant

Director, Division of Program Coordination and Management. In this interview he shall be instructed to make satisfactory arrangements for the payment of his debt immediately and informed that failure to do so will be grounds for removal.

(d) When an employee is the subject of a letter of complaint regarding any other kind of indebtedness to a unit of government, Federal, State, or local, the procedure prescribed in paragraph (c) of this section shall be observed.

(e) When a creditor who holds a legal judgment against an employee requests that the Council assist in collecting the debt, the employee shall be interviewed by the Assistant Director, Division of Program Coordination and Management. In this interview he shall be instructed to pay the debt in full within 90 days, or within whatever longer period is specified by the Assistant Director, Division of Program Coordination and Management if he determines that a 90-day limit would impose undue hardship on the employee, and informed that failure to do so will be grounds for removal.

(f) When an employee is the subject of a letter of complaint from a creditor who does not hold a legal judgment against the employee, the Assistant Director, Division of Program Coordination and Management shall forward a copy of the letter to the employee together with a memorandum calling the employee's attention to the provisions of this section. However, the Council will not assist the creditor in collecting the debt.

§ 706.209 Gambling, betting, and lotteries.

An employee shall not participate, while on Government-owned or leased property or while on duty for the Government, in any gambling activity, including the operation of a gambling device, in conducting a lottery or pool, in a game for money or property, or in selling or purchasing a numbers slip or ticket.

§ 706.210 Coercion.

An employee shall not use his Government employment to coerce, or give the appearance of coercing, a person to provide financial benefit to himself or another person, particularly one with whom he has family, business, or financial ties.

§ 706.211 General conduct prejudicial to the Government.

An employee shall not engage in criminal, infamous, dishonest, immoral, or notoriously disgraceful conduct, or other conduct prejudicial to the Government.

§ 706.212 Miscellaneous statutory provisions.

The attention of each employee is directed to the following statutory provisions:

(a) House Concurrent Resolution 175, 85th Congress, 2d Session, 72 Stat. B12, the Code of Ethics for Government Service.

(b) Chapter 11 of Title 18, United States Code, relating to bribery, graft and conflicts of interest.

(c) The prohibition against lobbying with appropriated funds (18 U.S.C. 1913).

(d) The prohibitions against disloyalty and striking (E.O. 10450, 18 U.S.C. 1918).

(e) The prohibition against the employment of a member of a Communist organization (50 U.S.C. 784).

(f) The prohibitions against:

(1) The disclosure of classified information (18 U.S.C. 798, 50 U.S.C. 783); and

(2) The disclosure of confidential information (18 U.S.C. 1905).

(g) The provision relating to the habitual use of intoxicants to excess (5 U.S.C. 7352).

(h) The prohibition against the misuse of a Government vehicle (31 U.S.C. 638a(c)).

(i) The prohibition against the misuse of the franking privilege (18 U.S.C. 1719).

(j) The prohibition against the use of deceit in an examination or personnel action in connection with Government employment (18 U.S.C. 1917).

(k) The prohibition against fraud or false statements in a Government matter (18 U.S.C. 1001).

(l) The prohibition against mutilating or destroying a public record (18 U.S.C. 2071).

(m) The prohibition against counterfeiting and forging transportation requests (18 U.S.C. 508).

(n) The prohibitions against:

(1) Embezzlement of Government money or property (18 U.S.C. 641);

(2) Failing to account for public money (18 U.S.C. 643); and

(3) Embezzlement of the money or property of another person in the possession of an employee by reason of his employment (18 U.S.C. 654).

(o) The prohibition against unauthorized use of documents relating to claims from or by the Government (18 U.S.C. 285).

(p) The prohibitions against political activities in Subchapter III of Chapter 73 of Title 5, United States Code and 18 U.S.C. 602, 603, 607, and 608.

(q) The provision relating to the denial of the right to petition Congress (5 U.S.C. 7102).

(r) The prohibition against an employee acting as the agent of a foreign principal registered under the Foreign Agents Registration Act (18 U.S.C. 219).

(s) The prohibition against a public official appointing or promoting a relative, or advocating such an appointment or promotion (5 U.S.C. 3110).

(t) The prohibition against the employment of an individual convicted of felonious rioting or related offenses (5 U.S.C. 7313).

(u) The tax imposed on certain employees (e.g., Presidential appointees, employees excepted under Schedule C, employees in GS–16 or above, or a comparable pay level) who knowingly engage in self-dealing with a private foundation (26 U.S.C. 4941, 4946). "Self-dealing" is defined in the statute to include certain transactions involving an employee's receipt of pay, a loan, or reimbursement for travel or other expenses from, or his sale to or purchase of property from a private foundation.

Subpart C—Conduct and Responsibilities of Special Government Employees

§706.301 Use of Government employment.

A special Government employee shall not use his Government employment for a purpose that is, or gives the appearance of being, motivated by the desire for private gain for himself or another person, particularly one with whom he has family, business, or financial ties.

§706.302 Use of inside information.

(a) A special Government employee shall not use inside information obtained as a result of his Government employment for private gain for himself or another person either by direct action on his part or by counsel, recommendation, or suggestion to another person, particularly one with whom he has family, business, or financial ties. For the purpose of this section, "inside information" means information obtained under Government authority which has not become part of the body of public information.

(b) A special Government employee may engage in teaching, lecturing, and writing to the same extent, and subject to the same restrictions, as provided in §706.303(b) for employees.

§706.303 Gifts, entertainment, and favors.

(a) Except as provided in paragraph (b) of this section a special Government employee, while so employed or in connection with his employment, shall not receive or solicit from a person having business with the Council anything of value as a gift, gratuity, loan, entertainment, or favor for himself or another person, particularly one with whom he has family, business, or financial ties.

(b) The exceptions from the restrictions as set forth in §706.202(b) for employees apply in the same manner to special Government employees.

§706.304 Applicability of other provisions.

The provisions of §§706.206 through 706.211 apply to special Government employees in the same manner as to employees.

Subpart D—Statements of Employment and Financial Interests

§706.401 Employees required to submit statements.

(a) Employees in the following named positions shall submit statements of employment and financial interst to the Director:

(1) Employees in Grade GS–16 or above of the General Schedule established by the Classification Act of 1949, as amended;

(2) The General Counsel and Administrative Officer;

(3) The Staff Specialists assigned to review applications by States for planning grants under Title III of the Water Resources Planning Act;

(4) Special Government employees, as defined in § 706.102; and

(5) Employees classified at GS–13 or above under 5 U.S.C. 5332, or at a comparable pay level under another authority, who are in positions which the Director may determine have duties and responsibilities which require the incumbent to report employment and financial interests in order to avoid involvement in possible conflicts-of-interest situation and carry out the purpose of law, Executive order, and Council regulations.

(b) A statement of employment and financial interest is required from the Director and shall be submitted by the Director to the Chairman of the Council.

§ 706.402 Employee's complaint on filing requirements.

An employee who feels that his position has been improperly included in the list in § 706.401 as one requiring the submission of a statement of employment and financial interests may obtain a review of his complaint under the Council's internal grievance procedure.

§ 706.403 Form of statements.

An employee required to submit a statement of employment and financial interests shall submit that statement in the format prescribed by the Division of Management.

§ 706.404 Time for submission of statements.

An employee required to submit a statement of employment and financial intersts by § 706.401 shall submit that statement no later than 30 days after the date of entrance on duty in the position covered by § 706.401.

§ 706.405 Supplementary statements.

Changes in, or additions to, the information contained in an employee's statement of employment and financial interests shall be reported in a supplementary statement, in the format prescribed by the Division of Management, as of June 30 each year. If no changes or additions occur, a negative report is required. Notwithstanding the filing of the annual report required by this section, each employee shall at all times avoid acquiring a financial interest that could result, or taking an action that would result in a violation of the conflicts-of-interest provisions of section 18 U.S.C. 208, or subpart B of this part.

§ 706.406 Interests of employees' relatives.

The interests of a spouse, minor child, or other member of an employee's immediate household are considered to be interests of the employee. For the purpose of this section, "member of an employee's immediate household" means those blood relations who are residents of the employee's household.

§ 706.407 Information not known by employees.

If any information required to be included on a statement of employment and financial interests or on a supplementary statement, including holdings placed in trust, is not known to the employee but is known to another person, the employee shall request that other person to submit the information in his behalf.

§ 706.408 Information not required.

An employee is not required to submit on a statement of employment and financial interests, or on a supplementary statement, any information relating to the employee's connection with, or interest in, a professional society or a charitable, religious, social, fraternal, recreational, public service, civic, or political organization or a similar organization not conducted as a business enterprise. For the purpose of this section, educational and other institutions doing research and development or related work involving grants of money from or contracts with the Government are deemed "business enterprises" and are required to be included in an employee's statement of employment and financial interests.

§ 706.409 Opportunity for explanation of conflict or appearance of conflict.

When a statement submitted under § 706.401 indicates a conflict or an appearance of conflict, between the interests of an employee and the performance of his services for the Government, the employee concerned shall be given an opportunity to explain the conflict or appearance of conflict before remedial action is initiated.

§ 706.410 Confidentiality of statements.

Each statement of employment and financial interests, and each supplementary statement, shall be held in confidence and retained in limited access files of the reviewing official. The use of information on the statements shall be limited to that necessary to carry out the purposes of this part. Information from a statement or a supplementary statement shall not be disclosed except by decision of the Director for good cause shown: *Provided,* That information from a statement or a supplementary statement of the Director shall not be disclosed except by decision of the Chairman for good cause shown.

§ 706.411 Effect of statements on other requirements.

The statements of employment and financial interests and supplementary statements required of employees are in addition to, and not in substitution for or in derogation of any similar requirement imposed by law, order, or regulation. The submission of a statement or supplementary statement by an employee does not permit him or any other person to participate in a matter in which he or the other person's participation is prohibited by law, order, or regulation.

§ 706.412 Submission of statements by special Government employees.

(a) Each special Government employee shall submit a statement of employment and financial interests not later than the time of his employment.

Each special Government employee shall keep his statement current throughout his period of employment by the submission of supplementary statements.

(b) A special Government employee shall submit his statement of employment and financial interests in the format prescribed by the Division of Management. The statement will be filed with the Division of Management and is accorded the confidentiality prescribed in § 706.410.

(c) The provisions of §§ 706.406 through 706.411 apply to special Government employees in the same manner as to employees.

(d) The Director may waive the requirement in paragraph (a) of this section for the submission of a statement of employment and financial interests in the case of a special Government employee who is not a consultant or an expert when he finds that the duties of the position held by that special Government employee are of a nature and at such a level of responsibility that the submission of the statement by the incumbent is not necessary to protect the integrity of the Government. For the purposes of this paragraph "consultant" and "expert" have the meanings given those terms by Chapter 304 of the Federal Personnel Manual.

§ 706.413 Submission of statements by River Basin Commission Chairmen.

A statement of employment and financial interest is not required under this part from Chairmen of River Basin Commissions created by the President pursuant to Title II of the U.S. Water Resources Planning Act. The Commission Chairmen are subject to section 401 of Executive Order 11222, as amended, and are required to file a statement with the Chairman of the Civil Service Commission.

PART 707—COMPLIANCE WITH THE NATIONAL ENVIRONMENTAL POLICY ACT (NEPA)

Subpart A—General

707.5 Policy.

Subpart B—Water Resources Council Implementing Procedures

707.6 Early involvement in private, State, local, and other non-Federal activities requiring Federal action.
707.7 Ensuring that environmental documents are actually considered in agency decisionmaking.
707.8 Typical classes of action requiring similar treatment under NEPA.
707.9 Tiering.
707.10 Scoping.
707.11 Environmental information.

AUTHORITY: National Environmental Policy Act of 1969 (42 U.S.C. 4321 *et seq.*); E.O. 11991, 42 FR 26967; 3 CFR 1977 Compl. p. 123.

SOURCE: 44 FR 69922, Dec. 5, 1979, unless otherwise noted.

Subpart A—General

§ 707.1 Background.

(a) The National Environmental Policy Act (NEPA) of 1969 (42 U.S.C. 4321 *et seq.*) establishes national policies and goals for the protection and enhancement of the environment. Section 102(2) of NEPA contains certain policy statements and procedural requirements directed toward the attainment of such goals. In particular, all Federal agencies are required to give appropriate consideration to the environmental effects of their proposed actions in their decisionmaking and to prepare detailed environmental statements on recommendations or reports on proposals for legislation and other major Federal actions significantly affecting the quality of the human environment.

(b) Executive Order 11991 of May 24, 1977, amended E.O. 11514 and directed the Council on Environmental Quality (CEQ) to issue regulations to implement the procedural provisions of NEPA. Accordingly, CEQ issued final NEPA regulations (40 CFR Parts 1500–1508) on November 29, 1978, which are binding on all Federal agencies as of July 30, 1979. Section 1507.3(a) of CEQ regulations provides that each Federal agency shall as necessary adopt implementing procedures to supplement the regulations. Section 1507.3(b) of the CEQ NEPA regulations identifies those sections of the regulations which must be addressed in agency procedures.

§ 707.2 Purpose.

The purpose of this NEPA rule is to establish Water Resources Council (WRC) policy and procedures which supplement the CEQ NEPA regulations by making them more specifically applicable to our activities and which implement § 1507.3 (a) and (b) of the CEQ NEPA regulations. This rule will be revised to incorporate detailed procedures integrating NEPA and the Principles and Standards (P&S) and applicable parts of the procedures for Federal participants in the preparation of comprehensive regional or river basin plans when these procedures are developed. This NEPA rule must be used in conjunction with the CEQ NEPA regulations. Compliance with both the CEQ NEPA regulations and this NEPA rule is required. Information in the CEQ NEPA regulations generally is not repeated here to avoid needless duplication. This NEPA rule supersedes WRC Policy Statement No. 2—Environmental Statements-Framework Studies and Assessments and Regional or River Basin Plans.

§ 707.3 Applicability.

This NEPA rule applies to the WRC as an independent executive agency and to Title II river basin commissions (RBC's) and other entities (such as interagency committees) preparing studies and plans for WRC review and transmittal to the President. Although Title III State planning grants do not normally require environmental assessments or statements (§ 707.8 (a)(3)), the WRC will encourage States receiving grants to give appropriate consideration to the environmental effects of their proposed actions and to incorporate suitable environmental conditions, to the extent permitted by State law. The preamble to the WRC Title III guidelines will reflect this policy.

§ 707.4 Definitions.

(a) *Responsible Federal Official (RFO)*. The "Responsible Federal Official (RFO)" is the official of the Federal Government designated by this rule who shall be responsible for the implementation of NEPA, including regulations issued by the CEQ (40 CFR parts 1500 through 1508) and the rule. Of particular importance, the RFO determines the need for an Environmental Assessment or Environmental Impact Statement (EIS) in accordance with §707.8 (a)(2) and (b), and if an EIS is required, files the draft and final EIS, makes the Record of Decision and assures appropriate public involvement in accordance with 40 CFR 1506.6. The Chairman of the RBC's are the RFO's for the purpose of ensuring compliance with the provisions of NEPA and the P&S for those activities which are funded in whole or in part through the WRC and carried out by the RBC's, such as framework studies, special studies, comprehensive coordinated joint plans, regional or river basin (Level B) plans and revisions thereof. The Chairman of the WRC, or his designee, is the RFO for complying with the provisons of NEPA and the P&S for those framework studies, regional or river basin plans, comprehensive coordinated joint plans, and special studies which are funded by the WRC and carried out by WRC interagency committees and WRC coordinating committees; principles, standards and procedures for planning water and related land resources; rules and regulations of the WRC, and other activities of the WRC.

(b) *Major Federal Action.* "Major Federal action" as defined in the CEQ NEPA regulations (40 CFR 1508.18) includes actions with effects that may be major and which are potentially subject to Federal control and responsibility. Such actions include WRC interagency committee, and WRC coordinating committee adoption, approval or submittal of plans for water and related land resources. For the purpose of this rule, RBC adoption, approval or submittal of a plan for water and related land resources is considered a major Federal action by virtue of the scope and significant environmental consequences of such actions, the participation of Federal officials in these RBC actions, and the WRC requirements for Federal agency consistency with approved regional water resource management plans (WRC Policy State-

ment No. 4—The Utilization of Comprehensive Regional Water Resource Management Plans).

§707.5 **Policy.**

(a) *General.* The WRC and the RBC's administer certain programs that must comply with both NEPA and the P&S. Generally, the environmental analysis done during the development of the Environmental Quality (EQ) account under the P&S partially overlaps the analysis required in an EIS, presenting an opportunity for integration. The requirements of NEPA and the P&S will be carried out by integrating the two processes to the fullest extent practicable and by combining to the fullest extent practicable the Environmental Assessment or, when required, Environmental Impact Statement, with each study or plan into a single document that will comply fully with the requirements of both processes, as provided by the CEQ NEPA regulations (40 CFR 1502.10 and 1506.4).

(b) *Public participation.* For each environmental assessment and impact statement, the appropriate RFO will establish a specific program and schedule for public participation of all interested parties in the NEPA process, and shall otherwise provide for public involvement in accordance with the CEQ NEPA regulations (40 CFR 1506.6).

(c) *Environmental Impact Statements.* Environmental Impact Statements (EIS's) as required under Section 102(2)(C) of NEPA will be prepared by river basin commissions, interagency committee, or WRC coordinating committees for comprehensive coordinated joint plans and regional or river basin (Level B) plans, or revisions thereof. The Environmental Impact Statement will be prepared concurrently with the preparation of the study or plan. The statement will reflect the level of planning involved and will address those environmental considerations and alternatives relevant to decisionmaking at that level (see §707.9 Tiering). Review and comment on the draft study or plan and the incorporated draft environmental impact statement will be performed simultaneously, and the final combined report will incorporate and discuss the comments received on the draft.

Subpart B—Water Resources Council Implementing Procedures

§ 707.6 Early involvement in private, State, local, and other non-Federal activities requiring Federal action.

(a) Section 1501.2(d) of the CEQ NEPA regulations requires Federal agencies to provide for early involvement in activities which, while planned by private or other non-Federal entities, requires some subsequent form of Federal approval or action to which NEPA applies. Such activities for which early involvement is appropriate include those private, local, State, or regional water and related land resources plans, projects or programs which should be included in a regional water resources management plan or Level B plan, since the plans normally required an EIS or assessment as provided in § 707.8(a) of this NEPA rule.

(b) To facilitate the implementation of 40 CFR 1501.2(d), the appropriate RFO shall publish and distribute in the region or basin in which a comprehensive or Level B study is conducted, guidelines for non-Federal entities of the types of plans, projects, and programs which shall be included in such comprehensive or Level B plan. The RFO shall advise non-Federal entities on the scope and level of environmental information and analysis needed for environmental documents.

§ 707.7 Ensuring that environmental documents are actually considered in agency decisionmaking.

(a) Section 1505.1 of the NEPA regulations contains requirements to ensure adequate consideration of the environmental documents in agency decisionmaking. To implement these requirements, the RFO shall:

(1) Consider relevant environmental documents in evaluating actions proposed in plans and studies.

(2) Make relevant environmental documents, comments, and responses part of the record in any formal rulemaking or adjudicatory proceedings.

(3) Ensure that relevant environmental documents, comments and responses accompany the proposed actions through existing review processes.

(4) Consider only those alternatives encompassed by the range of alternatives discussed in the relevant environmental documents when evaluating proposals for agency action.

(5) Where an EIS has been prepared, consider the specific alternatives analyzed in the EIS when evaluating the proposal which is the subject of the EIS.

(b) The NEPA process begins at the earliest possible stage of the planning process and is completed when the RFO makes a finding of significant impact or a record of decision. In cases where the Chairman of a River Basin Commission, or regional Federal official has been designated as the RFO, and a plan or report is submitted to WRC for review and comment after completion of the NEPA process, the environmental documents incorporated into such plans or reports, or submitted with them, shall be fully considered by WRC when it prepares its views, comments, and recommendations for transmittal to the President and Congress. The RFO shall include the Findings of No Significant Impact, or the Record of Decision, with the documents submitted to WRC for review.

§ 707.8 Typical classes of action requiring similar treatment under NEPA.

(a) Section 1507.3(b)(2) of the CEQ NEPA regulations in conjunction with § 1508.4 requires agencies to establish three typical classes of action for similar treatment under NEPA. These typical classes of actions are set forth below:

(1) Actions normally requiring EIS's:

(i) Adoption, approval or submittal of regional water resources management plans (comprehensive, coordinated, joint plans or elements thereof).

(ii) Adoption, approval or submittal of Level B plans.

(2) Actions normally requiring assessments but not necessarily EIS's:

(i) Establishment and implementing guidance (including significant changes) in principles, standards, and procedures for planning water and related land resources.

(ii) Adoption, approval or submittal of framework studies and special studies which include recommendations for future actions.

(iii) Any action not in paragraph (a) (1) or (3) of this section.

(3) Actions normally not requiring assessments or EIS's (categorical exclusions):

(i) Approval of Title III State planning grants.

(ii) Adoption, approval or transmittal or priorities reports.

(iii) Preparation of the National Water Assessment.

(iv) Recommendations to the President with the respect to Federal policies and programs, except for transmittal of plans described in paragraph (a) (1) or (2) of this section for which the original EIS or Environmental Assessment (EA) will be transmitted with the plan. A second EIS is not required.

(v) Framework studies and assessments and special studies which do not include recommendations for future actions.

(b) Where the presence of extraordinary circumstances indicates that an action normally excluded may have a significant environmental effect, the appropriate RFO shall independently determine whether an EIS or an environmental assessment is required.

§ 707.9 Tiering.

In accordance with the CEQ NEPA regulations 40 CFR 1502.4(d) and 1508.28(a), this NEPA rule emphasizes the use of tiering to relate broad and narrow actions. The level of detail in EIS's and EA's prepared by RBC's, WRC interagency committees or WRC coordinating committees will reflect the level of detail in the plans, particularly the comprehensive and policy nature of comprehensive, coordinated, joint plans or elements or revisions thereof. These EIS's are not intended to substitute for individual statements on individual projects as more detailed planning and analysis will be required for major Federal actions proposed in these plans. The "policy" or "overview" EIS should serve as the framework and introduction for a more site-specific project EIS developed by the implementing Federal agency. Environmental impact statements for regional water resource management and Level B plans will generally address the items in the recommended format (40 CFR 1502.10) on the basis of water

and related land resources of an entire region or river basin. This is the level of consideration at which the environmental issues and considerations are most relevant to decisionmaking. They may also address groups of interrelated or individual plan elements where these involve significant environmental considerations.

§ 707.10 Scoping.

Scoping will be used to determine the extent of issues to be addressed by the EIS and to identify significant issues related to the proposed action. Scoping will be conducted as described by the CEQ NEPA regulations, §§ 1501.7 and 1508.25.

§ 707.11 Environmental information.

Interested persons may contact the Director, U.S. Water Resources Council, 2120 L Street, NW., Washington, DC 20037, for information regarding the Council's compliance with NEPA.

PART 708—UPPER MISSISSIPPI RIVER BASIN COMMISSION: PUBLIC PARTICIPATION IN UPPER MISSISSIPPI RIVER SYSTEM MASTER PLAN

AUTHORITY: Title II, sec. 204, Pub. L. 89–80, Water Resources Planning Act of 1965; Title I, sec. 101(b), Pub. L. 95–502, Inland Waterways Authorization Act of 1978.

SOURCE: 44 FR 14537, Mar. 13, 1979, unless otherwise noted.

§ 708.1 Definitions.

As used in the part, the term:

(a) *Act* means the Inland Waterways Authorization Act of 1978, Pub. L. 95–502.

(b) *Commission* means the Upper Mississippi River Basin Commission, with headquarters at Fort Snelling, Twin Cities, Minnesota.

(c) *Master Plan* means the Upper Mississippi River System Comprehensive Master Management Plan mandated by Title I of the Act.

(d) *GREAT* refers to studies conducted by Great River Environmental Action Teams pursuant to section 117 of the Water Resources and Development Act of 1976 (Pub. L. 94–587) for purposes of developing balanced management strategies for multipurpose use of the Upper Mississippi River.

(e) *System* means those Upper Mississippi River reaches containing commercial navigation channels on the Mississippi River main stem north of Cairo, Illinois; the Minnesota River, Minnesota; Black River, Wisconsin; Saint Croix River, Minnesota and Wisconsin; Illinois River and Waterway, Illinois; and Kaskaskia River, Illinois.

(f) *Public meeting* means a meeting to provide individuals and representatives of interested organizations opportunities to present their opinions and suggestions by means of an informally structured format.

(g) *Public hearing* means a formally structured public meeting scheduled to provide adequate time for each testimony, which will be recorded, transcribed, published, and made available to the public.

§ 708.2 **Scope.**

(a) This part describes minimum guidelines for public participation in the development, revision, and implementation of the Master Plan specified in the Act.

(b) This part applies to the following organizations with references to the activities described in § 708.2(a):

(1) The Commission, including its staff and persons, organizations, and agencies under contract to it for work within the scope of the Master Plan.

(2) Such Federal departments and agencies as are directed under section 101(3) of the Act to conduct studies pursuant to the Master Plan, for any work carried out for purposes of developing, revising, and implementing the Master Plan.

(3) Such departments and agencies of any state or local government as are authorized and/or directed to carry out studies and analyses under direction or advice of the Commission as stipulated in section 101 of the Act.

(c) The guidelines referred to in this part shall be considered general requirements applicable to all studies, procedures, programs, regulations, or other administrative devices carried out under § 708.2(b), but only for those Master Plan Activities under authority of the Act.

§ 708.3 **Policy, objectives, and standards.**

(a) *Policy.* (1) Congress has directed the Commission to prepare a comprehensive Master Plan for management of the System in cooperation with appropriate Federal, state, and local officials. In developing the plan, the Commission is required to identify various economic, recreational, and environmental objectives of the System, recommend guidelines to achieve such objectives, and propose methods to assure compliance with such guidelines and coordination of future management decisions affecting the System, and include with the proposed plan any legislative proposals which may be necessary to carry out such recommendations and achieve such objectives.

(2) The Commission is required to provide for public participation in the development, revision, and implementation of the Master Plan and to encourage and assist such participation. In doing this, the Commission seeks to foster a spirit of openness and a sense of mutual trust between the public and the planners. Public participation is expected to result in greater responsiveness of the Master Plan to public concerns and priorities, as well as improved popular understanding of official studies, planning processes, and decisions.

(3) In order for public participation to be effective, it must be timely and integrated into the planning process. The Commission shall seek public participation prior to any decision-making on the Master Plan or any of its components. Such public participation will ordinarily include informational output about the plan, public response and input, two-way discussions or exchange, and Commission consideration of public expressions.

(4) Neither the Master Plan as a whole nor any component of it shall be formulated without incorporation of a program of public participation involving fair representation of all segments of the public. The public participation

section of the Master Plan—Plan of Study shall be developed consistent with the guidelines described in this part.

(5) Public participation processes utilized by the Commission in developing the Master Plan shall aim for the highest achievable standards of objectivity and thoroughness consistent with other requirements of the Act and the intent, concepts, ideas, and basic tenets of the Principles and Standards for Planning Water and Related Land Resources published by the Water Resources Council in the FEDERAL REGISTER, Volume 38, Number 174, part III, September 10, 1973 and any forthcoming revisions. Public participation programs shall include monitoring procedures to maintain an acceptable degree of responsiveness and accountability.

(b) *Objectives.* Objectives of the public participation program developed by the Commission as part of the Master Plan are:

(1) To develop awareness of public preferences by those responsible for preparation and approval of the Master Plan.

(2) To anticipate and help resolve conflicts arising during the study,

(3) To improve information transfer and public awareness of the study,

(4) To provide for periodic reviews in the development of the Master Plan as well as the final review required by the Act, and

(5) To provide for evaluation of public participation in the planning process.

(c) *Standards.* The Commission in meeting the above objectives recognizes that:

(1) Inputs from the public are important for development of the Master Plan;

(2) Participants are to include individual citizens as well as organizations;

(3) The public participation program is to assume the existence of numerous publics and their interests—identified and delineated according to a number of socioeconomic, demographic, geographic, person, and ideological variables;

(4) The public participation process must be continuous: it is to be provided for, encouraged, and assisted throughout the planning process;

(5) The public participation process is to have as a product measurable sets of opinion and other manifestations of the public will in regard to details of the Master Plan;

(6) Inputs from the public into the Master Plan through avenues other than the Commission public participation program should be facilitated; and

(7) Desires expressed by the public are likely to be conflicting and therefore, public participation cannot be substituted for the decision-making responsibility.

§ 708.4 Required programs and reports.

(a) The Commission shall prepare a work plan for public participation as part of the Master Plan—Plan of Study. The work plan shall satisfy minimum standards described in this part. The work plan shall describe all substantive administrative and management arrangements to elicit public participation, shall delineate Commission member and staff responsibilities, and shall identify budgetary provisions.

(b) In addition to public meetings and hearings, the public participation program shall include survey research, program evaluation, and information/education activities as described in § 708.5.

(c) The Commission shall recommend long-term public participation activities and programs related to implementation of the Master Plan. These recommendations shall be based on evaluation of procedures and results mandated in this part and carried out during the Master Plan preparation.

(d) The Commission shall issue reports describing the participation program as developed or implemented during the designated reporting period. Each such report shall include as a minimum a brief description of the main participation elicited, the costs of the effort, and the use that was made of the elicited information in the planning process. The reporting periods shall be arranged so as to correspond generally with the main sequential segments of the overall planning process.

§ 708.5 Program objectives implementation.

(a) The continuing public participation program shall contain mechanisms or activities for each objective listed in § 708.3(b). The listing of specific measures in this section shall not preclude additional techniques for obtaining, encouraging, or assisting public participation. Special efforts shall be made to simplify the planning process and products for public and media use. Variances may occur in the use of any given program element, according to the nature of the planning issues, the budgetary resources accorded the participation process, and the effectiveness of the participation actually elicited and measured in the field.

(b) To obtain data in regard to plan-relevant public opinion, methods, shall include but not be limited to survey research.

(1) The survey research process shall be developed and utilized in connection with the Master Plan as a whole and its components. Whereas public meetings are organized to elicit unstructured participation and opinion changes, surveys shall be targeted on carefully selected samples of functionally defined publics located throughout the System.

(2) The Commission shall evaluate the effectiveness of the information/education program on the part of the surveyed publics. This is necessary for continued and sustained participation in the decision-making steps of the planning process.

(3) If a gap is found between the desired and actual effectiveness, the Commission shall develop and implement a short-term narrow-focus information and education program targeted at the specific problem areas in question.

(4) On completion of the short-term information/education program, re-surveys shall be made among the affected publics. The results shall constitute a measure of the effectiveness of the short-term information/education program.

(c) To improve information transfer and public awareness of the study, two levels of information and education activities shall be pursued. The first shall have the general public as its target audience and shall emphasize methods that foster general awareness and understanding of plan issues and the nature of the ongoing planning process. The second level of information and education activities shall focus on public interest groups, agency representatives, and elected officials and shall emphasize the creation of plan component data and information in a form that can be utilized by these groups in the plan decision-making process. The information presented shall be broadly representative of the relevant perspectives and issues.

(d) Throughout the period of study and the succeeding period of implementation of the Master Plan, the Commission shall provide a centralized capability for acting as an information/education center. The Commission shall provide a central source of media-directed information about the Master Plan, its components, future expected planning needs in the System, current program-related activities, and other relevant subject areas. Special efforts shall be made to summarize complex technical materials for public and media use. The Commission shall have standing arrangements for early consultation and exchange of views with interested or affected persons and organizations on development or revisions of plans, programs, or other significant actions prior to decision-making. Survey research methods and other procedures will be used to determine the content and emphasis of information and education activities and products.

(e) The Commission shall provide for periodic reviews of the development of the Master Plan as well as the final review required by the Act. Activities to accomplish this shall include:

(1) *Public meetings.* (i) Public meetings shall be organized at locations in parts of the System most significantly affected by the possible outcomes. These open meetings shall be timed to coincide with sequential elements of the planning process.

(ii) The meetings shall provide citizens and representatives of interested organizations an opportunity to utilize an informally-structured format to air their suggestions and grievances in regard to the subject matter of the Master Plan.

(iii) When the Commission deems a formal public hearing is necessary, it may coincide with the pulic meeting. When this is the case, a clear distinction shall be made between the formal and open segments of the meeting/hearing.

(iv) Documents and data pertaining to the agenda for each public meeting shall be made available to the public for a reasonable time prior to the public meeting, at a location convenient to the expected participants. In addition, the Commission shall prepare outlines of major issues including brief descriptions of the issues, alternatives, and sources of additional information.

(2) *Public hearings.* (i) The Commission is required to publish a preliminary plan not later than January 1, 1981 and to hold public hearings in each state which would be affected by the plan. The Commission is required to review all comments presented at such hearings or submitted in writing to the Commission, and, after making any revisions in the plan it decides are necessary, to submit to Congress a final Master Plan not later than January 1, 1982.

(ii) The public hearings on the preliminary plan and any other public hearings deemed necessary by the Commission are to be consistent with the provisions of sec. 205 of Pub. L. 89-80 in conformity with this part. If conflict exists between the minimum guidelines of this part and requirements of state or Federal law or other regulations pertaining to a particular hearing, the more stringent requirements shall be observed.

(iii) In addition to any other formal legal requirements, the public hearings are to be well publicized and notices of each hearing will be mailed to interested or affected persons at least 30 calendar days before the hearings.

(iv) In determining locations and times for hearings, consideration will be given to travel and to facilitating attendance and testimony by a cross-section of interested or affected persons and organizations. Accessibility of hearing sites by public transportation will be considered.

(v) The preliminary plan and any supporting reports, documents, and data to be discussed at the public hear-

ings are to be made available to the public at least 30 days prior to the public hearings. Information concerning availability of the preliminary plan, reports, documents, and data will be provided in public hearing notices.

(vi) The elements of the public hearings, proposed time schedules, and any constraints on statements shall be specified in public hearing notices.

(vii) Testimony of witnesses at public hearings shall be scheduled in advance when necessary to ensure maximum participation and allotment of adequate time for testimony, provided that such scheduling is not used as a bar to unscheduled testimony. Blocks of time shall be considered for major categories of witnesses.

(viii) Public hearing procedures shall not inhibit free expression of views by requirements of more than one legible copy of any statement submitted, or for qualifications of witnesses beyond that needed for identification.

(ix) A record of public hearing proceedings shall be made promptly available to the public at cost. The Commission shall invite, receive, and consider comments in writing from any interested or affected persons and organizations. All such comments shall be part of the public record.

(f) To provide mechanisms for evaluation of public participations in the Master Plan:

(1) The Commission shall conduct periodic evaluations of the public participation program. The purpose of this evaluation is to determine the following:

(i) The extent of actual participation elicited from each of the process phases—public meetings, public hearings, survey research, direct input from organizations, and other sources.

(ii) The degree to which participation elicited from each process phase was actually utilized in the planning process.

(iii) Regional/local differences in effectiveness of public participation methods and procedures.

(iv) The need to modify the public participation process during the Master Plan.

(2) Public participation evaluations shall be incorporated into the Master Plan. Recommendations resulting from

this overall evaluation shall be utilized to draft new guidelines and plans of study for public participation programs to be implemented after the Master Plan has been adopted.

PART 725—IMPLEMENTATION OF EXECUTIVE ORDERS 11988, FLOODPLAIN MANAGEMENT AND 11990, PROTECTION OF WETLANDS

Subpart A—Introduction

AUTHORITY: The Water Resources Planning Act of 1965, sec. 402, Pub. L. 89–80, 79 Stat. 245 (42 U.S.C. 1962d–1), the National Environmental Policy Act of 1969, as amended (42 U.S.C. 4321 *et seq.*), the National Flood Insurance Act of 1968, as amended (42 U.S.C. 4001 *et seq.*), the Flood Disaster Protection Act of 1973, as amended (87 Stat. 975), E.O. 11988 and E.O. 11990 (42 FR 26951).

SOURCE: 45 FR 76683, Nov. 20, 1980, unless otherwise noted.

Subpart A—Introduction

§ 725.0 Purpose.

This rule establishes the procedures to be followed by the U.S. Water Resources Council for applying Executive Order 11988, Floodplain Management, and Executive Order 11990, Wetlands Protection, to the water resources planning assistance activities that it performs.

§ 725.1 Authority.

This rule is being promulgated pursuant to the Water Resources Planning Act of 1965, section 402, Pub. L. 89–90, 79 Stat. 245 (42 U.S.C. 1962d–1). In addition, Executive Order 11988, *Floodplain Management*, at section 2(d); directs the preparation of procedures imple-

menting its provisions, as does Executive Order 11990, *Protection of Wetlands*, at section 6. Each of these Orders was prepared in furtherance of the National Environmental Policy Act of 1969, as amended (42 U.S.C. 4321 *et seq.*). The floodplain management Order is also based on the National Flood Insurance Act of 1968, as amended (42 U.S.C. 4001 *et seq.*), and the Flood Disaster Protection Act of 1977, as amended (87 Stat. 975).

§ 725.2 Policy.

It is the policy of the Council to provide leadership in floodplain management and the protection of wetlands. Further, the Council shall integrate the goals of the Orders to the greatest possible degree into its procedures for implementing the National Environmental Policy Act. The Council shall take action to:

(a) Avoid long- and short-term adverse impacts associated with the occupancy and modification of floodplains and the destruction or modification of wetlands;

(b) Avoid direct and indirect support of floodplain development and new construction in wetlands wherever there is a practicable alternative;

(c) Reduce the risk of flood loss;

(d) Promote the use of nonstructural loss reduction methods to reduce the risk of flood loss;

(e) Minimize the impact of floods on human health, safety and welfare;

(f) Minimize the destruction, loss or degradation of wetlands;

(g) Restore and preserve the natural and beneficial values served by floodplains;

(h) Preserve and enhance the natural and beneficial values served by wetlands;

(i) Involve the public throughout the floodplain management and wetlands protection decisionmaking process;

(j) Adhere to the objectives of the Unified National Program for Floodplain Management;

(k) Continually analyze existing and new policies of the Council to ensure consistency between them and the provisions of E.O. 11988 and 11990; and

(l) Improve and coordinate the Council's plans, programs, functions and resources so that the Nation may attain the widest range of beneficial uses of the environment without degradation or risk to health and safety.

§725.3 Applicability.

These regulations apply to all Council actions which have the potential to affect floodplains or wetlands or which would be subject to potential harm if they were located in floodplains or wetlands. The basic test of the potential of an action to affect floodplains or wetlands is the action's potential to result in the long- or short-term adverse impacts associated with:

(a) The occupancy or modification of floodplains, or the direct and indirect support of floodplain development; or

(b) The destruction or modification of wetlands or the direct or indirect support of new construction in wetlands.

These procedures apply to Level A and B regional or river basin planning activities carried out by regional planning sponsors including consideration of inclusion of site specific projects in Level A or B regional or river basin plans. These procedures do not apply to site specific Level C planning carried out by individual Federal agencies. Each Federal agency shall use its own procedures promulgated pursuant to these Orders for such Level C planning.

§725.4 Definitions.

The following definitions shall apply throughout this regulation:

(a) All definitions from section 6 of E.O. 11988 (42 FR 26951); all definitions from section 7 of E.O. 11990 (42 FR 26951); and all definitions listed in the Glossary of the Council's Floodplain Management Guidelines for Implementing E.O. 11988 (43 FR 6030) from the term *base flood* through the term *structures*.

(b) *Action* means all Council activities including but not limited to plan review, study preparation, preparation and modifications to the Council's Principles, Standards and Procedures (P,S,&P), provision of financial assistance for State, regional, and river basin planning and reviews of compliance.

(c) *Council* means the U.S. Water Resources Council.

(d) *Enhance* means to increase, heighten, or improve the natural and beneficial values associated with wetlands.

(e) *Regional planning sponsors* means Federal agencies, states, groups of States, river basin commissions, interstate compact commissions and interagency committees.

Subpart B—Responsibilities

§725.5 Council studies.

All studies and appraisals performed by the Council pursuant to section 102 of Pub. L. 89-80 and any recommendations based on these activities shall include specific analyses for reflection of and opportunities to meet the objectives of E.O. 11988 and E.O. 11990. The Council's Floodplain Management Guidelines (43 FR 6030), E.O. 11988 and E.O. 11990 provide the basic evaluation tools for these analyses.

§725.6 Principles, standards and procedures.

The Principles, Standards and Procedures established by the Council pursuant to section 103 of Pub. L. 89-80 shall reflect the provisions of the Executive Orders. These Principles, Standards and Procedures are found in 18 CFR parts 710 through 717.

§725.7 Regional or river basin planning.

(a) In agreements between river basin commissions or other regional planning sponsors and the Council for the preparation and revision of regional and river basin Level B Studies and regional water resource management plans, the responsible official representing the river basin commission or regional planning sponsor shall certify to the Council that the following criteria have been or will be utilized as part of the planning process:

(1) Determination of whether proposed activities would be located in floodplains or wetlands, or, even if located outside of them, would have the potential to affect floodplains or wetlands;

(2) Avoidance of performing activities within floodplains or wetlands wherever there is a practicable alternative;

(3) Where avoidance of floodplains cannot be achieved, minimization of adverse impacts and support of floodplain development, and preservation and restoration of natural and beneficial floodplain values;

(4) Where avoidance of wetlands cannot be achieved, minimization of adverse impacts and support of new construction in wetlands, and preservation and enhancement of natural and beneficial wetlands values; and

(5) Involvement of the public in the floodplain management and wetlands protection decisionmaking process.

(b) The Council's Floodplain Management Guidelines (43 FR 6030) shall be used as the basis for implementing the criteria in § 725.7(a)(1) through (5).

(c) The responsible official representing the regional planning sponsor shall, to the fullest extent of his or her authority, ensure that any activities carried out under his or her plans and programs meet the criteria in § 725.7(a)(1) through (5).

§ 725.8 Report, plan and recommendation development and review.

All reports, plans and recommendations received under section 104 of Pub. L. 89–80 shall be reviewed by the Council for reflection of and opportunities to meet the objectives of E.O. 11988 and 11990. This review shall be based on the criteria in § 725.7(a)(1) through (5), on E.O. 11988 and 11990, and on the Council's Floodplain Management Guidelines (43 FR 6030).

§ 725.9 Reviews of compliance.

Reviews of compliance performed pursuant to section 304 of Pub. L. 89–80 shall include analysis of each program's treatment of floodplain management and wetland protection in accordance with the manner in which these concepts are expressed in E.O. 11988, 11990, and the Council's Floodplain Management Guidelines (43 FR 6030).

PART 740—STATE WATER MANAGEMENT PLANNING PROGRAM

Sec.

AUTHORITY: Water Resources Planning Act of 1965 (as amended), Pub. L. 89–80, 79 Stat. 244, 42 U.S.C. 1962c; Federal Grant and Cooperative Agreement Act of 1977, Pub. L. 95–224, 92 Stat. 3, 41 U.S.C. 501 et seq.; E.O. 12044, 43 FR 12660.

SOURCE: 45 FR 72010, Oct. 30, 1980, unless otherwise noted.

§ 740.1 Purpose and scope.

(a) In recognition of the role of the States as the focal point for the management of water and related land resources, this part establishes guidelines for financial and program assistance to States for water management planning programs which address each State's particular needs, which are based on established State goals and objectives, and which take into consideration national goals and objectives.

(b) The purpose of the State Water Management Planning Program (Program) is to provide financial and program assistance to participating States to support the development and modification of comprehensive water management planning programs.

(c) Funds made available under this part shall be used to establish, develop or enhance existing or proposed State water resources management and planning programs that are designed to address pertinent State and national goals and objectives, as well as the goals and objectives of Title III of the Water Resources Planning Act (Act), Pub. L. 89–80, as amended, by addressing in the Program the following:

(1) Coordination of the program authorized by the Act and those related programs of other Federal agencies;

(2) Integration of water conservation with State water management planning;

(3) Integration of water quantity and water quality planning;

(4) Integration of ground and surface water planning;

(5) Planning for protection and management of groundwater supplies;

(6) Planning for protection and management of instream values; and

(7) Enhanced cooperation and coordination between Federal, regional State and local governmental entities involved in water and related land resources planning and management.

§740.2 Definitions.

Act means the Water Resources Planning Act (as amended), Pub. L. 89–80, 42 U.S.C. 1962 *et seq.*

Activities means a series of actions and operations which address the water management problems of the State and have a specific purpose or objective. Activities are further characterized by one or more major tasks and milestones.

Affected interests means public and private organizations, local, tribal, State and Federal governments that may be potentially affected by the State water management planning program.

Application means a document submitted by a Governor or designee for consideration by the Council for a grant.

Council means the Water Resources Council established by section 101 of the Act.

Designated agency means an entity of a State designated by the Governor to act as the grant recipient and to act as liaison with the Council for this Program.

Fiscal year means a 12-month period ending on September 30, unless otherwise specified.

Governor means the chief executive officer of a State, including the Mayor of the District of Columbia.

Grant agreement means a document executed by the authorized official of the Water Resources Council and by the authorized representative of the State agency designated as the grant recipient containing the agreed terms and conditions of the approved grant offer and award.

Grant period means a 12-month period specified in the grant agreement, which shall begin during the fiscal year as defined above, during which program funds are authorized to be expended, obligated, or firmly committed by the

grantee for the purposes specified in the Act, in the grant agreement and in these guidelines.

Land area of a State means the land and inland water area of a State as defined and set forth in the publication "Boundaries of the United States and the Several States" Geological Survey Professional Paper 909, U.S. Government Printing Office, Washington, DC issued in 1976, or revisions thereof.

Local government means a local unit of government including a county municipality, city, town, township, local public authority, school district, special district, intrastate district, council of governments, sponsor group representative organization (as defined in 7 CFR 620.2, 40 FR 12472, March 19, 1975) and other regional or interstate government entity; or any agency or instrumentality of a local government exclusive of institutions of higher education and hospitals.

Milestones mean key events in the activity implementation schedule. Milestones indicate important dates for design implementation and monitoring tasks. Examples of milestones include but are not limited to hiring of key staff, publication dates, workshop dates, or the completion of specific phases of the implementation schedule.

Obligation means orders placed, contracts awarded, grants issued, services received and similar transactions during a given period that require the disbursement of money.

Per capita income of a State means the most recent year of official U.S. Department of Commerce per capita income figures for the State.

Program period means the period beginning on October 1, 1980, and extending through the authorized life of the Program.

Program funds means grant funds provided under the Act, non-Federal funds and the value of in-kind contributions used for matching purposes.

Population of a State means the latest official resident population estimate by the U.S. Department of Commerce available on or before January 1, of the year preceding the fiscal year for which funds under this part are appropriated.

Related land resources means any land affected by present or projected management practices causing significant effects on the quantity or quality of the water resource.

State means each of the 50 States, the District of Columbia, the Commonwealth of Puerto Rico, the Virgin Islands, Guam, or the Commonwealth of the Northern Mariana Islands.

State water management planning means those activities necessary to effect coordinated decisions for the use of water and related resources within a State or interstate region; which provide for the correction or prevention, respectively, of present and future water and related land resources problems; which consider the potential for water and related land resources use from the standpoint of present and future needs; and which provide for involvement of affected interests. Water management planning activities may include, but are not limited to, planning, data collection and analysis, studies and investigations, program design and coordination, development of regulation and enforcement programs, information dissemination, public meetings, and the coordination of the program with other related programs.

Task means a specific action or operation which comprises a part of the implementation effort for an activity.

Water conservation means activities designed to (1) reduce the demand for water, (2) improve efficiency in use and reduce losses and waste of water, or (3) improve land management practices to conserve water.

Water management planning need is defined as the basis for establishing criteria for assessing each State's need for assistance under the Program.

Work Plan means a document listing the major program elements to be performed under the program during each grant period which presents, in chronological order, the major activities and tasks in the program element; which targets major milestones or proposed accomplishments by activity, cost and date; and which will be used in preparing reports to reflect accomplishment of goals and objectives under the participating State's comprehensive program.

§ 740.3 State applications.

(a) The Council shall invite the Governor of each State to submit a State application.

(b) To be eligible for financial assistance under this part, a State shall submit to the Council an original and two copies of a State application executed by the Governor or designee. The State application shall be submitted not later than 90 days from the date of the Council's invitation.

(c) The program application package shall consist of:

(1) The forms and instructions for completing the application;

(2) The criteria to be used by the Council in assessing need for water management planning funds;

(3) Information on the applicable Federal requirements for administering the program; and

(4) Other information pertinent to the application.

(d) A State application shall contain:

(1) The name and address of the designated State agency;

(2) A description of the comprehensive State water management planning program, or modifications thereto, as required by § 740.4(a);

(3) A work plan of the major program activities of the State water management planning program which targets milestones on a semi-annual basis;

(4) A budget and corresponding narrative in accordance with the forms and instructions provided by the Council;

(5) A notice of concurrence by the State clearinghouse in accordance with the Office of Management and Budget (OMB) Circular A-95;

(6) The manner in which the general public is involved in the development and modification of the State program; and

(7) A brief description of activities, in order of priority, which would be carried out if additional funds were made available during the grant period under the provisions of § 740.6(e). This may include supplementing or complementing ongoing activities described in paragraph (d)(3) of this section.

(e) The Governor or designee may request an extension to the submission date by submitting a written request to the Council not less than 30 days prior to the date referred to in paragraph (b) of this section. The extension shall be granted only if, in the Council's judgment, acceptable and substantial justification is shown and the extension would further the objectives of the Act. An extension shall not be granted for more than 30 days.

§740.4 State water management planning program.

(a) A State shall submit a description of its proposed State program with the State application, which shall:

(1) Describe water and related land resources problems, needs and opportunities, and the priorities proposed for their resolution;

(2) Specify the goals and objectives which reflect the water resources policy of the State and which address the major problems which are of concern to the State;

(3) Describe the major elements of the State water management program, which should address but not be limited to:

(i) The integration of water quantity and water quality planning and management;

(ii) The protection and management of instream values;

(iii) The protection and management of groundwater supplies;

(iv) The integration of ground and surface water planning and management; and

(v) Water conservation.

(4) Identify Federal, State, or local government, or public or private organizations that will participate and a general description of how they are involved in the management planning process;

(5) If provisions are made for pass-through of funds, describe the *process* by which recipients will be selected, and the purpose of the pass-through; and

(6) List existing or proposed administrative, legal and/or institutional arrangements to be used in coordinating intrastate, interstate and regional water resources planning activities involving State, local and/or the Federal Government with the proposed water management planning program of the State to assure that all such activities

are considered in program implementation.

§740.5 Review and approval of State applications and programs.

(a) The Council shall review and approve each State application for financial assistance if it is determined that:

(1) The State water management planning program meets the objectives of the Act;

(2) The State application and the State water management planning program meet the requirements of this part; and

(3) Progress on the previous grant period's work plan is satisfactory, based on the requirements set forth by the Council.

(b) Based on the review of the application, the Council shall determine the amount of funds to be made available pursuant to §740.6 and shall notify the designated agency in each participating State of the grant award as soon as possible after funds are apportioned for Council use.

(c) If an application is not approved by the Council, it shall be returned by registered mail with a full explanation of the reasons for that determination. The State shall then be allowed the opportunity to submit a revised application within 30 days after receipt by the State of such notification. Should the State determine that further review is required by the State clearinghouse under OMB Circular A-95, an additional 30 days will be allowed.

(d) If the grant amount requested by a State differs from the grant amount offered by the Council, the Council will request the designated State agency to submit a revised budget and work plan with the acceptance of the grant offer.

(e) The State, upon acceptance of the terms and conditions of the notice of grant award, as presented by the Council, will be granted financial assistance in the amount of the approved final budget.

(f) The work plan for the State water management planning program may be revised at any time by submitting revisions to the work plan and budget to the Council for approval in connection with any proposed significant change (an addition or deletion of major activities specified in the approved work plan) with appropriate provision for A–95 State clearinghouse review. The Council will review the proposed revision and notify the State of its decision no later than 30 days from the date of receipt of the request.

§ 740.6 Financial assistance.

(a) The Council shall provide financial assistance from funds available for each fiscal year to each State having an approved application pursuant to § 740.5.

(b) Within the provisions prescribed by paragraphs (c) and (d) of this section, the Council may grant up to 50 percent of the cost for a State program.

(c) The funds appropriated pursuant to the Act for the fiscal year shall be allocated among the participating States as follows, except that under paragraphs (d) (2) through (4) of this section no State shall be granted a greater or lesser sum of funds which shall be based upon a procedure in which each of the factors of population, land area, and the reciprocal of per capital income, are adjusted such that:

(1) Those States having observations two standard deviations below the mean of each respective factor are equated to the mean-minus-two standard deviations, and

(2) Those States having observations two standard deviations above the mean of each respective factor are equated to the mean-plus-two standard deviations.

(d) Financial assistance for the Program shall be allocated among the participating States from funds available for any fiscal year based on the following formula:

(1) An equal share not to exceed $100,000, the total of which shares shall not exceed 10 percent of the funds available for any fiscal year;

(2) One-third of the remaining balance of the funds after accounting for paragraph (d)(1) of this section in the ratio that the population of each State bears to the population of all States;

(3) One-third of the remaining balance of the funds after accounting for paragraphs (d)(1) and (2) of this section in the ratio that the land area of each State bears to the land area of all the States;

(4) One-third of the remaining balance of funds after accounting for paragraphs (d)(1), (2), and (3) of this section in the ratio that the reciprocal of all per capital income of a State bears to the sum of the reciprocals for all States; and

(5) The remainder of the funds according to the need for water management planning in each State as expressed by the State and assessed by the Council. In assessing need for water management, the Council shall utilize established criteria, the proposed program, and information made available during program review.

(e) Redistribution of grant funds may occur:

(1) If a State fails to apply for a grant within the period specified in § 740.3, or is unable to match the total allocation reserved under § 740.6(d) for that State, that portion of the reserved allocation will be withdrawn by the Council;

(2) If a State fails to obligate Federal funds within the grant period of the approved or amended grant agreement as prescribed in § 740.7(c), such funds shall be returned to the Council not later than 30 days after submission of the Financial Statement for the grant period unless the Council, based on written request, grants an exception or extension to this time limitation;

(3) Funds available under paragraph (e)(1) of this section shall be available for redistribution to those States requesting additional funds pursuant to § 740.3(d)(7). These funds shall be distributed on the basis of proposals in the application, and the relationship of the State's original allocation to the original allocation of other States requesting redistribution funds; and

(4) Funds available under paragraph (e)(2) of this section shall be added to funds available for distribution for the next fiscal year, if the appropriation legislation for the current year allows such action.

§ 740.7 Administration of financial assistance.

(a) Grants under this part shall comply with the requirements of:

(1) Office of Management and Budget (OMB) Circular A–102, Revised, (34 CFR

part 256), entitled "Uniform Administrative Requirements for Grants-in-Aid to State and Local Governments;"

(2) Federal Management Circular (FMC) 74-4 (34 CFR part 255), entitled "Cost Principles Applicable to Grants and Contracts with State and Local Governments;"

(3) OMB Circular A-73 (34 CFR part 251), entitled "Audit of Federal Operations and Programs;"

(4) OMB Circular A-95, entitled "Evaluation, Review and Coordination of Federal and Federally assisted Programs and Projects;"

(5) Treasury Circular (TC) 1075, entitled "Regulations Governing Withdrawals of Cash from the Treasury for Advances under Federal Grants and other Programs;"

(6) TC 1082, entitled, "Notification to States of Grants-in-Aid Information"; and

(7) Other procedures which the Council may from time to time prescribe for the administration of financial assistance.

(b) The planning process as required by these guidelines and assisted by WRC Title III program funds shall reflect the concepts of the Council's 1979 publication, *A Unified National Program for Floodplain Management*, and the concepts of floodplain and wetlands identification, avoidance and mitigation as described in the Council's *Floodplain Management Guidelines* (43 FR 6030). In the application for financial assistance, the State shall assure the Council that the following planning concepts have been or will be integrated into the planning process:

(1) Determination of whether proposed activities would be located in floodplains or wetlands, or, even if located outside of them, would have the potential to affect floodplains or wetlands;

(2) Avoidance of performing activities within floodplains or wetlands wherever there is a practicable alternative;

(3) Where avoidance of floodplains cannot be achieved, minimization of adverse impacts and support of floodplain development, and preservation and restoration of natural and beneficial floodplain values; and

(4) Where avoidance of wetlands cannot be achieved, minimization of adverse impacts and support of new construction in wetlands, and preservation and enhancement of natural and beneficial wetlands values.

(c) Program funds must be obligated within the grant period unless the Council, based on written request, grants an exception or extension to this time limitation. The repeated occurrence of unobligated program funds at the end of the grant period will be considered in determining the need for assistance in subsequent years pursuant to §740.6(d)(5).

(d) The procurement standards, practices, rules and policies of the State as customarily applied, if in accordance with Attachment O of OMB Circular A-102, shall govern for procurement costs incurred in an approved program.

(e) For all matching funds the sources of a State's cost share shall have no bearing on whether or not such costs can be matched by Federal funds except that:

(1) Other Federal funds or property cannot be used for matching purposes unless specifically permitted by Federal law;

(2) Program funds shall not be used to match Federal funds under any other federally aided program;

(3) Non-Federal funds used to match other federally aided programs shall not be used to match funds provided under the Act; and

(4) Federal funds provided through this program, if duly matched through the requirements of this part, may be used as non-Federal contributions for Level B studies beginning in Fiscal Year 1981.

(f) Any cost incurred for water management planning may be employed for matching a grant awarded under the Act except as specified in this section. Such expenditures must be reasonable, documentable, and directly applicable to the approved program.

(g) Program funds may not be used for:

(1) Items whose costs are not allowable under the provision of FMC 74-4;

(2) Contributions, dues or assessments to support headquarters offices of interstate commissions, compacts,

councils, interagency committees, or other similar organizations;

(3) Scholarly or scientific investigations for purposes other than addressing water management problems, needs, concerns or interests specifically identified and explained in the approved program as a priority consideration;

(4) Construction, payment of subsidies, or purchase of land or easements;

(5) Purchase of equipment with a unit cost of $1,500 or more without prior approval of the Council; and

(6) Purchase of equipment with a unit cost of less than $1,500 when the cumulative cost of such equipment in any one grant period exceeds 1 percent of the grant award, without prior approval of the Council.

(h) Federal funds may not be used to substitute for State and local funds that would have been made available for water management planning programs in the absence of the grant funds provided under this part. Federal funds may be used to supplement and complement existing water management planning programs. It does not prevent drawing matching shares from individual programs or from existing agency appropriations, budgets, or resources so long as expenditures are not substituted by Federal funds for the purposes of the Act.

(i) Payments shall be made in accordance with Attachment J of OMB Circular A-102 and TC 1075. Grant funds shall be requested only on an as needed basis.

(j) Financial management procedures shall comply with Attachment G of OMB Circular A-102 and with TC 1075. The applicable Federal requirements shall apply to the State and to local governments or non-governmental entities that receive funds as a sub-grantee for the purposes of the Act.

§ 740.8   Reporting.

(a) The designated agency shall submit program status reports and financial statements in accordance with procedures established by the Council. Instructions and a description of the content of these reports and the appropriate forms will be provided by the Council and will be in accordance with Attachments H, I and K of OMB Circular A-102 and TC 1075.

(b) The annual program report shall be due 90 days after the end of the grant period, as specified in the grant agreement, and shall contain:

(1) A summary description of the major accomplishments and results of the water management planning activities for the year, and an explanation of any work proposed in the work plan that has not been completed;

(2) An updated activity milestone chart, for each major activity in the work plan, showing the completion dates of major tasks;

(3) For those States implementing an evaluation system, a summary of the results of the evaluation efforts on the overall program effectiveness and key water management activities;

(4) A list of publications, public information materials, and other documents prepared in whole or in part with program funds which must duly note the use of Council grant funds in the printing of these documents;

(5) Other pertinent information, including any specific need for assistance; and

(6) An annual Financial Status Report.

(c) The Report of Federal Cash Transactions, as required under the provisions of Treasury Circular 1075, is due 30 days after the end of each quarter of the grant period, as specified in the grant agreement.

§ 740.9   Recordkeeping.

Each State or other entity within a State receiving financial assistance under this part shall make and retain records required by the Council, including records which fully disclose the amount and disposition of financial assistance received; the cost of administration; the total cost of all activities for which assistance is given or used; and any data and information which the Council determines are necessary to protect the interests of the United States and to facilitate an effective financial audit and performance evaluation. The Council and the Comptroller General of the United States shall have access to any books, documents, records or receipts which the Council determines are relevant or pertinent, either directly or indirectly, to any financial assistance provided under this part. Such records shall be retained for a period of three years, which starts from the date of the submission of the annual financial status report for the grant period.

§740.10 Program review and assistance.

(a) Each State's program will be reviewed annually by the Council to evaluate program management and accomplishments relative to the approved work plan. The Council shall:

(1) Review progam information including the application, annual reports, and other relevant information; and

(2) Make onsite visits as frequently as practicable to review the State program to:

(i) Provide assistance in the administration of the program, and at the request of the State, specific technical assistance in water resources management;

(ii) Determine whether Council policies, procedures or guidelines need revision to more effectively administer the grant; and

(iii) Gather information on practical or innovative techniques, methodologies, or other relevant information on the program.

(b) Based on the Council's annual review of each State program, the following may occur:

(1) If the program conforms to the requirements of the Act, the State will be advised of its continued eligibility for a grant;

(2) If it appears that the program does not comply with the requirements of the Act in either design or administration, the Council shall ascertain all the relevant facts. The State shall be notified immediately of the apparent inadequacies of the program with citation of specific requirements of the Act, this part, or other relevant instructions which apparently have not been met. The State shall be given timely opportunity to be heard through the filing of written statements and personal presentations in support of their position. If the Council is satisfied that sufficient adjustments have been made in the design and operation of the program, payments to the State will be continued; and

(3) If the Council determines on the basis of all the facts that the program still does not meet the requirements of the Act, the Governor shall be notified of the decision and the reasons therefore, and that no further payments shall be made until the noted inadequacies are satisfactorily resolved.

§740.11 Federal/State coordination.

The Council will coordinate the program under this part with similar or related programs of other Federal agencies in an effort to achieve consistency and compatibility in the administration of Federal programs.

§740.12 Amendments.

The Council may amend all or portions of these guidelines in accordance with established procedures. If it does, it will:

(a) Consult with appropriate advisory groups;

(b) Publish such proposed rulemaking in the FEDERAL REGISTER; and

(c) Simultaneously provide a copy of such proposed changes to each designated agency.

§740.13 Supplemental instructions.

As deemed appropriate, the Council may amplify the guidelines in this part by means of supplemental instructions, and may clarify program or administrative requirements set forth in these guidelines by the means of policy bulletins.

PARTS 741–799 [RESERVED]

CHAPTER VIII—SUSQUEHANNA RIVER BASIN COMMISSION

PART 800 [RESERVED]

PART 801—GENERAL POLICIES

AUTHORITY: Secs. 3.1, 3.4, 3.5(1), 15.1 and
15.2, Pub. L. 91–575 (84 Stat. 1509 *et seq.*).

SOURCE: 38 FR 4662, Feb. 20, 1973, unless
otherwise noted.

§ 801.0 Introduction.

(a) The Governors of the States of
New York, Pennsylvania, and Maryland, and a representative of the President of the United States are members
of the Susquehanna River Basin Commission. The Commission is a regional
governmental agency whose purpose is
to effect comprehensive multiple purpose planning for the conservation, utilization, development, management,
and control of the water and related
natural resources of the basin, which
includes part of New York, Pennsylvania, and Maryland.

(b) The Susquehanna River Basin
Compact provides broad authority for
the Commission to carry out basinwide
planning programs and projects, and to
take independent action as it determines essential to fulfill its statutory
regional governmental role.

(c) The objectives of the Commission
are to:

(1) Develop cooperative and coordinated Federal, State, local, and private
water and related natural resources
planning within the basin,

(2) Formulate, adopt, effectuate, and
keep current a comprehensive plan and
a water resources program for the immediate and long-range use and development of the water resources of the
basin,

(3) Provide for orderly collection and
evaluation of data, and for the continuing promotion and conduct of appropriate research relating to water resources problems,

(4) Establish priorities for planning,
financing subject to applicable laws,
development and use of projects and facilities essential to effectively meet
identified water resource needs,

(5) And to maintain these resources
in a viable state.

(d) The Commission shall employ a
multiobjective approach recognizing
national economy, regional development and environmental quality in
planning for the use and development
of the water resources of the basin.

(e) It is the purpose of this document
to set forth the objectives of the Commission and to present certain basic
policies that (1) have basinwide application, (2) are specifically pertinent to
the formulation of a comprehensive
plan, (3) will serve as guidelines for all
agencies or individuals with planning
responsibilities for the development
and use of the water resources of the
basin, (4) form the basis for working relationship between the Commission
and other agencies having related responsibilities in the basin. This statement will be amended and updated
from time to time.

§ 801.1 Standard definitions.

(a) Many terms that will be used in
official Commission documents may
have slightly different meanings to
various groups. To avoid confusion and
to increase the clarity of the meaning
the Commission applies to frequently
used terms standard definitions will be
utilized.

(b) The Commission will use the
standard definitions set forth for the
terms shown in section 1.2 of the Compact,[1] and will add terms and appropriate definitions as deemed necessary.

---

[1] Filed as part of FR Doc. 72–17234, Oct. 7,
1972.

§ 801.2 Coordination, cooperation, and intergovernmental relations.

(a) The interstate nature of the Susquehanna River Basin and the broad regional authority of the Commission require clear and effective working relationships with the States, Federal Government, and local and private sectors in all matters relating to the water resources of the basin.

(1) The Federal Government will be encouraged and asked to participate in water resources projects and programs having national or broad regional significance. The Commission will act to encourage local initiative to solve water resources problems within a local and regional context, but when faced with obviously needed action that is not forthcoming from other sources will act, in accordance with the Compact, on its own.

(2) The Compact provides authority for the Commission to serve in a regulatory capacity and also to act as a managing and operating agency. The Commission will exercise its regulatory authority mainly in interstate matters or where signatory authority is not being effectively exercised or where the signatory has little or no authority to act. Similarly, the Commission may manage and operate various facilities if it is determined that this is an area in which an important and necessary service can be rendered.

(3) Should it become necessary for the Commission to undertake development, management and operation of projects, arrangements for repayment of all project costs and eventual operation and maintenance costs will be appropriately prorated among the signatories or otherwise financed in accordance with the Compact.

(4) The Commission will utilize the functions, powers, and duties of the existing offices and agencies of government to the extent consistent with the Compact.

(5) In its actions the Commission will maintain a high level of public visibility. Broad government, public, and private sector commentary on Commission proposals and findings will be invited, and to the extent possible be incorporated and reflected in decisions for finalization of plans, projects, and programs having significant effect on the water resources of the basin. A concerted effort will be made to keep the Commission and its activities readily available to government and public scrutiny, and responsive to their concerns.

(b) The Commission shall exercise its regional jurisdiction in an effort to avoid and minimize conflicts and duplication of effort and shall:

(1) Cooperate with and help coordinate Federal, State, local government, and private sector efforts in all matters relating to the planning, conservation, preservation, use, development, management and control of the water resources of the basin.

(2) Develop administrative agreements, as needed, with appropriate agencies of the signatories and other agencies to facilitate achievement of the Commission's objectives and related responsibilities of other agencies by minimizing duplication of effort and maximizing the contributions the respective agencies are best able to make.

(3) Build upon present water resources planning and related activities of the signatory parties, local government, other public bodies, and the private sector and fully consider their recommendations and suggestions.

(4) Establish advisory committees as needed for specific assignments and seek meaningful liaison with sources of technical and scientific expertise.

(5) Share with interested parties results of investigations, studies, tests, and research undertaken by the Commission in an appropriate manner and form.

(6) Conduct its regular meetings announced in advance and open to the public.

(7) Depend upon existing public and private agencies for the construction, operation, and maintenance of projects except when the project is necessary to further the comprehensive plan and the responsible agency does not act or when the Commission is asked to act by one or more signatories, one or more local governments, or other responsible entities.

(8) Require that the planning of projects affecting the water resources of the basin by Federal, State, local agencies and private organizations be

undertaken in coordination with the Commission and in accordance with the Compact.

(9) Require that periodic reports of projects affecting water resources within the basin and listings of discharge permits granted, and similar activities undertaken by offices or agencies of the signatory parties, be submitted to the Commission.

§801.3 Allocations, diversions, withdrawals and release.

(a) The extremes in availability of water in the basin means that water will not always be available when and where it is needed. One of the responsibilities of the Commission is to act upon requests for allocations, withdrawals, or diversions of water for in-basin or out-of-basin use. Water emergencies may be expected to develop in portions of the basin due to drought conditions or other causes. The Commission will act promptly to effect alleviation of the condition to the extent possible.

(b) The Commission will require evidence that proposed interbasin transfers of water will not jeopardize, impair or limit the efficient development and management of the Susquehanna River Basin's water resources, or any aspects of these resources for in-basin use, or have a significant unfavorable impact on the resources of the basin and the receiving waters of the Chesapeake Bay.

(c) The Commission may, in making decisions on allocations, diversions, withdrawals, and releases, consider the following principles among others:

(1) That allocations, diversions, or withdrawals of water be based on the common law principles of riparian rights which entitles landholders in any watershed to draw upon the natural stream flow in reasonable amounts and be entitled to the stream flow not unreasonably diminished in quality or quantity by upstream use or diversion of water; and on the maintenance of the historic seasional variations of the flows into Chesapeake Bay.

(d) When the need arises for action on requests for allocations, diversions, or withdrawals of water from either surface or ground waters of the basin the Commission shall:

(1) Allocate waters of the basin to and among the signatory States to the Compact as the need appears, and impose related conditions, obligations, and release requirements.

(2) Determine if a proposed allocation, withdrawal or diversion is in conflict with or will significantly affect the comprehensive plan, and assure existing immediate and projected long term local and regional uses are protected.

(3) Impose conditions, obligations and release requirements for dams and/or diversion structures to protect prior local interests, downstream interests, and environmental quality.

(4) In the matter of drought, disasters or catastrophes, natural or man-made, which cause actual and immediate shortage of available and usable water supply, determine and delineate the area of shortage and by unanimous vote declare a state of water supply emergency therein, and impose direct controls on any and all allocations, diversions and uses of water to meet the emergency condition.

(5) In water emergencies coordinate the efforts of Federal, State, local, and other persons and entities in dealing with the emergency.

(6) Determine and delineate, after public hearing, areas within the basin wherein the demands upon supply made by water users have developed or threaten to develop to such a degree as to create a water shortage or impair or conflict with the comprehensive plan.

(7) When areas in need of protection from overdemand of safe yield of the supply have been delineated, declare such areas protected from further depletion, with the consent of the member or members from the affected State or States.

(8) Require that no person divert or withdraw from any protected area water for domestic, municipal, agricultural, or industrial uses in excess of such quantities as the Commission may prescribe by general regulation or pursuant to a permit granted heretofore under the laws of any of the signatory States.

§ 801.4 Project review.

(a) The Compact provides generally that no project affecting the water resources of the basin shall be undertaken by any person, governmental authority, or other entity prior to approval by the Commission.

(b) In many instances, one or more of the signatory parties will exercise project review authority regarding proposed projects in the basin coming under the review of the Commission. Accordingly the Commission will direct its attention to reviewing the completeness and effectiveness of the review procedures of the signatories and will endeavor to minimize duplication of staff effort, and time and cost to the applicant.

(c) The Commission will establish exempt categories in accordance with the section 3.10-3 of the Compact, and for projects determined not to have a substantial effect on the water resources of the basin. In dealing with Federal or federally licensed projects, the Commission will take the provisions of reservations (r) and (w) of United States Pub. L. 91-575 (84 Stat. 1509) and provisions of the Compact into account.

(d) It is expected that project review procedures will be modified following adoption of the comprehensive plan. In the meantime the Commission will:

(1) Base its review and comments pertaining to proposed projects within the basin coming under the purview of the Commission, on review and comments of signatory parties. In general, the Commission review will seek to ascertain the completeness of procedures followed by the signatory parties in their review, and will refrain from specifically rechecking detailed evaluations. (Susquehanna River Basin Commission Resolution No. 72-5)

(2) Require as it determines necessary, submission of pertinent project plans and documents for its independent review and approval. The purpose of this review will be to ascertain whether all relevant provisions of the Compact and actions taken pursuant thereto have been observed:

(i) When the Commission has determined that a project may have significant effect on the water resources of the basin.

(ii) When a proposed project does not fall under the review jurisdiction of any agency of the signatory parties.

§ 801.5 Comprehensive plan.

(a) The Compact requires that the Commission formulate and adopt a comprehensive plan for the immediate and long-range development and use of the water resources of the basin.

(1) The plan will include existing and proposed public and private programs, projects, and facilities which are required, in the judgment of the Commission, to meet present and future water resources needs of the basin. Consideration shall be given to the effect of the plan, or any part of the plan, on the receiving waters of the Chesapeake Bay. The Commission shall consult with interested public bodies and public utilities and fully consider the findings and recommendations of the signatory parties, their various subdivisions and interested groups. Prior to adoption of the plan the Commission shall conduct at least one public hearing in each signatory State.

(2) The plan will reflect consideration, of the multiobjectives of national economy, regional development and environmental quality; and multipurpose use of projects.

(3) Water quantity and water quality planning will be studied together and correlated to the extent feasible, with existing and proposed land uses. The development of a basinwide land use study to enable full consideration of basic and alternative proposals to meet water resources needs will be explored.

(4) An important phase of the plan formulation process is a thorough review and evaluation of the Susquehanna River Basin Coordinating Committee Study report, pertinent plans and reports of the signatories, including water quality standards and other data available. The findings and recommendations presented in the Susquehanna River Basin Coordinating Committee Study report will be considered for incorporation in the Commission's plan to the extent they are feasible and compatible with the current and projected needs and interests.

(5) Essentially the comprehensive plan will reflect the findings of an analysis of a mix of alternative futures

for industrial, agricultural, residential, and recreational development in the basin.

(6) The Commission will act diligently to promote Federal, State, local governmental, and private sector cooperation and coordination in the implementation of the adopted plan. It is expected that recommended development programs will be undertaken by the signatories, local governmental agencies, or private interests. If expeditious action by others is not forthcoming or is not possible the Commission will act in accordance with the Compact to implement programs, projects, and standards to the extent necessary to further the aims of the comprehensive plan.

(b) The comprehensive plan shall provide for the immediate and long-range use, development, conservation, preservation, and management of the water resources of the basin. The plan will be presented in a form and order as determined by the Commission and shall include, but not be limited to the following:

(1) Statement of authority, purpose, objectives, and scope.

(2) Description of the physical and human environment.

(3) Inventory of the basin's water resources and existing developments and facilities.

(4) Projection of immediate and long-range water resources needs of the basin.

(5) Description of a general system of measures and programs, including water quality and other standards as determined necessary, and reasonable alternatives considered essential to and capable of satisfying water resources needs into the reasonably foreseeable future.

(6) Criteria used for review and acceptance of projects within the plan.

(7) Procedures for updating and modifying the plan.

(8) Necessary appendices.

§801.6 Water supply.

(a) The Susquehanna River Basin is rich in water resources. With proper planning and management, and with adequate public and private investment in treatment, storage, and distribution facilities, the high potential of the basin to provide water of suitable quality for a wide array of public and private purposes into the foreseeable future should be possible.

(b) The Commission may regulate the withdrawal of waters of the basin not regulated by the signatory parties for domestic, municipal, industrial, and agricultural uses if regulation is considered essential to further the aims set forth in the comprehensive plan.

(c) The Commission shall study the basin's water supply needs, the potential surface and ground water resources, and the interrelationships to meet these needs through existing and new facilities and projects. Efficient use and management of existing facilities with emphasis on the full utilization of known technology will be explored in meeting water supply needs for domestic, municipal, agricultural, and industrial water supply before new programs or projects are approved.

§801.7 Water quality.

(a) The signatory States have the primary responsibility in the basin for water quality management and control. However, protection of the water resources of the basin from pollution, and actions by the signatory parties to achieve abatement and control of pollution are important to the Commission.

(b) The signatory parties have adopted water quality standards for the intra and interstate waters of the basin. Initially these standards will serve as the basis for the Commission's water quality program in the comprehensive plan.

(c) The Commission's role in water quality management and control essentially will be one of coordination to ensure water quality standards are adequate to protect broad public water resources interests, and that uniform policies and enforcement are affected by the signatories.

(d) The Commission shall:

(1) Encourage and coordinate efforts of the signatory parties to prevent, reduce, control, and eliminate water pollution and to maintain water quality in accordance with established standards.

(2) Promote government and private sector implementation of maximum

practical use of waste utilization and treatment technology.

(3) Promote and encourage State and local governments and industry to plan for regional waste water treatment and management.

(4) In cooperation with appropriate agencies of the signatory parties, make periodic inspections to ascertain the state of compliance with appropriate water quality standards, and as needed establish and operate water quality monitoring stations.

[38 FR 4662, Feb. 20, 1973, as amended at 38 FR 6386, Mar. 9, 1973]

§ 801.8 Flood plain management and protection.

(a) Periodic inundation of lands along waterways has not discouraged development of flood hazards areas. Major floods cause loss of life, extensive damages, and other conditions not in the public interest. A balanced flood plain management and protection program is needed to reduce the flood hazard to a minimum.

(b) The Commission may regulate the use of flood prone lands with approval of the appropriate signatory party, to safeguard public health, welfare, safety and property, and to sustain economic development.

(c) To foster sound flood plain controls, as an essential part of water resources management, the Commission shall:

(1) Encourage and coordinate the efforts of the signatory parties to control modification of the Susquehanna River and its tributaries by encroachment.

(2) Plan and promote implementation of projects and programs of a structural and nonstructural nature for the protection of flood plains subject to frequent flooding.

(3) Assist in the study and classification of flood prone lands to ascertain the relative risk of flooding, and establish standards for flood plain management.

(4) Promote the use of flood insurance by helping localities qualify for the national program.

(5) Assist in the development of a modern flood forecasting and warning system.

§ 801.9 Watershed management.

(a) The character, extent, and quality of water resources of a given watershed are strongly affected by the land use practices within that watershed. Accordingly the Commission will maintain close liaison with Federal, State, and local highway, mining, soil, forest, fish and wildlife, and recreation agencies and with government agencies dealing with urban and residential development programs.

(b) The Commission shall:

(1) Promote sound practices of watershed management including soil and water conservation measures, land restoration and rehabilitation, erosion control, forest management, improvement of fish and wildlife habitat, and land use in highway, urban, and residential development as related to water resources.

§ 801.10 Recreation.

(a) The use of surface water resources of the basin for recreation purposes is extensive. Swimming, fishing, boating, and other water oriented activities have regional and local economic benefit as well as recreational benefit.

(b) The Commission shall cooperate with public and private agencies in the planning and development of water-related recreation and fish and wildlife programs and projects within the basin and shall:

(1) Promote public access to and recreational use of existing and future public water areas.

(2) Promote recreational use of public water supply reservoirs and lakes where adequate treatment of water is provided, and/or where recreational uses are compatible with primary project purposes.

(3) Include recreation as a purpose where feasible, in multipurpose water use planning of reservoirs and other water bodies.

§ 801.11 Public values.

(a) The basin has many points of archeological and historic interest, and is well endowed with vistas of aesthetic significance.

(b) The Commission fully recognizes that the value of these areas cannot be measured simply in economic terms and will strive to preserve and promote them for the enjoyment and enrichment of present and future generations.

(c) The Commission shall:

(1) Seek the advice and assistance of appropriate societies and governmental agencies in the identification of archeological, historic, and scenic areas and unique lands in any planning or development affecting these attributes of the basin.

§ 801.12   Electric power generation.

(a) Significant uses are presently being made of the waters of the basin for the generation of electric power at hydro, pumped storage, and thermoelectric generating stations. Increased demands for electric power throughout the East Coast can be expected to result in proposals for the development of additional electric power generating stations located either in the basin or nearby its borders.

(b) There appears to be limited site potential in the basin for additional hydroelectric generation, and considerable potential for additional pumped storage and thermoelectric generation. The direct and indirect effects of existing and proposed electric generation projects will be considered by the Commission. Items of concern will include consumptive uses of water, alteration of natural stream regimen, effects on water quality, and on the other uses of the streams affected.

(c) The Commission, in cooperation with appropriate agencies of the signatory parties, and with other public and private agencies shall:

(1) Conduct a thorough review of applications to relicense existing electric power generating projects and facilities, and applications to amend existing licenses to determine if the proposal is in accord with the comprehensive plan.

(2) Require that the proposed siting and location in the basin of any type of electric generating facility or any facility located outside the basin having an effect on the waters of the basin, shall be planned in direct consultation with the Commission to enable advance consideration of the possible effects of such installation on the water resources of the basin.

§ 801.13   Proviso.

(a) This part is promulgated pursuant to sections 3.1, 3.5(1), and 15.2 of the Compact and shall be construed and applied subject to all of the terms and conditions of the Compact and of the provisions of Pub. L. 91–575, 84 Stat. 1509: *Provided,* Any provision in this statement of general policies that is inconsistent with the Compact itself shall be null and void.

§ 801.14   Public access to records.

(a) *Purpose.* The Commission, as an independent compact agency, is not subject to any of its member jurisdictions' laws regarding public access to records. Nevertheless, the Commission wishes to assure, to the maximum extent practicable, the availability of Commission records consistent with the Susquehanna River Basin Compact. The Commission shall maintain an "Access to Records Policy" that outlines the details and procedures related to public access to the Commission's records. Any revisions to this policy shall be consistent with this section and undertaken in accordance with appropriate public notice and comment consistent with requirements of 18 CFR 808.1(b).

(b) *Scope.* This section shall apply to all recorded information, regardless of whether the information exists in written or electronic format. There is a strong presumption that records shall be public, except where considerations of privacy, confidentiality, and security must be considered and require thoughtful balancing. The Commission shall identify types of records that are not subject to public access:

(1) Personnel or employment records, excluding salary information;

(2) Trade secrets, copyrighted material, or any other confidential business information;

(3) Records exempted from disclosure by statute, regulation, court order, or recognized privilege;

(4) Records reflecting internal predecisional deliberations, including deliberations between the commission and representatives of member jurisdictions;

(5) Records reflecting employee medical information, evaluations, tests or other identifiable health information;

(6) Records reflecting employee personal information, such as social security number, driver's license number, personal financial information, home addresses, home or personal cellular numbers, confidential personal information, spouse names, marital status or dependent information;

(7) Investigatory or enforcement records that would interfere with active enforcement proceedings or individual due process rights, disclose the identity of public complainants or confidential sources or investigative techniques or endanger the life or safety of Commission personnel; or

(8) Records related to critical infrastructure, excluding financial records, emergency procedures, or facilities.

(c) *Procedures.* The Access to Records Policy will detail the necessary procedures for requesting records and processing records requests:

(1) Requests shall be in writing and shall be reasonably specific;

(2) The Commission shall identify an Access to Records Officer to handle requests;

(3) The Commission shall respond to a records request within a reasonable time and in consideration of available resources and the nature of the request;

(4) The Commission shall not be required to create a record that does not already exist, or to compile, maintain, format or organize a public record in a manner in which the Commission does not currently practice;

(5) A procedure shall be identified for electronic transfer, copying or otherwise providing records in a manner that maintains the integrity of the Commission's files; and

(6) A procedure shall be identified for handling review of requests that seek access to information that has been identified as confidential and for notifying the person(s) who submitted the confidential information that it is subject to a records request.

(d) *Fees.* The Commission shall adopt and maintain a "Records Processing Fee Schedule." The fees shall be calculated to reflect the actual costs to the Commission for processing records requests and may include the costs of reproducing records and the cost to search, prepare and/or redact records for extraordinary requests.

(e) *Appeals.* Any person aggrieved by a Commission action on a records request shall have 30 days to appeal a decision in accordance with 18 CFR 808.2.

(f) *Disclosure to consultants, advisory committees, and State and local government officials and employees.* Data and information otherwise exempt from public disclosure may be disclosed to Commission consultants, advisory committees, and state and local government officials and employees for use only in their work in cooperation with the Commission. Such persons are thereafter subject to the same restrictions with respect to the disclosure of such data and information as any other Commission employee.

[83 FR 11876, Mar. 19, 2018]

PARTS 803–805 [RESERVED]

PART 806—REVIEW AND APPROVAL OF PROJECTS

Subpart A—General Provisions

806.25 Water conservation standards.

AUTHORITY: Secs. 3.4, 3.5 (5), 3.8, 3.10, and 15.2, Pub. L. 91–575, 84 Stat. 1509, *et seq.*

SOURCE: 71 FR 78579, Dec. 29, 2006, unless otherwise noted.

Subpart A—General Provisions

§ 806.1 Scope.

(a) This part establishes the scope and procedures for review and approval of projects under section 3.10 of the Susquehanna River Basin Compact, Pub. L. 91–575, 84 Stat. 1509, *et seq.*, (the compact) and establishes special standards under section 3.4(2) of the compact governing water withdrawals, the consumptive use of water, and diversions. The special standards established pursuant to section 3.4(2) shall be applicable to all water withdrawals and consumptive uses in accordance with the terms of those standards, irrespective of whether such withdrawals and uses are also subject to project review under section 3.10. This part, and every other part of 18 CFR chapter VIII, shall also be incorporated into and made a part of the comprehensive plan.

(b) When projects subject to Commission review and approval are sponsored by governmental authorities, the Commission shall submit recommendations and findings to the sponsoring agency, which shall be included in any report submitted by such agency to its respective legislative body or to any committee thereof in connection with any request for authorization or appropria-

tion therefor. The Commission review will ascertain the project's compatibility with the objectives, goals, guidelines and criteria set forth in the comprehensive plan. If determined compatible, the said project will also be incorporated into the comprehensive plan, if so required by the compact. For the purposes of avoiding conflicts of jurisdiction and of giving full effect to the Commission as a regional agency of the member jurisdictions, no expenditure or commitment shall be made by any governmental authority for or on account of the construction, acquisition or operation of any project or facility unless it first has been included by the Commission in the comprehensive plan.

(c) If any portion of this part, or any other part of 18 CFR Chapter VIII, shall, for any reason, be declared invalid by a court of competent jurisdiction, all remaining provisions shall remain in full force and effect.

(d) Except as otherwise stated in this part, this part shall be effective on January 1, 2007.

(e) When any period of time is referred to in this part, such period in all cases shall be so computed as to exclude the first and include the last day of such period. Whenever the last day of any such period shall fall on Saturday or Sunday, or on any day made a legal holiday by the law of the United States, such day shall be omitted from the computation.

(f) Any Commission forms or documents referenced in this part may be obtained from the Commission at 4423 North Front Street, Harrisburg, PA 17110, or from the Commission's Web site at *www.srbc.net.*

[71 FR 78579, Dec. 29, 2006, as amended at 82 FR 29390, June 29, 2017]

§ 806.2 Purposes.

(a) The general purposes of this part are to advance the purposes of the compact and include, but are not limited to:

(1) The promotion of interstate comity;

(2) The conservation, utilization, development, management and control of water resources under comprehensive, multiple purpose planning; and

(3) The direction, supervision and coordination of water resources efforts and programs of federal, state and local governments and of private enterprise.

(b) In addition, §§ 806.22, 806.23 and 806.24 of this part contain the following specific purposes: Protection of public health, safety and welfare; stream quality control; economic development; protection of fisheries and aquatic habitat; recreation; dilution and abatement of pollution; the regulation of flows and supplies of ground and surface waters; the avoidance of conflicts among water users; the prevention of undue salinity; and protection of the Chesapeake Bay.

(c) The objective of all interpretation and construction of this part and all subsequent parts is to ascertain and effectuate the purposes and the intention of the Commission set out in this section. These regulations shall not be construed in such a way as to limit the authority of the Commission, the enforcement actions it may take, or the remedies it may prescribe.

§ 806.3 Definitions.

For purposes of parts 806, 807 and 808, unless the context indicates otherwise, the words listed in this section are defined as follows:

Agricultural water use. A water use associated primarily with the raising of food, fiber or forage crops, trees, flowers, shrubs, turf products, livestock and poultry. The term shall include aquaculture.

Application. A written request for action by the Commission including without limitation thereto a letter, referral by any agency of a member jurisdiction, or an official form prescribed by the Commission.

Basin. The area of drainage of the Susquehanna River and its tributaries into the Chesapeake Bay to the southern edge of the Pennsylvania Railroad bridge between Havre de Grace and Perryville, Maryland.

Change of Ownership. A change in ownership shall mean any transfer by sale or conveyance of the real or personal property comprising a project.

Commission. The Susquehanna River Basin Commission, as established in Article 2 of the compact, including its commissioners, officers, employees, or

duly appointed agents or representatives.

Commissioner. Member or Alternate Member of the Susquehanna River Basin Commission as prescribed by Article 2 of the compact.

Compact. The Susquehanna River Basin Compact, Pub. L. 91–575; 84 Stat. 1509 *et seq.*

Comprehensive plan. The comprehensive plan prepared and adopted by the Commission pursuant to Articles 3 and 14 of the compact.

Construction. To physically initiate assemblage, installation, erection or fabrication of any facility, involving or intended for the withdrawal, conveyance, storage or consumptive use of the waters of the basin. For purposes of unconventional natural gas development projects subject to review and approval pursuant to § 806.4(a)(8), initiation of construction shall be deemed to commence upon the drilling (spudding) of a gas well, or the initiation of construction of any water impoundment or other water-related facility to serve the project, whichever comes first.

Consumptive use. The loss of water transferred through a manmade conveyance system or any integral part thereof (including such water that is purveyed through a public water supply or wastewater system), due to transpiration by vegetation, incorporation into products during their manufacture, evaporation, injection of water or wastewater into a subsurface formation from which it would not reasonably be available for future use in the basin, diversion from the basin, or any other process by which the water is not returned to the waters of the basin undiminished in quantity.

Diversion. The transfer of water into or out of the basin.

Drilling pad site. The area occupied by the equipment or facilities necessary for or incidental to drilling, production or plugging of one or more hydrocarbon development wells and upon which such drilling has or is intended to occur.

Executive Director. The chief executive officer of the Commission appointed pursuant to Article 15, Section 15.5, of the compact.

Facility. Any real or personal property, within or without the basin, and improvements thereof or thereon, and any and all rights of way, water, water rights, plants, structures, machinery, and equipment acquired, constructed, operated, or maintained for the beneficial use of water resources or related land uses or otherwise including, without limiting the generality of the foregoing, any and all things and appurtenances necessary, useful, or convenient for the control, collection, storage, withdrawal, diversion, release, treatment, transmission, sale, or exchange of water; or for navigation thereon, or the development and use of hydroelectric energy and power, and public recreational facilities; of the propagation of fish and wildlife; or to conserve and protect the water resources of the basin or any existing or future water supply source, or to facilitate any other uses of any of them.

Flowback. The return flow of water and formation fluids recovered from the wellbore of an unconventional natural gas or hydrocarbon development well following the release of pressures induced as part of the hydraulic fracture stimulation of a target geologic formation, and until the well is placed into production.

Formation fluids. Fluids in a liquid or gaseous physical state, present within the pore spaces, fractures, faults, vugs, caverns, or any other spaces of formations, whether or not naturally occurring or injected therein.

Governmental authority. A federal or state government, or any political subdivision, public corporation, public authority, special purpose district, or agency thereof.

Groundwater. Water beneath the surface of the ground within a zone of saturation, whether or not flowing through known and definite channels or percolating through underground geologic formations, and regardless of whether the result of natural or artificial recharge. The term includes water contained in quarries, pits and underground mines having no significant surface water inflow, aquifers, underground water courses and other bodies of water below the surface of the earth. The term also includes a spring in which the water level is sufficiently lowered by pumping or other means of drainage to eliminate the surface flow.

All other springs are considered to be surface water.

Hydrocarbon development project. A project undertaken for the purpose of extraction of liquid or gaseous hydrocarbons from geologic formations, including but not limited to the drilling, casing, cementing, stimulation and completion of unconventional natural gas development wells, and all other activities and facilities associated with the foregoing or with the production, maintenance, operation, closure, plugging and restoration of such wells or drilling pad sites that require water for purposes including but not limited to, re-stimulation and/or re-completion of wells, fresh water injection of production tubing, use of coiled tubing units, pumping, cement hydration, dust suppression, and hydro-seeding or other revegetation activities, until all post-plugging restoration is completed in accordance with all applicable member jurisdiction requirements. The project includes water used for hydro-seeding or other revegetation activities, dust suppression and hydro-excavation of access roads and underground lines, as well as cleaning of tanks, related to a drilling pad site and centralized impoundments.

Hydrocarbon water storage facility. An engineered barrier or structure, including but not limited to tanks, pits or impoundments, constructed for the purpose of storing water, flowback or production fluids for use in hydrocarbon development.

Member jurisdiction. The signatory parties as defined in the compact, comprised of the States of Maryland and New York, the Commonwealth of Pennsylvania, and the United States of America.

Member state. The States of Maryland and New York, and the Commonwealth of Pennsylvania.

Person. An individual, corporation, partnership, unincorporated association, and the like and shall have no gender and the singular shall include the plural. The term shall include a governmental authority and any other entity which is recognized by law as the subject of rights and obligations.

Pre-compact consumptive use. The maximum average daily quantity or volume of water consumptively used over any consecutive 30-day period prior to January 23, 1971.

Production fluids. Water or formation fluids recovered at the wellhead of a producing hydrocarbon well as a by-product of the production activity.

Project. Any work, service, activity or facility undertaken, which is separately planned, financed or identified by the Commission, or any separate facility undertaken or to be undertaken by the Commission or otherwise within a specified area, for the conservation, utilization, control, development, or management of water resources, which can be established and utilized independently, or as an addition to an existing facility, and can be considered as a separate entity for purposes of evaluation.

Project sponsor. Any person who owns, operates or proposes to undertake a project. The singular shall include the plural.

Public water supply. A system, including facilities for collection, treatment, storage and distribution, that provides water to the public for human consumption, that:

(1) Serves at least 15 service connections used by year-round residents of the area served by the system; or

(2) Regularly serves at least 25 year-round residents.

Surface water. Water on the surface of the ground, including water in a perennial or intermittent watercourse, lake, reservoir, pond, spring, wetland, estuary, swamp or marsh, or diffused surface water, whether such body of water is natural or artificial.

Tophole water. Water that is brought to the surface while drilling through the strata containing fresh groundwater. Tophole water may contain drill cuttings typical of the formation being penetrated but may not be polluted or contaminated by additives, brine, oil or man induced conditions.

Unconventional natural gas development project. A hydrocarbon development project undertaken for the purpose of extraction of gaseous hydrocarbons from low permeability geologic formations utilizing enhanced drilling, stimulation or recovery techniques.

Undertake. Except for activities related to site evaluation, the initiation of construction or operation of a new or expanded project, or the operation of an existing project, that is subject to Commission review and approval.

Water or waters of the basin. Groundwater or surface water, or both, within the basin either before or after withdrawal.

Water resources. Includes all waters and related natural resources within the basin.

Wetlands. Those areas that are inundated or saturated by surface or groundwater at a frequency and duration sufficient to support, and that under normal circumstances do support, a prevalence of vegetation typically adapted for life in saturated soil conditions. Wetlands generally include swamps, marshes, bogs, and similar areas.

Withdrawal. A taking or removal of water from any source within the basin for use within the basin.

[71 FR 78579, Dec. 29, 2006, as amended at 73 FR 1273, Jan. 8, 2008; 73 FR 78619, Dec. 23, 2008; 77 FR 8098, Feb. 14, 2012; 79 FR 75429, Dec. 18, 2014; 82 FR 29390, June 29, 2017]

§ 806.4 Projects requiring review and approval.

(a) Except for activities relating to site evaluation, to aquifer testing under § 806.12 or to those activities authorized under § 806.34, no person shall undertake any of the following projects without prior review and approval by the Commission. The project sponsor shall submit an application in accordance with subpart B of this part and shall be subject to the applicable standards in subpart C of this part.

(1) *Consumptive use of water.* Any consumptive use project described below shall require an application to be submitted in accordance with § 806.13, and shall be subject to the standards set forth in § 806.22, and, to the extent that it involves a withdrawal from groundwater or surface water, shall also be subject to the standards set forth in § 806.23. Except to the extent that they involve the diversion of the waters of the basin, public water supplies shall be exempt from the requirements of this section regarding consumptive use; provided, however, that nothing in this section shall be construed to exempt individual consumptive users connected to any such public water

supply from the requirements of this section. Provided the commission determines that low flow augmentation projects sponsored by the commission's member states provide sufficient mitigation for agricultural water use to meet the standards set forth in § 806.22, and except as otherwise provided below, agricultural water use projects shall not be subject to the requirements of this paragraph (a)(1). Notwithstanding the foregoing, an agricultural water use project involving a diversion of the waters of the basin shall be subject to such requirements unless the property, or contiguous parcels of property, upon which the agricultural water use project occurs is located at least partially within the basin.

(i) Any project initiated on or after January 23, 1971, involving a consumptive water use of an average of 20,000 gallons per day (gpd) or more in any consecutive 30-day period.

(ii) With respect to projects previously approved by the Commission for consumptive use, any project that will involve an increase in a consumptive use above that amount which was previously approved.

(iii) With respect to projects that existed prior to January 23, 1971, any project:

(A) Registered in accordance with subpart E of this part that increases its consumptive use by any amount over the quantity determined under § 806.44;

(B) Increasing its consumptive use to an average of 20,000 gpd or more in any consecutive 30-day period; or

(C) That fails to register its consumptive use in accordance with subpart E of this part.

(iv) Any project, regardless of when initiated, involving a consumptive use of an average of 20,000 gpd or more in any 30-day period, and undergoing a change of ownership, unless such project satisfies the requirements of paragraphs (b) or (c) of this section or the existing Commission approval for such project is transferred pursuant to § 806.6.

(2) *Withdrawals.* Any project, including all of its sources, described below shall require an application to be submitted in accordance with § 806.13, and shall be subject to the standards set forth in §§ 806.21 and 806.23. Hydro-electric projects, except to the extent that such projects involve a withdrawal, shall be exempt from the requirements of this section regarding withdrawals; provided, however, that nothing in this paragraph (a)(2) shall be construed as exempting hydro-electric projects from review and approval under any other category of project requiring review and approval as set forth in this section, § 806.5, or part 801 of this chapter. The taking or removal of water by a public water supplier indirectly through another public water supply system or another water user's facilities shall constitute a withdrawal hereunder.

(i) Any project initiated on or after the applicable dates specified in paragraph (a)(2)(iv) below, withdrawing a consecutive 30-day average of 100,000 gpd or more from a groundwater or surface water source, or a combination of such sources.

(ii) With respect to projects previously approved by the Commission, any project that increases a withdrawal above that amount which was previously approved and any project that will add a source or increase withdrawals from an existing source which did not require approval prior to January 1, 2007.

(iii) Any project which involves a withdrawal from a groundwater or surface water source and which is subject to the requirements of paragraph (a) of this section regarding consumptive use.

(iv) With respect to groundwater projects that existed prior to July 13, 1978, surface water projects that existed prior to November 11, 1995, or projects that existed prior to January 1, 2007, with multiple sources involving a withdrawal of a consecutive 30-day average of 100,000 gpd or more that did not require Commission review and approval, any project:

(A) Registered in accordance with subpart E of this part that increases its withdrawal by any amount over the quantity determined under § 806.44;

(B) Increasing its withdrawal individually or cumulatively from all sources to an average of 100,000 gpd or more in any consecutive 30-day period; or

(C) That fails to register its withdrawals in accordance with subpart E of this part.

(v) Any project, regardless of when initiated, involving a withdrawal of a consecutive 30-day average of 100,000 gpd or more, from either groundwater or surface water sources, or in combination from both, and undergoing a change of ownership, unless such project satisfies the requirements of paragraphs (b) or (c) of this section or the existing Commission approval for such project is transferred pursuant to § 806.6.

(3) *Diversions.* Except with respect to agricultural water use projects not subject to the requirements of paragraph (a)(1) of this section, the projects described in paragraphs (a)(3)(i) through (a)(3)(iv) of this section shall require an application to be submitted in accordance with § 806.13, and shall be subject to the standards set forth in § 806.24. The project sponsors of out-of-basin diversions shall also comply with all applicable requirements of this part relating to consumptive uses and withdrawals. The projects identified in paragraphs (a)(3)(v) and (a)(3)(vi) of this section shall be subject to regulation pursuant to § 806.22(f).

(i) Any project initiated on or after January 23, 1971, involving the diversion of water into the basin, or involving a diversion of water out of the basin of an average of 20,000 gallons of water per day or more in any consecutive 30-day period.

(ii) With respect to diversions previously approved by the Commission, any project that will increase a diversion above the amount previously approved.

(iii) With respect to diversions initiated prior to January 23, 1971, any project that will increase a diversion into the basin by any amount, or increase the diversion of water out of the basin by an average of 20,000 gpd or more in any consecutive 30-day period.

(iv) Any project, regardless of when initiated, involving the diversion of water into the basin or involving a diversion of an average of 20,000 gallons of water per day or more in any consecutive 30-day period out of the basin, and undergoing a change of ownership, unless such project satisfies the requirements of paragraphs (b) or (c) of this section or the Commission approval for such project is transferred pursuant to § 806.6.

(v) The interbasin diversion of any flowback or production fluids from hydrocarbon development projects from one drilling pad site to another drilling pad site for use in hydrofracture stimulation, provided it is handled, transported and stored in compliance with all standards and requirements of the applicable member jurisdiction, shall not be subject to separate review and approval as a diversion under this paragraph if the generating or receiving pad site is subject to an Approval by Rule issued pursuant to § 806.22(f) and provided all monitoring and reporting requirements applicable to such approval are met.

(vi) The diversion of flowback or production fluids from a hydrocarbon development project for which an Approval by Rule has been issued pursuant to § 806.22(f), to an out-of-basin treatment or disposal facility authorized under separate governmental approval to accept flowback or production fluids, shall not be subject to separate review and approval as a diversion under this paragraph, provided all monitoring and reporting requirements applicable to the Approval by Rule are met and it is handled, transported and stored in compliance with all standards and requirements of the applicable member jurisdiction.

(vii) The diversion of any flowback or production fluids from hydrocarbon development projects located outside the basin to an in-basin treatment or disposal facility authorized under separate government approval to accept flowback or production fluids, shall not be subject to separate review and approval as a diversion under this paragraph (c)(3), provided the fluids are handled, transported and stored in compliance with all standards and requirements of the applicable member jurisdiction.

(4) Any project on or crossing the boundary between two member states.

(5) Any project in a member state having a significant effect on water resources in another member state.

(6) Any project which has been or is required to be included by the Commission in its comprehensive plan, or will have a significant effect upon the comprehensive plan.

(7) Any other project so determined by the commissioners or Executive Director pursuant to §806.5 or 18 CFR part 801. Such project sponsors shall be notified in writing by the Executive Director.

(8) Any unconventional natural gas development project in the basin involving a withdrawal, diversion or consumptive use, regardless of the quantity.

(9) Any project subject to coverage under a general permit issued under §806.17.

(b) Any project that did not require Commission approval prior to January 1, 2007, and undergoing a change of ownership, shall be exempt from the requirements of paragraph (a)(1)(iv), (a)(2)(v) or (a)(3)(iv) of this section if it satisfies any of the following categories:

(1) A corporate reorganization of the following types:

(i) Where property is transferred to a corporation by one or more corporations solely in exchange for stock or securities of the transferee corporation, provided that immediately after the exchange the transferor corporation(s) own 80 percent of the voting stock and 80 percent of all other stock of the transferee corporation.

(ii) Where the corporate reorganization is merely a result of a change of the name, identity, internal corporate structure or place of organization and does not affect ownership or control.

(2) Transfer of a project to the transferor's spouse or one or more lineal descendents, or any spouse of such lineal descendents, or to a corporation owned or controlled by the transferor, or the transferor's spouse or lineal descendents, or any spouse of such lineal descendents, for so long as the combined ownership interest of the transferor, the transferor's spouse and/or the transferor's lineal descendent(s) and their spouses, continues to be 51 percent or greater.

(3) Transfer of land used primarily for the raising of food, fiber or forage crops, trees, flowers, shrubs, turf products, livestock, or poultry, or for aquaculture, to the extent that, and for so long as, the project's water use continues to be for such agricultural water use purposes.

(c) Any project that did not require Commission approval prior to January 1, 2007, and not otherwise exempt from the requirements of paragraph (a)(1)(iv), (a)(2)(v), or (a)(3)(iv) of this section, pursuant to paragraph (b) of this section, may be undertaken by a new project sponsor upon a change of ownership pending action on a transfer application under §806.6.

[71 FR 78579, Dec. 29, 2006, as amended at 73 FR 1273, Jan. 8, 2008; 73 FR 78620, Dec. 23, 2008; 75 FR 60620, Oct. 1, 2010; 77 FR 8099, Feb. 14, 2012; 80 FR 76857, Dec. 11, 2015; 82 FR 29390, June 29, 2017]

§806.5 Projects that may require review and approval.

(a) The following projects, if not otherwise requiring review and approval under §806.4, and provided that the project sponsor is notified in writing by the Executive Director, may be subject to Commission review and approval as determined by the Commission or the Executive Director:

(1) Projects that may affect interstate water quality.

(2) Projects within a member state that have the potential to affect waters within another member state. This includes, but is not limited to, projects which have the potential to alter the physical, biological, chemical or hydrological characteristics of water resources of interstate streams designated by the Commission under separate resolution.

(3) Projects that may have a significant effect upon the comprehensive plan.

(4) Projects not included in paragraphs (a)(1) through (a)(3) of this section, but which could have an adverse, adverse cumulative, or interstate effect on the water resources of the basin.

(b) Determinations by the Executive Director may be appealed to the Commission within 30 days after receipt of notice of such determination as set forth in §808.2.

§ 806.6 Transfer of approvals.

(a) An existing Commission approval may be transferred to a new project sponsor by the Executive Director provided:

(1) The application for transfer is submitted within 90 days of a transfer or change in ownership of a project.

(2) The new project sponsor operates the project subject to the same terms and conditions of the existing approval pending approval of the transfer application.

(3) Any noncompliance by the existing project sponsor associated with the project or by the new project sponsor associated with other projects is resolved to the Commission's satisfaction.

(4) If the existing approval is greater than 10 years old, the transfer shall be conditioned to require the submission of an updated metering and monitoring plan consistent with the requirements of § 806.30.

(5) If the existing project has an unapproved withdrawal, consumptive use and/or diversion listed in paragraph (b) of this section, the transfer shall be conditioned to require the submission of a new application for review and approval of the unapproved withdrawal, consumptive use and/or diversion consistent with §§ 806.4 and 806.14.

(6) Any modifications proposed by the new project sponsor shall be subject to a separate application and review process under §§ 806.14 and 806.18.

(b) Previously unapproved activities associated with a project subject to transfer under paragraph (a) of this section include:

(1) The project has an associated pre-compact consumptive water use that has not been subject to approval or had mitigation approved by the Commission.

(2) The project has an associated diversion that was initiated prior to January 23, 1971.

(3) The project has an associated groundwater withdrawal that was initiated prior to July 13, 1978, and that has not been approved by the Commission.

(4) The project has an associated surface water withdrawal that was initiated prior to November 11, 1995, and that has not been approved by the Commission.

(5) The project has a consumptive water use approval and has an associated withdrawal that has not been approved by the Commission.

(6) The project is registered under subpart E of this part.

(c) Upon undergoing a change of name that does not affect ownership or control of the project, the project sponsor must request a reissuance of the project's approval by the Executive Director within 90 days from the date of the change.

[80 FR 76857, Dec. 11, 2015, as amended at 82 FR 29390, June 29, 2017]

§ 806.7 Concurrent project review by member jurisdictions.

(a) The Commission recognizes that agencies of the member jurisdictions will exercise their review and approval authority and evaluate many proposed projects in the basin. The Commission will adopt procedures to assure compatibility between jurisdictional review and Commission review.

(b) To avoid duplication of work and to cooperate with other government agencies, the Commission may develop administrative agreements or other cooperative arrangements, in accordance with the procedures outlined in this part, with appropriate agencies of the member jurisdictions regarding joint review of projects. These agreements or arrangements may provide for joint efforts by staff, delegation of authority by an agency or the Commission, or any other matter to support cooperative review activities. Permits issued by a member jurisdiction agency shall be considered Commission approved if issued pursuant to an administrative agreement or other cooperative arrangement with the Commission specifically providing therefor.

[71 FR 78579, Dec. 29, 2006, as amended at 75 FR 60620, Oct. 1, 2010]

§ 806.8 Waiver/modification.

The Commission may, in its discretion, waive or modify any of the requirements of this or any other part of its regulations if the essential purposes set forth in § 806.2 continue to be served.

Subpart B—Application Procedure

§ 806.10 Purpose of this subpart.

The purpose of this subpart is to set forth procedures governing applications required by §§ 806.4, 806.5, 806.6 and 18 CFR part 801.

§ 806.11 Preliminary consultations.

(a) Any project sponsor of a project that is or may be subject to the Commission's jurisdiction is encouraged, prior to making application for Commission review, to request a preliminary consultation with the Commission staff for an informal discussion of preliminary plans for the proposed project. To facilitate preliminary consultations, it is suggested that the project sponsor provide a general description of the proposed project, a map showing its location and, to the extent available, data concerning dimensions of any proposed structures, anticipated water needs, and the environmental impacts.

(b) Except for project sponsors of electric power generation projects under § 801.12(c)(2) of this chapter, preliminary consultation is optional for the project sponsor (except with respect to aquifer test plans under § 806.12) but shall not relieve the sponsor from complying with the requirements of the compact or with this part.

[71 FR 78579, Dec. 29, 2006, as amended at 82 FR 29390, June 29, 2017]

§ 806.12 Constant-rate aquifer testing.

(a) Prior to submission of an application pursuant to § 806.13, a project sponsor seeking approval for a new groundwater withdrawal, a renewal of an expiring groundwater withdrawal, or an increase of a groundwater withdrawal shall perform a constant-rate aquifer test in accordance with this section.

(b) The project sponsor shall prepare a constant-rate aquifer test plan for prior review and approval by Commission staff before testing is undertaken. Such plan shall include a groundwater availability analysis to determine the availability of water during a 1-in-10-year recurrence interval.

(c) Unless otherwise specified, approval of a test plan is valid for two years from the date of approval.

(d) Approval of a test plan shall not be construed to limit the authority of the Commission to require additional testing or monitoring.

(e) The project sponsor may be required, at its expense, to provide temporary water supply if an aquifer test results in interference with an existing water use.

(f) Review of submittals under this section may be terminated by the Commission in accordance with the procedures set forth in § 806.16.

[71 FR 78579, Dec. 29, 2006, as amended at 82 FR 29390, June 29, 2017]

§ 806.13 Submission of application.

Sponsors of projects subject to review and approval of the Commission under § 806.4, § 806.5 or § 806.6, or project sponsors seeking renewal of an existing approval of the Commission, shall submit an application and applicable fee to the Commission, in accordance with this subpart.

[77 FR 8099, Feb. 14, 2012]

§ 806.14 Contents of application.

(a) Applications for a new project or a major modification to an existing approved project shall include, but not be limited to, the following information and, where applicable, shall be subject to the requirements in paragraph (b) of this section and submitted on forms and in the manner prescribed by the Commission.

(1) Identification of project sponsor including any and all proprietors, corporate officers or partners, the mailing address of the same, and the name of the individual authorized to act for the sponsor.

(2) Project location, including latitude and longitude coordinates in decimal degrees accurate to within 10 meters, the project location displayed on a map with a 7.5-minute USGS topographic base, and evidence of legal access to the property upon which the project is proposed.

(3) Project description, including: Purpose, proposed quantity to be withdrawn or consumed, if applicable, and identification of all water sources related to the project including location and date of initiation of each source.

(4) Anticipated impact of the project, including impacts on existing water withdrawals, nearby surface waters, and threatened or endangered species and their habitats.

(5) The reasonably foreseeable need for the proposed quantity of water to be withdrawn or consumed, including supporting calculations, and the projected demand for the term of the approval.

(6) A metering plan that adheres to § 806.30.

(7) Evidence of coordination and compliance with member jurisdictions regarding all necessary permits or approvals required for the project from other federal, state or local government agencies having jurisdiction over the project.

(8) Project estimated completion date and estimated construction schedule.

(9) Draft notices required by § 806.15.

(10) The Commission may also require the following information as deemed necessary:

(i) Engineering feasibility.

(ii) Ability of the project sponsor to fund the project.

(b) Additional information is required for a new project or a major modification to an existing approved project as follows.

(1) *Surface water.* (i) Water use and availability.

(ii) Project setting, including surface water characteristics, identification of wetlands, and site development considerations.

(iii) Description and design of intake structure.

(iv) Anticipated impact of the proposed project on local flood risk, recreational uses, fish and wildlife, and natural environment features.

(v) For new projects and major modifications to increase a withdrawal, alternatives analysis for a withdrawal proposed in settings with a drainage area of 50 miles square or less, or in a waterway with exceptional water quality, or as required by the Commission.

(2) *Groundwater*—(i) With the exception of mining related withdrawals solely for the purpose of dewatering; construction dewatering withdrawals and withdrawals for the sole purpose of groundwater or below water table re-

mediation generally which are addressed in paragraph (b)(6) of this section, the project sponsor shall provide an interpretative report that includes all monitoring and results of a constant-rate aquifer test consistent with § 806.12 and an updated groundwater availability estimate if changed from the aquifer test plan, unless a request for a waiver of the requirements of § 806.12 is granted. The project sponsor shall obtain Commission approval of the test procedures prior to initiation of the constant-rate aquifer test.

(ii) Water use and availability.

(iii) Project setting, including nearby surface water features.

(iv) Groundwater elevation monitoring plan for all production wells.

(v) Alternatives analysis as required by the Commission.

(3) *Consumptive use.* (i) Consumptive use calculations, and a mitigation plan consistent with § 806.22(b).

(ii) Water conservation methods, design or technology proposed or considered.

(iii) Alternatives analysis as required by the Commission.

(4) *Into basin diversions.* (i) Provide the necessary information to demonstrate that the proposed project will meet the standards in § 806.24(c).

(ii) Identification of the source and water quality characteristics of the water to be diverted.

(5) *Out of basin diversions.* (i) Provide the necessary information to demonstrate that the proposed project will meet the standards in § 806.24(b).

(ii) Project setting.

(6) *Other projects.* Other projects, including without limitation, mine dewatering, construction dewatering, water resources remediation projects, and AMD remediation facilities that qualify as a withdrawal.

(i) In lieu of aquifer testing, report(s) prepared for any other purpose or as required by other governmental regulatory agencies that provides a demonstration of the hydrogeologic and/or hydrologic effects and limits of said effects due to operation of the proposed project and effects on local water availability.

(ii) [Reserved]

(c) All applications for renewal of expiring approved projects, including those with minor or major modifications, shall include, but not be limited to, the following information, and, where applicable, shall be subject to the requirements in paragraph (d) of this section and submitted on forms and in the manner prescribed by the Commission.

(1) Identification of project sponsor including any and all proprietors, corporate officers or partners, the mailing address of the same, and the name of the individual authorized to act for the sponsor.

(2) Project location, including latitude and longitude coordinates in decimal degrees accurate to within 10 meters, the project location displayed on map with a 7.5-minute USGS topographic base, and evidence of legal access to the property upon which the project is located.

(3) Project description, to include, but not be limited to: Purpose, proposed quantity to be withdrawn or consumed if applicable, identification of all water sources related to the project including location and date of initiation of each source, and any proposed project modifications.

(4) The reasonably foreseeable need for the requested renewal of the quantity of water to be withdrawn or consumed, including supporting calculations, and the projected demand for the term of the approval.

(5) An as-built and approved metering plan.

(6) Copies of permits from member jurisdictions regarding all necessary permits or approvals obtained for the project from other federal, state, or local government agencies having jurisdiction over the project.

(7) Copy of any approved mitigation or monitoring plan and any related as-built for the expiring project.

(8) Demonstration of registration of all withdrawals or consumptive uses in accordance with the applicable state requirements.

(9) Draft notices required by § 806.15.

(d) Additional information is required for the following applications for renewal of expiring approved projects.

(1) *Surface water.* (i) Historic water use quantities and timing of use.

(ii) Changes to stream flow or quality during the term of the expiring approval.

(iii) Changes to the facility design.

(iv) Any proposed changes to the previously authorized purpose.

(2) *Groundwater*—(i) The project sponsor shall provide an interpretative report that includes all monitoring and results of any constant-rate aquifer testing previously completed or submitted to support the original approval. In lieu of a testing report, historic operational data pumping and elevation data may be considered, as a request for waiver of the requirements of § 806.12. Those projects that did not have constant-rate aquifer testing completed for the original approval that was consistent with § 806.12 or sufficient historic operational pumping and groundwater elevation data may be required to complete constant-rate aquifer testing consistent with § 806.12, prepare and submit an interpretative report that includes all monitoring and results of any constant-rate aquifer test.

(ii) An interpretative report providing analysis and comparison of current and historic water withdrawal and groundwater elevation data with previously completed hydrogeologic report.

(iii) Current groundwater availability analysis assessing the availability of water during a 1-in-10 year recurrence interval under the existing conditions within the recharge area and predicted for term of renewal (*i.e.*, other users, discharges, and land development within the groundwater recharge area).

(iv) Groundwater elevation monitoring plan for all production wells.

(v) Changes to the facility design.

(vi) Any proposed changes to the previously authorized purpose.

(3) *Consumptive use.* (i) Consumptive use calculations, and a copy of the approved plan or method for mitigation consistent with § 806.22.

(ii) Changes to the facility design.

(iii) Any proposed changes to the previously authorized purpose.

(4) *Into basin diversion.* (i) Provide the necessary information to demonstrate that the proposed project will meet the standards in § 806.24(c).

(ii) Identification of the source and water quality characteristics of the water to be diverted.

(iii) Changes to the facility design.

(iv) Any proposed changes to the previously authorized purpose.

(5) *Out of basin diversion.* (i) Historic water use quantities and timing of use.

(ii) Changes to stream flow or quality during the term of the expiring approval.

(iii) Changes to the facility design.

(iv) Any proposed changes to the previously authorized purpose,

(6) *Other projects.* Other projects, including without limitation, mine dewatering, water resources remediation projects, and AMD facilities that qualify as a withdrawal.

(i) Copy of approved report(s) prepared for any other purpose or as required by other governmental regulatory agencies that provides a demonstration of the hydrogeologic and/or hydrologic effects and limits of said effects due to operation of the project and effects on local water availability.

(ii) Any data or reports that demonstrate effects of the project are consistent with those reports provided in paragraph (d)(6)(i) of this section.

(iii) Demonstration of continued need for expiring approved water source and quantity.

(iv) Changes to the facility design.

(v) Any proposed changes to the previously authorized purpose.

(e) A report about the project prepared for any other purpose, or an application for approval prepared for submission to a member jurisdiction, may be accepted by the Commission provided the said report or application addresses all necessary items on the Commission's form or listed in this section, as appropriate.

(f) Applications for minor modifications must be complete and will be on a form and in a manner prescribed by the Commission. Applications for minor modifications must contain the following:

(1) Description of the project;

(2) Description of all sources, consumptive uses and diversions related to the project;

(3) Description of the requested modification;

(4) Statement of the need for the requested modification; and

(5) Demonstration that the anticipated impact of the requested modification will not adversely impact the water resources of the basin.

(g) For any applications, the Executive Director or Commission may require other information not otherwise listed in this section.

[82 FR 29390, June 29, 2017]

§ 806.15 Notice of application.

(a) Except with respect to paragraphs (h) and (i) of this section, any project sponsor submitting an application to the Commission shall provide notice thereof to the appropriate agency of the member State, each municipality in which the project is located, and the county and the appropriate county agencies in which the project is located. The project sponsor shall also publish notice of submission of the application at least once in a newspaper of general circulation serving the area in which the project is located. The project sponsor shall also meet any of the notice requirements set forth in paragraphs (b) through (f) of this section, if applicable. All notices required under this section shall be provided or published no later than 20 days after submission of the application to the Commission and shall contain a description of the project, its purpose, the requested quantity of water to be withdrawn, obtained from sources other than withdrawals, or consumptively used, and the address, electronic mail address, and phone number of the project sponsor and the Commission. All such notices shall be in a form and manner as prescribed by the Commission.

(b) For withdrawal applications submitted pursuant to § 806.4(a)(2), the project sponsor shall also provide the notice required under paragraph (a) of this section to each property owner listed on the tax assessment rolls of the county in which such property is located and identified as follows:

(1) For groundwater withdrawal applications, the owner of any property that is located within a one-half mile radius of the proposed withdrawal location.

(2) For surface water withdrawal applications, the owner of any property that is riparian or littoral to the body of water from which the proposed withdrawal will be taken and is within a one-half mile radius of the proposed withdrawal location.

(3) For groundwater withdrawal applications, the Commission or Executive Director may allow notification of property owners through alternate methods where the property of such property owner is served by a public water supply.

(c) For projects involving a diversion of water out of the basin, the project sponsor shall also publish a notice of the submission of its application at least once in a newspaper of general circulation serving the area outside the basin where the project proposing to use the diverted water is located. For projects involving a diversion of water into the basin, the project sponsor shall also publish a notice of the submission of its application at least once in a newspaper of general circulation serving the area outside the basin where the withdrawal of water proposed for diversion is located.

(d) For applications submitted under §806.22(f)(13) for a public water supply source, the newspaper notice requirement contained in paragraph (a) of this section shall be satisfied by publication in a newspaper of general circulation in the area served by the public water supply.

(e) For applications submitted under §806.22(f)(13) for a wastewater discharge source, the newspaper notice requirement contained in paragraph (a) of this section shall be satisfied by publication in a newspaper of general circulation in each area within which the water obtained from such source will initially be used for hydrocarbon development.

(f) For applications submitted under §806.22(f)(14) for a hydrocarbon water storage facility, the newspaper notice requirement contained in paragraph (a) of this section shall be satisfied by publication in a newspaper of general circulation in the area in which the facility is located.

(g) The project sponsor shall provide the Commission with a copy of the United States Postal Service return receipt or the verified return receipt from a comparable delivery service for the notifications to agencies of member States, municipalities and appropriate county agencies required under paragraph (a) of this section. The project sponsor shall also provide certification on a form provided by the Commission that it has published the newspaper notice(s) required by this section and made the landowner notifications as required under paragraph (b) of this section, if applicable. Until these items are provided to the Commission, processing of the application will not proceed. The project sponsor shall maintain all proofs of publication and records of notices sent under this section for the duration of the approval related to such notices.

(h) For Notices of Intent (NOI) seeking coverage under a general permit, the project sponsor shall provide the NOI to the appropriate agency of the member State and each municipality and county planning agency in which the project is located and any additional notice identified in the general permit.

(i) For applications for minor modifications, the project sponsor shall provide notice of the application to the appropriate agency of the member State and each municipality and county planning agency in which the project is located.

[75 FR 60620, Oct. 1, 2010, as amended at 77 FR 8099, Feb. 14, 2012; 79 FR 75430, Dec. 18, 2014; 80 FR 76858, Dec. 11, 2015; 82 FR 29392, June 29, 2017]

§806.16 Completeness of application.

(a) The Commission's staff shall review the application, and if necessary, request the project sponsor to provide any additional information that is deemed pertinent for proper evaluation of the project.

(b) An application deemed administratively incomplete will be returned to the project sponsor, who shall have 30 days to cure the administrative deficiencies. An application deemed technically deficient may be returned to the project sponsor, who shall have a period of time prescribed by Commission staff to cure the technical deficiencies. Failure to cure either administrative or technical deficiencies within the prescribed time may result in termination of the application process and forfeiture of any fees submitted.

(c) The project sponsor has a duty to provide information reasonably necessary for the Commission's review of the application. If the project sponsor fails to respond to the Commission's request for additional information, the Commission may terminate the application process, close the file and so notify the project sponsor. The project sponsor may reapply without prejudice by submitting a new application and fee.

§ 806.17 General permits.

(a) *Coverage and purpose.* The Commission may issue a general permit, in lieu of issuing individual approvals, for a specifically described category of diversions, water withdrawals and consumptive uses that:

(1) Involve the same or substantially similar types of operations or activities;

(2) Require the same limitations or operating conditions, or both;

(3) Require the same or similar monitoring and reporting; and

(4) Will result in minimal adverse impacts consistent with §§ 806.21 through 806.24.

(b) *Procedure for issuance.* (1) At least 30 days prior to the issuance of a general permit, the Commission shall publish notice in the FEDERAL REGISTER and the member jurisdiction administrative bulletins of the intent to issue a general permit.

(2) At least 30 days shall be provided for interested members of the public and Federal, State and local agencies to provide written comments on a proposed general permit.

(3) The Commission or Executive Director may, in its discretion, hold a public hearing on a proposed general permit, taking into account the level of public interest and likelihood of controversy.

(4) The issuance of a general permit adopted by the Commission will be published in the FEDERAL REGISTER and the member jurisdiction adminis-

trative bulletins. This notice shall set forth the effective date of the general permit.

(c) *Administration of general permits.* General permits may be issued, amended, suspended, revoked, reissued or terminated under this section.

(1) Any general permit issued under this section shall set forth the applicability of the permit and the conditions that apply to any diversion, withdrawal or consumptive use authorized by such general permit.

(2) The Commission may fix a term to any general permit issued.

(3) A project sponsor shall obtain permission to divert, withdraw or consumptively use water in accordance with a general permit by filing a Notice of Intent (NOI) with the Commission, in a form and manner determined by the Commission.

(4) Approval of coverage under a general permit shall be determined by the Executive Director or by any other manner that the Commission shall establish for any general permit.

(5) The Commission may set a fee for NOIs to any general permit.

(6) A project sponsor shall provide notice for NOIs in accordance with § 806.15(h) and any additional notice requirements that the Commission may adopt for any general permit.

(7) The requirements of § 806.16 apply to the review of NOIs to any general permit.

(8) Upon reissuance or amendment of a general permit, all project sponsors permitted to divert, withdraw or consumptively use water in accordance with the previous general permit shall be permitted to continue to operate with the renewed or modified general permit unless otherwise notified by the Commission.

(9) Notice of receipt of NOIs shall be published on the Commission's Web site and in any other manner that the Commission shall establish for any general permit.

(d) *Denial of coverage.* The Executive Director will deny or revoke coverage under a general permit when one or more of the following conditions exist:

(1) The project or project sponsor does not or can no longer meet the criteria for coverage under a general permit.

(2) The diversion, withdrawal or consumptive use, individually or in combination with other similar Commission regulated activities, is causing or has the potential to cause adverse impacts to water resources or competing water users.

(3) The project does not comport with § 806.21(a) or (b).

(4) The project includes other diversions, withdrawals or consumptive uses that require an individual approval and the issuance of both an individual approval and a general permit for the project would constitute an undue administrative burden on the Commission.

(5) The Executive Director determines that a project cannot be effectively regulated under a general permit and is more effectively regulated under an individual approval.

(e) *Requiring an individual approval.* If coverage is denied or revoked under paragraph (d) of this section, the project sponsor shall be notified in writing. The notice will include a brief statement for the reasons for the decision. If coverage under a general permit was previously granted, the notice will also include a deadline for submission of an application for an individual approval. Timely submission of a complete application will result in continuation of coverage of the applicable withdrawal, consumptive use or diversion under the general permit, until the Commission takes final action on the pending individual approval application.

(f) *Action of the Commission.* Action by the Executive Director denying or revoking coverage under a general permit under paragraph (d) of this section, or requiring an individual approval under paragraph (e) of this section, is not a final action of the Commission until the project sponsor submits and the Commission takes final action on an individual approval application.

[80 FR 76858, Dec. 11, 2015]

§ 806.18 Approval modifications.

(a) *General.* A project sponsor shall submit an application for modification of a current approval prior to making a change in the design, operational plans, or use as presented in the application upon which the approval was originally issued, and that will affect the terms and conditions of the current approval.

(b) *Applications for modification.* A project sponsor may apply for a modification of a current approval by submitting an application for modification to the Commission.

(c) *Minor modifications.* The following are minor modifications:

(1) Correction of typographical errors;

(2) Changes to monitoring or metering conditions;

(3) Addition of sources of water for consumptive use;

(4) Changes to the authorized water uses;

(5) Changes to conditions setting a schedule for developing, implementing, and/or reporting on monitoring, data collection and analyses;

(6) Changes to the design of intakes;

(7) Increases to total system limits that were established based on the projected demand of the project; and

(8) Modifications of extraction well network used for groundwater remediation systems.

(d) *Major modifications.* Major modifications are changes not considered to be minor modifications. Major modifications may include, but are not limited to:

(1) Increases in the quantity of water withdrawals, consumptive uses or diversions;

(2) Increases to peak day consumptive water use;

(3) Increases to the instantaneous withdrawal rate or changes from a single withdrawal rate to a varied withdrawal rate;

(4) Changes affecting passby flow requirements; and

(5) Changes that have the potential for adverse impacts to water resources or competing water users.

(e) *Notice and approval.* (1) Applications for modifications are subject to the notice requirements of § 806.15.

(2) The Commission or Executive Director may approve, approve with conditions or deny an application for minor modification, or direct that an application for major modification be made.

133

(3) The Commission may approve, approve with conditions or deny an application for major modification.

[80 FR 76859, Dec. 11, 2015]

Subpart C—Standards for Review and Approval

§ 806.20 Purpose of this subpart.

The purpose of this subpart is to set forth general standards that shall be used by the Commission to evaluate all projects subject to review and approval by the Commission pursuant to §§ 806.4, 806.5 and 806.6, and to establish special standards applicable to certain water withdrawals, consumptive uses and diversions. This subpart shall not be construed to limit the Commission's authority and scope of review. These standards are authorized under Sections 3.4(2), 3.4(8), 3.4(9), and 3.10 of the compact and are based upon, but not limited to, the goals, objectives, guidelines and criteria of the comprehensive plan.

§ 806.21 General standards.

(a) A project shall be feasible and not be detrimental to the proper conservation, development, management, or control of the water resources of the basin.

(b) The Commission may modify and approve as modified, or may disapprove, a project if it determines that the project is not in the best interest of the conservation, development, management, or control of the basin's water resources, or is in conflict with the comprehensive plan.

(c) *Disapprovals—other governmental jurisdictions.* (1) The Commission may suspend the review of any application under this part if the project is subject to the lawful jurisdiction of any member jurisdiction or any political subdivision thereof, and such member jurisdiction or political subdivision has disapproved or denied the project. Where such disapproval or denial is reversed on appeal, the appeal is final, and the project sponsor provides the Commission with a certified copy of the decision, the Commission shall resume its review of the application. Where, however, an application has been suspended hereunder for a period

greater than three years, the Commission may terminate its review. Thereupon, the Commission shall notify the project sponsor of such termination and that the application fee paid by the project sponsor is forfeited. The project sponsor may reactivate the terminated application by reapplying to the Commission, providing evidence of its receipt of all necessary governmental approvals and, at the discretion of the Commission, submitting new or updated information.

(2) The Commission may modify, suspend or revoke a previously granted approval if the project sponsor fails to obtain or maintain the approval of a member jurisdiction or political subdivision thereof having lawful jurisdiction over the project.

[71 FR 78579, Dec. 29, 2006, as amended at 82 FR 29392, June 29, 2017]

§ 806.22 Standards for consumptive uses of water.

(a) The project sponsors of all consumptive water uses subject to review and approval under § 806.4, § 806.5 or § 806.6 of this part shall comply with this section.

(b) *Mitigation.* All project sponsors whose consumptive use of water is subject to review and approval under § 806.4, § 806.5, § 806.6, or § 806.17 shall mitigate such consumptive use. Except to the extent that the project involves the diversion of the waters out of the basin, public water supplies shall be exempt from the requirements of this section regarding consumptive use; provided, however, that nothing in this section shall be construed to exempt individual consumptive users connected to any such public water supply from the requirements of this section. Mitigation may be provided by one or a combination of the following:

(1) During low flow periods as may be designated by the Commission for consumptive use mitigation.

(i) Reduce withdrawal from the approved source(s), in an amount equal to the project's total consumptive use, and withdraw water from alternative surface water storage or aquifers or other underground storage chambers or facilities approved by the Commission, from which water can be withdrawn for a period of 90 days without impact to surface water flows.

(ii) Release water for flow augmentation, in an amount equal to the project's total consumptive use, from surface water storage or aquifers, or other underground storage chambers or facilities approved by the Commission, from which water can be withdrawn for a period of 90 days without impact to surface water flows.

(iii) Discontinue the project's consumptive use, except that reduction of project sponsor's consumptive use to less than 20,000 gpd during periods of low flow shall not constitute discontinuance.

(2) Use, as a source of consumptive use water, surface storage that is subject to maintenance of a conservation release acceptable to the Commission. In any case of failure to provide the specified conservation release, such project shall provide mitigation in accordance with paragraph (3), below, for the calendar year in which such failure occurs, and the Commission will re-evaluate the continued acceptability of the conservation release.

(3) Provide monetary payment to the Commission, for all water consumptively used over the course of a year, in an amount and manner prescribed by the Commission.

(4) Implement other alternatives approved by the Commission.

(c) *Determination of manner of mitigation.* The Commission will, in its sole discretion, determine the acceptable manner of mitigation to be provided by project sponsors whose consumptive use of water is subject to review and approval. Such a determination will be made after considering the project's location, source characteristics, anticipated amount of consumptive use, proposed method of mitigation and their effects on the purposes set forth in §806.2 of this part, and any other pertinent factors. The Commission may modify, as appropriate, the manner of mitigation, including the magnitude and timing of any mitigating releases, required in a project approval.

(d) *Quality of water released for mitigation.* The physical, chemical and biological quality of water released for mitigation shall at all times meet the quality required for the purposes listed in §806.2, as applicable.

(e) *Approval by rule for consumptive uses*—(1) *General rule.* Except with respect to projects involving hydrocarbon development subject to the provisions of paragraph (f) of this section, any project who is solely supplied water for consumptive use by public water supply may be approved by the Executive Director under this paragraph (e) in accordance with the following, unless the Executive Director determines that the project cannot be adequately regulated under this approval by rule.

(2) *Notification of intent.* Prior to undertaking a project or increasing a previously approved quantity of consumptive use, the project sponsor shall submit a notice of intent (NOI) on forms prescribed by the Commission, and the appropriate application fee, along with any required attachments.

(3) *Time of notice.* Within 20 days after submittal of an NOI under paragraph (e)(2) of this section, the project sponsor shall satisfy the notice requirements set forth in §806.15.

(4) *Metering, daily use monitoring, and quarterly reporting.* The project sponsor shall comply with metering, daily use monitoring, and quarterly reporting as specified in §806.30.

(5) *Standard conditions.* The standard conditions set forth in §806.21 shall apply to projects approved by rule.

(6) *Mitigation.* The project sponsor shall comply with mitigation in accordance with paragraph (b)(2) or (3) of this section.

(7) *Compliance with other laws.* The project sponsor shall obtain all necessary permits or approvals required for the project from other federal, state or local government agencies having jurisdiction over the project. The Commission reserves the right to modify, suspend or revoke any approval under this paragraph (e) if the project sponsor fails to obtain or maintain such approvals.

(8) *Decision.* The Executive Director may grant, deny, suspend, revoke, modify or condition an approval to operate under this approval by rule, or

renew an existing approval by rule previously granted hereunder, and will notify the project sponsor of such determination, including the quantity of consumptive use approved.

(9) *Term.* Approval by rule shall be effective upon written notification from the Executive Director to the project sponsor, shall expire 15 years from the date of such notification, and shall be deemed to rescind any previous consumptive use approvals.

(f) *Approval by rule for consumptive use related to unconventional natural gas and other hydrocarbon development projects.* (1) Any unconventional natural gas development project subject to review and approval under § 806.4(a)(8), or any other hydrocarbon development project subject to review and approval under § 806.4, § 806.5, or § 806.6, shall be subject to review and approval by the Executive Director under this paragraph (f) regardless of the source or sources of water being used consumptively.

(2) Notification of Intent: Prior to undertaking a project or increasing a previously approved quantity of consumptive use, the project sponsor shall submit a Notice of Intent (NOI) on forms prescribed by the Commission, and the appropriate application fee, along with any required attachments.

(3) Within 20 days after submittal of an NOI under paragraph (f)(2) of this section, the project sponsor shall satisfy the notice requirements set forth in § 806.15.

(4) The project sponsor shall comply with metering, daily use monitoring and quarterly reporting as specified in § 806.30, or as otherwise required by the approval by rule. Daily use monitoring shall include amounts delivered or withdrawn per source, per day, and amounts used per oil or gas well or drilling pad site, per day, for well drilling, hydrofracture stimulation, hydrostatic testing, and other project-related activity. The foregoing shall apply to all water, including stimulation additives, flowback, drilling fluids, formation fluids and production fluids, utilized by the project. The project sponsor shall also submit a post-hydrofracture report in a form and manner as prescribed by the Commission.

(5) The project sponsor shall comply with the mitigation requirements set forth in § 806.22(b).

(6) Any flowback or production fluids utilized by the project sponsor for hydrofracture stimulation undertaken at the project shall be separately accounted for, but shall not be included in the daily consumptive use amount calculated for the project, or be subject to the mitigation requirements of § 806.22(b).

(7) The project sponsor shall obtain all necessary permits or approvals required for the project from other federal, state, or local government agencies having jurisdiction over the project. The Executive Director reserves the right to modify, suspend or revoke any approval under this paragraph (f) if the project sponsor fails to obtain or maintain such approvals.

(8) The project sponsor shall certify to the Commission that all flowback and production fluids have been re-used or treated and disposed of in accordance with applicable state and federal law.

(9) The Executive Director may grant, deny, suspend, revoke, modify or condition an approval to operate under this approval by rule, or renew an existing approval by rule granted hereunder, and will notify the project sponsor of such determination, including the sources and quantity of consumptive use approved. The issuance of any approval hereunder shall not be construed to waive or exempt the project sponsor from obtaining Commission approval for any water withdrawals or diversions subject to review pursuant to § 806.4(a). Any sources of water approved pursuant to this section shall be further subject to any approval or authorization required by the member jurisdiction.

(10) Approval by rule shall be effective upon issuance by the Executive Director to the project sponsor, shall expire five years from the date of such issuance, and supersede any previous consumptive use approvals to the extent applicable to the project.

(11) In addition to water sources approved for use by the project sponsor pursuant to § 806.4 or this section, a project sponsor issued an approval by rule pursuant to paragraph (f)(9) of this

section may utilize any of the following water sources at the drilling pad site, subject to such monitoring and reporting requirements as the Commission may prescribe:

(i) Tophole water encountered during the drilling process, provided it is used only for drilling or hydrofracture stimulation.

(ii) Precipitation or stormwater collected on the drilling pad site, provided it is used only for drilling or hydrofracture stimulation.

(iii) Drilling fluids, formation fluids, flowback or production fluids obtained from a drilling pad site, production well site or hydrocarbon water storage facility, provided it is used only for hydrofracture stimulation, and is handled, transported and stored in compliance with all standards and requirements of the applicable member jurisdiction.

(iv) Water obtained from a hydrocarbon water storage facility associated with an approval issued by the Commission pursuant to §806.4(a) or by the Executive Director pursuant to this section, provided it is used only for the purposes authorized therein, and in compliance with all standards and requirements of the applicable member jurisdiction.

(12) A project sponsor issued an approval by rule pursuant to paragraph (f)(9) of this section may utilize a source of water approved by the Commission pursuant to §806.4(a), or by the Executive Director pursuant to paragraph (f)(14) of this section, and issued to persons other than the project sponsor, provided any such source is approved for use in hydrocarbon development, the project sponsor has an agreement for its use, and at least 10 days prior to use, the project sponsor registers such source with the Commission on a form and in the manner prescribed by the Commission.

(13) A project sponsor issued an approval by rule pursuant to paragraph (f)(9) of this section may also utilize other sources of water, including but not limited to, public water supply or wastewater discharge not otherwise associated with an approval issued by the Commission pursuant to §806.4(a) or an approval by rule issued pursuant to paragraph (f)(9) of this section, provided such sources are first approved by the Executive Director. Any request for approval shall be submitted on a form and in the manner prescribed by the Commission, shall satisfy the notice requirements set forth in §806.15, and shall be subject to review pursuant to the standards set forth in subpart C of this part.

(14) A project sponsor issued an approval by rule pursuant to paragraph (f)(9) of this section may utilize water obtained from a hydrocarbon water storage facility that is not otherwise associated with an approval issued by the Commission pursuant to §806.4(a), or an approval by rule issued pursuant to paragraph (f)(9) of this section, provided such sources are first approved by the Executive Director and are constructed and maintained in compliance with all standards and requirements of the applicable member jurisdiction. The owner or operator of any such facility shall submit a request for approval on a form and in the manner prescribed by the Commission, shall satisfy the notice requirements set forth in §806.15, and shall be subject to review pursuant to the standards set forth in subpart C of this part.

(15) The project sponsor shall provide a copy of any registration or source approval issued pursuant to this section to the appropriate agency of the applicable member jurisdiction. The project sponsor shall record on a daily basis, and report quarterly on a form and in a manner prescribed by the Commission, the quantity of water obtained from any source registered or approved hereunder. Any source approval issued hereunder shall also be subject to such monitoring and reporting requirements as may be contained in such approval or otherwise required by this part.

[71 FR 78579, Dec. 29, 2006, as amended at 73 FR 78620, Dec. 23, 2008; 74 FR 49812, Sept. 29, 2009; 75 FR 60621, Oct. 1, 2010; 77 FR 8099, Feb. 14, 2012; 79 FR 75430, Dec. 18, 2014; 82 FR 29393, June 29, 2017]

§806.23 Standards for water withdrawals.

(a) The project sponsors of all withdrawals subject to review and approval under §806.4, §806.5 or §806.6 of this part shall comply with the following standards, in addition to those required pursuant to § 806.21.

(b) *Limitations on withdrawals.* (1) The Commission may limit withdrawals to the amount (quantity and rate) of water that is needed to meet the reasonably foreseeable needs of the project sponsor.

(2) The Commission may deny an application, limit or condition an approval to ensure that the withdrawal will not cause significant adverse impacts to the water resources of the basin. The Commission may consider, without limitation, the following in its consideration of adverse impacts: Lowering of groundwater or stream flow levels; groundwater and surface water availability, including cumulative uses; rendering competing supplies unreliable; affecting other water uses; causing water quality degradation that may be injurious to any existing or potential water use; affecting fish, wildlife or other living resources or their habitat; causing permanent loss of aquifer storage capacity; affecting wetlands; or affecting low flow of perennial or intermittent streams.

(3) The Commission may impose limitations or conditions to mitigate impacts, including without limitation:

(i) Limit the quantity, timing or rate of withdrawal or level of drawdown, including requiring a total system limit.

(ii) Require the project sponsor to provide, at its own expense, an alternate water supply or other mitigating measures.

(iii) Require the project sponsor to implement and properly maintain special monitoring measures.

(iv) Require the project sponsor to implement and properly maintain stream flow protection measures.

(v) Require the project sponsor to develop and implement an operations plan acceptable to the Commission.

(4) The Commission may require the project sponsor to undertake the following, to ensure its ability to meet its present or reasonably foreseeable water needs from available groundwater or surface water without limitation:

(i) Investigate additional sources or storage options to meet the demand of the project.

(ii) Submit a water resource development plan that shall include, without limitation, sufficient data to address any supply deficiencies, identify alternative water supply options, and support existing and proposed future withdrawals.

(5) For projects consisting of mine dewatering, water resources remediation, and AMD facilities that qualify as a withdrawal, review of adverse impacts will have limited consideration of groundwater availability, causing permanent loss of aquifer storage and lowering of groundwater levels provided these projects are operated in accordance with the laws and regulations of the member jurisdictions.

[71 FR 78579, Dec. 29, 2006, as amended at 82 FR 29393, June 29, 2017]

§ 806.24 **Standards for diversions.**

(a) The project sponsors of all diversions subject to review and approval under § 806.4, § 806.5 or § 806.6 of this part shall comply with the following standards.

(b) For projects involving out-of-basin diversions, the following requirements shall apply.

(1) Project sponsors shall:

(i) Demonstrate that they have made good faith efforts to develop and conserve sources of water within the importing basin, and have considered other reasonable alternatives to the diversion.

(ii) Comply with the general standards set forth in §§ 801.3, 806.21, and 806.22, and the applicable requirements of this part relating to consumptive uses and withdrawals.

(2) In deciding whether to approve a proposed diversion out of the basin, the Commission shall also consider and the project sponsor shall provide information related to the following factors:

(i) Any adverse effects and cumulative adverse effects the project may have on the ability of the Susquehanna River Basin, or any portion thereof, to meet its own present and future water needs.

(ii) The location, amount, timing, purpose and duration of the proposed diversion and how the project will individually and cumulatively affect the flow of any impacted stream or river, and the freshwater inflow of the Chesapeake Bay, including the extent to which any diverted water is being returned to the basin or the bay.

(iii) Whether there is a reasonably foreseeable need for the quantity of water requested by the project sponsor and how that need is measured against reasonably foreseeable needs in the Susquehanna River Basin.

(iv) The amount and location of water being diverted to the Susquehanna River Basin from the importing basin.

(v) The proximity of the project to the Susquehanna River Basin.

(vi) The project sponsor's pre-compact member jurisdiction approvals to withdraw or divert the waters of the basin.

(vii) Historic reliance on sources within the Susquehanna River Basin.

(3) In deciding whether to approve a proposed diversion out of the basin, the Commission may also consider, but is not limited to, the factors set forth in paragraphs (i) through (v) of this paragraph (b)(3). The decision whether to consider the factors in this paragraph (b) and the amount of information required for such consideration, if undertaken, will depend upon the potential for the proposed diversion to have an adverse impact on the ability of the Susquehanna River Basin, or any portion thereof, to meet its own present and future needs.

(i) The impact of the diversion on economic development within the Susquehanna River Basin, the member states or the United States of America.

(ii) The cost and reliability of the diversion versus other alternatives, including certain external costs, such as impacts on the environment or water resources.

(iii) Any policy of the member jurisdictions relating to water resources, growth and development.

(iv) How the project will individually and cumulatively affect other environmental, social and recreational values.

(v) Any land use and natural resource planning being carried out in the importing basin.

(c) For projects involving into-basin diversions, the following requirements shall apply.

(1) Project sponsors shall:

(i) Provide information on the source, amount, and location of the water being diverted to the Susquehanna River Basin from the importing basin.

(ii) Provide information on the water quality classification, if any, of the Susquehanna River Basin stream to which diverted water is being discharged and the discharge location or locations.

(iii) Demonstrate that they have applied for or received all applicable withdrawal or discharge permits or approvals related to the diversion, and demonstrate that the diversion will not result in water quality degradation that may be injurious to any existing or potential ground or surface water use.

(2) In deciding whether to approve a proposed diversion into the basin, the Commission shall also consider and the project sponsor shall provide information related to the following factors:

(i) Any adverse effects and cumulative adverse effects the project may have on the Susquehanna River Basin, or any portion thereof, as a result of the introduction or potential introduction of invasive or exotic species that may be injurious to the water resources of the basin.

(ii) The extent to which the proposed diversion satisfies all other applicable general and specific standards set forth in subpart C of this part pertaining to withdrawals and consumptive use.

[71 FR 78579, Dec. 29, 2006, as amended at 75 FR 60621, Oct. 1, 2010]

§ 806.25 Water conservation standards.

Any project sponsor whose project is subject to Commission approval under this part proposing to withdraw water either directly or indirectly (through another user) from groundwater or surface water sources, or both, shall comply with the following requirements:

(a) *Public water supply.* As circumstances warrant, a project sponsor of a public water supply shall:

(1) Reduce distribution system losses to a level not exceeding 20 percent of the gross withdrawal.

(2) Install meters for all users.

(3) Establish a program of water conservation that will:

(i) Require installation of water conservation devices, as applicable, by all classes of users.

(ii) Prepare and distribute literature to customers describing available water conservation techniques.

(iii) Implement a water pricing structure which encourages conservation.

(iv) Encourage water reuse.

(b) *Industrial.* Project sponsors who use water for industrial purposes shall:

(1) Designate a company representative to manage plant water use.

(2) Install meters or other suitable devices or utilize acceptable flow measuring methods for accurate determination of water use by various parts of the company operation.

(3) Install flow control devices which match the needs of the equipment being used for production.

(4) Evaluate and utilize applicable recirculation and reuse practices.

(c) *Irrigation.* Project sponsors who use water for irrigation purposes shall utilize irrigation systems properly designed for the sponsor's respective soil characteristics, topography and vegetation.

(d) *Effective date.* Notwithstanding the effective date for other portions of this part, this section shall apply to all groundwater and surface water withdrawals initiated on or after January 11, 1979.

Subpart D—Terms and Conditions of Approval

§ 806.30 Monitoring.

The Commission, as part of the project review, shall evaluate the proposed methodology for monitoring consumptive uses, water withdrawals and mitigating flows, including flow metering devices, stream gages, and other facilities used to measure the withdrawals or consumptive use of the project or the rate of stream flow. If the Commission determines that additional flow measuring, metering or monitoring devices are required, these shall be provided at the expense of the project sponsor, installed in accordance with a schedule set by the Commission, and installed per the specifications and recommendations of the manufacturer of the device, and shall

be subject to inspection by the Commission at any time.

(a) Project sponsors of projects that are approved under this part shall:

(1) Measure and record on a daily basis, or such other frequency as may be approved by the Commission, the quantity of all withdrawals, using meters or other methods approved by the Commission.

(2) Certify, at the time of installation and no less frequently than once every 5 years, the accuracy of all measuring devices and methods to within 5 percent of actual flow, unless specified otherwise by the Commission.

(3) Maintain metering or other approved methods so as to provide a continuous, accurate record of the withdrawal or consumptive use.

(4) Measure groundwater levels in all approved production and other wells, as specified by the Commission.

(5) Measure groundwater levels at additional monitoring locations, as specified by the Commission.

(6) Measure water levels in surface storage facilities, as specified by the Commission.

(7) Measure stream flows, passby flows or conservation releases, as specified by the Commission, using methods and at frequencies approved by the Commission.

(8) Perform other monitoring for impacts to water quantity, water quality and aquatic biological communities, as specified by the Commission.

(b) *Reporting.* (1) Project sponsors whose projects are approved under this section shall report to the Commission on a quarterly basis on forms and in a manner prescribed by the Commission all information recorded under paragraph (a) of this section, unless otherwise specified by the Commission.

(2) Project sponsors whose projects are approved under this section shall report to the Commission:

(i) Violations of withdrawal limits and any conditions of approvals, within 5 days of such violation.

(ii) Loss of measuring or recording capabilities required under paragraph (a)(1) of this section, within 5 days after any such loss.

[71 FR 78579, Dec. 29, 2006, as amended at 82 FR 29393, June 29, 2017]

§806.31 Term of approvals.

(a) Approvals issued under this part shall have a term equal to the term of any accompanying member jurisdiction approval regulating the same subject matter, but not longer than 15 years, unless an alternate period is provided for in the Commission approval. If there is no such accompanying member jurisdiction approval, or if no term is specified in such accompanying member jurisdiction approval, the term of a Commission approval issued under this part shall be no longer than 15 years or the anticipated life of the project, whichever is less, unless an alternate period is provided for in the Commission approval.

(b) Commission approval of a project shall expire three years from the date of such approval if the withdrawal, diversion or consumptive use has not been commenced, unless an alternate period is provided for in the docket approval or such 3-year period is extended in writing by the Commission upon written request from the project sponsor submitted no later than 120 days prior to such expiration. The Commission may grant an extension, for a period not to exceed two years, only upon a determination that the delay is due to circumstances beyond the project sponsor's control and that there is a likelihood of project implementation within a reasonable period of time. The Commission may also attach conditions to the granting of such extensions, including modification of any terms of approval that the Commission may deem appropriate.

(c) If a withdrawal, diversion or consumptive use approved by the Commission for a period of five consecutive years, the approval shall be null and void, unless a waiver is granted in writing by the Commission, upon written request by the project sponsor demonstrating due cause and with notification thereof to the member jurisdiction in which the project is located, prior to the expiration of such period.

(d) If the Commission determines that a project has been abandoned, by evidence of nonuse for a period of time and under such circumstances that an abandonment may be inferred, the Commission may revoke the approval for such withdrawal, diversion or consumptive use.

(e) If a project sponsor submits an application to the Commission no later than six months prior to the expiration of its existing Commission docket approval or no later than one month prior to the expiration of its existing ABR or NOI approval, the existing approval will be deemed extended until such time as the Commission renders a decision on the application, unless the existing approval or a notification in writing from the Commission provides otherwise.

[71 FR 78579, Dec. 29, 2006, as amended at 82 FR 29394, June 29, 2017]

§806.32 Reopening/modification.

(a) Once a project is approved, the Commission, upon its own motion, or upon petition of the project sponsor or any interested party, may at any time reopen any project approval and make additional orders or otherwise modify or impose such additional conditions that may be necessary to mitigate or avoid adverse impacts or to otherwise protect the public health, safety, and welfare or water resources. Whenever a petition for reopening is filed by an interested party, the burden shall be upon that interested party to show, by a preponderance of the evidence, that a significant adverse impact or a threat to the public health, safety and welfare or water resources exists that warrants reopening of the docket. Notwithstanding the foregoing, any petition filed by a party who previously sought the same or functionally equivalent relief identified in the petition pursuant to the administrative appeals process under §808.2 will not be eligible for consideration by the Commission absent new facts not known or readily discernable at the time of consideration of the petitioner's previous request for administrative appeal filed pursuant to §808.2.

(b) If the project sponsor fails to comply with any term or condition of a Commission approval, the Commission may issue an order suspending, modifying or revoking its approval of the project. The Commission may also, in its discretion, suspend, modify or revoke its approval if the project sponsor fails to obtain or maintain other federal, state or local approvals.

(c) For any previously approved project where interference occurs, the Commission may require a project sponsor to provide a temporary source of potable water at the project sponsor's expense, pending a final determination of causation by the Commission.

(d) The Commission, upon its own motion, may at any time reopen any project approval and make additional corrective modifications that may be necessary.

[71 FR 78579, Dec. 29, 2006, as amended at 74 FR 49813, Sept. 29, 2009]

§ 806.33 Interest on fees.

The Executive Director may establish interest to be paid on all overdue or outstanding fees of any nature that are payable to the Commission.

§ 806.34 Emergencies.

(a) *Emergency certificates.* The other requirements of these regulations notwithstanding, in the event of an emergency requiring immediate action to protect the public health, safety and welfare or to avoid substantial and irreparable injury to any person, property, or water resources when circumstances do not permit a review and determination in the regular course of the regulations in this part, the Executive Director, with the concurrence of the chairperson of the Commission and the commissioner from the affected member state, may issue an emergency certificate authorizing a project sponsor to take such action as the Executive Director may deem necessary and proper in the circumstances, pending review and determination by the Commission as otherwise required by this part. In the exercise of such authority, consideration should be given to actions deemed necessary to sustain human life, health and safety, or that of livestock or food, fiber or forage crops, the maintenance of electric system reliability to serve such needs, to avoid significant disruption of employment, or any other such priorities that the Commission may establish from time to time utilizing its authority under Section 11.4 of the Compact related to drought emergencies.

(b) *Notification and application.* A project sponsor shall notify the Commission, prior to commencement of the project, that an emergency certificate is needed. In the case of a project operating under an existing Commission approval seeking emergency approval to modify, waive or partially waive one or more conditions of such approval, notice shall be provided to the Commission prior to initiating the operational changes associated with the request. If immediate action, as defined by this section, is required by a project sponsor and prior notice to the Commission is not possible, then the project sponsor must contact the Commission within one (1) business day of the action. Notification may be by certified mail, facsimile, telegram, mailgram, electronic mail or other form of written communication. This notification must be followed within one (1) business day by submission of the following:

(1) A completed emergency application form or copy of the State or Federal emergency water use application if the project sponsor also is requesting emergency approval from either a state or federal agency.

(2) At a minimum, the application shall contain:

(i) Contact information.

(ii) Justification for emergency action (purpose).

(iii) Location map and schematic of proposed project, or in the case of a project operating under an existing Commission approval, the project approval reference and a description of the operational changes requested.

(iv) Desired term of emergency use.

(v) Source(s) of the water.

(vi) Quantity of water.

(vii) Flow measurement system (such as metering).

(viii) Use restrictions in effect (or planned).

(ix) Description of potential adverse impacts and mitigating measures.

(x) Appropriate fee, unless reduced, waived or delayed with the approval of the Executive Director.

(c) *Emergency certificate issuance.* The Executive Director shall:

(1) Review and act on the emergency request as expeditiously as possible

upon receipt of all necessary information stipulated in paragraph (b)(2) of this section.

(2) With the concurrence of the chairperson of the Commission and the commissioner from the affected member state, issue an emergency certificate for a term not to extend beyond the next regular business meeting of the Commission.

(3) Include conditions in the emergency certificate which may include, without limitation, monitoring of withdrawal and/or consumptive use amounts, measurement devices, public notification, and reporting, to assure minimal adverse impacts to the environment and other users.

(d) *Post approval.* Actions following issuance of emergency certificates may include, but are not limited to, the following:

(1) The Commission may, by resolution, extend the term of the emergency certificate, upon presentation of a request from the project sponsor accompanied by appropriate evidence that the conditions causing the emergency persist.

(2) If the condition is expected to persist longer than the specified extended term, the project sponsor must submit an application to the Commission for applicable water withdrawal or consumptive use, or the emergency certificate will terminate as specified. If the project sponsor has a prior Commission approval for the project, the project sponsor must submit an application to modify the existing docket accordingly.

(e) *Early termination.* With the concurrence of the chairperson of the Commission and the commissioner from the affected member state, the Executive Director may terminate an emergency certificate earlier than the specified duration if it is determined that an emergency no longer exists and/or the certificate holder has not complied with one or more special conditions for the emergency withdrawal or consumptive water use.

(f) *Restoration or mitigation.* Project sponsors are responsible for any necessary restoration or mitigation of environmental damage or interference with another user that may occur as a result of the emergency action.

[71 FR 78579, Dec. 29, 2006, as amended at 79 FR 15909, Mar. 24, 2014]

§806.35 Fees.

Project sponsors shall have an affirmative duty to pay such fees as established by the Commission to cover its costs of administering the regulatory program established by this part, including any extraordinary costs associated with specific projects.

[71 FR 78579, Dec. 29, 2006, as amended at 75 FR 60622, Oct. 1, 2010]

Subpart E—Registration of Grandfathered Projects

SOURCE: 82 FR 29394, June 29, 2017, unless otherwise noted.

§806.40 Applicability.

(a) This subpart is applicable to the following projects, which shall be known as grandfathered projects:

(1) The project has an associated average consumptive use of 20,000 gpd or more in any consecutive 30-day period all or part of which is a pre-compact consumptive use that has not been approved by the Commission pursuant to §806.4.

(2) The project has an associated groundwater withdrawal average of 100,000 gpd or more in any consecutive 30-day period all or part of which was initiated prior to July 13, 1978, that has not been approved by the Commission pursuant to §806.4.

(3) The project has an associated surface water withdrawal average of 100,000 gpd or more in any consecutive 30-day period all or part of which was initiated prior to November 11, 1995, that has not been approved by the Commission pursuant to §806.4.

(4) The project (or an element of the project) has been approved by the Commission but has an associated consumptive use or water withdrawal that has not been approved by the Commission pursuant to §806.4.

(5) Any project not included in paragraphs (a)(2) through (4) of this section that has a total withdrawal average of 100,000 gpd or more in any consecutive 30-day average from any combination

143

of sources which was initiated prior to January 1, 2007, that has not been approved by the Commission pursuant to § 806.4.

(6) Any source associated with a project included in paragraphs (a)(2) through (5) of this section regardless of quantity.

(b) A project, including any source of the project, that can be determined to have been required to seek Commission review and approval under the pertinent regulations in place at the time is not eligible for registration as a grandfathered project.

§ 806.41 Registration and eligibility.

(a) Project sponsors of grandfathered projects identified in § 806.40 shall submit a registration to the Commission, on a form and in a manner prescribed by the Commission, by December 31, 2019.

(b) Any grandfathered project that fails to register under paragraph (a) of this section shall be subject to review and approval under § 806.4.

(c) Any project that is not eligible to register under paragraph (a) of this section shall be subject to review and approval under § 806.4.

(d) The Commission may establish fees for obtaining and maintaining registration in accordance with § 806.35.

(e) A registration under this subpart may be transferred pursuant to § 806.6.

§ 806.42 Registration requirements.

(a) Registrations shall include the following information:

(1) Identification of project sponsor including any and all proprietors, corporate officers or partners, the mailing address of the same, and the name of the individual authorized to act for the sponsor.

(2) Description of the project and site in terms of:

(i) Project location, including latitude and longitude coordinates in decimal degrees accurate to within 10 meters.

(ii) Project purpose.

(3) Identification of all sources of water, including the date the source was put into service, each source location (including latitude and longitude coordinates in decimal degrees accu-

rate to within 10 meters), and if applicable, any approved docket numbers.

(4) Identification of current metering and monitoring methods for water withdrawal and consumptive use.

(5) Identification of current groundwater level or elevation monitoring methods at groundwater sources.

(6) All quantity data for water withdrawals and consumptive use for a minimum of the previous five calendar years. If the project sponsor registering submitted the water withdrawal and consumptive use data for the previous five calendar years to a member jurisdiction, that data will satisfy this requirement. A project sponsor registering may provide supplementary data related to water withdrawals and consumptive use quantities. If quantity data are not available, any information available upon which a determination of quantity could be made.

(7) For consumptive use, description of processes that use water, identification of water returned to the Basin, history of the use, including process changes, expansions and other actions that would have an impact on the amount of water consumptively used during the past five calendar years.

(8) Based on the data provided, the quantity of withdrawal for each individual source and consumptive use the project sponsor requests to be grandfathered by the Commission.

(9) Any ownership or name changes to the project since January 1, 2007.

(b) The Commission may require any other information it deems necessary for the registration process or waive any information required under paragraph (a) of this section for projects relying on a prior determination of the Commission.

§ 806.43 Metering and monitoring requirements.

(a) As a part of the registration process, the Commission shall review the current metering and monitoring for grandfathered withdrawals and consumptive uses.

(b) The Commission may require a metering and monitoring plan for the project sponsor to follow.

(c) Project sponsors, as an ongoing obligation of their registration, shall report to the Commission all information specified in the grandfathering determination under § 806.44 in a form and manner determined by the Commission. If water withdrawal and consumptive use quantity reporting is required by the member jurisdiction where the project is located, the Commission shall accept that reported quantity to satisfy the requirements of this paragraph (c), unless the Commission finds that additional data is needed that is not required by the member jurisdiction.

(d) Any data generated or collected under paragraph (c) of this section will be made available to the member jurisdictions in a manner and timeframe mutually agreeable to both the Commission and the jurisdiction.

§ 806.44 Determination of grandfathered quantities.

(a) For each registration submitted, the Executive Director shall determine the grandfathered quantity for each withdrawal source and consumptive use.

(b) In making a determination, the following factors should be considered:

(1) The withdrawal and use data and the peak consecutive 30-day average shown by the data;

(2) The reliability and accuracy of the data and/or the meters or measuring devices;

(3) Determination of reasonable and genuine usage of the project, including any anomalies in the usage;

(4) Whether the grandfathered amount includes an operational margin of safety; and

(5) Other relevant factors.

(c) The Executive Director, in lieu of a determination under paragraph (b) of this section, may accept a previous grandfathering determination by the Commission at the request of the project sponsor.

§ 806.45 Appeal of determination.

(a) A final determination of the grandfathered quantity by the Executive Director must be appealed to the Commission within 30 days from actual notice of the determination.

(b) The Commission shall appoint a hearing officer to preside over appeals under this section. Hearings shall be governed by the procedures set forth in part 808 of this chapter.

PART 807—WATER WITHDRAWAL REGISTRATION

Sec.
807.1 Requirement.
807.2 Time limits.
807.3 Administrative agreements.
807.4 Effective date.
807.5 Definitions.

AUTHORITY: Secs. 3.4(2) and (9), 3.8, 3.10 and 15.2, Pub. L. 91–575, 84 Stat. 1509 et seq.

SOURCE: 71 FR 78588, Dec. 29, 2006, unless otherwise noted.

§ 807.1 Requirement.

In addition to any other requirements of Commission regulations, and subject to the consent of the affected member state to this requirement, any person withdrawing or diverting in excess of an average of 10,000 gpd for any consecutive 30-day period, from ground or surface water sources, as defined in part 806 of this chapter, shall register the amount of this withdrawal with the Commission and provide such other information as requested on forms prescribed by the Commission.

§ 807.2 Time limits.

(a) Except for agricultural water use projects, all registration forms shall be submitted within one year after May 11, 1995, or within six months of initiation of the water withdrawal or diversion, whichever is later; provided, however, that nothing in this section shall limit the responsibility of a project sponsor to apply for and obtain an approval as may be required under part 806 of this chapter. All registered withdrawals shall re-register with the Commission within five years of their initial registration, and at five-year intervals thereafter, unless the withdrawal is sooner discontinued. Upon notice by the Executive Director, compliance with a registration or reporting requirement, or both, of a member state that is substantially equivalent to this requirement shall be considered compliance with this requirement.

(b) Project sponsors whose existing agricultural water use projects i.e., projects coming into existence prior to March 31, 1997) withdraw or divert in excess of an average of 10,000 gpd for any consecutive 30-day period from a ground or surface water source shall register their use no later than March 31, 1997. Thereafter, project sponsors of new projects proposing to withdraw or divert in excess of 10,000 gpd for any consecutive 30-day period from a ground or surface water source shall be registered prior to project initiation.

§ 807.3 Administrative agreements.

The Commission may complete appropriate administrative agreements or arrangements to carry out this registration requirement through the offices of member jurisdictions. Forms developed by the Commission shall apprise registrants of any such agreements or arrangements, and provide appropriate instructions to complete and submit the form.

§ 807.4 Effective date.

This part shall be effective on January 1, 2007.

§ 807.5 Definitions.

Terms used in this part shall be defined as set forth in § 806.3 of this chapter.

PART 808—HEARINGS AND ENFORCEMENT ACTIONS

Subpart A—Conduct of Hearings

AUTHORITY: Secs. 3.4 (9), 3.5 (5), 3.8, 3.10 and 15.2, Pub. L. 91–575, 84 Stat. 1509 *et seq.*

SOURCE: 71 FR 78589, Dec. 29, 2006, unless otherwise noted.

Subpart A—Conduct of Hearings

§ 808.1 Public hearings.

(a) *Required hearings.* A public hearing shall be conducted in the following instances:

(1) Addition of projects or adoption of amendments to the comprehensive plan, except as otherwise provided by section 14.1 of the compact.

(2) Review and approval of diversions.

(3) Imposition or modification of rates and charges.

(4) Determination of protected areas.

(5) Drought emergency declarations.

(6) Hearing requested by a member jurisdiction.

(7) As otherwise required by sections 3.5(4), 4.4, 5.2(e), 6.2(a), 8.4, and 10.4 of the compact.

(b) *Optional hearings.* A public hearing may be conducted by the Commission or the Executive Director in any form or style chosen by the Commission or Executive Director in the following instances:

(1) Proposed rulemaking.

(2) Consideration of projects, except projects approved pursuant to memoranda of understanding with member jurisdictions.

(3) Adoption of policies and technical guidance documents.

(4) When it is determined that a hearing is necessary to give adequate consideration to issues related to public health, safety and welfare, or protection of the environment, or to gather additional information for the record or consider new information on a matter before the Commission.

(c) *Notice of public hearing.* At least 20 days before any public hearing required by the compact, notices stating the date, time, place and purpose of the hearing including issues of interest to the Commission shall be published at least once in a newspaper of general circulation in the area affected. In all other cases, at least 20 days prior to the hearing, notice shall be posted on the Commission Web site, sent to the parties who, to the Commission's knowledge, will participate in the hearing, and sent to persons, organizations and news media who have made requests to the Commission for notices of hearings or of a particular hearing.

With regard to rulemaking, hearing notices need only be forwarded to the directors of the *New York Register,* the *Pennsylvania Bulletin,* the *Maryland Register* and the FEDERAL REGISTER, and it is sufficient that this notice appear in the FEDERAL REGISTER at least 20 days prior to the hearing and in each individual state publication at least 10 days prior to any hearing scheduled in that state.

(d) *Standard public hearing procedure.* (1) Hearings shall be open to the public. Participants may be any person, including a project sponsor, wishing to appear at the hearing and make an oral or written statement. Statements shall be made a part of the record of the hearing, and written statements may be received up to and including the last day on which the hearing is held, or within 10 days or a reasonable time thereafter as may be specified by the presiding officer.

(2) Participants are encouraged to file with the Commission at its headquarters written notice of their intention to appear at the hearing. The notice should be filed at least three days prior to the opening of the hearing.

(e) *Representative capacity.* Participants wishing to be heard at a public hearing may appear in person or be represented by an attorney or other representative. A governmental authority may be represented by one of its officers, employees or by a designee of the governmental authority.

(f) *Description of project.* When notice of a public hearing is issued, there shall be available for inspection, consistent with the Commission's Access to Records Policy, all plans, summaries, maps, statements, orders or other supporting documents which explain, detail, amplify, or otherwise describe the project the Commission is considering. Instructions on where and how the documents may be obtained will be included in the notice.

(g) *Presiding officer.* A public hearing shall be presided over by the Commission chair, the Executive Director, or any member or designee of the Commission or Executive Director. The presiding officer shall have full authority to control the conduct of the hearing and make a record of the same.

(h) *Transcript.* Whenever a project involving a diversion of water is the subject of a public hearing, and at all other times deemed necessary by the Commission or the Executive Director, a written transcript of the hearing shall be made. A certified copy of the transcript and exhibits shall be available for review during business hours at the Commission's headquarters to anyone wishing to examine them. Persons wishing to obtain a copy of the transcript of any hearing shall make arrangements to obtain it directly from the recording stenographer at their expense.

(i) *Joint hearings.* The Commission may conduct any public hearings in concert with any other agency of a member jurisdiction.

[82 FR 29395, June 29, 2017]

§808.2 Administrative appeals.

(a) A project sponsor or other person aggrieved by a final action or decision of the Executive Director shall file a written appeal with the Commission within 30 days of the receipt of actual notice by the project sponsor or within 30 days of publication of the action in the FEDERAL REGISTER. Appeals shall be filed on a form and in a manner prescribed by the Commission and the petitioner shall have 20 days from the date of filing to amend the appeal. The following is a non-exclusive list of actions by the Executive Director that are subject to an appeal to the Commission:

(1) A determination that a project requires review and approval under §806.5;

(2) An approval or denial of an application for transfer under §806.6;

(3) An approval of a Notice of Intent under a general permit under §806.17;

(4) An approval of a minor modification under §806.18;

(5) A determination regarding an approval by rule under §806.22(e) or (f);

(6) A determination regarding an emergency certificate under §806.34;

(7) Enforcement orders issued under §808.14;

(8) A finding regarding a civil penalty under §808.15(c);

(9) A determination of grandfathered quantity under §806.44;

(10) A decision to modify, suspend or revoke a previously granted approval; and

(11) A records access determination made pursuant to Commission policy.

(b) The appeal shall identify the specific action or decision being appealed, the date of the action or decision, the interest of the person requesting the hearing in the subject matter of the appeal, and a statement setting forth the basis for objecting to or seeking review of the action or decision.

(c) Any request not filed on or before the applicable deadline established in paragraph (a) of this section hereof will be deemed untimely and such request for a hearing shall be considered denied unless the Commission, upon written request and for good cause shown, grants leave to make such filing nunc pro tunc; the standard applicable to what constitutes good cause shown being the standard applicable in analogous cases under Federal law. Receipt of requests for hearings pursuant to this section, whether timely filed or not, shall be submitted by the Executive Director to the commissioners for their information.

(d) Petitioners shall be limited to a single filing that shall set forth all matters and arguments in support thereof, including any ancillary motions or requests for relief. Issues not raised in this single filing shall be considered waived for purposes of the instant proceeding. Where the petitioner is appealing a final determination on a project application and is not the project sponsor, the petitioner shall serve a copy of the appeal upon the project sponsor within five days of its filing.

(e) The Commission will determine the manner in which it will hear the appeal. If a hearing is granted, the Commission shall serve notice thereof upon the petitioner and project sponsor and shall publish such notice in the FEDERAL REGISTER. The hearing shall not be held less than 20 days after publication of such notice. Hearings may be conducted by one or more members of the Commission, or by such other hearing officer as the Commission may designate.

(1) The petitioner may also request a stay of the action or decision giving rise to the appeal pending final disposition of the appeal, which stay may be granted or denied by the Executive Director after consultation with the Commission chair and the member from the affected member State. The decision of the Executive Director on the request for stay shall not be appealable to the Commission under this section and shall remain in full force and effect until the Commission acts on the appeal.

(2) In addition to the contents of the request itself, the Executive Director, in granting or denying the request for stay, will consider the following factors:

(i) Irreparable harm to the petitioner.

(ii) The likelihood that the petitioner will prevail.

(f) The Commission shall grant the hearing request pursuant to this section if it determines that an adequate record with regard to the action or decision is not available, or that the Commission has found that an administrative review is necessary or desirable. If the Commission denies any request for a hearing, the party seeking such hearing shall be limited to such remedies as may be provided by the compact or other applicable law or court rule. If a hearing is granted, the Commission shall refer the matter for hearing to be held in accordance with § 808.3, and appoint a hearing officer.

(g) If a hearing is not granted, the Commission may set a briefing schedule and decide the appeal based on the record before it. The Commission may, in its discretion, schedule and hear oral argument on an appeal.

(h)(1) A request for intervention may be filed with the Commission by persons other than the petitioner within 20 days of the publication of a notice of the granting of such hearing in the FEDERAL REGISTER. The request for intervention shall state the interest of the person filing such notice, and the specific grounds of objection to the action or decision or other grounds for appearance. The hearing officer(s) shall determine whether the person requesting intervention has standing in the matter that would justify their admission as an intervener to the proceedings in accordance with Federal case law.

(2) Interveners shall have the right to be represented by counsel, to present evidence and to examine and cross-examine witnesses.

(i) Where a request for an appeal is made, the 90-day appeal period set forth in section 3.10 (6) and Federal reservation (o) of the compact shall not commence until the Commission has either denied the request for or taken final action on an administrative appeal.

[82 FR 29396, June 29, 2017]

§808.3 Hearings on administrative appeal.

(a) Unless otherwise agreed to by the Commission and the party requesting an administrative appeal under §808.2 of this part, the following procedures shall govern the conduct of hearing on an administrative appeal.

(b) *Hearing procedure.* (1) The hearing officer shall have the power to rule upon offers of proof and the admissibility of evidence, to regulate the course of the hearing, to set the location or venue of the hearing, to hold conferences for the settlement or simplification of issues and the stipulation of facts, to determine the proper parties to the hearing, to determine the scope of any discovery procedures, to delineate the hearing issues to be adjudicated, and to take notice of judicially cognizable facts and general, technical, or scientific facts. The hearing officer may, with the consent of the parties, conduct all or part of the hearing or related proceedings by telephone conference call or other electronic means.

(2) The hearing officer shall cause each witness to be sworn or to make affirmation.

(3) Any party to a hearing shall have the right to present evidence, to examine and cross-examine witnesses, submit rebuttal evidence, and to present summation and argument.

(4) When necessary, in order to prevent undue prolongation of the hearing, the hearing officer may limit the number of times any witness may testify, the repetitious examination or cross-examination of witnesses, or the extent of corroborative or cumulative testimony.

(5) The hearing officer shall exclude irrelevant, immaterial or unduly repetitious evidence, but the parties shall not be bound by technical rules of evidence, and all relevant evidence of reasonably probative value may be received provided it shall be founded upon competent, material evidence which is substantial in view of the entire record.

(6) Any party may appear and be heard in person or be represented by an attorney at law who shall file an appearance with the Commission.

(7) Briefs and oral argument may be required by the hearing officer and may be permitted upon request made prior to the close of the hearing by any party. They shall be part of the record unless otherwise ordered by the presiding officer.

(8) The hearing officer may, as he/she deems appropriate, issue subpoenas in the name of the Commission requiring the appearance of witnesses or the production of books, papers, and other documentary evidence for such hearings.

(9) A record of the proceedings and evidence at each hearing shall be made by a qualified stenographer designated by the Executive Director. Where demanded by the petitioner, or any other person who is a party to the appeal proceedings, or where deemed necessary by the Hearing Officer, the testimony shall be transcribed. In those instances where a transcript of proceedings is made, two copies shall be delivered to the Commission. The petitioner or other persons who desire copies shall obtain them from the stenographer at such price as may be agreed upon by the stenographer and the person desiring the transcript.

(c) *Staff and other expert testimony.* The Executive Director shall arrange for the presentation of testimony by the Commission's technical staff and other experts, as he/she may deem necessary or desirable, to be incorporated in the record to support the administrative action, determination or decision which is the subject of the hearing.

(d) *Written testimony.* If the direct testimony of an expert witness is expected to be lengthy or of a complex, technical nature, the presiding officer may order that such direct testimony be submitted to the Commission in sworn, written form. Copies of said testimony shall be served upon all parties appearing at the hearing at least 10 days prior to said hearing. Such written testimony, however, shall not be admitted whenever the witness is not present and available for cross-examination at the hearing unless all parties have waived the right of cross-examination.

(e) *Assessment of costs.* (1) Whenever a hearing is conducted, the costs thereof, as herein defined, shall be assessed by the presiding officer to the petitioner or such other party as the hearing officer deems equitable. For the purposes of this section, costs include all incremental costs incurred by the Commission, including, but not limited to, hearing officer and expert consultants reasonably necessary in the matter, stenographic record, rental of the hall and other related expenses.

(2) Upon the scheduling of a matter for hearing, the hearing officer shall furnish to the petitioner a reasonable estimate of the costs to be incurred under this section. The project sponsor may be required to furnish security for such costs either by cash deposit or by a surety bond of a corporate surety authorized to do business in a member state.

(3) A party to an appeal under this section who desires to proceed in forma pauperis shall submit an affidavit to the Commission requesting the same and showing in detail the assets possessed by the party, and other information indicating the reasons why that party is unable to pay costs incurred under this section or to give security for such costs. The Commission may grant or refuse the request based upon the contents of the affidavit or other factors, such as whether it believes the appeal or intervention is taken in good faith.

(f) *Findings and report.* The hearing officer shall prepare a report of his/her findings and recommendations based on the record of the hearing. The report shall be served by personal service or certified mail (return receipt requested) upon each party to the hearing or its counsel. Any party may file objections to the report. Such objections shall be filed with the Commission and served on all parties within 20 days after the service of the report. A brief shall be filed together with objections. Any replies to the objections shall be filed and served on all parties within 10 days of service of the objections. Prior to its decision on such objections, the Commission may grant a request for oral argument upon such filing.

(g) *Action by the Commission.* The Commission will act upon the findings and recommendations of the presiding officer pursuant to law. The determination of the Commission will be in writing and shall be filed in Commission records together with any transcript of the hearing, report of the hearing officer, objections thereto, and all plans, maps, exhibits and other papers, records or documents relating to the hearing.

§ 808.4 Optional joint hearing.

(a) The Commission may order any two or more public hearings involving a common or related question of law or fact to be consolidated for hearing on any or all of the matters at issue in such hearings.

(b) Whenever designated by a department, agency or instrumentality of a member jurisdiction, and within any limitations prescribed by the designation, a hearing officer designated pursuant to § 808.2 may also serve as a hearing officer, examiner or agent pursuant to such additional designation and may conduct joint hearings for the Commission and for such other department, agency or instrumentality. Pursuant to the additional designation, a hearing officer shall cause to be filed with the department, agency, or instrumentality making the designation, a certified copy of the transcript of the evidence taken before him/her and, if requested, of his/her findings and recommendations. Neither the hearing officer nor the Susquehanna River Basin Commission shall have or exercise any power or duty as a result of such additional designation to decide the merits of any matter arising under the separate laws of a member jurisdiction (other than the compact).

Subpart B—Compliance and Enforcement

§ 808.10 Scope of subpart.

This subpart shall be applicable where there is reason to believe that a person may have violated any provision of the compact, or the Commission's rules, regulations, orders, approvals, docket conditions, or any other requirements of the Commission. The said person shall hereinafter be referred to as the alleged violator.

§ 808.11 Duty to comply.

It shall be the duty of any person to comply with any provision of the compact, or the Commission's rules, regulations, orders, approvals, docket conditions, staff directives or any other requirement of the Commission.

[82 FR 29396, June 29, 2017]

§ 808.12 Investigative powers.

(a) The Commission or its agents or employees, at any reasonable time and upon presentation of appropriate credentials, may inspect or investigate any person or project to determine compliance with any provisions of the compact, or the Commission's rules, regulations, orders, approvals, docket conditions, or any other requirements of the Commission. Such employees or agents are authorized to conduct tests or sampling; to take photographs; to perform measurements, surveys, and other tests; to inspect the methods of construction, operation, or maintenance; to inspect all measurement equipment; and to audit, examine, and copy books, papers, and records pertinent to any matter under investigation. Such employees or agents are authorized to take any other action necessary to assure that any project is constructed, operated and maintained in accordance with any provisions of the compact, or the Commission's rules, regulations, orders, approvals, docket conditions, or any other requirements of the Commission.

(b) Any person shall allow authorized employees or agents of the Commission, without advance notice, at any reasonable time and upon presentation of appropriate credentials, and without delay, to have access to and to inspect all areas where a project is being constructed, operated, or maintained.

(c) Any person shall provide such information to the Commission as the Commission may deem necessary to determine compliance with any provisions of the compact, or the Commission's rules, regulations, orders, approvals, docket conditions, or any other requirements of the Commission. The person submitting information to the Commission shall verify that it is true and accurate to the best of the knowledge, information, and belief of the person submitting such information. Any person who knowingly submits false information to the Commission shall be subject to civil penalties as provided in the compact and criminal penalties under the laws of the member jurisdictions relating to unsworn falsification to authorities.

§ 808.13 Notice of violation.

When the Executive Director or his/her designee issues a Notice of Violation (NOV) to an alleged violator, such NOV will:

(a) List the violations that are alleged to have occurred.

(b) State a date by which the alleged violator shall respond to the NOV.

§ 808.14 Orders.

(a) Whether or not an NOV has been issued, the Executive Director may issue an order directing an alleged violator to cease and desist any action or activity to the extent such action or activity constitutes an alleged violation, or may issue any other order related to the prevention of further violations, or the abatement or remediation of harm caused by the action or activity.

(b) If the project sponsor fails to comply with any term or condition of a docket or other approval, the commissioners or Executive Director may issue an order suspending, modifying or revoking approval of the docket. The commissioners may also, in their discretion, suspend, modify or revoke a docket approval if the project sponsor fails to obtain or maintain other federal, state or local approvals.

(c) The commissioners or Executive Director may issue such other orders as may be necessary to enforce any provision of the compact, the Commission's rules or regulations, orders, approvals, docket conditions, or any other requirements of the Commission.

(d) It shall be the duty of any person to proceed diligently to comply with any order issued pursuant to this section.

(e) The Commission or Executive Director may enter into a Consent Order and Agreement with an alleged violator to resolve non-compliant operations and enforcement proceedings in conjunction with or separately from settlement agreements under § 808.18.

[82 FR 29396, June 29, 2017]

§ 808.15 Show cause proceeding.

(a) The Executive Director may issue an order requiring an alleged violator to show cause why a penalty should not be assessed in accordance with the provisions of this chapter and section 15.17 of the compact. The order to the alleged violator shall:

(1) Specify the nature and duration of violation(s) that is alleged to have occurred.

(2) Set forth the date by which the alleged violator must provide a written response to the order.

(3) Identify the civil penalty recommended by Commission staff.

(b) The written response by the project sponsor should include the following:

(1) A statement whether the project sponsor contests that the violations outlined in the Order occurred;

(2) If the project sponsor contests the violations, then a statement of the relevant facts and/or law providing the basis for the project sponsor's position;

(3) Any mitigating factors or explanation regarding the violations outlined in the Order; and

(4) A statement explaining what the appropriate civil penalty, if any, should be utilizing the factors at § 808.16.

(c) Based on the information presented and any relevant policies, guidelines or law, the Executive Director shall make a written finding affirming or modifying the civil penalty recommended by Commission staff.

[82 FR 29397, June 29, 2017]

§ 808.16 Civil penalty criteria.

(a) In determining the amount of any civil penalty or any settlement of a violation, the Commission and Executive Director shall consider:

(1) Previous violations, if any, of any provision of the compact, the Commission's rules or regulations, orders, approvals, docket conditions or any other requirements of the Commission.

(2) The intent of the alleged violator.

(3) The extent to which the violation caused adverse consequences to public health, safety and welfare or to water resources.

(4) The costs incurred by the Commission or any member jurisdiction relating to the failure to comply with any provision of the compact, the Commission's rules or regulations, orders, approvals, docket conditions or any other requirements of the Commission.

(5) The extent to which the violator has cooperated with the Commission in correcting the violation and remediating any adverse consequences or harm that has resulted therefrom.

(6) The extent to which the failure to comply with any provision of the compact, the Commission's rules or regulations, orders, approvals, docket conditions or any other requirements of the Commission was economically beneficial to the violator.

(7) The length of time over which the violation occurred and the amount of water used, diverted or withdrawn during that time period.

(8) The punitive effect of a civil penalty.

(b) The Commission and/or Executive Director retains the right to waive any penalty or reduce the amount of the penalty recommended by the Commission staff under § 808.15(a)(3) should it be determined, after consideration of the factors in paragraph (a) of this section, that extenuating circumstances justify such action.

[71 FR 78689, Dec. 29, 2006, as amended at 82 FR 29397, June 29, 2017]

§808.17 Enforcement of penalties, abatement or remedial orders.

Any penalty imposed or abatement or remedial action ordered by the Commission or the Executive Director shall be paid or completed within such time period as shall be specified in the civil penalty assessment or order. The Executive Director and Commission counsel are authorized to take such additional action as may be necessary to assure compliance with this subpart. If a proceeding before a court becomes necessary, the penalty amount determined in accordance with this part shall constitute the penalty amount recommended by the Commission to be fixed by the court pursuant to section 15.17 of the compact.

[82 FR 29397, June 29, 2017]

§808.18 Settlement by agreement.

(a) An alleged violator may offer to settle an enforcement action by agreement. The Executive Director may enter into settlement agreements to resolve an enforcement action. The Commission may, by Resolution, require certain types of enforcement actions or settlements to be submitted to the Commission for action or approval.

(b) In the event the violator fails to carry out any of the terms of the settlement agreement, the Commission or Executive Director may reinstitute a civil penalty action and any other applicable enforcement action against the alleged violator.

[82 FR 29397, June 29, 2017]

§808.19 Effective date.

This part shall be effective on January 1, 2007.

PARTS 809–899 [RESERVED]

CHAPTER XIII—TENNESSEE VALLEY AUTHORITY

PART 1300—STANDARDS OF CONDUCT FOR EMPLOYEES OF TENNESSEE VALLEY AUTHORITY

AUTHORITY: 16 U.S.C. 831–831dd; 18 U.S.C. 208(b)(2).

SOURCE: 61 FR 20118, May 6, 1996, unless otherwise noted.

§ 1300.101 Cross references to employee ethical conduct standards and other applicable regulations.

Employees of the Tennessee Valley Authority (TVA) are subject to the executive branch-wide standards of ethical conduct at 5 CFR part 2635 and to the TVA regulations at 5 CFR part 7901 which supplement the executive branch-wide standards. In addition, certain TVA employees are subject to executive branch-wide financial disclosure regulations at 5 CFR part 2634.

§ 1300.102 Gambling, betting, and lotteries.

An employee shall not participate, while on Government- or TVA-owned or leased property or while on TVA duty, in any gambling activity including the operation of a gambling device, in conducting a lottery or pool, in a game for money or property, or in selling or purchasing a numbers slip or ticket. However, this section does not preclude activities:

(a) Necessitated by an employee's law enforcement duties; or

(b) Under section 7 of Executive Order 12353 (47 FR 12785, 3 CFR, 1982 Comp., p. 139) and similar TVA-approved activities.

§ 1300.103 General conduct prejudicial to TVA.

An employee shall not engage in criminal, infamous, dishonest, immoral, or notoriously disgraceful conduct, or other conduct prejudicial to TVA.

§ 1300.104 Sexual harassment.

It is TVA policy that all TVA employees are responsible for assuring that the workplace is free from sexual harassment. Accordingly, all employees must avoid any action or conduct which could be viewed as sexual harassment including:

(a) Unwelcome sexual advances;

(b) Requests for sexual favors; and

(c) Other verbal or physical conduct of a sexual nature when:

(1) Submission to such conduct is made either explicitly or implicitly a term or condition of an individual's employment;

(2) Submission to or rejection of such conduct by an individual is used as the basis for employment decisions affecting such individual; or

(3) Such conduct has the purpose or effect of unreasonably interfering with an individual's work performance or creating an intimidating, hostile, or offensive working environment.

§ 1300.105 National origin harassment.

It is TVA policy that all TVA employees are responsible for assuring that the workplace is free from national origin harassment. Accordingly, all employees must avoid any action or conduct which could be viewed as national origin harassment, including ethnic slurs and other verbal or physical conduct relating to an individual's national origin when such conduct:

(a) Has the purpose or effect of creating an intimidating, hostile, or offensive working environment;

(b) Has the purpose or effect of unreasonably interfering with an individual's work performance; or

(c) Otherwise adversely affects an individual's employment opportunities.

§ 1300.106 Harassment on the basis of race, color, religion, age, or disability.

It is TVA policy that all TVA employees are responsible for assuring that the workplace is free from harassment on the basis of race, color, religion, age, or disability. Accordingly, all employees must avoid any action or conduct which could be viewed as harassment on these bases, including any verbal or physical conduct relating to an individual's race, color, religion, age, or disability when such conduct:

(a) Has the purpose or effect of creating an intimidating, hostile, or offensive working environment;

(b) Has the purpose or effect of unreasonably interfering with an individual's work performance; or

(c) Otherwise adversely affects an individual's employment opportunities.

§ 1300.107 Financial interest exemptions.

In accordance with the provisions of 18 U.S.C. 208(b)(2), TVA has exempted the following financial interests of its employees from the requirements of 18 U.S.C. 208(a) upon the ground that such interests are too remote or too inconsequential to affect the integrity of such employees' services. When any of the following exemptions applies only to a limited range of official actions, rather than all official acts, the range of actions will be specified within the language of the exemption.

(a) An investment in a business enterprise in the form of ownership of bonds, notes, and other evidences of indebtness which are not convertible into shares of preferred or common stock and have no warrants attached entitling the holder to purchase stock provided that the estimated market value of the interest does not exceed $5,000;

(b) An investment in the form of shares in the ownership of enterprises, including preferred and common stocks whether voting or nonvoting, or warrants to purchase such shares, or evidences of indebtedness convertible into such shares provided that the estimated market value of the interest does not exceed $5,000 and does not exceed 1 percent of the estimated market value of all the outstanding shares of the enterprise;

(c) Shares or investments in a well-diversified money market or mutual fund;

(d) Vested interests in a pension fund arising out of former employment and to which no further contributions are being made in the employee's behalf, provided that, if the pension plan is a defined benefit plan, the assets of the plan are diversified. For the purpose of this provision, payments are not considered to be made "in the employee's behalf" if they are made solely to maintain adequate plan funding rather than to provide specific benefits for the employee; or

(e) The interest an employee has by virtue of his or her personal or family use of electric power or through his or her interests in an organization using electric power generated or distributed by TVA, for purposes of his or her official actions at TVA in the process of developing or approving TVA power rate schedules.

PART 1301—PROCEDURES

Subpart A—Freedom of Information Act

Subpart C—Government in the Sunshine Act

Subpart D—Testimony by TVA Employees, Production of Official Records, and Disclosure of Official Information in Legal Proceedings

Subpart E—Protection of National Security Classified Information

AUTHORITY: 5 U.S.C. 552 and 552a; 16 U.S.C. 831–831dd.

SOURCE: 64 FR 4044, Jan. 27, 1999, unless otherwise noted.

Subpart A—Freedom of Information Act

SOURCE: 82 FR 41511, Sept. 1, 2017, unless otherwise noted.

§ 1301.1 General provisions.

(a) This subpart contains the rules that the Tennessee Valley Authority (TVA) follows in processing requests for records under the Freedom of Information Act (FOIA), 5 U.S.C. 552. These rules should be read in conjunction with the text of the FOIA and the Uniform Freedom of Information Fee Schedule and Guidelines published by the Office of Management and Budget ("OMB Guidelines"). Requests made by individuals for records about themselves under the Privacy Act of 1974, 5 U.S.C. 552a, are processed in accordance with TVA's Privacy Act regulations as well as under this subpart.

(a) [Reserved]

§ 1301.2 Proactive disclosures.

Records that the FOIA requires agencies to make available for public inspection in an electronic format may be accessed through the TVA Web site. Each TVA organization is responsible for determining which of its records must be made publicly available, for identifying additional records of interest to the public that are appropriate for public disclosure, and for posting and indexing such records. Each TVA organization shall ensure that its posted records and indices are reviewed and updated on an ongoing basis. TVA has a FOIA Requester Service Center and a FOIA Public Liaison who can assist individuals in locating TVA records. Contact information for the FOIA Requester Service Center and Public Liaison is available at *https://www.tva.com/ Information/Freedom-of-Information/ FOIA-Contacts.*

§ 1301.3 Requirements for making requests.

(a) *General information.* (1) TVA has a centralized system for responding to FOIA requests. To make a request for records, a requester should write directly to the Tennessee Valley Authority, FOIA Officer, 400 W. Summit Hill Drive (WT 7D), Knoxville, TN 37902-1401. TVA's Guide to Information, which may be accessed on the TVA Web site at *https://www.tva.com/Information/Freedom-of-Information/A-Guide-to-Information-About-The-Tennessee-Valley-Authority* may be helpful in making your request.

(2) If you are making a request about yourself, see subpart B Privacy Act for additional requirements.

(3) Where a request for records pertains to another individual, a requester may receive greater access by submitting either a notarized authorization signed by that individual or a declaration made in compliance with the requirements set forth in 28 U.S.C. 1746

by that individual authorizing disclosure of the records to the requester, or by submitting proof that the individual is deceased (*e.g.*, a copy of a death certificate or an obituary). As an exercise of administrative discretion, TVA may require a requester to supply additional information if necessary in order to verify that a particular individual has consented to disclosure.

(b) *Description of records sought.* Requesters must describe the records sought in sufficient detail to enable TVA personnel to locate them with a reasonable amount of effort. To the extent possible, requesters should include specific information that may help TVA identify the requested records, such as the date, title or name, author, recipient, subject matter of the record, case number, file designation, or reference number. Before submitting their requests, requesters may contact the TVA's FOIA Officer or FOIA Public Liaison to discuss the records they seek and to receive assistance in describing the records. If after receiving a request the agency determines that the request does not reasonably describe the records sought, the agency shall inform the requester of what additional information is needed or why the request is otherwise insufficient. Requesters who are attempting to reformulate or modify such a request may discuss their request with the agency's FOIA Officer or FOIA Public Liaison. If a request does not reasonably describe the records sought, the agency's response to the request may be delayed.

(c) *Format of records sought.* Requests may specify the preferred form or format (including electronic formats) for the records you seek. TVA will accommodate your request if the record is readily reproducible in that form or format.

(d) *Requester contact information.* Requesters must provide contact information, such as their phone number, email address, and/or mailing address, to assist the agency in communicating with them and providing released records.

§ 1301.4 Responsibility for responding to requests.

(a) *In general.* TVA's FOIA Officer or the FOIA Officer's designee is responsible for responding to all FOIA requests. In determining which records are responsive to a request, TVA ordinarily will include only records in its possession as of the date that it begins its search. If any other date is used, the agency will inform the requester of that date. A record that is excluded from the requirements of the FOIA pursuant to 5 U.S.C. 552(c), is not considered responsive to a request.

(b) *Authority to grant or deny requests.* TVA's FOIA Officer or the FOIA Officer's designee is authorized to grant or to deny any requests for records that are maintained by TVA.

(c) *Consultation, referral and coordination.* When reviewing records located by TVA in response to a request, TVA will determine whether another agency of the Federal Government is better able to determine whether the record is exempt from disclosure under the FOIA. As to any such record, TVA shall proceed in one of the following ways:

(1) *Consultation.* When records originated with the agency processing the request, but contain within them information of interest to another agency or other Federal Government office, the agency processing the request should typically consult with that other entity prior to making a release determination.

(2) *Referral.* (i) When the agency processing the request believes that a different agency or component is best able to determine whether to disclose the record, the agency typically should refer the responsibility for responding to the request regarding that record to that agency. Ordinarily, the agency that originated the record is presumed to be the best agency to make the disclosure determination. However, if the agency processing the request and the originating agency jointly agree that the agency processing the request is in the best position to respond regarding the record, then the record may be handled as a consultation.

(ii) Whenever an agency refers any part of the responsibility for responding to a request to another agency, it must document the referral, maintain a copy of the record that it refers, and notify the requester of the referral, informing the requester of the name(s) of the agency to which the record was referred, including that agency's FOIA contact information.

(3) *Coordination.* The standard referral procedure is not appropriate where disclosure of the identity of the agency to which the referral would be made could harm an interest protected by an applicable exemption, such as the exemptions that protect personal privacy or national security interests. For example, if a non-law enforcement agency responding to a request for records on a living third party locates within its files records originating with a law enforcement agency, and if the existence of that law enforcement interest in the third party was not publicly known, then to disclose that law enforcement interest could cause an unwarranted invasion of the personal privacy of the third party. Similarly, if an agency locates within its files material originating with an Intelligence Community agency, and the involvement of that agency in the matter is classified and not publicly acknowledged, then to disclose or give attribution to the involvement of that Intelligence Community agency could cause national security harms. In such instances, in order to avoid harm to an interest protected by an applicable exemption, the agency that received the request should coordinate with the originating agency to seek its views on the disclosability of the record. The release determination for the record that is the subject of the coordination should then be conveyed to the requester by the agency that originally received the request.

(d) *Classified information.* On receipt of any request involving classified information, the agency must determine whether the information is currently and properly classified in accordance with applicable classification rules. Whenever a request involves a record containing information that has been classified or may be appropriate for classification by another agency under any applicable executive order concerning the classification of records, the receiving agency must refer the responsibility for responding to the request regarding that information to the agency that classified the information, or that should consider the information for classification. Whenever an

agency's record contains information that has been derivatively classified (for example, when it contains information classified by another agency), the agency must refer the responsibility for responding to that portion of the request to the agency that classified the underlying information.

(e) *Timing of responses to consultations and referrals.* All consultations and referrals received by TVA will be handled according to the date that the first agency received the perfected FOIA request.

(f) *Agreements regarding consultations and referrals.* TVA may establish agreements with other agencies to eliminate the need for consultations or referrals with respect to particular types of records.

§1301.5 Timing of responses to requests.

(a) *In general.* TVA ordinarily will respond to requests according to their order of receipt and placement in an appropriate processing track as follows.

(b) *Multitrack processing.* TVA has established three tracks for handling requests and the track to which a request is assigned will depend on the nature of the request and the estimated processing time. Among the factors TVA may consider are the number of records requested, the number of pages involved in processing the request and the need for consultations or referrals. TVA will also designate a specific track for requests that are granted expedited processing, in accordance with the standards set forth in paragraph (e) of this section. TVA will advise requesters of the track into which their request falls and, when appropriate, will offer the requesters an opportunity to narrow or modify their request so that it can be placed in a different processing track.

(1) *Track 1.* Requests that can be answered with readily available records or information. These are the fastest to process. These requests ordinarily will be responded to within 20 working days of receipt of a proper request by the FOIA Officer. The 20 working day time limit provided in this paragraph may be extended by TVA for unusual circumstances, as defined in paragraph (c)

of this section, upon written notice to the person requesting the records.

(2) *Track 2.* Requests where we need records or information from other offices throughout TVA, where we must consult with other Government agencies, or when we must process a submitter notice as described in § 1301.8(d), but we do not expect that the decision on disclosure will be as time consuming as for requests in Track 3.

(3) *Track 3.* Requests which require a decision or input from another office or agency, extensive submitter notifications because of the presence of Business Information as defined in § 1301.8(b)(1), and a considerable amount of time will be needed for that, or the request is complicated or involves a large number of records. Usually, these requests will take the longest to process.

(c) *Unusual circumstances.* Whenever the statutory time limit for processing a request cannot be met because of "unusual circumstances," and TVA extends the time limit on that basis, TVA will, before expiration of the 20-day period to respond, notify the requester in writing of the unusual circumstances involved and of the date by which TVA estimates processing of the request will be completed. Where the extension exceeds 10 working days, TVA will, as described by the FOIA, provide the requester with an opportunity to modify the request or arrange an alternative time period for processing the original or modified request. TVA will make available its FOIA Officer or its FOIA Public Liaison for this purpose. A list of agency FOIA Public Liaisons is available at *https://www.foia.gov/report-makerequest.html.* TVA will also alert requesters to the availability of the Office of Government Information Services (OGIS) to provide dispute resolution services. As used in this paragraph, "unusual circumstances" means, but only to the extent reasonable necessary to the proper processing of the particular requests:

(1) The need to search for and collect the requested records from field facilities or other establishments that are separate from the office processing the request;

(2) The need to search for, collect, and appropriately examine a voluminous amount of separate and distinct records which are demanded in a single request; or

(3) The need for consultation, which shall be conducted with all practicable speed, with another agency having a substantial interest in the determination of the request or among two or more components of the agency having substantial subject-matter interest therein.

(d) *Aggregating requests.* To satisfy unusual circumstances under the FOIA, TVA may aggregate requests in cases where it reasonably appears that multiple requests, submitted either by a requester or by a group of requesters acting in concert, constitute a single request that would otherwise involve unusual circumstances. TVA cannot aggregate multiple requests that involve unrelated matters.

(e) *Expedited processing.* (1) TVA will process requests and appeals on an expedited basis whenever it is determined that they involve:

(i) Circumstances in which the lack of expedited processing could reasonably be expected to pose an imminent threat to the life or physical safety of an individual;

(ii) An urgency to inform the public about an actual or alleged Federal Government activity, if made by a person who is primarily engaged in disseminating information;

(iii) The loss of substantial due process rights.

(2) A request for expedited processing may be made at any time. For a prompt determination, requests based on paragraphs (e)(1)(i) and (ii) of this section should be submitted to the TVA FOIA Officer. Requests based on paragraph (e)(1)(iii) of this section should be submitted in accordance with the agency's requirements as described in § 1301.3. When making a request for expedited processing of an administrative appeal, the request should be submitted to the TVA Chief FOIA Officer and Appeals Official.

(3) A requester who seeks expedited processing must submit a statement, certified to be true and correct, explaining in detail the basis for making the request for expedited processing.

For example, under paragraph (e)(1)(ii) of this section, a requester who is not a full-time member of the news media must establish that the requester is a person whose primary professional activity or occupation is information dissemination, though it need not be the requester's sole occupation. Such a requester also must establish a particular urgency to inform the public about the government activity involved in the request—one that extends beyond the public's right to know about government activity generally. The existence of numerous articles published on a given subject can be helpful in establishing the requirement that there be an "urgency to inform" the public on the topic. As a matter of administrative discretion, TVA may waive the formal certification requirement.

(4) TVA will notify the requester within 10 calendar days of the receipt of a request for expedited processing of its decision whether to grant or deny expedited processing. If expedited processing is granted, the request must be given priority, placed in the processing track for expedited requests, and must be processed as soon as practicable. If a request for expedited processing is denied, the agency must act on any appeal of that decision expeditiously.

§ 1301.6 Responses to requests.

(a) *In general.* TVA, to the extent practicable, will communicate with requesters having access to the Internet electronically, such as email.

(b) *Acknowledgments of requests.* TVA will acknowledge the request in writing and assign it an individualized tracking number if it will take longer than 10 working days to process. TVA will include in the acknowledgment a brief description of the records sought to allow requesters to more easily keep track of their requests.

(c) *Estimated dates of completion and interim responses.* Upon request, TVA will provide an estimated date by which the agency expects to provide a response to the requester. If a request involves a voluminous amount of material, or searches in multiple locations, TVA may provide interim responses, releasing the records on a rolling basis.

(d) *Grants of requests.* Once TVA determines it will grant a request in full or in part, it will notify the requester in writing. TVA will also inform the requester of any fees charged under § 1301.11 of this subpart and will disclose the requested records to the requester promptly upon payment of any applicable fees.

(e) *Adverse determinations of requests.* If TVA makes an adverse determination denying a request in any respect, it will notify the requester of that determination in writing. Adverse determinations, or denials of requests, include decisions that: the requested record is exempt, in whole or in part; the request does not reasonably describe the records sought; the information requested is not a record subject to the FOIA; the requested record does not exist, cannot be located, or has been destroyed; or the requested record is not readily reproducible in the form or format sought by the requester. Adverse determinations also include denials involving fees or fee waiver matters or denials of requests for expedited processing. In the event of an adverse determination, TVA will inform the requester of the availability of its FOIA Public Liaison to offer assistance to requesters.

(f) *Content of denial.* The denial must be signed by the head of the agency or their designee and must include:

(1) The name and title or position of the person responsible for the denial;

(2) A brief statement of the reasons for the denial, including any FOIA exemption applied by the agency in denying the request;

(3) An estimate of the volume of any records or information withheld, such as the number of pages or some other reasonable form of estimation, although such an estimate is not required if the volume is otherwise indicated by deletions marked on records that are disclosed in part or if providing an estimate would harm an interest protected by an applicable exemption; and

(4) A statement that the denial may be appealed under § 1301.9(a) of this subpart, and a description of the appeal requirements.

(5) A statement notifying the requester of the assistance available

163

from the agency's FOIA Public Liaison and the dispute resolution services offered by OGIS.

(g) *Markings on released documents.* Records disclosed in part must be marked clearly to show the amount of information deleted and the exemption under which the deletion was made unless doing so would harm an interest protected by an applicable exemption. The location of the information deleted must also be indicated on the record, if technically feasible.

(h) *Use of record exclusions.* (1) In the event that TVA identifies records that may be subject to exclusion from the requirements of the FOIA pursuant to 5 U.S.C. 552(c), TVA will confer with the Department of Justice, Office of Information Policy, to obtain approval to apply the exclusion.

(2) If an exclusion is invoked, TVA will maintain an administrative record of the process of invocation and approval of the exclusion by OIP.

§ 1301.7   Exempt records.

(a) TVA's records will be disclosed to any person upon request as provided in this section, except records that are exempt and are not made available if they are:

(1)(i) Specifically authorized under criteria established by an Executive order to be kept secret in the interest of national defense or foreign policy, and

(ii) Are in fact properly classified pursuant to such Executive order;

(2) Related solely to the internal personnel rules and practices of an agency;

(3) Specifically exempted from disclosure by statute (other than section 552b of this title), if that statute—

(i)(A) Requires that the matters be withheld from the public in such a manner as to leave no discretion on the issue; or

(B) Establishes particular criteria for withholding or refers to particular types of matters to be withheld; and

(ii) If enacted after the date of enactment of the OPEN FOIA Act of 2009, specifically cites to this paragraph.

(4) Trade secrets and commercial or financial information obtained from a person and privileged or confidential;

(5) Inter-agency or intra-agency memorandums or letters that would not be available by law to a party other than an agency in litigation with the agency, provided that the deliberative process privilege shall not apply to records created 25 years or more before the date on which the records were requested;

(6) Personnel and medical files and similar files the disclosure of which would constitute a clearly unwarranted invasion of personal privacy;

(7) Records or information compiled for law enforcement purposes, but only to the extent that the production of such law enforcement records or information—

(i) Could reasonably be expected to interfere with enforcement proceedings,

(ii) Would deprive a person of a right to a fair trial or an impartial adjudication,

(iii) Could reasonably be expected to constitute an unwarranted invasion of personal privacy,

(iv) Could reasonably be expected to disclose the identity of a confidential source, including a State, local, or foreign agency or authority or any private institution which furnished information on a confidential basis, and, in the case of a record or information compiled by a criminal law enforcement authority in the course of a criminal investigation or by an agency conducting a lawful national security intelligence investigation, information furnished by a confidential source,

(v) Would disclose techniques and procedures for law enforcement investigations or prosecutions, or would disclose guidelines for law enforcement investigations or prosecutions if such disclosure could reasonably be expected to risk circumvention of the law, or

(vi) Could reasonably be expected to endanger the life or physical safety of any individual;

(8) Contained in or related to examination, operating, or condition reports prepared by, on behalf of, or for the use of an agency responsible for the regulation or supervision of financial institutions; or

(9) Geological and geophysical information and data, including maps, concerning wells.

(b) The availability of certain classes of nonexempt records is deferred for such time as TVA may determine is reasonable necessary to avoid interference with the accomplishment of its statutory responsibilities. Such records include bids and information concerning the identity and number of bids received prior to bid opening and award; and all negotiations in progress involving contracts or agreements for the acquisition or disposal of real or personal property by TVA prior to the conclusion of such negotiations. Any reasonably segregable portion of an available record shall be provided to any person requesting such record after deletion of the portions which are exempt under this paragraph.

§1301.8 Confidential commercial information.

(a) *Definitions*—(1) *Confidential commercial information* means commercial or financial information obtained by TVA from a submitter that may be protected from disclosure under Exemption 4 of the FOIA, 5 U.S.C. 552(b)(4).

(2) *Submitter* means any person or entity, including a corporation, State, or foreign government, but not including another Federal Government entity, that provides confidential commercial information, either directly or indirectly to the Federal Government.

(b) *Designation of confidential commercial information.* A submitter of confidential commercial information must use good faith efforts to designate by appropriate markings, at the time of submission, any portion of its submission that it considers to be protected from disclosure under Exemption 4. These designations expire 10 years after the date of the submission unless the submitter requests and provides justification for a longer designation period.

(c) *When notice to submitters is required.* (1) TVA will promptly provide written notice to the submitter of confidential commercial information whenever records containing such information are requested under the FOIA if TVA determines that it may be required to disclose the records, provided:

(i) The requested information has been designated in good faith by the submitter as information considered protected from disclosure under Exemption 4; or

(ii) TVA has a reason to believe that the requested information may be protected from disclosure under Exemption 4, but has not yet determined whether the information is protected from disclosure.

(2) The notice must either describe the commercial information requested or include a copy of the requested records or portions of records containing the information. In cases involving a voluminous number of submitters, the agency may post or publish a notice in a place or manner reasonably likely to inform the submitters of the proposed disclosure, instead of sending individual notifications.

(d) *Exceptions to submitter notice requirements.* The notice requirements of this section do not apply if:

(1) TVA determines that the information is exempt under the FOIA, and therefore will not be disclosed;

(2) The information has been lawfully published or has been officially made available to the public;

(3) Disclosure of the information is required by a statute other than the FOIA or by a regulation issued in accordance with the requirements of Executive Order 12600 of June 23, 1987; or

(4) The designation made by the submitter under paragraph (b) of this section appears obviously frivolous. In such case, TVA will give the submitter written notice of any final decision to disclose the information within a reasonable number of days prior to a specified disclosure date.

(e) *Opportunity to object to disclosure.* (1) TVA will specify a reasonable time period within which the submitter must respond to the notice referenced under paragraph (c)(1) of this section.

(2) If a submitter has any objections to disclosure, it should provide TVA a detailed written statement that specifies all grounds for withholding the particular information under any exemption of the FOIA. In order to rely on Exemption 4 as basis for nondisclosure, the submitter must explain why

the information constitutes a trade secret or commercial or financial information that is confidential.

(3) A submitter who fails to respond within the time period specified in the notice will be considered to have no objection to disclosure of the information. TVA is not required to consider any information received after the date of any disclosure decision. Any information provided by a submitter under this subpart may itself be subject to disclosure under the FOIA.

(f) *Analysis of objections.* TVA will consider a submitter's objections and specific grounds for nondisclosure in deciding whether to disclose the requested information.

(g) *Notice of intent to disclose.* Whenever TVA decides to disclose information over the objection of a submitter, TVA will provide the submitter written notice, which will include:

(1) A statement of the reasons why each of the submitter's disclosure objections was not sustained;

(2) A description of the information to be disclosed or copies of the records as TVA intends to release them; and

(3) A specified disclosure date, which must be a reasonable time after the notice.

(h) *Notice of FOIA lawsuit.* Whenever a requester files a lawsuit seeking to compel the disclosure of confidential commercial information, TVA will promptly notify the submitter.

(i) *Requester notification.* TVA will notify the requester whenever it provides the submitter with notice and an opportunity to object to disclosure; whenever it notifies the submitter of its intent to disclose the requested information; and whenever a submitter files a lawsuit to prevent the disclosure of the information.

§ 1301.9 Appeals.

(a) *Requirements for making an appeal.* A requester may appeal any adverse determinations to TVA's office designated to receive FOIA appeals (FOIA Appeals Office). Examples of adverse determinations are provided in § 1301.6(e) of this subpart. Requesters can submit appeals by mail to TVA FOIA Appeals Official, Tennessee Valley Authority, 400 W. Summit Hill Drive (WT 7C), Knoxville, TN 37902–

1401. The requester must make the appeal in writing and to be considered timely it must be postmarked within 90 calendar days after the date of the initial response. The appeal should clearly identify the agency determination that is being appealed and the assigned request number. To facilitate handling, the requester should mark both the appeal letter and envelope "Freedom of Information Act Appeal."

(b) *Adjudication of appeals.* (1) The TVA Chief FOIA Officer and FOIA Appeals Official or designee will act on all appeals under this section.

(2) An appeal ordinarily will not be adjudicated if the request becomes a matter of FOIA litigation.

(3) On receipt of any appeal involving classified information, the Chief FOIA Officer and FOIA Appeals Official will take appropriate action to ensure compliance with applicable classification rules.

(c) *Decisions on appeals.* TVA will provide its decision on an appeal in writing. A decision that upholds TVA's determination in whole or in part must contain a statement that identifies the reasons for the affirmance, including any FOIA exemptions applied. The decision must provide the requester with notification of the statutory right to file a lawsuit and will inform the requester of the dispute resolution services offered by the Office of Government Information Services (OGIS) of the National Archives and Records Administration as a non-exclusive alternative to litigation. If TVA's decision is remanded or modified on appeal, TVA will notify the requester of that determination in writing. TVA will then further process the request in accordance with that appeal determination and will respond directly to the requester.

(d) *Engaging in dispute resolution services provided by OGIS.* Dispute resolution is a voluntary process. If TVA agrees to participate in the dispute resolution services provided by OGIS, it will actively engage as a partner to the process in an attempt to resolve the dispute.

(e) *When appeal is required.* Before seeking review by a court of TVA's adverse determination, a requester generally must first submit a timely administrative appeal.

§1301.10 Preservation of records.

TVA will preserve all correspondence pertaining to the requests that it receives under this subpart, as well as copies of all requested records, until disposition or destruction is authorized pursuant to title 44 of the United States Code or the General Records Schedule 4.2 of the National Archives and Records Administration. TVA will not dispose of or destroy records while they are the subject of a pending request, appeal, or lawsuit under the FOIA.

§1301.11 Fees.

(a) *In general.* (1) TVA will charge for processing requests under the FOIA in accordance with the provisions of this section and with the OMB Guidelines. For purposes of assessing fees, the FOIA establishes three categories of requesters:

(i) Commercial use requesters;

(ii) Non-commercial scientific or educational institutions or news media requesters; and

(iii) All other requesters.

(2) Different fees are assessed depending on the category. Requesters may seek a fee waiver. TVA will consider requests for fee waivers in accordance with the requirements in paragraph (k) of this section. To resolve any fee issues that arise under this section, TVA may contact a requester for additional information. TVA will ensure that searches, review, and duplication are conducted in the most efficient and the least expensive manner. TVA ordinarily will collect all applicable fees before sending copies of records to a requester. Requesters must pay fees by check or money order made payable to the Tennessee Valley Authority, or by another method as determined by TVA.

(b) *Definitions.* For purposes of this section:

(1) Commercial use request is a request that asks for information for a use or a purpose that furthers a commercial, trade, or profit interest, which can include furthering those interests through litigation. TVA's decision to place a requester in the commercial use category will be made on a case-by-case basis based on the requester's intended use of the information. TVA will notify requesters of their placement in this category.

(2) Direct costs are those expenses that TVA incurs in searching for and duplicating (and, in the case of commercial use requests, reviewing) records in order to respond to a FOIA request. For example, direct costs include the salary of the employee performing the work (*i.e.*, the basic rate of pay for the employee, plus 16 percent of that rate to cover benefits) and the cost of operating computers and other electronic equipment, such as photocopiers and scanners. Direct costs do not include overhead expenses such as the costs of space, and of heating or lighting a facility.

(3) Duplication is reproducing a copy of a record, or of the information contained in it, necessary to respond to a FOIA request. Copies can take the form of paper, audiovisual materials, or electronic records, among others.

(4) Educational institution is any school that operates a program of scholarly research. A requester in this fee category must show that the request is made in connection with his or her role at the educational institution. TVA may seek verification from the requester that the request is in furtherance of scholarly research and TVA will advise requesters of their placement in this category.

Example 1. A request from a professor of geology at a university for records relating to soil erosion, written on letterhead of the Department of Geology, would be presumed to be from an educational institution.

Example 2. A request from the same professor of geology seeking drug information from the Food and Drug Administration in furtherance of a murder mystery he is writing would not be presumed to be an institutional request, regardless of whether it was written on institutional stationery.

Example 3. A student who makes a request in furtherance of their coursework or other school-sponsored activities and provides a copy of a course syllabus or other reasonable documentation to indicate the research purpose for the request, would qualify as part of this fee category.

(5) Noncommercial scientific institution is an institution that is not operated on a "commercial" basis, as defined in paragraph (b)(1) of this section and that is operated solely for the purpose of conducting scientific research the results of which are not intended to promote any particular product or industry. A requester in this category must show that the request is authorized by and is made under the auspices of a qualifying institution and that the records are sought to further scientific research and are not for a commercial use. TVA will advise requesters of their placement in this category.

(6) Representative of the news media is any person or entity that gathers information of potential interest to a segment of the public, uses its editorial skills to turn the raw materials into a distinct work, and distributes that work to an audience. The term "news" means information that is about current events or that would be of current interest to the public. Examples of news media entities include television or radio stations that broadcast "news" to the public at large and publishers of periodicals that disseminate "news" and make their products available through a variety of means to the general public, including news organizations that disseminate solely on the Internet. A request for records supporting the news-dissemination function of the requester will not be considered to be for a commercial use. "Freelance" journalists who demonstrate a solid basis for expecting publication through a news media entity will be considered as a representative of the news media. A publishing contract would provide the clearest evidence that publication is expected; however, agencies can also consider a requester's past publication record in making this determination. TVA will advise requesters of their placement in this category.

(7) Search is the process of looking for and retrieving records or information responsive to a request. Search time includes page-by-page or line-by-line identification of information within records and the reasonable efforts expended to locate and retrieve information from electronic records.

(8) Review is the examination of a record located in response to a request in order to determine whether any portion of it is exempt from disclosure. Review time includes processing any record for disclosure, such as doing all that is necessary to prepare the record for disclosure, including the process of redacting the record and marking the appropriate exemptions. Review costs are properly charged even if a record ultimately is not disclosed. Review time also includes time spent both obtaining and considering any formal objection to disclosure made by a confidential commercial information submitter under § 1301.7 of this subpart, but it does not include time spent resolving general legal or policy issues regarding the application of exemptions.

(c) *Charging fees.* In responding to FOIA requests, TVA will charge the following fees unless a waiver or reduction of fees has been granted under paragraph (k) of this section. Because the fee amounts provided below already account for the direct costs associated with a given fee type, agencies should not add any additional costs to charges calculated under this section.

(1) *Search.* (i) Requests made by educational institutions, noncommercial scientific institutions, or representatives of the news media are not subject to search fees. TVA will charge search fees for all other requesters, subject to the restrictions of paragraph (d) of this section. TVA may properly charge for time spent searching even if they do not locate any responsive records or if they determine that the records are entirely exempt from disclosure.

(ii) For each hour spent by personnel searching for requested records, including electronic searches that do not require new programming, the fees will be charged as follows: For time spent by clerical employees, the charge is $14.90 per hour. For time spent by supervisory and professional employees, the charge is $34.30 per hour.

(iii) TVA will charge the direct costs associated with conducting any search that requires the creation of a new computer program to locate the requested records. TVA must notify the requester of the costs associated with creating such a program, and the requester must agree to pay the associated costs before the costs may be incurred.

(iv) For requests that require the retrieval of records stored by TVA at a Federal records center operated by the National Archives and Records Administration (NARA), TVA will charge additional costs in accordance with the Transactional Billing Rate Schedule established by NARA.

(2) *Duplication.* TVA will charge duplication fees to all requesters, subject to the restrictions of paragraph (d) of this section. TVA must honor a requester's preference for receiving a record in a particular form or format where TVA can readily reproduce it in the form or format requested. Where photocopies are supplied, TVA will provide one copy per request at the cost of 10 cents per page for sheets no larger than 8½ by 14 inches. For copies of records produced on tapes, disks, or other media, TVA will charge the direct costs of producing the copy, including operator time. Where paper documents must be scanned in order to comply with a requester's preference to receive the records in an electronic format, the requester must also pay the direct costs associated with scanning those materials. For other forms of duplication, TVA will charge the direct costs.

(3) *Review.* TVA will charge review fees to requesters who make commercial use requests. Review fees will be assessed in connection with the initial review of the record, *i.e.*, the review conducted by TVA to determine whether an exemption applies to a particular record or portion of a record. No charge will be made for review at the administrative appeal stage of exemptions applied at the initial review stage. However, if a particular exemption is deemed to no longer apply, any costs associated with an agency's re-review of the records in order to consider the use of other exemptions may be assessed as review fees. Review fees will be charged at the same rates as those charged for a search under paragraph (c)(1)(ii) of this section.

(d) *Restrictions on charging fees.* (1) When TVA determines that a requester is an educational institution, non-com-

mercial scientific institution, or representative of the news media, and the records are not sought for commercial use, it will not charge search fees.

(2)(i) If TVA fails to comply with the FOIA's time limits in responding to a request, it may not charge search fees, or, in the instances of requests from requesters described in paragraph (d)(1) of this section, may not charge duplication fees, except as described in paragraphs (d)(2)(ii) through (iv) of this section.

(ii) If TVA has determined that unusual circumstances, as defined by the FOIA, apply and the agency provided timely written notice to the requester in accordance with the FOIA, a failure to comply with the time limit shall be excused for an additional 10 days.

(iii) If TVA has determined that unusual circumstances, as defined by the FOIA, apply and more than 5,000 pages are necessary to respond to the request, TVA may charge search fees, or, in the case of requesters described in paragraph (d)(1) of this section, may charge duplication fees, if the following steps are taken. TVA must have provided timely written notice of unusual circumstances to the requester in accordance with the FOIA and TVA must have discussed with the requester via written mail, email, or telephone (or made not less than three good-faith attempts to do so) how the requester could effectively limit the scope of the request in accordance with 5 U.S.C. 552(a)(6)(B)(ii). If this exception is satisfied, TVA may charge all applicable fees incurred in the processing of the request.

(iv) If a court has determined that exceptional circumstances exist, as defined by the FOIA, a failure to comply with the time limits shall be excused for the length of time provided by the court order.

(3) No search or review fees will be charged for a quarter-hour period unless more than half of that period is required for search or review.

(4) Except for requesters seeking records for a commercial use, TVA must provide without charge:

(i) The first 100 pages of duplication (or the cost equivalent for other media); and

(ii) The first two hours of search.

(5) No fee will be charged when the total fee, after deducting the 100 free pages (or its cost equivalent) and the first two hours of search, is equal to or less than $25.

(e) *Notice of anticipated fees in excess of $25.00.* (1) When TVA determines or estimates that the fees to be assessed in accordance with this section will exceed $25.00, TVA will notify the requester of the actual or estimated amount of the fees, including a breakdown of the fees for search, review or duplication, unless the requester has indicated a willingness to pay fees as high as those anticipated. If only a portion of the fee can be estimated readily, TVA will advise the requester accordingly. If the request is not for noncommercial use, the notice will specify that the requester is entitled to the statutory entitlements of 100 pages of duplication at no charge and, if the requester is charged search fees, two hours of search time at no charge, and will advise the requester whether those entitlements have been provided.

(2) If TVA notifies the requester that the actual or estimated fees are in excess of $25.00, the request will not be considered received and further work will not be completed until the requester commits in writing to pay the actual or estimated total fee, or designates some amount of fees the requester is willing to pay, or in the case of a noncommercial use requester who has not yet been provided with the requester's statutory entitlements, designates that the requester seeks only that which can be provided by the statutory entitlements. The requester must provide the commitment or designation in writing, and must, when applicable, designate an exact dollar amount the requester is willing to pay. TVA is not required to accept payments in installments.

(3) If the requester has indicated a willingness to pay some designated amount of fees, but TVA estimates that the total fee will exceed that amount, TVA will toll the processing of the request when it notifies the requester of the estimated fees in excess of the amount the requester has indicated a willingness to pay. TVA will inquire whether the requester wishes to revise the amount of fees the requester

is willing to pay or modify the request. Once the requester responds, the time to respond will resume from where it was at the date of the notification.

(4) TVA will make available its FOIA Officer or FOIA Public Liaison to assist any requester in reformulating a request to meet the requester's needs at a lower cost.

(f) *Charges for other services.* Although not required to provide special services, if TVA chooses to do so as a matter of administrative discretion, the direct costs of providing the service will be charged. Examples of such services include certifying that records are true copies, providing multiple copies of the same document, or sending records by means other than first class mail.

(g) *Charging interest.* TVA may charge interest on any unpaid bill starting on the 31st day following the date of billing the requester. Interest charges will be assessed at the rate provided in 31 U.S.C. 3717 and will accrue from the billing date until payment is received by TVA. TVA must follow the provisions of the Debt Collection Act of 1982 (Pub. L. 97–365, 96 Stat. 1749), as amended, and its administrative procedures, including the use of consumer reporting agencies, collection agencies, and offset.

(h) *Aggregating requests.* When TVA reasonably believes that a requester or a group of requesters acting in concert is attempting to divide a single request into a series of requests for the purpose of avoiding fees, TVA may aggregate those requests and charge accordingly. TVA may presume that multiple requests of this type made within a 30-day period have been made in order to avoid fees. For requests separated by a longer period, TVA will aggregate them only where there is a reasonable basis for determining that aggregation is warranted in view of all the circumstances involved. Multiple requests involving unrelated matters cannot be aggregated.

(i) *Advance payments.* (1) For requests other than those described in paragraphs (i)(2) or (i)(3) of this section, TVA cannot require the requester to make an advance payment before work is commenced or continued on a request. Payment owed for work already completed (*i.e.,* payment before copies are sent to a requester) is not an advance payment.

(2) When TVA determines or estimates that a total fee to be charged under this section will exceed $250.00, it may require that the requester make an advance payment up to the amount of the entire anticipated fee before beginning to process the request. TVA may elect to process the request prior to collecting fees when it receives a satisfactory assurance of full payment from a requester with a history of prompt payment.

(3) Where a requester has previously failed to pay a properly charged FOIA fee to any agency within 30 calendar days of the billing date, TVA may require that the requester pay the full amount due, plus any applicable interest on that prior request, and TVA may require that the requester make an advance payment of the full amount of any anticipated fee before TVA begins to process a new request or continues to process a pending request or any pending appeal. Where TVA has a reasonable basis to believe that a requester has misrepresented the requester's identity in order to avoid paying outstanding fees, it may require that the requester provide proof of identity.

(4) In cases in which TVA requires advance payment, the request will not be considered received and further work will not be completed until the required payment is received. If the requester does not pay the advance payment within 30 calendar days after the date of TVA's fee determination, the request will be closed.

(j) *Other statutes specifically providing for fees.* The fee schedule of this section does not apply to fees charged under any statute that specifically requires an agency to set and collect fees for particular types of records. In instances where records responsive to a request are subject to a statutorily-based fee schedule program, TVA will inform the requester of the contact information for that program.

(k) *Requirements for waiver or reduction of fees.* (1) Requesters may seek a waiver of fees by submitting a written application demonstrating how disclosure of the requested information is in the public interest because it is likely to contribute significantly to public understanding of the operations or activities of the government and is not primarily in the commercial interest of the requester.

(2) TVA will furnish records responsive to a request without charge or at a reduced rate when it determines, based on all available information, that the factors described in paragraphs (k)(2)(i) through (iii) of this section are satisfied:

(i) Disclosure of the requested information would shed light on the operations or activities of the government. The subject of the request must concern identifiable operations or activities of the Federal Government with a connection that is direct and clear, not remote or attenuated.

(ii) Disclosure of the requested information is likely to contribute significantly to public understanding of those operations or activities. This factor is satisfied when the following criteria are met:

(A) Disclosure of the requested records must be meaningfully informative about government operations or activities. The disclosure of information that already is in the public domain, in either the same or a substantially identical form, would not be meaningfully informative if nothing new would be added to the public's understanding.

(B) The disclosure must contribute to the understanding of a reasonably broad audience of persons interested in the subject, as opposed to the individual understanding of the requester. A requester's expertise in the subject area as well as the requester's ability and intention to effectively convey information to the public must be considered. TVA will presume that a representative of the news media will satisfy this consideration.

(iii) The disclosure must not be primarily in the commercial interest of the requester. To determine whether disclosure of the requested information is primarily in the commercial interest of the requester, TVA will consider the following criteria:

(A) TVA must identify whether the requester has any commercial interest that would be furthered by the requested disclosure. A commercial interest includes any commercial, trade, or profit interest. Requesters will be given an opportunity to provide explanatory information regarding this consideration.

(B) If there is an identified commercial interest, TVA must determine whether that is the primary interest furthered by the request. A waiver or reduction of fees is justified when the requirements of paragraphs (k)(2)(i) and (ii) of this section are satisfied and any commercial interest is not the primary interest furthered by the request. TVA ordinarily will presume that when a news media requester has satisfied factors paragraphs (k)(2)(i) and (ii), the request is not primarily in the commercial interest of the requester. Disclosure to data brokers or others who merely compile and market government information for direct economic return will not be presumed to primarily serve the public interest.

(3) Where only some of the records to be released satisfy the requirements for a waiver of fees, a waiver must be granted for those records.

(4) Requests for a waiver or reduction of fees should be made when the request is first submitted to TVA and should address the criteria referenced above. A requester may submit a fee waiver request at a later time so long as the underlying record request is pending or on administrative appeal. When a requester who has committed to pay fees subsequently asks for a waiver of those fees and that waiver is denied, the requester must pay any costs incurred up to the date the fee waiver request was received.

§ 1301.12 Other rights and services.

Nothing in this subpart shall be construed to entitle any person, as of right, to any service or to the disclosure of any record to which such person is not entitled under the FOIA.

Subpart B—Privacy Act

AUTHORITY: 16 U.S.C. 831–831ee, 5 U.S.C. 552a.

SOURCE: 40 FR 45313, Oct. 1, 1975, unless otherwise noted. Redesignated at 44 FR 30682, May 29, 1979.

§ 1301.21 Purpose and scope.

(a) The regulations in §§ 1301.21 to 1301.34 implement section 3 of the Privacy Act of 1974, 5 U.S.C. 552a, with respect to systems of records maintained by TVA. They provide procedures by which an individual may exercise the rights granted by the Act to determine whether a TVA system contains a record pertaining to him; to gain access to such records; to have a copy made of all or any portion thereof; and to request administrative correction or amendment of such records. They prescribe fees to be charged for copying records; establish identification requirements; list penalties provided by statute for certain violations of the Act; and establish exemptions from certain requirements of the Act for certain TVA systems or components thereof.

(b) Nothing in §§ 1301.21 to 1301.34 entitles an individual to any access to any information or record compiled in reasonable anticipation of a civil action or proceeding.

(c) Certain records of which TVA may have physical possession are the official records of another government agency which exercises dominion and control over the records, their content, and access thereto. In such cases, TVA's maintenance of the records is subject to the direction of the other government agency. Except for a request for a determination of the existence of the record, when TVA receives requests related to these records, TVA will immediately refer the request to the controlling agency for all decisions regarding the request, and will notify the individual making the request of the referral.

[40 FR 45313, Oct. 1, 1975. Redesignated at 44 FR 30682, May 29, 1979, and further redesignated and amended at 82 FR 51757, Nov. 8, 2017]

§ 1301.22 Definitions.

For purposes of §§ 1301.21 to 1301.34:

(a) The *Act* means section 3 of the Privacy Act of 1974, 5 U.S.C. 552a;

(b) The terms *individual, maintain, record, system of records, statistical record,* and *routine use* have the meaning provided for by the Act;

(c) The term *TVA system* means a system of records maintained by TVA;

(d) The term *TVA system notice* means a notice of a TVA system published in the FEDERAL REGISTER pursuant to the Act. TVA has published TVA system notices about the following TVA systems:

Apprentice Training Records—TVA.
Personnel Files—TVA.
Discrimination Complaint Files—TVA.
Work Injury Illness System—TVA.
Employee Accounts Receivable—TVA.
Health Records—TVA.
Payroll Records—TVA.
Travel History Records—TVA.
Employment Applicant Files—TVA.
Grievance Records—TVA.
Employee Supplementary Vacancy Announcement Records—TVA.
Consultant and Contractor Records—TVA.
Nuclear Quality Assurance Personnel Records—TVA.
Questionnaire—Land Use Surveys in Vicinity of Proposed or Licensed Nuclear Power Plant—TVA.
Radiation Dosimetry Personnel Monitoring Records—TVA.
Retirement System Records—TVA.
Energy Program Participant Records—TVA.
OIG Investigative Records—TVA.
Call Detail Records—TVA.
Project/Tract Files—TVA.
Section 26a Permit Application Records—TVA.
U.S. TVA Police Records—TVA.
Wholesale, Retail, and Emergency Data Files—TVA.
Nuclear Access Authorization and Fitness for Duty Records—TVA.

(e) The term *appellant* means an individual who has filed an appeal pursuant to §1301.29(a) from an initial determination refusing to amend a record on request of the individual;

(f) The term *reviewing official* means TVA's Senior Vice President, Chief Human Resources Officer (or incumbent of a successor position), or another TVA official designated by the Senior Vice President in writing to decide an appeal pursuant to §1301.29;

(g) The term *day*, when used in computing a time period, excludes Saturdays, Sundays, and legal public holidays.

[40 FR 45313, Oct. 1, 1975. Redesignated at 44 FR 30682, May 29, 1979, and amended at 53 FR 30252, Aug. 11, 1988; 56 FR 9288, Mar. 6, 1991; 57 FR 33634, July 30, 1992; 57 FR 59803, Dec. 16, 1992; 75 FR 11736, Mar. 12, 2010; 81 FR 88999, Dec. 9, 2016. Redesignated and amended at 82 FR 51757, Nov. 8, 2017]

§1301.23 Procedures for requests pertaining to individual records in a record system.

(a) An individual may, in accordance with this section (1) request a TVA determination whether a record retrieved by the individual's name or other personal identifier is maintained in a TVA system, and (2) request access to such a record. A request for determination may be combined with a request for access.

(b) Requests under this section shall:

(1) Be in writing and signed by the individual seeking the determination or access;

(2) Include the individual's mailing address;

(3) Name the TVA system as listed in the TVA system notice;

(4) Include any additional identifying information specified in the paragraph headed "Notification procedure" in the applicable TVA system notice;

(5) Specify whether the request is for determination only or for both determination and access; and

(6) Include such proof of identity as may be required by §1301.24 and the applicable system notice. Requests may be presented in person or by mail. In-person requests shall be presented during normal TVA business hours, as set out in §1301.24(g).

(c) Requests for determination only shall be presented to the official designated in the paragraph headed "Notification procedure" in the TVA system notice for the TVA system concerned. Requests for both determination and access shall be presented to the official designated in the paragraph headed "Access procedure" in the TVA system notice for the TVA system concerned. Certain TVA system notices designate officials at field locations of TVA systems. With respect to such TVA systems, an individual who believes his record is located at the field location may present a request to the designated official at the field location. If the record is not available at that field location, the request will be forwarded to the appropriate TVA office.

(d) If a request is for determination only, the determination will normally be made within 10 days after receipt of the request. If the determination cannot be made within 10 days after receipt of a request, the designated official will acknowledge the request in writing and state when the determination will be made. Upon making a determination, the designated official will notify the individual making the request whether the record exists. The notice will include any additional information necessary to enable the individual to request access to the record.

(e) A request which includes a request for access will be acknowledged within 10 days after receipt. If access can be granted as requested, the acknowledgment will provide a time and place for disclosure of the requested record. Disclosure will normally be made within 30 days of the date of the acknowledgement, but the designated official may extend the 30-day period for reasons found by him to be good cause. In case of an extension, TVA will notify the individual, in writing, that disclosure will be delayed, the reasons for delay, and the anticipated date on which the individual may expect the record to be disclosed. TVA will attempt to accommodate reasonable requests for disclosure at specified times and dates, as set forth in a request for access, so far as compatible with the conduct of TVA business.

[40 FR 45313, Oct. 1, 1975. Redesignated at 44 FR 30682, May 29, 1979, and further redesignated and amended at 82 FR 51757, Nov. 8, 2017]

§ 1301.24 Times, places, and requirements for identification of individuals making requests.

(a) TVA will require proof of identity, in accordance with this section, before it will disclose a record under § 1301.25 of this part to an individual requesting access to the record, and before it will disclose the existence of a record to a requester under § 1301.23 of this part, if TVA determines that disclosure of the existence of such record would constitute an unwarranted invasion of personal privacy.

(b) Identification normally required would be an identification card such as a valid state driver's license or TVA or other employee identification card. A comparison of the signature of the requester with either the signature on the card or a signature in the record may be used to confirm identity.

(c) Because of the sensitivity of the subject matter in a TVA system, a TVA system notice may prescribe special identification requirements for the disclosure of the existence of or access to records in that TVA system. In such case, the special identification requirements prescribed in the TVA system notice shall apply in lieu of those prescribed by paragraph (b) of this section.

(d) If TVA deems it warranted by the nature of identification presented, the subject matter of the material to be disclosed, or other reasons found by TVA to be sufficient, TVA may require the individual requesting access to sign a statement asserting identity and stating that the individual understands that knowingly or willfully seeking or obtaining access to records about another person under false pretenses is punishable by a fine of up to $5,000.

(e) Where TVA is requested to provide access to records by mailing copies of records to the requester, the request shall contain or be accompanied by adequate identifying information to make it likely the requester is the person he purports to be and a notarized statement asserting identity and stating that the individual understands that knowingly or willfully seeking or obtaining access to records about another person under false pretenses is punishable by a fine of up to $5,000.

(f) Where sensitivity of record information may warrant (i.e., unauthorized access could cause harm or embarrassment to the individual) or disclosure by mail to third persons is requested, TVA may require in-person confirmation of identity. If in-person confirmation of identity is required, the individual may arrange with the designated TVA official to provide such identification at any of these TVA locations convenient to the individual: Knoxville, Nashville, and Chattanooga, Tennessee; Muscle Shoals, Alabama; Washington, DC, or another location agreed upon by the individual and the designated TVA official. Upon request the TVA official will provide an address and an appropriate time for such identification to be presented.

(g) In general, TVA offices located in the Eastern Time zone are open 8 a.m.

to 4:45 p.m., and those in the Central Time zone 7:30 a.m. to 4:15 p.m. Offices are closed on Saturdays, Sundays, and the following holidays: New Year's Day, Birthday of Martin Luther King, Jr., Presidents' Day, Memorial Day, Independence Day, Labor Day, Columbus Day, Veterans Day, Thanksgiving Day, and Christmas Day.

[40 FR 45313, Oct. 1, 1975. Redesignated at 44 FR 30682, May 29, 1979, and amended at 53 FR 30253, Aug. 11, 1988; 75 FR 11736, Mar. 12, 2010. Redesignated and amended at 82 FR 51757, Nov. 8, 2017]

§1301.25 Disclosure of requested information to individuals.

(a) All disclosure and examination of records shall normally be made in the presence of a TVA representative. If an individual wishes to be accompanied by a third person of the individual's choosing when the record is disclosed, TVA may require the individual to furnish TVA, in advance of disclosure of the record, a statement signed by the individual authorizing discussion and disclosure of the record in the presence of the accompanying person. If desired by the individual, TVA shall provide copies of any documents reviewed in the record which are requested at the time of review. Fees shall be charged for such copies in accordance with the fee schedule in §1301.31, and shall be payable prior to delivery of the copies to the individual.

(b) Where permitted by §1301.24, copies of an individual's record will be made available by mail. A charge for copies will be made in accordance with §1301.31 of this part. All fees due shall be paid prior to mailing of the materials. However, if TVA is unable to allow in-person review of the record, the first copy will be made available without charge.

[40 FR 45313, Oct. 1, 1975. Redesignated at 44 FR 30682, May 29, 1979, and further redesignated and amended at 82 FR 51757, Nov. 8, 2017]

§1301.26 Special procedures—medical records.

If, in the judgment of TVA, the transmission of medical records, including psychological records, directly to a requesting individual could have an adverse effect upon such individual, TVA may refuse to disclose such information directly to the individual. TVA will, however, disclose this information to a licensed health care provider or legal representative designated by the individual in writing who should then provide the records to the individual along with any necessary interpretations.

[75 FR 11736, Mar. 12, 2010. Redesignated at 82 FR 51757, Nov. 8, 2017]

§1301.27 Requests for correction or amendment of record.

(a) An individual may request amendment of records pertaining to him in a TVA system to the extent permitted by the Act in accordance with this section. A request for amendment shall:

(1) Be in writing and signed by the individual seeking the amendment;

(2) Name the TVA system in which the record is maintained;

(3) Describe the item or items of information to be amended;

(4) Describe the nature of the amendment requested; and

(5) Give the reasons for the requested change.

(b) Requests shall be made to the official designated in the paragraph headed "Contesting record procedures" in the TVA system notice for the TVA system concerned. Before considering a request, TVA may require proof of identity of the requester similar to that required under §1301.24 to gain access to the record.

(c) The individual requesting amendment has the responsibility of providing TVA with evidence of why his record should be amended, and must provide adequate evidence to TVA to justify his request.

(d) The provisions of §§1301.21 to 1301.34 of this part do not permit the alteration of evidence presented or to be presented in the course of judicial or administrative proceedings; neither do they permit collateral attack on a prior judicial or administrative action, or provide a collateral remedy for a matter otherwise judicially or administratively cognizable.

[40 FR 45313, Oct. 1, 1975. Redesignated at 44 FR 30682, May 29, 1979, and amended at 53 FR 30253, Aug. 11, 1988. Redesignated and amended at 82 FR 51757, 51758, Nov. 8, 2017]

§ 1301.28 TVA review of request for correction or amendment of record.

(a) TVA will acknowledge a request for amendment within 10 days of receipt. The acknowledgement will be in writing, will request any additional information TVA requires to determine whether to make the requested correction or amendment, and will indicate the date by which TVA expects to make its initial determination.

(b) TVA will, except in unusual circumstances, complete its consideration of requests to amend records within 30 days. If more time is deemed necessary, TVA will notify the individual of the delay and of the expected date of completion of the review.

(c) If TVA determines that a record should be corrected or amended, in whole or in part, in accordance with a request, it will advise the requesting individual in writing of its determination, and correct or amend the record accordingly. If an accounting of disclosures has been made, TVA will, to the extent of the accounting, inform prior recipients of the record of the fact that the correction was made and the substance of the correction.

(d) If TVA, after initial consideration of a request, determines that a record should not be corrected or amended, in whole or in part, in accordance with a request, it will notify the individual in writing of its refusal to amend the record and the reasons therefor. The notification will inform the individual that the refusal may be appealed administratively and will advise the individual of the procedures for such appeals.

[40 FR 45313, Oct. 1, 1975. Redesignated at 44 FR 30682, May 29, 1979, and further redesignated at 82 FR 51757, Nov. 8, 2017]

§ 1301.29 Appeals on initial adverse agency determination on correction or amendment.

(a) An individual may appeal an initial determination refusing to amend that individual's record in accordance with this section. An appeal must be taken within 20 days of receipt of notice of TVA's initial refusal to amend the record and is taken by delivering a written notice of appeal to the Privacy Act Reviewing Official, Tennessee Valley Authority, Knoxville, Tennessee

37902-1401. Such notice shall be signed by the appellant and shall state:

(1) That it is an appeal from a denial of a request to amend the individual's records under these regulations and under the Privacy Act of 1974;

(2) The reasons why the appellant believes the denial to have been erroneous;

(3) The date on which the denial was issued; and

(4) The date on which the denial was received by the appellant.

(b) Appeals shall be determined by a reviewing official. Such determination may be based on information provided for the initial determination; any additional information which TVA or the appellant may desire to provide; and any other material the reviewing official deems relevant to the determination. The reviewing official, in his sole discretion, may request TVA or the appellant to provide additional information deemed relevant to the appeal. The appellant will be given an opportunity to respond to any information provided by TVA or independently procured by the reviewing official. If in the sole discretion of the reviewing official a hearing is deemed necessary for resolution of the appeal, the reviewing official may conduct a hearing upon notice to TVA and the appellant, at which both TVA and the appellant shall be afforded an opportunity to be heard on the appeal. The rules governing any hearing will be set forth in the notice of hearing.

(c) The reviewing official shall make final determination on the appeal within 30 days after it is received unless such period is extended for good cause. If the reviewing official finds good cause for an extension, TVA will inform the appellant in writing of the reason for the delay and of the approximate date on which the reviewing official expects to complete his determination of the appeal.

(d) If the reviewing official determines that a record should be amended in whole or in part in accordance with an appellant's request, TVA will inform the appellant in writing of its determination and correct or amend the record. If an accounting of disclosures has been made, TVA will, to the extent of the accounting, inform prior recipients of the record of the fact that the correction was made and of the substance of the correction.

(e) If the reviewing official determines not to amend a record, in whole or in part, in accordance with a request, TVA will advise the individual:

(1) Of its refusal to amend and the reasons therefor;

(2) Of the appellant's right to file a concise statement of reasons for disagreement with the refusal as set out in paragraph (f) of this section;

(3) Of the procedures for filing a statement of disagreement;

(4) That any statement of disagreement will be made available to anyone to whom the record is subsequently disclosed together with any statement by TVA summarizing its reasons for refusing to amend the record;

(5) That prior recipients of the disputed record will be provided a copy of any statement of dispute to the extent that an accounting of disclosures was maintained; and

(6) Of his or her right to seek judicial review of the agency's refusal to amend a record.

(f) If the reviewing official's final determination of an appeal is a refusal to correct or amend a record, in whole or in part, in accordance with the request, the appellant may file with TVA a concise statement setting forth the reasons for his or her disagreement with the refusal of TVA to amend the records. Such statements normally should not exceed 100 words. A statement of disagreement should be submitted within 30 days of receipt of notice of the reviewing official's decision on the appeal, and should be sent to system manager. In any disclosure containing information about which the individual has filed a statement of disagreement which occurs after the filing of the statement, TVA will clearly note any portion of the record which is disputed and provide copies of the statement with the disclosure. Copies of the statement will also be furnished to persons or other agencies to whom the record has been disclosed to the extent that an accounting of disclosures was made. TVA may attach to the statement of disagreement a brief summary of TVA's reasons for refusing to amend

the record. Such summaries will be disclosed to the individual, but are not subject to amendment.

[40 FR 45313, Oct. 1, 1975. Redesignated at 44 FR 30682, May 29, 1979, and amended at 53 FR 30253, Aug. 11, 1988; 57 FR 33634, July 30, 1992; 75 FR 11736, Mar. 12, 2010. Redesignated at 82 FR 51757, Nov. 8, 2017]

§ 1301.30 Disclosure of record to persons other than individual to whom it pertains.

For purposes of §§ 1301.21 to 1301.34, the parent of any minor or the legal guardian of any individual who has been declared incompetent due to physical or mental incapacity or age by a court of competent jurisdiction may act on behalf of the individual. TVA may require proof of the relationship prior to allowing such action. The parent or legal guardian may not act where the individual concerned objects to the action of the parent or legal guardian, unless a court otherwise orders.

[40 FR 45313, Oct. 1, 1975. Redesignated at 44 FR 30682, May 29, 1979, and further redesignated and amended at 82 FR 51757, 51758, Nov. 8, 2017]

§ 1301.31 Fees.

(a) Fees to be charged, if any, to any individual for making copies of his or her record exclude the cost of any search and review of the record. The following fees are applicable:

(1) For reproduction of material consisting of sheets no larger than 8½ by 14 inches, ten cents per page; and

(2) For reproduction of other materials, the direct cost of photostats or other means necessarily used for duplication.

(b) [Reserved]

[40 FR 45313, Oct. 1, 1975. Redesignated at 44 FR 30682, May 29, 1979, and further redesignated at 82 FR 51757, Nov. 8, 2017]

§ 1301.32 Penalties.

Section 552a(i), Title 5, United States Code provides that:

(1) *Criminal Penalties.* Any officer or employee of an agency, who by virtue of his employment or official position, has possession of, or access to, agency records which contain individually identifiable information the disclosure of which is prohibited by this section or by rules or regulations established

thereunder, and who knowing that disclosure of the specific material is so prohibited, willfully discloses the material in any manner to any person or agency not entitled to receive it, shall be guilty of a misdemeanor and fined not more than $5,000.

(2) Any officer or employee of any agency who willfully maintains a system of records without meeting the notice requirements of subsection (e)(4) of this section shall be guilty of a misdemeanor and fined not more than $5,000.

(3) Any person who knowingly and willfully requests or obtains any record concerning an individual from an agency under false pretenses shall be guilty of a misdemeanor and fined not more than $5,000.

[40 FR 45313, Oct. 1, 1975. Redesignated at 44 FR 30682, May 29, 1979, and further redesignated at 82 FR 51757, Nov. 8, 2017]

§ 1301.33 General exemptions.

Individuals may not have access to records maintained by TVA but which were provided by another agency which has determined by regulation that such information is subject to general exemption under 5 U.S.C. 552a(j). If such exempt records are within a request for access, TVA will advise the individual of their existence and of the name and address of the source agency. For any further information concerning the record and the exemption, the individual must contact that source agency.

[75 FR 11736, Mar. 12, 2010. Redesignated at 82 FR 51757, Nov. 8, 2017]

§ 1301.34 Specific exemptions.

(a) The TVA system Nuclear Access Authorization and Fitness for Duty Records is exempt from subsections (d); (e)(4)(H); and (f)(2), (3), and (4) of 5 U.S.C. 522a (section 3 of the Privacy Act of 1974) to the extent that disclosure of material would reveal the identity of a source who furnished information to the Government under an express promise that the identity of the source would be held in confidence, and to the extent that disclosure of testing or examination material would compromise the objectivity or fairness of the testing or examination process. This exemption is pursuant to 5 U.S.C. 552a (k)(5) and (6).

(b)(1) The TVA systems "Apprentice Training Record System-TVA," "Consultant and Contractor Records-TVA,"

"Employment Applicant Files-TVA," "Personnel Files-TVA," and "Nuclear Quality Assurance Personnel Records-TVA" are exempted from subsections (d); (e)(4)(H); (f)(2), (3), and (4) of 5 U.S.C. 552a and corresponding sections of these rules to the extent that disclosure of material would reveal the identity of a source who furnished information to the Government under an express promise that the identity of the source would be held in confidence, or prior to September 27, 1975, under an implied promise that the identity of the source would be held in confidence. These TVA systems are exempted pursuant to section (k)(5) of 5 U.S.C. 552a (section 3 of the Privacy Act).

(2) Each of these TVA systems contain reference letters and information concerning employees and other individuals who perform services for TVA. TVA has received this information in the past under both express and implied promises of confidentiality and consistent with the Privacy Act these promises will be honored. Pledges of confidentiality will be necessary in the future to ensure that unqualified or unsuitable individuals are not selected for TVA positions. Without the ability to make these promises, a potential source of information may be unwilling to provide needed information, or may not be sufficiently frank to be of value in personnel screening.

(c)(1) The TVA systems "Apprentice Training Record System-TVA," "Consultant and Contractor Records-TVA," "Employment Applicant Files-TVA," and "Personnel Files-TVA," are exempted from subsections (d); (e)(4)(H); (f)(2), (3), and (4) of 5 U.S.C. 552a and corresponding sections of these rules to the extent that disclosure of testing or examination material used solely to determine individual qualifications for appointment or promotion in the Federal service would compromise the objectivity or fairness of the testing or examination process. These systems are exempted pursuant to section (k)(6) of 5 U.S.C. 552a (section 3 of the Privacy Act).

(2) This material is exempted because its disclosure would reveal information about the testing process which would potentially give an individual an unfair

competitive advantage in selection based on test performance.

(d) The TVA system OIG Investigative Records is exempt from subsections (c)(3), (d), (e)(1), (e)(4), (G), (H), and (I) and (f) of 5 U.S.C. 552a (section 3 of the Privacy Act) and corresponding sections of these rules pursuant to 5 U.S.C. 552a(k)(2). The TVA system OIG Investigative Records is exempt from subsections (c)(3), (d), (e)(1), (e)(2), (e)(3), (e)(4)(G), (H), and (I), (e)(5), (e)(8), and (g) pursuant to 5 U.S.C. 552a(j)(2). This system is exempt because application of these provisions might alert investigation subjects to the existence or scope of investigations, lead to suppression, alteration, fabrication, or destruction of evidence, disclose investigative techniques or procedures, reduce the cooperativeness or safety of witnesses, or otherwise impair investigations.

(e) The TVA system TVA Police Records is exempt from subsections (c)(3), (d), (e)(1), (e)(4), (G), (H), and (I) and (f) of 5 U.S.C. 552a (section 3 of the Privacy Act) and corresponding sections of these rules pursuant to 5 U.S.C. 552a(k)(2). The TVA system Police Records is exempt from subsections (c)(3), (d), (e)(1), (e)(2), (e)(3), (e)(4)(G), (H), and (I), (e)(5), (e)(8), and (g) pursuant to 5 U.S.C. 552a(j)(2). This system is exempt because application of these provisions might alert investigation subjects to the existence or scope of investigations, lead to suppression, alteration, fabrication, or destruction of evidence, disclose investigative techniques or procedures, reduce the cooperativeness or safety of witnesses, or otherwise impair investigations.

[40 FR 45313, Oct. 1, 1975. Redesignated at 44 FR 30682, May 29, 1979, and amended at 53 FR 30253, Aug. 11, 1988; 56 FR 9288, Mar. 6, 1991; 61 FR 2111, Jan. 25, 1996; 62 FR 4644, Jan. 31, 1997; 75 FR 11736, Mar. 12, 2010; 81 FR 88999, Dec. 9, 2016. Redesignated at 82 FR 51757, Nov. 8, 2017]

Subpart C—Government in the Sunshine Act

AUTHORITY: 16 U.S.C. 831–831ee, 5 U.S.C. 552b.

SOURCE: 42 FR 14086, Mar. 15, 1977, unless otherwise noted. Redesignated at 44 FR 30682, May 29, 1979.

§1301.41 Purpose and scope.

(a) The provisions of this subpart are intended to implement the requirements of section 3(a) of the Government in the Sunshine Act, 5 U.S.C. 552b, consistent with the purposes and provisions of the Tennessee Valley Authority Act of 1933, 16 U.S.C. 831–831dd.

(b) Nothing in this subpart expands or limits the present rights of any person under the Freedom of Information Act (5 U.S.C. 552) and the provisions of Subpart A of this part, except that the exemptions set forth in §1301.46 shall govern in the case of any request made pursuant to the Freedom of Information Act and Subpart A to copy or inspect the transcripts, recordings, or minutes described in §1301.47.

(c) Nothing in this subpart authorizes TVA to withhold from any individual any record, including transcripts, recordings, or minutes required by this subpart, which is otherwise accessible to such individual under the Privacy Act (5 U.S.C. 552a) and the provisions of Subpart B.

(d) The requirements of Chapter 33 of Title 44 of the United States Code shall not apply to the transcripts, recordings, and minutes described in §1301.47.

§1301.42 Definitions.

For the purposes of this subpart:

(a) The term *Board* means the Board of Directors of the Tennessee Valley Authority;

(b) The term *meeting* means the deliberations of five or more members of the TVA Board where such deliberations determine or result in the joint conduct or disposition of official TVA business, but the term does not include deliberations required or permitted by §1301.44 or §1301.45;

(c) The term *member* means an individual who is a member of the TVA Board; and

(d) The term *TVA* means the Tennessee Valley Authority.

[42 FR 14086, Mar. 15, 1977, as amended at 75 FR 11737, Mar. 12, 2010]

§ 1301.43 Open meetings.

Members shall not jointly conduct or dispose of TVA business other than in accordance with this subpart. Except as provided in § 1301.46, every portion of every meeting of the agency shall be open to public observation, and TVA shall provide suitable facilities therefor, but participation in the deliberations at such meetings shall be limited to members and certain TVA personnel. The public may make reasonable use of electronic or other devices or cameras to record deliberations or actions at meetings so long as such use is not disruptive of the meetings.

[42 FR 21470, Apr. 27, 1977. Redesignated at 44 FR 30682, May 29, 1979]

§ 1301.44 Notice of meetings.

(a) TVA shall make a public announcement of the time, place, and subject matter of each meeting, whether it is to be open or closed to the public, and the name and telephone number of a TVA official who can respond to requests for information about the meeting.

(b) Such public announcement shall be made at least one week before the meeting unless a majority of the members determines by a recorded vote that TVA business requires that such meeting be called at an earlier date. If an earlier date is so established, TVA shall make such public announcement at the earliest practicable time.

(c) Following a public announcement required by paragraph (a) of this section, the time or place of the meeting may be changed only if TVA publicly announces the change at the earliest practicable time. The subject matter of a meeting or the determination to open or close a meeting or portion of a meeting to the public may be changed following the public announcement required by paragraph (a) of this section only if a majority of the entire membership determines by a recorded vote that TVA business so requires and that no earlier announcement of the change was possible and if TVA publicly announces such change and the vote of each member upon such change at the earliest, practicable time.

(d) Immediately following each public announcement required by this section, notice of the time, place, and subject matter of a meeting, whether the meeting is open or closed, any change in one of the preceding, and the name and phone number of the TVA official designated to respond to requests for information about the meeting shall be submitted for publication in the FEDERAL REGISTER.

[42 FR 14087, Mar. 15, 1977, as amended at 75 FR 11737, Mar. 12, 2010]

§ 1301.45 Procedure for closing meetings.

(a) Action under § 1301.46 to close a meeting shall be taken only when a majority of the members vote to take such action. A separate vote shall be taken with respect to each meeting a portion or portions of which are proposed to be closed to the public pursuant to § 1301.46 or with respect to any information which is proposed to be withheld under § 1301.46. A single vote may be taken with respect to a series of meetings, a portion or portions of which are proposed to be closed to the public, or with respect to any information concerning such series of meetings, so long as each meeting in such series involves the same particular matters and is scheduled to be held no more than 30 days after the initial meeting in such series. The vote of each member participating in such vote shall be recorded and no proxies shall be allowed.

(b) Notwithstanding that the members may have already voted not to close a meeting, whenever any person whose interests may be directly affected by a portion of a meeting requests that the agency close such portion to the public for any of the reasons referred to in paragraphs (e), (f), or (g) of § 1301.46, the Board, upon request of any one of its members made prior to the commencement of such portion, shall vote by recorded vote whether to close such portion of the meeting.

(c) Within one day of any vote taken pursuant to this section, TVA shall make publicly available in accordance with § 1301.48 a written copy of such vote reflecting the vote of each member on the question. If a portion of a meeting is to be closed to the public, TVA shall, within one day of the vote taken pursuant to this section, make publicly available in accordance with § 1301.48 a full written explanation of this action closing the portion together with a list of all persons expected to attend the meeting and their affiliation.

(d) Prior to every meeting closed pursuant to § 1301.46, there shall be a certification by the General Counsel of TVA stating whether, in his or her opinion, the meeting may be closed to the public and each relevant exemptive provision. A copy of such certification shall be retained by TVA and shall be made publicly available in accordance with § 1301.48.

[42 FR 14087, Mar. 15, 1977, as amended at 75 FR 11737, Mar. 12, 2010]

§ 1301.46 Criteria for closing meetings.

Except in a case where the Board finds that the public interest requires otherwise, the second sentence of § 1301.43 shall not apply to any portion of a meeting and such portion may be closed to the public, and the requirements of §§ 1301.44 and 1301.45(a), (b), and (c) shall not apply to any information pertaining to such meeting otherwise required by this subpart to be disclosed to the public, where the Board properly determines that such portion or portions of its meeting or the disclosure of such information is likely to:

(a) Disclose matters that are (1) specifically authorized under criteria established by an Executive order to be kept secret in the interests of national defense or foreign policy and (2) in fact properly classified pursuant to such Executive order;

(b) Relate solely to the internal personnel rules and practices of an agency;

(c) Disclose matters specifically exempted from disclosure by statute (other than 5 U.S.C. 552), provided that such statute (1) requires that the matters be withheld from the public in such a manner as to leave no discretion on the issue, or (2) establishes particular criteria for withholding or refers to particular types of matters to be withheld;

(d) Disclose trade secrets and commercial or financial information obtained from a person and privileged or confidential;

(e) Involve accusing any person of a crime, or formally censuring any person;

(f) Disclose information of a personal nature where disclosure would constitute a clearly unwarranted invasion of personal privacy;

(g) Disclose investigatory records compiled for law enforcement purposes, or information which if written would be contained in such records, but only to the extent that the production of such records or information would:

(1) Interfere with enforcement proceedings,

(2) Deprive a person of a right to a fair trial or an impartial adjudication,

(3) Constitute an unwarranted invasion of personal privacy,

(4) Disclose the identity of a confidential source and, in the case of a record compiled by a criminal law enforcement authority in the course of a criminal investigation, or by an agency conducting a lawful national security intelligence investigation, confidential information furnished only by the confidential source,

(5) Disclose investigative techniques and procedures, or

(6) Endanger the life or physical safety of law enforcement personnel;

(h) Disclose information contained in or related to examination, operating, or condition reports prepared by, on behalf of, or for the use of any agency responsible for the regulation or supervision of financial institutions;

(i) Disclose information the premature disclosure of which would:

(1) In the case of any agency which regulates currencies, securities, commodities, or financial institutions, be likely to (i) lead to significant financial speculation in currencies, securities, or commodities, or (ii) significantly endanger the stability of any financial institution; or

(2) In the case of any agency, be likely to significantly frustrate implementation of a proposed agency action, except that this provision shall not apply in any instance where the agency has already disclosed to the public the content or nature of its proposed action, or where the agency is required by law to make such disclosure on its own initiative prior to taking final action on such proposal; or

(j) Specifically concern an agency's issuance of a subpena, or its participation in a civil action or proceeding, an action in a foreign court or international tribunal, or an arbitration, or the initiation, conduct, or disposition by an agency of a particular case of formal agency adjudication pursuant to the procedures in 5 U.S.C. 554 or otherwise involving a determination on the record after opportunity for a hearing.

§ 1301.47 Transcripts of closed meetings.

(a) For every meeting closed pursuant to § 1301.46, the presiding officer of the meeting shall prepare a statement setting forth the time and place of the meeting, and the persons present, and such statement shall be retained by TVA.

(b) TVA shall maintain a complete transcript or electronic recording adequate to record fully the proceedings of each meeting, or portion of a meeting, closed to the public, except that in the case of a meeting, or portion of a meeting, closed to the public pursuant to paragraph (h), (i)(1), or (j) of § 1301.46, TVA shall maintain either such a transcript or recording, or a set of minutes. Such minutes shall fully and clearly describe all matters discussed and shall provide a full and accurate summary of any actions taken, and the reasons therefor, including a description of each of the views expressed on any item and the record of any rollcall vote (reflecting the vote of each member on the question). All documents considered in connection with any action shall be identified in such minutes.

(c) TVA shall maintain a complete verbatim copy of the transcript, a complete copy of the minutes, or a complete electronic recording of each meeting, or portion of a meeting, closed to the public, for a period of at least two years after such meeting, or until one year after the conclusion of any TVA proceeding with respect to which the meeting or portion was held, whichever occurs later.

§ 1301.48 Public availability of transcripts and other documents.

(a) Public announcements of meetings pursuant to § 1301.44, written copies of votes to change the subject matter of meetings made pursuant to § 1301.44(c), written copies of votes to close meetings and explanations of such closings made pursuant to § 1301.45(c), and certifications of the General Counsel made pursuant to § 1301.45(d) shall be available for public inspection during regular business hours in the TVA Research Library, 400 W. Summit Hill Drive, Knoxville, Tennessee 37902–1401.

(b) TVA shall make promptly available to the public at the location described in paragraph (a) of this section the transcript, electronic recording, or minutes (as required by § 1301.47(b)) of the discussion of any item on the agenda, or of any item of the testimony of any witness received at the meeting, except for such item or items of such discussion or testimony as TVA determines to contain information which may be withheld under § 1301.46. Each request for such material shall be made to the Manager, Media Relations, Tennessee Valley Authority, Knoxville, Tennessee 37902–1499; state that it is a request for records pursuant to the Government in the Sunshine Act and this subpart; and reasonably describe the discussion or item of testimony, and the date of the meeting, with sufficient specificity to permit TVA to identify the item requested.

(c) In the event the person making a request under paragraph (b) of this section has reason to believe that all transcripts, electronic recordings, or minutes or portions thereof requested by that person and required to be made available under paragraph (b) of this section were not made available, the person shall make a written request to the Senior Manager, Media Relations, for such additional transcripts, electronic recordings, or minutes or portions thereof as that person believes should have been made available under paragraph (b) of this section and shall set forth in the request the reasons why such additional material is required to be made available with sufficient particularity for the Senior Manager, Media Relations, to determine the validity of such request. Promptly after a request pursuant to this paragraph is received, the Senior Manager, Media Relations, or his/her designee shall make a determination as to whether to comply with the request, and shall immediately give written notice of the determination to the person making the request. If the determination is to deny the request, the notice to the person making the request shall include a statement of the reasons for the denial, a notice of the right of the person making the request to appeal the denial to TVA's Senior Vice President, Communications, and the time limits thereof.

(d) If the determination pursuant to paragraph (c) of this section is to deny the request, the person making the request may appeal such denial to TVA's Senior Vice President, Communications. Such an appeal must be taken within 30 days after the person's receipt of the determination by the Senior Manager, Media Relations, and is taken by delivering a written notice of appeal to the Senior Vice President, Communications, Tennessee Valley Authority, Knoxville, Tennessee 37902–1401. Such notice shall include a statement that it is an appeal from a denial of a request under § 1301.48(c) and the Government in the Sunshine Act and shall indicate the date on which the denial was issued and the date on which the denial was received by the person making the request. Promptly after such an appeal is received, TVA's Senior Vice President, Communications, or the Senior Vice President's designee shall make a final determination on the appeal. In making such a determination, TVA will consider whether or not to waive the provisions of any exemption contained in § 1301.46. TVA shall immediately give written notice of the final determination to the person making the request. If the final determination on the appeal is to deny the request, the notice to the person making the request shall include a statement of the reasons for the denial and a notice of the person's right to judicial review of the determination.

(e) Copies of materials available for public inspection under this section shall be furnished to any person at the actual cost of duplication or transcription.

[42 FR 14086, Mar. 15, 1977. Redesignated at 44 FR 30682, May 29, 1979, and amended at 56 FR 55452, Oct. 28, 1991; 75 FR 11737, Mar. 12, 2010]

Subpart D—Testimony by TVA Employees, Production of Official Records, and Disclosure of Official Information in Legal Proceedings

SOURCE: 72 FR 60548, Oct. 25, 2007, unless otherwise noted.

§ 1301.51 Purpose and scope.

(a) *Purpose.* This part sets forth the procedures to be followed when TVA or a TVA employee is served with a demand to provide testimony and/or produce or disclose official information or records in a legal proceeding in which TVA or the United States is not a party, and where such appearance arises out of, or is related to, the individual's employment with TVA.

(b) *Scope.* This part applies when, in a judicial, administrative, legislative, or other legal proceeding, a TVA employee is served with a demand to provide testimony concerning information acquired in the course of performing official duties or because of official status and/or to produce official information and/or records.

§ 1301.52 Definitions.

The following definitions apply to this part:

(a) *Appearance* means testimony or production of documents or other material, including an affidavit, deposition, interrogatory, declaration, or other required written submission.

(b) *Demand* means a subpoena, order, or other demand of a court of competent jurisdiction, or other specific authority (e.g. an administrative or State legislative body), for the production, disclosure, or release of TVA records or information or for the appearance of TVA personnel as witnesses in their official capacities.

(c) *Employee* means any members of the Board of Directors, officials, officers, directors, employees or agents of TVA, except as TVA may otherwise determine in a particular case, and includes former TVA employees to the extent that the information sought was acquired in the performance of official duties for TVA.

(d) *General Counsel* means the General Counsel of TVA or a person to whom the General Counsel has delegated authority under this part.

(e) *Legal proceeding* means any and all pre-trial, trial, and post-trial stages of all judicial or administrative actions, hearings, investigations, or similar proceedings before courts, commissions, boards, or other judicial or quasi-judicial bodies or tribunals, whether criminal, civil, or administrative in nature.

(f) *Records* or *official records and information* means all information in the custody and control of TVA, relating to information in the custody and control of TVA, or acquired by a TVA employee in performance of his or her official duties or because of his or her official status while the individual was employed by TVA.

(g) *Testimony* means any written or oral statements, including depositions, answers to interrogatories, affidavits, declarations, interviews, and statements made by an individual in connection with a legal proceeding.

§ 1301.53   General.

(a) No employee shall appear, in response to a demand for official records or information, in any proceeding to which this part applies to provide testimony and/or produce records or other official information without prior authorization as set forth in this part.

(b) This part is intended only to provide procedures for responding to demands for testimony or production of records or other official information, and is not intended to, does not, and may not be relied upon to, create any right or benefit, substantive or procedural, enforceable by any party against TVA and the United States.

§ 1301.54   Requirements for a demand for records or testimony.

(a) *Service of demands.* Only TVA's General Counsel or his/her designee is authorized to receive and accept demands sought to be served upon TVA or its employees. All such documents should be delivered in person or by United States mail to the Office of the General Counsel, Tennessee Valley Authority, 400 W. Summit Hill Drive, Knoxville, Tennessee 37902.

(b) *Time limit for serving demands.* The demand must be served at least 30 days

prior to the scheduled date of testimony or disclosure of records, in order to ensure that the General Counsel has adequate time to consider the demand and prepare a response, except in cases of routine requests for personnel and payroll records located on-site in Knoxville, where service 15 days prior will normally be considered sufficient. The General Counsel may, upon request and for good cause shown, waive the requirement of this paragraph.

(c) *Form of Demand.* A demand for testimony or production of records or other official information must comply with the following requirements:

(1) The demand must be in writing and submitted to the General Counsel.

(2) The demand must include the following information:

(i) The caption of the legal proceeding, docket number, and name and address of the court or other authority involved.

(ii) If production or records or other official information is sought, a list of categories of records sought, a detailed description of how the information sought is relevant to the issues in the legal proceeding, and a specific description of the substance of the records sought.

(iii) If testimony is sought, a description of the intended use of the testimony, a detailed description of how the testimony sought is relevant to the issues in the legal proceeding, and a specific description of the substance of the testimony sought.

(iv) A statement as to how the need for the information outweighs any need to maintain the confidentiality of the information and outweighs the burden on TVA to produce the documents or testimony.

(v) A statement indicating that the information sought is not available from another source, from other persons or entities, or from the testimony of someone other than a TVA employee, such as a retained expert.

(vi) The name, address, and telephone number of counsel to each party in the case.

(d) *Additional information.* TVA reserves the right to require additional information to complete the request where appropriate or to waive any of the requirements of this section at its sole discretion.

§1301.55 Responding to demands.

Generally, authorization to provide the requested material or testimony shall not be withheld unless their disclosure is prohibited by law or for other compelling reasons, provided the request is reasonable and in compliance with the requirements of this part, and subject to the following conditions:

(a) *Demands for testimony.* TVA's practice is to provide requested testimony of TVA employees by affidavit only. TVA will provide affidavit testimony in response to demands for such testimony, provided all requirements of this part are met and there is no compelling factor under paragraph (c) of this section that requires the testimony to be withheld. The General Counsel may waive this restriction when necessary.

(b) *Demands for production of records or official information.* TVA's practice is to provide requested records or official information, provided all requirements of this part are met and there is no compelling factor under paragraph (c) of this section that requires the records or official information to be withheld.

(c) *Factors to be considered in determining whether requested testimony or records or official information must be withheld.* The General Counsel shall consider the following factors, among others, in deciding whether requested testimony or materials must be withheld:

(1) Whether production is appropriate in light of any relevant privilege;

(2) Whether production is appropriate under the applicable rules of discovery or the procedures governing the case or matter in which the demand arose;

(3) Whether the material requested is relevant to the matter at issue;

(4) Whether allowing such testimony or production of records would be necessary to prevent a miscarriage of justice;

(5) Whether disclosure would violate a statute, Executive Order, or regulation, including, but not limited to, the Privacy Act of 1974, as amended, 5 U.S.C. 552a;

(6) Whether disclosure would impede or interfere with an ongoing law enforcement investigation or proceeding, or compromise constitutional rights or national security interests;

(7) Whether disclosure would improperly reveal trade secrets or proprietary confidential information without the owner's consent;

(8) Whether disclosure would unduly interfere with the orderly conduct of TVA's functions;

(9) Whether the records or testimony can be obtained from other sources;

(10) Whether disclosure would result in TVA appearing to favor one litigant over another;

(11) Whether the demand or request is within the authority of the party making it; and

(12) Whether a substantial Government interest is implicated.

(d) *Restrictions on testimony or production of records or official information.* When necessary or appropriate, the General Counsel may impose restrictions or conditions on the production of testimony or records or official information. These restrictions may include, but are not limited to:

(1) Limiting the area of testimony;

(2) Requiring that the requester and other parties to the legal proceeding agree to keep the testimony under seal;

(3) Requiring that the testimony be used or made available only in the legal proceeding for which it was requested;

(4) Requiring that the parties to the legal proceeding obtain a protective order or execute a confidentiality agreement to limit access and any further disclosure of produced records or official information.

(e) *Fees for Production.* Fees will be charged for production of TVA records and information. The fees will be the same as those charged by TVA pursuant to its Freedom of Information Act regulations, 16 CFR 1301.10.

§1301.56 Final determination.

The General Counsel makes the final determination whether a demand for testimony or production of records or official testimony in a legal proceeding in which TVA is not a party shall be granted. All final determinations are within the sole discretion of the General Counsel. The General Counsel will notify the requesting party and, when necessary, the court or other authority of the final determination, the reasons for the grant or denial of the request, and any conditions that the General Counsel may impose on the production of testimony or records or official information.

§ 1301.57 Waiver.

The General Counsel may grant a waiver of any procedure described by this part where a waiver is considered necessary to promote a significant interest of TVA or the United States, or for other good cause.

Subpart E—Protection of National Security Classified Information

SOURCE: 76 FR 39261, July 6, 2011, unless otherwise noted.

§ 1301.61 Purpose and scope.

(a) *Purpose.* These regulations, taken together with the Information Security Oversight Office's implementing directive at 32 CFR part 2001, Classified National Security Information, provide the basis for TVA's security classification program implementing Executive Order 13526, "Classified National Security Information," as amended ("the Executive Order").

(b) *Scope.* These regulations apply to TVA employees, contractors, and individuals who serve in advisory, consultant, or non-employee affiliate capacities who have been granted access to classified information.

§ 1301.62 Definitions.

The following definitions apply to this part:

(a) "Original classification" is the initial determination that certain information requires protection against unauthorized disclosure in the interest of national security (i.e., national defense or foreign relations of the United States), together with a designation of the level of classification.

(b) "Classified national security information" or "classified information" means information that has been determined pursuant to Executive Order

13526 or any predecessor order to require protection against unauthorized disclosure and is marked to indicate its classified status when in documentary form.

§ 1301.63 Senior agency official.

(a) The Executive Order requires that each agency that originates or handles classified information designate a senior agency official to direct and administer its information security program. TVA's senior agency official is the Director, Enterprise Information Security & Policy.

(b) Questions with respect to the Information Security Program, particularly those concerning the classification, declassification, downgrading, and safeguarding of classified information, shall be directed to the Senior Agency Official.

§ 1301.64 Original classification authority.

(a) Original classification authority is granted by the Director of the Information Security Oversight Office. TVA does not have original classification authority.

(b) If information is developed that appears to require classification, or is received from any foreign government information as defined in section 6.1(s) of Executive Order 13526, the individual in custody of the information shall immediately notify the Senior Agency Official and appropriately protect the information.

(c) If the Senior Agency Official believes the information warrants classification, it shall be sent to the appropriate agency with original classification authority over the subject matter, or to the Information Security Oversight Office, for review and a classification determination.

(d) If there is reasonable doubt about the need to classify information, it shall be safeguarded as if it were classified pending a determination by an original classification authority. If there is reasonable doubt about the appropriate level of classification, it shall be safeguarded at the higher level of classification pending a determination by an original classification authority.

§1301.65 Derivative classification.

(a) In accordance with Part 2 of Executive Order 13526 and directives of the Information Security Oversight Office, the incorporation, paraphrasing, restating or generation in new form of information that is already classified, and the marking of newly developed material consistent with the classification markings that apply to the source information, is derivative classification.

(1) Derivative classification includes the classification of information based on classification guidance.

(2) The duplication or reproduction of existing classified information is not derivative classification.

(b) Authorized individuals applying derivative classification markings shall:

(1) Observe and respect original classification decisions; and

(2) Carry forward to any newly created documents the pertinent classification markings.

(3) For information derivatively classified based on multiple sources, the authorized individuals shall carry forward:

(i) The date or event for declassification that corresponds to the longest period of classification among the sources; and

(ii) A listing of these sources on or attached to the official file or record copy.

(c) Documents classified derivatively shall bear all markings prescribed by 32 CFR 2001.20 through 2001.23 and shall otherwise conform to the requirements of 32 CFR 2001.20 through 2001.23.

§1301.66 General declassification and downgrading policy.

(a) TVA does not have original classification authority.

(b) TVA personnel may not declassify information originally classified by other agencies.

§1301.67 Mandatory review for declassification.

(a) Reviews and referrals in response to requests for mandatory declassification shall be conducted in compliance with section 3.5 of Executive Order 13526, 32 CFR 2001.33, and 32 CFR 2001.34.

(b) Any individual may request a review of classified information and material in possession of TVA for declassification. All information classified under Executive Order 13526 or a predecessor Order shall be subject to a review for declassification by TVA, if:

(1) The request describes the documents or material containing the information with sufficient specificity to enable TVA to locate it with a reasonable amount of effort. Requests with insufficient description of the material will be returned to the requester for further information.

(2) The information requested is not the subject of pending litigation.

(c) Requests shall be in writing, and shall be sent to: Director, Enterprise Information Security & Policy, Tennessee Valley Authority, 1101 Market St., Chattanooga, TN 37402.

§1301.68 Identification and marking.

(a) Classified information shall be marked pursuant to the standards set forth in section 1.6, Identification and Marking, of the Executive Order; Information Security Oversight Office implementing directives in 32 CFR part 2001, subpart B; and internal TVA procedures.

(b) Foreign government information shall retain its original classification markings or be marked and classified at a U.S. classification level that provides a degree of protection at least equivalent to that required by the entity that furnished the information. Foreign government information retaining its original classification markings need not be assigned a U.S. classification marking provided the responsible agency determines that the foreign government markings are adequate to meet the purposes served by U.S. classification markings.

(c) Information assigned a level of classification under predecessor executive orders shall be considered as classified at that level of classification.

§1301.69 Safeguarding classified information.

(a) All classified information shall be afforded a level of protection against unauthorized disclosure commensurate with its level of classification.

(b) The Executive Order and the Information Security Oversight Office implementing directive provides information on the protection of classified information. Specific controls on the use, processing, storage, reproduction, and transmittal of classified information within TVA to provide protection for such information and to prevent access by unauthorized persons are contained in internal TVA procedures.

(c) Any person who discovers or believes that a classified document is lost or compromised shall immediately report the circumstances to their supervisor and the Senior Agency Official, who shall conduct an immediate inquiry into the matter.

PART 1302—NONDISCRIMINATION IN FEDERALLY ASSISTED PROGRAMS OF TVA—EFFECTUATION OF TITLE VI OF THE CIVIL RIGHTS ACT OF 1964

AUTHORITY: TVA Act, 48 Stat. 58 (1933) as amended, 16 U.S.C. 831–831dd, and sec. 602 of the Civil Rights Act of 1964, 78 Stat. 252, 42 U.S.C. 2000d–1.

SOURCE: 30 FR 311, Jan. 9, 1965, unless otherwise noted. Redesignated at 44 FR 30682, May 29, 1979.

§ 1302.1   Purpose.

The purpose of this part is to effectuate the provisions of Title VI of the Civil Rights Act 1964 (hereafter referred to as the "Act") to the end that no person in the United States shall, on the ground of race, color, or national origin, be excluded from participation in, be denied the benefits of, or be otherwise subjected to discrimination under any program or activity receiving financial assistance from TVA.

§ 1302.2   Application of this part.

This part applies to any program for which financial assistance is provided by TVA. The types of Federal financial assistance to which this part applies are listed in appendix A of this part. Financial assistance, as used in this part, includes the grant or loan of money; the donation of real or personal property; the sale, lease, or license of real or personal property for a consideration which is nominal or reduced for the purpose of assisting the recipient; the waiver of charges which would normally be made, in order to assist the recipient; the entry into a contract where a purpose is to give financial assistance to the contracting party; and similar transactions. This part does not apply to:

(a) Any financial assistance by way of insurance or guaranty contracts,

(b) Money paid, property transferred, or other assistance extended before the effective date of this part,

(c) Any assistance to any individual who is the ultimate beneficiary, or

(d) Any employment practice, under any such program, of any employer, employment agency, or labor organization, unless such practice exists in a program where a primary objective of the TVA financial assistance is to provide employment; or where such practice subjects persons to discrimination in the provision of services and benefits on the grounds of race, color, or national origin in a program or activity receiving Federal financial assistance from TVA.

The fact that a type of Federal financial assistance is not listed in appendix A shall not mean, if Title VI of the Act is otherwise applicable, that a program is not covered. Other types of Federal financial assistance may be added to this list by notice published in the FEDERAL REGISTER.

[30 FR 311, Jan. 9, 1965. Redesignated at 44 FR 30682, May 29, 1979, and amended at 49 FR 20481, May 15, 1984; 68 FR 51355, Aug. 26, 2003]

§1302.3 Definitions.

(a) *TVA* as used in these regulations, refers to the Tennessee Valley Authority, as created by the Tennessee Valley Authority Act of 1933, 48 Stat. 58, *as amended*, 16 U.S.C. 831–831dd. *See also* paragraph (e) of §1302.6.

(b) *Recipient* refers to any person, group, or other entity which either receives financial assistance from TVA, or which has been denied such assistance.

(c) *Assistant Attorney General* refers to the Assistant Attorney General, Civil Rights Division, Department of Justice.

(d) *Title VI* refers to Title VI of the Civil Rights Act of 1964, 42 U.S.C. 2000d, *et seq.*

(e) *Program or activity* and *program* refer to all of the operations of any entity described in paragraphs (e)(1) through (4) of this section, any part of which is extended Federal financial assistance:

(1)(i) A department, agency, special purpose district, or other instrumentality of a State or of a local government; or

(ii) The entity of such State or local government that distributes such assistance and each such department or agency (and each other State or local government entity) to which the assistance is extended, in the case of assistance to a State or local government;

(2)(i) A college, university, or other postsecondary institution, or a public system of higher education; or

(ii) A local educational agency (as defined in 20 U.S.C. 7801), system of vocational education, or other school system;

(3)(i) An entire corporation, partnership, or other private organization, or an entire sole proprietorship—

(A) If assistance is extended to such corporation, partnership, private organization, or sole proprietorship as a whole; or

(B) Which is principally engaged in the business of providing education, health care, housing, social services, or parks and recreation; or

(ii) The entire plant or other comparable, geographically separate facility to which Federal financial assistance is extended, in the case of any other corporation, partnership, private organization, or sole proprietorship; or

(4) Any other entity which is established by two or more of the entities described in paragraph (e)(1), (2), or (3) of this section.

[49 FR 20481, May 15, 1984; 49 FR 47383, Dec. 4, 1984, as amended at 68 FR 51355, Aug. 26, 2003]

§1302.4 Discrimination prohibited.

(a) *General.* No person in the United States shall, on the ground of race, color, or national origin, be excluded from participation in, be denied the benefits of, or be otherwise subjected to discrimination under any program or activity receiving Federal financial assistance from TVA. For the purposes of this part, the following definitions of race and ethnic group apply:

(1) *Black, not of Hispanic origin.* A person having origins in any of the black racial groups of Africa;

(2) *Hispanic.* A person of Mexican, Puerto Rican, Cuban, Central or South American, or other Spanish culture or origin, regardless of race;

(3) *Asian or Pacific Islander.* A person having origin in any of the original peoples of the Far East, Southeast Asia, the Indian Subcontinent, or the Pacific Islands. This area includes, for example, China, Japan, Korea, the Philippine Islands, and Samoa;

(4) *American Indian or Alaskan Native.* A person having origins in any of the original peoples of North America, and who maintains cultural identification through tribal affiliation or community recognition;

(5) *White, not of Hispanic origin.* A person having origins in any of the original peoples of Europe, North Africa, or the Middle East.

Additional subcategories based on national origin or primary language spoken may be used where appropriate.

(b) *Specific discriminatory actions prohibited.* (1) A recipient receiving Federal financial assistance from TVA may not, directly or through contractual or other arrangements, on ground of race, color, or national origin:

(i) Deny an individual any service, financial aid, or other benefit provided under the program;

(ii) Provide any service, financial aid or other benefit to an individual which is different, or is provided in a different manner, from that provided to others under the program;

(iii) Subject an individual to segregation or separate treatment in any manner related to that individual's receipt of any service, financial aid, or other benefit under the program;

(iv) Restrict an individual in any way in the enjoyment of any advantage or privilege enjoyed by others receiving any service, financial aid, or other benefit under the program;

(v) Treat an individual differently from others in determining whether any admission, enrollment, quota, eligibility, membership, or other requirement or condition which individuals must meet in order to be provided any service, financial aid, or other benefit provided under the program has been satisfied.

(vi) Deny an individual an opportunity to participate in the program through the provision of services or otherwise or afford that individual an opportunity to do so which is different from that afforded others under the program.

(2) A recipient, in determining the types of services, financial aid, or other benefits, or facilities which will be provided under any such program, or the class of individuals to whom, or the situations in which, such services, financial aid, other benefits, or facilities will be provided under any such program, or the class of individuals to be afforded an opportunity to participate in any such program, may not, directly or through contractual or other arrangements, utilize criteria or methods of administration which have the effect of subjecting individuals to discrimination because of their race, color, or national origin, or have the effect of defeating or substantially impairing accomplishment of the objectives of the program as respect individuals of a particular race, color, or national origin.

(3) In determining the site or location of facilities, a recipient may not make selections with the purpose or effect of excluding individuals from, denying them the benefits of, or subjecting them to discrimination under any program to which this regulation applies, on the grounds of race, color, or national origin; or with the purpose or effect of defeating or substantially

impairing the accomplishment of the objectives of the Act or this regulation.

(4) As used in this section the services, financial aid, or other benefits provided under a program receiving financial assistance shall be deemed to include any service, financial aid, or other benefit provided in or through a facility provided with the aid of the financial assistance.

(5) The enumeration of specific forms of prohibited discrimination in this paragraph does not limit the generality of the prohibition in paragraph (a) of this section.

(6) This regulation does not prohibit the consideration of race, color, or national origin if the purpose and effect are to remove or overcome the consequences of practices or impediments which have restricted the availability of, or participation in, the program or activity receiving Federal financial assistance, on the grounds of race, color, or national origin. Where previous discriminatory practice or usage tends, on the grounds of race, color, or national origin, to exclude individuals from participation in, to deny them the benefits of, or to subject them to discrimination under any program or activity to which this regulation applies, the recipient has an obligation to take reasonable action to remove or overcome the consequences of the prior discriminatory practice or usage, and to accomplish the purposes of the Act.

[30 FR 311, Jan. 9, 1965, as amended at 38 FR 17944, July 5, 1973. Redesignated at 44 FR 30682, May 29, 1979. Redesignated and amended at 49 FR 20481, May 15, 1984; 68 FR 51355, Aug. 26, 2003]

§ 1302.5 Assurances required.

(a) TVA contributes financial assistance only under agreements which contain a provision which specifically requires compliance with this part in programs or activities receiving Federal financial assistance from TVA. If the financial assistance involves the furnishing of real property, the agreement shall obligate the recipient, or in the case of a subsequent transfer, the transferee, for the period during which the real property is used for a purpose for which the financial assistance is extended or for another purpose involving the provision of similar services or benefits. Where the financial assistance involves the furnishing of personal property, the agreement shall obligate the recipient for the period during which the recipient retains ownership or possession of the property. In all other cases the agreement shall obligate the recipient for the period during which financial assistance is extended pursuant to the agreement. TVA shall specify the form of the foregoing agreements, and the extent to which an agreement shall be applicable to subgrantees, contractors and subcontractors, transferees, successors in interest, and other participants.

(b) In the case of real property, structures or improvements thereon, or interests therein, which is acquired with Federal financial assistance, or in the case where Federal financial assistance is provided in the form of a transfer by TVA of real property or interest therein, the instrument effecting or recording the transfer of title shall contain a covenant running with the land assuring nondiscrimination for the period during which the real property is used for a purpose for which the Federal financial assistance is extended or for another purpose involving the provision of similar services or benefits. Where no transfer of property is involved, but property is improved with Federal financial assistance, the recipient shall agree to include such a covenant in any subsequent transfer of such property. Where the property is obtained by transfer from TVA, the covenant against discrimination may also include a condition coupled with a right to be reserved by TVA to revert title to the property in the event of a breach of the covenant where, in the discretion of TVA, such a condition and right of reverter is appropriate to the statute under which the real property is obtained and to the nature of the grant and the grantee. In such event if a transferee of real property proposes to mortgage or otherwise encumber the real property as security for financing construction of new, or improvement of existing, facilities on such property for the purposes for which the property was transferred, TVA may agree, upon request of the transferee and if necessary to accomplish such financing, and upon such

conditions as it deems appropriate, to forbear the exercise of such right to revert title for so long as the lien of such mortgage or other encumbrance remains effective.

[30 FR 311, Jan. 9, 1965, as amended at 38 FR 17944, July 5, 1973. Redesignated at 44 FR 30682, May 29, 1979. Redesignated and amended at 49 FR 20481, May 15, 1984; 68 FR 51355, Aug. 26, 2003]

§1302.6 **Compliance information.**

(a) *Cooperation and assistance.* TVA shall to the fullest extent practicable seek the cooperation of recipients in obtaining compliance with this part and shall provide assistance and guidance to recipients to help them comply voluntarily with this part.

(b) *Compliance reports.* Each recipient shall keep such records and submit to TVA timely, complete and accurate compliance reports at such times, and in such form and containing such information, as TVA may determined to be necessary to enable it to ascertain whether the recipient has complied or is complying with this part. In the case in which a primary recipient extends Federal financial assistance to any other recipient, such other recipient shall also submit such compliance reports to the primary recipient as may be necessary to enable the primary recipient to carry out its obligations under this part.

(c) *Access to sources of information.* Each recipient shall permit access by TVA during normal business hours to such of its books, records, accounts, and other sources of information, and its facilities as may be pertinent to ascertain compliance with this part. Where any information required of a recipient is in the exclusive possession of any other agency, institution or person and this agency, institution or person shall fail or refuse to furnish this information, the recipient shall so certify in its report and shall set forth what efforts it has made to obtain the information.

(d) *Information to beneficiaries and participants.* Each recipient shall make available to participants, beneficiaries, and other interested persons such information regarding the provisions of this part and its applicability to the program for which the recipient receives financial assistance, and make such information available to them in such manner as TVA finds necessary to apprise such persons of the protections against discrimination assured them by the Act and this part.

(Information collection requirements appearing in § 1302.6 were approved by the Office of Management and Budget under control number 3316–0077)

[30 FR 311, Jan. 9, 1965. Redesignated at 44 FR 30682, May 29, 1979. Redesignated at 49 FR 20481, May 15, 1984, and amended at 51 FR 9649, Mar. 20, 1986; 68 FR 51355, Aug. 26, 2003]

§ 1302.7 Compliance reviews and conduct of investigations.

(a) *Preaward compliance reviews.* (1) Prior to approval of financial assistance, TVA will make a determination as to whether the proposed recipient is in compliance with Title VI and the requirements of this part with respect to a program or activity for which it is seeking Federal financial assistance from TVA. The basis for such a determination shall be submission of an assurance of compliance and a review of the data and information submitted by the proposed recipient, any relevant compliance review reports on file with TVA, and any other information available to TVA. Where a determination cannot be made from this data, TVA will require the submission of necessary additional information and may take additional steps. Such additional steps may include, for example, communicating with local government officials, protected class organizations, and onsite reviews.

(2) No proposed recipient shall be approved unless it is determined that the proposed recipient is in compliance with Title VI and this part or has agreed in writing to take necessary specified steps within a stated period of time to come into compliance with Title VI and this part. Such an agreement must be approved by TVA and made a part of the conditions of the agreement under which the financial assistance is provided.

(3)(i) Where TVA finds that a proposed recipient may not be in compliance with Title VI and this part, TVA shall notify the proposed recipient and the Assistant Attorney General for Civil Rights in writing of:

(A) The preliminary findings setting forth the alleged noncompliance;

(B) Suggested actions for correcting the alleged noncompliance; and

(C) The fact that the proposed recipient has 10 days to correct the alleged noncompliance or to provide during this time a written submission responding to or rebutting the preliminary findings or suggested corrective actions set forth in the notice.

(ii) If within this 10-day period the proposed recipient has not agreed to the suggested actions set forth or to other actions that would correct the alleged noncompliance under paragraph (a)(3)(i)(B) of this section, or the preliminary findings set forth in paragraph (a)(3)(i)(A) of this section have not been rebutted to TVA's satisfaction, or voluntary compliance has not been otherwise secured, TVA shall make a formal determination of compliance or noncompliance, notify the proposed recipient, and the Assistant Attorney General for Civil Rights and institute proceedings (including provision of an opportunity for a hearing) under § 1302.8 of this part.

(b) *Postaward compliance reviews.* (1) TVA may periodically conduct compliance reviews of selected recipients in their programs or activities receiving TVA financial assistance, including the request of data and information, and may conduct onsite reviews where it has reason to believe that discrimination may be occurring in such programs or activities.

(2) Selection for review shall be made on the basis of the following criteria among others:

(i) The number and nature of discrimination complaints filed against a recipient with TVA or other Federal agencies;

(ii) The scope of the problem revealed by an investigation commenced on the basis of a complaint filed with TVA against a recipient; and

(iii) The amount of assistance provided to the recipient.

(3) Within 15 days after selection of a recipient for review, TVA shall inform the recipient that it has been selected for review. The review will ordinarily be initiated by a letter requesting data

pertinent to the review and advising the recipient of:

(i) The practices to be reviewed;

(ii) The programs or activities affected by the review;

(iii) The opportunity to make, at any time prior to receipt of the final TVA findings with respect to the review pursuant to paragraph (b)(6) of this section, a documentary submission responding to TVA which explains, validates, or otherwise addresses the practices under review; and

(iv) The schedule under which the review will be conducted and a determination of compliance or noncompliance made.

(4) Within 180 days of initiation of a review, TVA shall advise the recipient, in writing of:

(i) Its preliminary findings;

(ii) Where appropriate, recommendations for achieving voluntary compliance;

(iii) The opportunity to request TVA to engage in voluntary compliance negotiations prior to TVA's final determination of compliance or noncompliance. TVA shall notify the Assistant Attorney General at the time it notifies the recipient of any matter where recommendations for achieving voluntary compliance are made.

(5) TVA's General Manager may extend the 180-day period set out in paragraph (b)(4) of this section for good cause shown.

(6) If, within 50 days of the recipient's notification under paragraph (b)(4) of this section, TVA's recommendations for compliance are not met or voluntary compliance is not secured, and the preliminary findings have not been rebutted to TVA's satisfaction, TVA shall make a final determination of compliance or noncompliance. The determination is to be made no later than 14 days after the conclusion of the 50-day negotiation period. TVA's General Manager may extend the 14-day period for good cause shown.

(7) Where TVA makes a formal determination of noncompliance on a postaward review, the recipient and the Assistant Attorney General shall be immediately notified in writing of the determination and of the fact that the recipient has an additional 10 days in which to come into voluntary compli-

ance. If voluntary compliance has not been achieved within the 10 days, TVA shall institute proceedings under § 1302.8 of this part.

(8) All agreements to come into voluntary compliance shall be in writing and signed by TVA and an official who has authority to legally bind the recipient.

(c) *Complaint investigation.* (1) TVA shall investigate complaints of discrimination in a program or activity receiving Federal financial assistance from TVA that allege a violation of Title VI or this part.

(2) No complaint will be investigated if it is received by TVA more than 180 days after the date of the alleged discrimination unless the time for filing is extended by TVA for good cause shown. Where a complaint is accepted for investigation, TVA will initiate an investigation. The complainant shall be notified in writing as to whether the complaint has been accepted or rejected.

(3) TVA shall conduct investigations of complaints as follows:

(i) Within 10 days of receipt of a complaint, the Director of Equal Opportunity Compliance shall:

(A) Determine whether TVA has jurisdiction under paragraphs (c) (1) and (2) of this section;

(B) If jurisdiction is not found, wherever possible refer the complaint to the Federal agency with such jurisdiction and advise the complainant;

(C) If jurisdiction is found, notify the recipient alleged to be in violation of the receipt and acceptance of the complaint; and

(D) Initiate the investigation.

(ii) The investigation will ordinarily be initiated by a letter to the recipient requesting data pertinent to the complaint and informing the recipient of:

(A) The nature of the complaint, and with the written consent of the complainant, the identity of the complainant;

(B) The programs or activities affected by the complaint;

(C) The opportunity to make, at any time prior to receipt of TVA's final findings under paragraph (c)(5) of this section, a documentary submission, responding to, rebutting, or denying the allegations made in the complaint; and

(D) The schedule under which the complaint will be investigated and a determination of compliance or noncompliance made.

(iii) Within 180 days of the initiation of a complaint investigation, TVA shall advise the recipient, in writing, of:

(A) Preliminary findings;

(B) Where appropriate, recommendations for achieving voluntary compliance; and

(C) The opportunity to request TVA to engage in voluntary compliance negotiations prior to TVA's final determination of compliance or noncompliance. TVA shall notify the Assistant Attorney General at the time the recipient is notified of any matter where recommendations for achieving voluntary compliance are made.

(4) If, within 50 days of the recipient's notification under paragraph (c) of this section, TVA's recommendations for compliance are not met, or voluntary compliance is not secured, and the preliminary findings have not been rebutted to TVA's satisfaction, TVA shall make a formal determination of compliance or noncompliance. The determination is to be made no later than 14 days after conclusion of a 50-day negotiation period. TVA's General Manager may extend the 14-day period for good cause shown.

(5) Where TVA makes a formal determination of noncompliance, the complainant, the recipient, and the Assistant Attorney General shall be immediately notified in writing of the determination and of the fact that the recipient has an additional 10 days in which to come into compliance. If voluntary compliance has not been achieved within the 10 days, TVA shall institute proceedings under § 1302.8 of this part. The complainant shall also be notified of any action taken including the closing of the complaint or the achievement of voluntary compliance. All agreements to come into voluntary compliance shall be in writing and signed by TVA and an official who has authority to legally bind the recipient and shall be made available to the complainant on request.

(6) If the complainant or party other than TVA has filed suit in Federal or State court alleging the same discrimination as alleged in a complaint pending before TVA, and if during TVA's investigation the trial of that suit would be in progress, TVA will consult with the Assistant Attorney General and court records to determine the need to continue or suspend the investigation and will monitor the litigation through the court docket and contacts with the complainant. Upon receipt of notice that the court has made a finding of discrimination against a recipient that would constitute a violation of this part, TVA shall institute proceedings as specified in § 1302.8 of this part. All agreements to come into voluntary compliance shall be in writing and signed by TVA and an official who has authority to legally bind the recipient.

(7) The time limits listed in paragraphs (c) (3) through (5) of this section shall be appropriately adjusted where TVA requests another Federal agency to act on the complaint. TVA shall monitor the progress of the matter through liaison with the other agency. Where the request to act does not result in timely resolution of the matter, TVA shall institute appropriate proceedings as required by this part.

(d) *Intimidatory or retaliatory acts prohibited.* No recipient or other person shall intimidate, threaten, coerce, or discriminate against any individual for the purpose of interfering with any right or privilege secured by section 601 of Title VI or this part, or because such individual has made a complaint, testified, assisted, or participated in any manner in an investigation, proceeding, or hearing under this part. The identity of complainants shall be kept confidential except to the extent necessary to carry out the purposes of this regulation, including the conduct of any investigation, hearing, or judicial proceeding arising thereunder.

(e) *Enforcement authority.* TVA's Director of Equal Opportunity Compliance, or a successor as designated by TVA's Board of Directors, will be responsible for all decisions about initiating compliance reviews and complaint investigations. TVA's General Manager, or a successor as designated by TVA's Board of Directors, shall be responsible for all decisions about initiating compliance actions under §1302.8(a) of this part.

(Information collection requirements appearing in §1302.7 were approved by the Office of Management and Budget under control number 3316–0077)

[49 FR 20481, May 15, 1984, as amended at 49 FR 47383, Dec. 4, 1984; 51 FR 9649, Mar. 20, 1986; 68 FR 51355, Aug. 26, 2003]

§1302.8 Procedure for effecting compliance.

(a) *General.* If there appears to be a failure or threatened failure to comply with this part, and if the noncompliance or threatened noncompliance cannot be corrected by informal means, compliance with this regulation may be effected by the suspension or termination of or refusal to grant or to continue financial assistance or by any other means authorized by law. Such other means may include, but are not limited to,

(1) A reference to the Department of Justice with a recommendation that appropriate proceedings be brought to enforce any rights of the United States under any law of the United States (including other titles of the Act),

(2) Institution of appropriate proceedings by TVA to enforce the provisions of the agreement of financial assistance or of any deed or instrument relating thereto, and

(3) Any applicable proceeding under State or local law.

The Assistant Attorney General, Civil Rights Division, Department of Justice, will be notified of all findings of probable noncompliance at the same time the recipient or applicant is notified.

(b) *Noncompliance with §1302.5.* If anyone requesting financial assistance declines to furnish the assurance required under §1302.5 of this part, or otherwise fails or refuses to comply with a requirement imposed by or pursuant to that section, financial assistance may be refused in accordance with the procedures of paragraph (c) of this section and for such purposes, the term "recipient" shall be deemed to include one which has been denied financial assistance. TVA shall not be required to provide assistance in such a case during the pendency of the administrative proceedings under such paragraph except that TVA shall continue assistance during the pendency of such proceedings where such assistance is due and payable pursuant to an agreement therefor entered into with TVA prior to the effective date of this part.

(c) *Termination of or refusal to grant or to continue financial assistance.* No order suspending, terminating or refusing to grant or continue financial assistance shall become effective until (1) TVA has advised the recipient of his failure to comply and has determined that compliance cannot be secured by voluntary means, (2) there has been an express finding on the record, after opportunity for hearing, or a failure by the recipient to comply with a requirement imposed by or pursuant to this part, (3) the action has been approved by the TVA Board pursuant to §1302.9, and (4) the expiration of 30 days after the TVA Board has filed with the committee of the House and the committee of the Senate having legislative jurisdiction over the program involved, a full written report of the circumstances and the grounds for such action. Any action to suspend or terminate or to refuse to grant or to continue financial assistance shall be limited to the particular political entity, or part thereof, or recipient as to whom such a finding has been made and shall be limited in its effect to the particular program, or part thereof, in which such noncompliance has been so found.

(d) *Other means authorized by law.* No action to effect compliance by any other means authorized by law shall be taken until (1) TVA has determined that compliance cannot be secured by voluntary means, (2) the recipient or other person has been notified of its failure to comply and of the action to be taken to effect compliance, and (3) the expiration of at least 10 days from the mailing of such notice to the recipient or other person. During this period of at least 10 days additional efforts shall be made to persuade the recipient or other person to comply with the regulation and to take such corrective action as may be appropriate.

[30 FR 311, Jan. 9, 1965, as amended at 38 FR 17945, July 5, 1973. Redesignated at 44 FR 30682, May 29, 1979. Redesignated and amended at 49 FR 20483, May 15, 1984; 49 FR 47384, Dec. 4, 1984]

§ 1302.9 Hearings.

(a) *Opportunity for hearing.* Whenever an opportunity for a hearing is required by § 1302.7(b), reasonable notice shall be given by registered or certified mail, return receipt requested, to the affected recipient. This notice shall advise the recipient of the action proposed to be taken, the specific provision under which the proposed action against it is to be taken, and the matters of fact or law asserted as the basis for this action, and either (1) fix a date not less than 20 days after the date of such notice within which the recipient may request of TVA that the matter be scheduled for hearing or (2) advise the recipient that the matter in question has been set down for hearing at a stated time and place. The time and place so fixed shall be reasonable and shall be subject to change for cause. The complainant, if any, shall be advised of the time and place of the hearing. A recipient may waive a hearing and submit written information and argument for the record. The failure of a recipient to request a hearing under this subsection or to appear at a hearing for which a date has been set shall be deemed to be a waiver of the right to a hearing under section 602 of the Act and § 1302.7(b) and consent to the making of a decision on the basis of such information as is available.

(b) *Time and place of hearing.* Hearings shall be held at the time and place fixed by TVA unless it determines that the convenience of the recipient requires that another place be selected. Hearings shall be held before the TVA Board, or a member thereof, or, at the discretion of the Board, before a hearing examiner designated in accordance with section 11 of the Administrative Procedure Act.

(c) *Right to counsel.* In all proceedings under this section, the recipient and TVA shall have the right to be represented by counsel.

(d) *Procedures, evidence, and record.* (1) The hearing, decision, and any administrative review thereof shall be conducted in conformity with the procedures contained in 5 U.S.C. 554–557 (sections 5–8 of the Administrative Procedure Act) and in accordance with such rules of procedure as are proper (and not inconsistent with this section) relating to the conduct of the hearing, giving of notices subsequent to those provided for in paragraph (a) of this section, taking of testimony, exhibits, arguments and briefs, requests for findings, and other related matters. Both TVA and the recipient shall be entitled to introduce all relevant evidence on the issues as stated in the notice for hearing or as determined by the officer conducting the hearing at the outset of or during the hearing.

(2) Technical rules of evidence shall not apply to hearings conducted pursuant to this part, but rules or principles designed to assure production of the most credible evidence available and to subject testimony to test by cross-examination shall be applied where reasonably necessary by the officer conducting the hearing. The hearing officer may exclude irrelevant, immaterial, or unduly repetitious evidence. All documents and other evidence offered or taken for the record shall be open to examination by the parties and opportunity shall be given to refute facts and arguments advanced on either side of the issues. A transcript shall be made of the oral evidence except to the extent the substance thereof is stipulated for the record. All decisions shall be based upon the hearing record and written findings shall be made.

(e) *Consolidated or Joint Hearings.* In cases in which the same or related facts are asserted to constitute noncompliance with this part with respect to two or more Federal statutes, authorities, or other means by which Federal financial assistance is extended and to which this part applies, or noncompliance with this part and the regulations of one or more other Federal departments or agencies issued under Title VI of the Act, the TVA Board may, by agreement with such other departments or agencies where applicable, provide for the conduct of consolidated or joint hearings, and for the application to such hearings of rules of procedure not inconsistent with this part. Final decisions in such cases, insofar as this part is concerned, shall be made in accordance with §1302.9.

[30 FR 311, Jan. 9, 1965, as amended at 38 FR 17945, July 5, 1973. Redesignated at 44 FR 30682, May 29, 1979, and 49 FR 20483, May 15, 1984; 68 FR 51355, Aug. 26, 2003]

§1302.10 Decisions and notices.

(a) *Decision by a member of the TVA Board or a hearing examiner.* A member of the TVA Board or a hearing examiner who holds the hearing shall either make an initial decision or certify the entire record, including the Board member's or examiner's recommended findings and proposed decision, to the TVA Board for a final decision. A copy of such initial decision or certification shall be mailed to the recipient. Where the initial decision is made by a member of the TVA Board or a hearing examiner, the recipient may file exceptions to the initial decision, together with a statement of reasons therefor. Such exceptions and statement shall be filed with the TVA Board within 30 days of the date the notice of initial decision was mailed to the recipient. In the absence of exceptions, the TVA Board may on its own motion within 45 days after the initial decision serve on the recipient a notice that the TVA Board will review the decision. Upon the filing of such exceptions or of such notice of review, the TVA Board shall review the initial decision and issue its own decision thereon including the reasons therefor. In the absence of either exceptions or a notice of review, the initial decision shall constitute the final decision of the TVA Board.

(b) *Decisions on record or review by the TVA Board.* Whenever a record is certified to the TVA Board for decision or it reviews the decision of a member of the TVA Board or a hearing examiner pursuant to paragraph (a) of this section, or whenever the TVA Board conducts the hearing, the recipient shall be given reasonable opportunity to file with the Board briefs or other written statements of its contentions, and a copy of the final decision of the Board shall be given in writing to the recipient and to the complainant, if any.

(c) *Decisions on record where a hearing is waived.* Whenever a hearing is waived pursuant to §1302.8(a) a decision shall be made by the TVA Board on the record and a copy of such decision shall be given to the recipient, and to the complainant, if any.

(d) *Rulings required.* Each decision shall set forth a ruling on each finding, conclusion, or exception presented, and shall identify the requirement or requirements imposed by or pursuant to this part with which it is found that the recipient has failed to comply.

(e) *Approval by TVA Board.* Any final decision (other than a decision by the TVA Board) which provides for the suspension or termination of, or the refusal to grant or continue financial assistance, or the imposition of any other sanction available under this regulation or the Act, shall promptly be transmitted to the TVA Board, which may approve such decision, may vacate it, or remit or mitigate any sanction imposed.

(f) *Content of orders.* The final decision may provide for suspension or termination of, or refusal to grant or continue financial assistance, in whole or in part, to which this regulation applies, and may contain such terms, conditions, and other provisions as are consistent with and will effectuate the purposes of the Act and this part, including provisions designed to assure that no financial assistance to which this regulation applies will thereafter be extended to the recipient determined by such decision to have failed to comply with this part, unless and until it corrects its noncompliance and satisfies TVA that it will fully comply with this part.

(g) *Posttermination proceedings.* (1) A recipient adversely affected by an order issued under paragraph (f) of this section shall be restored to full eligibility to receive Federal financial assistance if it satisfies the terms and conditions of that order for such eligibility or if it brings itself into compliance with this regulation and provides reasonable assurance that it will fully comply with this regulation.

(2) Any recipient or proposed recipient adversely affected by an order entered pursuant to paragraph (f) of this section may at any time request TVA

to restore fully the recipient's eligibility to receive Federal financial assistance. Any such request shall be supported by information showing that the recipient has met the requirements of paragraph (g)(1) of this section. If TVA determines that those requirements have been satisfied, TVA shall restore such eligibility.

(3) If TVA denies any such request, the recipient may submit a written request for a hearing specifying why it believes TVA to have been in error. The recipient shall thereupon be given an expeditious hearing, with a decision on the record, in accordance with rules of procedure issued by TVA. The recipient will be restored to such eligibility if the recipient proves at such a hearing that it satisfied the requirements of paragraph (g)(1) of this section. While proceedings under this paragraph are pending, the sanctions imposed by the order issued under paragraph (f) of this section shall remain in effect.

[30 FR 311, Jan. 9, 1965. Redesignated at 44 FR 30682, May 29, 1979. Redesignated and amended at 45 FR 20483, May 15, 1983; 68 FR 51355, Aug. 26, 2003]

§ 1302.11   Judicial review.

Action taken pursuant to section 602 of the Act is subject to judicial review as provided in section 603 of the Act.

[30 FR 311, Jan. 9, 1965. Redesignated at 44 FR 30682, May 29, 1979, and 49 FR 47384, Dec. 4, 1984]

§ 1302.12   Effect on other regulations; supervision and coordination.

(a) *Effect on other regulations.* All regulations, orders, or like directions heretofore issued by TVA which impose requirements designed to prohibit any discrimination against individuals on the ground of race, color, or national origin to which this regulation applies, and which authorize the suspension or termination of or refusal to grant or to continue financial assistance to any recipient of such assistance under such program for failure to comply with such requirements, are hereby superseded to the extent that such discrimination is prohibited by this part, except that nothing in this part shall be deemed to relieve any person of any obligation assumed or imposed under any such superseded regulation, order, instruction, or like direction prior to the effective date of this part. Nothing in this part, however, shall be deemed to supersede any of the following (including future amendments thereof):

(1) Executive Order 12250 and regulations issued thereunder, or

(2) Any other regulations or instructions, insofar as they prohibit discrimination on the ground of race, color, or national origin in any program or situation to which this regulation is inapplicable, or prohibit discrimination on any other ground.

(b) *Supervision and coordination.* TVA may from time to time assign to officials of other departments or agencies of the Government with the consent of such departments or agencies, responsibilities in connection with the effectuation of the purposes of Title VI of the Act and this part (other than responsibility for final decision as provided in § 1302.9), including the achievement of effective coordination and maximum uniformity within the Executive Branch of the Government in the application of Title VI and this part to similar programs and in similar situations. Any action taken, determination made, or requirement imposed by an official of another department or agency acting pursuant to an assignment of responsibility under this subsection shall have the same effect as though such action had been taken by TVA.

[38 FR 17945, July 5, 1973. Redesignated at 44 FR 30682, May 29, 1979. Redesignated and amended at 49 FR 20484, May 15, 1984; 68 FR 51355, Aug. 26, 2003]

APPENDIX A TO PART 1302—FEDERAL FINANCIAL ASSISTANCE TO WHICH THESE REGULATIONS APPLY

1. Transfers, leases and licenses of real property for nominal consideration to states, counties, municipalities, and other public agencies for development for public recreation.

2. Furnishing funds, property and services to state agencies, local governments and citizen organizations to advance economic growth in watersheds of Tennessee River tributaries through cooperative resource development programs.

3. Furnishing funds, property and services to land grant colleges for use in a cooperative program utilizing test-demonstration farms to test experimental fertilizers developed by TVA and to educate farmers and other interested persons concerning these

new fertilizers. This program also includes the furnishing of fertilizers at reduced prices by TVA, through its fertilizer distributors, to such test-demonstration farms.

4. Furnishing space and utilities without charge under agreements with state agencies for use in accordance with the Vending Stands for Blind Act.

[30 FR 311, Jan. 9, 1965, as amended at 38 FR 17945, July 5, 1973. Redesignated at 44 FR 30682, May 29, 1979]

PART 1303—PROPERTY MANAGEMENT

Subpart A—General Information

Subpart B—Tobacco Products

AUTHORITY: 16 U.S.C. 831–831dd.

SOURCE: 61 FR 6110, Feb. 16, 1996, unless otherwise noted.

Subpart A—General Information

§ 1303.1   Applicability.

This part sets out certain regulations applicable to buildings, structures, and other property under TVA control.

Subpart B—Tobacco Products

§ 1303.2   Definition.

Tobacco product means cigarettes, cigars, little cigars, pipe tobacco, smokeless tobacco, snuff, and chewing tobacco.

[61 FR 6110, Feb. 16, 1996; 61 FR 54849, Oct. 22, 1996]

§ 1303.3   Prohibition on tobacco products.

(a) Sale of tobacco products by vending machine on TVA property is prohibited. Tobacco product vending machines already in place on TVA property as of November 15, 1995, may continue in operation for one year from February 16, 1996 while TVA completes review of whether such machines should be exempted under paragraph (c) of this section.

(b) Distribution of free samples of tobacco products on TVA property is prohibited.

(c) TVA may, as appropriate, designate areas not subject to this section if individuals under the age of 18 are not allowed in such areas.

PART 1304—APPROVAL OF CONSTRUCTION IN THE TENNESSEE RIVER SYSTEM AND REGULATION OF STRUCTURES AND OTHER ALTERATIONS

Subpart A—Procedures for Approval of Construction

Subpart B—Regulation of Nonnavigable Houseboats

Subpart C—TVA-Owned Residential Access Shoreland

199

Subpart D—Activities on TVA Flowage Easement Shoreland

1304.300   Scope and intent.
1304.301   Utilities.
1304.302   Vegetation management on flowage easement shoreland.
1304.303   Channel excavation.

Subpart E—Miscellaneous

1304.400   Flotation devices and material, all floating structures.
1304.401   Marine sanitation devices.
1304.402   Wastewater outfalls.
1304.403   Marina sewage pump-out stations and holding tanks.
1304.404   Commercial marina harbor limits.
1304.405   Fuel storage tanks and handling facilities.
1304.406   Removal of unauthorized, unsafe, and derelict structures or facilities.
1304.407   Development within flood control storage zones of TVA reservoirs.
1304.408   Variances.
1304.409   Indefinite or temporary moorage of recreational vessels.
1304.410   Navigation restrictions.
1304.411   Fish attractor, spawning, and habitat structures.
1304.412   Definitions.

AUTHORITY: 16 U.S.C. 831–831ee.

SOURCE: 68 FR 46936, Aug. 7, 2003, unless otherwise noted.

Subpart A—Procedures for Approval of Construction

§ 1304.1 Scope and intent.

The Tennessee Valley Authority Act of 1933 among other things confers on TVA broad authority related to the unified conservation and development of the Tennessee River Valley and surrounding area and directs that property in TVA's custody be used to promote the Act's purposes. In particular, section 26a of the Act requires that TVA's approval be obtained prior to the construction, operation, or maintenance of any dam, appurtenant works, or other obstruction affecting navigation, flood control, or public lands or reservations along or in the Tennessee River or any of its tributaries. By way of example only, such obstructions may include boat docks, piers, boathouses, buoys, floats, boat launching ramps, fills, water intakes, devices for discharging effluent, bridges, aerial cables, culverts, pipelines, fish attractors, shoreline stabilization projects,

channel excavations, and nonnavigable houseboats as defined in § 1304.101. Any person considering constructing, operating, or maintaining any such obstruction on a stream in the Tennessee River Watershed should carefully review the regulations in this part and the 26a Applicant's Package before doing so. The regulations also apply to certain activities on TVA-owned land alongside TVA reservoirs and to land subject to TVA flowage easements. TVA uses and permits use of the lands and land rights in its custody alongside and subjacent to TVA reservoirs and exercises its land rights to carry out the purposes and policies of the Act. In addition, the National Environmental Policy Act of 1969 (NEPA), as amended, 42 U.S.C. 4321 *et seq.*, and the Federal Water Pollution Control Act Amendments of 1972 (FWPCA), 33 U.S.C. 1251 *et seq.*, have declared it to be congressional policy that agencies should administer their statutory authorities so as to restore, preserve, and enhance the quality of the environment and should cooperate in the control of pollution. It is the intent of the regulations in this part 1304 to carry out the purposes of the Act and other statutes relating to these purposes, and this part shall be interpreted and applied to that end.

§ 1304.2 Application.

(a) If the facility is to be built on TVA land, the applicant must, in addition to the other requirements of this part, own the fee interest in or have an adequate leasehold or easement interest of sufficient tenure to cover the normal useful life of the proposed facility in land immediately adjoining the TVA land. If the facility is to be built on private land, the applicant must own the fee interest in the land or have an adequate leasehold or easement interest in the property where the facility will be located. TVA recognizes, however, that in some cases private property has been subdivided in a way that left an intervening strip of land between the upland boundary of a TVA flowage easement and the waters of the reservoir, or did not convey to the adjoining landowner the land underlying the waters of the reservoir. In some of these situations, the owner of the intervening strip or underlying land cannot be identified or does not object to construction of water-use facilities by the adjacent landowner. In these situations, TVA may exercise its discretion to permit the facility, provided there is no objection from the fee owner of the intervening strip or underlying land. A TVA permit conveys no property interest. The applicant is responsible for locating the proposed facility on qualifying land and ensuring that there is no objection from any owner of such land. TVA may require the applicant to provide appropriate verification of ownership and lack of objection, but TVA is not responsible for resolving ownership questions. In case of a dispute, TVA may require private parties requesting TVA action to grant or revoke a TVA permit to obtain a court order declaring respective land rights. TVA may exercise its discretion to permit a facility on TVA land that is located up or downstream from the land which makes the applicant eligible for consideration to receive a permit.

(b) Applications shall be addressed to the Tennessee Valley Authority at the appropriate Regional Watershed Office location using the addresses provided below. To contact an office, call 1–800–882–5263. Applications are available on TVA's internet Web site and at the addresses listed below.

(1) For Chickamauga and Nickajack Reservoirs: 1101 Market Street, PSC 1E–C, Chattanooga, TN 37402–2801;

(2) For Apalachia, Blue Ridge, Chatuge, Hiwassee, Nottely, and the Ocoee Reservoirs: 4800 US Highway 64 West, Suite 102, MLO 1A–MRN, Murphy, NC 28906;

(3) For Guntersville, Normandy, and Tims Ford Reservoirs: 3696 Alabama Highway 69, CAB 1A–GVA, Guntersville, AL 35976–7196;

(4) For Cherokee, Douglas, and Nolichucky Reservoirs and the French Broad River: 3726 E. Morris Boulevard, MOC 1A–MOT, Morristown, TN 37813–1270;

(5) For Boone, Fort Patrick Henry South Holston, Watauga, and Wilbur Reservoirs and the Bristol Project: 106 Tri-Cities Business Park Drive, WTR 1A–GRT, Gray, TN 37615;

(6) For the Beech River Project, Kentucky Reservoir, and the Lower Duck River: 2835–A East Wood Street, WTB 1A–PAT, Paris, TN 38242–5948;

(7) For Fontana, Fort Loudon, Great Falls, Melton Hill, Norris, Tellico, and Watts Bar Reservoirs, and the Little Tennessee, Clinch, and Powell Rivers: 260 Interchange Park Dr., LCB 1A–LCT, Lenoir City, TN 37772–5664;

(8) For Bear Creek, Cedar Creek, Little Bear Creek, Upper Bear Creek, and the Duck and Elk Rivers, and Pickwick, Wheeler and Wilson Reservoirs: P.O. Box 1010, MPB 1H–M, Muscle Shoals, AL 35662–1010.

(c) *Submittal of section 26a application.* Applicants must submit certain required information depending upon whether a proposed facility is a minor or major facility. Examples of the two categories are provided in paragraphs (c)(1) and (2) of this section. Most residential related facilities are minor facilities. Commercial or community facilities generally are major facilities. TVA shall determine whether a proposed facility is minor or major. An application shall not be complete until payment of the appropriate fee as determined in accordance with 18 CFR part 1310, and disclosed to the applicant in the materials provided with the application package or by such other means of disclosure as TVA shall from time to time adopt. For purposes of the information required to be submitted under this section and the determination of fees, a request for a variance to the size limitations for a residential-related facility (other than a waiver request under §1304.212 or §1304.300(a)) shall be regarded as an application for a major facility. In addition to the information required in paragraphs (c)(1) and (2) of this section, TVA may require the applicant to provide such other information as TVA deems necessary for adequate review of a particular application.

(1) *Information required for review of minor facility.* By way of example only, minor facilities may include: boat docks, piers, rafts, boathouses, fences,

steps, and gazebos. One copy of the application shall be prepared and submitted in accordance with the instructions included in the section 26a Applicant's Package. The application shall include:

(i) *Completed application form.* One (1) copy of the application shall be prepared and submitted. Application forms are available from TVA at the locations identified at the beginning of this section. The application shall include a project description which indicates what is to be built, removed, or modified, and the sequence of the work.

(ii) *Project, plan, or drawing.* The project plan/drawing shall:

(A) Be prepared on paper suitable for reproduction (8½ by 11 inches);

(B) Identify the kind of structure, purpose/intended use;

(C) Show principal dimensions, size, and location in relation to shoreline;

(D) Show the elevation of the structure above the full summer pool; and

(E) Indicate the river or reservoir name, river mile, locator landmarks, and direction of water flow if known.

(iii) *A site photograph.* The photograph shall be at least 3 by 5 inches in size and show the location of the proposed structure or alteration and the adjacent shoreline area.

(iv) *Location map.* The location map shall clearly show the location of the proposed facility and the extent of any site disturbance for the proposed project. An 8½ by 11-inch copy of one of the following is ideal: a TVA land map, a subdivision map, or a portion of a United States Geological Survey topographic map. The subdivision name and lot number and the map number or name shall be included, if available.

(v) *Environmental consultations and permits.* To the fullest extent possible the applicant shall obtain or apply for other required environmental permits and approvals before or at the same time as applying for section 26a approvals. Consultations under the National Historic Preservation Act of 1966 and the Endangered Species Act of 1973 shall take place, and permits from the U. S. Army Corps of Engineers and State agencies for water or air regulation shall be obtained or applied for at the same time as or before application for section 26a approval. The applicant

shall provide TVA with copies of any such permits or approvals that are issued.

(2) *Information required for a major facility.* One (1) copy of the application shall be prepared and submitted according to instructions included in the section 26a Applicant's Package. By way of example only, major projects and facilities may include: marinas, community docks, barge terminals, utility crossings, bridges, culverts, roads, wastewater discharges, water intakes, dredging, and placement of fill. The application shall include:

(i) *Completed application form.* Application forms are available from TVA at the locations identified at the beginning of this section. The application shall include a narrative project description which indicates what is to be built, removed, or modified, and the sequence of the work.

(ii) *Project plan or drawing.* Adequate project plans or drawings shall accompany the application. They shall:

(A) Be prepared on paper suitable for reproduction (no larger than 11 by 17 inches) or contained on a 3½-inch floppy disc in "dxf" format.

(B) Contain the date; applicant name; stream; river or reservoir name; river mile; locator landmarks; and direction of water flow, if known;

(C) Identify the kind of structure, purpose/intended use;

(D) Include a plan and profile view of the structure;

(E) Show principal dimensions, size, and location in relation to shoreline;

(F) Show the elevations of the structure above full summer pool if located on a TVA reservoir or above the normal high water elevation if on a free-flowing stream or river; and

(G) Show the north arrow.

(iii) *Location map.* The location map must clearly indicate the exact location and extent of site disturbance for the proposed project. An 8½- by 11-inch copy of the appropriate portion of a United States Geological Survey topographic map is recommended. The map number or name shall be included. In addition, recent photos of the location are helpful for TVA's review and may be included.

(iv) *Other information where applicable.* The location of any material laydown or assembly areas, staging areas, equipment storage areas, new access roads, and road/access closure required by the project or needed for construction; the location of borrow or spoil areas on or off TVA land; the extent of soil and vegetative disturbance; and information on any special reservoir operations needed for the project, such as drawdown or water discharge restrictions.

(v) *Site plans.* Some projects, particularly larger ones, may require a separate site plan which details existing and proposed changes to surface topography and elevations (cut and fill, clearing, etc.), location of all proposed facilities, and erosion control plans.

(vi) *Environmental consultations and permits.* To the fullest extent possible the applicant shall obtain or apply for other required environmental permits and approvals before or at the same time as applying for section 26a approvals. Consultations under the National Historic Preservation Act of 1966 and the Endangered Species Act of 1973 shall take place, and permits from the U.S. Army Corps of Engineers and State agencies for water or air regulation shall be obtained or applied for at the same time as or before application for section 26a approval. The applicant shall provide TVA with copies of any such permits or approvals that are issued.

(d) *Discharges into navigable waters of the United States.* If construction, maintenance, or operation of the proposed structure or any part thereof, or the conduct of the activity in connection with which approval is sought, may result in any discharge into navigable waters of the United States, applicant shall also submit with the application, in addition to the material required by paragraph (c) of this section, a certification from the State in which such discharge would originate, or, if appropriate, from the interstate water pollution control agency having jurisdiction over the navigable waters at the point where the discharge would originate, or from the Environmental Protection Agency, that such State or interstate agency or the Environmental Protection Agency has determined that there is reasonable assurance that the applicant's proposed activity will be con-

ducted in a manner which will not violate applicable water quality standards. The applicant shall further submit such supplemental and additional information as TVA may deem necessary for the review of the application, including, without limitation, information concerning the amounts, chemical makeup, temperature differentials, type and quantity of suspended solids, and proposed treatment plans for any proposed discharges.

[68 FR 46936, Aug. 7, 2003, as amended at 79 FR 4621, Jan. 29, 2014]

EFFECTIVE DATE NOTE: At 68 FR 46936, Aug. 7, 2003, §1304.2 was revised. Paragraphs (b), (c), and (d) of this section contain information collection and recordkeeping requirements and will not become effective until approval has been given by the Office of Management and Budget.

§1304.3 Delegation of authority.

The power to approve or disapprove applications under this part is delegated to the Vice President, Natural Resources, or the designee thereof, subject to appeal to the Chief Executive Officer and discretionary review by a designated committee of the TVA Board, as provided in §1304.6. The administration of applications is delegated to the Natural Resources staff or the group with functionally equivalent responsibilities.

[79 FR 4621, Jan. 29, 2014]

§1304.4 Application review and approval process.

(a) TVA shall notify the U.S. Army Corps of Engineers (USACE) and other federal agencies with jurisdiction over the application as appropriate.

(b) If a hearing is held for any of the reasons described in paragraph (c) of this section, any interested person may become a party of record by following the directions contained in the hearing notice.

(c) Hearings concerning approval of applications are conducted (in accordance with §1304.5) when:

(1) TVA deems a hearing is necessary or appropriate in determining any issue presented by the application;

(2) A hearing is required under any applicable law or regulation;

(3) A hearing is requested by the USACE pursuant to the TVA/Corps

joint processing Memorandum of Understanding; or

(4) The TVA Investigating Officer directs that a hearing be held.

(d) Upon completion of the review of the application, including any hearing or hearings, the Vice President or the designee thereof shall issue an initial decision approving or disapproving the application. The basis for the decision shall be set forth in the decision.

(e) Promptly following the issuance of the decision, the Vice President or the designee thereof shall furnish a written copy of the decision to the applicant and to any parties of record. The initial decision shall become final unless an appeal is made pursuant to § 1304.6.

[79 FR 4621, Jan. 29, 2014]

§ 1304.5 Conduct of hearings.

(a) If a hearing is to be held for any of the reasons described in § 1304.4(c), TVA shall give notice of the hearing to interested persons. Such notice may be given by publication in a daily newspaper of general circulation in the area of the proposed structure, personal written notice, posting on TVA's Internet Web site, or by any other method reasonably calculated to come to the attention of interested persons. The notice shall provide to the extent feasible the place, date, and time of hearing; the particular issues to which the hearing will pertain; the manner of becoming a party of record; and any other pertinent information as appropriate. The applicant shall automatically be a party of record.

(b) Hearings may be conducted by any such person or persons as may be designated by the Vice President, the Vice President's designee, or the Chief Executive Officer. Hearings are public and are conducted in an informal manner. Parties of record may be represented by counsel or other persons of their choosing. Technical rules of evidence are not observed although reasonable bounds are maintained as to relevancy, materiality, and competency. Evidence may be presented orally or by written statement and need not be under oath. Cross-examination by parties of witnesses or others providing statements or testifying at a hearing shall not be allowed. After the

hearing has been completed, additional evidence will not be received unless it presents new and material matter that in the judgment of the person or persons conducting the hearing could not be presented at the hearing. The Vice President may arrange a joint hearing with another federal agency where the subject of an application will require the approval of and necessitate a hearing by or before that other agency. In TVA's discretion, the format of any such joint hearing may be that used by the other agency.

[79 FR 4621, Jan. 29, 2014]

§ 1304.6 Appeals.

(a) Decisions approving or disapproving an application may be appealed as provided in this section. Decisions by the Vice President's designee may be appealed to the Vice President and decisions by the Vice President may be appealed to the Chief Executive Officer, with the possibility of further discretionary review by a committee of the TVA Board.

(b) If a designee of the Vice President issues an initial decision disapproving an application or approving it with terms and conditions deemed unacceptable by the applicant, the applicant may obtain the Vice President's review of that decision by mailing within thirty (30) days after receipt of the designee's decision a written request to the Vice President, Natural Resources, Tennessee Valley Authority, 400 West Summit Hill Drive, Knoxville, Tennessee 37902. Otherwise, the initial decision of the Vice President's designee becomes final.

(c) If the Vice President, either initially or as the result of an appeal, disapproves an application or approves it with terms and conditions deemed unacceptable by the applicant, the applicant may obtain the Chief Executive Officer's review of that decision by mailing within thirty (30) days after receipt of the decision a written request to the Chief Executive Officer, Tennessee Valley Authority, 400 W. Summit Hill Drive, Knoxville, Tennessee 37902. Otherwise, the Vice President's decision becomes final.

(d) The decision of the Chief Executive Officer shall become final unless a request for discretionary review by a committee of the Board (Committee) is justified by extraordinary circumstances and mailed within thirty (30) days after receipt of the decision to the attention of Board Services, Tennessee Valley Authority, 400 West Summit Hill Drive, Knoxville, Tennessee 37902. If within 60 days of such a request, one or more members of the Committee indicate that there are extraordinary circumstances warranting further review, the matter will be reviewed by the Committee. Otherwise, the Chief Executive Officer's decision becomes final. The Committee will schedule a meeting not more often that twice a year as needed to hear discretionary appeals. The Committee decides what kind of process to use for these appeals. Deliberations and voting on the reviews will take place at these meetings.

(e) Any interested party who becomes a party of record at a hearing as set forth in §1304.4(b) and who is aggrieved or adversely affected by any decision approving an application may obtain review by the Vice President or Chief Executive Officer, as appropriate, and may request discretionary review by the Committee, in the same manner as an applicant by adhering to the requirements of paragraphs (b), (c), and (d) of this section.

(f) All requests for review shall fully explain the reasons the applicant or other aggrieved party of record contends that the decision below is in error, and shall include a signed certification that the request for review was mailed to each party of record at the same time that it was mailed to TVA. TVA shall maintain lists of parties of record and make those available upon request for this purpose.

(g) The applicant and any party of record requesting review by the Vice President or Chief Executive Officer may submit additional written material in support of their positions within thirty (30) days after mailing the request for review or during such additional period as the Vice President or Chief Executive Officer may allow.

(h) In considering an appeal, the Vice President or Chief Executive Officer may conduct or cause to be conducted such investigation of the application as he or she deems necessary or desirable,

and may appoint an Investigating Officer. The Investigating Officer may be a TVA employee or a person under contract to TVA, and shall not have been directly and substantially involved in the decision being appealed. The Investigating Officer may be the hearing officer for any hearing held during the appeal process. The Vice President or Chief Executive Officer shall render a decision approving or disapproving the application based on a review of the record and the information developed during any investigation and/or submitted by the applicant and any parties of record.

(i) No applicant or party of record shall contact the Chief Executive Officer, Committee members, or any other TVA Board member during the appeal process, except as specified in correspondence from the Chief Executive Officer or from the Committee Secretary. The appeal process runs from the date of an appeal to the Chief Executive Officer until a final resolution of the matter.

(j) A written copy of the decision by the Vice President or the Chief Executive Officer shall be furnished to the applicant and to all parties of record promptly following determination of the matter.

(k) In the event the Committee grants a request for discretionary review, notice of that decision and information about the review shall be provided to the person(s) requesting review and to other parties of record in accordance with the methods set forth in §1304.5(a). Written notice of the Committee's final determination of the appeal shall be provided to the applicant and to all parties of record in accordance with the methods set forth in §1304.5(a).

[79 FR 4622, Jan. 29, 2014]

§1304.7 Conditions of approvals.

Approvals of applications shall contain such conditions as are required by law and may contain such other general and special conditions as TVA deems necessary or desirable.

§1304.8 Denials.

TVA may, at its sole discretion, deny any application to construct, operate, conduct, or maintain any obstruction, structure, facility, or activity that in TVA's judgment would be contrary to the unified development and regulation of the Tennessee River system, would adversely affect navigation, flood control, public lands or reservations, the environment, or sensitive resources (including, without limitation, federally listed threatened or endangered species, high priority State-listed species, wetlands with high function and value, archaeological or historical sites of national significance, and other sites or locations identified in TVA Reservoir Land Management Plans as requiring protection of the environment), or would be inconsistent with TVA's Shoreline Management Policy. In lieu of denial, TVA may require mitigation measures where, in TVA's sole judgment, such measures would adequately protect against adverse effects.

§ 1304.9 Initiation of construction.

A permit issued pursuant to this part shall expire unless the applicant initiates construction within eighteen (18) months after the date of issuance.

§ 1304.10 Change in ownership of approved facilities or activities.

(a) When there is a change in ownership of the land on which a permitted facility or activity is located (or ownership of the land which made the applicant eligible for consideration to receive a permit when the facility or activity is on TVA land), the new owner shall notify TVA within sixty (60) days. Upon application to TVA by the new owner, the new owner may continue to use existing facilities or carry out permitted activities pending TVA's decision on reissuance of the permit. TVA shall reissue the permit upon determining that the facilities are in good repair and are consistent with the standards in effect at the time the permit was first issued.

(b) Subsequent owners are not required to modify existing facilities constructed and maintained in accordance with the standards in effect at the time the permit was first issued provided they:

(1) Maintain such facilities in good repair; and

(2) Obtain TVA approval for any repairs that would alter the size of the facility or for any new construction.

§ 1304.11 Little Tennessee River; date of formal submission.

As regards structures on the Little Tennessee River, applications are deemed by TVA to be formally submitted within the meaning of section 26a of the Act, on that date upon which applicant has complied in good faith with all applicable provisions of § 1304.2.

Subpart B—Regulation of Nonnavigable Houseboats

§ 1304.100 Scope and intent.

This subpart prescribes regulations governing existing nonnavigable houseboats that are moored, anchored, or installed in TVA reservoirs. No new nonnavigable houseboats shall be moored, anchored, or installed in any TVA reservoir.

§ 1304.101 Nonnavigable houseboats.

(a) Any houseboat failing to comply with the following criteria shall be deemed a non-navigable houseboat and may not be moored, anchored, installed, or operated in any TVA reservoir except as provided in paragraph (b) of this section:

(1) Built on a boat hull or on two or more pontoons;

(2) Equipped with a motor and rudder controls located at a point on the houseboat from which there is forward visibility over a 180-degree range;

(3) Compliant with all applicable State and Federal requirements relating to vessels;

(4) Registered as a vessel in the State of principal use; and

(5) State registration numbers clearly displayed on the vessel.

(b) Nonnavigable houseboats approved by TVA prior to February 15, 1978, shall be deemed existing houseboats and may remain on TVA reservoirs provided they remain in compliance with the rules contained in this part. Such houseboats shall be moored to mooring facilities contained within the designated and approved harbor limits of a commercial marina. Alternatively, provided the owner has obtained written approval from TVA pursuant to subpart A of this part authorizing mooring at such location, nonnavigable houseboats may be moored to the bank of the reservoir at locations where the owner of the houseboat is the owner or lessee (or the licensee of such owner or lessee) of the proposed mooring location, and at locations described by § 1304.201(a)(1), (2), and (3). All nonnavigable houseboats must be moored in such a manner as to:

(1) Avoid obstruction of or interference with navigation, flood control, public lands or reservations;

(2) Avoid adverse effects on public lands or reservations;

(3) Prevent the preemption of public waters when moored in permanent locations outside of the approved harbor limits of commercial marinas;

(4) Protect land and landrights owned by the United States alongside and subjacent to TVA reservoirs from trespass and other unlawful and unreasonable uses; and

(5) Maintain, protect, and enhance the quality of the human environment.

(c) All approved nonnavigable houseboats with toilets must be equipped as follows with a properly installed and operating Marine Sanitation Device (MSD) or Sewage Holding Tank and pumpout capability:

(1) Nonnavigable houseboats moored on "Discharge Lakes" must be equipped with a Type I or Type II MSD.

(2) Nonnavigable houseboats moored in: "No Discharge Lakes" must be equipped with holding tanks and pumpout capability. If a nonnavigable houseboat moored in a "No Discharge Lake" is equipped with a Type I or Type II MSD, it must be secured to prevent discharge into the lake.

(d) Approved nonnavigable houseboats shall be maintained in a good state of repair. Such houseboats may be structurally repaired or rebuilt without additional approval from TVA, but any expansion in length, width, or height is prohibited except as approved in writing by TVA.

(e) All nonnavigable houseboats shall comply with the requirements for flotation devices contained in § 1304.400.

(f) Applications for mooring of a nonnavigable houseboat outside of designated harbor limits will be disapproved if TVA determines that the proposed mooring location would be contrary to the intent of this subpart.

§ 1304.102 Numbering of nonnavigable houseboats and transfer of ownership.

(a) All approved nonnavigable houseboats shall display a number assigned by TVA. The owner of the nonnavigable houseboat shall paint or attach a facsimile of the number on a readily visible part of the outside of the facility in letters at least three inches high.

(b) The transferee of any nonnavigable houseboat approved pursuant to the regulations in this subpart shall, within thirty (30) days of the transfer transaction, report the transfer to TVA.

(c) A nonnavigable houseboat moored at a location approved pursuant to the regulations in this subpart shall not be relocated and moored at a different location without prior approval by TVA, except for movement to a new location within the designated harbor limits of a commercial dock or marina.

§ 1304.103 Approval of plans for structural modifications or rebuilding of approved nonnavigable houseboats.

Plans for the structural modification, or rebuilding of an approved nonnavigable houseboat shall be submitted to TVA for review and approval in advance of any structural modification which would increase the length, width, height, or flotation of the structure.

Subpart C—TVA-Owned Residential Access Shoreland

§ 1304.200 Scope and intent.

This subpart C applies to residential water-use facilities, specifically the construction of docks, piers, boathouses (fixed and floating), retaining walls, and other structures and alterations, including channel excavation and vegetation management, on or along TVA-owned residential access shoreland. TVA manages the TVA-owned residential access shoreland to conserve, protect, and enhance shoreland resources, while providing reasonable access to the water of the reservoir by qualifying adjacent residents.

§ 1304.201 Applicability.

This subpart addresses residential-related (all private, noncommercial uses) construction activities along and across shoreland property owned by the United States and under the custody and control of TVA. Individual residential landowners wishing to construct facilities, clear vegetation and/or maintain an access corridor on adjacent TVA-owned lands are required to apply for and obtain a permit from TVA before conducting any such activities.

(a) This subpart applies to the following TVA-reservoir shoreland classifications:

(1) TVA-owned shorelands over which the adjacent residential landowner holds rights of ingress and egress to the water (except where a particular activity is specifically excluded by an applicable real estate document), including, at TVA's discretion, cases where the applicant owns access rights across adjoining private property that borders on and benefits from rights of ingress and egress across TVA-owned shoreland.

(2) TVA-owned shorelands designated in current TVA Reservoir Land Management Plans as open for consideration of residential development; and

(3) On reservoirs not having a current approved TVA Reservoir Land Management Plan at the time of application, TVA-owned shorelands designated in TVA's property forecast system as "reservoir operations property," identified in a subdivision plat recorded prior to September 24, 1992, and containing at least one water-use facility developed prior to September 24, 1992.

(b) Construction of structures, access corridors, and vegetation management activities by owners of adjacent upland residential property shall not be allowed on any TVA-owned lands other than those described in one or more of the classifications identified in paragraph (a) of this section.

(c) Flowage easement shoreland. Except as otherwise specifically provided in subpart D of this part, this subpart C does not apply to shoreland where TVA's property interest is ownership of a flowage easement. The terms of the particular flowage easement and subparts A, B, D, and E of this part govern the use of such property.

§ 1304.202 General sediment and erosion control provisions.

(a) During construction activities, TVA shall require that appropriate erosion and sediment control measures be utilized to prevent pollution of the waters of the reservoir.

(b) All material which accumulates behind sediment control structures must be removed from TVA land and placed at an upland site above the 100-year floodplain elevation or the Flood Risk Profile Elevation (whichever is applicable).

(c) Disturbed sites must be promptly stabilized with seeding, vegetative planting, erosion control netting, and/or mulch material.

§ 1304.203 Vegetation management.

No vegetation management shall be approved on TVA-owned Residential Access Shoreland until a Vegetation Management Plan meeting the vegetation management standards contained in this section is submitted to and approved by TVA.

(a) Except for the mowing of lawns established and existing before November 1, 1999, all vegetation management activities on TVA-owned property subject to this subpart (including all such activities described in paragraphs (b) through (m) of this section as "allowed" and all activities undertaken in connection with a section 26a permit obtained before September 8, 2003) require TVA's advance written permission. Special site circumstances such as the presence of wetlands may result in a requirement for mitigative measures or alternative vegetation management approaches.

(b) Vegetation may be cleared to create and maintain an access corridor up to but not exceeding 20 feet wide. The corridor will extend from the common boundary between TVA and the adjacent landowner to the water-use facility.

(c) The access corridor will be located to minimize removal of trees or other vegetation on the TVA land.

(d) Grass may be planted and mowed within the access corridor, and stone, brick, concrete, mulch, or wooden paths, walkways and/or steps are allowed. Pruning of side limbs that extend into the access corridor from trees located outside the access corridor is allowed.

(e) A 50-foot-deep shoreline management zone (SMZ) shall be designated by TVA on TVA property; provided, however, that where TVA ownership is insufficient to establish a 50-foot-deep SMZ, the SMZ shall consist only of all of the TVA land at the location (private land shall not be included within the SMZ). Within the SMZ, no trees may be cut or vegetation removed, except that which is preapproved by TVA within the access corridor.

(f) Within the 50-foot SMZ and elsewhere on TVA land as defined in § 1304.201, clearing of specified understory plants (poison ivy, Japanese honeysuckle, kudzu, and other exotic plants on a list provided by TVA) is allowed.

(g) On TVA land situated above the SMZ, selective thinning of trees or other vegetation under three inches in diameter at the ground level is allowed.

(h) Removal of trees outside of the access corridor but within the SMZ may be approved to make the site suitable for approved shoreline erosion control projects.

(i) Vegetation removed for erosion control projects must be replaced with native species of vegetation.

(j) The forest floor must be left undisturbed, except as specified in this section. Mowing is allowed only within the access corridor.

(k) Planting of trees, shrubs, wildflowers, native grasses, and ground covers within the SMZ is allowed to create, improve, or enhance the vegetative cover, provided native plants are used.

(l) Fertilizers and herbicides shall not be applied within the SMZ or elsewhere on TVA land, except as specifically approved in the Vegetative Management Plan.

(m) Restricted use herbicides and pesticides shall not be applied on TVA-owned shoreland except by a State certified applicator. All herbicides and pesticides shall be applied in accordance with label requirements.

§ 1304.204 **Docks, piers, and boathouses.**

Applicants are responsible for submitting plans for proposed docks, piers, and boathouses that conform to the size standards specified in this section. Where and if site constraints at the proposed construction location preclude a structure of the maximum size, TVA shall determine the size of facility that may be approved. Applicants are required to submit accurate drawings with dimensions of all proposed facilities.

(a) Docks, piers, boathouses, and all other residential water-use facilities shall not exceed a total footprint area of greater than 1000 square feet.

(b) Docks, boatslips, piers, and fixed or floating boathouses are allowable. These and other water-use facilities associated with a lot must be sited within a 1000-square-foot rectangular or square area at the lakeward end of the access walkway that extends from the shore to the structure. Access walkways to the water-use structure are not included in calculating the 1000-foot area.

(c) Docks and walkway(s) shall not extend more than 150 feet from the shoreline, or more than one-third the distance to the opposite shoreline, whichever is less.

(d) All fixed piers and docks on Pickwick, Wilson, Wheeler, Guntersville, and Nickajack Reservoirs shall have deck elevations at least 18 inches above full summer pool level; facilities on all other reservoirs, shall be a minimum of 24 inches above full summer pool.

(e) All docks, piers, and other water-use facilities must be attached to the shore with a single walkway which must connect from land to the structure by the most direct route and must adjoin the access corridor.

(f) Docks, piers, and boathouses may be fixed or floating or a combination of the two types.

(g) Roofs are allowed on boatslips, except on Kentucky Reservoir where roofs are not allowed on fixed structures due to extreme water level fluctuations. Roofs over docks or piers to provide shade are allowed on all reservoirs.

(h) Docks proposed in subdivisions recorded after November 1, 1999, must be placed at least 50 feet from the neighbors' docks. When this density requirement cannot be met, TVA may require group or community facilities.

(i) Where the applicant owns or controls less than 50 feet of property adjoining TVA shoreline, the overall width of the facilities permitted along the shore shall be limited to ensure sufficient space to accommodate other property owners.

(j) Covered boatslips may be open or enclosed with siding.

(k) Access walkways constructed over water and internal walkways inside of boathouses shall not exceed six feet in width.

(l) Enclosed space shall be used solely for storage of water-use equipment. The outside dimensions of any completely enclosed storage space shall not exceed 32 square feet and must be located on an approved dock, pier, or boathouse.

(m) Docks, piers, and boathouses shall not contain living space or sleeping areas. Floor space shall not be considered enclosed if three of the four walls are constructed of wire or screen mesh from floor to ceiling, and the wire or screen mesh leaves the interior of the structure open to the weather.

(n) Except for nonnavigable houseboats approved in accordance with subpart B of this part, toilets and sinks are not permitted on water-use facilities.

(o) Covered docks, boatslips, and boathouses shall not exceed one story in height.

(p) Second stories on covered docks, piers, boatslips, or boathouses may be constructed as open decks with railing, but shall not be covered by a roof or enclosed with siding or screening.

(q) In congested areas or in other circumstances deemed appropriate by TVA, TVA may require an applicant's dock, pier, or boathouse to be located on an area of TVA shoreline not directly fronting the applicant's property.

§ 1304.205   Other water-use facilities.

(a) A marine railway or concrete boat launching ramp with associated driveway may be located within the access corridor. Construction must occur during reservoir drawdown. Excavated material must be placed at an upland site. Use of concrete is allowable; asphalt is not permitted.

(b) Tables or benches for cleaning fish are permitted on docks or piers.

(c) All anchoring cables or spud poles must be anchored to the walkway or to the ground in a way that will not accelerate shoreline erosion. Anchoring of cables, chains, or poles to trees on TVA property is not permitted.

(d) Electrical appliances such as stoves, refrigerators, freezers, and microwave ovens are not permitted on docks, piers, or boathouses.

(e) Mooring buoys/posts may be permitted provided the following requirements are met.

(1) Posts and buoys shall be placed in such a manner that in TVA's judgment they would not create a navigation hazard.

(2) Mooring posts must be a minimum 48 inches in height above the full summer pool elevation of the reservoir or higher as required by TVA.

(3) Buoys must conform to the Uniform State Waterway Marking system.

(f) Structures shall not be wider than the width of the lot.

(g) In congested areas, TVA may establish special permit conditions requiring dry-docking of floating structures when a reservoir reaches a specific drawdown elevation to prevent these structures from interfering with navigation traffic, recreational boating access, or adjacent structures during winter drawdown.

(h) Closed loop heat exchanges for residential heat pump application may be approved provided they are installed five feet below minimum winter water elevation and they utilize propylene glycol or water. All land-based pipes must be buried within the access corridor.

§ 1304.206   Requirements for community docks, piers, boathouses, or other water-use facilities.

(a) Community facilities where individual facilities are not allowed:

(1) TVA may limit water-use facilities to community facilities where physical or environmental constraints preclude approval of individual docks, piers, or boathouses.

(2) When individual water-use facilities are not allowed, no more than one slip for each qualified applicant will be approved for any community facility. TVA shall determine the location of the facility and the named permittees, taking into consideration the preferences of the qualified applicants and such other factors as TVA determines to be appropriate.

(3) In narrow coves or other situations where shoreline frontage is limited, shoreline development may be limited to one landing dock for temporary moorage of boats not to exceed the 1000-square-foot footprint requirement, and/or a boat launching ramp, if the site, in TVA's judgment, will accommodate such development.

(b) Private and community facilities at jointly-owned community outlots:

(1) Applications for private or community facilities to be constructed at a jointly-owned community outlot must be submitted either with 100 percent concurrence of all co-owners of such lot, or with concurrence of the authorized representatives of a State-chartered homeowners association with the authority to manage the common lot on behalf of all persons having an interest in such lot. If the community facility will serve five or more other lots, the application must be submitted by the authorized representatives of such an association. TVA considers an association to have the necessary authority to manage the common lot if all co-owners are eligible for membership in the association and a majority are members. TVA may request the association to provide satisfactory evidence of its authority.

(2) Size and number of slips at community water-use facilities lots shall be determined by TVA with consideration of the following:

(i) Size of community outlot;

(ii) Parking accommodations on the community outlot;

(iii) Length of shoreline frontage associated with the community outlot;

(iv) Number of property owners having the right to use the community outlot;

(v) Water depths fronting the community lot;

(vi) Commercial and private vessel navigation uses and restrictions in the vicinity of the community lot;

(vii) Recreational carrying capacity for water-based activities in the vicinity of the community lot, and

(viii) Other site specific conditions and considerations as determined by TVA.

(3) Vegetation management shall be in accordance with the requirements of § 1304.203 except that, at TVA's discretion, the community access corridor may exceed 20 feet in width, and thinning of vegetation outside of the corridor within or beyond the SMZ may be allowed to enhance views of the reservoir.

(c) TVA may approve community facilities that are greater in size than 1000 square feet. In such circumstances, TVA also may establish harbor limits.

§ 1304.207 Channel excavation on TVA-owned residential access shoreland.

(a) Excavation of individual boat channels shall be approved only when TVA determines there is no other practicable alternative to achieving sufficient navigable water depth and the action would not substantially impact sensitive resources.

(b) No more than 150 cubic yards of material shall be removed for any individual boat channel.

(c) The length, width, and depth of approved boat channels shall not exceed the dimensions necessary to achieve three-foot water depths for navigation of the vessel at the minimum winter water elevation.

(d) Each side of the channel shall have a slope ratio of at least 3:1.

(e) Only one boat channel or harbor may be considered for each abutting property owner.

(f) The grade of the channel must allow drainage of water during reservoir drawdown periods.

(g) Channel excavations must be accomplished during the reservoir drawdown when the reservoir bottom is exposed and dry.

(h) Spoil material from channel excavations must be placed in accordance with any applicable local, State, and Federal regulations at an upland site above the TVA Flood Risk Profile elevation. For those reservoirs that have no flood control storage, dredge spoil must be disposed of and stabilized above the limits of the 100-year floodplain and off of TVA property.

§ 1304.208 Shoreline stabilization on TVA-owned residential access shoreland.

TVA may issue permits allowing adjacent residential landowners to stabilize eroding shorelines on TVA-owned residential access shoreland. TVA will determine if shoreline erosion is sufficient to approve the proposed stabilization treatment.

(a) Biostabilization of eroded shorelines.

(1) Moderate contouring of the bank may be allowed to provide conditions suitable for planting of vegetation.

(2) Tightly bound bundles of coconut fiber, logs, or other natural materials may be placed at the base of the eroded site to deflect waves.

(3) Willow stakes and bundles and live cuttings of suitable native plant materials may be planted along the surface of the eroded area.

(4) Native vegetation may be planted within the shoreline management zone to help minimize further erosion.

(5) Riprap may be allowed along the base of the eroded area to prevent further undercutting of the bank.

(b) Use of gabions and riprap to stabilize eroded shorelines.

(1) The riprap material must be quarry-run stone, natural stone, or other material approved by TVA.

(2) Rubber tires, concrete rubble, or other debris salvaged from construction sites shall not be used to stabilize shorelines.

(3) Gabions (rock wrapped with wire mesh) that are commercially manufactured for erosion control may be used.

(4) Riprap material must be placed so as to follow the existing contour of the bank.

(5) Site preparation must be limited to the work necessary to obtain adequate slope and stability of the riprap material.

(c) Use of retaining walls for shoreline stabilization.

(1) Retaining walls shall be allowed only where the erosion process is severe and TVA determines that a retaining wall is the most effective erosion control option or where the proposed wall would connect to an existing TVA-approved wall on the lot or to an adjacent owner's TVA-approved wall.

(2) The retaining wall must be constructed of stone, concrete blocks, poured concrete, gabions, or other materials acceptable to TVA. Railroad ties, rubber tires, broken concrete (unless determined by TVA to be of adequate size and integrity), brick, creosote timbers, and asphalt are not allowed.

(3) Reclamation of land that has been lost to erosion is not allowed.

(4) The base of the retaining wall shall not be located more than an average of two horizontal feet lakeward of the existing full summer pool water. Riprap shall be placed at least two feet in depth along the footer of the retaining wall to deflect wave action and reduce undercutting that could eventually damage the retaining wall.

§ 1304.209 Land-based structures/alterations.

(a) Except for steps, pathways, boat launching ramps, marine railways located in the access corridor, bank stabilization along the shoreline, and other uses described in this subpart, no permanent structures, fills or grading shall be allowed on TVA land.

(b) Portable items such as picnic tables and hammocks may be placed on TVA land; permanent land-based structures and facilities such as picnic pavilions, gazebos, satellite antennas, septic tanks, and septic drainfields shall not be allowed on TVA land.

(c) Utility lines (electric, water-intake lines, etc.) may be placed within the access corridor as follows:

(1) Power lines, poles, electrical panel, and wiring must be installed:

(i) In a way that would not be hazardous to the public or interfere with TVA operations;

(ii) Solely to serve water-use facilities, and

(iii) In compliance with all State and local electrical codes (satisfactory evidence of compliance to be provided to TVA upon request).

(2) Electrical service must be installed with an electrical disconnect that is:

(i) Located above the 500-year floodplain or the flood risk profile, whichever is higher, and

(ii) Is accessible during flood events.

(3) TVA's issuance of a permit does not mean that TVA has determined the facilities are safe for any purpose or that TVA has any duty to make such a determination.

(d) Fences crossing TVA residential access shoreland may be considered only where outstanding agricultural rights or fencing rights exist and the land is used for agricultural purposes. Fences must have a built-in means for easy pedestrian passage by the public and they must be clearly marked.

§ 1304.210 Grandfathering of pre-existing shoreland uses and structures.

In order to provide for a smooth transition to new standards, grandfathering provisions shall apply as follows to pre-existing development and shoreland uses established prior to November 1, 1999, which are located along or adjoin TVA-owned access residential shoreland.

(a) Existing shoreline structures (docks, retaining walls, etc.) previously permitted by TVA are grandfathered.

(b) Grandfathered structures may continue to be maintained in accordance with previous permit requirements, and TVA does not require modification to conform to new standards.

(c) If a permitted structure is destroyed by fire or storms, the permit shall be reissued if the replacement facility is rebuilt to specifications originally permitted by TVA.

(d) Vegetation management at grandfathered developments shall be as follows:

(1) Mowing of lawns established on TVA-owned residential access shoreland prior to November 1, 1999, may be continued without regard to whether the lawn uses are authorized by a TVA permit.

(2) At sites where mowing of lawns established prior to November 1, 1999, is not specifically included as an authorized use in an existing permit, TVA will include mowing as a permitted use in the next permit action at that site.

(3) The SMZ is not required where established lawns existed prior to November 1, 1999.

(4) Any additional removal of trees or other vegetation (except for mowing of lawns established prior to November 1, 1999) requires TVA's approval in accordance with § 1304.203. Removal of trees greater than three inches in diameter at ground level is not allowed.

§ 1304.211 Change in ownership of grandfathered structures or alterations.

(a) When ownership of a permitted structure or other shoreline alteration changes, the new owner shall comply with § 1304.10 regarding notice to TVA.

(b) The new owner may, upon application to TVA for a permit, continue to use existing permitted docks and other shoreline alterations pending TVA action on the application.

(c) Subsequent owners are not required to modify to new standards existing shoreline alterations constructed and maintained in accordance with the standards in effect at the time the previous permit was first issued, and they may continue mowing established lawns that existed prior to November 1, 1999.

(d) New owners wishing to continue existing grandfathered activities and structures must:

(1) Maintain existing permitted docks, piers, boathouses, and other shoreline structures in good repair.

(2) Obtain TVA approval for any repairs that would alter the size of the facility, for any new construction, or for removal of trees or other vegetation (except for mowing of lawns established prior to November 1, 1999).

§ 1304.212 Waivers.

(a) Waivers of standards contained in this subpart may be requested when the following minimum criteria are established:

(1) The property is within a pre-existing development (an area where

shoreline development existed prior to November 1, 1999); and

(2) The proposed shoreline alterations are compatible with surrounding permitted structures and uses within the subdivision or, if there is no subdivision, within the immediate vicinity (one-fourth mile radius).

(b) In approving waivers of the standards of this subpart C, TVA will consider the following:

(1) The prevailing permitted practices within the subdivision or immediate vicinity; and

(2) The uses permitted under the guidelines followed by TVA before November 1, 1999.

Subpart D—Activities on TVA Flowage Easement Shoreland

§ 1304.300 Scope and intent.

Any structure built upon land subject to a flowage easement held by TVA shall be deemed an obstruction affecting navigation, flood control, or public lands or reservations within the meaning of section 26a of the Act. Such obstructions shall be subject to all requirements of this part except those contained in subpart C of this part, which shall apply as follows:

(a) All of § 1304.212 shall apply.

(b) Sections 1304.200, 1304.203, 1304.207, and 1304.209 shall not apply.

(c) Section 1304.201 shall not apply except for paragraph (c).

(d) Section 1304.202 shall apply except that TVA shall determine on a case-by-case basis whether it is necessary to remove materials accumulated behind sediment control structures to an upland site.

(e) Section 1304.204 shall apply except that the "50 feet" trigger of paragraph (i) of that section shall not apply. TVA may impose appropriate requirements to ensure accommodation of neighboring landowners.

(f) Section 1304.205 shall apply except that the facilities described in paragraph (a) are not limited to locations within an access corridor.

(g) Section 1304.206 shall apply except for paragraph (b)(3).

(h) Section 1304.208 shall apply except that TVA approval shall not be required to conduct the activities described in paragraph (a).

(i) Section 1304.210 shall apply except for paragraph (d).

(j) Section 1304.211 shall apply except to the extent that it would restrict mowing or other vegetation management.

(k) Nothing contained in this part shall be construed to be in derogation of the rights of the United States or of TVA under any flowage easement held by the United States or TVA.

§ 1304.301 Utilities.

Upon application to and approval by TVA, utility lines (electric, water-intake lines, etc.) may be placed within the flowage easement area as follows:

(a) Power lines, poles, electrical panels, and wiring shall be installed:

(1) In a way that would not be hazardous to the public or interfere with TVA operations; and

(2) In compliance with all State and local electrical codes (satisfactory evidence of compliance to be provided to TVA upon request).

(b) Electrical service shall be installed with an electrical disconnect that is located above the 500-year floodplain or the flood risk profile, whichever is higher, and is accessible during flood events.

(c) TVA's issuance of a permit does not mean that TVA has determined the facilities are safe for any purpose or that TVA has any duty to make such a determination.

§ 1304.302 Vegetation management on flowage easement shoreland.

Removal, modification, or establishment of vegetation on privately-owned shoreland subject to a TVA flowage easement does not require approval by TVA. When reviewing proposals for docks or other obstructions on flowage easement shoreland, TVA shall consider the potential for impacts to sensitive plants or other resources and may establish conditions in its approval of a proposal to avoid or minimize such impacts consistent with applicable laws and executive orders.

§ 1304.303 Channel excavation.

(a) Channel excavation of privately-owned reservoir bottom subject to a TVA flowage easement does not require approval by TVA under section 26a if:

(1) All dredged material is placed above the limits of the 100-year floodplain or the TVA flood risk profile elevation, whichever is applicable, and

(2) The dredging is not being accomplished in conjunction with the construction of a structure requiring a section 26a permit.

(b) Any fill material placed within the flood control zone of a TVA reservoir requires TVA review and approval.

(c) TVA shall encourage owners of flowage easement property to adopt the standards for channel excavation applicable to TVA-owned residential access shoreland.

Subpart E—Miscellaneous

§ 1304.400 Flotation devices and material, all floating structures.

(a) All flotation for docks, boat mooring buoys, and other water-use structures and facilities, shall be of materials commercially manufactured for marine use. Flotation materials shall be fabricated so as not to become water-logged, crack, peel, fragment, or be subject to loss of beads. Flotation materials shall be resistant to puncture, penetration, damage by animals, and fire. Any flotation within 40 feet of a line carrying fuel shall be 100 percent impervious to water and fuel. Styrofoam floatation must be fully encased. Reuse of plastic, metal, or other previously used drums or containers for encasement or flotation purpose is prohibited, except as provided in paragraph (c) of this section for certain metal drums already in use. Existing flotation (secured in place prior to September 8, 2003) in compliance with previous rules is authorized until in TVA's judgment the flotation is no longer serviceable, at which time it shall be replaced with approved flotation upon notification from TVA. For any float installed after September 8, 2003, repair or replacement is required when it no longer performs its designated function or exhibits any of the conditions prohibited by this subpart.

(b) Because of the possible release of toxic or polluting substances, and the hazard to navigation from metal drums that become partially filled with water and escape from docks, boathouses, houseboats, floats, and other water-use structures and facilities for which they are used for flotation, the use of metal drums in any form, except as authorized in paragraph (c) of this section, for flotation of any facilities is prohibited.

(c) Only metal drums which have been filled with plastic foam or other solid flotation materials and welded, strapped, or otherwise firmly secured in place prior to July 1, 1972, on existing facilities are permitted. Replacement of any metal drum flotation permitted to be used by this paragraph must be with a commercially manufactured flotation device or material specifically designed for marine applications (for example, pontoons, boat hulls, or other buoyancy devices made of steel, aluminum, fiberglass, or plastic foam, as provided for in paragraph (a) of this section).

(d) Every flotation device employed in the Tennessee River system must be firmly and securely affixed to the structure it supports with materials capable of withstanding prolonged exposure to wave wash and weather conditions.

§ 1304.401 Marine sanitation devices.

No person operating a commercial boat dock permitted under this part shall allow the mooring at such permitted facility of any watercraft or floating structure equipped with a marine sanitation device (MSD) unless such MSD is in compliance with all applicable statutes and regulations, including the FWPCA and regulations issued thereunder, and, where applicable, statutes and regulations governing "no discharge" zones.

§ 1304.402 Wastewater outfalls.

Applicants for a wastewater outfall shall provide copies of all Federal, State, and local permits, licenses, and approvals required for the facility prior to applying for TVA approval, or shall concurrently with the TVA application apply for such approvals. A section 26a permit shall not be issued until other required water quality approvals are obtained, and TVA reserves the right to impose additional requirements.

§ 1304.403 Marina sewage pump-out stations and holding tanks.

All pump-out facilities constructed after September 8, 2003 shall meet the following minimum design and operating requirements:

(a) Spill-proof connection with shipboard holding tanks;

(b) Suction controls or vacuum breaker capable of limiting suction to such levels as will avoid collapse of rigid holding tanks;

(c) Available fresh water facilities for tank flushing;

(d) Check valve and positive cut-off or other device to preclude spillage when breaking connection with vessel being severed;

(e) Adequate interim storage where storage is necessary before transfer to approved treatment facilities;

(f) No overflow outlet capable of discharging effluent into the reservoir;

(g) Alarm system adequate to notify the operator when the holding tank is full;

(h) Convenient access to holding tanks and piping system for purposes of inspection;

(i) Spill-proof features adequate for transfer of sewage from all movable floating pump-out facilities to shore-based treatment plants or intermediate transfer facilities;

(j) A reliable disposal method consisting of:

(1) An approved upland septic system that meets TVA, State, and local requirements; or

(2) Proof of a contract with a sewage disposal contractor; and

(k) A written statement to TVA certifying that the system shall be operated and maintained in such a way as to prevent any discharge or seepage of wastewater or sewage into the reservoir.

§ 1304.404 Commercial marina harbor limits.

The landward limits of commercial marina harbor areas are determined by the extent of land rights held by the dock operator. The lakeward limits of harbors at commercial marinas will be designated by TVA on the basis of the size and extent of facilities at the dock, navigation and flood control requirements, optimum use of lands and land rights owned by the United States, carrying capacity of the reservoir area in the vicinity of the marina, and on the basis of the environmental effects associated with the use of the harbor. Mooring buoys, slips, breakwaters, and permanent anchoring are prohibited beyond the lakeward extent of harbor limits. TVA may, at its discretion, reconfigure harbor limits based on changes in circumstances, including but not limited to, changes in the ownership of the land base supporting the marina.

§ 1304.405 Fuel storage tanks and handling facilities.

Fuel storage tanks and handling facilities are generally either underground (UST) or aboveground (AST) storage tank systems. An UST is any one or combination of tanks or tank systems defined in applicable Federal or State regulations as an UST. Typically (unless otherwise provided by applicable Federal or State rules), an UST is used to contain a regulated substance (such as a petroleum product) and has 10 percent or more of its total volume beneath the surface of the ground. The total volume includes any piping used in the system. An UST may be a buried tank, or an aboveground tank with buried piping if the piping holds 10 percent or more of the total system volume including the tank. For purposes of this part, an aboveground storage tank (AST) is any storage tank whose total volume (piping and tank) is less than 10 percent underground or any storage tank defined by applicable law or regulation as an AST.

(a) TVA requires the following to be included in all applications submitted after September 8, 2003 to install an UST or any part of an UST system below the 500-year flood elevation on a TVA reservoir, or regulated tailwater:

(1) A copy of the State approval for the UST along with a copy of the application sent to the State and any plans or drawings that were submitted for the State's review;

(2) Evidence of secondary containment for all piping or other systems associated with the UST;

(3) Evidence of secondary containment to contain leaks from gas pump(s);

(4) Calculations certified by a licensed, professional engineer in the relevant State showing how the tank will be anchored so that it does not float during flooding; and

(5) Evidence, where applicable, that the applicant has complied with all spill prevention, control and countermeasures (SPCC) requirements.

(b) The applicant must accept and sign a document stating that the applicant shall at all times be the owner of the UST system, that TVA shall have the right (but no duty) to prevent or remedy pollution or violations of law, including removal of the UST system, with costs charged to the applicant, that the applicant shall at all times maintain and operate the UST system in full compliance with applicable Federal, State, and local UST regulations, and that the applicant shall maintain eligibility in any applicable State trust fund.

(c) An application to install an AST or any part of an AST system below the 500-year elevation on a TVA reservoir or a regulated tailwater is subject to all of the requirements of paragraphs (a) and (b) of this section except that paragraph (a)(1) shall not apply in States that do not require application or approval for installation of an AST. Eligibility must be maintained for any applicable AST trust fund, and the system must be maintained and operated in accordance with any applicable AST regulations. The applicant must notify and obtain any required documents or permission from the State fire marshal's office prior to installation of the AST. The applicant must also follow the National Fire Protection Association Codes 30 and 30A for installation and maintenance of flammable and combustible liquids storage tanks at marine service stations.

(d) *Fuel handling on private, non-commercial docks and piers.* TVA will not approve the installation, operation, or maintenance of fuel handling facilities on any private, non-commercial dock or pier.

(e) *Floating fuel handling facilities.* TVA will not approve the installation of any floating fuel handling facility or fuel storage tank.

(f) *Demonstration of financial responsibility.* Applicants for a fuel handling fa-

cility to be located in whole or in part on TVA land shall be required to provide TVA, in a form and amount acceptable to TVA, a surety bond, irrevocable letter of credit, pollution liability insurance, or other evidence of financial responsibility in the event of a release.

§1304.406 Removal of unauthorized, unsafe, and derelict structures or facilities.

If, at any time, any dock, wharf, boathouse (fixed or floating), nonnavigable houseboat, outfall, aerial cable, or other fixed or floating structure or facility (including any navigable boat or vessel that has become deteriorated and is a potential navigation hazard or impediment to flood control) is anchored, installed, constructed, or moored in a manner inconsistent with this part, or is not constructed in accordance with plans approved by TVA, or is not maintained or operated so as to remain in accordance with this part and such plans, or is not kept in a good state of repair and in good, safe, and substantial condition, and the owner or operator thereof fails to repair or remove such structure (or operate or maintain it in accordance with such plans) within ninety (90) days after written notice from TVA to do so, TVA may cancel any license, permit, or approval and remove such structure, and/or cause it to be removed, from the Tennessee River system and/or lands in the custody or control of TVA. Such written notice may be given by mailing a copy thereof to the owner's address as listed on the license, permit, or approval or by posting a copy on the structure or facility. TVA may remove or cause to be removed any such structure or facility anchored, installed, constructed, or moored without such license, permit, or approval, whether such license or approval has once been obtained and subsequently canceled, or whether it has never been obtained. TVA's removal costs shall be charged to the owner of the structure, and payment of such costs shall be a condition of approval for any future facility proposed to serve the tract of land at issue or any tract derived therefrom whether or not the current owner caused such charges to be incurred. In addition, any applicant with an outstanding removal charge payable to TVA shall, until such time as the charge be paid in full, be ineligible to receive a permit or approval from TVA for any facility located anywhere along or in the Tennessee River or its tributaries. TVA shall not be responsible for the loss of property associated with the removal of any such structure or facility including, without limitation, the loss of any navigable boat or vessel moored at such a facility. Any costs voluntarily incurred by TVA to protect and store such property shall be removal costs within the meaning of this section, and TVA may sell such property and apply the proceeds toward any and all of its removal costs. Small businesses seeking expedited consideration of the economic impact of actions under this section may contact TVA's Supplier and Diverse Business Relations staff, TVA Procurement, 1101 Market Street, Chattanooga, Tennessee 37402–2801.

§ 1304.407   Development within flood control storage zones of TVA reservoirs.

(a) Activities involving development within the flood control storage zone on TVA reservoirs will be reviewed to determine if the proposed activity qualifies as a repetitive action. Under TVA's implementation of Executive Order 11988, Floodplain Management, repetitive actions are projects within a class of actions TVA has determined to be approvable without further review and documentation related to flood control storage, provided the loss of flood control storage caused by the project does not exceed one acre-foot. A partial list of repetitive actions includes:

(1) Private and public water-use facilities;

(2) Commercial recreation boat dock and water-use facilities;

(3) Water intake structures;

(4) Outfalls;

(5) Mooring and loading facilities for barge terminals;

(6) Minor grading and fills; and

(7) Bridges and culverts for pedestrian, highway, and railroad crossings.

(b) Projects resulting in flood storage loss in excess of one acre-foot will not be considered repetitive actions.

(c) For projects not qualifying as repetitive actions, the applicant shall be required, as appropriate, to evaluate alternatives to the placement of fill or the construction of a project within the flood control storage zone that would result in lost flood control storage. The alternative evaluation would either identify a better option or support and document that there is no reasonable alternative to the loss of flood control storage. If this determination can be made, the applicant must then demonstrate how the loss of flood control storage will be minimized.

(1) In addition, documentation shall be provided regarding:

(i) The amount of anticipated flood control storage loss;

(ii) The cost of compensation of the displaced flood control storage (how much it would cost to excavate material from the flood control storage zone, haul it to an upland site and dispose of it);

(iii) The cost of mitigation of the displaced flood control storage (how much it would cost to excavate material from another site within the flood control storage zone, haul it to the project site and use as the fill material);

(iv) The cost of the project; and

(v) The nature and significance of any economic and/or natural resource benefits that would be realized as a result of the project.

(2) TVA may, in its discretion, decline to permit any project that would result in the loss of flood control storage.

(d) Recreational vehicles parked or placed within flood control storage zones of TVA reservoirs shall be deemed an obstruction affecting navigation, flood control, or public lands or reservations within the meaning of section 26a of the Act unless they:

(1) Remain truly mobile and ready for highway use. The unit must be on its wheels or a jacking system and be attached to its site by only quick disconnect type utilities;

(2) Have no permanently attached additions, connections, foundations, porches, or similar structures; and

(3) Have an electrical cutoff switch that is located above the flood control zone and fully accessible during flood events.

§1304.408 Variances.

The Vice President or the designee thereof is authorized, following consideration whether a proposed structure or other regulated activity would adversely impact navigation, flood control, public lands or reservations, power generation, the environment, or sensitive environmental resources, or would be incompatible with surrounding uses or inconsistent with an approved TVA reservoir land management plan, to approve a structure or activity that varies from the requirements of this part in minor aspects.

§1304.409 Indefinite or temporary moorage of recreational vessels.

(a) Recreational vessels' moorage at unpermitted locations along the water's edge of any TVA reservoir may not exceed 14 consecutive days at any one place or at any place within one mile thereof.

(b) Recreational vessels may not establish temporary moorage within the limits of primary or secondary navigation channels.

(c) Moorage lines of recreational vessels may not be placed in such a way as to block or hinder boating access to any part of the reservoir.

(d) Permanent or extended moorage of a recreational vessel along the shoreline of any TVA reservoir without approval under section 26a of the TVA Act is prohibited.

§1304.410 Navigation restrictions.

(a) Except for the placement of riprap along the shoreline, structures, land based or water use, shall not be located within the limits of safety harbors and landings established for commercial navigation.

(b) Structures shall not be located in such a way as to block the visibility of navigation aids. Examples of navigation aids are lights, dayboards, and directional signs.

(c) The establishment of "no-wake" zones outside approved harbor limits is prohibited at marinas or community dock facilities that are adjacent to or near a commercial navigation channel. In such circumstances, facility owners may, upon approval from TVA, install a floating breakwater along the harbor limit to reduce wave and wash action.

§1304.411 Fish attractor, spawning, and habitat structures.

Fish attractors constitute potential obstructions and require TVA approval.

(a) Fish attractors may be constructed of anchored brush piles, log cribs, and/or spawning benches, stake beds, vegetation, or rock piles, provided they meet "TVA Guidelines for Fish Attractor Placement in TVA Reservoirs" (TVA 1997).

(b) When established in connection with an approved dock, fish attractors shall not project more than 30 feet out from any portion of the dock.

(c) Any floatable materials must be permanently anchored.

§1304.412 Definitions.

Except as the context may otherwise require, the following words or terms, when used in this part 1304, have the meaning specified in this section.

100-year floodplain means that area inundated by the one percent annual chance (or 100-year) flood.

500-year floodplain means that area inundated by the 0.2 percent annual chance (or 500-year) flood; any land susceptible to inundation during the 500-year or greater flood.

Act means the Tennessee Valley Authority Act of 1933, as amended.

Applicant means the person, corporation, State, municipality, political subdivision or other entity making application to TVA.

Application means a written request for the approval of plans pursuant to the regulations contained in this part.

Backlot means a residential lot not located adjacent to the shoreline but located in a subdivision associated with the shoreline.

Board means the Board of Directors of TVA.

Chief Executive Officer means the Chief Executive Officer, TVA.

Committee means a committee of the TVA Board of Directors that has been designated by the TVA Board to hear appeals under this regulation.

Community outlot means a subdivision lot located adjacent to the shoreline and designated by deed, subdivision covenant, or recorded plat as available for use by designated property owners within the subdivision.

Dredging means the removal of material from a submerged location, primarily for deepening harbors and waterways.

Enclosed structure means a structure enclosed overhead and on all sides so as to keep out the weather.

Flood control storage means the volume within an elevation range on a TVA reservoir that is reserved for the storage of floodwater.

Flood control storage zone means the area within an elevation range on a TVA reservoir that is reserved for the storage of floodwater. TVA shall, upon request, identify the contour marking the upper limit of the flood control storage zone at particular reservoir locations.

Flood risk profile elevation means the elevation of the 500-year flood that has been adjusted for surcharge at the dam. Surcharge is the ability to raise the water level behind the dam above the top-of-gates elevation.

Flowage easement shoreland means privately-owned properties where TVA has the right to flood the land.

Footprint means the total water surface area of either a square or rectangular shape occupied by an adjoining property owner's dock, pier, boathouse, or boatwells.

Full summer pool means the targeted elevation to which TVA plans to fill each reservoir during its annual operating cycle. Applicants are encouraged to consult the appropriate TVA Watershed Team or the TVA website to obtain the full summer pool elevation for the reservoir in question at the time the application is submitted.

Land-based structure means any structure constructed on ground entirely above the full summer pool elevation of a TVA reservoir but below the maximum shoreline contours of that reservoir.

Maximum shoreline contour means an elevation typically five feet above the top of the gates of a TVA dam. It is sometimes the property boundary between TVA property and adjoining private property.

Nonnavigable houseboat means any houseboat not in compliance with one or more of the criteria defining a navigable houseboat.

Owner or landowner ordinarily means all of the owners of a parcel of land. Except as otherwise specifically provided in this part, in all cases where TVA approval is required to engage in an activity and the applicant's eligibility to seek approval depends on status as an owner of real property, the owner or owners of only a fractional interest or of fractional interests totaling less than one in any such property shall not be considered, by virtue of such fractional interest or interests only, to be an owner and as such eligible to seek approval to conduct the activity without the consent of the other co-owners. In cases where the applicant owns water access rights across adjoining private property that borders TVA-owned shoreland, TVA may exercise its discretion to consider such person an owner, taking into account the availability of the shoreline to accommodate similarly situated owners and such other factors as TVA deems to be appropriate. In subdivisions where TVA had an established practice prior to September 8, 2003 of permitting individual or common water-use facilities on or at jointly-owned lots without the consent of all co-owners, TVA may exercise its discretion to continue such practice, taking into account the availability of the shoreline to accommodate similarly situated owners and other factors as TVA deems to be appropriate; provided, however, that the issuance of a TVA permit conveys no property interests, and the objections of a co-owner may be a basis for revocation of the permit.

Shoreland means the surface of land lying between minimum winter pool elevation of a TVA reservoir and the maximum shoreline contour.

Shoreline means the line where the water of a TVA reservoir meets the shore when the water level is at the full summer pool elevation.

Shoreline Management Zone (SMZ) means a 50-foot-deep vegetated zone designated by TVA on TVA-owned land.

TVA means the Tennessee Valley Authority.

TVA Investigating Officer means a TVA employee or a person under contract to TVA appointed by the Vice President or the CEO to investigate any issue concerning an appeal of a decision on an application under this part.

TVA property means real property owned by the United States and under the custody and control of TVA.

Vice President means the Vice President, Natural Resources, TVA, or a position with functionally equivalent supervisory responsibilities.

Water-based structure means any structure, fixed or floating, constructed on or in navigable waters of the United States.

Winter drawdown elevation means the elevation to which a reservoir water level is lowered during fall to provide storage capacity for winter and spring floodwaters.

Winter pool means the lowest level expected for the reservoir during the flood season.

[68 FR 46936, Aug. 7, 2003, as amended at 79 FR 4622, Jan. 29, 2014]

PART 1305 [RESERVED]

PART 1306—RELOCATION ASSISTANCE AND REAL PROPERTY ACQUISITION POLICIES

Subpart A—Regulations and Procedures

Sec.

Subpart B [Reserved]

AUTHORITY: Sec. 213, Uniform Relocation Assistance and Real Property Acquisition Policies Act of 1970, Pub. L. 91–646, 84 Stat. 1894 (42 U.S.C. 4601) as amended by the Surface Transportation and Uniform Relocation Assistance Act of 1987, Title IV of Pub. L. 100–17, 101 Stat. 246–256 (42 U.S.C. 4601 note); 48 Stat. 58, as amended (16 U.S.C. 831–831dd).

Subpart A—Regulations and Procedures

§1306.1 Purpose and applicability.

(a) *Purpose.* The purpose of the regulations and procedures in this Subpart

A is to implement Uniform Relocation Assistance and Real Property acquisition Policies Act of 1970 (Pub. L. 91–646, 84 Stat. 42 U.S.C. 4601) as amended by the Surface Transportation and Uniform Relocation Assistance Act of 1987 (Title IV of Pub. L. 100–17, Stat. 246–256, 42 U.S.C. 4601 note) (Uniform Act, as amended).

(b) *Applicability.* (1) Titles and I and II of the Uniform Act, as amended, govern relocation assistance by TVA. For TVA program activities undertaken after April 1, 1989, relocation assistance under those titles will be governed by implementing regulations set forth in Subpart A and Subparts C through G of 49 CFR part 24.

(2) Regulations and procedures for complying with the real property acquisition provisions of Title III of the Uniform Act, as amended, are set forth in this part.

[52 FR 48019, Dec. 17, 1987]

§1306.2 Uniform real property acquisition policy.

(a) Before negotiations are initiated for acquisition of real property, the Chief of TVA's Land Branch will cause the property to be appraised and establish an amount believed to be just compensation therefor. The appraiser shall afford the owner or his representative an opportunity to accompany him during his inspection of the property.

(b) When negotiations are initiated to acquire real property, the owner will be given a written statement of, and summary of the basis for, the amount estimated as just compensation. The statement will identify the property and the interest therein to be acquired, including buildings and other improvements to be acquired as a part of the real property, the amount of the estimated just compensation, and the basis therefor. If only a portion of the property is to be acquired, the statement will include a statement of damages and benefits, if any, to the remainder.

[38 FR 3592, Feb. 8, 1973. Redesignated at 52 FR 48019, Dec. 17, 1987]

§1306.3 Surrender of possession.

Possession of real property will not be taken until the owner has been paid the agreed purchase price or TVA's estimate of just compensation has been deposited in court in a condemnation proceeding. To the greatest extent practicable, no person will be required to move from property acquired by TVA without at least 90 days' written notice thereof.

[38 FR 3592, Feb. 8, 1973. Redesignated at 52 FR 48019, Dec. 17, 1987]

§ 1306.4 Rent after acquisition.

If TVA rents real property acquired by it to the former owner or former tenant, the amount of rent shall not exceed the fair rental value on a short-term basis.

[38 FR 3592, Feb. 8, 1973. Redesignated at 52 FR 48019, Dec. 17, 1987]

§ 1306.5 Tenants' rights in improvements.

Tenants of real property being acquired by TVA will be paid just compensation for any improvements owned by them, whether or not they might have a right to remove such improvements under the terms of their tenancy. Such payment will be made only upon the condition that all right, title, and interest of the tenant in such improvements shall be transferred to TVA and upon the further condition that the owner of the real property being acquired shall execute a disclaimer of any interest in said improvements.

[38 FR 3592, Feb. 8, 1973. Redesignated at 52 FR 48019, Dec. 17, 1987]

§ 1306.6 Expense of transfer of title and proration of taxes.

In connection with the acquisition of real property by TVA:

(a) TVA will, to the extent it deems fair and reasonable, bear all expenses incidental to the transfer of title to the United States, including penalty costs for the prepayment of any valid pre-existing recorded mortgage;

(b) Real property taxes shall be prorated to relieve the seller from paying taxes which are allocable to a period subsequent to vesting of title in the United States or the date of possession, whichever is earlier.

[38 FR 3592, Feb. 8, 1973. Redesignated at 52 FR 48019, Dec. 17, 1987]

Subpart B [Reserved]

PART 1307—NONDISCRIMINATION WITH RESPECT TO HANDICAP

AUTHORITY: TVA Act, 48 Stat. 58 (1933) as amended, 16 U.S.C. 831–831dd (1976) and sec. 504 of the Rehabilitation Act of 1973, Pub. L. 93–112, as amended, 29 U.S.C. 794 (1976; Supp. II 1978).

SOURCE: 45 FR 22895, Apr. 4, 1980, unless otherwise noted.

§ 1307.1 Definitions.

As used in this part, the following terms have the stated meanings, unless the context otherwise requires:

(a) *Section 504* means section 504 of the Rehabilitation Act of 1973, Pub. L. 93–112, as amended, 29 U.S.C. 794.

(b) *Recipient* means any individual, any State or its political subdivision, or any instrumentality of either, and any public or private agency, institution, organization, or other entity to which financial assistance is extended by TVA directly or through another recipient, including any successor, assignee, or transferee of a recipient as hereinafter set forth, but excluding the ultimate beneficiary of the assistance.

(c) *Financial assistance* means the grant or loan of money; the donation of real or personal property; the sale, lease, or license of real or personal property for a consideration which is nominal or reduced for the purpose of assisting the recipient; the waiver of charges which would normally be made, in order to assist the recipient; the entry into a contract where a purpose is to give financial assistance to the contracting party; and similar transactions.

(d) *Facility* means all or any portion of buildings, structures, equipment, roads, walks, parking lots, or other real or personal property or interest in such property.

(e) *Federal agency* means any department, agency, or instrumentality of the Government of the United States, other than TVA.

(f) *Handicapped person* means any individual who has a physical or mental impairment that substantially limits one or more major life activities, has a record of such an impairment, or is regarded as having such an impairment, as further defined below, except that, as related to employment, the term *handicapped individual* does not include any individual who is an alcoholic or drug abuser whose current use of alcohol or drugs prevents such individual from performing the duties of the job in question or whose employment, by reason of such current drug or alcohol abuse, would constitute a direct threat to property or the safety of others:

(1) *Physical or mental impairment* means (i) any physiological disorder or condition, cosmetic disfigurement, or anatomical loss affecting one or more of the following body systems: Neurological; musculoskeletal; special sense organs; respiratory, including speech organs; cardiovascular; reproductive; digestive; genitourinary; hemic and lymphatic; skin; and endocrine; or (ii) any mental or psychological disorder, such as mental retardation, organic brain syndrome, emotional or mental illness, and specific learning disabilities. The term *physical or mental impairment* includes, but is not limited to, such diseases and conditions as orthopedic, visual, speech, and hearing impairments; cerebral palsy; epilepsy; muscular dystrophy; multiple sclerosis; cancer; heart disease; diabetes; mental retardation; emotional illness; and drug addiction and alcoholism.

(2) *Major life activities* means functions such as caring for one's self, performing manual tasks, walking, seeing, hearing, speaking, breathing, learning, and working.

(3) *Has a record of such an impairment* means has a history of, or has been misclassified as having, a physical or mental impairment that substantially limits one or more major life activities.

(4) *Is regarded as having such an impairment* means (i) has a physical or mental impairment that does not substantially limit major life activities but which is treated by a recipient as constituting such a limitation; (ii) has a physical or mental impairment that substantially limits major life activities only as a result of the attitudes of others toward the impairment; or (iii) does not have a physical or mental impairment as defined in paragraph (f)(1) of this section but is treated by a recipient as having such an impairment.

(g) *Qualified handicapped person* means (1) with respect to employment, a handicapped person (except an alcoholic or drug abuser as defined in paragraph (f) of this section), who, with reasonable accommodation, can perform the essential functions of the job in question and (2) with respect to services, a handicapped person who meets the essential eligibility requirements for the receipt of such services.

(h) *Historic property* means an architecturally, historically, or culturally significant property listed in or eligible for listing in the National Register of Historic Places, or a property officially designated as having architectural, historic, or cultural significance under a statute of the appropriate State or local governmental body.

(i) *Building alterations* means those changes to existing conditions and equipment of a building which do not involve any structural changes, but which typically improve and upgrade a building, such as site improvements and alterations to stairways, doors, toilets or elevators.

(j) *Structural changes* shall mean those changes which alter the structure of a building, including but not limited to its load bearing walls and all types of post and beam systems in wood, steel, iron or concrete.

(k) *Program or activity* means all of the operations of any entity described in paragraphs (k)(1) through (4) of this section, any part of which is extended Federal financial assistance:

(1)(i) A department, agency, special purpose district, or other instrumentality of a State or of a local government; or

(ii) The entity of such State or local government that distributes such assistance and each such department or agency (and each other State or local government entity) to which the assistance is extended, in the case of assistance to a State or local government;

(2)(i) A college, university, or other postsecondary institution, or a public system of higher education; or

(ii) A local educational agency (as defined in 20 U.S.C. 7801), system of vocational education, or other school system;

(3)(i) An entire corporation, partnership, or other private organization, or an entire sole proprietorship—

(A) If assistance is extended to such corporation, partnership, private organization, or sole proprietorship as a whole; or

(B) Which is principally engaged in the business of providing education, health care, housing, social services, or parks and recreation; or

(ii) The entire plant or other comparable, geographically separate facility to which Federal financial assistance is extended, in the case of any other corporation, partnership, private organization, or sole proprietorship; or

(4) Any other entity which is established by two or more of the entities described in paragraph (k)(1), (2), or (3) of this section.

[45 FR 22895, Apr. 4, 1980, as amended at 68 FR 51356, Aug. 26, 2003]

§ 1307.2 Purpose.

The purpose of this part is to effectuate section 504 to the end that no otherwise qualified handicapped individual shall, solely by reason of his or her handicap, be excluded from the participation in, be denied the benefits of, or be subjected to discrimination under any program or activity receiving financial assistance from TVA.

§ 1307.3 Application.

This part applies to any program or activity for which financial assistance is provided by TVA, except that this part does not apply to any (a) TVA procurement contracts, contracts with other Federal agencies, or contracts of insurance or guaranty, (b) money paid, property transferred, or other assistance extended to a recipient before the effective date of this part, or (c) assistance to any individual or entity which is the ultimate beneficiary. Nothing in paragraph (b) of this section exempts any recipient of financial assistance under a contract in effect on the effective date of this part from compliance with this part.

[45 FR 22895, Apr. 4, 1980, as amended at 68 FR 51356, Aug. 26, 2003]

§ 1307.4 Discrimination prohibited.

(a) *General.* No qualified handicapped person, shall, on the basis of handicap, be excluded from participation in, be denied the benefits of, or otherwise be subjected to discrimination under any program or activity to which this part applies.

(b) *Specific discriminatory actions.* (1) A recipient to which this part applies shall not, directly or through contractual, licensing, or other arrangements, on the basis of handicap:

(i) Deny a qualified handicapped person the opportunity to participate in or benefit from the aid, benefit, or services available under the program or activity;

(ii) Afford a qualified handicapped person an opportunity to participate in or benefit from the aid, benefit, or service that is not equal to that afforded others under the program or activity;

(iii) Provide a qualified handicapped person with an aid, benefit, or service that is not as effective in affording equal opportunity to obtain the same result, to gain the same benefit, or to reach the same level of achievement as that provided to others under the program or activity;

(iv) Provide different or separate aid, benefits, or services to handicapped persons or to any class of handicapped persons than is provided to others, unless such action is necessary to provide qualified handicapped persons with aid, benefits, or services that are as effective as those provided to others under the program or activity;

(v) Aid or perpetuate discrimination against a qualified handicapped person by providing significant assistance to an agency, organization, or entity that discriminates on the basis of handicap in providing any aid, benefit, or service to beneficiaries of the recipient's program or activity;

(vi) Deny a qualified handicapped person the opportunity to participate as a member of planning or advisory boards with respect to the program or activity; or

(vii) Otherwise limit a qualified handicapped person in the enjoyment under the program of any right, privilege, advantage, or opportunity enjoyed by others under the program or activity.

(2) A recipient shall not deny a qualified handicapped person the opportunity to participate under the program or activity in aid, benefits, or services that are not separate or different, despite the existence of permissibly separate or different aid, benefits, or services.

(3) A recipient shall not, directly or through contractual or other arrangements, utilize criteria or methods of administration (i) that have the effect of subjecting qualified handicapped persons to discrimination on the basis of handicap, (ii) that have the purpose or effect of defeating or substantially impairing accomplishment of the objectives of the program or activity with respect to handicapped persons, or (iii) that perpetuate the discrimination of another recipient if both recipients are subject to common administrative control.

(4) A recipient shall not, in determining the site or location of a facility under the program or activity, make selections (i) that have the effect of excluding handicapped persons from, denying them the benefits of, or otherwise subjecting them to discrimination under the program or activity, or (ii) that have the purpose or effect of defeating or substantially impairing the accomplishment of the objectives of the program or activity with respect to handicapped persons.

(c) The exclusion of nonhandicapped persons from aid, benefits, or services limited by Federal statute or executive order to handicapped persons or the exclusion of a specific class of handicapped persons from aid, benefits, or services limited by Federal statute or executive order to a different class of handicapped persons is not prohibited by this part.

(d) Recipients shall administer programs or activities in the most integrated setting appropriate to the needs of qualified handicapped persons. A recipient who wishes to establish a policy of separate aid, benefits, or services or different treatment for handicapped and nonhandicapped persons shall request and receive written approval from TVA before instituting such policy or undertaking any such separate treatment.

(e) Recipients shall take appropriate steps to ensure that communications to their applicants, employees, and beneficiaries are available to such persons with impaired vision and hearing.

[45 FR 22895, Apr. 4, 1980, as amended at 68 FR 51356, Aug. 26, 2003]

§1307.5 **Employment discrimination.**

(a) *General.* No qualified handicapped person shall, on the basis of handicap, be subjected to discrimination in employment under any program or activity subject to this part.

(b) *Specific discriminatory actions.* With respect to a program or activity subject to this part, a recipient shall not limit, segregate, or classify applicants or employees in any way that adversely affects their opportunities or status because of handicap.

(c) A recipient shall make all decisions concerning employment under any program or activity subject to this part in a manner which ensures that discrimination on the basis of handicap does not occur, including the following activities:

(1) Recruitment, advertising, and processing of applications for employment;

(2) Hiring, upgrading, promotion, award of tenure, demotion, transfer, layoff, termination, right of return from layoff, and rehiring;

(3) Rates of pay or any other form of compensation and changes in compensation;

(4) Job assignments, job classifications, organizational structures, position descriptions, lines of progression, and seniority lists;

(5) Leaves of absence, sick leave, or any other leave;

(6) Fringe benefits available by virtue of employment, whether or not administered by the recipient;

(7) Selection and financial support for training, including apprenticeship, professional meetings, conferences, and other related activities, and selection for leaves of absence to pursue training;

(8) Employer sponsored activities, including those that are social or recreational; and

(9) Any other term, condition, or privilege of employment.

(d) A recipient shall not participate in a contractual or other relationship that has the effect of subjecting qualified handicapped applicants or employees to discrimination prohibited by this part, including relationships with employment and referral agencies, with labor unions, with organizations providing or administering fringe benefits to employees of the recipient, and with organizations providing training and apprenticeships.

(e) *Reasonable accommodation.* (1) A recipient shall make reasonable accommodation to the known physical or mental limitations of an otherwise qualified handicapped applicant or employee unless the recipient can demonstrate that the accommodation would impose an undue hardship on the operation of the program or activity subject to this part. Reasonable accommodation may include:

(i) Making facilities used by employees readily accessible to and usable by handicapped persons; and

(ii) Job restructuring, part-time or modified work schedules, acquisition or modification of equipment or devices, the provision of readers or interpreters, or other similar actions.

(2) In determining whether an accommodation would impose an undue hardship on the operation of a recipient's program or activity under this paragraph factors to be considered include but are not limited to:

(i) The nature and cost of the accommodation needed, and its effect, if any, on the recipient's programs or activities.

(ii) The kind of operation conducted by the recipient, including the com-

position and structure of the recipient's workforce; and

(iii) The overall size of the recipient's program or activity with respect to number of employees, number and type of facilities, and size of budget.

(3) It is not an undue hardship with respect to a qualified handicapped employee or applicant if the sole basis for the claim of hardship is the need to make an accommodation to the physical or mental limitations of the otherwise qualified employee or applicant and the accommodation is deemed by TVA to be reasonable.

(f) *Employment criteria.* A recipient shall not use employment tests or criteria that discriminate against handicapped persons and shall ensure that employment tests are adapted for use by persons who have handicaps that impair sensory, manual, or speaking skills.

(g) *Preemployment inquiries.* (1) A recipient shall not conduct a preemployment medical examination or make a preemployment inquiry as to whether an applicant is a handicapped person or as to the nature or severity of a handicap except as set out in this paragraph (g).

(2) A recipient may make a preemployment inquiry into an applicant's ability to perform job-related functions.

(3) When a recipient is taking remedial action to correct the effects of past discrimination, taking voluntary action to overcome the effects of conditions that resulted in limited participation in its TVA-assisted program or activity or is taking affirmative action pursuant to section 503 of the Rehabilitation Act of 1973, the recipient may invite applicants for employment to indicate whether and to what extent they are handicapped: *Provided,* That the recipient states clearly on any written questionnaire used for this purpose, or makes clear orally if no written questionnaire is so used, that:

(i) The information requested is intended for use solely in connection with such remedial, voluntary or affirmative action efforts;

(ii) The information is being requested on a voluntary basis and it will be kept confidential as provided in paragraph (g)(4) of this section;

(iii) Refusal to provide the information will not subject the applicant or employee to any adverse treatment; and

(iv) The information will be used only in accordance with this part.

(4) Nothing in this section shall prohibit a recipient from conditioning an offer of employment on the results of a medical examination conducted prior to the employee's entrance on duty: *Provided,* That:

(i) All entering employees are subjected to such an examination regardless of handicap; and

(ii) The results of such an examination are used only in accordance with the requirements of this part.

(5) Information obtained in accordance with this section as to the medical condition or history of an employee or applicant shall be collected and maintained on separate forms that shall be accorded confidentiality as medical records, except that:

(i) Supervisors and managers may be informed regarding restrictions on the work or duties of handicapped persons and regarding necessary accommodations;

(ii) First aid and safety personnel may be informed, where appropriate, if the condition might require emergency treatment; and

(iii) TVA officials investigating compliance with section 504 shall be provided information which they deem relevant upon request.

[45 FR 22895, Apr. 4, 1980, as amended at 68 FR 51356, Aug. 26, 2003]

§1307.6 **Accessibility.**

(a) *General.* No qualified handicapped person shall, because facilities are inaccessible to or unusable by handicapped persons, be denied the benefits of, be excluded from participation in, or otherwise be subjected to discrimination under any program or activity subject to this part.

(b) *Existing facilities.* (1) Each program or activity subject to this part shall be operated so that when each part is viewed in its entirety it is readily accessible to and usable by qualified handicapped persons. This paragraph does not necessarily require a recipient to make each of its existing facilities or every part of an existing facility ac-

cessible to and usable by handicapped persons. A recipient is not required to make building alterations or structural changes if other methods are effective in achieving accessibility. Such compliance methods may include (subject to the provisions of §§1307.4 and 1307.5), reassigning aid, benefits, or services to accessible locations within a facility; providing assistance to handicapped persons into or through an otherwise inaccessible facility; delivering programs or activities at other alternative sites which are accessible and are operated or available for use by the recipient; or other methods which comply with the intent of this paragraph.

(2) This paragraph governs the timing of development of transition plans and the completion of necessary building alterations and structural changes to existing facilities, including historic property covered by paragraph (c) of this section. If building alterations or structural changes will be necessary to comply with paragraph (b)(1) of this section, the recipient shall develop a transition plan setting forth the steps necessary to complete the alterations or changes in accordance with such standards as TVA may specify in the contract or agreement, and shall have the plan approved by TVA. If the financial assistance from TVA is expected to last for less than three years, the contract or agreement shall specify the date by which the transition plan shall be developed and approved. If the financial assistance from TVA is expected to last for at least three years, the transition plan shall be developed and submitted to TVA within six months from the effective date of the contract or agreement, subject to extension by TVA for an additional six month period, for good cause shown to it. A transition plan shall:

(i) Be developed with the assistance of interested persons or organizations representing handicapped persons;

(ii) Be available for public inspection after approval by TVA (or at any earlier time required by state or local law applicable to the recipient);

(iii) Identify the official responsible for implementation of the approved plan; and

(iv) Specify the date by which the required alterations or changes shall be completed, which shall be as soon as practicable and in no event later than three years after the effective date that financial assistance is extended by TVA.

(3) Alterations to existing facilities shall, to the maximum extent feasible, be designed and constructed to be readily accessible to and usable by handicapped persons.

(c) *Historic property.* If a recipient's program or activity uses an existing facility which is an historic property, the recipient shall endeavor to assure compliance with paragraph (b)(1) of this section by compliance methods which do not alter the historic character or architectural integrity of the historic property. The recipient must determine that accessibility cannot be accomplished by such alternative methods before considering building alterations as a compliance method. To the maximum extent possible any building alterations determined to be necessary shall be undertaken so as not to alter or destroy architecturally significant elements or features. A recipient may determine that structural changes are necessary to accomplish accessibility only if the recipient has determined that accessibility cannot feasibly be accomplished by any of the other foregoing methods. To the maximum extent possible, any structural changes determined to be necessary shall be undertaken so as not to alter or destroy architecturally significant elements or features.

(d) *New construction.* (1) New facilities required under a program or activity subject to this part shall be designed and constructed to be readily accessible to and usable by handicapped persons.

(2) Effective as of November 4, 1988, design, construction, or alteration of buildings in conformance with Sections 3–8 of the Uniform Federal Accessibility Standards (UFAS) (41 CFR Subpart 101–19.6 app. A) shall be deemed to comply with the requirements of this section with respect to those buildings. Departures from particular technical and scoping requirements of UFAS by the use of other methods are permitted where substantially equivalent or greater access to and usability of the building is provided.

(3) For purposes of this section, section 4.1.6(1)(g) of UFAS shall be interpreted to exempt from the requirements of UFAS only mechanical rooms and other spaces that, because of their intended use, will not require accessibility to the public or beneficiaries or result in the employment or residence therein of physically handicapped persons.

(4) This section does not require recipients to make building alterations that have little likelihood of being accomplished without removing or altering a load-bearing structural member.

[45 FR 22895, Apr. 4, 1980, as amended at 53 FR 39083, Oct. 5, 1988; 68 FR 51356, Aug. 26, 2003]

§ 1307.7 **Assurances required.**

(a) TVA contributes financial assistance only under agreements which contain a provision which specifically requires compliance with this part and compliance with such standards for construction and alteration of facilities as TVA may provide. If the financial assistance involves the furnishing of real property, the agreement shall obligate the recipient, or the transferee in the case of a subsequent transfer, for the period during which the real property is used for a purpose for which the financial assistance is extended or for another purpose involving the provision of similar services or benefits. Where the financial assistance involves the furnishing of personal property, the agreement shall obligate the recipient during the period for which ownership or possession of the property is retained. In all other cases the agreement shall obligate the recipient for the period during which financial assistance is extended pursuant to the agreement. TVA shall specify the form of the foregoing agreement, and the extent to which an agreement shall be applicable to subcontractors, transferees, successors in interest, and other participants.

(b) In the case of real property, structures or improvements thereon, or interests therein, acquired with TVA financial assistance, or in the case where financial assistance was provided in the form of a transfer by TVA of real property or interest therein, the instrument effecting or recording the transfer of title shall contain a covenant running with the land assuring compliance with this part and the guidelines contained herein for the period during which the real property is used for a purpose for which the TVA financial assistance is extended or for another purpose involving the provision of similar services or benefits. Where no transfer of property is involved, but property is improved with of TVA financial assistance, the recipient shall agree to include such a covenant in any subsequent transfer of such property. Where the property is obtained by transfer from TVA, the covenant against discrimination may also include a condition coupled with a right to be reserved by TVA to revert title to the property in the event of a breach of the covenant where, in the discretion of TVA, such a condition and right of reverter is appropriate to the statute under which the real property is obtained and to the nature of the grant and the grantee. In such event, if a transferee of real property proposes to mortgage or otherwise encumber the real property as security for financing construction of new, or improvement of existing, facilities on such property for the purposes for which the property was transferred, TVA may agree, upon request of the transferee and if necessary to accomplish such financing, and upon such conditions as it deems appropriate, to forbear the exercise of such right to revert title for so long as the lien of such mortgage or other encumbrance remains effective.

[45 FR 22895, Apr. 4, 1980, as amended at 68 FR 51356, Aug. 26, 2003]

§1307.8 **Compliance information.**

(a) *Cooperation and assistance.* TVA shall to the fullest extent practicable seek the cooperation of recipients in obtaining compliance with this part and shall provide assistance and guidance to recipients to help them comply voluntarily with this part.

(b) *Compliance reports.* Each recipient shall keep such records and submit to TVA timely, complete and accurate compliance reports at such times, and in such form and containing such information, as TVA may determine to be necessary to enable it to ascertain whether the recipient has complied or is complying with this part. In the case which a primary recipient extends financial assistance to any other recipient, such other recipient shall also submit such compliance reports to the primary recipient as may be necessary to enable the primary recipient to carry out its obligations under this part.

(c) *Access to sources of information.* Each recipient shall permit access by TVA during normal business hours to such of its books, records, accounts, and other sources of information, and its facilities, as TVA may require to ascertain compliance with this part. Where any information required of a recipient is in the exclusive possession of any other agency, institution or person and this agency, institution or person shall fail or refuse to furnish this information, the recipient shall so certify in its report and set forth the efforts it has made to obtain the information.

(d) *Information to employees, beneficiaries and participants.* Each recipient shall make available to employees, participants, beneficiaries, and other interested persons such information regarding the provisions of this part and its applicability to the program or activity for which the recipient receives financial assistance, and shall make such information available to them in such manner, as TVA finds necessary to apprise such persons of the protections against discrimination assured them by section 504 and this part.

[45 FR 22895, Apr. 4, 1980, as amended at 68 FR 51356, Aug. 26, 2003]

§1307.9 **Conduct of investigations.**

(a) *Periodic compliance reviews.* TVA shall from time to time review the practices of recipients to determine whether they are complying with this part.

(b) *Complaints.* Any individual who claims (individually or on behalf of any specific class of individuals) to have been subjected to discrimination prohibited by this part may, personally or by a representative, file with TVA a written complaint. A complaint must be filed not later than ninety (90) days from the date of the alleged discrimination, unless the time for filing is extended by TVA.

(c) *Investigations.* TVA will make a prompt investigation whenever a compliance review, report, complaint, or any other information indicates a possible failure to comply with this part. The investigation shall include, where appropriate, a review of the pertinent practices and policies of the recipient, the circumstances under which the possible noncompliance with this part occurred, and other factors relevant to a determination as to whether the recipient has failed to comply with this part.

(d) *Resolution of matters.* (1) If an investigation pursuant to paragraph (c) of this section indicates a failure to comply with this part, TVA will so inform the recipient and the matter will be resolved by informal means whenever possible. If TVA determines that the matter cannot be resolved by informal means, action will be taken as provided for in § 1307.10.

(2) If an investigation does not warrant action pursuant to paragraph (d) (1) of this section, TVA will so inform the recipient and the complainant, if any, in writing.

(e) *Intimidatory or retaliatory acts prohibited.* No recipient or other person shall intimidate, threaten, coerce, or discriminate against any individual for the purpose of interfering with any right or privilege secured by section 504 or this part, or because the individual had made a complaint, testified, assisted, or participated in any manner in an investigation, proceeding, or hearing under this part. The identity of complainants shall be kept confidential except to the extent necessary to carry out the purposes of this part, including the conduct of any investigation, hearing, or judicial proceeding arising thereunder.

§ 1307.10 Procedure for effecting compliance.

(a) *General.* If there appears to be a failure or threatened failure to comply with this part, and if the noncompliance or threatened noncompliance cannot be corrected by informal means, compliance with this part may be effected by the suspension or termination of or refusal to grant or to continue financial assistance or by any other means authorized by law. Such other means may include, but are not

to be limited to, (1) a reference to the Department of Justice with a recommendation that appropriate proceedings be brought to enforce any rights of the United States under any law of the United States, (2) institution of appropriate proceedings by TVA to enforce the provisions of the agreement of financial assistance or of any deed or instrument relating thereto, and (3) any applicable proceeding under State or local law.

(b) *Noncompliance with § 1307.7.* If any entity requesting financial assistance from TVA declines to furnish the assurance required under § 1307.7, or otherwise fails or refuses to comply with a requirement imposed by or pursuant to that section, financial assistance may be refused in accordance with the procedures of paragraph (c) of this section; and for such purposes, the term "recipient" includes one who has been denied financial assistance. TVA shall not be required to provide assistance in such a case during the pendency of the administrative proceedings under such paragraph except that TVA shall continue assistance during the pendency of such proceedings where such assistance was due and payable pursuant to an agreement therefor entered into with TVA prior to the effective date of this part.

(c) *Termination of or refusal to grant or to continue financial assistance.* No order suspending, terminating or refusing to grant or continue financial assistance shall become effective until (1) TVA has advised the recipient of the failure to comply and has determined that compliance cannot be secured by voluntary means, (2) there has been an express finding on the record, after opportunity for hearing, of a failure by the recipient to comply with a requirement imposed by or pursuant to this part, including any act of discrimination on the basis of handicap in violation of this part, and (3) the action has been approved by the TVA Board pursuant to § 1307.12. Any action to suspend or terminate or to refuse to grant or to continue financial assistance shall be limited to the particular recipient as to whom such a finding had been made and shall be limited in its effect to the particular program or activity, or part thereof, in which such noncompliance had been so found.

(d) *Other means authorized by law.* No action to effect compliance by any other means authorized by law shall be taken until (1) TVA has determined that compliance cannot be secured by voluntary means, (2) the recipient or other person has been notified of its failure to comply and of the action to be taken to effect compliance, and (3) the expiration of at least ten (10) days from the mailing of such notice to the recipient or other person. During this period of at least ten (10) days additional efforts will be made to persuade the recipient or other person to comply with this part and to take such corrective action as may be appropriate.

[45 FR 22895, Apr. 4, 1980, as amended at 68 FR 51356, Aug. 26, 2003]

§1307.11 Hearings.

(a) *Opportunity for hearing.* Whenever an opportunity for a hearing is required by §1307.10, reasonable notice shall be given by registered or certified mail, return receipt requested, to the affected recipient. This notice shall advise the recipient of the action proposed to be taken, the specific provision under which the proposed action against it is to be taken, and the matters of fact or law asserted as the basis for this action, and shall either (1) fix a date not less than twenty (20) days after the date of such notice within which the recipient may request of TVA that the matter be scheduled for hearing or (2) advise the recipient that the matter in question has been set down for hearing at a stated time and place. The time and place so fixed shall be reasonable and shall be subject to change for cause. The complainant, if any, shall be advised of the time and place of the hearing. A recipient may waive a hearing and submit written information and argument for the record. The failure of a recipient to request a hearing under this subsection or to appear at a hearing for which a date has been set shall be deemed to be a waiver of the right to a hearing and a consent to the making of a decision on the basis of such information as is available.

(b) *Time and place of hearing.* Hearings shall be held at the time and place fixed by TVA unless it determines that the convenience of the recipient requires that another place be selected. Hearings shall be held before the TVA Board or before a "hearing officer" who shall be either a member of the TVA Board or, at the discretion of the Board, a person designated by the Board who shall not be employed in or under the TVA division through or under which the financial assistance has been extended by TVA to the recipient involved in the hearing.

(c) *Right to counsel.* In all proceedings under this section, the recipient and TVA shall have the right to be represented by counsel.

(d) *Procedures, evidence, and record.* (1) The hearing, decision, and any administrative review thereof shall be conducted in accordance with such rules of procedure as are proper (and not inconsistent with this section) relating to the conduct of the hearing, giving of notices subsequent to those provided for in paragraph (a) of this section, taking of testimony, exhibits, arguments and briefs, requests for findings, and other related matters. Both TVA and the recipient shall be entitled to introduce all relevant evidence on the issues as stated in the notice for hearing or as determined by the officer conducting the hearing at the outset of or during the hearing.

(2) Technical rules of evidence will not apply to hearings conducted pursuant to this part, but rules or principles designed to assure production of the most credible evidence available and to subject testimony to test by cross-examination shall be applied where reasonably necessary by the officer conducting the hearing. That officer may exclude irrelevant, immaterial, or unduly repetitious evidence. All documents and other evidence offered or taken for the record shall be open to examination by the parties and opportunity shall be given to refute facts and arguments advanced on either side of the issues. A transcript shall be made of the oral evidence except to the extent the substance thereof is stipulated for the record. All decisions shall be based upon the hearing record and written findings shall be made.

(e) *Consolidated or joint hearings.* In cases in which the same or related facts are asserted to constitute noncompliance with this part with respect to two or more Federal statutes, authorities, or other means by which Federal financial assistance is extended and to which this part applies, or noncompliance with this part and the regulations of one or more other Federal agencies issued under section 504, the TVA Board may, by agreement with such other agency, provide for the conduct of consolidated or joint hearings, and for the application to such hearings of rules of procedure not inconsistent with this part. Final decisions in such cases, insofar as this part is concerned, shall be made in accordance with § 1307.12.

[45 FR 22895, Apr. 4, 1980, as amended at 68 FR 51356, Aug. 26, 2003]

§ 1307.12 Decisions and notices.

(a) *Decision by a member of the TVA Board or a hearing officer.* If the hearing is held before a "hearing officer" as defined in § 1307.11(b), that hearing officer shall either make an initial decision, if so authorized, or certify the entire record including recommended findings and proposed decision to the TVA Board for a final decision. A copy of such initial decision or certification shall be mailed to the recipient. Where the initial decision is made by a hearing officer, the recipient may file with the TVA Board exceptions to the initial decision, which shall include a statement of reasons therefor. Such exceptions shall be filed within thirty (30) days of the mailing of the notice of initial decision. In the absence of exceptions, the TVA Board may on its own motion within forty-five (45) days after the initial decision serve on the recipient a notice that it will review the decision. Upon the filing of such exceptions or of such notice of review, the TVA Board shall review the initial decision and issue its own decision thereon including the reasons therefor. In the absence of either exceptions or a notice of review, the initial decision shall constitute the final decision of the TVA Board.

(b) *Decisions on record or review by the TVA Board.* Whenever a record is certified to the TVA Board for decision or

it reviews the decision of a hearing officer pursuant to paragraph (a) of this section, or whenever the TVA Board conducts the hearing, the recipient shall be given reasonable opportunity to file with the Board briefs or other written statements of its contentions, and a copy of the final decision of the Board shall be given in writing to the recipient and to the complainant, if any.

(c) *Decisions on record where a hearing is waived.* Whenever a hearing is waived, a decision shall be made by the TVA Board on the record and a copy of such decision shall be given to the recipient, and to the complainant, if any.

(d) *Rulings required.* Each decision shall set forth a ruling on each finding, conclusion, or exception presented, and shall identify the requirement or requirements imposed by or pursuant to this part with which it is found that the recipient has failed to comply.

(e) *Approval by TVA Board.* Any final decision (other than a decision by the TVA Board) which provides for the suspension or termination of, or the refusal to grant or continue financial assistance, or the imposition of any other sanction available under this part or section 504 shall promptly be transmitted to the TVA Board which may approve such decision, vacate it, or remit or mitigate any sanction imposed.

(f) *Content of orders.* The final decision may provide for suspension or termination of, or refusal to grant or continue financial assistance, in whole or in part, to which this regulation applies, and may contain such terms, conditions, and other provisions as are consistent with and will effectuate the purposes of section 504 and this part, including provisions designed to assure that no financial assistance to which this regulation applies will thereafter be extended to the recipient determined by such decision to have failed to comply with this part, unless and until it corrects its noncompliance and satisfies TVA that it will fully comply with this part.

(g) *Posttermination proceedings.* (1) A recipient adversely affected by an order issued under paragraph (f) of this section shall be restored to full eligibility to receive financial assistance

upon satisfaction of the terms and conditions for such eligibility contained in
that order, or if the recipient otherwise
comes into compliance with this part
and provides reasonable assurance of
future full compliance with this part.

(2) Any recipient adversely affected
by an order entered pursuant to paragraph (f) of this section may at any
time request that TVA fully restore
the recipient's eligibility to receive financial assistance. Any such request
shall be supported by information
showing that the recipient has met the
requirements of paragraph (g)(1) of this
section. If TVA determines that those
requirements have been satisfied, it
shall restore such eligibility.

(3) If TVA denies any such request,
the recipient may submit a request for
a hearing in writing, specifying its reasons for believing TVA to have been in
error. The recipient shall thereupon be
given an expeditious hearing, with a
decision on the record, in accordance
with rules of procedure issued by TVA.
The recipient, upon proving at such a
hearing that the requirements of paragraph (g)(1) of this section are satisfied, will be restored to such eligibility. While proceedings under this
paragraph are pending, the sanctions
imposed by the order issued under
paragraph (f) of this section shall remain in effect.

[45 FR 22895, Apr. 4, 2003, as amended at 68
FR 51356, Aug. 26, 2003]

§ 1307.13 Effect on other regulations; supervision and coordination.

(a) *Effect on other regulations.* Nothing
in this part shall be deemed to supersede or affect any of the following (including future amendments thereof):
(1) Regulations by TVA and other Federal agencies issued with respect to
section 503 of the Rehabilitation Act of
1973, or (2) any other regulations or instructions, insofar as they prohibit discrimination on the ground of handicap
in any program or activity or situation
to which this part is inapplicable, or
which prohibit discrimination on any
other ground.

(b) *Supervison and coordination.* TVA
may from time to time assign to officials of other Federal agencies, with
the consent of such agencies, responsibilities in connection with the effectuation of the purposes of section 504
and this part (other than responsibility
for final decision as provided in
§ 1307.12), including the achievement of
effective coordination and maximum
uniformity within the Executive
Branch of the government in the application of section 504 and this part to
similar programs or activities and in
similar situations. Any action taken,
determination made, or requirement
imposed by an official of another federal agency acting pursuant to an assignment of responsibility under this
part shall have the same effect as
though such action had been taken by
TVA.

[45 FR 22895, Apr. 26, 1980, as amended at 68
FR 51356, Apr. 4, 2003]

PART 1308—CONTRACT DISPUTES

Subpart A—General Matters

AUTHORITY: Tennessee Valley Authority Act of 1933, as amended, 16 U.S.C. 831–831dd; Contract Disputes Act of 1978, 92 Stat. 2383–2391.

SOURCE: 44 FR 29648, May 22, 1979, unless otherwise noted. Redesignated at 44 FR 30682, May 29, 1979.

Subpart A—General Matters

§ 1308.1 Purpose and organization.

The regulations in this part implement the Contract Disputes Act of 1978 as it relates to TVA. This part consists of 5 subparts. Subpart A deals with matters applicable throughout the part, incuding definitions. Subpart B deals with Contracting Officers' decisions. Subpart C deals with general matters concerning the TVA Board of Contract Appeals. Subpart D deals with hearing and prehearing procedures, including discovery. Subpart E deals with subpoenas.

§ 1308.2 Definitions.

For the purposes of this part, unless otherwise provided:

(a) The term *Act* means the Contract Disputes Act of 1978, 92 Stat. 2383–91.

(b) The term *Board* means the TVA Board of Contract Appeals.

(c) The term *claim* means a written demand by a Contractor, in compliance with this paragraph, for a decision by a Contracting Officer under a disputes clause. A claim must:

(1) State the amount of monetary relief, or the kind of nonmonetary relief, sought, and identify the contract provision relied upon;

(2) Include sufficient supporting data to permit the Contracting Officer to decide the claim, or provide appropriate reference to previously submitted data;

(3) If monetary relief totalling more than $50,000 is involved, include a signed certification by the Contractor that the claim is made in good faith, that the supporting data are accurate and complete to the best of the Contractor's knowledge and belief, and that the amount requested accurately reflects the contract adjustment for which the Contractor believes TVA is liable;

(4) Be signed by the Contractor, or on its behalf if the Contractor is other than an individual. If signed on a Contractor's behalf, the claim must include evidence of the authority of the individual so signing it, and of the individual signing any certification required by this paragraph, unless such authority appears in the contract or contract file.

The Contracting Officer has no authority to waive any of the requirements of this paragraph.

(d) The term *contract* means an agreement in writing entered into by TVA for:

(1) The procurement of property, other than real property in being;

(2) The procurement of nonpersonal services;

(3) The procurement of construction, alteration, repair or maintenance of real property; or

(4) The disposal of personal property. The term "contract" does not include any TVA contract for the sale of fertilizer or electric power, or any TVA contract related to the conduct or operation of the electric power system.

(e) The term *Contracting Officer* means TVA's Director of Purchasing, or duly authorized representative acting within the limits of the representative's authority. The TVA Purchasing Agent who administers a contract for TVA is designated as the duly authorized representative of the Director of Purchasing to act as Contracting Officer for all purposes in the administration of the contract (including, without limitation, decision of claims under the disputes clause). Such a designation continues until it is revoked or modified by written notice to the Contractor and the Purchasing Agent from TVA's Director of Purchasing.

(f) The term *Contractor* means a party to a TVA contract which contains a disputes clause. The term "Contractor" does not include TVA.

(g) The term *disputes clause* means a clause in a TVA contract requiring that a contract dispute be resolved through a TVA-conducted administrative process. It does not include, for example, arbitration provisions, or provisions specifying an independent third party to decide certain kinds of matters or special mechanisms to establish prices or price adjustments in contracts.

(h) The term *Hearing Officer* means a member of the Board who has been designated to hear and determine a particular matter pending before the Board.

(i) The term *TVA* means the Tennessee Valley Authority.

(j) A term defined as in a contract subject to this part shall have the meaning given it in the contract.

§1308.3 Exclusions.

(a) This part does not apply to any TVA contract which does not contain a disputes clause.

(b) Except as otherwise specifically provided, this part does not apply to any TVA contract entered into prior to March 1, 1979, or to any dispute relating to such a contract.

§1308.4 Coverage of certain excluded Contractors.

(a) A Contractor whose contract is excluded from this part under §1308.3(b) may elect to proceed under this part and the Act with respect to any dispute pending before a Contracting Officer on March 1, 1979, or initiated thereafter. If the disputes clause in the contract is not an "all disputes" clause (*see Patton Wrecking & Dem. Co.* v. *Tennessee Valley Authority*, 465 F.2d 1073 (5th Cir. 1972)), a Contractor's election under this section shall cause the provisions of the first two sentences of section 6(a) of the Act to apply to the contract, and such an election shall be irrevocable.

(b) A Contractor makes an election under paragraph (a) of this section by giving written notice to the Contracting Officer stating that the Contractor elects to proceed with the dispute under the Act. For disputes pending on March 1, 1979, the notice shall be actually received by the Contracting

Officer within 30 days after the Contractor receives the Contracting Officer's decision. For disputes initiated thereafter, the notice shall be included in the document first requesting a decision by the Contracting Officer.

§1308.5 Interest.

TVA shall pay a Contractor interest on the amount found to be due on a claim:

(a) From the date payment is due under the contract or the Contracting Officer receives the claim, whichever is later, until TVA makes payment;

(b) At the rate payable pursuant to section 12 of the Act on the date from which interest runs pursuant to paragraph (a) of this section.

§1308.6 Fraudulent claims.

(a) If a Contractor is unable to support any part of a claim and it is determined that such inability is attributable to the Contractor's misrepresentation of fact or fraud, the Contractor shall be liable to TVA, as set out in section 5 of the Act, for:

(1) An amount equal to the unsupported part of the claim; plus

(2) All TVA's costs attributable to reviewing that part of the claim.

(b) The term "misrepresentation of fact" has the meaning given it in section 2(7) of the Act.

(c) Prior to TVA's filing suit for amounts due under this section, TVA shall provide the Contractor with a copy of any opinion under §1308.16 or §1308.37(b), and shall request the Contractor to pay voluntarily the amount TVA asserts is due to it.

(d) A determination by TVA that fraud or misrepresentation of the fact has been committed is not subject to decision under a disputes clause.

(e) The provisions of this section are in addition to whatever penalties or remedies may otherwise be provided by law.

§1308.7 Effective date.

Subject to §1308.3(a), this part applies to any TVA contract having an effective date on or after March 1, 1979.

Subpart B—Contracting Officers

§ 1308.11 Contractor's request for relief.

Any request for relief which a Contractor believes is due under a contract shall be submitted to the Contracting Officer in writing, in accordance with the terms of the contract, including applicable time limits.

§ 1308.12 Submission and decision of Contractor's claim.

(a) If Contractor and TVA are unable to resolve Contractor's request for relief by agreement within a reasonable time, Contractor may submit a claim to the Contracting Officer.

(b) The Contracting Officer shall issue a decision to the Contractor on a submitted claim in conformity with the contract's disputes clause. Specific findings of fact are not required, but may be made. Such findings are not binding in any subsequent proceeding except as provided in § 1308.15. The decision shall:

(1) Be in writing;

(2) State the reasons for the decision reached;

(3) Include information about the Contractor's rights of appeal under sections 7 and 10 of the Act (including time limits); and

(4) Notify the Contractor, as appropriate, of the special procedures available under §§ 1308.35 and 1308.36 at the Contractor's election. A copy of the provisions of this part shall be furnished with the decision.

§ 1308.13 Time limits for decisions.

(a) If a submitted claim involves $50,000 or less, the Contracting Officer shall issue the decision within 60 days from actual receipt of the claim. If a submitted claim involves more than $50,000, the Contracting Officer within 60 days from actual receipt shall either issue a decision or notify the Contractor of the date by which a decision shall be rendered, which shall be within a reasonable time. The Contracting Officer shall not be deemed to be in "actual receipt" of a claim until the claim meets all requirements of § 1308.2(c).

(b) The Contracting Officer shall issue a decision within any time limits set by an order under § 1308.24. If a

Hearing Officer grants a stay of an appeal pursuant to § 1308.25, the Contracting Officer shall issue a decision within any time limits specified by the stay order, or within a reasonable time after receipt of the stay, if it sets no time limits.

(c) As used in this subpart, the reasonableness of a time period depends on the amount or kind of relief involved and complexity of the issues raised, the adequacy of the Contractor's supporting data, contractual requirements for auditing of Contractor's cost or other data, and other relevant factors.

§ 1308.14 Request for relief by TVA.

When TVA believes it is due relief under a contract, the Contracting Officer shall make a request for relief against the Contractor, and shall attempt to resolve the request by agreement. If agreement cannot be reached within a reasonable time, the Contracting Officer shall issue a decision which complies with the requirements of § 1308.12(b).

§ 1308.15 Finality of decisions.

A decision by a Contracting Officer under the disputes clause of a contract subject to this part is final and conclusive and not subject to review by any forum, tribunal, or Government agency unless an appeal or suit is timely commenced under this part or section 10(a) (2) and (3) of the Act.

§ 1308.16 Decisions involving fraudulent claims.

If a Contracting Officer denies any part of a Contractor's claim for lack of support, and the Contracting Officer is of the opinion that the Contractor's inability to support that part of the claim is within § 1308.6 and section 5 of the Act, the Contracting Officer's decision shall not state that opinion, but, contemporaneously with the decision, the Contracting Officer shall separately notify TVA's General Counsel of that opinion and the reasons therefor.

§ 1308.17 Failure to render timely decision.

Any failure by Contracting Officer to issue a decision on a submitted claim within the period required or permitted by § 1308.13, will be deemed to be a decision by the Contracting Officer denying the claim and will authorize the commencement of an appeal on the claim under this part, or a suit on the claim as provided in section 10(a)(2) of the Act. If no appeal or suit pursuant to this section has been commenced at the time the Contracting Officer issues a decision, the right to sue or appeal and the time limits therefor shall be determined as otherwise provided in this part and the Act, and this section shall not authorize an appeal or suit from the decision.

Subpart C—Board of Contract Appeals

§ 1308.21 Jurisdiction and organization.

(a) The Board shall consider and determine timely appeals filed by Contractors from decisions of TVA Contracting Officers pursuant to a disputes clause.

(b) The Board shall consist of an indeterminate number of members, who shall serve on a part-time basis. The members of the Board shall all be attorneys at law duly licensed by any state, commonwealth, territory, or the District of Columbia. One of the members of the Board shall be designated as "Chairman" pursuant to section 8(b)(2) of the Act.

(c) Each appeal or other matter before the Board shall normally be assigned to a single Hearing Officer, to be designated by the Chairman. The Chairman may act as a Hearing Officer, and shall notify the Contractor and TVA of the name and mailing address of the person designated as Hearing Officer.

(d) If a member to whom an appeal has been assigned cannot perform in a timely manner the duties of Hearing Officer, because of unavailability or incapacity which would in the Chairman's judgment affect the expeditious and timely resolution of the appeal, or for any other reason deemed sufficient by the Chairman, the Chairman may take any action deemed appropriate to effectuate the disposition of the appeal and the rights of the parties under this part. The kind of action taken, and the manner thereof, shall be within the discretion of the Chairman, and may include, but is not limited to, action on pending motions, discovery, issuance of or ruling on objections to subpoenas, and reassignment of an appeal in whole or in part.

§ 1308.22 Representation.

(a) In any appeal to the Board, a Contractor may be represented by an attorney at law duly licensed by any state, commonwealth, territory, or the District of Columbia. A Contractor not an individual and not wishing to appear by an attorney may be represented by any member, partner, or officer duly authorized to act on Contractor's behalf, or if an individual, may appear personally.

(b) TVA shall be represented by attorneys from its Office of General Counsel.

§ 1308.23 Finality of decisions.

A decision by a Hearing Officer on an appeal shall be the decision of the Board and shall be final, subject only to amendment under § 1308.37(c), reconsideration under § 1308.38 or appeal pursuant to sections 8(g)(2) and 10(b) of the Act.

§ 1308.24 Undue delay in Contracting Officer's decision.

(a) If there is an undue delay by a Contracting Officer in issuing a decision on a claim, the Contractor may request the Chairman to direct the Contracting Officer to issue a decision within a specified period of time.

(b) A request under this section shall:

(1) Be in writing;

(2) State the date on which the claim was submitted to the Contracting Officer.

(3) State the date suggested for issuance of a decision by the Contracting Officer.

(c) TVA may reply to a motion under this section within 5 days after its receipt.

(d) The Chairman shall issue a written decision on the request. If granted, the decision shall specify the date by which the Contracting Officer's decision is to be rendered, and a copy shall be served on the Contracting Officer.

§ 1308.25 Stay of appeal for Contracting Officer's decision.

If an appeal has been taken because of a Contracting Officer's failure to render a timely decision, as provided by § 1308.17, the Hearing Officer, with or without a motion by a party, may stay proceedings on the appeal in order to obtain a decision on the matter appealed. Oral argument will not be heard on such a motion unless otherwise directed. The stay order will normally set a date certain by which the decision of the Contracting Officer will be rendered. Such date shall take into account the factors mentioned in § 1308.13(c), the length of time the matter has already been pending before the Contracting Officer, and the need for prompt and expeditious action on appeals.

§ 1308.26 Appeals.

(a) An appeal to the Board from a Contracting Officer's decision under § 1308.12 shall be initiated within 90 days from the Contractor's receipt of the Contracting Officer's decision and in the manner set forth in the disputes clause.

(b) An appeal from the Contracting Officer's failure to render a timely decison shall be taken within the time period provided by § 1308.17. The notice of appeal shall be in the form and filed in the manner specified in the disputes clause, but shall state that it is an appeal under § 1308.17, and shall include a copy of the claim which was submitted for decision.

§ 1308.27 Appeal files.

(a) Notices of appeal shall be filed as provided in the disputes clause, and shall be promptly transmitted by TVA to the Chairman.

(b) Following transmittal of the notice of appeal, TVA shall assemble and transmit to the Hearing Officer and the Contractor an appeal file consisting of:

(1) The Contracting Officer's decision, if any, from which the appeal is taken;

(2) The contract and pertinent amendments, specifications, plans, and drawings (a list of the documents submitted may be provided Contractor in lieu of copies);

(3) The claim;

(4) Any other matter pertinent to the appeal submitted to or considered by the Contracting Officer for reaching a decision.

(c) The appeal file shall be submitted within 30 days. Within 30 days after receipt of a copy, the Contractor may submit to the Hearing Officer and TVA's General Counsel any documents within the scope of paragraph (b) of this section which are not included in the appeal file but which the Contractor believes are pertinent to the appeal. Such documents are considered a part of the appeal file.

Subpart D—Prehearing and Hearing Procedures

§ 1308.31 Filing and service.

(a) All documents required to be served shall be served on TVA and Contractor and filed with the Board, except subpoenas.

(b) A request under § 1308.15 shall be directed to the General Manager, Tennessee Valley Authority, 400 Commerce Avenue, Knoxville, Tennessee 37902, and shall be transmitted to the Chairman.

(c) All other documents required to be filed shall be directed to the Hearing Officer assigned to the matter.

(d) Service on the opposing party may be made personally or by mail. The copy presented for filing shall bear an appropriate certificate or acknowledgment of service.

§ 1308.32 Prehearing procedures.

(a) Unless otherwise provided in this part, prehearing procedures, including discovery, shall be conducted in accordance with Rules 6, 7(b), 16, 26, 28–37, and 56 of the Federal Rules of Civil Procedure, except that the Hearing Officer may modify those Rules to meet the needs of the parties in a particular case.

(b) The term *court* as used in those Rules shall be deemed to mean "Hearing Officer"; the term *plaintiff* shall be deemed to mean "Contractor"; the term *defendant* shall be deemed to mean "TVA"; and the term *action* shall be deemed to mean the pending appeal.

(c) Discovery subpoenas are subject to Subpart E.

(d) The party giving notice of a deposition is responsible for securing a reporter.

(e) No appeal of counterclaim may be dismissed except by order of the Hearing Officer. The Hearing Officer may order at any time, with or without a motion by a party, that an appeal or counterclaim, or any part thereof, be dismissed because the matter has been settled, because the party no longer desires to pursue the matter, or because of the party's failure to prosecute the matter or to comply with the regulations in this part or with any order of the Hearing Officer. Any dismissal under this paragraph operates as an adjudication on the merits of the matter which is dismissed, and is a decision within the meaning of §1308.23, but does not affect the Hearing Officer's jurisdiction over any matter not so dismissed.

[44 FR 29648, May 22, 1979. Redesignated at 44 FR 30682, May 29, 1979, and amended at 49 FR 3845, Jan. 31, 1984]

§1308.33 Hearings.

(a) TVA shall arrange for the verbatim reporting of evidentiary hearings before the Hearing Officer, and shall provide the Hearing Officer with the original transcript. The parties shall make their own arrangements with the reporter for copies.

(b) Admissibility of evidence shall generally be governed by the Federal Rules of Evidence, subject, however, to the Hearing Officer's discretion. As used in those Rules, the term *court* shall be deemed to mean "Hearing Officer."

(c)(1) Conduct of hearings shall generally be governed by Rules 42–44, 44.1, and 46 of the Federal Rules of Civil Procedure, except that the Hearing Officer may modify those Rules to meet the needs of the parties in a particular case. The terms *court, plaintiff, defendant,* and *action* as used in those Rules shall be deemed to have the meaning given them in §1308.32.

(2) After the Contractor has completed the presentation of his evidence, TVA, without waiving the right to offer evidence in the event the motion is not granted, may move for a dismissal on the ground that upon the facts and the law the Contractor has

shown no right to relief. The Hearing Officer as the trier of the facts may then determine them and render a decision against the Contractor, or take the matter under advisement, or decline to render any decision until the close of all the evidence. Any decision rendered under this paragraph shall conform to §1308.37, and is a decision within the meaning of §1308.23.

(d) Hearings shall be as informal as may be reasonable and appropriate under the circumstances, and shall be held at a time and place to be specified by the Hearing Officer.

(e) Evidentiary subpoenas are subject to Subpart E of this part.

[44 FR 29648, May 22, 1979. Redesignated at 44 FR 30682, May 29, 1979, and amended at 49 FR 3845, Jan. 31, 1984]

§1308.34 Record on appeal.

Except as otherwise provided in this part, the appeal shall be decided on the basis of the record on appeal, which consists of the notice of appeal, the claim, any notice of election under §1308.35 or §1308.36, orders entered during the proceeding, admissions, transcripts of hearings, hearing exhibits and stipulations on file, all other documents admitted in evidence, and all briefs submitted by the parties.

§1308.35 Small claims procedure.

(a) The Contractor may elect to have the appeal processed under this section, if the amount in dispute is $10,000 or less. This amount shall be determined by totalling the amounts claimed by TVA and Contractor.

(b) Appeals under this section shall be decided, whenever possible, within 120 days after the Hearing Officer receives written notice that the Contractor has elected to proceed under this section. Such election may be made a part of the notice of appeal.

(c) An appeal under this section shall be determined on the basis of the record on appeal and those documents in the appeal file identified in §1308.27(b)(1), (2), and (3). Other documents may be considered in the determination of the appeal as may be stipulated to by the parties, or as the Hearing Officer may order on motion by a party. No evidentiary hearing shall be held unless the Hearing Officer directs testimony on a particular issue. Discovery and other prehearing procedures may be conducted under such time periods as the Hearing Officer may set to meet the 120-day period, and the Hearing Officer may reserve up to 30 days to prepare a decision. Upon request by either party, the Hearing Officer shall hear oral argument after the record is closed, and may direct oral argument on specified issues if the parties do not request it.

(d) The Hearing Officer's decision under this section will be short and contain only summary findings of fact and conclusions of law. The decision may, at the Hearing Officer's discretion, be rendered orally at the conclusion of any oral argument held. In such case, the Hearing Officer will promptly furnish the parties a typed copy of the decision, which shall constitute the final decision.

(e) Decisions under this section shall be final and conclusive except for fraud, and shall have no value as precedent for future appeals.

§ 1308.36 Accelerated appeal procedure.

(a) The Contractor may elect to have the appeal processed under this section if the amount in dispute is $50,000 or less. The amount shall be determined by totalling the amounts claimed by TVA and Contractor.

(b) Appeals under this section shall be decided, whenever possible, within 180 days after the Hearing Officer receives written notice that the Contractor has elected to proceed under this section. Such election may be made a part of the notice of appeal.

(c) In cases under this section, the parties are encouraged to limit discovery and briefing, consistent with adequate presentation of their positions. The Hearing Officer may shorten applicable time periods in order to meet the 180-day period, and may reserve 30 days to prepare a decision.

(d) The Hearing Officer's decision under this section will be short and may contain only summary findings of fact and conclusions of law. The decision may, at the Hearing Officer's election, be rendered orally at the conclusion of the evidentiary hearing, following such oral argument as may be permitted. In such case, the Hearing Officer will promptly furnish the parties a typed copy of the decision, which shall constitute the final decision.

§ 1308.37 Decisions.

(a) The Hearing Officer's decision shall be in writing. Except as provided by § 1308.35 or § 1308.36, the decision shall contain complete findings of fact and conclusions of law. The parties may be directed to submit proposed findings and conclusions. A decision against a Contractor on a claim shall include notice of the Contractor's rights under paragraphs (2) and (3) of section 10(a) of the Act.

(b) If the decision denies any part of a Contractor's claim for lack of support and the Hearing Officer is of the opinion that the Contractor's inability to support that part is within § 1308.6 and section 5 of the Act, the decision shall not state that opinion, but contemporaneously with the decision the Hearing Officer shall separately notify TVA's General Counsel of that opinion and the reasons therefor.

(c) Not later than 10 days after receipt of the decision, a party may move to alter or amend the findings or make additional findings and amend the conclusions and decision accordingly. Such a motion may be combined with a motion under § 1308.38. This time period cannot be extended.

§ 1308.38 Reconsideration.

Motions for reconsideration shall be served not later than 10 days after issuance of the Hearing Officer's decision. This time period cannot be extended. Such a motion shall be heard and decided in the manner provided by Rule 59 of the Federal Rules of Civil Procedure for motions for new trial in actions tried without a jury.

§ 1308.39 Briefs and motions.

(a) All motions shall be accompanied by a brief or memorandum setting forth supporting authorities. Briefs in opposition to a motion shall be served within 10 days after receipt of the motion, unless otherwise specified in this part, or by order of the Hearing Officer.

(b) The Hearing Officer shall set the schedule for service of prehearing and posthearing briefs on the merits.

(c) A motion to dismiss an appeal for lack of jurisdiction should be served seasonably, but may be served at any time. The issue of lack of jurisdiction may be raised by the Hearing Officer sua sponte, in which case the Hearing Officer shall set a briefing schedule on the issue in the document raising it to the parties.

(d) A motion for summary judgment may be made at any time after the appeal file has been transmitted under § 1308.26.

Subpart E—Subpoenas

§ 1308.51 Form.

(a) A subpoena shall state the name of the Board and the title of the appeal; shall command the person to whom it is directed to attend and give testimony at a deposition or hearing, as appropriate, and, if appropriate, to produce specified books, papers, documents, or tangible things at a time and place therein specified; and shall notify the person of the right to request that the subpoena be quashed or modified and of the penalties for contumacy or failure to obey.

(b) [Reserved]

§ 1308.52 Issuance.

(a) A deposition subpoena shall not issue except upon the filing of a notice of deposition of the person to be subpoenaed, which notice should normally be filed at least 15 days in advance of the scheduled deposition.

(b) A subpoena for the attendance of a witness at an evidentiary hearing shall not issue except upon the filing of a request for appearance at the hearing of the person to be subpoenaed, which request should normally be filed at least 30 days in advance of the scheduled hearing. The request should state:

(1) The name and address of the witness;

(2) The general scope of the witness' testimony;

(3) The books, records, papers, and other tangible things sought to be produced; and

(4) The general relevance of the matters sought to the case.

(c) Upon receipt of a notice of deposition or request for appearance at a hearing, the Hearing Officer shall fill in the name of the witness and sign and issue a subpoena otherwise in blank to the party seeking it, together with a duplicate for proof of service. The party requesting the subpoena shall fill in both copies before service.

(d) Letters rogatory may be issued by the Hearing Officer as provided in 28 U.S.C. 1781–1784.

§ 1308.53 Service.

A subpoena may be served at any place, and may be served by any individual not a party who is at least 18 years of age, or as otherwise provided by law. Service may be made by an attorney or employee of a party. Service shall be made by personal delivery of the subpoena to the individual named therein, together with tender of the amounts required by 5 U.S.C. 503 or other applicable law. The individual making service shall file with the Board the duplicate subpoena, filled out as served, with the return of service filled in, signed and notarized.

§ 1308.54 Requests to quash or modify.

The person served with a subpoena (or a party, if the person served is a party's employee) may request the Hearing Officer to quash or modify a subpoena. Such requests shall be made and determined in accordance with the time limits and principles of Rule 45(a), (b) and (d) of the Federal Rules of Civil Procedure.

§ 1308.55 Penalties.

In case of contumacy or refusal to obey a subpoena by a person who resides, is found, or transacts business within the jurisdiction of a United States District Court, the Board will apply to the court through the General Counsel of TVA for an order requiring the person to appear before the Hearing Officer, to produce evidence or give testimony, or both. Any failure of any such person to obey the order of the court may be punished by the court as a contempt thereof.

PART 1309—NONDISCRIMINATION WITH RESPECT TO AGE

Sec.

AUTHORITY: TVA Act of 1933, 48 Stat. 58 (1933), as amended, 16 U.S.C. 831–831dd (1976), and sec. 304 of the Age Discrimination Act of 1975, 89 Stat 729 (1975), as amended, 42 U.S.C. 6103 (1976).

SOURCE: 46 FR 30811, June 11, 1981, unless otherwise noted.

§ 1309.1 What are the defined terms in this part and what do they mean?

As used in this part the following terms have the stated meanings:

(a) *Act* means the Age Discrimination Act of 1975, as amended, 42 U.S.C. 6101, *et seq.* (Title III of Pub. L. 94–135).

(b) *Action* means any act, activity, policy, rule, standard, or method of administration; or the use of any policy, rule, standard, or method of administration.

(c) *Age* means how old a person is, or the number of elapsed years from the date of a person's birth.

(d) *Age distinction* means any action using age or an age-related term.

(e) *Age-related term* means a term which necessarily implies a particular age or range of ages (for example, "children," "adult," "older persons," but not "student").

(f) *Financial assistance* means any grant, entitlement, loan, cooperative agreement, contract (other than a procurement contract or a contract of insurance or guaranty), or any other arrangement, by which TVA provides or otherwise makes available to a recipient assistance in any of the following forms:

(1) Funds;

(2) Services of TVA personnel;

(3) Real and personal property or any interest in or use of property, including:

(i) Transfers or leases of property for less than fair market value or for reduced consideration; and

(ii) Proceeds from a subsequent transfer or lease of property if the share of its fair market value provided by TVA is not returned to TVA.

(g) For purposes of §§ 1309.6 and 1309.7, *normal operation* means the operation of a program or activity without significant changes that would impair its ability to meet it objectives.

(h) *Program or activity* means all of the operations of any entity described in paragraphs (h)(1) through (4) of this section, any part of which is extended Federal financial assistance:

(1)(i) A department, agency, special purpose district, or other instrumentality of a State or of a local government; or

(ii) The entity of such State or local government that distributes such assistance and each such department or agency (and each other State or local government entity) to which the assistance is extended, in the case of assistance to a State or local government;

(2)(i) A college, university, or other postsecondary institution, or a public system of higher education; or

(ii) A local educational agency (as defined in 20 U.S.C. 7801), system of vocational education, or other school system;

(3)(i) An entire corporation, partnership, or other private organization, or an entire sole proprietorship—

(A) If assistance is extended to such corporation, partnership, private organization, or sole proprietorship as a whole; or

(B) Which is principally engaged in the business of providing education, health care, housing, social services, or parks and recreation; or

(ii) The entire plant or other comparable, geographically separate facility to which Federal financial assistance is extended, in the case of any other corporation, partnership, private organization, or sole proprietorship; or

(4) Any other entity which is established by two or more of the entities described in paragraph (h)(1), (2), or (3) of this section.

(i) For purposes of §§ 1309.6 and 1309.7, *statutory objective* means any purpose of a program or activity expressly stated in any Federal statute, State statute, or local statute or ordinance adopted by an elected, general purpose legislative body.

(j) *Recipient* means any State or its political subdivision, any instrumentality of a State or its political subdivision, any State-created or recognized public or private agency, institution, organization, or other entity, or any person to which TVA extends financial assistance directly or through another recipient. Recipient includes any successor, assignee, or transferee, but excludes the ultimate beneficiary of the assistance.

(k) *Secretary* means the Secretary of the Department of Health, Education, and Welfare, and its successors.

(l) *United States* means the fifty States, the District of Columbia, Puerto Rico, the Virgin Islands, American Samoa, Guam, Wake Island, the Canal Zone, the Trust Territory of the Pacific Islands, the Northern Marianas, and the territories and possessions of the United States.

(m) *TVA* means the Tennessee Valley Authority.

[46 FR 30811, June 11, 1981, as amended at 68 FR 51357, Aug. 26, 2003]

§ 1309.2 What is the purpose of the Act?

The Act is designed to prohibit discrimination on the basis of age in programs or activities receiving Federal financial assistance. The Act also permits federally assisted programs or activities, and recipients of Federal funds, to continue to use certain age distinctions and factors other than age which meet the requirements of the Act and this part.

[46 FR 30811, June 11, 1981, as amended at 68 FR 51357, Aug. 26, 2003]

§ 1309.3 What is the purpose of this part?

The purpose of this part is to effectuate the Act in all programs or activities of recipients which receive financial assistance from TVA, and to inform the public and the recipients of financial assistance from TVA of the Act's requirements and how it will be enforced.

§ 1309.4 What programs or activities are covered by the Act and this part?

(a) The Act and this part apply to any program or activity receiving financial assistance from TVA.

(b) The Act and this part do not apply to:

(1) An age distinction contained in that part of a Federal, State or local statute or ordinance adopted by an elected, general purpose legislative body which:

(i) Provides any benefits or assistance to persons based on age; or

(ii) Establishes criteria for participation in age-related terms; or

(iii) Describes intended beneficiaries or target groups in age-related terms.

(2) Any employment practice of any employer, employment agency, labor organization, or any labor-management joint apprenticeship training program.

§ 1309.5 What are the rules against age discrimination?

(a) *General rule.* No person in the United States shall, on the basis of age, be excluded from participation in, be denied the benefits of, or be subjected to discrimination under, any program or activity receiving financial assistance from TVA.

(b) *Specific rules.* In any program or activity receiving financial assistance from TVA, a recipient may not directly or through contractual, licensing, or other arrangements, use age distinctions or take any other actions which have the effect, on the basis of age of:

(1) Excluding individuals from, denying them the benefits of, or subjecting them to discrimination under a program or activity receiving financial assistance from TVA, or

(2) Denying or limiting individuals in their opportunity to participate in any program or activity receiving financial assistance from TVA.

(c) The specific forms of age discrimination listed in paragraph (b) of this section do not necessarily constitute a complete list.

(d) The rules stated in this section are limited by the exceptions contained in §§ 1309.6 and 1309.7.

§ 1309.6 Is the normal operation or statutory objective of any program or activity an exception to the rules against age discrimination?

A recipient is permitted to take an action, otherwise prohibited by § 1309.5, if the action reasonably takes into account age as a factor necessary to the normal operation or the achievement of any statutory objective of a program or activity. An action reasonably takes into account age as a factor necessary to the normal operation or the achievement of any statutory objective of a program or activity, if:

(a) Age is used as a measure or approximation of one or more other characteristics; and

(b) The other characteristic(s) must be measured or approximated in order for the normal operation of the program or activity to continue, or to achieve any statutory objective of the program or activity; and

(c) The other characteristic(s) can be reasonably measured or approximated by the use of age; and

(d) It is impractical to measure the other characteristic(s) directly on an individual basis.

§ 1309.7 Is the use of reasonable factors other than age an exception to the rules against age discrimination?

A recipient is permitted to take an action otherwise prohibited by § 1309.5 which is based on a factor other than age, even though that action may have a disproportionate effect on persons of different ages. An action may be based on a factor other than age only if the factor bears a direct and substantial relationship to the normal operation of the program or activity or to the achievement of a statutory objective.

§ 1309.8 Who has the burden of proving that an action is excepted?

The burden of proving that an age distinction or other action falls within the exceptions outlined in §§ 1309.6 and 1309.7 is on the recipient of financial assistance from TVA.

§ 1309.9 How does TVA provide financial assistance in conformity with the Act?

(a) TVA contributes financial assistance only under agreements which contain a provision which specifically requires compliance with the Act and this part. If the financial assistance involves the furnishing of real property, the agreement shall obligate the recipient, or the transferee in the case of a subsequent transfer, for the period during which the real property is used for a purpose for which the financial assistance is extended or for another purpose involving the provision of similar services or benefits. Where the financial assistance involves the furnishing of personal property, the agreement shall obligate the recipient during the period for which ownership or possession of the property is retained. In all other cases the agreement shall obligate the recipient for the period during which financial assistance is extended pursuant to the agreement. TVA shall specify the form of the foregoing agreement, and the extent to which an agreement shall be applicable to subcontractors, transferees, successors in interest, and other participants.

(b) In the case of real property, structures or improvements thereon, or interests therein, acquired through a program of TVA financial assistance, or in the case where TVA financial assistance was provided in the form of a transfer by TVA of real property or an interest therein, the instrument effecting or recording the transfer of title shall contain a covenant running with the land assuring compliance with this part and the guidelines contained herein for the period during which the real property is used for a purpose for which the TVA financial assistance is extended or for another purpose involving the provision of similar services or benefits. Where no transfer of property is involved, but property is improved with TVA financial assistance, the recipient shall agree to include such a covenant in any subsequent transfer of such property. Where the property is obtained by transfer from TVA, the covenant against discrimination may also include a condition coupled with a right to be reserved by TVA to revert title to the property in the event of a breach of the covenant where, in the discretion of TVA, such a condition and right of reverter is appropriate to the nature of (1) the statute under which the real property is obtained, (2) the recipient, and (3) the instrument effecting or recording the transfer of title. In such event, if a transferee of real property proposes to mortgage or otherwise encumber the real property as security for financing construction of new, or improvement of existing, facilities on such property for the purposes for which the property was transferred, TVA may agree, upon request of the transferee and if necessary to accomplish such financing, and upon such conditions as it deems appropriate, to forbear the exercise of such right to revert title for so long as the lien of such mortgage or other encumbrance remains effective.

[46 FR 30811, June 11, 1981, as amended at 68 FR 51357, Aug. 26, 2003]

§1309.10 What general responsibilities do recipients and TVA have to ensure compliance with the Act?

(a) A recipient has primary responsibility to ensure that its programs or activities are in compliance with the Act and shall take steps to eliminate violations of the Act. A recipient also has responsibility to maintain records, provide information, and afford TVA

access to its records to the extent required by TVA to determine whether the recipient is in compliance with the Act.

(b) TVA has responsibility to attempt to secure a recipient's compliance with the Act by voluntary means, to the fullest extent practicable, and to provide assistance and guidance to recipients to help them comply voluntarily. TVA may use the services of appropriate Federal, State, local, or private organizations for this purpose. TVA also has the responsibility to enforce the Act when a recipient fails to eliminate violations of the Act.

[46 FR 30811, June 11, 1981, as amended at 68 FR 51357, Aug. 26, 2003]

§1309.11 What specific responsibilities do TVA and recipients have to ensure compliance with the Act?

(a) *Written notice, technical assistance, and educational materials.* TVA shall:

(1) Provide written notice to each recipient of its obligations under the Act. The notice shall include a requirement that where the recipient initially receiving funds makes the funds available to a subrecipient, the recipient must notify the subrecipient of its obligations under the Act. The notice may be made a part of the contract under which financial assistance is provided by TVA.

(2) Provide technical assistance to recipients, where necessary, to aid them in complying with the Act.

(3) Make available educational materials setting forth the rights and obligations of beneficiaries and recipients under the Act.

(b) [Reserved]

§1309.12 What are a recipient's responsibilities on compliance reports and access to information?

(a) *Compliance reports.* Each recipient shall keep such records and submit to TVA timely, complete and accurate compliance reports at such times and in such form and containing such information, as TVA may determine to be necessary to enable it to ascertain whether the recipient has complied or is complying with this part. In the case in which a primary recipient passes through financial assistance from TVA to any other recipient, such other recipient shall also submit such compliance reports to the primary recipient as may be necessary to enable the primary recipient to carry out its obligations under this part.

(b) *Access to sources of information.* Each recipient shall permit access by TVA during normal business hours to such of its books, records, accounts and other sources of information, and its facilities as may be pertinent to ascertain compliance with this part. Where any information required of a recipient is in the exclusive possession of any other agency, institution or person, and such agency, institution or person shall fail or refuse to furnish this information, the recipient shall so certify in its report and shall set forth what efforts it has made to obtain the information.

(c) *Information to beneficiaries and participants.* Each recipient shall make available to participants, beneficiaries, and other interested persons such information regarding the provisions of this part and its applicability to the program or activity for which the recipient receives financial assistance, and make such information available to them in such manner as TVA finds necessary to apprise such persons of the protections against discrimination assured them by the Act and this part.

[46 FR 30811, June 11, 1981, as amended at 68 FR 51357, Aug. 26, 2003]

§ 1309.13 What are the prohibitions against intimidation or retaliation?

No recipient or other person shall intimidate, threaten, coerce, or discriminate against any individual for the purpose of interfering with any right secured by the Act or this part, or because such individual has made a complaint, testified, assisted, or participated in any manner in an investigation, mediation, hearing, or other proceeding under this part. The identity of complainants shall be kept confidential except to the extent necessary to carry out the purposes of this part, including the conduct of any investigation, mediation, hearing, or judicial proceeding arising under the Act or this part.

§ 1309.14 How will complaints against recipients be processed?

(a) *Receipt of complaints.* Any individual who claims (individually or on behalf of any specific class of individuals) that he or she has been subjected to discrimination prohibited by this part (including § 1309.13) may file a written complaint with TVA. The written complaint must be filed not later than 90 days from the date of the alleged discrimination, unless the time for filing is extended by TVA for good cause shown. A complaint shall be signed by the complainant, give the name and mailing address of the complainant and the recipient, identify the TVA financial assistance involved, and state the facts and occurrences (including dates) which led the complainant to believe that an act of prohibited discrimination has occurred. Anonymous complaints will not be accepted or filed under this section, but may be the basis for a compliance review. TVA will reject any complaint which does not fall within the coverage of the Act and this part, and may reject or require supplementation or clarification of any complaint which does not contain sufficient information for further processing as set forth in this paragraph. A complaint shall not be deemed filed until all such information has been provided to TVA.

(b) *Prompt resolution of complaints.* The complaint shall be resolved promptly. To this end, TVA shall proceed with the complaint without undue delay so that the complaint is resolved within 180 calendar days after it is filed with TVA. The recipient and complainant involved in each complaint are required to cooperate in this effort. Failure to cooperate on the part of the complainant may result in cancellation of the complaint, while such failure on the part of the recipient may result in enforcement action as described in § 1309.15.

(c) *Mediation of complaints.* All complaints which fall within the coverage of the Act and this part will be referred to a mediation agency designated by the Secretary.

(1) The participation of the recipient and the complainant in the mediation

process is required, although both parties need not meet with the mediator at the same time.

(2) If the complainant and recipient reach a mutually satisfactory resolution of the complaint during the mediation period, they shall reduce the agreement to writing. The mediator shall send a copy of the settlement to TVA. No further action shall be taken based on that complaint unless it appears that the complainant or the recipient is failing to comply with the agreement.

(3) Not more than 60 days after the complaint is filed, the mediator shall return a still unresolved complaint to TVA for initial investigation. The mediator may return a complaint at any time before the end of the 60-day period if it appears that the complaint cannot be resolved through mediation.

(4) The mediator shall protect the confidentiality of all information obtained in the course of the mediation process. No mediator shall testify in any adjudicative proceeding, produce any document, or otherwise disclose any information obtained in the course of the mediation process without prior approval of the head of the agency appointing the mediator.

(d) *Investigation.* (1) TVA will make a prompt investigation whenever a complaint is unresolved within 60 days after it is filed with TVA or is reopened because of a violation of the mediation agreement. The investigation should include, where appropriate, a review of the pertinent practices and policies of the recipient, the circumstances under which the possible noncompliance with the Act and this part occurred, and other factors relevant to a determination as to whether the recipient has failed to comply with the Act and this part.

(2) As part of the initial investigation, TVA shall use informal fact finding methods including joint or individual discussions with the complainant and recipient to establish the facts, and, if possible, to resolve the complaint to the mutual satisfaction of the parties. TVA may seek the assistance of any involved State agency.

(3) If TVA cannot resolve the matter within 10 calendar days after the mediator returns the complaint, it shall complete the investigation, attempt to achieve voluntary compliance satisfactory to TVA, if the investigation indicates a violation, and arrange for enforcement as described in §1309.15, if necessary.

[46 FR 30811, June 11, 1981, as amended at 68 FR 51357, Aug. 26, 2003]

§1309.15 How will TVA enforce compliance with the Act and this part?

(a) If a compliance report, self-evaluation, or preaward review indicates a violation or threatened violation of the Act or this part, TVA shall attempt to secure the recipient's voluntary compliance with the Act and this part. If the violation or threatened violation cannot be corrected by informal means, compliance with the Act and this part may be effected by the following means:

(1) Termination of a recipient's financial assistance under the program or activity involved where the recipient has violated the Act or this part. The determination of the recipient's violation may be made only after a recipient has had an opportunity for a hearing on the record before an appropriate hearing officer.

(2) Any other means authorized by law including but not limited to:

(i) Referral to the Department of Justice for proceedings to enforce any rights of the United States or obligations of the recipient created by the Act or this part.

(ii) Use of any requirement of or referral to any Federal, State, or local government agency which will have the effect of correcting a violation of the Act or this part.

(iii) Commencement by TVA of proceedings to enforce any rights of TVA or obligations of the recipient created by the contract, the Act, or this part.

(b) Any termination under paragraph (a)(1) of this section shall be limited to the particular recipient and the particular program or activity (or portion thereof) receiving financial assistance from TVA which is found to be in violation of the Act or this part. No termination shall be based in whole or in part on a finding with respect to any program or activity which does not receive financial assistance from TVA.

(c) No assistance will be terminated under paragraph (a)(1) of this section until:

(1) TVA has advised the recipient of its failure to comply with the Act or this part and has determined that voluntary compliance cannot be obtained.

(2) Thirty days have elapsed after TVA has sent a written report of the circumstances and grounds of the termination of assistance to the committees of the Congress having legislative jurisdiction over the program or activity involved. A report shall be filed in each case in which TVA has determined that assistance will be terminated under paragraph (a)(1) of this section.

(d) TVA may defer granting new financial assistance to a recipient when termination proceedings under paragraph (a)(1) of this section are initiated.

(1) New financial assistance includes all assistance administered by or through TVA for which an application or approval, including renewal or continuation of existing activities, or authorization of new activities, is required during the deferral period. New financial assistance does not include assistance approved prior to the beginning of termination proceedings.

(2) A deferral may not begin until the recipient has received a notice of opportunity for a hearing under paragraph (a)(1) of this section. A deferral may not continue for more than 60 days unless a hearing has begun within that time or the time for beginning the hearing has been extended by mutual consent of the recipient and TVA. A deferral may not continue for more than 30 days after the close of the hearing, unless the hearing results in a finding against the recipient.

[46 FR 30811, June 11, 1981, as amended at 68 FR 51357, Aug. 26, 2003]

§ 1309.16 What is the alternate funds disbursal procedure?

When TVA withholds funds from a recipient under this part, TVA may contract to disburse the withheld funds directly to any public or nonprofit private organization or agency, or State or political subdivision of the State. These alternate recipients must demonstrate the ability to comply with

this part and to achieve the goals of the Federal financial assistance involved.

[46 FR 30811, June 11, 1981, as amended at 68 FR 51357, Aug. 26, 2003]

§ 1309.17 What is the procedure for hearings and issuance of TVA decisions required by this part?

(a) Opportunity for hearing. Whenever an opportunity for a hearing is required by § 1309.15(a)(1), reasonable notice shall be given by registered or certified mail, return receipt requested, to the affected recipient. This notice shall advise the recipient of the action proposed to be taken, the specific provision under which the proposed action against it is to be taken, and the matters of fact or law asserted as the basis for this action, and either (1) fix a date not less than 20 days after the date of such notice within which the recipient may request of TVA that the matter be scheduled for hearing or (2) advise the recipient that the matter in question has been set down for hearing at a stated time and place. The time and place so fixed shall be reasonable and shall be subject to change for cause. The complainant, if any, shall be advised of the time and place of the hearing. A recipient may waive a hearing and submit written information and argument for the record. The failure of a recipient to request a hearing under this subsection or to appear at a hearing for which a date has been set shall be deemed to be a waiver of the right to a hearing under the Act and § 1309.15(a)(1) and a consent to the making of a decision on the basis of such information as is available.

(b) Time and place of hearing. Hearings shall be held at the time and place fixed by TVA unless it determines that the convenience of the recipient requires that another place be selected. Hearings shall be held before a hearing officer who shall be designated by TVA's General Manager, and who shall not be a TVA employee.

(c) Right to counsel. In all proceedings under this section, the recipient and TVA shall have the right to be represented by counsel.

(d) Procedures, evidence, and record. (1) The hearing, decision, and any administrative review thereof by TVA's

Board of Directors shall be conducted in conformity with this part and in accordance with such rules of procedure as are proper (and not inconsistent with this section) relating to the conduct of the hearing, giving of notices subsequent to those provided for in paragraph (a) of this section, taking of testimony, exhibits, arguments and briefs, requests for findings, and other related matters, as prescribed by the hearing officer. Both TVA and the recipient shall be entitled to introduce all relevant evidence on the issues as stated in the notice for hearing or as determined by the hearing officer at the outset of or during the hearing.

(2) Technical rules of evidence shall not apply to hearings conducted pursuant to this part, but rules or principles designed to assure production of the most credible evidence available and to subject testimony to test by cross-examination shall be applied where reasonably necessary by the hearing officer. The hearing officer may exclude irrelevant, immaterial, or unduly repetitious evidence. All documents and other evidence offered or received for the record shall be open to examination by the parties and opportunity shall be given to refute facts and arguments advanced on either side of the issues. A transcript shall be made of the oral evidence except to the extent the substance thereof is stipulated for the record. All decisions shall be based upon the hearing record and written findings shall be made.

(e) *Consolidated or joint hearings.* In cases in which the same or related facts are asserted to constitute noncompliance with this part with respect to two or more Federal statutes, authorities, of other means by which Federal financial assistance is extended and to which this part applies, or noncompliance with this part and the regulations of one or more other Federal departments or agencies issued under the Act, the TVA Board may, by agreement with such other departments or agencies where applicable, provide for the conduct of consolidated or joint hearings, and for the application to such hearings of the rules of procedure applicable to such hearings by such other departments or agencies. Final decisions in such cases, insofar as this

part is concerned, shall be made in accordance with paragraph (f) of this section.

(f) *Decisions.* (1) After the hearing, or after the hearing is waived under paragraph (a) of this section, the hearing officer shall make an initial decision. The recipient may file exceptions to the decision with the TVA Board within 10 days of receipt of the decision. If exceptions are not filed within the specified time, the hearing officer's initial decision becomes the final TVA decision.

(2) Based on the hearing record, investigation, and any written submission to the hearing officer or the TVA Board, the Board shall render its decision accepting the initial decision, or rejecting it, in whole or part.

(3) The final decision may provide for suspension or termination of, or refusal to grant or continue financial assistance, in whole or in part, to which this regulation applies, and may contain such terms, conditions, and other provisions as are consistent with and will effectuate the purposes of the Act and this part, including provisions designed to assure that no financial assistance to which this regulations applies will thereafter be extended to the recipient determined by such decision to have failed to comply with this part, unless and until it corrects its noncompliance and satisfies TVA that it will fully comply with this part.

(g) *Posttermination proceedings.* (1) A recipient adversely affected by an order issued under paragraph (f) of this section shall be restored to full eligibility to receive financial assistance from TVA if it satisfies the terms and conditions of that order for such eligibility or if it brings itself into compliance with this part and provides reasonable assurance that it will fully comply with this part.

(2) Any recipient adversely affected by an order entered pursuant to paragraph (f) of this section may at any time request TVA to restore fully its eligibility to receive financial assistance from TVA. Any such request shall be supported by information showing

that the recipient has met the requirements of paragraph (g)(1) of this section. If TVA determines that those requirements have been satisfied, it shall restore such eligibility.

(3) If TVA denies any such request, the recipient may submit a written request for a hearing, specifying why it believes TVA to have been in error. The recipient shall thereupon be given an expeditious hearing, with a decision on the record, in accordance with rules of procedure issued by TVA. The recipient will be restored to such eligibility if it proves at such a hearing that it satisfied the requirements of paragraph (g)(1) of this section. While proceedings under this paragraph are pending, the sanctions imposed by the order issued under paragraph (f)(3) of this section shall remain in effect.

[46 FR 30811, June 11, 1981, as amended at 68 FR 51357, Aug. 26, 2003]

§ 1309.18 Under what circumstances must recipients take remedial or affirmative action?

(a) Where a recipient is found to have discriminated on the basis of age, the recipient shall take any remedial action which TVA may require to overcome the effects of the discrimination, if another recipient exercises control over the recipient that has discriminated, both recipients may be required to take remedial action.

(b) Even in the absence of a finding of discrimination, a recipient may take affirmative action to overcome the effects of conditions that resulted in limited participation recipient's program or activity on the basis of age.

(c) If a recipient operating a program or activity which serves the elderly or children, in addition to persons of other ages, provides special benefits to the elderly or to children, the provision of those benefits shall be presumed to be voluntary affirmative action provided that it does not have the effect of excluding otherwise eligible persons from participation in the program or activity.

[46 FR 30811, June 11, 1981, as amended at 68 FR 51357, Aug. 26, 2003]

§ 1309.19 When may a complainant file a civil action?

(a) A complainant may file a civil action following the exhaustion of administrative remedies under the Act. Administrative remedies are exhausted if:

(1) 180 days have elapsed since the complainant filed the complaint and TVA has made no finding with regard to the complaint; or

(2) TVA issues any finding in favor of the recipient.

(b) If either of the conditions set forth in paragraph (a) of this section is satisfied, TVA shall:

(1) Promptly advise the complainant of this fact; and

(2) Advise the complainant of his or her right, under Section 305(e) of the Act, to bring a civil action for injunctive relief that will effect the purposes of the Act; and

(3) Inform the complainant:

(i) That a civil action can only be brought in a United States district court for the district in which the recipient is found or transacts business;

(ii) That a complainant prevailing in a civil action has the right to be awarded the costs of the action, including reasonable attorney's fees, but that these costs must be demanded in the complaint;

(iii) That before commencing the action the complainant shall give 30 days' notice by registered mail to the Secretary, the Attorney General of the United States, TVA, and the recipient;

(iv) That the notice shall state: the alleged violation of the Act; the relief requested; the court in which the action will be brought; and whether or not attorney's fees are demanded in the event the complainant prevails; and

(v) That no action shall be brought if the same alleged violation of the Act by the same recipient is the subject of a pending action in any court of the United States.

PART 1310—ADMINISTRATIVE COST RECOVERY

Sec.
1310.1   Purpose.
1310.2   Application.
1310.3   Assessment of administrative charge.

AUTHORITY: 16 U.S.C. 831–831dd; 31 U.S.C. 9701.

SOURCE: 60 FR 8196, Feb. 13, 1995, unless otherwise noted.

§ 1310.1 Purpose.

The purpose of the regulations in this part is to establish a schedule of fees to be charged in connection with the disposition and uses of, and activities affecting, real property in TVA's custody or control; approval of plans under section 26a of the Tennessee Valley Authority Act of 1933, as amended (16 U.S.C. 831y–1); and certain other activities in order to help ensure that such activities are self-sustaining to the full extent possible.

§ 1310.2 Application.

(a) *General.* TVA will undertake the following actions only upon the condition that the applicant pay to TVA such administrative charges as the Senior Manager of the TVA organization that administers the land or permit being considered (hereinafter "responsible land manager"), as appropriate, shall assess in accordance with § 1310.3; provided, however, that the responsible land manager may waive payment where he/she determines that there is a corresponding benefit to TVA or that such waiver is otherwise in the public interest.

(1) Conveyances and abandonment of TVA land or landrights.

(2) Licenses and other uses of TVA land not involving the disposition of TVA real property or interests in real property.

(3) Actions taken to suffer the presence of unauthorized fills and structures over, on, or across TVA land or landrights, and including actions not involving the abandonment or disposal of TVA land or landrights.

(4) Actions taken to approve fills, structures, or other obstructions under section 26a of the Tennessee Valley Authority Act of 1933, as amended (16 U.S.C. 831y–1), and TVA's regulations issued thereunder at part 1304 of this chapter.

(b) *Exemption.* An administrative charge shall not be made for the following actions:

(1) Releases of unneeded mineral right options.

(2) TVA mineral transactions.

(c) *Quota deer hunt and turkey hunt applications.* Quota deer hunt and turkey hunt permit applications will be processed by TVA if accompanied by the fee prescribed in § 1310.3(d).

[60 FR 8196, Feb. 13, 1995, as amended at 72 FR 18118, Apr. 11, 2007]

§ 1310.3 Assessment of administrative charge.

(a) *Range of charges.* Except as otherwise provided herein, the responsible land manager shall assess a charge which he/she determines in his/her sole judgment to be approximately equal to the administrative costs incurred by TVA for each action including both the direct cost to TVA and applicable overheads. In determining the amount of such charge, the responsible land manager may establish a standard charge for each category of action rather than determining the actual administrative costs for each individual action. The standard charge shall be an amount approximately equal to TVA's actual average administrative costs for the category of action. Charges shall be not less than the minimum or greater than the maximum amount specified herein, except as otherwise provided in paragraph (c) of this section.

(1) Land transfers—$500–$10,000.

(2) Use permits or licenses–$50–$5,000.

(3) Actions taken to approve plans for fills, structures, or other obstructions under section 26a of the TVA Act—$100–$5,000.

(4) Abandonment of transmission line easements and rights-of-way—$100–$1,500.

(5) Quota deer hunt or turkey hunt applications—$5–$25.

(b) *Basis of charge.* The administrative charge assessed by the responsible land manager shall, to the extent applicable, include the following costs:

(1) Appraisal of the land or landrights affected;

(2) Assessing applicable rental fees;

(3) Compliance inspections and other field investigations;

(4) Title and record searches;

(5) Preparation for and conducting public auction and negotiated sales;

(6) Mapping and surveying;

(7) Preparation of conveyance instrument, permit, or other authorization or approval instrument;

(8) Coordination of the proposed action within TVA and with other Federal, State, and local agencies;

(9) Legal review; and

(10) Administrative overheads associated with the transaction.

(c) *Assessment of charge when actual administrative costs significantly exceed established range.* When the responsible land manager determines that the actual administrative costs are expected to significantly exceed the range of costs established in paragraph (a) of this section, such manager shall not proceed with the TVA action until agreement is reached on payment of a charge calculated to cover TVA's actual administrative cost.

(d) *Quota deer hunt and turkey hunt application fees.* A fee for each person in the amount prescribed by the responsible land manager must accompany the complete application form for a quota deer hunt and turkey hunt permit. Applications will not be processed unless accompanied by the correct fee amount. No refunds will be made to unsuccessful applicants, except that fees received after the application due date will be refunded.

(e) *Additional charges.* In addition to the charges assessed under these regulations, TVA may impose a charge in connection with environmental reviews or other environmental investigations it conducts under its policies or procedures implementing the National Environmental Policy Act (42 U.S.C. 4321 *et seq.*).

PART 1311—INTERGOVERNMENTAL REVIEW OF TENNESSEE VALLEY AUTHORITY FEDERAL FINANCIAL ASSISTANCE AND DIRECT FEDERAL DEVELOPMENT PROGRAMS AND ACTIVITIES

AUTHORITY: Tennessee Valley Authority Act of 1933, 48 Stat. 58, as amended, 16 U.S.C. 831–831dd (1976; Supp. V, 1981); E. O. 12372, July 14, 1982 (47 FR 30,959), amended April 8, 1983 (48 FR 15,887); sec. 401 of the Intergovernmental Cooperation Act of 1968, as amended.

SOURCE: 48 FR 29399, June 24, 1983, unless otherwise noted.

§ 1311.1 What is the purpose of these regulations?

(a) The regulations in this part implement Executive Order 12372, "Intergovernmental Review of Federal Programs," issued July 14, 1982, and amended on April 8, 1983. These regulations also implement applicable provisions of section 401 of the Intergovernmental Cooperation Act of 1968 and are intended to assist TVA in carrying out its responsibilities under the TVA Act.

(b) These regulations are intended to foster an intergovernmental partnership and a strengthened Federalism by relying on state processes and on state, areawide, regional, and local coordination for review of proposed federal financial assistance and direct federal development.

(c) These regulations are intended to aid the internal management of TVA, and are not intended to create any right or benefit enforceable at law by a party against TVA or its officers.

§ 1311.2 What definitions apply to these regulations?

TVA means the Tennessee Valley Authority, a wholly owned corporation and independent instrumentality of the United States.

Order means Executive Order 12372, issued July 14, 1982, and amended April 8, 1983, and titled "Intergovernmental Review of Federal Programs."

State means any of the 50 states, the District of Columbia, the Commonwealth of Puerto Rico, the Commonwealth of the Northern Mariana Islands, Guam, American Samoa, the U.S. Virgin Islands, or the Trust Territory of the Pacific Islands.

§ 1311.3 What programs and activities of TVA are subject to these regulations?

TVA publishes in the FEDERAL REGISTER a list of TVA's federal financial assistance and direct federal development programs and activities that are subject to these regulations.

§ 1311.4 [Reserved]

§ 1311.5 What is TVA's obligation with respect to federal interagency coordination?

TVA, to the extent practicable, consults with and seeks advice from all other substantially affected federal departments and agencies in an effort to assure full coordination between such agencies and TVA regarding programs and activities covered under these regulations.

§ 1311.6 What procedures apply to the selection of programs and activities under these regulations?

(a) A state may select any program or activity published in the FEDERAL REGISTER in accordance with § 1311.3 of this part for intergovernmental review under these regulations. Each state, before selecting programs and activities, shall consult with local elected officials.

(b) Each state that adopts a process shall notify TVA of the programs and activities selected for that process.

(c) A state may notify TVA of changes in its selections at any time. For each change, the state shall submit to TVA an assurance that the state has consulted with local elected officials regarding the change. TVA may establish deadlines by which states are required to inform TVA of changes in their program selections.

(d) TVA uses a state's process as soon as feasible, depending on individual programs and activities, after TVA is notified of the states selections.

§ 1311.7 How does TVA communicate with state, regional, and local officials concerning TVA's programs and activities?

(a) For those programs and activities covered by a state process under § 1311.6, TVA, to the extent permitted by law:

(1) Uses the official state process to determine views of state and local elected officials, and

(2) Communicates with state and local elected officials, through the official state process, as early in a program planning cycle as is reasonably feasible to explain specific plans and actions.

(b) TVA provides notice to directly affected state, areawide, regional, and local entities in a state of proposed Federal financial assistance or direct federal development if:

(1) The state has not adopted a process under the Order;

(2) The assistance or development involves a program or activity not selected for the state process; or

(3) The particular government entity is not part of or involved in the state process.

This notice may be made by a publication widely available in the potentially affected area or other appropriate means, which TVA in its discretion deems appropriate.

§ 1311.8 How does TVA provide states an opportunity to comment on proposed federal financial assistance and direct federal development?

(a) Except in unusual circumstances, TVA gives state processes or directly affected state, areawide, regional, and local officials and entities:

(1) [Reserved]

(2) At least 60 days from the date established by TVA to comment on proposed direct Federal development or federal financial assistance.

(b) This section also applies to comments in cases in which the review, coordination, and communication with TVA have been delegated or when TVA provides notice directly to potentially affected state, areawide, regional, or local entities under § 1311.7(b).

§ 1311.9 How does TVA receive and respond to comments?

(a) TVA follows the procedures in § 1311.10 if:

(1) A state office or official is designated to act as a single point of contact between a state process and all federal agencies, and

(2) That office or official transmits a state process recommendation for a program selected under § 1311.6.

(b)(1) The single point of contact is not obligated to transmit comments from state, areawide, regional, or local officials and entities where there is no state process recommendation; however, these officials or entities may submit comments directly to TVA for TVA's consideration.

(2) If a state process recommendation is transmitted by a single point of contact, all comments from state, areawide, regional, and local officials and entities that differ from it must also be transmitted.

(c) If a state has not established a process, or is unable to submit a state process recommendation, state, areawide, regional, and local officials and entities may submit comments to TVA.

(d) If a program or activity is not selected for a state process, state, areawide, regional, and local officials and entities may submit comments to TVA. In addition, if a state process recommendation for a nonselected program or activity is transmitted to TVA by the single point of contact, TVA follows the procedures of § 1311.10 of this part.

(e) TVA considers comments which do not constitute a state process recommendation submitted under these regulations and for which TVA is not required to apply the procedures of § 1311.10 of this part, when such comments are provided by a single point of contact or directly to TVA by a state, areawide, regional, or local government.

§ 1311.10 How does TVA make efforts to accommodate intergovernmental viewpoints?

(a) If a state process provides a state process recommendation to TVA through its single point contact, TVA either:

(1) Accepts the recommendation;

(2) Reaches a mutually agreeable solution with the state process; or

(3) Provides the single point of contact (including any regional or local office delegated a review and comment role by the state process) with written explanation of the decision in such form as TVA in its discretion deems appropriate. TVA may also supplement the written explanation by providing the explanation to the single point of contact by telephone, other telecommunications, meeting with the single point of contact, and, as appropriate, other interested officials or offices, or other means.

(b) In any explanation under paragraph (a)(3) of this section, TVA informs the single point of contact that:

(1) TVA will not implement its decision for at least 10 days after the single point of contact receives the explanation; or

(2) TVA's General Manager has reviewed the decision and determined that, because of unusual circumstances, the waiting period of at least 10 days is not feasible.

(c) For purposes of computing the waiting period under paragraph (b)(1) of this section, the explanation is presumed to have been received five days after the date of mailing of such notification.

§ 1311.11 What are TVA's obligations in interstate situations?

(a) TVA is responsible for:

(1) Identifying proposed Federal financial assistance and direct Federal development that potentially impact on interstate areas;

(2) Notifying appropriate officials and entities in states which have adopted a process and which select TVA's program or activity;

(3) In accordance with § 1311.7(b), making efforts to identify and notify the affected state, areawide, regional and local officials and entities in those states that have not adopted a process under the Order or do not select TVA's program or activity;

(4) Responding pursuant to § 1311.10 of this part if TVA receives a recommendation from a designated areawide agency transmitted by a single point of contact, in cases in which

254

the review, coordination, and communication with TVA have been delegated.

(b) TVA uses the procedures in §1311.10 if a state process provides a state process recommendation to TVA through a single point of contact.

§1311.12 [Reserved]

§1311.13 May TVA waive any provision of these regulations?

In an emergency, TVA may waive any provision of these regulations.

PART 1312—PROTECTION OF ARCHAEOLOGICAL RESOURCES: UNIFORM REGULATIONS

AUTHORITY: Pub. L. 96–95, 93 Stat. 721, as amended, 102 Stat. 2983 (16 U.S.C. 470aa–mm) (Sec. 10(a) & (b)); 16 U.S.C. 831–831ee (2012). Related Authority: Pub. L. 59–209, 34 Stat. 225 (16 U.S.C. 432, 433); Pub. L. 86–523, 74 Stat. 220, 221 (16 U.S.C. 469), as amended, 88 Stat. 174 (1974); Pub. L. 89–665, 80 Stat. 915 (16 U.S.C. 470a–t), as amended, 84 Stat. 204 (1970), 87 Stat. 139 (1973), 90 Stat. 1320 (1976), 92 Stat. 3467 (1978), 94 Stat. 2987 (1980); Pub. L. 95–341, 92 Stat. 469 (42 U.S.C. 1996).

SOURCE: 49 FR 1028, Jan. 6, 1984, unless otherwise noted.

§1312.1 Purpose.

(a) The regulations in this part implement provisions of the Archaeological Resources Protection Act of 1979, as amended (16 U.S.C. 470aa-mm) by establishing the uniform definitions, standards, and procedures to be followed by all Federal land managers in providing protection for archaeological resources, located on public lands and Indian lands of the United States. These regulations enable Federal land managers to protect archaeological resources, taking into consideration provisions of the American Indian Religious Freedom Act (92 Stat. 469; 42 U.S.C. 1996), through permits authorizing excavation and/or removal of archaeological resources, through civil penalties for unauthorized excavation and/or removal, through provisions for the preservation of archaeological resource collections and data, and through provisions for ensuring confidentiality of information about archaeological resources when disclosure would threaten the archaeological resources. The regulations in this part also enable TVA's law enforcement agents to issue petty offense citations for violations of any provision of 16 U.S.C. 470ee or 16 U.S.C. 433.

(b) The regulations in this part do not impose any new restrictions on activities permitted under other laws, authorities, and regulations relating to mining, mineral leasing, reclamation, and other multiple uses of the public lands.

[49 FR 1028, Jan. 6, 1984, as amended at 60 FR 5259, 5260, Jan. 26, 1995; 81 FR 54499, Aug. 16, 2016]

§1312.2 Authority.

(a) The regulations in this part are promulgated pursuant to section 10(a) of the Archaeological Resources Protection Act of 1979 (16 U.S.C. 470ii), which requires that the Secretaries of the Interior, Agriculture and Defense and the Chairman of the Board of the Tennessee Valley Authority jointly develop uniform rules and regulations for carrying out the purposes of the Act.

(b) In addition to the regulations in this part, section 10(b) of the Act (16

U.S.C. 470ii) provides that each Federal land manager shall promulgate such rules and regulations, consistent with the uniform rules and regulations in this part, as may be necessary for carrying out the purposes of the Act.

(c) Provisions pertaining to the issuance of petty offense citations are based on the duties and powers assigned to TVA's law enforcement agents under 16 U.S.C. 831–831ee.

[49 FR 1028, Jan. 6, 1984, as amended at 81 FR 54499, Aug. 16, 2016]

§ 1312.3 Definitions.

As used for purposes of this part:

(a) *Archaeological resource* means any material remains of human life or activities which are at least 100 years of age, and which are of archaeological interest.

(1) *Of archaeological interest* means capable of providing scientific or humanistic understandings of past human behavior, cultural adaptation, and related topics through the application of scientific or scholarly techniques such as controlled observation, contextual measurement, controlled collection, analysis, interpretation and explanation.

(2) *Material remains* means physical evidence of human habitation, occupation, use, or activity, including the site, location, or context in which such evidence is situated.

(3) The following classes of material remains (and illustrative examples), if they are at least 100 years of age, are of archaeological interest and shall be considered archaeological resources unless determined otherwise pursuant to paragraph (a)(4) or (5) of this section:

(i) Surface or subsurface structures, shelters, facilities, or features (including, but not limited to, domestic structures, storage structures, cooking structures, ceremonial structures, artificial mounds, earthworks, fortifications, canals, reservoirs, horticultural/agricultural gardens or fields, bedrock mortars or grinding surfaces, rock alignments, cairns, trails, borrow pits, cooking pits, refuse pits, burial pits or graves, hearths, kilns, post molds, wall trenches, middens);

(ii) Surface or subsurface artifact concentrations or scatters;

(iii) Whole or fragmentary tools, implements, containers, weapons and weapon projectiles, clothing, and ornaments (including, but not limited to, pottery and other ceramics, cordage, basketry and other weaving, bottles and other glassware, bone, ivory, shell, metal, wood, hide, feathers, pigments, and flaked, ground, or pecked stone);

(iv) By-products, waste products, or debris resulting from manufacture or use of human-made or natural materials;

(v) Organic waste (including, but not limited to, vegetal and animal remains, coprolites);

(vi) Human remains (including, but not limited to, bone, teeth, mummified flesh, burials, cremations);

(vii) Rock carvings, rock paintings, intaglios and other works of artistic or symbolic representation;

(viii) Rockshelters and caves or portions thereof containing any of the above material remains;

(ix) All portions of shipwrecks (including, but not limited to, armaments, apparel, tackle, cargo);

(x) Any portion or piece of any of the foregoing.

(4) The following material remains shall not be considered of archaeological interest, and shall not be considered to be archaeological resources for purposes of the Act and this part, unless found in a direct physical relationship with archaeological resources as defined in this section:

(i) Paleontological remains;

(ii) Coins, bullets, and unworked minerals and rocks.

(5) The Federal land manager may determine that certain material remains, in specified areas under the Federal land manager's jurisdiction, and under specified circumstances, are not or are no longer of archaeological interest and are not to be considered archaeological resources under this part. Any determination made pursuant to this subparagraph shall be documented. Such determination shall in no way affect the Federal land manager's obligations under other applicable laws or regulations.

(6) For the disposition following lawful removal or excavations of Native American human remains and "cultural items", as defined by the Native

American Graves Protection and Repatriation Act (NAGPRA; Pub. L. 101–601; 104 Stat. 3050; 25 U.S.C. 3001–13), the Federal land manager is referred to NAGPRA and its implementing regulations.

(b) *Arrowhead* means any projectile point which appears to have been designed for use with an arrow.

(c) *Federal land manager* means:

(1) With respect to any public lands, the secretary of the department, or the head of any other agency or instrumentality of the United States, having primary management authority over such lands, including persons to whom such management authority has been officially delegated;

(2) In the case of Indian lands, or any public lands with respect to which no department, agency or instrumentality has primary management authority, such term means the Secretary of the Interior;

(3) The Secretary of the Interior, when the head of any other agency or instrumentality has, pursuant to section 3(2) of the Act and with the consent of the Secretary of the Interior, delegated to the Secretary of the Interior the responsibilities (in whole or in part) in this part.

(d) *Public lands* means:

(1) Lands which are owned and administered by the United States as part of the national park system, the national wildlife refuge system, or the national forest system; and

(2) All other lands the fee title to which is held by the United States, except lands on the Outer Continental Shelf, lands under the jurisdiction of the Smithsonian Institution, and Indian lands.

(e) *Indian lands* means lands of Indian tribes, or Indian individuals, which are either held in trust by the United States or subject to a restriction against alienation imposed by the United States, except for subsurface interests not owned or controlled by an Indian tribe or Indian individual.

(f) *Indian tribe* as defined in the Act means any Indian tribe, band, nation, or other organized group or community, including any Alaska village or regional or village corporation as defined in, or established pursuant to, the Alaska Native Claims Settlement Act (85 Stat. 688). In order to clarify this statutory definition for purposes of this part, "Indian tribe" means:

(1) Any tribal entity which is included in the annual list of recognized tribes published in the FEDERAL REGISTER by the Secretary of the Interior pursuant to 25 CFR part 54;

(2) Any other tribal entity acknowledged by the Secretary of the Interior pursuant to 25 CFR part 54 since the most recent publication of the annual list; and

(3) Any Alaska Native village or regional or village corporation as defined in or established pursuant to the Alaska Native Claims Settlement Act (85 Stat. 688), and any Alaska Native village or tribe which is recognized by the Secretary of the Interior as eligible for services provided by the Bureau of Indian Affairs.

(g) *Person* means an individual, corporation, partnership, trust, institution, association, or any other private entity, or any officer, employee, agent, department, or instrumentality of the United States, or of any Indian tribe, or of any State or political subdivision thereof.

(h) *State* means any of the fifty states, the District of Columbia, Puerto Rico, Guam, and the Virgin Islands.

(i) *Act* means the Archaeological Resources Protection Act of 1979 (16 U.S.C. 470aa–mm).

(j) *Director* means the Director of TVA Police and Emergency Management assigned the function and responsibility of supervising TVA employees designated as law enforcement agents under 16 U.S.C. 831c–3(a).

[49 FR 1028, Jan. 6, 1984; 49 FR 5923, Feb. 16, 1984, as amended at 60 FR 5259, 5260, Jan. 26, 1995; 81 FR 54499, Aug. 16, 2016]

§1312.4 Prohibited acts and criminal penalties.

(a) Under section 6(a) of the Act, no person may excavate, remove, damage, or otherwise alter or deface, or attempt to excavate, remove, damage, or otherwise alter or deface any archaeological resource located on public lands or Indian lands unless such activity is pursuant to a permit issued under §1312.8 or exempted by §1312.5(b) of this part.

(b) No person may sell, purchase, exchange, transport, or receive any archaeological resource, if such resource was excavated or removed in violation of:

(1) The prohibitions contained in paragraph (a) of this section; or

(2) Any provision, rule, regulation, ordinance, or permit in effect under any other provision of Federal law.

(c) Under section (d) of the Act, any person who knowingly violates or counsels, procures, solicits, or employs any other person to violate any prohibition contained in section 6 (a), (b), or (c) of the Act will, upon conviction, be fined not more than $10,000.00 or imprisoned not more than one year, or both: provided, however, that if the commercial or archaeological value of the archaeological resources involved and the cost of restoration and repair of such resources exceeds the sum of $500.00, such person will be fined not more than $20,000.00 or imprisoned not more than two years, or both. In the case of a second or subsequent such violation upon conviction such person will be fined not more than $100,000.00, or imprisoned not more than five years, or both.

[49 FR 1028, Jan. 6, 1984, as amended at 60 FR 5259, 5260, Jan. 26, 1995]

§ 1312.5 Permit requirements and exceptions.

(a) Any person proposing to excavate and/or remove archaeological resources from public lands or Indian lands, and to carry out activities associated with such excavation and/or removal, shall apply to the Federal land manager for a permit for the proposed work, and shall not begin the proposed work until a permit has been issued. The Federal land manager may issue a permit to any qualified person, subject to appropriate terms and conditions, provided that the person applying for a permit meets conditions in § 1312.8(a) of this part.

(b) Exceptions:

(1) No permit shall be required under this part for any person conducting activities on the public lands under other permits, leases, licenses, or entitlements for use, when those activities are exclusively for purposes other than the excavation and/or removal of archaeological resources, even though those activities might incidentally result in the disturbance of archaeological resources. General earth-moving excavation conducted under a permit or other authorization shall not be construed to mean excavation and/or removal as used in this part. This exception does not, however, affect the Federal land manager's responsibility to comply with other authorities which protect archaeological resources prior to approving permits, leases, licenses, or entitlements for use; any excavation and/or removal of archaeological resources required for compliance with those authorities shall be conducted in accordance with the permit requirements of this part.

(2) No permit shall be required under this part for any person collecting for private purposes any rock, coin, bullet, or mineral which is not an archaeological resource as defined in this part, provided that such collecting does not result in disturbance of any archaelogical resource.

(3) No permit shall be required under this part or under section 3 of the Act of June 8, 1906 (16 U.S.C. 432), for the excavation or removal by any Indian tribe or member thereof of any archaeological resource located on Indian lands of such Indian tribe, except that in the absence of tribal law regulating the excavation or removal or archaeological resources on Indian lands, an individual tribal member shall be required to obtain a permit under this part;

(4) No permit shall be required under this part for any person to carry out any archaeological activity authorized by a permit issued under section 3 of the Act of June 8, 1906 (16 U.S.C. 432), before the enactment of the Archaeological Resources Protection Act of 1979. Such permit shall remain in effect according to its terms and conditions until expiration.

(5) No permit shall be required under section 3 of the Act of June 8, 1906 (16 U.S.C. 432) for any archaeological work for which a permit is issued under this part.

(c) Persons carrying out official agency duties under the Federal land manager's direction, associated with the management of archaeological resources, need not follow the permit application procedures of § 1312.6. However, the Federal land manager shall insure that provisions of §§ 1312.8 and 1312.9 have been met by other documented means, and that any official duties which might result in harm to or destruction of any Indian tribal religious or cultural site, as determined by the Federal land manager, have been the subject of consideration under § 1312.7.

(d) Upon the written request of the Governor of any State, on behalf of the State or its educational institutions, the Federal land manager shall issue a permit, subject to the provisions of §§ 1312.5(b)(5), 1312.7, 1312.8(a)(3), (4), (5), (6), and (7), 1312.9, 1312.10, 1312.12, and 1312.13(a) to such Governor or to such designee as the Governor deems qualified to carry out the intent of the Act, for purposes of conducting archaeological research, excavating and/or removing archaeological resources, and safeguarding and preserving any materials and data collected in a university, museum, or other scientific or educational institution approved by the Federal land manager.

(e) Under other statutory, regulatory, or administrative authorities governing the use of public lands and Indian lands, authorizations may be required for activities which do not require a permit under this part. Any person wishing to conduct on public lands or Indian lands any activities related to but believed to fall outside the scope of this part should consult with the Federal land manager, for the purpose of determining whether any authorization is required, prior to beginning such activities.

§ 1312.6 Application for permits and information collection.

(a) Any person may apply to the appropriate Federal land manager for a permit to excavate and/or remove archaeological resources from public lands or Indian lands and to carry out activities associated with such excavation and/or removal.

(b) Each application for a permit shall include:

(1) The nature and extent of the work proposed, including how and why it is proposed to be conducted, proposed time of performance, locational maps, and proposed outlet for public written dissemination of the results.

(2) The name and address of the individual(s) proposed to be responsible for conducting the work, institutional affiliation, if any, and evidence of education, training, and experience in accord with the minimal qualifications listed in § 1312.8(a).

(3) The name and address of the individual(s), if different from the individual(s) named in paragraph (b)(2) of this section, proposed to be responsible for carrying out the terms and conditions of the permit.

(4) Evidence of the applicant's ability to initiate, conduct, and complete the proposed work, including evidence of logistical support and laboratory facilities.

(5) Where the application is for the excavation and/or removal of archaeological resources on public lands, the names of the university, museum, or other scientific or educational institution in which the applicant proposes to store all collections, and copies of records, data, photographs, and other documents derived from the proposed work. Applicants shall submit written certification, signed by an authorized official of the institution, of willingness to assume curatorial responsibility for the collections, records, data, photographs and other documents and tm safeguard and preserve these materials as property of the United States.

(6) Where the application is for the excavation and/or removal of archaeological resources on Indian lands, the name of the university, museum, or other scientific or educational institution in which the applicant proposes to store copies of records, data, photographs, ald other documents derived from the proposed work, and all collections in the event the Indian owners do not wish tm take custody or otherwise dispose of the archaeological resources. Applicants shall submit written certification, signed by an authorized official of the institution, or willingness tm assume curatorial responsibility for the collections, if applicable, and/or the records, data, photographs, and other documents derived from the proposed work.

(c) The Federal land manager may require additional information, pertinent to land management responsibilities, to be included in the application for permit and shall so inform the applicant.

(d) *Paperwork Reduction Act.* The information collection requirement contained in § 1312.6 of these regulations has been approved by the Office of Management and Budget under 44 U.S.C. 3501 *et seq.* and assigned clearance number 1024–0037. The purpose of the information collection is to meet statutory and administrative requirements in the public interest. The information will be used to assist Federal land managers in determining that applicants for permits are qualified, that the work proposed would further archaeological knowledge, that archaeological resources and associated records and data will be properly preserved, and that the permitted activity would not conflict with the management of the public lands involved. Response to the information requirement is necessary in order for an applicant to obtain a benefit.

(Approved by the Office of Management and Budget under control number 1024–0037)

§ 1312.7 Notification to Indian tribes of possible harm to, or destruction of, sites on public lands having religious or cultural importance.

(a) If the issuance of a permit under this part may result in harm to, or destruction of, any Indian tribal religious or cultural site on public lands, as determined by the Federal land manager, at least 30 days before issuing such a permit the Federal land manager shall notify any Indian tribe which may consider the site as having religious or cultural importance. Such notice shall not be deemed a disclosure to the public for purposes of section 9 of the Act.

(1) Notice by the Federal land manager to any Indian tribe shall be sent to the chief executive officer or other designated official of the tribe. Indian tribes are encouraged to designate a tribal official to be the focal point for any notification and discussion between the tribe and the Federal land manager.

(2) The Federal land manager may provide notice to any other Native American group that is known by the Federal land manager to consider sites potentially affected as being of religious or cultural importance.

(3) Upon request during the 30-day period, the Federal land manager may meet with official representatives of any Indian tribe or group to discuss their interests, including ways to avoid or mitigate potential harm or destruction such as excluding sites from the permit area. Any mitigation measures which are adopted shall be incorporated into the terms and conditions of the permit under § 1312.9.

(4) When the Federal land manager detemines that a permit applied for under this part must be issued immediately because of an imminent threat of loss or destruction of an archaeological resource, the Federal land manager shall so notify the appropriate tribe.

(b)(1) In order to identify sites of religious or cultural importance, the Federal land manager shall seek to identify all Indian tribes having aboriginal or historic ties to the lands under the Federal land manager's jurisdiction and seek to determine, from the chief executive officer or other designated official of any such tribe, the location and nature of specific sites of religious or cultural importance so that such information may be on file for land management purposes. Information on sites eligible for or included in the National Register of Historic Places may be withheld from public disclosure pursuant to section 304 of the Act of October 15, 1966, as amended (16 U.S.C. 470w–3).

(2) If the Federal land manager becomes aware of a Native American group that is not an Indian tribe as defined in this part but has aboriginal or historic ties to public lands under the Federal land manager's jurisdiction, the Federal land manager may seek to communicate with official representatives of that group to obtain information on sites they may consider to be of religious or cultural importance.

(3) The Federal land manager may enter into agreement with any Indian tribe or other Native American group for determining locations for which such tribe or group wishes to receive notice under this section.

(4) The Federal land manager should also seek to determine, in consultation with official representatives of Indian tribes or other Native American groups, what circumstances should be the subject of special notification to the tribe or group after a permit has been issued. Circumstances calling for notification might include the discovery of human remains. When circumstances for special notification have been determined by the Federal land manager, the Federal land manager will include a requirement in the terms and conditions of permits, under §1312.9(c), for permittees to notify the Federal land manger immediately upon the occurrence of such circumstances. Following the permittee's notification, the Federal land manager will notify and consult with the tribe or group as appropriate. In cases involving Native American human remains and other "cultural items", as defined by NAGPRA, the Federal land manager is referred to NAGPRA and its implementing regulations.

[49 FR 1028, Jan. 6, 1984, as amended at 60 FR 5259, 5261, Jan. 26, 1995]

§1312.8 Issuance of permits.

(a) The Federal land manager may issue a permit, for a specified period of time appropriate to the work to be conducted, upon determining that:

(1) The applicant is appropriately qualified, as evidenced by training, education, and/or experience, and possesses demonstrable competence in archaeological theory and methods, and in collecting, handling, analyzing, evaluating, and reporting archaeological data, relative to the type and scope of the work proposed, and also meets the following minimum qualifications:

(i) A graduate degree in anthropology or archaeology, or equivalent training and experience;

(ii) The demonstrated ability to plan, equip, staff, organize, and supervise activity of the type and scope proposed;

(iii) The demonstrated ability to carry research to completion, as evidenced by timely completion of theses, research reports, or similar documents;

(iv) Completion of at least 16 months of professional experience and/or specialized training in archaeological field, laboratory, or library research, administration, or management, including at least 4 months experience and/or specialized training in the kind of activity the individual proposes to conduct under authority of a permit; and

(v) Applicants proposing to engage in historical archaeology should have had at least one year of experience in research concerning archaeological resources of the historic period. Applicants proposing to engage in prehistoric archaeology should have had at least one year of experience in research concerning archaeological resources of the prehistoric period.

(2) The proposed work is to be undertaken for the purpose of furthering archaeological knowledge in the public interest, which may include but need not be limited to, scientific or scholarly research, and preservation of archaeological data;

(3) The proposed work, including time, scope, location, and purpose, is not inconsistent with any management plan or established policy, objectives, or requirements applicable to the management of the public lands concerned;

(4) Where the proposed work consists of archaelogical survey and/or data recovery undertaken in accordance with other approved uses of the public lands or Indian lands, and the proposed work has been agreed to in writing by the Federal land manager pursuant to section 106 of the National Historic Preservation Act (16 U.S.C. 470f), paragraphs (a)(2) and (3) shall be deemed satisfied by the prior approval.

(5) Written consent has been obtained, for work proposed on Indian lands, from the Indian landowner and the Indian tribe having jurisdiction over such lands;

(6) Evidence is submitted to the Federal land manager that any university, museum, or other scientific or educational institution proposed in the application as the repository possesses adequate curatorial capability for safeguarding and preserving the archaeological resources and all associated records; and

(7) The applicant has certified that, not later than 90 days after the date the final report is submitted to the Federal land manager, the following

will be delivered to the appropriate official of the approved university, museum, or other scientific or educational institution, which shall be named in the permit:

(i) All artifacts, samples, collections, and copies of records, data, photographs, and other documents resulting from work conducted under the requested permit where the permit is for the excavation and/or removal of archaeological resources from public lands.

(ii) All artifacts, samples and collections resulting from work under the requested permit for which the custody or disposition is not undertaken by the Indian owners, and copies of records, data, photographs, and other documents resulting from work conducted under the requested permit, where the permit is for the excavation and/or removal of archaeological resources from Indian lands.

(b) When the area of the proposed work would cross jurisdictional boundaries, so that permit applications must be submitted to more than one Federal land manager, the Federal land managers shall coordinate the review and evaluation of applications and the issuance of permits.

[49 FR 1028, Jan. 6, 1984; 49 FR 5923, Feb. 16, 1984]

§ 1312.9 Terms and conditions of permits.

(a) In all permits issued, the Federal land manager shall specify:

(1) The nature and extent of work allowed and required under the permit, including the time, duration, scope, location, and purpose of the work;

(2) The name of the individual(s) responsible for conducting the work and, if different, the name of the individual(s) responsible for carrying out the terms and conditions of the permit;

(3) The name of any university, museum, or other scientific or educational insitutions in which any collected materials and data shall be deposited; and

(4) Reporting requirements.

(b) The Federal land manager may specify such terms and conditions as deemed necessary, consistent with this part, to protect public safety and other values and/or resources, to secure work areas, to safeguard other legitimate land uses, and to limit activities incidental to work authorized under a permit.

(c) The Federal land manager shall include in permits issued for archaeological work on Indian lands such terms and conditions as may be requested by the Indian landowner and the Indian tribe having jurisdiction over the lands, and for archaeological work on public lands shall include such terms and conditions as may have been developed pursuant to § 1312.7.

(d) Initiation of work or other activities under the authority of a permit signifies the permittee's acceptance of the terms and conditions of the permit.

(e) The permittee shall not be released from requirements of a permit until all outstanding obligations have been satisfied, whether or not the term of the permit has expired.

(f) The permittee may request that the Federal land manager extend or modify a permit.

(g) The permittee's performance under any permit issued for a period greater than 1 year shall be subject to review by the Federal land manager, at least annually.

§ 1312.10 Suspension and revocation of permits.

(a) *Suspension or revocation for cause.* (1) The Federal land manager may suspend a permit issued pursuant to this part upon determining that the permittee has failed to meet any of the terms and conditions of the permit or has violated any prohibition of the Act or § 1312.4. The Federal land manager shall provide written notice to the permittee of the suspension, the cause thereof, and the requirements which must be met before the suspension will be removed.

(2) The Federal land manager may revoke a permit upon assessment of a civil penalty under § 1312.15 upon the permittee's conviction under section 6 of the Act, or upon determining that the permittee has failed after notice under this section to correct the situation which led to suspension of the permit.

(b) *Suspension or revocation for management purposes.* The Federal land manager may suspend or revoke a permit, without liability to the United

States, its agents, or employees, when continuation of work under the permit would be in conflict with management requirements not in effect when the permit was issued. The Federal land manager shall provide written notice to the permittee stating the nature of and basis for the suspension or revocation.

[49 FR 1028, Jan. 6, 1984; 49 FR 5923, Feb. 16, 1984]

§ 1312.11 Appeals relating to permits.

Any affected person may appeal permit issuance, denial of permit issuance, suspension, revocation, and terms and conditions of a permit through existing administrative appeal procedures, or through procedures which may be established by the Federal land manager pursuant to section 10(b) of the Act and this part.

§ 1312.12 Relationship to section 106 of the National Historic Preservation Act.

Issuance of a permit in accordance with the Act and this part does not constitute an undertaking requiring compliance with section 106 of the Act of October 15, 1966 (16 U.S.C. 470f). However, the mere issuance of such a permit does not excuse the Federal land manager from compliance with section 106 where otherwise required.

§ 1312.13 Custody of archaeological resources.

(a) Archaeological resources excavated or removed from the public lands remain the property of the United States.

(b) Archaeological resources excavated or removed from Indian lands remain the property of the Indian or Indian tribe having rights of ownership over such resources.

(c) The Secretary of the Interior may promulgate regulations providing for the exchange of archaeological resources among suitable universities, museums, or other scientific or educational institutions, for the ultimate disposition of archaeological resources, and for standards by which archaeological resources shall be preserved and maintained, when such resources have been excavated or removed from public lands and Indian lands.

(d) In the absence of regulations referenced in paragraph (c) of this section, the Federal land manager may provide for the exchange of archaeological resources among suitable universities, museums, or other scientific or educational institutions, when such resources have been excavated or removed from public lands under the authority of a permit issued by the Federal land manager.

(e) Notwithstanding the provisions of paragraphs (a) through (d) of this section, the Federal land manager will follow the procedures required by NAGPRA and its implementing regulations for determining the disposition of Native American human remains and other "cultural items", as defined by NAGPRA, that have been excavated, removed, or discovered on public lands.

[49 FR 1028, Jan. 6, 1984, as amended at 60 FR 5259, 5261, Jan. 26, 1995]

§ 1312.14 Determination of archaeological or commercial value and cost of restoration and repair.

(a) *Archaeological value.* For purposes of this part, the archaeological value of any archaeological resource involved in a violation of the prohibitions in § 1312.4 of this part or conditions of a permit issued pursuant to this part shall be the value of the information associated with the archaeological resource. This value shall be appraised in terms of the costs of the retrieval of the scientific information which would have been obtainable prior to the violation. These costs may include, but need not be limited to, the cost of preparing a research design, conducting field work, carrying out laboratory analysis, and preparing reports as would be necessary to realize the information potential.

(b) *Commercial value.* For purposes of this part, the commercial value of any archaeological resource involved in a violation of the prohibitions in § 1312.4 of this part or conditions of a permit issued pursuant to this part shall be its fair market value. Where the violation has resulted in damage to the archaeological resource, the fair market value should be determined using the condition of the archaeological resource prior to the violation, to the extent that its prior condition can be ascertained.

(c) *Cost of restoration and repair.* For purposes of this part, the cost of restoration and repair of archaeological resources damaged as a result of a violation of prohibitions or conditions pursuant to this part, shall be the sum of the costs already incurred for emergency restoration or repair work, plus those costs projected to be necessary to complete restoration and repair, which may include, but need not be limited to, the costs of the following:

(1) Reconstruction of the archaeological resource;

(2) Stabilization of the archaeological resource;

(3) Ground contour reconstruction and surface stabilization;

(4) Research necessary to carry out reconstruction or stabilization;

(5) Physical barriers or other protective devices, necessitated by the disturbance of the archaeological resource, to protect it from further disturbance;

(6) Examination and analysis of the archaeological resource including recording remaining archaeological information, where necessitated by disturbance, in order to salvage remaining values which cannot be otherwise conserved;

(7) Reinterment of human remains in accordance with religious custom and State, local, or tribal law, where appropriate, as determined by the Federal land manager.

(8) Preparation of reports relating to any of the above activities.

§ 1312.15 Assessment of civil penalties.

(a) The Federal land manager may assess a civil penalty against any person who has violated any prohibition contained in § 1312.4 or who has violated any term or condition included in a permit issued in accordance with the Act and this part.

(b) *Notice of violation.* The Federal land manager shall serve a notice of violation upon any person believed to be subject to a civil penalty, either in person or by registered or certified mail (return receipt requested). The Federal land manager shall include in the notice:

(1) A concise statement of the facts believed to show a violation;

(2) A specific reference to the provision(s) of this part or to a permit issued pursuant to this part allegedly violated;

(3) The amount of penalty proposed to be assessed, including any initial proposal to mitigate or remit where appropriate, or a statement that notice of a proposed penalty amount will be served after the damages associated with the alleged violation have been ascertained;

(4) Notification of the right to file a petition for relief pursuant to paragraph (d) of this section, or to await the Federal land manager's notice of assessment, and to request a hearing in accordance with paragraph (g) of this section. The notice shall also inform the person of the right to seek judicial review of any final administrative decision assessing a civil penalty.

(c) The person served with a notice of violation shall have 45 calendar days from the date of its service (or the date of service of a proposed penalty amount, if later) in which to respond. During this time the person may:

(1) Seek informal discussions with the Federal land manager;

(2) File a petition for relief in accordance with paragraph (d) of this section;

(3) Take no action and await the Federal land manager's notice of assessment;

(4) Accept in writing or by payment the proposed penalty, or any mitigation or remission offered in the notice. Acceptance of the proposed penalty or mitigation or remission shall be deemed a waiver of the notice of assessment and of the right to request a hearing under paragraph (g) of this section.

(d) *Petition for relief.* The person served with a notice of violation may request that no penalty be assessed or that the amount be reduced, by filing a petition for relief with the Federal land manager within 45 calendar days of the date of service of the notice of violation (or of a proposed penalty amount, if later). The petition shall be in writing and signed by the person served with the notice of violation. If the person is a corporation, the petition must be signed by an officer authorized to sign such documents. The petition shall set forth in full the legal or factual basis for the requested relief.

(e) *Assessment of penalty*. (1) The Federal land manager shall assess a civil penalty upon expiration of the period for filing a petition for relief, upon completion of review of any petition filed, or upon completion of informal discussions, whichever is later.

(2) The Federal land manager shall take into consideration all available information, including information provided pursuant to paragraphs (c) and (d) of this section or furnished upon further request by the Federal land manager.

(3) If the facts warrant a conclusion that no violation has occurred, the Federal land manager shall so notify the person served with a notice of violation, and no penalty shall be assessed.

(4) Where the facts warrant a conclusion that a violation has occurred, the Federal land manager shall determine a penalty amount in accordance with § 1312.16.

(f) *Notice of assessment*. The Federal land manager shall notify the person served with a notice of violation of the penalty amount assessed by serving a written notice of assessment, either in person or by registered or certified mail (return receipt requested). The Federal land manager shall include in the notice of assessment:

(1) The facts and conclusions from which it was determined that a violation did occur;

(2) The basis in § 1312.16 for determining the penalty amount assessed and/or any offer to mitigate or remit the penalty; and

(3) Notification of the right to request a hearing, including the procedures to be followed, and to seek judicial review of any final administrative decision assessing a civil penalty.

(g) *Hearings*. (1) Except where the right to request a hearing is deemed to have been waived as provided in paragraph (c)(4) of this section, the person served with a notice of assessment may file a written request for a hearing with the adjudicatory body specified in the notice. The person shall enclose

with the request for hearing a copy of the notice of assessment, and shall deliver the request as specified in the notice of assessment, personally or by registered or certified mail (return receipt requested).

(2) Failure to deliver a written request for a hearing within 45 days of the date of service of the notice of assessment shall be deemed a waiver of the right to a hearing.

(3) Any hearing conducted pursuant to this section shall be held in accordance with 5 U.S.C. 554. In any such hearing, the amount of civil penalty assessed shall be determined in accordance with this part, and shall not be limited by the amount assessed by the Federal land manager under paragraph (f) of this section or any offer of mitigation or remission made by the Federal land manager.

(h) *Final administrative decision*. (1) Where the person served with a notice of violation has accepted the penalty pursuant to paragraph (c)(4) of this section, the notice of violation shall constitute the final administrative decision;

(2) Where the person served with a notice of assessment has not filed a timely request for a hearing pursuant to paragraph (g)(1) of this section, the notice of assessment shall constitute the final administrative decision;

(3) Where the person served with a notice of assessment has filed a timely request for a hearing pursuant to paragraph (g)(1) of this section, the decision resulting from the hearing or any applicable administrative appeal therefrom shall constitute the final administrative decision.

(i) *Payment of penalty*. (1) The person assessed a civil penalty shall have 45 calendar days from the date of issuance of the final administrative decision in which to make full payment of the penalty assessed, unless a timely request for appeal has been filed with a U.S. District Court as provided in section 7(b)(1) of the Act.

(2) Upon failure to pay the penalty, the Federal land manager may request the Attorney General to institute a civil action to collect the penalty in a U.S. District Court for any district in

which the person assessed a civil penalty is found, resides, or transacts business. Where the Federal land manager is not represented by the Attorney General, a civil action may be initiated directly by the Federal land manager.

(j) *Other remedies not waived.* Assessment of a penalty under this section shall not be deemed a waiver of the right to pursue other available legal or administrative remedies.

§ 1312.16 Civil penalty amounts.

(a) *Maximum amount of penalty.* (1) Where the person being assessed a civil penalty has not committed any previous violation of any prohibition in § 1312.4 or of any term or condition included in a permit issued pursuant to this part, the maximum amount of the penalty shall be the full cost of restoration and repair of archaeological resources damaged plus the archaeological or commercial value of archaeological resources destroyed or not recovered.

(2) Where the person being assessed a civil penalty has committed any previous violation of any prohibition in § 1312.4 or of any term or condition included in a permit issued pursuant to this part, the maximum amount of the penalty shall be double the cost of restoration and repair plus double the archaeological or commercial value of archaeological resources destroyed or not recovered.

(3) Violations limited to the removal of arrowheads located on the surface of the ground shall not be subject to the penalties prescribed in this section.

(b) *Determination of penalty amount, mitigation, and remission.* The Federal land manager may assess a penalty amount less than the maximum amount of penalty and may offer to mitigate or remit the penalty.

(1) Determination of the penalty amount and/or a proposal to mitigate or remit the penalty may be based upon any of the following factors:

(i) Agreement by the person being assessed a civil penalty to return to the Federal land manager archaeological resources removed from public lands or Indian lands;

(ii) Agreement by the person being assessed a civil penalty to assist the Federal land manager in activity to preserve, restore, or otherwise contribute to the protection and study of archaeological resources on public lands or Indian lands;

(iii) Agreement by the person being assessed a civil penalty to provide information which will assist in the detection, prevention, or prosecution of violations of the Act or this part;

(iv) Demonstration of hardship or inability to pay, provided that this factor shall only be considered when the person being assessed a civil penalty has not been found to have previously violated the regulations in this part;

(v) Determination that the person being assessed a civil penalty did not willfully commit the violation;

(vi) Determination that the proposed penalty would constitute excessive punishment under the circumstances;

(vii) Determination of other mitigating circumstances appropriate to consideration in reaching a fair and expeditious assessment.

(2) When the penalty is for a violation on Indian lands, the Federal land manager shall consult with and consider the interests of the Indian landowner and the Indian tribe having jurisdiction over the Indian lands prior to proposing to mitigate or remit the penalty.

(3) When the penalty is for a violation which may have had an effect on a known Indian tribal religious or cultural site on public lands, the Federal land manager should consult with and consider the interests of the affected tribe(s) prior to proposing to mitigate or remit the penalty.

[49 FR 1028, Jan. 6, 1984, as amended at 52 FR 47721, Dec. 16, 1987]

§ 1312.17 Other penalties and rewards.

(a) Section 6 of the Act contains criminal prohibitions and provisions for criminal penalties. Section 8(b) of the Act provides that archaeological resources, vehicles, or equipment involved in a violation may be subject to forfeiture.

(b) Section 8(a) of the Act provides for rewards to be made to persons who furnish information which leads to conviction for a criminal violation or to assessment of a civil penalty. The Federal land manager may certify to the

Secretary of the Treasury that a person is eligible to receive payment. Officers and employees of Federal, State, or local government who furnish information or render service in the performance of their official duties, and persons who have provided information under § 1312.16(b)(1)(iii) shall not be certified eligible to receive payment of rewards.

(c) In cases involving Indian lands, all civil penalty monies and any item forfeited under the provisions of this section shall be transferred to the appropriate Indian or Indian tribe.

§ 1312.18 **Confidentiality of archaeological resource information.**

(a) The Federal land manager shall not make available to the public, under Subchapter II of Chapter 5 of Title 5 of the U.S. Code or any other provision of law, information concerning the nature and location of any archaeological resource, with the following exceptions:

(1) The Federal land manager may make information available, provided that the disclosure will further the purposes of the Act and this part, or the Act of June 27, 1960, as amended (16 U.S.C. 469–469c), without risking harm to the archaeological resource or to the site in which it is located.

(2) The Federal land manager shall make information available, when the Governor of any State has submitted to the Federal land manager a written request for information, concerning the archaeological resources within the requesting Governor's State, provided that the request includes:

(i) The specific archaeological resource or area about which information is sought;

(ii) The purpose for which the information is sought; and

(iii) The Governor's written commitment to adequately protect the confidentiality of the information.

(b) [Reserved]

[49 FR 1028, Jan. 6, 1984; 49 FR 5923, Feb. 16, 1984]

§ 1312.19 **Report.**

(a) Each Federal land manager, when requested by the Secretary of the Interior, will submit such information as is necessary to enable the Secretary to comply with section 13 of the Act and

comprehensively report on activities carried out under provisions of the Act.

(b) The Secretary of the Interior will include in the annual comprehensive report, submitted to the Committee on Interior and Insular Affairs of the United States House of Representatives and to the Committee on Energy and Natural Resources of the United States Senate under section 13 of the Act, information on public awareness programs submitted by each Federal land manager under § 1312.20(b). Such submittal will fulfill the Federal land manager's responsibility under section 10(c) of the Act to report on public awareness programs.

(c) The comprehensive report by the Secretary of the Interior also will include information on the activities carried out under section 14 of the Act. Each Federal land manager, when requested by the Secretary, will submit any available information on surveys and schedules and suspected violations in order to enable the Secretary to summarize in the comprehensive report actions taken pursuant to section 14 of the Act.

[60 FR 5259, 5261, Jan. 26, 1995]

§ 1312.20 **Public awareness programs.**

(a) Each Federal land manager will establish a program to increase public awareness of the need to protect important archaeological resources located on public and Indian lands. Educational activities required by section 10(c) of the Act should be incorporated into other current agency public education and interpretation programs where appropriate.

(b) Each Federal land manager annually will submit to the Secretary of the Interior the relevant information on public awareness activities required by section 10(c) of the Act for inclusion in the comprehensive report on activities required by section 13 of the Act.

[60 FR 5259, 5261, Jan. 26, 1995]

§ 1312.21 **Surveys and schedules.**

(a) The Secretaries of the Interior, Agriculture, and Defense and the Chairman of the Board of the Tennessee Valley Authority will develop plans for surveying lands under each agency's control to determine the nature and extent of archaeological resources pursuant to section 14(a) of the Act. Such activities should be consistent with Federal agency planning policies and other historic preservation program responsibilities required by 16 U.S.C. 470 *et seq.* Survey plans prepared under this section will be designed to comply with the purpose of the Act regarding the protection of archaeological resources.

(b) The Secretaries of the Interior, Agriculture, and Defense and the Chairman of the Tennessee Valley Authority will prepare schedules for surveying lands under each agency's control that are likely to contain the most scientifically valuable archaeological resources pursuant to section 14(b) of the Act. Such schedules will be developed based on objectives and information identified in survey plans described in paragraph (a) of this section and implemented systematically to cover areas where the most scientifically valuable archaeological resources are likely to exist.

(c) Guidance for the activities undertaken as part of paragraphs (a) through (b) of this section is provided by the Secretary of the Interior's Standards and Guidelines for Archeology and Historic Preservation.

(d) Other Federal land managing agencies are encouraged to develop plans for surveying lands under their jurisdictions and prepare schedules for surveying to improve protection and management of archaeological resources.

(e) The Secretaries of the Interior, Agriculture, and Defense and the Chairman of the Tennessee Valley Authority will develop a system for documenting and reporting suspected violations of the various provisions of the Act. This system will reference a set of procedures for use by officers, employees, or agents of Federal agencies to assist them in recognizing violations, documenting relevant evidence, and reporting assembled information to the appropriate authorities. Methods employed to document and report such violations should be compatible with existing agency reporting systems for documenting violations of other appropriate Federal statutes and regula-

tions. Summary information to be included in the Secretary's comprehensive report will be based upon the system developed by each Federal land manager for documenting suspected violations.

[60 FR 5259, 5261, Jan. 26, 1995]

§ 1312.22   Issuance   of   citations   for petty offenses.

Any person who violates any provision contained in 16 U.S.C. 470ee or 16 U.S.C. 433 in the presence of a TVA law enforcement agent may be tried and sentenced in accordance with the provisions of section 3401 of Title 18, United States Code. Law enforcement agents designated by the Director for that purpose shall have the authority to issue a petty offense citation for any such violation, requiring any person charged with the violation to appear before a United States Magistrate Judge within whose jurisdiction the archaeological resource impacted by the violation is located. The term "petty offense" has the same meaning given that term under section 19 of Title 18, United States Code.

[81 FR 54499, Aug. 16, 2016]

PART 1313—ENFORCEMENT OF NONDISCRIMINATION ON THE BASIS OF HANDICAP IN PROGRAMS OR ACTIVITIES CONDUCTED BY THE TENNESSEE VALLEY AUTHORITY

1313.170 Compliance procedures.

AUTHORITY: 29 U.S.C. 794.

SOURCE: 51 FR 22889, 22896, June 23, 1986, unless otherwise noted.

§ 1313.101 Purpose.

This part effectuates section 119 of the Rehabilitation, Comprehensive Services, and Developmental Disabilities Amendments of 1978, which amended section 504 of the Rehabilitation Act of 1973 to prohibit discrimination on the basis of handicap in programs or activities conducted by Executive agencies or the United States Postal Service.

§ 1313.102 Application.

This part applies to all programs or activities conducted by the agency.

§ 1313.103 Definitions.

For purposes of this part, the term—

Assistant Attorney General means the Assistant Attorney General, Civil Rights Division, United States Department of Justice.

Auxiliary aids means services or devices that enable persons with impaired sensory, manual, or speaking skills to have an equal opportunity to participate in, and enjoy the benefits of, programs or activities conducted by the agency. For example, auxiliary aids useful for persons with impaired vision include readers, brailled materials, audio recordings, telecommunications devices and other similar services and devices. Auxiliary aids useful for persons with impaired hearing include telephone handset amplifiers, telephones compatible with hearing aids, telecommunication devices for deaf persons (TDD's), interpreters, notetakers, written materials, and other similar services and devices.

Complete complaint means a written statement that contains the complainant's name and address and describes the agency's alleged discriminatory action in sufficient detail to inform the agency of the nature and date of the alleged violation of section 504. It shall be signed by the complainant or by someone authorized to do so on his or her behalf. Complaints filed on behalf of classes or third parties shall describe or identify (by name, if possible) the alleged victims of discrimination.

Facility means all or any portion of buildings, structures, equipment, roads, walks, parking lots, rolling stock or other conveyances, or other real or personal property.

Handicapped person means any person who has a physical or mental impairment that substantially limits one or more major life activities, has a record of such an impairment, or is regarded as having such an impairment.

As used in this definition, the phrase:

(1) *Physical or mental impairment* includes—

(i) Any physiological disorder or condition, cosmetic disfigurement, or anatomical loss affecting one or more of the following body systems: Neurological; musculoskeletal; special sense organs; respiratory, including speech organs; cardiovascular; reproductive; digestive; genitourinary; hemic and lymphatic; skin; and endocrine; or

(ii) Any mental or psychological disorder, such as mental retardation, organic brain syndrome, emotional or mental illness, and specific learning disabilities. The term "physical or mental impairment" includes, but is not limited to, such diseases and conditions as orthopedic, visual, speech, and hearing impairments, cerebral palsy, epilepsy, muscular dystrophy, multiple sclerosis, cancer, heart disease, diabetes, mental retardation, emotional illness, and drug addiction and alcoholism.

(2) *Major life activities* includes functions such as caring for one's self, performing manual tasks, walking, seeing, hearing, speaking, breathing, learning, and working.

(3) *Has a record of such an impairment* means has a history of, or has been misclassified as having, a mental or physical impairment that substantially limits one or more major life activities.

(4) *Is regarded as having an impairment* means—

(i) Has a physical or mental impairment that does not substantially limit major life activities but is treated by the agency as constituting such a limitation;

(ii) Has a physical or mental impairment that substantially limits major life activities only as a result of the attitudes of others toward such impairment; or

(iii) Has none of the impairments defined in paragraph (1) of this definition but is treated by the agency as having such an impairment.

Historic preservation programs means programs conducted by the agency that have preservation of historic properties as a primary purpose.

Historic properties means those properties that are listed or eligible for listing in the National Register of Historic Places or properties designated as historic under a statute of the appropriate State or local government body.

Qualified handicapped person means—

(1) With respect to preschool, elementary, or secondary education services provided by the agency, a handicapped person who is a member of a class of persons otherwise entitled by statute, regulation, or agency policy to receive education services from the agency.

(2) With respect to any other agency program or activity under which a person is required to perform services or to achieve a level of accomplishment, a handicapped person who meets the essential eligibility requirements and who can acheive the purpose of the program or activity without modifications in the program or activity that the agency can demonstrate would result in a fundamental alteration in its nature;

(3) With respect to any other program or activity, a handicapped person who meets the essential eligibility requirements for participation in, or receipt of benefits from, that program or activity; and

(4) *Qualified handicapped person* is defined for purposes of employment in 29 CFR 1613.702(f), which is made applicable to this part by § 1313.140.

Section 504 means section 504 of the Rehabilitation Act of 1973 (Pub. L. 93–112, 87 Stat. 394 (29 U.S.C. 794)), as amended by the Rehabilitation Act Amendments of 1974 (Pub. L. 93–516, 88 Stat. 1617), and the Rehabilitation, Comprehensive Services, and Developmental Disabilities Amendments of 1978 (Pub. L. 95–602, 92 Stat. 2955). As used in this part, section 504 applies only to programs or activities conducted by Executive agencies and not to federally assisted programs.

Substantial impairment means a significant loss of the integrity of finished materials, design quality, or special character resulting from a permanent alteration.

§§ 1313.104–1313.109 [Reserved]

§ 1313.110 Self-evaluation.

(a) The agency shall, by August 24, 1987, evaluate its current policies and practices, and the effects thereof, that do not or may not meet the requirements of this part, and, to the extent modification of any such policies and practices is required, the agency shall proceed to make the necessary modifications.

(b) The agency shall provide an opportunity to interested persons, including handicapped persons or organizations representing handicapped persons, to participate in the self-evaluation process by submitting comments (both oral and written).

(c) The agency shall, until three years following the completion of the self-evaluation, maintain on file and make available for public inspection:

(1) A description of areas examined and any problems identified, and

(2) A description of any modifications made.

§ 1313.111 Notice.

The agency shall make available to employees, applicants, participants, beneficiaries, and other interested persons such information regarding the provisions of this part and its applicability to the programs or activities conducted by the agency, and make such information available to them in such manner as the head of the agency finds necessary to apprise such persons of the protections against discrimination assured them by section 504 and this regulation.

§§ 1313.112–1313.129 [Reserved]

§ 1313.130 General prohibitions against discrimination.

(a) No qualified handicapped person shall, on the basis of handicap, be excluded from participation in, be denied the benefits of, or otherwise be subjected to discrimination under any program or activity conducted by the agency.

(b)(1) The agency, in providing any aid, benefit, or service, may not, directly or through contractual, licensing, or other arrangements, on the basis of handicap—

(i) Deny a qualified handicapped person the opportunity to participate in or benefit from the aid, benefit, or service;

(ii) Afford a qualified handicapped person an opportunity to participate in or benefit from the aid, benefit, or service that is not equal to that afforded others;

(iii) Provide a qualified handicapped person with an aid, benefit, or service that is not as effective in affording equal opportunity to obtain the same result, to gain the same benefit, or to reach the same level of achievement as that provided to others;

(iv) Provide different or separate aid, benefits, or services to handicapped persons or to any class of handicapped persons than is provided to others unless such action is necessary to provide qualified handicapped persons with aid, benefits, or services that are as effective as those provided to others;

(v) Deny a qualified handicapped person the opportunity to participate as a member of planning or advisory boards; or

(vi) Otherwise limit a qualified handicapped person in the enjoyment of any right, privilege, advantage, or opportunity enjoyed by others receiving the aid, benefit, or service.

(2) The agency may not deny a qualified handicapped person the opportunity to participate in programs or activities that are not separate or different, despite the existence of permissibly separate or different programs or activities.

(3) The agency may not, directly or through contractual or other arrangments, utilize criteria or methods of administration the purpose or effect of which would—

(i) Subject qualified handicapped persons to discrimination on the basis of handicap; or

(ii) Defeat or substantially impair accomplishment of the objectives of a program or activity with respect to handicapped persons.

(4) The agency may not, in determining the site or location of a facility, make selections the purpose or effect of which would—

(i) Exclude handicapped persons from, deny them the benefits of, or otherwise subject them to discrimination under any program or activity conducted by the agency; or

(ii) Defeat or substantially impair the accomplishment of the objectives of a program or activity with respect to handicapped persons.

(5) The agency, in the selection of procurement contractors, may not use criteria that subject qualified handicapped persons to discrimination on the basis of handicap.

(6) The agency may not administer a licensing or certification program in a manner that subjects qualified handicapped persons to discrimination on the basis of handicap, nor may the agency establish requirements for the programs or activities of licensees or certified entities that subject qualified handicapped persons to discrimination on the basis of handicap. However, the programs or activities of entities that are licensed or certified by the agency are not, themselves, covered by this part.

(c) The exclusion of nonhandicapped persons from the benefits of a program limited by Federal statute or Executive order to handicapped persons or the exclusion of a specific class of handicapped persons from a program limited by Federal statute or Executive order to a different class of handicapped persons is not prohibited by this part.

(d) The agency shall administer programs and activities in the most integrated setting appropriate to the needs of qualified handicapped persons.

§§ 1313.131–1313.139 [Reserved]

§ 1313.140 Employment.

No qualified handicapped person shall, on the basis of handicap, be subjected to discrimination in employment under any program or activity conducted by the agency. The definitions, requirements, and procedures of section 501 of the Rehabilitation Act of

1973 (29 U.S.C. 791), as established by the Equal Employment Opportunity Commission in 29 CFR part 1613, shall apply to employment in federally conducted programs or activities.

§§ 1313.141–1313.148　[Reserved]

§ 1313.149　Program accessibility: Discrimination prohibited.

Except as otherwise provided in § 1313.150, no qualified handicapped person shall, because the agency's facilities are inaccessible to or unusable by handicapped persons, be denied the benefits of, be excluded from participation in, or otherwise be subjected to discrimination under any program or activity conducted by the agency.

§ 1313.150　Program accessibility: Existing facilities.

(a) *General.* The agency shall operate each program or activity so that the program or activity, when viewed in its entirety, is readily accessible to and usable by handicapped persons. This paragraph does not—

(1) Necessarily require the agency to make each of its existing facilities accessible to and usable by handicapped persons;

(2) In the case of historic preservation programs, require the agency to take any action that would result in a substantial impairment of significant historic features of an historic property; or

(3) Require the agency to take any action that it can demonstrate would result in a fundamental alteration in the nature of a program or activity or in undue financial and administrative burdens. In those circumstances where agency personnel believe that the proposed action would fundamentally alter the program or activity or would result in undue financial and administrative burdens, the agency has the burden of proving that compliance with § 1313.150(a) would result in such alteration or burdens. The decision that compliance would result in such alteration or burdens must be made by the agency head or his or her designee after considering all agency resources available for use in the funding and operation of the conducted program or activity, and must be accompanied by a written statement of the reasons for reaching that conclusion. If an action would result in such an alteration or such burdens, the agency shall take any other action that would not result in such an alteration or such burdens but would nevertheless ensure that handicapped persons receive the benefits and services of the program or activity.

(b) *Methods*—(1) *General.* The agency may comply with the requirements of this section through such means as redesign of equipment, reassignment of the services to accessible buildings, assignment of aides to beneficiaries, home visits, delivery of services at alternate accessible sites, alteration of existing facilities and construction of new facilities, use of accessible rolling stock, or any other methods that result in making its programs or activities readily accessible to and usable by handicapped persons. The agency is not required to make structural changes in existing facilities where other methods are effective in achieving compliance with this section. The agency, in making alterations to existing buildings, shall meet accessibility requirements to the extent compelled by the Architectural Barriers Act of 1968, as amended (42 U.S.C. 4151–4157), and any regulations implementing it. In choosing among available methods for meeting the requirements of this section, the agency shall give priority to those methods that offer programs and activities to qualified handicapped persons in the most integrated setting appropriate.

(2) *Historic preservation programs.* In meeting the requirements of § 1313.150(a) in historic preservation programs, the agency shall give priority to methods that provide physical access to handicapped persons. In cases where a physical alteration to an historic property is not required because of § 1313.150(a)(2) or (a)(3), alternative methods of achieving program accessibility include—

(i) Using audio-visual materials and devices to depict those portions of an historic property that cannot otherwise be made accessible;

(ii) Assigning persons to guide handicapped persons into or through portions of historic properties that cannot otherwise be made accessible; or

(iii) Adopting other innovative methods.

(c) *Time period for compliance.* The agency shall comply with the obligations established under this section by October 21, 1986, except that where structural changes in facilities are undertaken, such changes shall be made by August 22, 1989, but in any event as expeditiously as possible.

(d) *Transition plan.* In the event that structural changes to facilities will be undertaken to achieve program accessibility, the agency shall develop, by February 23, 1987, a transition plan setting forth the steps necessary to complete such changes. The agency shall provide an opportunity to interested persons, including handicapped persons or organizations representing handicapped persons, to participate in the development of the transition plan by submitting comments (both oral and written). A copy of the transition plan shall be made available for public inspection. The plan shall, at a minimum—

(1) Identify physical obstacles in the agency's facilities that limit the accessibility of its programs or activities to handicapped persons;

(2) Describe in detail the methods that will be used to make the facilities accessible;

(3) Specify the schedule for taking the steps necessary to achieve compliance with this section and, if the time period of the transition plan is longer than one year, identify steps that will be taken during each year of the transition period; and

(4) Indicate the official responsible for implementation of the plan.

§1313.151 Program accessibility: New construction and alterations.

Each building or part of a building that is constructed or altered by, on behalf of, or for the use of the agency shall be designed, constructed, or altered so as to be readily accessible to and usable by handicapped persons. The definitions, requirements, and standards of the Architectural Barriers Act (42 U.S.C. 4151–4157), as established

in 41 CFR 101–19.600 to 101–19.607, apply to buildings covered by this section.

§§1313.152–1313.159 [Reserved]

§1313.160 Communications.

(a) The agency shall take appropriate steps to ensure effective communication with applicants, participants, personnel of other Federal entities, and members of the public.

(1) The agency shall furnish appropriate auxiliary aids where necessary to afford a handicapped person an equal opportunity to participate in, and enjoy the benefits of, a program or activity conducted by the agency.

(i) In determining what type of auxiliary aid is necessary, the agency shall give primary consideration to the requests of the handicapped person.

(ii) The agency need not provide individually prescribed devices, readers for personal use or study, or other devices of a personal nature.

(2) Where the agency communicates with applicants and beneficiaries by telephone, telecommunication devices for deaf person (TDD's) or equally effective telecommunication systems shall be used.

(b) The agency shall ensure that interested persons, including persons with impaired vision or hearing, can obtain information as to the existence and location of accessible services, activities, and facilities.

(c) The agency shall provide signage at a primary entrance to each of its inaccessible facilities, directing users to a location at which they can obtain information about accessible facilities. The international symbol for accessibility shall be used at each primary entrance of an accessible facility.

(d) This section does not require the agency to take any action that it can demonstrate would result in a fundamental alteration in the nature of a program or activity or in undue financial and adminstrative burdens. In those circumstances where agency personnel believe that the proposed action would fundamentally alter the program or activity or would result in undue financial and administrative burdens, the agency has the burden of proving that compliance with §1313.160 would result in such alteration or burdens.

The decision that compliance would result in such alteration or burdens must be made by the agency head or his or her designee after considering all agency resources available for use in the funding and operation of the conducted program or activity, and must be accompanied by a written statement of the reasons for reaching that conclusion. If an action required to comply with this section would result in such an alteration or such burdens, the agency shall take any other action that would not result in such an alteration or such burdens but would nevertheless ensure that, to the maximum extent possible, handicapped persons receive the benefits and services of the program or activity.

§§ 1313.161–1313.169   [Reserved]

§ 1313.170   Compliance procedures.

(a) Except as provided in paragraph (b) of this section, this section applies to all allegations of discrimination on the basis of handicap in programs or activities conducted by the agency.

(b) The agency shall process complaints alleging violations of section 504 with respect to employment according to the procedures established by the Equal Employment Opportunity Commission in 29 CFR part 1613 pursuant to section 501 of the Rehabilitation Act of 1973 (29 U.S.C. 791).

(c) The Supervisor, Contracting and Community Assistance, shall be responsible for coordinating implementation of this section. Complaints may be sent to Supervisor, Contracting and Community Assistance, Tennessee Valley Authority, E5 B30, 400 West Summit Hill Drive, Knoxville, Tennessee 37902.

(d) The agency shall accept and investigate all complete complaints for which it has jurisdiction. All complete complaints must be filed within 180 days of the alleged act of discrimination. The agency may extend this time period for good cause.

(e) If the agency receives a complaint over which it does not have jurisdiction, it shall promptly notify the complainant and shall make reasonable efforts to refer the complaint to the appropriate government entity.

(f) The agency shall notify the Architectural and Transportation Barriers Compliance Board upon receipt of any complaint alleging that a building or facility that is subject to the Architectural Barriers Act of 1968, as amended (42 U.S.C. 4151–4157), or section 502 of the Rehabilitation Act of 1973, as amended (29 U.S.C. 792), is not readily accessible to and usable by handicapped persons.

(g) Within 180 days of the receipt of a complete complaint for which it has jurisdiction, the agency shall notify the complainant of the results of the investigation in a letter containing—

(1) Findings of fact and conclusions of law;

(2) A description of a remedy for each violation found; and

(3) A notice of the right to appeal.

(h) Appeals of the findings of fact and conclusions of law or remedies must be filed by the complainant within 90 days of receipt from the agency of the letter required by § 1313.170(g). The agency may extend this time for good cause.

(i) Timely appeals shall be accepted and processed by the head of the agency.

(j) The head of the agency shall notify the complainant of the results of the appeal within 60 days of the receipt of the request. If the head of the agency determines that additional information is needed from the complainant, he or she shall have 60 days from the date of receipt of the additional information to make his or her determination on the appeal.

(k) The time limits cited in paragraphs (g) and (j) of this section may be extended with the permission of the Assistant Attorney General.

(l) The agency may delegate its authority for conducting complaint investigations to other Federal agencies, except that the authority for making the final determination may not be delegated to another agency.

[51 FR 22889, 22896, June 23, 1986, as amended at 51 FR 22890, June 23, 1986]

PART 1314—BOOK-ENTRY PROCEDURES FOR TVA POWER SECURITIES ISSUED THROUGH THE FEDERAL RESERVE BANKS

Sec.

AUTHORITY: 16 U.S.C. 831–831dd.

SOURCE: 62 FR 920, Jan. 7, 1997, unless otherwise noted.

§ 1314.1 Applicability and effect.

(a) *Applicability.* The regulations in this part govern the issuance of, and transactions in, all TVA Power Securities issued by TVA in book-entry form through the Reserve Banks.

(b) *Effect.* The TVA Power Securities to which the regulations in this part apply are obligations which, by the terms of their issue, are available exclusively in book-entry form through the Reserve Banks' Book-entry System.

§ 1314.2 Definition of terms.

Unless the context requires otherwise, terms used in this part 1314 that are not defined in this section have the meanings as set forth in 31 CFR 357.2. Definitions and terms used in 31 CFR part 357 should be read as though modified to effectuate their application to Book-entry TVA Power Securities where applicable.

(a) *Book-entry System* means the automated book-entry system operated by the Reserve Banks acting as the fiscal agent for TVA on which Book-entry TVA Power Securities are issued, recorded, transferred, and maintained in book-entry form.

(b) *Book-entry TVA Power Security* means any TVA Power Security issued or maintained in the Book-entry System of the Reserve Banks.

(c) *CUSIP Number* is a unique identification for each security issue established by the Committee on Uniform Security Identification Procedures.

(d) *Depository Institution* means any Participant.

(e) *Entitlement Holder* means a Person to whose account an interest in a Book-entry TVA Power Security is credited on the records of a Securities Intermediary.

(f) *Funds Account* means a reserve and/or clearing account at a Reserve Bank to which debits or credits are posted for transfers against payment, book-entry securities transaction fees, or principal and interest payments.

(g) *Other TVA Power Evidences of Indebtedness* means any TVA Power Security issued consistent with section 2.5 of the TVA Basic Bond Resolution (see paragraph (r) of this section).

(h) *Participant* (also called "holder" in the TVA Basic Bond Resolution and in other resolutions adopted by the TVA Board of Directors relating to Book-entry TVA Power Securities) means a Person that maintains a Participant's Security Account with a Reserve Bank.

(i) *Participant's Security Account* means an account in the name of a Participant at a Reserve Bank to which Book-entry TVA Power Securities held for a Participant are or may be credited.

(j) *Person* means and includes an individual, corporation, company, governmental entity, association, firm, partnership, trust, estate, representative, and any other similar organization, but does not mean or include the United States or a Reserve Bank.

(k) *Reserve Banks* means the Federal Reserve Banks of the Federal Reserve System and their branches.

(l) *Reserve Bank Operating Circular* means the publication issued by each Reserve Bank that sets forth the terms and conditions under which the Reserve Bank maintains book-entry securities accounts and transfers book-entry securities.

(m) *Securities Documentation* means the applicable documents establishing the terms of a Book-entry TVA Power Security.

(n) *Securities Intermediary* means:

(1) A Person that is registered as a "clearing agency" under the Federal securities law; a Reserve Bank; any other Person that provides clearance or settlement services with respect to a Book-entry TVA Power Security that would require it to register as a clearing agency under the Federal securities laws but for an exclusion or exemption from the registration requirement, if its activities as a clearing corporation, including promulgation of rules, are subject to regulation by a Federal or State governmental authority; or

(2) A Person (other than an individual, unless such individual is registered as a broker or dealer under the Federal securities laws), including a bank or broker, that in the ordinary course of business maintains securities accounts for others and is acting in that capacity.

(o) *Security Entitlement* means the rights and property interests of an Entitlement Holder with respect to a Book-entry TVA Power Security.

(p) *State* means any State of the United States, the District of Columbia, Puerto Rico, the Virgin Islands, or any other territory or possession of the United States.

(q) *TVA* means the Tennessee Valley Authority, a wholly owned corporate agency and instrumentality of the United States of America created and existing under the Tennessee Valley Authority Act of 1933, as amended (16 U.S.C. 831–831dd).

(r) *TVA Basic Bond Resolution* means the Basic Tennessee Valley Authority Power Bond Resolution[1] adopted by the TVA Board of Directors on October 6, 1960, as heretofore and hereafter amended.

(s) *TVA Power Bond* means any TVA Power Security issued by TVA under section 2.2 of the TVA Basic Bond Resolution and the supplemental resolution adopted by the TVA Board of Directors authorizing the issuance thereof.

(t) *TVA Power Bond Anticipation Obligation* means any TVA Power Security

issued consistent with section 2.4 of the TVA Basic Bond Resolution.

(u) *TVA Power Note* means any Other TVA Power Evidences of Indebtedness in the form of a note having a maturity at the date of issue of less than one year.

(v) *TVA Power Security* means a TVA Power Bond, TVA Power Bond Anticipation Obligation, TVA Power Note, or Other TVA Power Evidence of Indebtedness issued by TVA under Section 15d of the TVA Act, as amended.

[62 FR 920, Jan. 7, 1997; 62 FR 4833, Jan. 31, 1997, as amended at 62 FR 29288, May 30, 1997]

§ 1314.3 Authority of Reserve Banks.

(a) Each Reserve Bank is hereby authorized as fiscal agent of TVA to perform the following functions with respect to the issuance of Book-entry TVA Power Securities offered and sold by TVA to which this part 1314 applies, in accordance with the Securities Documentation, Reserve Bank Operating Circulars, this part 1314, and procedures established by the Secretary of the United States Treasury consistent with these authorities:

(1) To service and maintain Book-entry TVA Power Securities in accounts established for such purposes;

(2) To make payments with respect to such securities, as directed by TVA;

(3) To effect transfer of Book-entry TVA Power Securities between Participants' Security Accounts as directed by the Participants;

(4) To perform such other duties as fiscal agent as may be requested by TVA.

(b) Each Reserve Bank may issue Reserve Bank Operating Circulars not inconsistent with this part 1314, governing the details of its handling of Book-entry TVA Power Securities, Security Entitlements, and the operation of the Book-entry System under this part 1314.

[62 FR 920, Jan. 7, 1997, as amended at 62 FR 29288, May 30, 1997]

[1] A copy of the TVA Basic Bond Resolution may be obtained upon request directed to TVA, 400 West Summit Hill Drive, Knoxville, Tennessee 37902–1499, Attn.: Treasurer.

§1314.4 Law governing the rights and obligations of TVA and Reserve Banks; law governing the rights of any Person against TVA and Reserve Banks; law governing other interests.

(a) Except as provided in paragraph (b) of this section, the following rights and obligations are governed solely by the book-entry regulations contained in this part 1314, the Securities Documentation (but not including any choice of law provisions in such documentation), and Reserve Bank Operating Circulars:

(1) The rights and obligations of TVA and Reserve Banks with respect to:

(i) A Book-entry TVA Power Security or Security Entitlement; and

(ii) The operation of the Book-entry System as it applies to TVA Power Securities; and

(2) The rights of any Person, including a Participant, against TVA and Reserve Banks with respect to:

(i) A Book-entry TVA Power Security or Security Entitlement; and

(ii) The operation of the Book-entry System as it applies to TVA Power Securities.

(b) A security interest in a Security Entitlement that is in favor of a Reserve Bank from a Participant and that is not recorded on the books of a Reserve Bank pursuant to §1314.5(c) is governed by the law (not including the conflict-of-law rules) of the jurisdiction where the head office of the Reserve Bank maintaining the Participant's Security Account is located. A security interest in a Security Entitlement that is in favor of a Reserve Bank from a Person that is not a Participant, and that is not recorded on the books of a Reserve Bank pursuant to §1314.5(c), is governed by the law determined in the manner specified in paragraph (d) of this section.

(c) If the jurisdiction specified in the first sentence of paragraph (b) of this section is a State that has not adopted Revised Article 8, then the law specified in paragraph (b) of this section shall be the law of that State as though Revised Article 8 had been adopted by that State.

(d) To the extent not otherwise inconsistent with this part 1314, and notwithstanding any provision in the Se-

curities Documentation setting forth a choice of law, the provisions set forth in 31 CFR 357.11 regarding law governing other interests apply and should be read as though modified to effectuate the application of 31 CFR 357.11 to Book-entry TVA Power Securities.

[62 FR 920, Jan. 7, 1997; 62 FR 8619, Feb. 26, 1997, as amended at 62 FR 29288, May 30, 1997]

§1314.5 Creation of Participant's Security Entitlement; security interests.

(a) A Participant's Security Entitlement is created when a Reserve Bank indicates by book-entry that a Book-entry TVA Power Security has been credited to a Participant's Security Account.

(b) A security interest in a Security Entitlement of a Participant in favor of the United States to secure deposits of public money, including without limitation deposits to the Treasury tax and loan accounts, or other security interest in favor of the United States that is required by Federal statute, regulation or agreement, and that is marked on the books of a Reserve Bank, is thereby effected and perfected, and has priority over any other interest in the securities. Where a security interest in favor of the United States in a Security Entitlement of a Participant is marked on the books of a Reserve Bank, such Reserve Bank may rely, and is protected in relying, exclusively on the order of an authorized representative of the United States directing the transfer of the security. For purposes of this paragraph, an "authorized representative of the United States" is the official designated in the applicable regulations or agreement to which a Reserve Bank is a party governing the security interest.

(c) TVA and Reserve Banks have no obligation to agree to act on behalf of any Person or to recognize the interest of any transferee of a security interest or other limited interest in favor of any Person except to the extent of any specific requirement of Federal law or regulation or to the extent set forth in any specific agreement with the Reserve Bank on whose books the interest of the Participant is recorded. To the extent required by such law or regulation or set forth in an agreement with a Reserve Bank or in a Reserve Bank Operating Circular, a security interest in a Security Entitlement that is in favor of a Reserve Bank or a Person may be created and perfected by a Reserve Bank marking its books to record the security interest. Subject to paragraph (b) of this section with respect to a security interest in favor of the United States, a security interest in a Security Entitlement marked on the books of a Reserve Bank shall have priority over any other interest in the securities.

(d) In addition to the method provided in paragraph (c) of this section, a security interest, including a security interest in favor of a Reserve Bank, may be perfected by any method by which a security interest may be perfected under applicable law as described in § 1314.4(b) or (d). The perfection, effect of perfection or non-perfection, and priority of a security interest are governed by such applicable law. A security interest in favor of a Reserve Bank shall be treated as a security interest in favor of a clearing corporation in all respects under such law, including with respect to the effect of perfection and priority of such security interest. A Reserve Bank Operating Circular shall be treated as a rule adopted by a clearing corporation for such purposes.

[62 FR 920, Jan. 7, 1997; 62 FR 4833, Jan. 31, 1997; 62 FR 8619, Feb. 26, 1997]

§ 1314.6 Obligations of TVA.

(a) Except in the case of a security interest in favor of the United States or a Reserve Bank or otherwise as provided in § 1314.5(c), for the purposes of this part 1314, TVA and Reserve Banks shall treat the Participant to whose securities account an interest in a Book-entry TVA Power Security has been credited as the Person exclusively entitled to issue a transfer message, to receive interest and other payments with respect thereof, and otherwise to exercise all the rights and powers with respect to such security, notwithstanding any information or notice to the contrary. Neither TVA nor the Reserve Banks are liable to a Person asserting or having an adverse claim to a Security Entitlement or to a Book-entry TVA Power Security in a Par-

ticipant's Security Account, including any such claim arising as a result of the transfer or disposition of a Book-entry TVA Power Security by a Reserve Bank pursuant to a transfer message that the Reserve Bank reasonably believes to be genuine.

(b) The obligation of TVA to make payments with respect to Book-entry TVA Power Securities is discharged at the time payment in the appropriate amount is made as follows:

(1) Interest or other payments on Book-entry TVA Power Securities are either credited by a Reserve Bank to a Funds Account maintained at such bank or otherwise paid as directed by the Participant.

(2) Book-entry TVA Power Securities are redeemed in accordance with their terms by a Reserve Bank withdrawing the securities from the Participant's Security Account in which they are maintained and by either crediting the amount of the redemption proceeds, including both principal and interest, where applicable, to a Funds Account at such bank or otherwise paying such principal and interest as directed by the Participant. No action by the Participant ordinarily is required in connection with the redemption of a Book-entry TVA Power Security.

[62 FR 920, Jan. 7, 1997; 62 FR 8619, 8620, Feb. 26, 1997]

§ 1314.7 Liability of TVA and Reserve Banks.

TVA and the Reserve Banks may rely on the information provided in a transfer message and are not required to verify the information. TVA and the Reserve Banks shall not be liable for any action taken in accordance with the information set out in a transfer message or evidence submitted in support thereof.

[62 FR 920, Jan. 7, 1997; 62 FR 4833, Jan. 31, 1997]

§ 1314.8 Identification of accounts.

Book-entry accounts may be established in such form or forms as customarily permitted by the entity (e.g., Depository Institution, Securities Intermediary, etc.) maintaining them, except that each account established by such entity (other than a Reserve

Bank) should include data to permit both customer identification by name, address, and taxpayer identifying number, as well as a determination of the Book-entry TVA Power Securities being held in such account by amount, maturity, date, and CUSIP Number, and of transactions relating thereto.

[62 FR 920, Jan. 7, 1997; 62 FR 8620, Feb. 26, 1997]

§ 1314.9 Waiver of regulations.

TVA reserves the right in TVA's discretion to waive any provision of the regulations in this part in any case or class of cases for the convenience of TVA or in order to relieve any Person of unnecessary hardship, if such action is not inconsistent with law and does not adversely affect any substantial existing rights, and TVA is satisfied that such action will not subject TVA to any substantial expense or liability.

§ 1314.10 Additional provisions.

(a) *Additional requirements.* In any case or any class of cases arising under the regulations in this part, TVA may require such additional evidence and a bond of indemnity, with or without surety, as may in the judgment of TVA be necessary for the protection of the interests of TVA.

(b) *Notice of attachment for TVA Power Securities in Book-entry System.* The interest of a debtor in a Security Entitlement may be reached by a creditor only by legal process upon the Securities Intermediary with whom the debtor's securities account is maintained, except where a Security Entitlement is maintained in the name of a secured party, in which case the debtor's interest may be reached by legal process upon the secured party. The regulations in this part do not purport to establish whether a Reserve Bank is required to honor an order or other notice of attachment in any particular case or class of cases.

PART 1315—NEW RESTRICTIONS ON LOBBYING

Subpart A—General

Sec.
1315.100 Conditions on use of funds.
1315.105 Definitions.

1315.110 Certification and disclosure.

Subpart B—Activities by Own Employees

1315.200 Agency and legislative liaison.
1315.205 Professional and technical services.
1315.210 Reporting.

Subpart C—Activities by Other Than Own Employees

1315.300 Professional and technical services.

Subpart D—Penalties and Enforcement

1315.400 Penalties.
1315.405 Penalty procedures.
1315.410 Enforcement.

Subpart E—Exemptions

1315.500 Secretary of Defense.

Subpart F—Agency Reports

1315.600 Semi-annual compilation.
1315.605 Inspector General report.
APPENDIX A TO PART 1315—CERTIFICATION REGARDING LOBBYING
APPENDIX B TO PART 1315—DISCLOSURE FORM TO REPORT LOBBYING

AUTHORITY: 16 U.S.C. 831–831ee; 31 U.S.C. 1352.

SOURCE: 55 FR 6737, 6748, Feb. 26, 1990, unless otherwise noted.

CROSS REFERENCE: See also Office of Management and Budget notice published at 54 FR 52306, December 20, 1989.

Subpart A—General

§ 1315.100 Conditions on use of funds.

(a) No appropriated funds may be expended by the recipient of a Federal contract, grant, loan, or cooperative ageement to pay any person for influencing or attempting to influence an officer or employee of any agency, a Member of Congress, an officer or employee of Congress, or an employee of a Member of Congress in connection with any of the following covered Federal actions: the awarding of any Federal contract, the making of any Federal grant, the making of any Federal loan, the entering into of any cooperative agreement, and the extension, continuation, renewal, amendment, or modification of any Federal contract, grant, loan, or cooperative agreement.

(b) Each person who requests or receives from an agency a Federal contract, grant, loan, or cooperative

279

agreement shall file with that agency a certification, set forth in appendix A, that the person has not made, and will not make, any payment prohibited by paragraph (a) of this section.

(c) Each person who requests or receives from an agency a Federal contract, grant, loan, or a cooperative agreement shall file with that agency a disclosure form, set forth in appendix B, if such person has made or has agreed to make any payment using nonappropriated funds (to include profits from any covered Federal action), which would be prohibited under paragraph (a) of this section if paid for with appropriated funds.

(d) Each person who requests or receives from an agency a commitment providing for the United States to insure or guarantee a loan shall file with that agency a statement, set forth in appendix A, whether that person has made or has agreed to make any payment to influence or attempt to influence an officer or employee of any agency, a Member of Congress, an officer or employee of Congress, or an employee of a Member of Congress in connection with that loan insurance or guarantee.

(e) Each person who requests or receives from an agency a commitment providing for the United States to insure or guarantee a loan shall file with that agency a disclosure form, set forth in appendix B, if that person has made or has agreed to make any payment to influence or attempt to influence an officer or employee of any agency, a Member of Congress, an officer or employee of Congress, or an employee of a Member of Congress in connection with that loan insurance or guarantee.

§ 1315.105 Definitions.

For purposes of this part:

(a) *Agency*, as defined in 5 U.S.C. 552(f), includes Federal executive departments and agencies as well as independent regulatory commissions and Government corporations, as defined in 31 U.S.C. 9101(1).

(b) *Covered Federal action* means any of the following Federal actions:

(1) The awarding of any Federal contract;

(2) The making of any Federal grant;

(3) The making of any Federal loan;

(4) The entering into of any cooperative agreement; and,

(5) The extension, continuation, renewal, amendment, or modification of any Federal contract, grant, loan, or cooperative agreement.

Covered Federal action does not include receiving from an agency a commitment providing for the United States to insure or guarantee a loan. Loan guarantees and loan insurance are addressed independently within this part.

(c) *Federal contract* means an acquisition contract awarded by an agency, including those subject to the Federal Acquisition Regulation (FAR), and any other acquisition contract for real or personal property or services not subject to the FAR.

(d) *Federal cooperative agreement* means a cooperative agreement entered into by an agency.

(e) *Federal grant* means an award of financial assistance in the form of money, or property in lieu of money, by the Federal Government or a direct appropriation made by law to any person. The term does not include technical assistance which provides services instead of money, or other assistance in the form of revenue sharing, loans, loan guarantees, loan insurance, interest subsidies, insurance, or direct United States cash assistance to an individual.

(f) *Federal loan* means a loan made by an agency. The term does not include loan guarantee or loan insurance.

(g) *Indian tribe* and *tribal organization* have the meaning provided in section 4 of the Indian Self-Determination and Education Assistance Act (25 U.S.C. 450B). Alaskan Natives are included under the definitions of Indian tribes in that Act.

(h) *Influencing or attempting to influence* means making, with the intent to influence, any communication to or appearance before an officer or employee or any agency, a Member of Congress, an officer or employee of Congress, or an employee of a Member of Congress in connection with any covered Federal action.

(i) *Loan guarantee* and *loan insurance* means an agency's guarantee or insurance of a loan made by a person.

(j) *Local government* means a unit of government in a State and, if chartered, established, or otherwise recognized by a State for the performance of a governmental duty, including a local public authority, a special district, an intrastate district, a council of governments, a sponsor group representative organization, and any other instrumentality of a local government.

(k) *Officer or employee of an agency* includes the following individuals who are employed by an agency:

(1) An individual who is appointed to a position in the Government under title 5, U.S. Code, including a position under a temporary appointment;

(2) A member of the uniformed services as defined in section 101(3), title 37, U.S. Code;

(3) A special Government employee as defined in section 202, title 18, U.S. Code; and,

(4) An individual who is a member of a Federal advisory committee, as defined by the Federal Advisory Committee Act, title 5, U.S. Code appendix 2.

(l) *Person* means an individual, corporation, company, association, authority, firm, partnership, society, State, and local government, regardless of whether such entity is operated for profit or not for profit. This term excludes an Indian tribe, tribal organization, or any other Indian organization with respect to expenditures specifically permitted by other Federal law.

(m) *Reasonable compensation* means, with respect to a regularly employed officer or employee of any person, compensation that is consistent with the normal compensation for such officer or employee for work that is not furnished to, not funded by, or not furnished in cooperation with the Federal Government.

(n) *Reasonable payment* means, with respect to perfessional and other technical services, a payment in an amount that is consistent with the amount normally paid for such services in the private sector.

(o) *Recipient* includes all contractors, subcontractors at any tier, and subgrantees at any tier of the recipient of funds received in connection with a Federal contract, grant, loan, or coop-

erative agreement. The term excludes an Indian tribe, tribal organization, or any other Indian organization with respect to expenditures specifically permitted by other Federal law.

(p) *Regularly employed* means, with respect to an officer or employee of a person requesting or receiving a Federal contract, grant, loan, or cooperative agreement or a commitment providing for the United States to insure or guarantee a loan, an officer or employee who is employed by such person for at least 130 working days within one year immediately preceding the date of the submission that initiates agency consideration of such person for receipt of such contract, grant, loan, cooperative agreement, loan insurance commitment, or loan guarantee commitment. An officer or employee who is employed by such person for less than 130 working days within one year immediately preceding the date of the submission that initiates agency consideration of such person shall be considered to be regularly employed as soon as he or she is employed by such person for 130 working days.

(q) *State* means a State of the United States, the District of Columbia, the Commonwealth of Puerto Rico, a territory or possession of the United States, an agency or instrumentality of a State, and a multi-State, regional, or interstate entity having governmental duties and powers.

§1315.110 Certification and disclosure.

(a) Each person shall file a certification, and a disclosure form, if required, with each submission that initiates agency consideration of such person for:

(1) Award of a Federal contract, grant, or cooperative agreement exceeding $100,000; or

(2) An award of a Federal loan or a commitment providing for the United States to insure or guarantee a loan exceeding $150,000.

(b) Each person shall file a certification, and a disclosure form, if required, upon receipt by such person of:

(1) A Federal contract, grant, or cooperative agreement exceeding $100,000; or

(2) A Federal loan or a commitment providing for the United States to insure or guarantee a loan exceeding $150,000,

Unless such person previously filed a certification, and a disclosure form, if required, under paragraph (a) of this section.

(c) Each person shall file a disclosure form at the end of each calendar quarter in which there occurs any event that requires disclosure or that materially affects the accuracy of the information contained in any disclosure form previously filed by such person under paragraphs (a) or (b) of this section. An event that materially affects the accuracy of the information reported includes:

(1) A cumulative increase of $25,000 or more in the amount paid or expected to be paid for influencing or attempting to influence a covered Federal action; or

(2) A change in the person(s) or individual(s) influencing or attempting to influence a covered Federal action; or,

(3) A change in the officer(s), employee(s), or Member(s) contacted to influence or attempt to influence a covered Federal action.

(d) Any person who requests or receives from a person referred to in paragraphs (a) or (b) of this section:

(1) A subcontract exceeding $100,000 at any tier under a Federal contract;

(2) A subgrant, contract, or subcontract exceeding $100,000 at any tier under a Federal grant;

(3) A contract or subcontract exceeding $100,000 at any tier under a Federal loan exceeding $150,000; or,

(4) A contract or subcontract exceeding $100,000 at any tier under a Federal cooperative agreement,

Shall file a certification, and a disclosure form, if required, to the next tier above.

(e) All disclosure forms, but not certifications, shall be forwarded from tier to tier until received by the person referred to in paragraphs (a) or (b) of this section. That person shall forward all disclosure forms to the agency.

(f) Any certification or disclosure form filed under paragraph (e) of this section shall be treated as a material representation of fact upon which all receiving tiers shall rely. All liability arising from an erroneous representation shall be borne solely by the tier filing that representation and shall not be shared by any tier to which the erroneous representation is forwarded. Submitting an erroneous certification or disclosure constitutes a failure to file the required certification or disclosure, respectively. If a person fails to file a required certification or disclosure, the United States may pursue all available remedies, including those authorized by section 1352, title 31, U.S. Code.

(g) For awards and commitments in process prior to December 23, 1989, but not made before that date, certifications shall be required at award or commitment, covering activities occurring between December 23, 1989, and the date of award or commitment. However, for awards and commitments in process prior to the December 23, 1989 effective date of these provisions, but not made before December 23, 1989, disclosure forms shall not be required at time of award or commitment but shall be filed within 30 days.

(h) No reporting is required for an activity paid for with appropriated funds if that activity is allowable under either subpart B or C.

Subpart B—Activities by Own Employees

§ 1315.200 Agency and legislative liaison.

(a) The prohibition on the use of appropriated funds, in § 1315.100 (a), does not apply in the case of a payment of reasonable compensation made to an officer or employee of a person requesting or receiving a Federal contract, grant, loan, or cooperative agreement if the payment is for agency and legislative liaison activities not directly related to a covered Federal action.

(b) For purposes of paragraph (a) of this section, providing any information specifically requested by an agency or Congress is allowable at any time.

(c) For purposes of paragraph (a) of this section, the following agency and legislative liaison activities are allowable at any time only where they are not related to a specific solicitation for any covered Federal action:

(1) Discussing with an agency (including individual demonstrations) the qualities and characteristics of the person's products or services, conditions or terms of sale, and service capabilities; and,

(2) Technical discussions and other activities regarding the application or adaptation of the person's products or services for an agency's use.

(d) For purposes of paragraph (a) of this section, the following agencies and legislative liaison activities are allowable only where they are prior to formal solicitation of any covered Federal action:

(1) Providing any information not specifically requested but necessary for an agency to make an informed decision about initiation of a covered Federal action;

(2) Technical discussions regarding the preparation of an unsolicited proposal prior to its official submission; and,

(3) Capability presentations by persons seeking awards from an agency pursuant to the provisions of the Small Business Act, as amended by Public Law 95-507 and other subsequent amendments.

(e) Only those activities expressly authorized by this section are allowable under this section.

§ 1315.205 Professional and technical services.

(a) The prohibition on the use of appropriated funds, in § 1315.100 (a), does not apply in the case of a payment of reasonable compensation made to an officer or employee of a person requesting or receiving a Federal contract, grant, loan, or cooperative agreement or an extension, continuation, renewal, amendment, or modification of a Federal contract, grant, loan, or cooperative agreement if payment is for professional or technical services rendered directly in the preparation, submission, or negotiation of any bid, proposal, or application for that Federal contract, grant, loan, or cooperative agreement or for meeting requirements imposed by or pursuant to law as a condition for receiving that Federal contract, grant, loan, or cooperative agreement.

(b) For purposes of paragraph (a) of this section, "professional and technical services" shall be limited to advice and analysis directly applying any professional or technical discipline. For example, drafting of a legal document accompanying a bid or proposal by a lawyer is allowable. Similarly, technical advice provided by an engineer on the performance or operational capability of a piece of equipment rendered directly in the negotiation of a contract is allowable. However, communications with the intent to influence made by a professional (such as a licensed lawyer) or a technical person (such as a licensed accountant) are not allowable under this section unless they provide advice and analysis directly applying their professional or technical expertise and unless the advice or analysis is rendered directly and solely in the preparation, submission or negotiation of a covered Federal action. Thus, for example, communications with the intent to influence made by a lawyer that do not provide legal advice or analysis directly and solely related to the legal aspects of his or her client's proposal, but generally advocate one proposal over another are not allowable under this section because the lawyer is not providing professional legal services. Similarly, communications with the intent to influence made by an engineer providing an engineering analysis prior to the preparation or submission of a bid or proposal are not allowable under this section since the engineer is providing technical services but not directly in the preparation, submission or negotiation of a covered Federal action.

(c) Requirements imposed by or pursuant to law as a condition for receiving a covered Federal award include those required by law or regulation, or reasonably expected to be required by law or regulation, and any other requirements in the actual award documents.

(d) Only those services expressly authorized by this section are allowable under this section.

§ 1315.210 Reporting.

No reporting is required with respect to payments of reasonable compensation made to regularly employed officers or employees of a person.

Subpart C—Activities by Other Than Own Employees

§ 1315.300 Professional and technical services.

(a) The prohibition on the use of appropriated funds, in § 1315.100 (a), does not apply in the case of any reasonable payment to a person, other than an officer or employee of a person requesting or receiving a covered Federal action, if the payment is for professional or technical services rendered directly in the preparation, submission, or negotiation of any bid, proposal, or application for that Federal contract, grant, loan, or cooperative agreement or for meeting requirements imposed by or pursuant to law as a condition for receiving that Federal contract, grant, loan, or cooperative agreement.

(b) The reporting requirements in § 1315.110 (a) and (b) regarding filing a disclosure form by each person, if required, shall not apply with respect to professional or technical services rendered directly in the preparation, submission, or negotiation of any commitment providing for the United States to insure or guarantee a loan.

(c) For purposes of paragraph (a) of this section, "professional and technical services" shall be limited to advice and analysis directly applying any professional or technical discipline. For example, drafting or a legal document accompanying a bid or proposal by a lawyer is allowable. Similarly, technical advice provided by an engineer on the performance or operational capability of a piece of equipment rendered directly in the negotiation of a contract is allowable. However, communications with the intent to influence made by a professional (such as a licensed lawyer) or a technical person (such as a licensed accountant) are not allowable under this section unless they provide advice and analysis directly applying their professional or technical expertise and unless the advice or analysis is rendered directly

and solely in the preparation, submission or negotiation of a covered Federal action. Thus, for example, communications with the intent to influence made by a lawyer that do not provide legal advice or analysis directly and solely related to the legal aspects of his or her client's proposal, but generally advocate one proposal over another are not allowable under this section because the lawyer is not providing professional legal services. Similarly, communications with the intent to influence made by an engineer providing an engineering analysis prior to the preparation or submission of a bid or proposal are not allowable under this section since the engineer is providing technical services but not directly in the preparation, submission or negotiation of a covered Federal action.

(d) Requirements imposed by or pursuant to law as a condition for receiving a covered Federal award include those required by law or regulation, or reasonably expected to be required by law or regulation, and any other requirements in the actual award documents.

(e) Persons other than officers or employees of a person requesting or receiving a covered Federal action include consultants and trade associations.

(f) Only those services expressly authorized by this section are allowable under this section.

Subpart D—Penalties and Enforcement

§ 1315.400 Penalties.

(a) Any person who makes an expenditure prohibited herein shall be subject to a civil penalty of not less than $12,000 and not more than $120,000 for each such expenditure.

(b) Any person who fails to file or amend the disclosure form (see appendix B) to be filed or amended if required herein, shall be subject to a civil penalty of not less than $12,000 and not more than $120,000 for each such failure.

(c) A filing or amended filing on or after the date on which an administrative action for the imposition of a civil penalty is commenced does not prevent the imposition of such civil penalty for a failure occurring before that date. An administrative action is commenced with respect to a failure when an investigating official determines in writing to commence an investigation of an allegation of such failure.

(d) In determining whether to impose a civil penalty, and the amount of any such penalty, by reason of a violation by any person, the agency shall consider the nature, circumstances, extent, and gravity of the violation, the effect on the ability of such person to continue in business, any prior violations by such person, the degree of culpability of such person, the ability of the person to pay the penalty, and such other matters as may be appropriate.

(e) First offenders under paragraph (a) or (b) of this section shall be subject to a civil penalty of $12,000, absent aggravating circumstances. Second and subsequent offenses by persons shall be subject to an appropriate civil penalty between $12,000 and $120,000, as determined by the agency head or his or her designee.

(f) An imposition of a civil penalty under this section does not prevent the United States from seeking any other remedy that may apply to the same conduct that is the basis for the imposition of such civil penalty.

[55 FR 6737, 6748, Feb. 26, 1990, as amended at 61 FR 55098, Oct. 24, 1996; 67 FR 9925, Mar. 5, 2002]

§1315.405 Penalty procedures.

Agencies shall impose and collect civil penalties pursuant to the provisions of the Program Fraud and Civil Remedies Act, 31 U.S.C. sections 3803 (except subsection (c)), 3804, 3805, 3806, 3807, 3808, and 3812, insofar as these provisions are not inconsistent with the requirements herein.

§1315.410 Enforcement.

The head of each agency shall take such actions as are necessary to ensure that the provisions herein are vigorously implemented and enforced in that agency.

Subpart E—Exemptions

§1315.500 Secretary of Defense.

(a) The Secretary of Defense may exempt, on a case-by-case basis, a covered Federal action from the prohibition whenever the Secretary determines, in writing, that such an exemption is in the national interest. The Secretary shall transmit a copy of each such written exemption to Congress immediately after making such a determination.

(b) The Department of Defense may issue supplemental regulations to implement paragraph (a) of this section.

Subpart F—Agency Reports

§1315.600 Semi-annual compilation.

(a) The head of each agency shall collect and compile the disclosure reports (see appendix B) and, on May 31 and November 30 of each year, submit to the Secretary of the Senate and the Clerk of the House of Representatives a report containing a compilation of the information contained in the disclosure reports received during the six-month period ending on March 31 or September 30, respectively, of that year.

(b) The report, including the compilation, shall be available for public inspection 30 days after receipt of the report by the Secretary and the Clerk.

(c) Information that involves intelligence matters shall be reported only to the Select Committee on Intelligence of the Senate, the Permanent Select Committee on Intelligence of the House of Representatives, and the Committees on Appropriations of the Senate and the House of Representatives in accordance with procedures agreed to by such committees. Such information shall not be available for public inspection.

(d) Information that is classified under Executive Order 12356 or any successor order shall be reported only to the Committee on Foreign Relations of the Senate and the Committee on Foreign Affairs of the House of Representatives or the Committees on Armed Services of the Senate and the House of Representatives (whichever such committees have jurisdiction of matters involving such information) and to the

Committees on Appropriations of the Senate and the House of Representatives in accordance with procedures agreed to by such committees. Such information shall not be available for public inspection.

(e) The first semi-annual compilation shall be submitted on May 31, 1990, and shall contain a compilation of the disclosure reports received from December 23, 1989 to March 31, 1990.

(f) Major agencies, designated by the Office of Management and Budget (OMB), are required to provide machine-readable compilations to the Secretary of the Senate and the Clerk of the House of Representatives no later than with the compilations due on May 31, 1991. OMB shall provide detailed specifications in a memorandum to these agencies.

(g) Non-major agencies are requested to provide machine-readable compilations to the Secretary of the Senate and the Clerk of the House of Representatives.

(h) Agencies shall keep the originals of all disclosure reports in the official files of the agency.

§ 1315.605   Inspector General report.

(a) The Inspector General, or other official as specified in paragraph (b) of this section, of each agency shall prepare and submit to Congress each year, commencing with submission of the President's Budget in 1991, an evaluation of the compliance of that agency with, and the effectiveness of, the requirements herein. The evaluation may include any recommended changes that may be necessary to strengthen or improve the requirements.

(b) In the case of an agency that does not have an Inspector General, the agency official comparable to an Inspector General shall prepare and submit the annual report, or, if there is no such comparable official, the head of the agency shall prepare and submit the annual report.

(c) The annual report shall be submitted at the same time the agency submits its annual budget justifications to Congress.

(d) The annual report shall include the following: All alleged violations relating to the agency's covered Federal actions during the year covered by the report, the actions taken by the head of the agency in the year covered by the report with respect to those alleged violations and alleged violations in previous years, and the amounts of civil penalties imposed by the agency in the year covered by the report.

APPENDIX A TO PART 1315—
CERTIFICATION REGARDING LOBBYING

Certification for Contracts, Grants, Loans, and Cooperative Agreements

The undersigned certifies, to the best of his or her knowledge and belief, that:

(1) No Federal appropriated funds have been paid or will be paid, by or on behalf of the undersigned, to any person for influencing or attempting to influence an officer or employee of an agency, a Member of Congress, an officer or employee of Congress, or an employee of a Member of Congress in connection with the awarding of any Federal contract, the making of any Federal grant, the making of any Federal loan, the entering into of any cooperative agreement, and the extension, continuation, renewal, amendment, or modification of any Federal contract, grant, loan, or cooperative agreement.

(2) If any funds other than Federal appropriated funds have been paid or will be paid to any person for influencing or attempting to influence an officer or employee of any agency, a Member of Congress, an officer or employee of Congress, or an employee of a Member of Congress in connection with this Federal contract, grant, loan, or cooperative agreement, the undersigned shall complete and submit Standard Form-LLL, "Disclosure Form to Report Lobbying," in accordance with its instructions.

(3) The undersigned shall require that the language of this certification be included in the award documents for all subawards at all tiers (including subcontracts, subgrants, and contracts under grants, loans, and cooperative agreements) and that all subrecipients shall certify and disclose accordingly.

This certification is a material representation of fact upon which reliance was placed when this transaction was made or entered into. Submission of this certification is a prerequisite for making or entering into this transaction imposed by section 1352, title 31, U.S. Code. Any person who fails to file the required certification shall be subject to a civil penalty of not less than $10,000 and not more than $100,000 for each such failure.

Statement for Loan Guarantees and Loan Insurance

The undersigned states, to the best of his or her knowledge and belief, that:

If any funds have been paid or will be paid to any person for influencing or attempting to influence an officer or employee of any agency, a Member of Congress, an officer or employee of Congress, or an employee of a Member of Congress in connection with this commitment providing for the United States to insure or guarantee a loan, the undersigned shall complete and submit Standard Form-LLL, "Disclosure Form to Report Lobbying," in accordance with its instructions.

Submission of this statement is a prerequisite for making or entering into this transaction imposed by section 1352, title 31, U.S. Code. Any person who fails to file the required statement shall be subject to a civil penalty of not less than $10,000 and not more than $100,000 for each such failure.

APPENDIX B TO PART 1315—DISCLOSURE FORM TO REPORT LOBBYING

DISCLOSURE OF LOBBYING ACTIVITIES

Complete this form to disclose lobbying activities pursuant to 31 U.S.C. 1352
(See reverse for public burden disclosure.)

Approved by OMB
0348-0046

1. Type of Federal Action:	2. Status of Federal Action:	3. Report Type:
☐ a. contract ☐ b. grant c. cooperative agreement d. loan e. loan guarantee f. loan insurance	☐ a. bid/offer/application b. initial award c. post-award	☐ a. initial filing b. material change **For Material Change Only:** year _____ quarter _____ date of last report _____

4. Name and Address of Reporting Entity:
☐ Prime   ☐ Subawardee
Tier _____ , if known:

Congressional District, if known:

5. If Reporting Entity in No. 4 is Subawardee, Enter Name and Address of Prime:

Congressional District, if known:

6. Federal Department/Agency:

7. Federal Program Name/Description:

CFDA Number, if applicable: _____

8. Federal Action Number, if known:

9. Award Amount, if known:
$

10. a. Name and Address of Lobbying Entity
(if individual, last name, first name, MI):

b. Individuals Performing Services (including address if different from No. 10a)
(last name, first name, MI):

(attach Continuation Sheet(s) SF-LLL-A, if necessary)

11. Amount of Payment (check all that apply):
$ _____   ☐ actual ☐ planned

12. Form of Payment (check all that apply):
☐ a. cash
☐ b. in-kind; specify: nature _____
value _____

13. Type of Payment (check all that apply):
☐ a. retainer
☐ b. one-time fee
☐ c. commission
☐ d. contingent fee
☐ e. deferred
☐ f. other; specify: _____

14. Brief Description of Services Performed or to be Performed and Date(s) of Service, including officer(s), employee(s), or Member(s) contacted, for Payment Indicated in Item 11:

(attach Continuation Sheet(s) SF-LLL-A, if necessary)

15. Continuation Sheet(s) SF-LLL-A attached: ☐ Yes   ☐ No

16. Information requested through this form is authorized by title 31 U.S.C. section 1352. This disclosure of lobbying activities is a material representation of fact upon which reliance was placed by the tier above when this transaction was made or entered into. This disclosure is required pursuant to 31 U.S.C. 1352. This information will be reported to the Congress semi-annually and will be available for public inspection. Any person who fails to file the required disclosure shall be subject to a civil penalty of not less than $10,000 and not more than $100,000 for each such failure.

Signature: _____
Print Name: _____
Title: _____
Telephone No.: _____ Date: _____

Federal Use Only:

Authorized for Local Reproduction
Standard Form - LLL

288

INSTRUCTIONS FOR COMPLETION OF SF-LLL, DISCLOSURE OF LOBBYING ACTIVITIES

This disclosure form shall be completed by the reporting entity, whether subawardee or prime Federal recipient, at the initiation or receipt of a covered Federal action, or a material change to a previous filing, pursuant to title 31 U.S.C. section 1352. The filing of a form is required for each payment or agreement to make payment to any lobbying entity for influencing or attempting to influence an officer or employee of any agency, a Member of Congress, an officer or employee of Congress, or an employee of a Member of Congress in connection with a covered Federal action. Use the SF-LLL-A Continuation Sheet for additional information if the space on the form is inadequate. Complete all items that apply for both the initial filing and material change report. Refer to the implementing guidance published by the Office of Management and Budget for additional information.

1. Identify the type of covered Federal action for which lobbying activity is and/or has been secured to influence the outcome of a covered Federal action.

2. Identify the status of the covered Federal action.

3. Identify the appropriate classification of this report. If this is a followup report caused by a material change to the information previously reported, enter the year and quarter in which the change occurred. Enter the date of the last previously submitted report by this reporting entity for this covered Federal action.

4. Enter the full name, address, city, state and zip code of the reporting entity. Include Congressional District, if known. Check the appropriate classification of the reporting entity that designates if it is, or expects to be, a prime or subaward recipient. Identify the tier of the subawardee, e.g., the first subawardee of the prime is the 1st tier. Subawards include but are not limited to subcontracts, subgrants and contract awards under grants.

5. If the organization filing the report in item 4 checks "Subawardee", then enter the full name, address, city, state and zip code of the prime Federal recipient. Include Congressional District, if known.

6. Enter the name of the Federal agency making the award or loan commitment. Include at least one organizational level below agency name, if known. For example, Department of Transportation, United States Coast Guard.

7. Enter the Federal program name or description for the covered Federal action (item 1). If known, enter the full Catalog of Federal Domestic Assistance (CFDA) number for grants, cooperative agreements, loans, and loan commitments.

8. Enter the most appropriate Federal identifying number available for the Federal action identified in item 1 (e.g., Request for Proposal (RFP) number; Invitation for Bid (IFB) number; grant announcement number; the contract, grant, or loan award number; the application/proposal control number assigned by the Federal agency). Include prefixes, e.g., "RFP-DE-90-001."

9. For a covered Federal action where there has been an award or loan commitment by the Federal agency, enter the Federal amount of the award/loan commitment for the prime entity identified in item 4 or 5.

10. (a) Enter the full name, address, city, state and zip code of the lobbying entity engaged by the reporting entity identified in item 4 to influence the covered Federal action.

   (b) Enter the full names of the individual(s) performing services, and include full address if different from 10 (a). Enter Last Name, First Name, and Middle Initial (MI).

11. Enter the amount of compensation paid or reasonably expected to be paid by the reporting entity (item 4) to the lobbying entity (item 10). Indicate whether the payment has been made (actual) or will be made (planned). Check all boxes that apply. If this is a material change report, enter the cumulative amount of payment made or planned to be made.

12. Check the appropriate box(es). Check all boxes that apply. If payment is made through an in-kind contribution, specify the nature and value of the in-kind payment.

13. Check the appropriate box(es). Check all boxes that apply. If other, specify nature.

14. Provide a specific and detailed description of the services that the lobbyist has performed, or will be expected to perform, and the date(s) of any services rendered. Include all preparatory and related activity, not just time spent in actual contact with Federal officials. Identify the Federal official(s) or employee(s) contacted or the officer(s), employee(s), or Member(s) of Congress that were contacted.

15. Check whether or not a SF-LLL-A Continuation Sheet(s) is attached.

16. The certifying official shall sign and date the form, print his/her name, title, and telephone number.

Public reporting burden for this collection of information is estimated to average 30 mintues per response, including time for reviewing instructions, searching existing data sources, gathering and maintaining the data needed, and completing and reviewing the collection of information. Send comments regarding the burden estimate or any other aspect of this collection of information, including suggestions for reducing this burden, to the Office of Management and Budget, Paperwork Reduction Project (0348-0046), Washington, D.C. 20503.

DISCLOSURE OF LOBBYING ACTIVITIES
CONTINUATION SHEET

Approved by OM
0348-0046

Reporting Entity: _____   Page _____ of _____

Authorized for Local Reproduction
Standard Form – LLL-A

PART 1316—GENERAL CONDITIONS AND CERTIFICATIONS FOR INCORPORATION IN CONTRACT DOCUMENTS OR ACTIONS

Subpart A—General Information

Sec.
1316.1 Applicability.

Subpart B—Text of Conditions and Certifications

1316.2 Affirmative action and equal opportunity.
1316.3 Anti-kickback procedures.
1316.4 Buy American Act supply contracts.
1316.5 Clean Air and Water Acts.
1316.6 Discrimination on the basis of age.
1316.7 Drug-free workplace.
1316.8 Employee protected activities.
1316.9 Nuclear energy hazards and nuclear incidents.
1316.10 Officials not to benefit.

AUTHORITY: 16 U.S.C. 831–831dd.

SOURCE: 58 FR 25930, Apr. 29, 1993, unless otherwise noted.

Subpart A—General Information

§1316.1 Applicability.

This part sets out the text of certain conditions and certifications which may be included by reference in certain TVA contract documents or actions. The provisions set out in this part are not automatically incorporated in all TVA actions.

Subpart B—Text of Conditions and Certifications

§1316.2 Affirmative action and equal opportunity.

When so indicated in TVA contract documents or actions, the following clause is included by reference in such documents or actions:

AFFIRMATIVE ACTION AND EQUAL OPPORTUNITY

(a) To the extent applicable, contract incorporates the following provisions: "Affirmative Action for Disabled Veterans and Veterans of the Vietnam Era" clause, 41 CFR 60–250.4; the "Affirmative Action for Handicapped Workers" clause, 41 CFR 60–741.4; and the "Equal Opportunity" clause, 41 CFR 60–1.4. Contractor complies with applicable regulatory requirements, including information reports and affirmative action programs.

(b) *Certification of Nonsegregated Facilities:* (1) By submission of its offer, the offeror certifies that it does not and will not maintain or provide for employees any segregated facilities at any of its establishments, and that it does not and will not permit employees to perform their services at any location under its control where segregated facilities are maintained. The offeror agrees that a breach of this certification is a violation of the Equal Opportunity clause in this contract.

(2) As used in this certification, the term "segregated facilities" means any waiting rooms, work areas, restrooms and washrooms, restaurants and other eating areas, timeclocks, locker rooms and other storage or dressing areas, parking lots, drinking fountains, recreation or entertainment areas, transportation, or housing facilities provided to employees which are segregated by explicit directive or are in fact segregated on the basis of race, religion, color, or national origin, because of habit, local custom, or otherwise.

(3) Contractor further agrees that (except where it has obtained identical certifications from proposed subcontractors for specific time periods) identical certifications will be obtained from proposed subcontractors prior to the award of subcontracts exceeding $10,000 which are not exempt from the provisions of the Equal Opportunity clause; that it will retain such certifications in its files; and that it will forward the following notice to such proposed subcontractors (except where the proposed subcontractors have submitted identical certifications for specific time periods):

Notice to Prospective Subcontractors of Requirement for Certifications of Nonsegregated Facilities. A Certification of Nonsegregated Facilities must be submitted prior to the award of a subcontract exceeding $10,000 which is not exempt from the provision of the Equal Opportunity clause. The certification may be submitted either for each subcontract or for all subcontracts during a period (*i.e.*, quarterly, semiannually, or annually).

(4) NOTE: The penalty for making false statements in offers is prescribed in Title 18 U.S.C. 1001.

(End of clause)

§1316.3 Anti-kickback procedures.

When so indicated in TVA contract documents or actions, the following clause is included by reference in such documents or actions:

ANTI-KICKBACK PROCEDURES

Contractor shall comply with the following:
(a) *Definitions.* As used in this clause, terms shall have the meanings defined in the

Anti-Kickback Act of 1986 (41 U.S.C. 51–58) (the Act).

(b) The Act prohibits any person from—

(1) Providing or attempting to provide or offering to provide any kickback;

(2) Soliciting, accepting, or attempting to accept any kickback; or

(3) Including, directly or indirectly, the amount of any kickback in the contract price charged by a prime contractor to TVA or in the contract price charged by the subcontractor to a prime contractor or higher tier subcontractor.

(c)(1) Contractor shall have in place and follow reasonable procedures designed to prevent and detect possible violations described in section (b) of this clause in its own operations and direct business relationships.

(2) When Contractor has reasonable grounds to believe that a violation described in section (b) of this clause may have occurred, Contractor shall promptly report in writing the possible violation. Such reports shall be made to the TVA Inspector General.

(3) Contractor shall cooperate fully with TVA or any other Federal agency investigating a possible violation described in section (b) of this clause.

(4) (i) Regardless of the contract tier at which a kickback was provided, accepted, or charged under the contract in violation of section (b) of this clause, the Contracting Officer may—

(A) Offset the amount of the kickback against any monies owed by TVA under this contract; and/or

(B) Direct that Contractor withhold from sums owed the subcontractor the amount of the kickback.

(ii) The Contracting Officer may order that monies withheld under subsection (c)(4)(i)(B) of this clause be paid over to TVA unless TVA has already offset those monies under subsection (c)(4)(i)(A) of this clause. In the latter case, Contracting shall notify the Contracting Officer when the monies are withheld.

(5) Contractor agrees to incorporate the substance of this clause, including this subsection (c)(5), in all subcontracts under this contract.

(End of clause)

§ 1316.4   Buy American Act supply contracts.

When so indicated in TVA contract documents or actions, the following clause is included by reference in such documents or actions:

BUY AMERICAN ACT SUPPLY CONTRACTS

(a) In TVA's acquisition of end products, the Buy American Act (41 U.S.C. 10a–10d) provides that preference be given to domestic end products. A domestic end product means:

(1) An unmanufactured end product which has been mined or produced in the United States; and

(2) An end product manufactured in the United States if the cost of components thereof which are mined, produced, or manufactured in the United States exceeds 50 percent of the cost of all its components.

(b) Contractor agrees that there will be delivered under this contract only domestic end products, except end products:

(1) Which are for use outside the United States;

(2) Which TVA determines are not mined, produced, or manufactured in the United States in sufficient and reasonably available commercial quantities and of a satisfactory quality;

(3) As to which TVA determines the domestic preference to be inconsistent with the public interest; or

(4) As to which TVA determines the cost to be unreasonable.

(End of clause)

§ 1316.5   Clean Air and Water Acts.

When so indicated in TVA contract documents or actions, the following clause is included by reference in such documents or actions:

CLEAN AIR AND WATER ACTS

(a) If performance of this contract would involve the use of facilities which have given rise to a conviction under section 113(c)(1) of the Clean Air Act (42 U.S.C. 7413) or section 309(c) of the Federal Water Pollution Control Act (33 U.S.C. 1319), offeror shall include in its offer a statement clearly setting forth the facts and circumstances of said conviction and shall list the facilities which gave rise to said conviction. If no such statement is submitted, submission of an offer constitutes certification by the offeror that performance of this contract will not involve the use of facilities which have given rise to a conviction under section 113(c)(1) of the Clean Air Act or section 309(c) of the Federal Water Pollution Control Act. As used in this clause "facilities" shall have the meaning set forth in 40 CFR 15.4.

(b) TVA will not award a contract to any offeror whose performance would involve the use of any facility or facilities which have given rise to a conviction as set forth in paragraph (a) of this clause except to the extent TVA, in its sole judgment, determines that such contract is exempt at the time of contract award from the provisions of 40 CFR part 15 as set forth therein.

(c) A condition of award of this contract is that contractor shall notify the Contracting

Officer in writing of the receipt of any communication from the U.S. Environmental Protection Agency (EPA) indicating that a facility to be utilized for this contract is under consideration to be listed on the EPA List of Violating Facilities. Prompt notification shall be required prior to contract award.

(End of clause)

§ 1316.6 Discrimination on the basis of age.

When so indicated in TVA contract documents or actions, the following clause is included by reference in such documents or actions:

DISCRIMINATION ON THE BASIS OF AGE

Executive Order 11141, 3 CFR, 1964–1965 Comp., p. 179, states that it is the policy of the Executive Branch of the United States that: Contractors and subcontractors engaged in the performance of Federal contracts shall not, in connection with the employment, advancement, or discharge of employees, or in connection with the terms, conditions, or privileges of their employment, discriminate against persons because of their age except upon the basis of a bona fide occupational qualification, retirement plan, or statutory requirement; and that contractors and subcontractors, or persons acting on their behalf, shall not specify, in solicitations or advertisements for employees to work on Government contracts, a maximum age limit for such employment unless the specified maximum age limit is based upon a bona fide occupational qualification, retirement plan, or statutory requirement.

(End of clause)

§ 1316.7 Drug-free workplace.

When so indicated in TVA contract documents or actions, the following clause is included by reference in such documents or actions:

DRUG-FREE WORKPLACE

(a) *Definitions.* As used in this provision:

Controlled substance means a controlled substance in schedules I through V of Section 202 of the Controlled Substances Act (21 U.S.C. 812) and as further defined in regulations at 21 CFR 1308.11 through 1308.15

Conviction means a finding of guilt (including a plea of nolo contendere) or imposition of sentence, or both, by any judicial body charged with the responsibility to determine violations of the Federal or State criminal drug statutes.

Criminal drug statute means a Federal or non-Federal criminal statute involving the manufacture, distribution, dispensing, possession, or use of any controlled substance.

Drug-free workplace means a site, including TVA premises, for the performance of work done in connection with a specific contract at which employees of Contractor are prohibited from engaging in the unlawful manufacture, distribution, dispensing, possession, or use of a controlled substance.

Employee means an employee of a contractor directly engaged in the performance of work under a Government contract.

Individual means an offeror/contractor that has no more than one employee, including the offeror/contractor.

(b) *Offerors Other than Individuals.* By submission of its offer, the offeror, if other than an individual, who is making an offer that equals or exceeds $25,000, certifies and agrees that, with respect to all employees of the offeror to be employed under a contract resulting from this solicitation, it will—

(1) Publish a statement notifying such employees that the unlawful manufacture, distribution, dispensing, possession, or use of a controlled substance is prohibited in Contractor's workplace and specifying the actions that will be taken against employees for violations of such prohibition;

(2) Establish a drug-free awareness program to inform such employees about—

(i) The dangers of drug abuse in the workplace;

(ii) Contractor's policy of maintaining a drug-free workplace;

(iii) Any available drug counseling, rehabilitation, and employee assistance programs; and

(iv) The penalties that may be imposed upon employees for drug abuse violations occurring in the workplace;

(3) Provide all employees engaged in performance of the contract with a copy of the statement required by paragraph (b)(1) of this section;

(4) Notify such employees in the statement required by paragraph (b)(1) of this section that, as a condition of continued employment on the contract resulting from this solicitation, the employee will—

(i) Abide by the terms of the statement; and

(ii) Notify Contractor of any criminal drug statute conviction for a violation occurring in the workplace no later than 5 days after such conviction;

(5) Notify the Contracting Officer within 10 days after receiving notice under paragraph (b)(4)(ii) of this section from an employee or otherwise receiving actual notice of such conviction;

(6) Within 30 days after receiving notice under subsection (b)(4) of this section of a conviction, impose the following sanctions or remedial measures on any employee who is convicted of drug abuse violations occurring in the workplace:

(i) Take appropriate personnel action against such employee, up to and including termination; or

(ii) Require such employee to satisfactorily participate in a drug abuse assistance or rehabilitation program approved for such purposes by a Federal, State, or local health, law enforcement, or other appropriate agency;

(7) Make a good-faith effort to maintain a drug-free workplace through implementation of subsections (b)(1) through (b)(6) of this provision.

(c) *Individuals.* By submission of its offer, the offeror, if an individual who is making an offer of any dollar value, certifies and agrees that the offeror will not engage in the unlawful manufacture, distribution, dispensing, possession, or use of a controlled substance in the performance of the contract resulting from this solicitation.

(d) *Enforcement.* Failure of the offeror to provide the certification required by section (b) or (c) of this provision, renders the offeror unqualified and ineligible for award. Failure of Contractor to comply with the requirements of subsections (b)(1) through (b)(7) or section (c) shall constitute a material breach of contract entitling TVA to suspend payments, terminate the contract, suspend or debar Contractor from Government contracting in accordance with subsection 5152(b)(2) of the Drug-Free Workplace Act of 1988 (41 U.S.C. 701(b)(2)), or take such other action as may be in accordance with law or the contract.

(e) In addition to other remedies available to the Government, the certification in sections (b) and (c) of this provision concerns a matter within the jurisdiction of an agency of the United States, and making of a false, fictitious, or fraudulent certification may render the maker subject to prosecution under 18 U.S.C. 1001.

(End of clause)

§ 1316.8 Employee protected activities.

When so indicated in TVA contract documents or actions, the following clause is included by reference in such documents or actions:

Employee Protected Activities

(Applicable to contracts for goods or services delivered to nuclear facilities or otherwise relating to Nuclear Regulatory Commission (NRC) licensed activities.)

(a) Contractor shall comply with Section 211 of the Energy Reorganization Act of 1974 (42 U.S.C. 5851), as amended, which prohibits discrimination against employees for engaging in certain protected activities. The Secretary of Labor has determined that "discrimination" means discharge or any other adverse actions that relate to compensation, terms, conditions, and privileges of employment; the term "protected activities" includes, among other things, employees raising nuclear safety or quality controls complaints either internally to their employer or to the NRC. Contractor shall aggressively pursue any employee allegation of discrimination and shall fully investigate such allegations. Contractor shall notify the TVA Concerns Resolution Staff Site Representative of such allegation or complaint in writing, together with a copy of any complaint. Contractor shall provide TVA any investigative reports that it may prepare and shall also provide to TVA a full written description of any management action taken in response to any such allegation or complaint. In circumstances where any such allegation or complaint also charges TVA employees with involvement in any discriminatory activities, contractor shall cooperate fully with TVA counsel in its representation.

(b) Contractor shall ensure that no agreement affecting compensation, terms, conditions, and privileges of employment, including, but not limited to, any agreement to settle a complaint filed by an employee or former employee of the Contractor with the Department of Labor pursuant to Section 211 of the Energy Reorganization Act of 1974, as amended, may contain any provision which would prohibit, restrict, or otherwise discourage an employee or former employee from participating in any protected activity as described in the "Employee Protection" regulations of NRC, 10 CFR 50.7, including, but not limited to, providing information to NRC on potential violations of the NRC's regulations or other matters within NRC's regulatory responsibilities.

(c) Any breach of this provision shall be a material breach of the contract. In the event NRC imposes a civil penalty against TVA as a result of a breach of this provision, such a civil penalty is considered by the parties to be direct and not special or consequential damages.

(d) Contractor agrees to place this provision, along with the flow-down requirement of this sentence, in all subcontracts of any tier entered into pursuant to this contract.

(End of clause)

§ 1316.9 Nuclear energy hazards and nuclear incidents.

When so indicated in TVA contract documents or actions, the following clause is included by reference in such documents or actions:

NUCLEAR ENERGY HAZARDS AND NUCLEAR INCIDENTS

(Applicable only to contracts for goods or services delivered to nuclear plants.)

(a) Prior to, or at the time of shipment of the first nuclear fuel to the TVA nuclear facility, TVA will furnish nuclear liability protection in accordance with Section 170 of the Atomic Energy Act (42 U.S.C. 2210) and applicable regulations of the Nuclear Regulatory Commission. Should this system of protection be repealed or changed, TVA would undertake to maintain in effect during the period of operation of the plant, to the extent available on reasonable terms, liability protection which would not result in a material impairment of the protection afforded to Contractor and its suppliers under existing system.

(b) TVA waives any claim it might have against Contractor or its subcontractors because of damage to, loss of, or loss of use of any property at the site of the TVA nuclear facility resulting from nuclear energy hazards or nuclear incidents. This provision shall not affect Contractor's obligation under the "Warranty" provision of this contract.

(c) TVA will indemnify Contractor and its subcontractors and save them harmless from any claims, losses, or liability arising as a result of damage to, loss of, or loss of use of any property at the site of the TVA nuclear facility resulting from nuclear energy hazards or nuclear incidents. In return for this indemnification, Contractor waives any claim it might have against any third party because of damage to, loss of, or loss of use of its property at the site of the TVA nuclear facility resulting from nuclear energy hazards or nuclear incidents.

(d) The foregoing waiver and indemnification provisions will apply to the full extent permitted by law and regardless of fault. The subcontractors referred to above include any of Contractor's suppliers of material, equipment, or services for the work, regardless of tier.

(e) For purposes of these provisions, the following definitions shall apply: Nuclear energy hazards shall mean the hazardous properties of nuclear material. Hazardous properties shall include radioactive, toxic, or explosive properties of nuclear material. Nuclear material shall include source material, special nuclear material or by-product material as those are defined in the Atomic Energy Act (42 U.S.C. 2014). Nuclear incident shall have the meaning given that term in the Atomic Energy Act (42 U.S.C. 2014(q)).

(End of clause)

§ 1316.10   Officials not to benefit.

When so indicated in TVA contract documents or actions, the following clause is included by reference in such documents or actions:

OFFICIALS NOT TO BENEFIT

No member of or delegate to Congress or Resident Commissioner, or any officer, employee, special Government employee, or agent of TVA shall be admitted to any share or part of this agreement or to any benefit that may arise therefrom unless it be made with a corporation for its general benefit; nor shall Contractor offer or give, directly or indirectly, to any officer, employee, special Government employee, or agent of TVA, any gift, gratuity, favor, entertainment, loan, or any other thing of monetary value, except as provided in 5 CFR part 2635. Breach of this clause shall constitute a material breach of this contract, and TVA shall have the right to exercise all remedies provided in this contract or at law.

(End of clause)

PART 1317—NONDISCRIMINATION ON THE BASIS OF SEX IN EDUCATION PROGRAMS OR ACTIVITIES RECEIVING FEDERAL FINANCIAL ASSISTANCE

Subpart A—Introduction

AUTHORITY: 20 U.S.C. 1681, 1682, 1683, 1685, 1686, 1687, 1688.

SOURCE: 65 FR 52865, 52877, Aug. 30, 2000, unless otherwise noted.

Subpart A—Introduction

§ 1317.100   Purpose and effective date.

The purpose of these Title IX regulations is to effectuate Title IX of the Education Amendments of 1972, as amended (except sections 904 and 906 of those Amendments) (20 U.S.C. 1681, 1682, 1683, 1685, 1686, 1687, 1688), which is designed to eliminate (with certain exceptions) discrimination on the basis of sex in any education program or activity receiving Federal financial assistance, whether or not such program or activity is offered or sponsored by an educational institution as defined in these Title IX regulations. The effective date of these Title IX regulations shall be September 29, 2000.

§ 1317.105   Definitions.

As used in these Title IX regulations, the term:

Administratively separate unit means a school, department, or college of an educational institution (other than a local educational agency) admission to which is independent of admission to any other component of such institution.

Admission means selection for part-time, full-time, special, associate, transfer, exchange, or any other enrollment, membership, or matriculation in or at an education program or activity operated by a recipient.

Applicant means one who submits an application, request, or plan required to be approved by an official of the Federal agency that awards Federal financial assistance, or by a recipient, as a condition to becoming a recipient.

Designated agency official means Manager, Supplier and Diverse Business Relations.

Educational institution means a local educational agency (LEA) as defined by 20 U.S.C. 8801(18), a preschool, a private elementary or secondary school, or an applicant or recipient that is an institution of graduate higher education, an institution of undergraduate higher education, an institution of professional education, or an institution of vocational education, as defined in this section.

Federal financial assistance means any of the following, when authorized and extended under a law administered by the Federal agency that awards such assistance:

(1) A grant or loan of Federal financial assistance, including funds made available for:

(i) The acquisition, construction, renovation, restoration, or repair of a building or facility or any portion thereof; and

(ii) Scholarships, loans, grants, wages, or other funds extended to any entity for payment to or on behalf of students admitted to that entity, or extended directly to such students for payment to that entity.

(2) A grant of Federal real or personal property or any interest therein, including surplus property, and the proceeds of the sale or transfer of such property, if the Federal share of the fair market value of the property is not, upon such sale or transfer, properly accounted for to the Federal Government.

(3) Provision of the services of Federal personnel.

(4) Sale or lease of Federal property or any interest therein at nominal consideration, or at consideration reduced for the purpose of assisting the recipient or in recognition of public interest to be served thereby, or permission to use Federal property or any interest therein without consideration.

(5) Any other contract, agreement, or arrangement that has as one of its purposes the provision of assistance to any education program or activity, except a contract of insurance or guaranty.

Institution of graduate higher education means an institution that:

(1) Offers academic study beyond the bachelor of arts or bachelor of science degree, whether or not leading to a certificate of any higher degree in the liberal arts and sciences;

(2) Awards any degree in a professional field beyond the first professional degree (regardless of whether the first professional degree in such field is awarded by an institution of undergraduate higher education or professional education); or

(3) Awards no degree and offers no further academic study, but operates ordinarily for the purpose of facilitating research by persons who have received the highest graduate degree in any field of study.

Institution of professional education means an institution (except any institution of undergraduate higher education) that offers a program of academic study that leads to a first professional degree in a field for which there is a national specialized accrediting agency recognized by the Secretary of Education.

Institution of undergraduate higher education means:

(1) An institution offering at least two but less than four years of college-level study beyond the high school level, leading to a diploma or an associate degree, or wholly or principally creditable toward a baccalaureate degree; or

(2) An institution offering academic study leading to a baccalaureate degree; or

(3) An agency or body that certifies credentials or offers degrees, but that may or may not offer academic study.

Institution of vocational education means a school or institution (except an institution of professional or graduate or undergraduate higher education) that has as its primary purpose preparation of students to pursue a technical, skilled, or semiskilled occupation or trade, or to pursue study in a technical field, whether or not the school or institution offers certificates, diplomas, or degrees and whether or not it offers full-time study.

Recipient means any State or political subdivision thereof, or any instrumentality of a State or political subdivision thereof, any public or private agency, institution, or organization, or other entity, or any person, to whom Federal financial assistance is extended directly or through another recipient and that operates an education program or activity that receives such assistance, including any subunit, successor, assignee, or transferee thereof.

Student means a person who has gained admission.

Title IX means Title IX of the Education Amendments of 1972, Public Law 92–318, 86 Stat. 235, 373 (codified as amended at 20 U.S.C. 1681–1688) (except sections 904 and 906 thereof), as amended by section 3 of Public Law 93–568, 88 Stat. 1855, by section 412 of the Education Amendments of 1976, Public Law 94–482, 90 Stat. 2234, and by Section 3 of Public Law 100–259, 102 Stat. 28, 28–29 (20 U.S.C. 1681, 1682, 1683, 1685, 1686, 1687, 1688).

Title IX regulations means the provisions set forth at §§1317.100 through 1317.605.

Transition plan means a plan subject to the approval of the Secretary of Education pursuant to section 901(a)(2) of the Education Amendments of 1972,

20 U.S.C. 1681(a)(2), under which an educational institution operates in making the transition from being an educational institution that admits only students of one sex to being one that admits students of both sexes without discrimination.

[65 FR 52865, 52877, 52878, Aug. 30, 2000]

§ 1317.110 Remedial and affirmative action and self-evaluation.

(a) *Remedial action.* If the designated agency official finds that a recipient has discriminated against persons on the basis of sex in an education program or activity, such recipient shall take such remedial action as the designated agency official deems necessary to overcome the effects of such discrimination.

(b) *Affirmative action.* In the absence of a finding of discrimination on the basis of sex in an education program or activity, a recipient may take affirmative action consistent with law to overcome the effects of conditions that resulted in limited participation therein by persons of a particular sex. Nothing in these Title IX regulations shall be interpreted to alter any affirmative action obligations that a recipient may have under Executive Order 11246, 3 CFR, 1964–1965 Comp., p. 339; as amended by Executive Order 11375, 3 CFR, 1966–1970 Comp., p. 684; as amended by Executive Order 11478, 3 CFR, 1966–1970 Comp., p. 803; as amended by Executive Order 12086, 3 CFR, 1978 Comp., p. 230; as amended by Executive Order 12107, 3 CFR, 1978 Comp., p. 264.

(c) *Self-evaluation.* Each recipient education institution shall, within one year of September 29, 2000:

(1) Evaluate, in terms of the requirements of these Title IX regulations, its current policies and practices and the effects thereof concerning admission of students, treatment of students, and employment of both academic and nonacademic personnel working in connection with the recipient's education program or activity;

(2) Modify any of these policies and practices that do not or may not meet the requirements of these Title IX regulations; and

(3) Take appropriate remedial steps to eliminate the effects of any discrimination that resulted or may have resulted from adherence to these policies and practices.

(d) *Availability of self-evaluation and related materials.* Recipients shall maintain on file for at least three years following completion of the evaluation required under paragraph (c) of this section, and shall provide to the designated agency official upon request, a description of any modifications made pursuant to paragraph (c)(2) of this section and of any remedial steps taken pursuant to paragraph (c)(3) of this section.

§ 1317.115 Assurance required.

(a) *General.* Either at the application stage or the award stage, Federal agencies must ensure that applications for Federal financial assistance or awards of Federal financial assistance contain, be accompanied by, or be covered by a specifically identified assurance from the applicant or recipient, satisfactory to the designated agency official, that each education program or activity operated by the applicant or recipient and to which these Title IX regulations apply will be operated in compliance with these Title IX regulations. An assurance of compliance with these Title IX regulations shall not be satisfactory to the designated agency official if the applicant or recipient to whom such assurance applies fails to commit itself to take whatever remedial action is necessary in accordance with § 1317.110(a) to eliminate existing discrimination on the basis of sex or to eliminate the effects of past discrimination whether occurring prior to or subsequent to the submission to the designated agency official of such assurance.

(b) *Duration of obligation.* (1) In the case of Federal financial assistance extended to provide real property or structures thereon, such assurance shall obligate the recipient or, in the case of a subsequent transfer, the transferee, for the period during which the real property or structures are used to provide an education program or activity.

(2) In the case of Federal financial assistance extended to provide personal property, such assurance shall obligate the recipient for the period during

which it retains ownership or possession of the property.

(3) In all other cases such assurance shall obligate the recipient for the period during which Federal financial assistance is extended.

(c) *Form.* (1) The assurances required by paragraph (a) of this section, which may be included as part of a document that addresses other assurances or obligations, shall include that the applicant or recipient will comply with all applicable Federal statutes relating to nondiscrimination. These include but are not limited to: Title IX of the Education Amendments of 1972, as amended (20 U.S.C. 1681–1683, 1685–1688).

(2) The designated agency official will specify the extent to which such assurances will be required of the applicant's or recipient's subgrantees, contractors, subcontractors, transferees, or successors in interest.

§1317.120 Transfers of property.

If a recipient sells or otherwise transfers property financed in whole or in part with Federal financial assistance to a transferee that operates any education program or activity, and the Federal share of the fair market value of the property is not upon such sale or transfer properly accounted for to the Federal Government, both the transferor and the transferee shall be deemed to be recipients, subject to the provisions of §§ 1317.205 through 1317.235(a).

§1317.125 Effect of other requirements.

(a) *Effect of other Federal provisions.* The obligations imposed by these Title IX regulations are independent of, and do not alter, obligations not to discriminate on the basis of sex imposed by Executive Order 11246, 3 CFR, 1964–1965 Comp., p. 339; as amended by Executive Order 11375, 3 CFR, 1966–1970 Comp., p. 684; as amended by Executive Order 11478, 3 CFR, 1966–1970 Comp., p. 803; as amended by Executive Order 12087, 3 CFR, 1978 Comp., p. 230; as amended by Executive Order 12107, 3 CFR, 1978 Comp., p. 264; sections 704 and 855 of the Public Health Service Act (42 U.S.C. 295m, 298b-2); Title VII of the Civil Rights Act of 1964 (42 U.S.C. 2000e *et seq.*); the Equal Pay Act of 1963

(29 U.S.C. 206); and any other Act of Congress or Federal regulation.

(b) *Effect of State or local law or other requirements.* The obligation to comply with these Title IX regulations is not obviated or alleviated by any State or local law or other requirement that would render any applicant or student ineligible, or limit the eligibility of any applicant or student, on the basis of sex, to practice any occupation or profession.

(c) *Effect of rules or regulations of private organizations.* The obligation to comply with these Title IX regulations is not obviated or alleviated by any rule or regulation of any organization, club, athletic or other league, or association that would render any applicant or student ineligible to participate or limit the eligibility or participation of any applicant or student, on the basis of sex, in any education program or activity operated by a recipient and that receives Federal financial assistance.

§1317.130 Effect of employment opportunities.

The obligation to comply with these Title IX regulations is not obviated or alleviated because employment opportunities in any occupation or profession are or may be more limited for members of one sex than for members of the other sex.

§1317.135 Designation of responsible employee and adoption of grievance procedures.

(a) *Designation of responsible employee.* Each recipient shall designate at least one employee to coordinate its efforts to comply with and carry out its responsibilities under these Title IX regulations, including any investigation of any complaint communicated to such recipient alleging its noncompliance with these Title IX regulations or alleging any actions that would be prohibited by these Title IX regulations. The recipient shall notify all its students and employees of the name, office address, and telephone number of the employee or employees appointed pursuant to this paragraph.

(b) *Complaint procedure of recipient.* A recipient shall adopt and publish grievance procedures providing for prompt and equitable resolution of student and employee complaints alleging any action that would be prohibited by these Title IX regulations.

§ 1317.140   Dissemination of policy.

(a) *Notification of policy.* (1) Each recipient shall implement specific and continuing steps to notify applicants for admission and employment, students and parents of elementary and secondary school students, employees, sources of referral of applicants for admission and employment, and all unions or professional organizations holding collective bargaining or professional agreements with the recipient, that it does not discriminate on the basis of sex in the educational programs or activities that it operates, and that it is required by Title IX and these Title IX regulations not to discriminate in such a manner. Such notification shall contain such information, and be made in such manner, as the designated agency official finds necessary to apprise such persons of the protections against discrimination assured them by Title IX and these Title IX regulations, but shall state at least that the requirement not to discriminate in education programs or activities extends to employment therein, and to admission thereto unless §§ 1317.300 through 1317.310 do not apply to the recipient, and that inquiries concerning the application of Title IX and these Title IX regulations to such recipient may be referred to the employee designated pursuant to § 1317.135, or to the designated agency official.

(2) Each recipient shall make the initial notification required by paragraph (a)(1) of this section within 90 days of September 29, 2000 or of the date these Title IX regulations first apply to such recipient, whichever comes later, which notification shall include publication in:

(i) Newspapers and magazines operated by such recipient or by student, alumnae, or alumni groups for or in connection with such recipient; and

(ii) Memoranda or other written communications distributed to every student and employee of such recipient.

(b) *Publications.* (1) Each recipient shall prominently include a statement of the policy described in paragraph (a) of this section in each announcement, bulletin, catalog, or application form that it makes available to any person of a type, described in paragraph (a) of this section, or which is otherwise used in connection with the recruitment of students or employees.

(2) A recipient shall not use or distribute a publication of the type described in paragraph (b)(1) of this section that suggests, by text or illustration, that such recipient treats applicants, students, or employees differently on the basis of sex except as such treatment is permitted by these Title IX regulations.

(c) *Distribution.* Each recipient shall distribute without discrimination on the basis of sex each publication described in paragraph (b)(1) of this section, and shall apprise each of its admission and employment recruitment representatives of the policy of nondiscrimination described in paragraph (a) of this section, and shall require such representatives to adhere to such policy.

Subpart B—Coverage

§ 1317.200   Application.

Except as provided in §§ 1317.205 through 1317.235(a), these Title IX regulations apply to every recipient and to each education program or activity operated by such recipient that receives Federal financial assistance.

§ 1317.205   Educational institutions and other entities controlled by religious organizations.

(a) *Exemption.* These Title IX regulations do not apply to any operation of an educational institution or other entity that is controlled by a religious organization to the extent that application of these Title IX regulations would not be consistent with the religious tenets of such organization.

(b) *Exemption claims.* An educational institution or other entity that wishes to claim the exemption set forth in paragraph (a) of this section shall do so by submitting in writing to the designated agency official a statement by the highest-ranking official of the institution, identifying the provisions of these Title IX regulations that conflict with a specific tenet of the religious organization.

§1317.210 **Military and merchant marine educational institutions.**

These Title IX regulations do not apply to an educational institution whose primary purpose is the training of individuals for a military service of the United States or for the merchant marine.

§1317.215 **Membership practices of certain organizations.**

(a) *Social fraternities and sororities.* These Title IX regulations do not apply to the membership practices of social fraternities and sororities that are exempt from taxation under section 501(a) of the Internal Revenue Code of 1954, 26 U.S.C. 501(a), the active membership of which consists primarily of students in attendance at institutions of higher education.

(b) *YMCA, YWCA, Girl Scouts, Boy Scouts, and Camp Fire Girls.* These Title IX regulations do not apply to the membership practices of the Young Men's Christian Association (YMCA), the Young Women's Christian Association (YWCA), the Girl Scouts, the Boy Scouts, and Camp Fire Girls.

(c) *Voluntary youth service organizations.* These Title IX regulations do not apply to the membership practices of a voluntary youth service organization that is exempt from taxation under section 501(a) of the Internal Revenue Code of 1954, 26 U.S.C. 501(a), and the membership of which has been traditionally limited to members of one sex and principally to persons of less than nineteen years of age.

§1317.220 **Admissions.**

(a) Admissions to educational institutions prior to June 24, 1973, are not covered by these Title IX regulations.

(b) *Administratively separate units.* For the purposes only of this section, §§1317.225 and 1317.230, and §§1317.300 through 1317.310, each administratively separate unit shall be deemed to be an educational institution.

(c) *Application of §§1317.300 through .310.* Except as provided in paragraphs (d) and (e) of this section, §§1317.300 through 1317.310 apply to each recipient. A recipient to which §§1317.300

through 1317.310 apply shall not discriminate on the basis of sex in admission or recruitment in violation of §§1317.300 through 1317.310.

(d) *Educational institutions.* Except as provided in paragraph (e) of this section as to recipients that are educational institutions, §§1317.300 through 1317.310 apply only to institutions of vocational education, professional education, graduate higher education, and public institutions of undergraduate higher education.

(e) *Public institutions of undergraduate higher education.* §§1317.300 through 1317.310 do not apply to any public institution of undergraduate higher education that traditionally and continually from its establishment has had a policy of admitting students of only one sex.

§1317.225 **Educational institutions eligible to submit transition plans.**

(a) *Application.* This section applies to each educational institution to which §§1317.300 through 1317.310 apply that:

(1) Admitted students of only one sex as regular students as of June 23, 1972; or

(2) Admitted students of only one sex as regular students as of June 23, 1965, but thereafter admitted, as regular students, students of the sex not admitted prior to June 23, 1965.

(b) *Provision for transition plans.* An educational institution to which this section applies shall not discriminate on the basis of sex in admission or recruitment in violation of §§1317.300 through 1317.310.

§1317.230 **Transition plans.**

(a) *Submission of plans.* An institution to which §1317.225 applies and that is composed of more than one administratively separate unit may submit either a single transition plan applicable to all such units, or a separate transition plan applicable to each such unit.

(b) *Content of plans.* In order to be approved by the Secretary of Education, a transition plan shall:

(1) State the name, address, and Federal Interagency Committee on Education Code of the educational institution submitting such plan, the administratively separate units to which the

plan is applicable, and the name, address, and telephone number of the person to whom questions concerning the plan may be addressed. The person who submits the plan shall be the chief administrator or president of the institution, or another individual legally authorized to bind the institution to all actions set forth in the plan.

(2) State whether the educational institution or administratively separate unit admits students of both sexes as regular students and, if so, when it began to do so.

(3) Identify and describe with respect to the educational institution or administratively separate unit any obstacles to admitting students without discrimination on the basis of sex.

(4) Describe in detail the steps necessary to eliminate as soon as practicable each obstacle so identified and indicate the schedule for taking these steps and the individual directly responsible for their implementation.

(5) Include estimates of the number of students, by sex, expected to apply for, be admitted to, and enter each class during the period covered by the plan.

(c) *Nondiscrimination.* No policy or practice of a recipient to which § 1317.225 applies shall result in treatment of applicants to or students of such recipient in violation of §§ 1317.300 through 1317.310 unless such treatment is necessitated by an obstacle identified in paragraph (b)(3) of this section and a schedule for eliminating that obstacle has been provided as required by paragraph (b)(4) of this section.

(d) *Effects of past exclusion.* To overcome the effects of past exclusion of students on the basis of sex, each educational institution to which § 1317.225 applies shall include in its transition plan, and shall implement, specific steps designed to encourage individuals of the previously excluded sex to apply for admission to such institution. Such steps shall include instituting recruitment programs that emphasize the institution's commitment to enrolling students of the sex previously excluded.

§ 1317.235 Statutory amendments.

(a) This section, which applies to all provisions of these Title IX regula-tions, addresses statutory amendments to Title IX.

(b) These Title IX regulations shall not apply to or preclude:

(1) Any program or activity of the American Legion undertaken in connection with the organization or operation of any Boys State conference, Boys Nation conference, Girls State conference, or Girls Nation conference;

(2) Any program or activity of a secondary school or educational institution specifically for:

(i) The promotion of any Boys State conference, Boys Nation conference, Girls State conference, or Girls Nation conference; or

(ii) The selection of students to attend any such conference;

(3) Father-son or mother-daughter activities at an educational institution or in an education program or activity, but if such activities are provided for students of one sex, opportunities for reasonably comparable activities shall be provided to students of the other sex;

(4) Any scholarship or other financial assistance awarded by an institution of higher education to an individual because such individual has received such award in a single-sex pageant based upon a combination of factors related to the individual's personal appearance, poise, and talent. The pageant, however, must comply with other nondiscrimination provisions of Federal law.

(c) *Program or activity* or *program* means:

(1) All of the operations of any entity described in paragraphs (c)(1)(i) through (iv) of this section, any part of which is extended Federal financial assistance:

(i)(A) A department, agency, special purpose district, or other instrumentality of a State or of a local government; or

(B) The entity of such State or local government that distributes such assistance and each such department or agency (and each other State or local government entity) to which the assistance is extended, in the case of assistance to a State or local government;

(ii)(A) A college, university, or other postsecondary institution, or a public system of higher education; or

(B) A local educational agency (as defined in section 8801 of title 20), system of vocational education, or other school system;

(iii)(A) An entire corporation, partnership, or other private organization, or an entire sole proprietorship—

(1) If assistance is extended to such corporation, partnership, private organization, or sole proprietorship as a whole; or

(2) Which is principally engaged in the business of providing education, health care, housing, social services, or parks and recreation; or

(B) The entire plant or other comparable, geographically separate facility to which Federal financial assistance is extended, in the case of any other corporation, partnership, private organization, or sole proprietorship; or

(iv) Any other entity that is established by two or more of the entities described in paragraphs (c)(1)(i), (ii), or (iii) of this section.

(2)(i) *Program or activity* does not include any operation of an entity that is controlled by a religious organization if the application of 20 U.S.C. 1681 to such operation would not be consistent with the religious tenets of such organization.

(ii) For example, all of the operations of a college, university, or other postsecondary institution, including but not limited to traditional educational operations, faculty and student housing, campus shuttle bus service, campus restaurants, the bookstore, and other commercial activities are part of a "program or activity" subject to these Title IX regulations if the college, university, or other institution receives Federal financial assistance.

(d)(1) Nothing in these Title IX regulations shall be construed to require or prohibit any person, or public or private entity, to provide or pay for any benefit or service, including the use of facilities, related to an abortion. Medical procedures, benefits, services, and the use of facilities, necessary to save the life of a pregnant woman or to address complications related to an abortion are not subject to this section.

(2) Nothing in this section shall be construed to permit a penalty to be imposed on any person or individual because such person or individual is seeking or has received any benefit or service related to a legal abortion. Accordingly, subject to paragraph (d)(1) of this section, no person shall be excluded from participation in, be denied the benefits of, or be subjected to discrimination under any academic, extracurricular, research, occupational training, employment, or other educational program or activity operated by a recipient that receives Federal financial assistance because such individual has sought or received, or is seeking, a legal abortion, or any benefit or service related to a legal abortion.

Subpart C—Discrimination on the Basis of Sex in Admission and Recruitment Prohibited

§1317.300   Admission.

(a) *General.* No person shall, on the basis of sex, be denied admission, or be subjected to discrimination in admission, by any recipient to which §§1317.300 through 1317.310 apply, except as provided in §§1317.225 and 1317.230.

(b) *Specific prohibitions.* (1) In determining whether a person satisfies any policy or criterion for admission, or in making any offer of admission, a recipient to which §§1317.300 through 1317.310 apply shall not:

(i) Give preference to one person over another on the basis of sex, by ranking applicants separately on such basis, or otherwise;

(ii) Apply numerical limitations upon the number or proportion of persons of either sex who may be admitted; or

(iii) Otherwise treat one individual differently from another on the basis of sex.

(2) A recipient shall not administer or operate any test or other criterion for admission that has a disproportionately adverse effect on persons on the basis of sex unless the use of such test or criterion is shown to predict validly success in the education program or activity in question and alternative tests or criteria that do not have such a disproportionately adverse effect are shown to be unavailable.

(c) *Prohibitions relating to marital or parental status.* In determining whether a person satisfies any policy or criterion for admission, or in making any offer of admission, a recipient to which §§ 1317.300 through 1317.310 apply:

(1) Shall not apply any rule concerning the actual or potential parental, family, or marital status of a student or applicant that treats persons differently on the basis of sex;

(2) Shall not discriminate against or exclude any person on the basis of pregnancy, childbirth, termination of pregnancy, or recovery therefrom, or establish or follow any rule or practice that so discriminates or excludes;

(3) Subject to § 1317.235(d), shall treat disabilities related to pregnancy, childbirth, termination of pregnancy, or recovery therefrom in the same manner and under the same policies as any other temporary disability or physical condition; and

(4) Shall not make pre-admission inquiry as to the marital status of an applicant for admission, including whether such applicant is "Miss" or "Mrs." A recipient may make pre-admission inquiry as to the sex of an applicant for admission, but only if such inquiry is made equally of such applicants of both sexes and if the results of such inquiry are not used in connection with discrimination prohibited by these Title IX regulations.

§ 1317.305 **Preference in admission.**

A recipient to which §§ 1317.300 through 1317.310 apply shall not give preference to applicants for admission, on the basis of attendance at any educational institution or other school or entity that admits as students only or predominantly members of one sex, if the giving of such preference has the effect of discriminating on the basis of sex in violation of §§ 1317.300 through 1317.310.

§ 1317.310 **Recruitment.**

(a) *Nondiscriminatory recruitment.* A recipient to which §§ 1317.300 through 1317.310 apply shall not discriminate on the basis of sex in the recruitment and admission of students. A recipient may be required to undertake additional recruitment efforts for one sex as remedial action pursuant to § 1317.110(a), and

may choose to undertake such efforts as affirmative action pursuant to § 1317.110(b).

(b) *Recruitment at certain institutions.* A recipient to which §§ 1317.300 through 1317.310 apply shall not recruit primarily or exclusively at educational institutions, schools, or entities that admit as students only or predominantly members of one sex, if such actions have the effect of discriminating on the basis of sex in violation of §§ 1317.300 through 1317.310.

Subpart D—Discrimination on the Basis of Sex in Education Programs or Activities Prohibited

§ 1317.400 **Education programs or activities.**

(a) *General.* Except as provided elsewhere in these Title IX regulations, no person shall, on the basis of sex, be excluded from participation in, be denied the benefits of, or be subjected to discrimination under any academic, extracurricular, research, occupational training, or other education program or activity operated by a recipient that receives Federal financial assistance. Sections 1317.400 through 1317.455 do not apply to actions of a recipient in connection with admission of its students to an education program or activity of a recipient to which §§ 1317.300 through 1317.310 do not apply, or an entity, not a recipient, to which §§ 1317.300 through 1317.310 would not apply if the entity were a recipient.

(b) *Specific prohibitions.* Except as provided in §§ 1317.400 through 1317.455, in providing any aid, benefit, or service to a student, a recipient shall not, on the basis of sex:

(1) Treat one person differently from another in determining whether such person satisfies any requirement or condition for the provision of such aid, benefit, or service;

(2) Provide different aid, benefits, or services or provide aid, benefits, or services in a different manner;

(3) Deny any person any such aid, benefit, or service;

(4) Subject any person to separate or different rules of behavior, sanctions, or other treatment;

(5) Apply any rule concerning the domicile or residence of a student or

applicant, including eligibility for in-state fees and tuition;

(6) Aid or perpetuate discrimination against any person by providing significant assistance to any agency, organization, or person that discriminates on the basis of sex in providing any aid, benefit, or service to students or employees;

(7) Otherwise limit any person in the enjoyment of any right, privilege, advantage, or opportunity.

(c) *Assistance administered by a recipient educational institution to study at a foreign institution.* A recipient educational institution may administer or assist in the administration of scholarships, fellowships, or other awards established by foreign or domestic wills, trusts, or similar legal instruments, or by acts of foreign governments and restricted to members of one sex, that are designed to provide opportunities to study abroad, and that are awarded to students who are already matriculating at or who are graduates of the recipient institution; *Provided,* that a recipient educational institution that administers or assists in the administration of such scholarships, fellowships, or other awards that are restricted to members of one sex provides, or otherwise makes available, reasonable opportunities for similar studies for members of the other sex. Such opportunities may be derived from either domestic or foreign sources.

(d) *Aids, benefits or services not provided by recipient.* (1) This paragraph (d) applies to any recipient that requires participation by any applicant, student, or employee in any education program or activity not operated wholly by such recipient, or that facilitates, permits, or considers such participation as part of or equivalent to an education program or activity operated by such recipient, including participation in educational consortia and cooperative employment and student-teaching assignments.

(2) Such recipient:

(i) Shall develop and implement a procedure designed to assure itself that the operator or sponsor of such other education program or activity takes no action affecting any applicant, student, or employee of such recipient that

these Title IX regulations would prohibit such recipient from taking; and

(ii) Shall not facilitate, require, permit, or consider such participation if such action occurs.

§1317.405 Housing.

(a) *Generally.* A recipient shall not, on the basis of sex, apply different rules or regulations, impose different fees or requirements, or offer different services or benefits related to housing, except as provided in this section (including housing provided only to married students).

(b) *Housing provided by recipient.* (1) A recipient may provide separate housing on the basis of sex.

(2) Housing provided by a recipient to students of one sex, when compared to that provided to students of the other sex, shall be as a whole:

(i) Proportionate in quantity to the number of students of that sex applying for such housing; and

(ii) Comparable in quality and cost to the student.

(c) *Other housing.* (1) A recipient shall not, on the basis of sex, administer different policies or practices concerning occupancy by its students of housing other than that provided by such recipient.

(2)(i) A recipient which, through solicitation, listing, approval of housing, or otherwise, assists any agency, organization, or person in making housing available to any of its students, shall take such reasonable action as may be necessary to assure itself that such housing as is provided to students of one sex, when compared to that provided to students of the other sex, is as a whole:

(A) Proportionate in quantity; and

(B) Comparable in quality and cost to the student.

(ii) A recipient may render such assistance to any agency, organization, or person that provides all or part of such housing to students of only one sex.

§1317.410 Comparable facilities.

A recipient may provide separate toilet, locker room, and shower facilities on the basis of sex, but such facilities provided for students of one sex shall be comparable to such facilities provided for students of the other sex.

§ 1317.415 Access to course offerings.

(a) A recipient shall not provide any course or otherwise carry out any of its education program or activity separately on the basis of sex, or require or refuse participation therein by any of its students on such basis, including health, physical education, industrial, business, vocational, technical, home economics, music, and adult education courses.

(b)(1) With respect to classes and activities in physical education at the elementary school level, the recipient shall comply fully with this section as expeditiously as possible but in no event later than one year from September 29, 2000. With respect to physical education classes and activities at the secondary and post-secondary levels, the recipient shall comply fully with this section as expeditiously as possible but in no event later than three years from September 29, 2000.

(2) This section does not prohibit grouping of students in physical education classes and activities by ability as assessed by objective standards of individual performance developed and applied without regard to sex.

(3) This section does not prohibit separation of students by sex within physical education classes or activities during participation in wrestling, boxing, rugby, ice hockey, football, basketball, and other sports the purpose or major activity of which involves bodily contact.

(4) Where use of a single standard of measuring skill or progress in a physical education class has an adverse effect on members of one sex, the recipient shall use appropriate standards that do not have such effect.

(5) Portions of classes in elementary and secondary schools, or portions of education programs or activities, that deal exclusively with human sexuality may be conducted in separate sessions for boys and girls.

(6) Recipients may make requirements based on vocal range or quality that may result in a chorus or choruses of one or predominantly one sex.

§ 1317.420 Access to schools operated by LEAs.

A recipient that is a local educational agency shall not, on the basis of sex, exclude any person from admission to:

(a) Any institution of vocational education operated by such recipient; or

(b) Any other school or educational unit operated by such recipient, unless such recipient otherwise makes available to such person, pursuant to the same policies and criteria of admission, courses, services, and facilities comparable to each course, service, and facility offered in or through such schools.

§ 1317.425 Counseling and use of appraisal and counseling materials.

(a) *Counseling.* A recipient shall not discriminate against any person on the basis of sex in the counseling or guidance of students or applicants for admission.

(b) *Use of appraisal and counseling materials.* A recipient that uses testing or other materials for appraising or counseling students shall not use different materials for students on the basis of their sex or use materials that permit or require different treatment of students on such basis unless such different materials cover the same occupations and interest areas and the use of such different materials is shown to be essential to eliminate sex bias. Recipients shall develop and use internal procedures for ensuring that such materials do not discriminate on the basis of sex. Where the use of a counseling test or other instrument results in a substantially disproportionate number of members of one sex in any particular course of study or classification, the recipient shall take such action as is necessary to assure itself that such disproportion is not the result of discrimination in the instrument or its application.

(c) *Disproportion in classes.* Where a recipient finds that a particular class contains a substantially disproportionate number of individuals of one sex, the recipient shall take such action as is necessary to assure itself that such disproportion is not the result of discrimination on the basis of sex in counseling or appraisal materials or by counselors.

§ 1317.430 Financial assistance.

(a) *General.* Except as provided in paragraphs (b) and (c) of this section, in providing financial assistance to any of its students, a recipient shall not:

(1) On the basis of sex, provide different amounts or types of such assistance, limit eligibility for such assistance that is of any particular type or source, apply different criteria, or otherwise discriminate;

(2) Through solicitation, listing, approval, provision of facilities, or other services, assist any foundation, trust, agency, organization, or person that provides assistance to any of such recipient's students in a manner that discriminates on the basis of sex; or

(3) Apply any rule or assist in application of any rule concerning eligibility for such assistance that treats persons of one sex differently from persons of the other sex with regard to marital or parental status.

(b) *Financial aid established by certain legal instruments.* (1) A recipient may administer or assist in the administration of scholarships, fellowships, or other forms of financial assistance established pursuant to domestic or foreign wills, trusts, bequests, or similar legal instruments or by acts of a foreign government that require that awards be made to members of a particular sex specified therein; *Provided,* that the overall effect of the award of such sex-restricted scholarships, fellowships, and other forms of financial assistance does not discriminate on the basis of sex.

(2) To ensure nondiscriminatory awards of assistance as required in paragraph (b)(1) of this section, recipients shall develop and use procedures under which:

(i) Students are selected for award of financial assistance on the basis of nondiscriminatory criteria and not on the basis of availability of funds restricted to members of a particular sex;

(ii) An appropriate sex-restricted scholarship, fellowship, or other form of financial assistance is allocated to each student selected under paragraph (b)(2)(i) of this section; and

(iii) No student is denied the award for which he or she was selected under paragraph (b)(2)(i) of this section because of the absence of a scholarship, fellowship, or other form of financial assistance designated for a member of that student's sex.

(c) *Athletic scholarships.* (1) To the extent that a recipient awards athletic scholarships or grants-in-aid, it must provide reasonable opportunities for such awards for members of each sex in proportion to the number of students of each sex participating in interscholastic or intercollegiate athletics.

(2) A recipient may provide separate athletic scholarships or grants-in-aid for members of each sex as part of separate athletic teams for members of each sex to the extent consistent with this paragraph (c) and § 1317.450.

§ 1317.435 Employment assistance to students.

(a) *Assistance by recipient in making available outside employment.* A recipient that assists any agency, organization, or person in making employment available to any of its students:

(1) Shall assure itself that such employment is made available without discrimination on the basis of sex; and

(2) Shall not render such services to any agency, organization, or person that discriminates on the basis of sex in its employment practices.

(b) *Employment of students by recipients.* A recipient that employs any of its students shall not do so in a manner that violates §§ 1317.500 through 1317.550.

§ 1317.440 Health and insurance benefits and services.

Subject to § 1317.235(d), in providing a medical, hospital, accident, or life insurance benefit, service, policy, or plan to any of its students, a recipient shall not discriminate on the basis of sex, or provide such benefit, service, policy, or plan in a manner that would violate §§ 1317.500 through 1317.550 if it were provided to employees of the recipient. This section shall not prohibit a recipient from providing any benefit or service that may be used by a different proportion of students of one sex than of the other, including family planning services. However, any recipient that provides full coverage health service shall provide gynecological care.

§ 1317.445   Marital or parental status.

(a) *Status generally.* A recipient shall not apply any rule concerning a student's actual or potential parental, family, or marital status that treats students differently on the basis of sex.

(b) *Pregnancy and related conditions.* (1) A recipient shall not discriminate against any student, or exclude any student from its education program or activity, including any class or extracurricular activity, on the basis of such student's pregnancy, childbirth, false pregnancy, termination of pregnancy, or recovery therefrom, unless the student requests voluntarily to participate in a separate portion of the program or activity of the recipient.

(2) A recipient may require such a student to obtain the certification of a physician that the student is physically and emotionally able to continue participation as long as such a certification is required of all students for other physical or emotional conditions requiring the attention of a physician.

(3) A recipient that operates a portion of its education program or activity separately for pregnant students, admittance to which is completely voluntary on the part of the student as provided in paragraph (b)(1) of this section, shall ensure that the separate portion is comparable to that offered to non-pregnant students.

(4) Subject to § 1317.235(d), a recipient shall treat pregnancy, childbirth, false pregnancy, termination of pregnancy and recovery therefrom in the same manner and under the same policies as any other temporary disability with respect to any medical or hospital benefit, service, plan, or policy that such recipient administers, operates, offers, or participates in with respect to students admitted to the recipient's educational program or activity.

(5) In the case of a recipient that does not maintain a leave policy for its students, or in the case of a student who does not otherwise qualify for leave under such a policy, a recipient shall treat pregnancy, childbirth, false pregnancy, termination of pregnancy, and recovery therefrom as a justification for a leave of absence for as long a period of time as is deemed medically necessary by the student's physician, at the conclusion of which the student shall be reinstated to the status that she held when the leave began.

§ 1317.450   Athletics.

(a) *General.* No person shall, on the basis of sex, be excluded from participation in, be denied the benefits of, be treated differently from another person, or otherwise be discriminated against in any interscholastic, intercollegiate, club, or intramural athletics offered by a recipient, and no recipient shall provide any such athletics separately on such basis.

(b) *Separate teams.* Notwithstanding the requirements of paragraph (a) of this section, a recipient may operate or sponsor separate teams for members of each sex where selection for such teams is based upon competitive skill or the activity involved is a contact sport. However, where a recipient operates or sponsors a team in a particular sport for members of one sex but operates or sponsors no such team for members of the other sex, and athletic opportunities for members of that sex have previously been limited, members of the excluded sex must be allowed to try out for the team offered unless the sport involved is a contact sport. For the purposes of these Title IX regulations, contact sports include boxing, wrestling, rugby, ice hockey, football, basketball, and other sports the purpose or major activity of which involves bodily contact.

(c) *Equal opportunity.* (1) A recipient that operates or sponsors interscholastic, intercollegiate, club, or intramural athletics shall provide equal athletic opportunity for members of both sexes. In determining whether equal opportunities are available, the designated agency official will consider, among other factors:

(i) Whether the selection of sports and levels of competition effectively accommodate the interests and abilities of members of both sexes;

(ii) The provision of equipment and supplies;

(iii) Scheduling of games and practice time;

(iv) Travel and per diem allowance;

(v) Opportunity to receive coaching and academic tutoring;

(vi) Assignment and compensation of coaches and tutors;

(vii) Provision of locker rooms, practice, and competitive facilities;

(viii) Provision of medical and training facilities and services;

(ix) Provision of housing and dining facilities and services;

(x) Publicity.

(2) For purposes of paragraph (c)(1) of this section, unequal aggregate expenditures for members of each sex or unequal expenditures for male and female teams if a recipient operates or sponsors separate teams will not constitute noncompliance with this section, but the designated agency official may consider the failure to provide necessary funds for teams for one sex in assessing equality of opportunity for members of each sex.

(d) *Adjustment period.* A recipient that operates or sponsors interscholastic, intercollegiate, club, or intramural athletics at the elementary school level shall comply fully with this section as expeditiously as possible but in no event later than one year from September 29, 2000. A recipient that operates or sponsors interscholastic, intercollegiate, club, or intramural athletics at the secondary or postsecondary school level shall comply fully with this section as expeditiously as possible but in no event later than three years from September 29, 2000.

§1317.455 Textbooks and curricular material.

Nothing in these Title IX regulations shall be interpreted as requiring or prohibiting or abridging in any way the use of particular textbooks or curricular materials.

Subpart E—Discrimination on the Basis of Sex in Employment in Education Programs or Activities Prohibited

§1317.500 Employment.

(a) *General.* (1) No person shall, on the basis of sex, be excluded from participation in, be denied the benefits of, or be subjected to discrimination in employment, or recruitment, consideration, or selection therefor, whether full-time or part-time, under any education program or activity operated by a recipient that receives Federal financial assistance.

(2) A recipient shall make all employment decisions in any education program or activity operated by such recipient in a nondiscriminatory manner and shall not limit, segregate, or classify applicants or employees in any way that could adversely affect any applicant's or employee's employment opportunities or status because of sex.

(3) A recipient shall not enter into any contractual or other relationship which directly or indirectly has the effect of subjecting employees or students to discrimination prohibited by §§1317.500 through 1317.550, including relationships with employment and referral agencies, with labor unions, and with organizations providing or administering fringe benefits to employees of the recipient.

(4) A recipient shall not grant preferences to applicants for employment on the basis of attendance at any educational institution or entity that admits as students only or predominantly members of one sex, if the giving of such preferences has the effect of discriminating on the basis of sex in violation of these Title IX regulations.

(b) *Application.* The provisions of §§1317.500 through 1317.550 apply to:

(1) Recruitment, advertising, and the process of application for employment;

(2) Hiring, upgrading, promotion, consideration for and award of tenure, demotion, transfer, layoff, termination, application of nepotism policies, right of return from layoff, and rehiring;

(3) Rates of pay or any other form of compensation, and changes in compensation;

(4) Job assignments, classifications, and structure, including position descriptions, lines of progression, and seniority lists;

(5) The terms of any collective bargaining agreement;

(6) Granting and return from leaves of absence, leave for pregnancy, childbirth, false pregnancy, termination of pregnancy, leave for persons of either sex to care for children or dependents, or any other leave;

(7) Fringe benefits available by virtue of employment, whether or not administered by the recipient;

(8) Selection and financial support for training, including apprenticeship, professional meetings, conferences, and other related activities, selection for tuition assistance, selection for sabbaticals and leaves of absence to pursue training;

(9) Employer-sponsored activities, including social or recreational programs; and

(10) Any other term, condition, or privilege of employment.

§ 1317.505 Employment criteria.

A recipient shall not administer or operate any test or other criterion for any employment opportunity that has a disproportionately adverse effect on persons on the basis of sex unless:

(a) Use of such test or other criterion is shown to predict validly successful performance in the position in question; and

(b) Alternative tests or criteria for such purpose, which do not have such disproportionately adverse effect, are shown to be unavailable.

§ 1317.510 Recruitment.

(a) *Nondiscriminatory recruitment and hiring.* A recipient shall not discriminate on the basis of sex in the recruitment and hiring of employees. Where a recipient has been found to be presently discriminating on the basis of sex in the recruitment or hiring of employees, or has been found to have so discriminated in the past, the recipient shall recruit members of the sex so discriminated against so as to overcome the effects of such past or present discrimination.

(b) *Recruitment patterns.* A recipient shall not recruit primarily or exclusively at entities that furnish as applicants only or predominantly members of one sex if such actions have the effect of discriminating on the basis of sex in violation of §§ 1317.500 through 1317.550.

§ 1317.515 Compensation.

A recipient shall not make or enforce any policy or practice that, on the basis of sex:

(a) Makes distinctions in rates of pay or other compensation;

(b) Results in the payment of wages to employees of one sex at a rate less than that paid to employees of the opposite sex for equal work on jobs the performance of which requires equal skill, effort, and responsibility, and that are performed under similar working conditions.

§ 1317.520 Job classification and structure.

A recipient shall not:

(a) Classify a job as being for males or for females;

(b) Maintain or establish separate lines of progression, seniority lists, career ladders, or tenure systems based on sex; or

(c) Maintain or establish separate lines of progression, seniority systems, career ladders, or tenure systems for similar jobs, position descriptions, or job requirements that classify persons on the basis of sex, unless sex is a bona fide occupational qualification for the positions in question as set forth in § 1317.550.

§ 1317.525 Fringe benefits.

(a) *"Fringe benefits" defined.* For purposes of these Title IX regulations, *fringe benefits* means: Any medical, hospital, accident, life insurance, or retirement benefit, service, policy or plan, any profit-sharing or bonus plan, leave, and any other benefit or service of employment not subject to the provision of § 1317.515.

(b) *Prohibitions.* A recipient shall not:

(1) Discriminate on the basis of sex with regard to making fringe benefits available to employees or make fringe benefits available to spouses, families, or dependents of employees differently upon the basis of the employee's sex;

(2) Administer, operate, offer, or participate in a fringe benefit plan that does not provide for equal periodic benefits for members of each sex and for equal contributions to the plan by such recipient for members of each sex; or

(3) Administer, operate, offer, or participate in a pension or retirement plan that establishes different optional or compulsory retirement ages based on sex or that otherwise discriminates in benefits on the basis of sex.

§ 1317.530 Marital or parental status.

(a) *General.* A recipient shall not apply any policy or take any employment action:

(1) Concerning the potential marital, parental, or family status of an employee or applicant for employment that treats persons differently on the basis of sex; or

(2) Which is based upon whether an employee or applicant for employment is the head of household or principal wage earner in such employee's or applicant's family unit.

(b) *Pregnancy.* A recipient shall not discriminate against or exclude from employment any employee or applicant for employment on the basis of pregnancy, childbirth, false pregnancy, termination of pregnancy, or recovery therefrom.

(c) *Pregnancy as a temporary disability.* Subject to § 1317235(d), a recipient shall treat pregnancy, childbirth, false pregnancy, termination of pregnancy, recovery therefrom, and any temporary disability resulting therefrom as any other temporary disability for all job-related purposes, including commencement, duration, and extensions of leave, payment of disability income, accrual of seniority and any other benefit or service, and reinstatement, and under any fringe benefit offered to employees by virtue of employment.

(d) *Pregnancy leave.* In the case of a recipient that does not maintain a leave policy for its employees, or in the case of an employee with insufficient leave or accrued employment time to qualify for leave under such a policy, a recipient shall treat pregnancy, childbirth, false pregnancy, termination of pregnancy, and recovery therefrom as a justification for a leave of absence without pay for a reasonable period of time, at the conclusion of which the employee shall be reinstated to the status that she held when the leave began or to a comparable position, without decrease in rate of compensation or loss of promotional opportunities, or any other right or privilege of employment.

§ 1317.535 Effect of state or local law or other requirements.

(a) *Prohibitory requirements.* The obligation to comply with §§ 1317.500 through 1317.550 is not obviated or alleviated by the existence of any State or local law or other requirement that imposes prohibitions or limits upon employment of members of one sex that are not imposed upon members of the other sex.

(b) *Benefits.* A recipient that provides any compensation, service, or benefit to members of one sex pursuant to a State or local law or other requirement shall provide the same compensation, service, or benefit to members of the other sex.

§ 1317.540 Advertising.

A recipient shall not in any advertising related to employment indicate preference, limitation, specification, or discrimination based on sex unless sex is a bona fide occupational qualification for the particular job in question.

§ 1317.545 Pre-employment inquiries.

(a) *Marital status.* A recipient shall not make pre-employment inquiry as to the marital status of an applicant for employment, including whether such applicant is "Miss" or "Mrs."

(b) *Sex.* A recipient may make pre-employment inquiry as to the sex of an applicant for employment, but only if such inquiry is made equally of such applicants of both sexes and if the results of such inquiry are not used in connection with discrimination prohibited by these Title IX regulations.

§ 1317.550 Sex as a bona fide occupational qualification.

A recipient may take action otherwise prohibited by §§ 1317.500 through 1317.550 provided it is shown that sex is a bona fide occupational qualification for that action, such that consideration of sex with regard to such action is essential to successful operation of the employment function concerned. A recipient shall not take action pursuant to this section that is based upon alleged comparative employment characteristics or stereotyped characterizations of one or the other sex, or upon preference based on sex of the recipient, employees, students, or other persons, but nothing contained in this section shall prevent a recipient from considering an employee's sex in relation

311

to employment in a locker room or toilet facility used only by members of one sex.

Subpart F—Procedures

§ 1317.600 Notice of covered programs.

Within 60 days of September 29, 2000, each Federal agency that awards Federal financial assistance shall publish in the FEDERAL REGISTER a notice of the programs covered by these Title IX regulations. Each such Federal agency shall periodically republish the notice of covered programs to reflect changes in covered programs. Copies of this no-

tice also shall be made available upon request to the Federal agency's office that enforces Title IX.

§ 1317.605 Enforcement procedures.

The investigative, compliance, and enforcement procedural provisions of Title VI of the Civil Rights Act of 1964 (42 U.S.C. 2000d) ("Title VI") are hereby adopted and applied to these Title IX regulations. These procedures may be found at 18 CFR part 1302.

[65 FR 52878, Aug. 30, 2000]

PARTS 1318–1399 [RESERVED]

FINDING AIDS

A list of CFR titles, subtitles, chapters, subchapters and parts and an alphabetical list of agencies publishing in the CFR are included in the CFR Index and Finding Aids volume to the Code of Federal Regulations which is published separately and revised annually.

Table of CFR Titles and Chapters
Alphabetical List of Agencies Appearing in the CFR
List of CFR Sections Affected

Table of CFR Titles and Chapters

(Revised as of April 1, 2018)

Title 1—General Provisions

Title 2—Grants and Agreements

Title 2—Grants and Agreements—Continued

Title 3—The President

Title 4—Accounts

Title 5—Administrative Personnel

Title 5—Administrative Personnel—Continued

Title 5—Administrative Personnel—Continued

Title 6—Domestic Security

Title 7—Agriculture

Title 7—Agriculture—Continued

319

Title 8—Aliens and Nationality

Title 9—Animals and Animal Products

Title 10—Energy

Title 11—Federal Elections

Title 12—Banks and Banking

Title 15—Commerce and Foreign Trade—Continued

Title 16—Commercial Practices

Title 17—Commodity and Securities Exchanges

Title 18—Conservation of Power and Water Resources

Title 19—Customs Duties

Title 20—Employees' Benefits

Title 20—Employees' Benefits—Continued

III   Social Security Administration (Parts 400—499)

IV   Employees' Compensation Appeals Board, Department of Labor (Parts 500—599)

V   Employment and Training Administration, Department of Labor (Parts 600—699)

VI   Office of Workers' Compensation Programs, Department of Labor (Parts 700—799)

VII   Benefits Review Board, Department of Labor (Parts 800—899)

VIII   Joint Board for the Enrollment of Actuaries (Parts 900—999)

IX   Office of the Assistant Secretary for Veterans' Employment and Training Service, Department of Labor (Parts 1000—1099)

Title 21—Food and Drugs

I   Food and Drug Administration, Department of Health and Human Services (Parts 1—1299)

II   Drug Enforcement Administration, Department of Justice (Parts 1300—1399)

III   Office of National Drug Control Policy (Parts 1400—1499)

Title 22—Foreign Relations

I   Department of State (Parts 1—199)

II   Agency for International Development (Parts 200—299)

III   Peace Corps (Parts 300—399)

IV   International Joint Commission, United States and Canada (Parts 400—499)

V   Broadcasting Board of Governors (Parts 500—599)

VII   Overseas Private Investment Corporation (Parts 700—799)

IX   Foreign Service Grievance Board (Parts 900—999)

X   Inter-American Foundation (Parts 1000—1099)

XI   International Boundary and Water Commission, United States and Mexico, United States Section (Parts 1100—1199)

XII   United States International Development Cooperation Agency (Parts 1200—1299)

XIII   Millennium Challenge Corporation (Parts 1300—1399)

XIV   Foreign Service Labor Relations Board; Federal Labor Relations Authority; General Counsel of the Federal Labor Relations Authority; and the Foreign Service Impasse Disputes Panel (Parts 1400—1499)

XV   African Development Foundation (Parts 1500—1599)

XVI   Japan-United States Friendship Commission (Parts 1600—1699)

XVII   United States Institute of Peace (Parts 1700—1799)

Title 23—Highways

I   Federal Highway Administration, Department of Transportation (Parts 1—999)

Title 23—Highways—Continued

Title 24—Housing and Urban Development

Title 24—Housing and Urban Development—Continued

XXIV Board of Directors of the HOPE for Homeowners Program (Parts 4000—4099) [Reserved]

XXV Neighborhood Reinvestment Corporation (Parts 4100—4199)

Title 25—Indians

I Bureau of Indian Affairs, Department of the Interior (Parts 1—299)

II Indian Arts and Crafts Board, Department of the Interior (Parts 300—399)

III National Indian Gaming Commission, Department of the Interior (Parts 500—599)

IV Office of Navajo and Hopi Indian Relocation (Parts 700—899)

V Bureau of Indian Affairs, Department of the Interior, and Indian Health Service, Department of Health and Human Services (Parts 900—999)

VI Office of the Assistant Secretary, Indian Affairs, Department of the Interior (Parts 1000—1199)

VII Office of the Special Trustee for American Indians, Department of the Interior (Parts 1200—1299)

Title 26—Internal Revenue

I Internal Revenue Service, Department of the Treasury (Parts 1—End)

Title 27—Alcohol, Tobacco Products and Firearms

I Alcohol and Tobacco Tax and Trade Bureau, Department of the Treasury (Parts 1—399)

II Bureau of Alcohol, Tobacco, Firearms, and Explosives, Department of Justice (Parts 400—699)

Title 28—Judicial Administration

I Department of Justice (Parts 0—299)

III Federal Prison Industries, Inc., Department of Justice (Parts 300—399)

V Bureau of Prisons, Department of Justice (Parts 500—599)

VI Offices of Independent Counsel, Department of Justice (Parts 600—699)

VII Office of Independent Counsel (Parts 700—799)

VIII Court Services and Offender Supervision Agency for the District of Columbia (Parts 800—899)

IX National Crime Prevention and Privacy Compact Council (Parts 900—999)

XI Department of Justice and Department of State (Parts 1100—1199)

Title 29—Labor

Title 30—Mineral Resources

Title 31—Money and Finance: Treasury

Title 31—Money and Finance: Treasury—Continued

Title 32—National Defense

Title 33—Navigation and Navigable Waters

Title 34—Education

Title 34—Education—Continued

Title 35 [Reserved]

Title 36—Parks, Forests, and Public Property

Title 37—Patents, Trademarks, and Copyrights

Title 38—Pensions, Bonuses, and Veterans' Relief

Title 39—Postal Service

Title 40—Protection of Environment

Title 41—Public Contracts and Property Management

Title 41—Public Contracts and Property Management—Continued

Chap.

Title 42—Public Health

Title 43—Public Lands: Interior

Title 44—Emergency Management and Assistance

Title 45—Public Welfare

54 Defense Logistics Agency, Department of Defense (Parts 5400—5499)

57 African Development Foundation (Parts 5700—5799)

61 Civilian Board of Contract Appeals, General Services Administration (Parts 6100—6199)

99 Cost Accounting Standards Board, Office of Federal Procurement Policy, Office of Management and Budget (Parts 9900—9999)

Title 49—Transportation

SUBTITLE A—OFFICE OF THE SECRETARY OF TRANSPORTATION (PARTS 1—99)

SUBTITLE B—OTHER REGULATIONS RELATING TO TRANSPORTATION

I Pipeline and Hazardous Materials Safety Administration, Department of Transportation (Parts 100—199)

II Federal Railroad Administration, Department of Transportation (Parts 200—299)

III Federal Motor Carrier Safety Administration, Department of Transportation (Parts 300—399)

IV Coast Guard, Department of Homeland Security (Parts 400—499)

V National Highway Traffic Safety Administration, Department of Transportation (Parts 500—599)

VI Federal Transit Administration, Department of Transportation (Parts 600—699)

VII National Railroad Passenger Corporation (AMTRAK) (Parts 700—799)

VIII National Transportation Safety Board (Parts 800—999)

X Surface Transportation Board (Parts 1000—1399)

XI Research and Innovative Technology Administration, Department of Transportation (Parts 1400—1499) [Reserved]

XII Transportation Security Administration, Department of Homeland Security (Parts 1500—1699)

Title 50—Wildlife and Fisheries

I United States Fish and Wildlife Service, Department of the Interior (Parts 1—199)

II National Marine Fisheries Service, National Oceanic and Atmospheric Administration, Department of Commerce (Parts 200—299)

III International Fishing and Related Activities (Parts 300—399)

IV Joint Regulations (United States Fish and Wildlife Service, Department of the Interior and National Marine Fisheries Service, National Oceanic and Atmospheric Administration, Department of Commerce); Endangered Species Committee Regulations (Parts 400—499)

V Marine Mammal Commission (Parts 500—599)

Alphabetical List of Agencies Appearing in the CFR

(Revised as of April 1, 2018)

Agency	CFR Title, Subtitle or Chapter
Administrative Committee of the Federal Register	1, I
Administrative Conference of the United States	1, III
Advisory Council on Historic Preservation	36, VIII
Advocacy and Outreach, Office of	7, XXV
Afghanistan Reconstruction, Special Inspector General for	5, LXXXIII
African Development Foundation	22, XV
Federal Acquisition Regulation	48, 57
Agency for International Development	2, VII; 22, II
Federal Acquisition Regulation	48, 7
Agricultural Marketing Service	7, I, IX, X, XI
Agricultural Research Service	7, V
Agriculture Department	2, IV; 5, LXXIII
Advocacy and Outreach, Office of	7, XXV
Agricultural Marketing Service	7, I, IX, X, XI
Agricultural Research Service	7, V
Animal and Plant Health Inspection Service	7, III; 9, I
Chief Financial Officer, Office of	7, XXX
Commodity Credit Corporation	7, XIV
Economic Research Service	7, XXXVII
Energy Policy and New Uses, Office of	2, IX; 7, XXIX
Environmental Quality, Office of	7, XXXI
Farm Service Agency	7, VII, XVIII
Federal Acquisition Regulation	48, 4
Federal Crop Insurance Corporation	7, IV
Food and Nutrition Service	7, II
Food Safety and Inspection Service	9, III
Foreign Agricultural Service	7, XV
Forest Service	36, II
Grain Inspection, Packers and Stockyards Administration	7, VIII; 9, II
Information Resources Management, Office of	7, XXVII
Inspector General, Office of	7, XXVI
National Agricultural Library	7, XLI
National Agricultural Statistics Service	7, XXXVI
National Institute of Food and Agriculture	7, XXXIV
Natural Resources Conservation Service	7, VI
Operations, Office of	7, XXVIII
Procurement and Property Management, Office of	7, XXXII
Rural Business-Cooperative Service	7, XVIII, XLII
Rural Development Administration	7, XLII
Rural Housing Service	7, XVIII, XXXV
Rural Telephone Bank	7, XVI
Rural Utilities Service	7, XVII, XVIII, XLII
Secretary of Agriculture, Office of	7, Subtitle A
Transportation, Office of	7, XXXIII
World Agricultural Outlook Board	7, XXXVIII
Air Force Department	32, VII
Federal Acquisition Regulation Supplement	48, 53
Air Transportation Stabilization Board	14, VI
Alcohol and Tobacco Tax and Trade Bureau	27, I
Alcohol, Tobacco, Firearms, and Explosives, Bureau of	27, II
AMTRAK	49, VII
American Battle Monuments Commission	36, IV
American Indians, Office of the Special Trustee	25, VII

337

Agency	CFR Title, Subtitle or Chapter
Indian Arts and Crafts Board	25, II
Indian Health Service	25, V
Industry and Security, Bureau of	15, VII
Information Resources Management, Office of	7, XXVII
Information Security Oversight Office, National Archives and Records Administration	32, XX
Inspector General	
Agriculture Department	7, XXVI
Health and Human Services Department	42, V
Housing and Urban Development Department	24, XII, XV
Institute of Peace, United States	22, XVII
Inter-American Foundation	5, LXIII; 22, X
Interior Department	2, XIV
American Indians, Office of the Special Trustee	25, VII
Endangered Species Committee	50, IV
Federal Acquisition Regulation	48, 14
Federal Property Management Regulations System	41, 114
Fish and Wildlife Service, United States	50, I, IV
Geological Survey	30, IV
Indian Affairs, Bureau of	25, I, V
Indian Affairs, Office of the Assistant Secretary	25, VI
Indian Arts and Crafts Board	25, II
Land Management, Bureau of	43, II
National Indian Gaming Commission	25, III
National Park Service	36, I
Natural Resource Revenue, Office of	30, XII
Ocean Energy Management, Bureau of	30, V
Reclamation, Bureau of	43, I
Safety and Enforcement Bureau, Bureau of	30, II
Secretary of the Interior, Office of	2, XIV; 43, Subtitle A
Surface Mining Reclamation and Enforcement, Office of	30, VII
Internal Revenue Service	26, I
International Boundary and Water Commission, United States and Mexico, United States Section	22, XI
International Development, United States Agency for	22, II
Federal Acquisition Regulation	48, 7
International Development Cooperation Agency, United States	22, XII
International Joint Commission, United States and Canada	22, IV
International Organizations Employees Loyalty Board	5, V
International Trade Administration	15, III; 19, III
International Trade Commission, United States	19, II
Interstate Commerce Commission	5, XL
Investment Security, Office of	31, VIII
James Madison Memorial Fellowship Foundation	45, XXIV
Japan–United States Friendship Commission	22, XVI
Joint Board for the Enrollment of Actuaries	20, VIII
Justice Department	2, XXVIII; 5, XXVIII; 28, I, XI; 40, IV
Alcohol, Tobacco, Firearms, and Explosives, Bureau of	27, II
Drug Enforcement Administration	21, II
Federal Acquisition Regulation	48, 28
Federal Claims Collection Standards	31, IX
Federal Prison Industries, Inc.	28, III
Foreign Claims Settlement Commission of the United States	45, V
Immigration Review, Executive Office for	8, V
Independent Counsel, Offices of	28, VI
Prisons, Bureau of	28, V
Property Management Regulations	41, 128
Labor Department	2, XXIX; 5, XLII
Employee Benefits Security Administration	29, XXV
Employees' Compensation Appeals Board	20, IV
Employment and Training Administration	20, V
Employment Standards Administration	20, VI
Federal Acquisition Regulation	48, 29
Federal Contract Compliance Programs, Office of	41, 60

Agency	CFR Title, Subtitle or Chapter
Workers' Compensation Programs, Office of	20, I, VII
World Agricultural Outlook Board	7, XXXVIII

List of CFR Sections Affected

All changes in this volume of the Code of Federal Regulations (CFR) that were made by documents published in the FEDERAL REGISTER since January 1, 2013 are enumerated in the following list. Entries indicate the nature of the changes effected. Page numbers refer to FEDERAL REGISTER pages. The user should consult the entries for chapters, parts and subparts as well as sections for revisions.

For changes to this volume of the CFR prior to this listing, consult the annual edition of the monthly List of CFR Sections Affected (LSA). The LSA is available at *www.fdsys.gov*. For changes to this volume of the CFR prior to 2001, see the "List of CFR Sections Affected, 1949–1963, 1964–1972, 1973–1985, and 1986–2000" published in 11 separate volumes. The "List of CFR Sections Affected 1986–2000" is available at *www.fdsys.gov*.

18 CFR—Continued

○

www.ingramcontent.com/pod-product-compliance
Lightning Source LLC
Chambersburg PA
CBHW061125220326
41599CB00024B/4175